The Best of

PARIS

4th Revised Edition

Adaptation and Translation: Sheila Mooney;
With the contribution of: Laurie Chamberlain, Pauline Ridel;
Coordination: Sophie Gayot; *Operations:* Alain Gayot.

Editorial Staff, French-language Guide
Editor-in-Chief: Christian Millau; *Coordination:* Gilles Plazy, assisted by Anne Yerly; *Editorial Assistance:* Françoise Avril, Bertrand Gauthey, Anna Köböl, Valérie Oger; *Contributors:* Abigaëlle, Fabienne Ancelle, Frédérique Basset, Françoise Boisard, François Cazenave, Pierre Crisol, Véronique Donnat, Alain Dreyfus, Isabelle Dumas-Vorzet, Jacques Dupont, Véronique Duthille, Charly Dupuis, Hélène Engrand, Alain Garrel, Herma Kervran, Marie-Hélène Laugier, Caroline Le Got, Josée Lochon, Lorris Murail, Angélique Négroni, Patrice de Nussac, Christophe Perrier, Jean-Louis Pinte, Alexandra Senes, Jean-Luc Toula-Breysse, Anne Valéry, Thomas Vié, Edith Zeitlin.

Gault

AN ANDRÉ GAYO ⎯**ᴀ⊤ION**

ANDRÉ GAYOT PUBLICATIONS

Bring You

The Best of Chicago	The Best of New England
The Best of Florida	The Best of New Orleans
The Best of France	The Best of New York
The Best of Germany	The Best of Paris
The Best of Hawaii	The Best of San Francisco
The Best of Hong Kong	The Best of Thailand
The Best of Italy	The Best of Toronto
The Best of London	The Best of Washington, D.C.
The Best of Los Angeles	The Best Wines of America

The Food Paper - Los Angeles
The Food Paper - San Francisco
Tastes Newsletter

Copyright © 1982, 1986, 1990, 1993 by Gault Millau, Inc.

Published by Gault Millau, Inc.
5900 Wilshire Blvd., 29th Floor
Los Angeles, CA 90036

Advertising Sales:
Alliance-Inter, 5bis, avenue Foch, 94160 Saint-Mandé, France (1) 43 28 20 20

Please address all comments regarding
The Best of Paris to:
Gault Millau, Inc.
P.O. Box 361144
Los Angeles, CA 90036

Library of Congress Cataloging-in-Publication Data

Guide Gault Millau Paris. English.
The Best of Paris / adaptation and translation, Sheila Mooney; with the contribution of Laurie
Chamberlain, Pauline Ridel; coordination, Sophie Gayot; operations, Alain Gayot; editorial
staff, French-language guide, editor-in-chief, Christian Millau.—4th revised ed.
p. cm.
Includes index.
ISBN 1-881066-03-7: $20.00

1. Paris (France)—Guidebooks.
I. Mooney, Sheila. II. Millau, Christian.
III. Gault Millau (Firm). IV. Title.
DC708.G3313 1993
914.4'36104839—dc20   92-41037
                                                                      CIP

Printed in the United States of America

Cover illustration by Dennis Ziemienski

CONTENTS

■ INTRODUCTION 5

■ RESTAURANTS 9

Gault Millau's penchant for observing everything that's good (and bad) about food and the dining experience is what made these guides so popular in the first place. Here you'll find candid, penetrating and often amusing reviews of the very, very best, the undiscovered and the undeserving. Listed by arrondissements of the city, including a section on the suburbs. Includes the Toque Tally.

■ HOTELS 99

A hotel guide to suit every taste. Where to spend a few days treated as royalty. Where to get the most for your money. Where to find the finest service, the most charm, the best location.

■ CAFES & QUICK BITES 131

Paris's palate may be found in its restaurants, but its heart and soul are found in its many cafés, wine bars and *salons de thé*. Where to hang out with a coffee and a copy of *Libération*, where to refresh yourself with a snack or a glass of wine.

■ NIGHTLIFE 153

A tour of some of the city's most amusing and exciting bars and nightspots, with discerning commentary on what goes on in Paris after dark. Where to go and where to avoid.

■ SHOPS 163

Discover in these pages why Paris is a shopper's dream. Where to buy anything and everything.

■ ARTS & LEISURE 283

Where to discover the lively arts in Paris, from avant-garde galleries to internationally acclaimed museums. How to enjoy your leisure time, indoors and out.

■ OUT OF PARIS 311

Everything you need to know to set off for a wonderful day (or three) in the country. Includes restaurants, hotels and sights in Paris's environs.

■ BASICS 331

Everything you need to know about getting around and about like a Parisian native.

■ MAPS 342

Includes an overview of the city.

■ INDEX 344

PARIS

A CITY ABOIL

City of Light, Stupefying Spectacle or Moveable Feast—call it what you will, Paris is as alive in the collective fantasies of the Western world as its streets are crawling with humanity of every imaginable origin, shape, shade, size and social station. From the crêpe-stand–studded rue Saint-André-des-Arts, which snakes through the Latin Quarter, to the silk-wrapped glamour and classic chic of the avenue Montaigne, to the Marché d'Aligre, which looks like it was lifted from downtown Algiers, Paris is one of those throbbing capitals that churns out legends—and spawns myths—like they were going out of style. As we dash to press, Paris is aboil: clubs, restaurants and even museums are popping up as fast as others are closing down. More than 11 million inhabitants (2.2 million within the old city walls) are this minute tearing along underground freeways, winging into busy airports and commuting to ultramodern, futuristic satellite business centers, making Paris shine among the world's most up-to-date cities. Yet nothing *seems* to have changed in decades, perhaps centuries: The familiar face of central Paris changes slowly indeed, almost imperceptibly. The bustling *grands boulevards* are still lined with giant sycamores that spread over crowded cafés. *Bouquinistes* go on hawking their books along the Seine's noisy *quais.* The open-air markets and specialty food shops in practically every *quartier* disgorge their wares on teeming sidewalks. And gardens lifted from Impressionist paintings, like the Luxembourg or Parc Monceau, continue to fill daily with armies of au pairs pushing babies in luxurious carriages down carefully raked gravel lanes. No wonder droves of urban trekkers, travel enthusiasts and pilgrims to the mecca of existentialism spend their days seeking the Paris of yore. Well, Paris is the quintessential Old World city, trussed up by an often boggling—and sometimes debilitating—cultural tradition and groaning under the weight of artistic wonders that are the envy of much of the civilized world. And it is old, old, old.

Since Day One, about 5,000 years ago, Parisian life has flowed along the Seine. Paris's twenty arrondissements spiral outward clockwise from the Ile de la Cité, its geographical and historical hub. The Cité, where Notre-Dame rears its Gothic bell towers, was the fortified capital of the Parisii, a Gallic tribe that Julius Caesar trounced circa 52 B.C. Then came the Gallo-Roman period, which lasted several centuries. Although this period left practically no monuments (save the baths at Cluny and the Arena, both in the Latin Quarter), the city was laid out once and for all. Fast forward: Clovis makes Paris the capital of his empire in 508. Fast forward again: Hugues Capet, the founding father of the Capetian dynasty, makes Paris (i.e., the Ile de la Cité) his capital. And here we are, 1,000 years later, and the Cité is still an island, detached in every sense from the life of the Left and Right Banks and from the nearby Ile Saint-Louis, famous nowadays as much for its ice cream as for its seventeenth-century architecture. Only place Dauphine, with its lovely triangular garden, antiques shops and brasseries, affords a backward glance of old Paris.

Way back in 1208, the cathedral schools of Paris were united into a single university on the Left Bank. As you might expect, students flooded into the neighborhood. And they have remained there ever since. From Jussieu in the fifth arrondissement to Saint-Germain-de-Prés in the sixth—commonly though inaccurately known as the *Quartier Latin*—the narrow, twisting streets are thronged by a decidedly young, casual crowd. So the concentration of late-night cafés, clubs, art galleries and bistros comes as no surprise. To many, the Latin Quarter is synonymous with The Real Paris: Saint-Michel, Saint-Germain, Odéon.

The Latin Quarter's sometimes snooty neighbor—still part of the Left Bank but altogether a different world—is the fashionable seventh arrondissement. The key words here are: Eiffel Tower, Invalides, Ecole Militaire and Palais Bourbon, plus at least a dozen ministries (don't get flustered when cabinet ministers and visiting dignitaries descend with their bullet-proof retinues). Some of Paris's finest restaurants, shops and hotels line the seventh's wide, handsome avenues.

At about the time the Latin Quarter was sprouting around the *civitas philosophorum*, the less-than-humble *Ville* on the Right Bank was lifting its patrician nose. Starting in the Middle Ages, merchants and the middle class settled into the *bourgs* around the villas and palaces of the nobility. Over time, the Louvre, the Tuileries, the Palais-Royal, place Louis-XV (now place de la Concorde), place Vendôme and place des Victoires became the landmarks that set the tone of the Right Bank. In the eighteenth and nineteenth centuries the well-bred and better-heeled built their major theaters there: the Opéra-Comique and Comédie-Française, the Palais Garnier Opéra and many others. They were soon flanked by the Grand Palais and Petit Palais. Napoléon's Arc de Triomphe crowns this upscale ensemble. Now, as then, the Champs-Elysées and surrounding grand avenues and boulevards of the first, eighth and sixteenth arrondissements are the best place to take a mink for a stroll or shop for diamonds before dining at the legendary Maxim's or Lucas-Carton, to name two of the most famous. But tennis shoes are equally at home: The Champs-Elysées—on every tourist itinerary—has also become the haunt of the *banlieusards*. These youngsters from the suburbs take the RER express subway to Etoile and spend hours at the Virgin mega–music store, or at the dozens of franchise *restos* and multiscreen movie theaters strung along the drag.

But many a Right Bank devotee will steer you off the thoroughfares and into the maze of nineteenth-century *passages*—passage des Panoramas or Galerie Vivienne, for example—scattered around the second, ninth and tenth arrondissements. Chockablock with boutiques, restaurants, food and wine shops and even hotels, these covered emporium-passageways are animated year-round, not just during a rainstorm. The soulful, industrious *faubourgs*— former working-class neighborhoods lying beyond the seventeenth-century city gates, now central Paris—whose higgledy-piggledy buildings snake out from the grand boulevards, are all too often overlooked. Likewise the garment district in the second and third arrondissements. A cross between Bangkok and lower Manhattan, it is a colorful hive of incessant activity and a great place to buy ready-to-wear and casual clothing direct from the factory.

The nearby Marais district, from the Centre Pompidou to the Musée Picasso and east to the place de la Bastille, used to be up and coming. Now it's up, up and away, a Parisian showcase of gentrification with a sky-high boutique-per-block ratio. Such venerable giants as the Brasserie Bofinger— the oldest and one of the handsomest in town—stand firm in the ebb and flow of new (and often excellent) restaurants and tea rooms. The Musée Carnavalet and Hôtel de Sully have been scrubbed and buttressed. The harmonious place des Vosges (1605) has been trimmed and returfed, its newly plumbed fountains splashing to the great delight of locals and tourists alike. The Marais is also home to France's distinguished and ancient Jewish population. Take a walk down the rue des Rosiers and discover any number of delicatessens and kosher food emporiums.

On the other side of the place de la Bastille, big bucks and revolutionary zeal (funneled in for the 1989 Bicentenary bash) have worked their magic on the neighborhood. The new Opéra de la Bastille is the turbo-charged motor that is transforming the faubourg Saint-Antoine, rue de la Roquette, rue de Lappe and rue de Charonne into the latest haven for hipsters, artists and restaurateurs with a flair for the profitably offbeat. High rents are becoming the rule in this former working-class neighborhood.

Above all, Paris is a city for walking, and this may be your best way to see Montmartre, although the newly refurbished funicular will carry those with sore feet to the top. Nowadays young night hawks haunt the notoriously naughty place Pigalle, where strip joints and porno shops are daily giving way to trendy late-night bars and discos. Speaking of dancing, the old Moulin Rouge still stands at the foot of Montmartre, a beacon for nostalgia buffs for whom the can-can remains the essence of gay Paree. But just a little farther up the hill, the steep steps and winding byways of Montmartre keep a village atmosphere alive in this most sophisticated of cities. Don't despise the droves of sightseers and would-be Picassos packed onto place du Tertre, a traditional stronghold of artists. Instead, duck into that wedding cake of a church, Sacré-Cœur, and most of all admire the stupendous view of Paris laid out at your feet.

Guidebooks invariably refer to unassailable authorities when serving up Paris in introductions like this one. We think that's swell, except for one small problem: What does *unassailable* mean? Ernest Hemingway, child of the tipsy Twenties and a dubious authority on Paris-beyond-La-Coupole, correctly called this sprawling metropolis "a moveable feast." Food—both spiritual and material—is indeed paramount here, from snails and scallops served with a cool Sancerre white to duck breast in a green-peppercorn sauce washed down with a brawny Bordeaux. While she doubtless enjoyed the feast, writer Katherine Anne Porter called Hemingway's Paris "shallow, trivial and silly." George Orwell was down and out in Paris, dreaming of a rare *steack frites*, while Henry Miller was discovering the tropics in brasseries around the seamy place Clichy. A gourmand at heart, Lawrence Durrell loved Paris because here he felt "on a par with a good cheese or a bad one." That's understandable, given the hundreds of varieties of cow, goat and sheep curd available here, and the millennial traditions attached to them.

Since selection is the rod by which guidebooks are measured, we will spare you the wisdom of Henry James, F. Scott Fitzgerald, Victor Hugo and company, ad infinitum. In short, you can find anything here: the great, the mediocre, the mundane, the sublime and the overrated. We hope the pages that follow will inspire you to seek—and help you to find—the best Paris has to offer.

André Gayot

RESTAURANTS

INTRODUCTION

A MANY-SPLENDORED EXPERIENCE

F or food-lovers, the lure of Paris's *haute cuisine* is at least as powerful as the temptations of *haute couture* for followers of fashion, or *haute culture* for the high-minded. In fact, we know of one American lady who planned her entire trip abroad around a dinner reservation (made months in advance, of course) *chez* mega-chef Joël Robuchon, so compelling was her craving for his langoustines aux morilles. Nor is it rare for people who have never even set foot in the French capital to know the names and specialties of all the city's fashionable chefs. Dining out in Paris is a many-splendored experience. Elegance reigns here to a degree not often attained in the restaurants of other cities; Le Grand Véfour, Maxim's and Lucas-Carton, for instance, are classified historical landmarks, with interiors of unparalleled beauty. These and the city's other top establishments also offer distinguished service: from the maître d'hôtel and the sommelier to the humblest busboy, the staffs are stylish and professional, a real *corps d'élite*. And the food, on a night when a chef like Alain Senderens is particularly inspired, can be memorable, even thrilling, a joy to the eye and a feast for the palate.

If your tastes (or finances!) lead you to prefer less exalted eating houses, we urge you to peruse our reviews for Paris's many marvelous bistros, brasseries and home-style restaurants, where prices are—usually—far lower than in *grands restaurants* and where the atmosphere veers more toward relaxed informality. Parisians are fiercely loyal to their neighborhood bistros where they regularly tuck into familiar, traditional dishes with pronounced regional accents (Gascon, Alsatian, Provençal)—if you go in for local color, those are the places to try. Brasseries are perfect when you want to eat just a single dish rather than a multicourse meal (but don't try ordering only a salad at Lipp!). And they offer sustenance at odd hours (that's important if you're jet-lagged!); brasseries tend to stay open late, and generally do not require reservations.

RESTAURANT SAVVY

• At top Parisian restaurants, you must **reserve a table** far in advance—at least three weeks, sometimes two or three months for such places as Robuchon and Taillevent. Reservation requests from abroad are taken much more seriously if they are accompanied by a deposit of, say, 300 francs (about $60). Tables at less celebrated spots can be reserved one or two days ahead, or even on the morning of the day you wish to dine. If you cannot honor your reservation, don't forget to call the restaurant and cancel.

• **Men should wear** a jacket and tie in any Parisian restaurant of some standing. **Women are well advised to dress up**, wearing pantsuits only if they are the highest in fashion. Luxury restaurants do not take the question of dress lightly, so be forewarned. At modest eateries, of course, more casual wear is perfectly acceptable (but jogging suits or running shorts and tank tops are looked at askance).

• When you go to a top restaurant, let the **headwaiter** suggest some possibilities from the menu (you'll find that they quite often speak English, though they always appreciate an attempt on the diner's part to speak French). Likewise, the **sommelier**'s job is to give diners expert advice on the choice of a suitable wine—regardless of price. Don't be afraid to seek his opinion, or to tell him your budget.

• **Dinner service** begins around 8 p.m. in most Paris restaurants. People start appearing in the finer restaurants about 9 p.m. **Luncheon is served** between 12:30 p.m. and 2 p.m. In addition to the standard carte, or **à la carte** menu, you will frequently be offered a choice of all-inclusive fixed-price meals called **menus**, which are generally a very good value. Also common in finer restaurants is the many-course sampling menu, or **menu dégustation**, a good (though not always economical) way to get an overview of a restaurant's specialties. Daily specials, or **plats du jour**, are usually reliable, inexpensive and prepared with fresh ingredients (whatever the chef found at the market that morning).

• French law mandates that the **service charge**, usually 15 percent, always be included in the menu prices. You are not obliged to leave an additional tip, but it is good form to leave a little more if the service was satisfactory.

• The **opening** and **closing times** we've quoted are always subject to change, particularly holiday closings, so be sure to call ahead.

• Many chefs have the bad habit of **changing restaurants frequently**, which means a restaurant can turn mediocre or even bad in just a few days. Chef-owned restaurants tend to be more stable, but even they can decline: A successful owner may be tempted to accept too many diners, which can result in a drop in quality. Should this be your experience, please don't hold us responsible!

ABOUT THE REVIEWS

RATINGS & TOQUES

Gault Millau ranks restaurants in the same manner that French students are graded: on a scale of zero to twenty, twenty being unattainable perfection. The rankings reflect *only* the quality of the cooking; decor, service, reception and atmosphere do not influence the rating, though they are explicitly commented on within the reviews. Restaurants ranked thirteen and above are distinguished with toques (chef's hats), according to the following table:

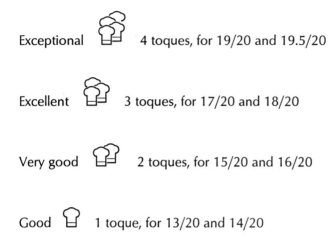

Exceptional   4 toques, for 19/20 and 19.5/20

Excellent   3 toques, for 17/20 and 18/20

Very good   2 toques, for 15/20 and 16/20

Good   1 toque, for 13/20 and 14/20

Toques in red denote restaurants serving modern, inventive cuisine; toques in black denote restaurants serving classic or traditional food.

Keep in mind that these ranks are *relative*. One toque for 13/20 is not a very good rating for a highly reputed (and very expensive) temple of fine dining, but it is quite complimentary for a small place without much pretension.

PRICES

At the end of each restaurant review, prices are given—either **A la carte** or **Menus** (fixed-price meals) or both. A la carte prices are those of an average meal (an appetizer, main course, dessert and coffee) for one person, including service and a half bottle of a relatively modest wine. Lovers of the great Bordeaux, Burgundies and Champagnes will, of course, face stiffer tabs. The menu prices quoted are for a complete multicourse meal for one person, including service but excluding wine, unless otherwise noted. These fixed-price menus often give diners on a budget a chance to sample the cuisine of an otherwise expensive restaurant.

The prices in this guide reflect what establishments were charging at press time.

TOQUE TALLY

Red toques: Modern cuisine
White toques: Traditional cuisine
The numbers following each restaurant refer to its arrondissement or suburban town.

Four Toques (19.5/20)

Lucas-Carton (Senderens), *Paris 8th*
Robuchon, *Paris 16th*

Four Toques (19/20)

L'Ambroisie, *Paris 4th*
Arpège (Alain Passard), *Paris 7th*
Taillevent, *Paris 8th*
Michel Rostang, *Paris 17th*
Guy Savoy, *Paris 17th*
Vivarois, *Paris 16th*

Three Toques (18/20)

Apicius, *Paris 17th*
Le Bourdonnais, *Paris 7th*
Jacques Cagna, *Paris 6th*
Carré des Feuillants, *Paris 1st*
Le Duc, *Paris 14th*
Faugeron, *Paris 16th*
Le Divellec, *Paris 7th*
Les Trois Marches, *Versailles*

Three Toques (18/20)

La Tour d'Argent, *Paris 5th*
La Vieille Fontaine, *Maisons-Laffite*

Three Toques (17/20)

Les Ambassadeurs, *Paris 8th*
Amphyclès, *Paris 17th*
A. Beauvilliers, *Paris 18th*
Chiberta, *Paris 8th*
Clos Longchamp, *Paris 17th*
Drouant, *Paris 2nd*
Duc d'Enghien, *Enghien*
Jean-Claude Ferrero, *Paris 16th*
Le Manoir de Paris, *Paris 17th*
Morot-Gaudry, *Paris 15th*
Au Petit Montmorency, *Paris 8th*
Le Pré Catelan, *Paris 16th*
Sormani, *Paris 17th*

Three Toques (17/20)

Gérard Besson, *Paris 1st*
Lasserre, *Paris 8th*

1st arrondissement

10/20 Joe Allen

30, rue P.-Lescot
42 36 70 13
Open daily until 1 a.m. Bar: until 2 a.m. Terrace dining. Air cond.
This small Franco-American club is a fine place to hoist a few beers and chat up a tall, dark and handsome stranger. Try the chef's salad, the chili burger, the barbecued spareribs and the apple pie.
A la carte: 150 F.

Armand au Palais-Royal

6, rue de Beaujolais
42 60 05 11
Closed Sat. lunch, Sun. & Aug. 15-30. Open until 11:30 p.m. Air cond.
Chefs Jean-Pierre Ferron and Bruno Roupie cook in an intelligent, sometimes even ingenious style that draws stockbrokers (at noon) and theater-goers (in the evening) to these handsomely renovated former stables (which once belonged to the maréchal-duc de Richelieu) facing the gardens of the Palais-Royal. Try the corn crêpe with warm foie gras, the shredded skate with cabbage or a lush Bresse chicken, and follow up with one of the delicate chocolate desserts. The cellar holds some notable Bordeaux.
A la carte: 320-530 F. Menus: 170 F (lunch only, except holidays), 240 F (dinner only), 290 F (weekdays dinner, Sat. and holidays).

Gérard Besson

5, rue Coq-Héron
42 33 14 74
Closed Sat. & Sun. Annual closings not available. Open until 10:30 p.m. Air cond.
Gérard Besson may not make front-page news like some other chefs, probably because he is too busy turning out masterpieces of classic cuisine. A disciple of Chapel, Garin and Jamin, Besson has brought his talent for elegant simplicity to such dishes as oyster flan with saffron-mussel cream, brioche of scrambled eggs with prawns, and warm rabbit pâté in flaky pastry. What might be a pompous exercise in style in less skilled hands here becomes light, flavorful and modern.
With his feet thus solidly set in tradition, Gérard Besson makes successful sorties into brave new territory: divinely moist sea bream baked in a crust of coarse salt with fresh herbs and napped with bell-pepper coulis; a fragrant fumet de coquilles Saint-Jacques dotted with plump pasta dumplings; fabulous sweet-and-sour pigeon (in a reduced sauce hinting of quince and cardamom); or sweetbread ragoût in a walnut-bread croûte.
The decor is dignified, despite some coy touches: bleached-wood furnishings, antique paintings, and vitrines filled with silver-plated carafes. Excellent desserts (chocolate sorbet, blanc-mange with strawberry coulis and almond milk). The service is less stiff now that Alain Delaveyne supervises the staff. The wine cellar boasts some 50,000 bottles, all of them costly.
A la carte: 600-750 F. Menu: 270 F (lunch only).

12/20 Brasserie Munichoise

5, rue D.-Casanova
42 61 47 16
Closed Sat. lunch, Sun., Dec. 24-Jan. 30 & Aug. Open until 12:30 a.m. Private room: 20.
A cozy little brasserie that serves famously good grilled veal sausages and pigs' knuckles, and one of the best choucroutes in Paris. Excellent Hacker-Pschorr beer on tap.
A la carte: 200-300 F.

Carré des Feuillants

Alain Dutournier
14, rue de Castiglione
42 86 82 82,
fax 42 86 07 71
Closed Sat. lunch (and dinner in July), Sun. & Aug. Open until 10:30 p.m. Private room: 14. Air cond.
You can take Alain Dutournier out of his native Landes but you cannot take the *Landais* out of Dutournier. Together with his wife Nicole, Dutournier regularly nips out to his birthplace in southwest France to sniff the cèpes and stimulate his appetite. Paris? The restaurant's sophisticated setting of stone and pale *trompe-l'œil* woodwork might as well be in Gascony.
Here you spread the terrine of foie gras on a slice of warm cornbread and savour vigorous yet elegant specialties such as warm pâté of cèpes enhanced by a fresh-tasting parsley jus, garbure (an earthy cabbage soup) with goose confit, free-range capon with a galette de cèpes, and a venison and foie gras terrine with cranberry jelly. Desserts include an exceptionally fine vanilla ice cream which is handmade to order, and an ethereal feuillantine sablée garnished with hazelnuts and glazed chestnuts.
Jean-Guy Loustau, the able steward of both the dining room and the cellar, dispenses in equal measure smiles, good counsel and marvelous bottles of wine (with a marked preference for vintages from the Pays d'Oc). Alas, as one might expect, there is nothing rustic about the prices.
A la carte: 600-800 F. Menus: 250 F (lunch only, except holidays), 550 F (except holidays).

Les Cartes Postales

7, rue Gomboust
42 61 02 93
Closed Sat. lunch, Sun., Dec. 23-Jan. 6 & July 31-Aug. 22. Open until 10:15 p.m. Air cond.
Blow-ups of photographs hang on the beige-and-white walls of this small, pretty, flower-filled restaurant. Yoshimasa Watanabe, disciple of the great Robuchon, creates outstanding cuisine with just the right pinch of the exotic. Since his arrival several years ago the restaurant has counted success upon success. Try his deliciously caramelized crab cake with grapefruit vinaigrette, spiced foie gras with broccoli, or the extraordinary Robuchon-style crème brûlée with vanilla and cinnamon. The cellar is improving, but still has a way to go.
A la carte: 350-400 F. Menus: 145 F (weekdays lunch), 345 F (wine incl.), 295 F.

12/20 Le Caveau du Palais

17-19, pl. Dauphine
43 26 04 28
Closed Sat. (except June-Sept.), Sun. & last 2 wks. of Dec. Open until 10:30 p.m. Terrace dining.
The good, solid cuisine (grilled andouillette, veal shanks with basil) is served in a charming place Dauphine cellar divided down the center by a wine bar.
A la carte: 275-350 F.

 ## Bernard Chirent

28, rue du Mont-Thabor
42 86 80 05
Closed Sat. lunch & Sun. Open until 10:30 p.m. Private room: 15. Air cond.
A few years back, chef Bernard Chirent moved from that high-society haunt, Castel, to open his own restaurant here on the ground floor of the Hôtel du Continent. The sober decor is brightened by a touch of pinkish beige. Famous for his sauces and his peerless prawns in an herbed broth, Chirent also excels with frogs' legs, boned young pigeon perfumed with tarragon, and an airy millefeuille—all richly deserving of a second toque. The wine list is modest but includes several interesting finds (Arbois, Rully, Saumur); some selections are available by the glass. The first prix-fixe menu (including wine) is marvelous.
A la carte: 300 F and up. Menus: 170 F and 250 F (wine incl.).

11/20 Le Comptoir

37, rue Berger
40 26 26 66
Open daily until 1 a.m. Terrace dining.
Sensational prices for tasty tapas (Spanish-style chicken, cold grilled vegetables, spinach-and-ricotta dumplings) served in a lively bistro atmosphere.
A la carte: 150 F.

 ## L'Espadon

Hôtel Ritz
15, pl. Vendôme
42 60 38 30
Closed Aug. Open daily until 11 p.m. Garden dining. Air cond. No pets. Heated pool. Valet parking
From the humble ham sandwich at 90 francs to the rack of lamb sprinkled with chopped parsley at 450 francs (OK, so it's for two), the grand Ritz style shines through. As one is entitled to expect, service is among the finest in the world, the clientele prodigiously prosperous. Owner El Fayed, ever fond of show, is breaking records for "ritziness" with his grandiose thermal baths, squash courts and rooftop heliport (for *deus ex machina* arrivals to the imperial suite—60,000 francs a night). From the most sumptuous kitchen in France award-winning chef Guy Legay conjures with increasing grace and inventiveness delightful dishes such as red mullet with tapenade, crispy-skinned sea bass and ris de veau meunière. The 120,000-bottle wine cellar is under the direction of virtuoso Georges Lepré.
A la carte: 700-900 F. Menus: 330 F (lunch only), 550 F (dinner only).

 ## La Fermette du Sud-Ouest

31, rue Coquillière
42 36 73 55
Closed Sun. Open until 10:30 p.m.
Christian Naulet has returned to his native Périgord, leaving a void behind him. But Jacky Mayer, the Fermette's new owner, has remained faithful to the restaurant's Gascon tradition and has kept the same chef on. Go for the perfect pork grattons, or the excellent duck breast with cèpes and garlicky potatoes. The menu is a bit short, but the welcome is warm.
A la carte: 200-280 F. Menu: 80 F (weekdays lunch only).

 ## Goumard-Prunier

9, rue Duphot
42 60 36 07
Closed Sun. & Mon. Open until 10:30 p.m. Private room: 25. Air cond.
Jean-Claude Goumard has transferred his restaurant to a celebrated Belle Epoque site (note the new address), but he still treks out at 3 a.m. to the Rungis market to net the very best sole and turbot, the fattest lobsters and prawns, for his chef Georges Landriot—fish and crustaceans so perfect that no flambé nor croûte shall ever be allowed to mar them. A pinch of turmeric to enliven the shellfish fricassée; a drop

15

of veal juice with soy sauce to accompany the braised sole; precious little butter all around: in short, nothing that might denature the marvelously fresh taste of the sea.

Unless of course you prefer the enormous Brittany prawns roasted in their shell, or red mullet dabbed with virgin olive oil and basil. Dessert brings excellent chocolate fondant with coffee sauce. Little remains, alas, of the original decor by Majorelle (the only vestiges are in the restrooms); and the less said about the present interior, the better.

A la carte: 500-700 F.

12/20 Le Grand Louvre

At the museum entrance, under the pyramid
40 20 53 41,
fax 42 86 04 63
Closed Tues. Open until 10 p.m. Private room: 100. Air cond.
Something is cooking under I.M. Pei's glass pyramid. In contrast with the chilly decor, the Louvre's restaurant, directed by the Gascon chef and culinary counselor André Daguin, serves reasonably priced country fare from the Southwest: walnut-studded pigeon terrine, hot foie gras with grapes, duck confit with spiced honey, prune nougat glacé. Non-stop service.

A la carte: 210-280 F.

Le Grand Véfour

17, rue de Beaujolais
42 96 56 27,
fax 42 86 80 71
Closed Sat., Sun. & Aug. Open until 10:15 p.m. Private room: 22. Air cond. Valet parking.
Guy Martin got off to a rough start here. Nearly every food critic in town greeted Martin's arrival at Le Grand Véfour with a cutting review. Well, we decided to give the fellow a chance to settle in before sitting in judgment, and for our money, Martin's cuisine is worth a solid double toque. Spiced roasted prawns, truffled potato terrine, Bresse pigeon tenderly enveloped in cabbage leaves and a delicious, lightly smoked chateaubriand prepared "à la ficelle" (poached in boiling broth) are just a few of the reasons we're so enthusiastic. As always, the magic of the Grand Véfour also resides in the fact that were every table empty you would still dine in perfect contentment, free to admire the exquisite surroundings that Jean Taittinger's good taste and family fortune have restored to their former glory: carved boiserie ceilings, graceful painted allegories under glass, lush carpeting, tables with white linens among black and gold Directoire chairs. The dining rooms evoke memories of such immortals as Napoléon, Jean Cocteau, Victor Hugo and Colette, who once lounged on these red velvet banquettes in the soft glow of the Palais-Royal gardens.

The service, under the expert and charming guidance of Béatrice Ruggieri, is as elegant as the clientele. The à la carte bill is astronomical, but the fixed-price lunch menu—which offers a wide variety of dishes—is pretty fair value: With a modest Bordeaux, you'll spend about 400 francs all told and walk away with an unforgettable memory.

A la carte: 700-1,000 F. Menu: 305 F (lunch only).

A la Grille Saint-Honoré

15, pl. du Marché-St-Honoré
42 61 00 93,
fax 47 03 31 64
Closed Sun., Mon., Aug. 7-23 & Dec. 24-31. Open until 10:30 p.m. Private room: 30. Terrace dining. Air cond.
The eyesore (a multiple-storey concrete garage) that currently mars the center of the place du Marché Saint-Honoré will soon be replaced by a glass gallery designed by Riccardo Bofill. Thus transformed, this historic market square will flourish once again. No surprise then that Jean Speyer, formerly cramped in an eighth-arrondissement basement restaurant, recently took over what was a shabby corner bistro and gave it a new lease on life. In the sparkling pink-and-gray decor Speyer serves tasty, imaginative "market cuisine": roast veal kidneys with anchovies, pumpkin-mussel soup, crispy mackerel with onion fondue, blanquette of young rabbit. The desserts and affordably priced wines are Speyer's strongest suit.

A la carte: 320-380 F. Menus: 180 F, 230 F.

11/20 Lescure

7, rue de Mondovi
42 60 18 91
Closed Sat. dinner, Sun., Aug. & Dec. 24-Jan. 1. Open until 10:15 p.m. Terrace dining. Air cond.
Tried-and-true French fare served in a feverishly *gai Paris* bistro atmosphere. Sample the rib-sticking veal sauté or duck confit. Game dishes are highlighted in the fall and winter hunting season.

A la carte: 150 F. Menu: 98 F (wine incl.).

11/20 Le Louchebem

10, rue des Prouvaires
42 33 12 99
Closed Sun. Open until 11:30 p.m. Terrace dining.
Carnivores can count on satisfaction here: huge portions of grilled or roasted beef, lamb and pork, tripe, pigs' trotters and the like are served forth in a butcher-shop

decor (rather cold, all that tile!). Modest, well-chosen wine list.
A la carte: 200 F. Menu: 85 F.

 La Main à la Pâte

35, rue St-Honoré
45 08 85 73
Closed Sun. Open until 12:30 a.m. Private room: 30. Garden dining. Air cond.
The plastic plants and conservatory decor may be ghastly, but the pasta from Annita Bassano's kitchen (10 eggs per kilo of pasta!) is *squisita*. So too are the rich polenta alla bolognese, the osso buco and one of the finest Italian wine cellars in Paris.
A la carte: 300-350 F. Menus: 114 F (weekdays lunch only), 176 F.

 Mercure Galant

15, rue des Petits-Champs
42 96 98 89
Closed Sat. lunch & Sun. Open until 10:30 p.m. Private room: 35.
The service in this grand old eating house is charming, the decor elegant and the cuisine better than ever. Chef Pierre Ferranti cooks with admirable brio, producing such delectable dishes as gratin of just-caught lobster, tournedos de lotte with herbed butter, pan-fried oysters with endive fondue, and for dessert, the famous "mille et une feuilles". Interesting cellar with a wide range of Bordeaux; smoothly impeccable service.
A la carte: 380-530 F. Menus: 250 F (lunch only), 280 F and 400 F (dinner only).

 La Passion

41, rue des Petits-Champs
42 97 53 41
Closed w.-e., holidays & July 24-Aug. 24. Open until 10:30 p.m.

Private room: 10. Air cond. No pets.
Gilles Zellenwarger's *trompe-l'œil* and woodwork decor is rather more elegant than passionate. And his rigorously correct cuisine enhanced by subtle sauces shows great respect for tradition. Notable progress is evident in his young pigeon with cabbage and foie gras, truffled blanc de volaille en vessie, and sole with fresh mint. Excellent fixed-price menus, improved wine list, with several selections available by the glass.
A la carte: 220-300 F. Menus: 170 F, 200 F, 360 F.

 Chez Pauline

5, rue Villedo
42 96 20 70
Closed Sat. dinner, Sun. & Aug. 1-17. Open until 10:30 p.m. Private room: 16. Air cond.
André Genin has taken over from his father Paul and slapped a fresh coat of paint on this wonderful old bistro, with its huge mirrors, glowing woodwork, zinc bar and red-velvet banquettes. An almost imperceptible touch of modernity has crept into the menu: old-time specialties like young rabbit in white-wine aspic, or daube of hogs' jowls now flank fresh steamed fish and fresh pasta with truffles and foie gras. The cellar holds memorable Burgundies, and there is an excellent selection of coffees.
A la carte: 400-450 F. Menu: 190 F (lunch only).

12/20 **Au Pied de Cochon**

6, rue Coquillière
42 36 11 75
Open daily, 24 hours. Private room: 50. Terrace dining. Air cond.
The atmosphere is at once feverish and euphoric in this Les Halles institution, renowned for serving forth

thundering herds of pigs' trotters (85,000 annually) and one ton of shellfish every blessed day and night of the year.
A la carte: 250-300 F.

 Pierre au Palais-Royal

Au Palais-Royal
10, rue de Richelieu
42 96 09 17
Closed Sat., Sun., holidays & Aug. Open until 10 p.m.
Country delights from the four corners of France fill the lovely handwritten menu of this traditional bistro. The cuisine is in the reliable hands of Roger Leplu, who uses top-quality ingredients to produce such pillars of French cooking as boudin with onions, mackerel in cider and bœuf à la ficelle, as well as stuffed cabbage bourguignonne or sheep's tripe and trotters à la marseillaise. Superb home-style desserts.
A la carte: 300-350 F. Menu: 250 F (wine incl.).

12/20 **La Pomme**

18, pl. Dauphine
43 25 74 93
Closed Wed. off-season & Dec. 20-Jan. Open until 10:30 p.m. Terrace dining.
This restaurant may become the apple of your eye. La Pomme, a modest and charming little establishment on the leafy place Dauphine, serves good, honest food (fish soup, tête de veau, pot-au-feu).
A la carte: 200-250 F.

 Le Poquelin

17, rue Molière
42 96 22 19,
fax 42 96 05 72
Closed Sat. lunch, Sun. & Aug. 1-20. Open until 10:30 p.m. Private room: 8. Air cond.
Habitués like us rejoice in the unfailing inventiveness of Michel Guillaumin, a tried-and-true chef renowned for his desserts (the honey ice cream

and nougat with apricot coulis are exquisite). Guillaumin lightens and updates traditional recipes such as wild-mushroom feuilleté and freshwater perch roasted in Saint-Pourçain wine. There are two eminently worthwhile fixed-price menus and many fine wines this side of 150 francs.
A la carte: 300-350 F. Menus: 154 F, 185 F.

11/20 La Providence

6, rue de la Sourdière
42 60 46 13
Closed Sat., Sun. & holidays. Open until 11 p.m. Air cond.
Hearty Alsatian specialties such as presskopf and baeckeoffe are providential for avid appetites. Bustling *winstub* atmosphere.
A la carte: 170 F. Menus: 78 F and 109 F (lunch only), 119 F (dinner only).

Saudade

34, rue des Bourdonnais
42 36 30 71
Closed Sun. Open until 10:30 p.m. (w.-e. 11 p.m.). Air cond. No pets.
Skillfully prepared Portuguese dishes have a pinch of nostalgia for Old Lusitania: marinated roast suckling pig alentejana, codfish (bacalhau) and robust boiled-beef cozido. Magnificent Portuguese wines and vintage ports.
A la carte: 220-320 F.

La Terrasse Fleurie

Hôtel Inter-Continental
3, rue de Castiglione
44 77 10 44,
fax 44 77 10 94
Closed Dec. 20-30. Open until 10:30 p.m. Private room: 15. Terrace dining. Air cond. No pets. Valet parking.
Dine amid flowers year round in the palatial decor of the Inter-Continental Hotel's candle-lit terrace. The service is excellent and the cuisine surprisingly fine. Try chef Jean-

Jacques Barbier's lightly smoked lotte in a warm vinaigrette, or the saddle of young rabbit with potato and celery gratin. The prices (unsurprisingly) are pretty stiff.
A la carte: 400-550 F. Menus: 270 F (lunch only), 450 F (dinner only).

Chez la Vieille

37, rue de l'Arbre-Sec
42 60 15 78
Open for lunch only. Closed Sat., Sun. & Aug. No pets.
The obsessive media cult that surrounds chef Adrienne Biasin hasn't corrupted her culinary talents. A regular circle of bankers, press barons and show-business personalities fill this tiny rustic-kitsch restaurant and worship Adrienne's legendary pot-au-feu, hachis Parmentier and sublime stuffed tomatoes.
A la carte: 300-350 F.

12/20 Willi's Wine Bar

13, rue des Petits-Champs
42 61 05 09,
fax 47 03 36 93
Closed Sun. Open until 11 p.m.
Mark Williamson, alias Willi, is an extremely knowledgeable British wine expert. He has wisely reverted to a low-price policy and simple cuisine. The food served in the smallish dining room (whiting with olives en croustade, ragoût d'encornets printanier, Stilton served with a glass of cream sherry) now makes a better match for the marvelous Côtes-du-Rhônes and other wines on offer. If you can't get a table, join the clients sitting chummily elbow-to-elbow at the polished wood bar.
A la carte: 220-300 F. Menu: 148 F.

Red toques signify modern cuisine; white toques signify traditional cuisine.

2nd arrondissement

12/20 Café Runtz

16, rue Favart
42 96 69 86
Closed Sat., Sun., holidays, 1 wk. in May & 3 wk. in Aug. Open until 11:30 p.m. Private room: 45. Air cond.
This is an 1880s Alsatian *winstub* whose classic fare ranges from foie gras to choucroute or potato salad with pork knuckle. Good French Rhine wines.
A la carte: 180-240 F.

Le Céladon

Hôtel Westminster
15, rue Daunou
47 03 40 42,
fax 47 60 30 66
Closed Sat., Sun., holidays & Aug. 1-29. Open until 10 p.m. Private room: 40. Air cond. Valet parking.
Well-lighted, flower-filled, and impeccably elegant dining rooms in what is possibly the loveliest *restaurant de palace* in Paris form the perfect setting for a romantic dinner. Le Céladon's remarkable young chef creates delicious and resolutely refined dishes such as scrambled eggs with sea urchins, grilled coquilles Saint-Jacques, smoked breast of duck, cumin-spiced sweetbreads with chicory. Desserts are generally less successful, but we liked the marvelously crisp lemon millefeuille.
A la carte: 450-600 F. Menu: 300 F.

La Corbeille

Hôtel Cyrnos
154, rue Montmartre
40 26 30 87
Closed Sat., Sun. & holidays. Open until 10:30 p.m. Private room: 20. Air cond.
When he abandons his penchant for "virtuoso" turns and manneristic touches, chef

Jean-Pierre Cario excels at such delightfully simple dishes as cold oysters with cabbage, monkfish bourride, or a perfect filet de bœuf à la ficelle. We heartily approve the Provençal lilt he has given his latest menu. Comfortable, lavishly lacquered 1930s decor. Superb wine cellar.

A la carte: 300-350 F. Menus: 280 F (dinner only), 150 F and 220 F.

12/20 Coup de Cœur

19, rue St-Augustin
47 03 45 70

Closed Sat. lunch & Sun. Open until 10:30 p.m. Private room: 60. Air cond.

The reception, service, and cuisine are thoroughly professional. Appetizing entrées (spinach salad with strips of smoked duck breast) lead into tasty "neo-bourgeois" main courses (pigeon gros sel) and the nice little house Bourgueil is a bargain. The atmosphere inclines to the trendy—there are no little gray men in the crowd, despite the monochromatic postmodern decor designed by Philippe Starck.

A la carte: 180-230 F. Menu: 170 F (wine incl.), 135 F.

Delmonico

39, av. de l'Opéra
42 61 44 26

Closed Sat., Sun. & Aug. Open until 10 p.m. Private room: 14. Terrace dining. Air cond.

The new manager of this old standby has lightened the decor and enlivened the ambience. In the kitchen, Alain Soltys (also a recent arrival) prepares fresh, modern dishes (artichoke and truffle salad, brill in puff pastry with sea-urchin cream) which we far prefer to the sad (veal chop flamed in Calvados) and distressing (kidneys cooked in whisky) offerings of yore. The service is uniformly charming.

And note that a fast pre-theater supper or business lunch can be served in 45 minutes.
A la carte: 250-350 F. Menu: 148 F.

Drouant

18, rue Gaillon
42 65 15 16,
fax 49 24 02 15

Open daily 10:30 pm (12:30 a.m. at Le Café). Private room: 50. Air cond. Valet parking.

Louis Grondard has descended from his eyrie at the Jules Verne (second storey of the Eiffel Tower), bringing with him well-deserved laurels and a repertoire of modern gastronomical classics. After his Robuchon-like success on high, Grondard is bidding fair to keep the 200 seats at Drouant (restaurant, Café, and salons) packed year-round. Appropriately enough, the Goncourt literary prize is awarded here each year, and the monthly literary luncheons of the jury are held in a handsome room with a charming Art Deco pastiche of a decor that features a splendid wrought-iron and marble staircase.

The masterly touch of the great sauce-maker is evident in Grondard's baby turbot with a beurre blanc redolent of lemongrass, the long-simmered curried suckling pig, or the pigeon in a potato crust. Few palates would fail to appreciate desserts like spiced vanilla crème brûlée, croquant aux marrons, and honey-gentian ice cream.

The Café Drouant is the haunt of businessmen in search of reasonably priced bourgeois cuisine.

The wine cellar's rare bottles at 5,000 francs are flanked by a selection of fine wines priced between 100 and 200 francs. Efficient, workmanlike service.

A la carte: 600-850 F. Menus: 320 F (weekdays

lunch only), 200 F (at Le Café; dinner only).

12/20 Gallopin

40, rue N.-D.-des-Victoires
42 36 45 38

Closed Sat. & Sun. Open until 11:30 p.m. Terrace dining.

The 1876 brassy Victorian decor is a feast for the eyes. The food at Gallopin isn't bad either. Try the house specialty: sole à la crème, a nice, fat fish done to a turn. Jolly service.

A la carte: 220-300 F. Menu: 150 F (dinner only, wine incl.).

11/20 Le Grand Colbert

2, rue Vivienne
42 86 87 88

Closed Aug. Open daily until 1 a.m. Air cond.

Classic brasserie cuisine (oysters and shellfish, andouillette ficelle, bœuf gros sel, and poached chicken) served in a freshly restored historic monument, with frescoes and ornate plasterwork, brass railings and painted glass panels.

A la carte: 200-250 F.

11/20 La Movida

14, rue M.-Stuart
42 21 98 60

Closed Sat., Sun. & Mon. Open until 2 a.m. Air cond.

Tattooed guitarists incite wild flamenco dancers barely visible through the haze of cigarette smoke. Unspectacular tapas, astonishingly good Spanish sweets.

A la carte: 150-200 F.

12/20 Pierre

A la Fontaine Gaillon
Pl. Gaillon
42 65 87 04

Closed Sat. lunch, Sun. & Aug. Open until 12:30 a.m. Private room: 30. Terrace dining. Air cond.

The menu is long, but short on ideas. You're better off sticking to the fresh daily specials, which are always ably prepared. The delightful

old *hôtel particulier* decor was recently restored, and the grand terrace's fountain is spectacular when lit at night.
A la carte: 250-400 F. Menu: 160 F (dinner only).

Pile ou Face
52 bis, rue N.-D.-des-Victoires
42 33 64 33
Closed Sat., Sun., holidays, Dec. 24-Jan. 1 & July 26-Aug. 22. Open until 10 p.m. Private room: 20. Air cond.
A pretty, if ruinously expensive, little establishment run by three associates proud of their success and determined to keep standards high. The stockbroker lunch crowd gives way in the evening to a pleasant mix of bourgeois provincials and foreigners. The first floor's red-and-gold decor, with *fin de siècle* touches, perfectly matches chef Claude Udron's cuisine. Sometimes slightly off the mark, but mostly on target, Udron scores with delicious duck liver coated with gingerbread crumbs, roast pigeon with truffled oil and the many other dishes on the "special" menu, which showcases the restaurant's farm products (rabbit, poultry). A very fine wine cellar.
A la carte: 400-450 F.

Le Saint-Amour
8, rue de Port-Mahon
47 42 63 82
Closed Sat. lunch, Sun. & holidays. Open until 10:15 p.m. Air cond.
Impeccable service and a simple, fresh, generous cuisine distinguish Le Saint Amour. The new chef has a pronounced penchant for fish and seafood: try, for example the tasty Marennes oysters, or the turbot baked in a salt crust and served with a chervil-scented beurre blanc. Concise but interesting wine list.
A la carte: 300-370 F.

Menus: 145 F (dinner only), 165 F (lunch only).

La Taverne du Nil
9, rue du Nil
42 33 51 82
Closed Sat. lunch, Sun. (except dinner in Aug.). Open until 11 p.m. Air cond.
The setting is rather down-at-heel but lightened and brightened by pink upholstery and *naïf* paintings representing the River Nile. Straightforward Lebanese country dishes (hummus with meat and pine nuts, mezes, keftedes with onions and parsley, delicious garlicky grilled chicken) at exceptional prices. Belly dancers sometimes shake things up on the weekend.
A la carte: 180-220 F. Menus: 45 F and 60 F (lunch only, except holidays), 120 F and 165 F (wine incl.), 80 F.

3rd arrondissement

Ambassade d'Auvergne
22, rue du Grenier-St-Lazare
42 72 31 22,
fax 42 78 85 47
Closed 15 days in summer. Open until 10:30 p.m. Private room: 35. Air cond.
Each visit to this embassy brings the same delightful experience. The Petrucci tribe's hospitality knows no bounds. The decor, featuring timbers festooned with hanging hams, is worn but authentic; the atmosphere is marvelously convivial.
Authenticity is equally present in the house specialties: real country ham, cabbage and Roquefort soup, boudin with chestnuts, cassoulet of lentils from Le Puy, legendary sausages served with slabs of delicious bread, duck daube with fresh pasta and smoky

bacon, and so forth. Good desserts (try the aumônière à l'orange, or the mousseline glacée à la verveine du Velay). The cellar is vast and boasts some little-known Auvergnat wines (Chanturgue, Saint-Pourçain) in a wide range of prices.
A la carte: 220-300 F.

L'Ami Louis
32, rue du Vertbois
48 87 77 48
Closed July 12-Aug. 30. Open until 11 p.m.
Despite its improbably shabby decor (note the peeling, brownish walls), L'Ami Louis jealously claims the title of "the world's costliest bistro". It is certainly dear to the hearts of the Americans, tourists, suicidal over-eaters and rail-thin fashion models who battle to book a table at this famous *lieu de mémoire*. The heirs of old Père Magnin carry on the house tradition of huge portions, but the ingredients are not so choice as once they were. And nowadays the sauces are sometimes thick or sticky, the frites oily and the meats overcooked. What a joy, though, to sit down to a Gargantuan serving of foie gras fresh from the Landes, giant escargots de Bourgogne, whole roast chickens, the incomparable gigot of baby Pyrénées lamb. The desserts are insignificant, the cellar respectable.
A la carte: 700-750 F.

12/20 Le Bar à Huîtres
33, bd Beaumarchais
48 87 98 92
See *14th arrondissement.*

12/20 Chez Janou
2, rue R.-Verlomme
42 72 28 41
Closed Sat. & Sun. Open until 11 p.m. Terrace dining.
An honest little old-fashioned bistro with turn-of-the-century decor and a

pleasant terrace. The neighborhood (place des Vosges/Bastille) has gone up-market and so have Janou's prices, but the country cuisine

ered tables. The cuisine has a regional (Southwestern) slant and is simple and carefully prepared (foie gras, magret, cassoulet). Try the copious

shelves, and a sumptuous seventeenth-century tapestry adorning the beige walls. Others may find the rigorous and restrained atmosphere rather "cold." We don't. It has the lived-in feel of a beautifully maintained private home, of which Danièle is the charming hostess. Don't expect to see much of Bernard, a retiring chef who prefers the sizzling sounds of his kitchen to the applause of an appreciative public. The influence of his mentor, Claude Peyrot, is everywhere felt in Bernard's chiseled, architectural cuisine. We used to find it a bit cool, but recently it has been warmed with sunny spices and herbs.

Market culture

A stroll round a Parisian *street market* **is one of the best ways to see, smell and sample French food. Start out early to admire the carefully constructed stacks of fruits and vegetables—and stick around for bargains when stallholders close up shop at about 1 p.m. The speed with which they dismantle their stalls and pack up their produce is a spectacle in itself. Most markets are held twice a week, some three times a week, and there are 57 sites to choose from. For contrasting views of Parisian shopping and eating habits, visit the resolutely upscale Saint-Didier market in the sixteenth arrondissement (go down the rue Mesnil from place Victor-Hugo) held on Tuesday, Thursday and Saturday, and the funky, multiracial market on the place de la Réunion in the twentieth arrondissement on Thursday or Sunday.**

---

here (Jerusalem artichokes tossed in hazelnut oil, duck confit) is still authentically homey and good. Improved wine list.

A la carte: 180-250 F. Menu: 160 F.

11/20 Chez Jenny
39, bd du Temple
42 74 75 75
Open daily until 1 a.m. Private room: 120. Terrace dining. Air cond.
This grand, historical monument of a brasserie, with lovely marquetry upstairs, is on the upswing. Many good "world-famous" choucroutes and superb Alsatian charcuteries.
A la carte: 220-270 F. Menu: 160 F (wine incl.).

12/20 Le Souvré
10, rue Fts-du-Temples
42 72 35 71
Closed Sat. lunch, Sun., holidays & Aug. Open until 10 p.m.
A somber decor is relieved by lovely candle-lit, lace-cov-

salmon with dill, or the boned saddle of young rabbit with parsley and garlic, followed by a strawberry pastry brimming with Chantilly cream. Smiling service.

A la carte: 250-300 F. Menu: 120 F.

4th arrondissement

L'Ambroisie
9, place des Vosges
42 78 51 45
Closed Sun., Mon., Feb. school holidays & 3 1st wks. of Aug. Open until 10:15 p.m. Air cond. No pets. Valet parking.
Bernard and Danièle Pacaud transformed this former goldsmith's shop under the arcades of the place des Vosges into the most gracious, charming and refined salon in the Marais. The dining room is worthy of a château, with high ceilings and inlaid stone and parquet floors, book-lined

For example, an almost imperceptible touch of aniseed gives a new, needed dimension to a highly concentrated jus of mushrooms and cream, made with baby meadow mushrooms, morels and chanterelles. Red mullet with cumin and carrots, curried prawns with sesame crêpes, calf's liver with sherry vinegar and a hint of honey have won us over and warmed our hearts.

Vive the new Pacaud! And hats off too for the fantastic profiteroles with vanilla ice cream and warm chocolate sauce, as well as for the florentines napped with a saffron-tinctured crème anglaise. Another round of applause for Pierre Le Moullac, the maître d'hôtel-sommelier, who seems to have countless magical bottles up his sleeve.
A la carte: 650-1,000 F.

11/20 Auberge de Jarente
7, rue de Jarente
42 77 49 35
Closed Sun., Mon., Aug. & 1 wk. beg. April. Open until 10:30 p.m. Air cond.
Here you'll find unpretentious Basque cuisine served in

a charming old Marais atmosphere (skip the prawns cooked in whisky and the sole au Noilly). The fixed-price menu, which includes pipérade de Saint-Jean, cassoulet, cheese and gâteau basque, is irreproachable. A la carte: 170 F. Menus: 120 F (wine incl.), 108 F, 160 F.

 Benoit

20, rue St-Martin
42 72 25 76
Closed Sat., Sun., & Aug. Open until 10 p.m. Private room: 18. Air cond.
The more things change, the more Benoit's solid, bourgeois cuisine stays the same. This is the archetypal Parisian bistro, with red-velvet banquettes, brass fixtures, lace curtains and a polished zinc bar. Chef Michel Petit (who is anything but!) continues the lusty tradition begun before the Great War by his grandfather. His repertoire consists of simple, modest marvels: bœuf mode, foie gras with lentils, beef tongue in port, salt cod with aïoli, accompanied by lush desserts (try the chocolate fondue). An excellent cellar is stacked with reasonably priced bottles from Mâcon, Sancerre, Beaujolais, Saumur-Champigny, and Burgundy. Benoit numbers among Paris's best—and most expensive—bistros.
A la carte: 420-570 F

10/20 Brasserie de l'Ile Saint-Louis

55, quai de Bourbon
43 54 02 59
Open daily until 1 a.m.
Choucroute, sausages and cassoulet terrine are washed down here with torrents of frothy draft Mutzig. This is a favorite haunt of both islanders and famished outlanders.
A la carte: 200 F.

 Coconnas

2 bis, pl. des Vosges
42 78 58 16
Closed Mon., Tues. & Jan. 13-Feb. 11. Open until 10:15 p.m. Terrace dining. Air cond.
Claude Terrail (La Tour d'Argent) saw a good thing coming when nearly 40 years ago he bought and transformed this old tourist bistro on the lovely place des Vosges. The tourists still flock here, but they're on to a good thing. In recent years the cuisine has become reliable and remarkably well-prepared. Sample traditional favorites such as poule au pot with a "garden of vegetables", salt-cured duck or tournedos in a gingerbread croûte. The fixed-price lunches offer excellent value.
A la carte: 280-400 F. Menus: 105 F (weekdays lunch and Sat., wine incl.), 150 F (weekdays lunch and Sat.).

12/20 Le Coin du Caviar

2, rue de la Bastille
48 04 82 93
Closed Sat. lunch & Sun. Open until midnight. Private room: 14. Air cond.
Greece, Russia, Iran and France meet here under the sign of the salmon. Upstairs, in the rather precious dining room, choose from among a variety of salmon dishes (raw and smoked) or an authentic beef Stroganov. In the noisier, more switched-on downstairs bar, savor bortsch, blini, smoked fish—or caviar! For dessert, there's a delicious apple strudel.
A la carte: 300-400 F (without caviar). Menu: 180 F (lunch only).

12/20 Au Franc Pinot

1, quai de Bourbon
43 29 46 98,
fax 42 77 28 16
Closed Sun. & Mon. Open until 11 p.m. Private room: 30. Air cond.
Napoleonic iron gates stand guard before this historic cave on the Ile Saint-Louis. We can't really fault the cuisine, which is serious enough, but we resent the recently inaugurated high-price policy: tourists shouldn't be taken for pigeons!
A la carte: 500-600 F. Menu: 195 F (weekdays lunch only).

10/20 Jo Goldenberg

7, rue des Rosiers
48 87 20 16
Open daily until midnight. Terrace dining.
This is the archetypal, and most picturesque, of the Goldenberg restaurants in Paris (see seventeenth arrondissement). The Central European Yiddish cuisine is served in the heart of the Marais's Jewish district. Prepared foods are sold in the take-out boutique.
A la carte: 200-250 F.

11/20 Au Gourmet de l'Isle

42, rue St-Louis-en-l'Ile
43 26 79 27
Closed Mon. & Tues. Open until 10 p.m.
The reception is charming, the crowd young and cheerful, the stone-and-beams decor suitably rustic. Au Gourmet de l'Isle has enjoyed over 40 years of deserved success for one of the city's surest-value set menus priced at 120 francs: boudin with apples, beef and lentil salad, andouillette with red beans.

We're always happy to hear about your discoveries and receive your comments on ours. We want to give your letters the attention they deserve, so when you write to Gault Millau, please state clearly what you liked or disliked. Be concise but convincing, and take the time to argue your point.

A la carte: 170 F. Menu: 120 F.

Miravile

72, quai de l'Hôtel-de-Ville
42 74 72 22,
fax 42 74 67 55
Closed Sat. lunch & Sun. Open until 10:30 p.m. Private room: 50. Terrace dining. Air cond. Valet parking.

Right, left, right: this remarkable establishment has shifted back and forth over the Seine several times, but is now permanently installed in a beautifully restored building on the quay between the Hôtel de Ville and Châtelet. Marble floors, *trompe-l'œil* paintings and warm colors give the surroundings—the comfortable creation of chef/owner Gilles Epié and his wife Muriel—a charming Mediterranean feel. The kitchen has been revamped and expanded, a good thing as the talented young Gilles needs plenty of elbow room. It comes as no surprise that Gilles's cuisine, which was shaped under the tutelage of Alain Passard, is now better than ever. Gilles is determined to join the ranks of the great toque-laden chefs. And his further ascent will doubtless be sped by such acutely flavorful, imaginative dishes as céleri rémoulade with duck foie gras, grilled red mullet with arugula, roast tuna with cumin and cèpes, saddle of rabbit with olives, or sea bream with roasted figs. The desserts are a delight (macaroons with raspberries, chocolate-caramel millefeuille, pistachio-cherry gratin), and the four-course lunch prix-fixe menu is an excellent value.
A la carte: 450-600 F. Menus: 150 F (weekdays lunch only), 280 F, 480 F.

Le Monde des Chimères

69, rue St-Louis-en-l'Ile
43 54 45 27
Closed Sun., Mon. & Feb. school holidays. Open until 10:30 p.m.

A delightful old "island bistro" now run by former TV personality Cécile Ibane. The cuisine is reminiscent of Sunday dinner *en famille*—if, that is, your family included a French granny who was also a marvelous cook! We recommend the oxtail terrine with its garnish of sweet-and-sour quince and cherries, the veal paupiettes with tomatoes, the chicken sautéed with 40 cloves of garlic, and a smooth, creamy brandade de morue gentled with milk and olive oil. Yummy homemade desserts and an expertly chosen wine list.
A la carte: 270-350 F. Menu: 150 F (lunch only).

Le Vieux Bistro

14, rue du Cloître-Notre-Dame
43 54 18 95
Closed at Christmas. Open daily until 11 p.m.

Shame on Gault Millau for neglecting this authentic old bistro (perhaps its façade was hidden by a hedge of tour buses). What unexpected pleasures lurk here, among the marble table-tops and velvet banquettes, the shady terrace in the shadow of Notre-Dame! A discovery indeed. The mustachioed owner, Fernand Fleury, is an old-fashioned host of rare warmth and good humor. Try the andouillette simmered in Sancerre, the beef fillet en papillote with bone marrow, the excellent potatoes au gratin and, for dessert, chocolate profiteroles. Accompanied by a famously good bottle of Henry Fessy Brouilly, your bill probably won't top 250 F. Be sure to book ahead.
A la carte: 200-350 F.

Wally Saharien

16, rue Le Regrattier
43 25 01 39
Closed Mon. lunch & Sun. Open until 11:30 p.m. Private room: 20. Air cond. No pets.

Wally's desert empire is the place to sample marvelous Saharan couscous—served dry and *sans* vegetables—and classic, festive delights such as harira, pigeon pastilla, stuffed sardines and North African pastries.
Menu: 300 F (wine incl.).

5th arrondissement

Auberge des Deux Signes

46, rue Galande
43 25 46 56,
fax 46 33 20 49
Closed Sat. lunch, Sun., May 1 & Aug. Open until 10:30 p.m. Private room: 70.

If there is one restaurant in Paris that must be seen to be believed, it is this marvelous medieval hostelry lovingly restored and run by Georges Dhulster. Solid oak beams, Gothic vaults and windows that frame Notre-Dame: the setting is nothing short of spectacular (despite the somewhat heavyhanded neo-Louis XIII touches). And now the menu, which was not always so appealing as the surroundings, is packed with delicate, imaginative dishes like boiled-beef ravioli with ginger-scented cabbage, mackerel tart with leek fondue, and warm pear croquant laced with Cointreau. Courteous service.
A la carte: 400-500 F. Menus: 140 F and 230 F (lunch only).

Find the address you are looking for, quickly and easily, in the index.

11/20 Le Balzar

49, rue des Ecoles
43 54 13 67
*Closed Dec. 24-Jan. 1 & Aug.
Open until 12:30 a.m.*
This Left-Bank/Sorbonne haunt, with its Art Deco woodwork and mirrors, is ever faithful to tried-and-true brasserie fare (calf's liver, choucroute).
A la carte: 200-250 F.

 ## La Bûcherie

41, rue de la Bûcherie
43 54 78 06
Open daily until 12:30 a.m. Private room: 45 Terrace dining. Air cond.
Bernard Bosque is built like a Breton buccaneer and has been running his "Hôtel du Bon Dieu" (the Bûcherie's name back in 1900) for over 30 years with winning talent and great success. Handsome woodwork and good contemporary engravings adorn the walls, and there are views of Notre-Dame through the windows of the comfortable covered terrace. The cuisine is rich and rather too predictable (poached eggs meurette, brandade de morue, lamb sauté with aubergines), but satisfying withal. The wine cellar boasts a magnificent selection of Bordeaux.
A la carte: 240-400 F. Menu: 220 F (wine incl.).

 ## Chieng-Mai

12, rue F.-Sauton
43 25 45 45
Closed Sun., Aug. 1-15 & Dec. 16-31. Open until 11:30 p.m. Air cond. No pets.
Its cool, stylized atmosphere, efficient service, and increasingly interesting Thai menu have won Chieng Mai a growing corps of admirers (it is therefore wise to reserve your table in advance). The repertoire features several delicious new dishes: shrimp and spiced roe salad, steamed spicy seafood served in a crab

shell, duck breast with basil and pepper buds, and a remarkable coconut-milk flan.
A la carte: 200-300 F. Menus: 91 F (lunch only), 136 F, 159 F, 173 F.

 ## Clavel

65, quai de la Tournelle
46 33 18 65
Closed Sun. dinner, Mon., Feb. school holidays & Aug. 7-30. Open until 10:30 p.m. Air cond.
Chef Frédéric Mignot is the new hand in the kitchen; he plans to update the repertoire of this small, quiet restaurant by the Seine. The decor has been redone in a spare Japanese style; the soft lights and pleasant service create a cozy, intimate atmosphere. The lunch menu is particularly appealing, the à la carte selections rather costly (especially the entrées). Try the generously served Brittany lobster ravioli with chives, the duck and foie gras tourte, and finish up with the dark, bewitching African chocolate cake.
A la carte: 400-450 F. Menus: 160 F (weekdays lunch and Sat.), 350 F.

 ## Les Colonies

10, rue St-Julien-le-Pauvre
43 54 31 33
Dinner only. Closed Sun. & Aug. Open until 1 a.m. Private room: 38. Air cond.
The decorator of L'Ambroisie took this old building, which faces the church of Saint-Julien-le-Pauvre, and transformed it with subtle refinements such as painted woodwork, luxurious fabrics and fine china. A mild breeze from the colonies stirs many of chef Spyros Vakanas's creations, witness his goat-cheese toasts enhanced with the warm flavor of nutmeg, the rib steak coated with crushed spices, or the chocolate "shell" with

sweet saffron cream sauce. Charming service and a high-society clientele. Book ahead for late dining.
A la carte: 280-350 F. Menu: 170 F.

11/20 Délices d'Aphrodite

4, rue Candolle
43 31 40 39
Closed Mon. Open until 11:30 p.m. Air cond.
You'll find a catering service, two take-out shops and a small, summery dining room at this likeable Greek spot. The food is hearty and authentic: pan-fried octopus, stuffed cabbage dolmades, moussaka.
A la carte: 200-220 F.

 ## Diapason

30, rue des Bernardins
43 54 21 13
Closed Sat. lunch, Sun. & Aug. 1-15. Open until 10:30 p.m.
A nicely kept, flower-filled establishment crowded with tiny tables pushed up to comfortable banquettes. The cuisine is rigorously classic (warm oysters with lemon butter, sole and salmon à l'orange, grenadin of young pigeon with truffles and foie gras). Good desserts, fine Loire wines.
A la carte: 350-400 F. Menus: 165 F, 300 F.

 ## Dodin-Bouffant

25, rue F.-Sauton
43 25 25 14,
fax 43 29 52 61
Closed Sun. Open until 11 p.m. Terrace dining. Air cond.
Prepare yourself for the sound and the fury of high and not-so-high-society diners jostling for a table in this cigar-box of a bistro. Dodin-Bouffant is renowned for its charming owners (Danièle and Maurice Cartier) and its delicious, no-nonsense cuisine (the work of chef Philippe Valin, disciple of the late Jacques Manière).

Two hundred souls feed here daily, enjoying the wonderful oysters and seafood (duo of lotte and lobster with mild garlic), the gutsy bistro fare (daube de joues de bœuf, calf's head) and the many special "market" dishes (sea bream with basil and fennel, roast kid with oyster mushrooms). The very fine wine cellar is in the manner of Manière—full of finds at the right price. Roughshod but cheerful service.
A la carte: 350-400 F. Menu: 170 F (lunch only).

 Les Fontaines
9, rue Soufflot
43 26 42 80
Closed Sun. & Aug. Open until 10:30 p.m.
Roger Lacipière was clever to set aside the back room of his otherwise banal corner café and turn it into a delightful restaurant. Jolly waiters bring on generously robust and reasonably priced dishes like fricasséed young rabbit, Dijon-style kidney, and Bresse pigeon in a sauce thickened with foie gras. Fine selection of Loire and Bordeaux wines, and Beaujolais by the carafe.
A la carte: 200-300 F.

 Moissonnier
28, rue des Fossés-St-Bernard
43 29 87 65
Closed Sun. dinner, Mon. & Aug.-Sept. 7. Open until 10 p.m.
Reserve your table on the ground floor, where Jeannine trots to and fro serving the regulars from the university nearby, her arms laden with rib-sticking Lyonnais specialties (tablier de sapeur, quenelles, andouillette au vin blanc) and *pots* of Morgon, Brouilly and other Beaujolais wines drawn from the barrel. A delightful bistro run by the Moissonnier family for the last 30 years.
A la carte: 220-280 F.

 Au Pactole
44, bd St-Germain
46 33 31 31,
fax 46 33 07 60
Closed Sat. lunch & Sun. Open until 10:30 p.m. Private room: 12. Terrace dining.
Roland Magne's policy of serving laudably lightened traditional fare at attractive prices has finally paid off. Au Pactole was for years an inexplicably under-appreciated restaurant, but now the lovely dining room is reliably full at lunch and dinner (perhaps the news that François Mitterrand and Helmut Kohl—both known for their love of fine food—had engaged in some dinner diplomacy here early in 1992 gave the restaurant a boost). Try the excellent beef-jowl terrine with onion confit, the perfect crab ravioli, or one of the best rib steaks in Paris (it's roasted in a salt crust), followed by a tasty apple tart with sabayon sauce for dessert. Nice but pricey wine list.
A la carte: 300 F. Menus: 139 F, 279 F.

11/20 Perraudin
157, rue Saint-Jacques
46 33 15 75
Closed Sat. lunch, Sun., Mon. lunch & last 2 wks. of Aug. Open until 10:15 p.m. Terrace dining. No cards.
This establishment is run by one of the city's top specialists in homey, country-style cooking, formerly of Le Polidor (see sixth arrondissement). Heartwarming Vouvray andouillette, bœuf bourguignon, and duck confit. Modest but charming early 1900s decor.
A la carte: 150 F. Menu: 59 F (lunch only).

12/20 Le Petit Navire
14, rue des Fossés-St-Bernard
43 54 22 52
Closed Sun., Mon., 1st wk. of Feb. school holidays & Aug. 1-16.

Open until 10 p.m. Terrace dining.
For over twenty years regulars have been flocking here for tapenade, garlicky shellfish soup, grilled sardines and delightful growers' wines that sell for under 80 francs.
A la carte: 400 F. Menu: 120 F.

11/20 Le Petit Prince
12, rue Lanneau
43 54 77 26
Open daily until 12:30 a.m.
A modest Latin-Quarter restaurant serving classic, honest food (confit and magret de canard, lamb curry) and good little wines at low prices.
Menus: 82 F, 146 F.

 Restaurant A
5, rue de Poissy
46 33 85 54
Closed Mon. Open until 11 p.m. Air cond.
Huynh-Kien regales clients with his spectacular vegetable and rice-paste sculptures and beguiles their taste buds with all-but-forgotten Chinese dishes from the eighteenth-century imperial court: duck cooked in mustard leaves, sautéed pork with spicy leeks, or the famous imperial chicken. By all means order the litchee-nut sorbet for dessert.
A la carte: 200-350 F. Menu: 108 F.

12/20 Rôtisserie du Beaujolais
19, quai de la Tournelle
43 54 17 47
Closed Mon. Open until 11:15 p.m. Terrace dining. Air cond.
Claude Terrail of the Tour d'Argent (across the road) opened this traditional Lyonnais bistro in 1989 to great fanfare. It's still a nice little place to spend an animated evening with friends. The roast Challans duck is a delight, the saucisson pistaché

and the salad of boiled beef and lentils are equally delicious. Exemplary Beaujolais from Dubœuf, impersonal service.

A la carte: 160-250 F. Menu: 150 F (weekdays lunch and Sat., wine incl.).

La Timonerie

35, quai de la Tournelle
43 25 44 42
Closed Sun., Mon., 1 wk. in Feb. & last wk. of Aug. Open until 10:30 p.m. Air cond.

La Timonerie is a handsome, lively little establishment taken over and redecorated a few years ago by Philippe de Givenchy, a disciple of Senderens and Chibois. Givenchy's technical precision is coupled with a knack for harmonizing flavors, as you will discover when you taste his potato and chèvre tart napped in chive cream, his freshwater perch with crisp fried cabbage and celery, or spiced crab with an orange brunoise. The tarte au chocolat is one of several enchanting desserts. Short, oft-changing menu, nice little wine cellar, attractive set lunch.

A la carte: 350-450 F. Menu: 185 F (lunch only).

La Tour d'Argent

15-17, quai de la Tournelle
43 54 23 31,
fax 44 07 12 04
Closed Mon. Open until 10 p.m. Private room: 60. Valet parking.

We hope the sight of those sweet little ducks and drakes bobbing on the Seine between the Ile Saint-Louis and your panoramic table doesn't take away your appetite for the best canard aux cerises you'll ever taste—a pressed duck paddling in a deeply flavorful sauce, which has been the house specialty for 100 years. Chef Manuel Martinez, now a Tour

d'Argent veteran, knows better than anyone how to work wonders with the web-footed fowl.

Don't expect any audacious novelties or revolutionary changes in the Tour d'Argent tradition. Claude Terrail, eternally youthful, charming and diplomatic, has chosen his field of honor once and for all. And what better aide-de-camp than Martinez, battle-tested at the Relais Louis XIII? Within the limits of a "noble"—but not boring—repertoire, he imbues his creations with such flavor and harmony that you might be too delightedly dazed to notice the astronomical bill. But then, who notices the bill when it comes time to buy the Rolls and the diamonds?

You can easily waste 400 francs on a ghastly meal elsewhere, and though it might seem galling to spend four or five times that here, you will never call into question the excellence of the repast. It might feature luscious, large prawns with tiny cèpes, tantalizing truffled brouillade sauce Périgourdine, lobster-stuffed cabbage escorted by lobster ravioli, or a voluptuously tender double veal chop. And what of the *nec plus ultra* of ice creams, the Tour d'Argent's vanilla or pistachio? A year from now you won't have forgotten it! Nor will you forget the sight of dusk's golden light on Notre-Dame, or the fantastical cityscape spread out before you.

The fabled cellar, skilfully stewarded by David Ridgway, harbors bottles with prices in four and even five digits—but it also holds unsung marvels tariffed at less than 200 francs. And do remember: the lunch menu costs only 375 F—put aside a franc and a centime each day for a year and there you are!

A la carte: 1,000 F and up.

Menu: 375 F (weekdays lunch and Sat.).

Chez Toutoune

5, rue de Pontoise
43 26 56 81
Closed Mon. lunch, Sun. & Aug. Open until 10:45 p.m. Terrace dining.

Owner Colette Dejean, alias Toutoune, has put her restaurant right. Charming service and a delicious prix-fixe menu which offers fragrant soups, tasty terrines, a hearty sauté of duck and artichokes, chocolate soufflé and riz au caramel. To drink, there's a perfectly decent wine from Roussillon priced at just 65 francs. Lively atmosphere.

A la carte: 220-320 F. Menu: 179 F.

6th arrondissement

Allard

41, rue St-André-des-Arts
43 26 48 23
Closed Sat., Sun., Dec. 23-Jan. 3 & Aug. Open until 9:45 p.m. Private room: 25. Air cond.

Fernande Allard would still feel right at home in the enchanting establishment that she and her husband founded several decades ago. For practically nothing has changed, from the decor to the handwritten daily menu of escargots, turbot au beurre blanc, pigeon aux petits pois, duck with olives, and gâteau moka for dessert. The charm and chic of Allard are alive, but the wines are overpriced and the bill often overblown.

A la carte: 370-420 F. Menu: 250 F (lunch only).

> *Remember to call ahead to reserve your table, and please, if you cannot honor your reservation, be courteous and let the restaurant know.*

Le Bélier

L'Hôtel
13, rue des Beaux-Arts
43 25 27 22,
fax 43 25 64 81
Open daily until 12:30 a.m. Private room: 80. Air cond.

The picturesque, theatrical setting features a tree trunk, a fountain, a huge bouquet of flowers and an elegant, cosmopolitan clientele. The chef acquits himself well of a rather classic repertoire, occasionally leavened with a spark of imagination (salmon sauté with eggplant caviar, sea bream touched with ginger, duck confit with tapenade). The à la carte offerings are considerably more tempting (and costly) than the dishes that make up the prosaic set menus.
A la carte: 300-400 F. Menus: 150 F (lunch only), 170 F (dinner only).

12/20 Bistro de la Grille

14, rue Mabillon
43 54 16 87
Open daily until 12:30 a.m. Terrace dining.

Fine shellfish at reasonable prices (offered at dinner only), appealing prix-fixe menus, and good home-style dishes (skate, pot-au-feu) attract a handsome Left-Bank crowd to this bustling bistro hung with photographs of early film stars.
Menu: 140 F (dinner only).

12/20 Brasserie Lutétia

Hôtel Lutétia
23, rue de Sèvres
49 54 46 76,
fax 49 54 46 64
Open daily until midnight. Air cond. Valet parking.

The no-nonsense country cooking is prepared with considerable finesse in the same kitchens as Le Paris. Superb seafood is available except for two months in summer. Brunch on Sundays.
A la carte: 200-250 F. Menus: 95 F (weekdays lunch and Sat.), 135 F (weekdays and Sat.), 165 F.

 Jacques Cagna

14, rue des Grands-Augustins
43 26 49 39,
fax 43 54 54 48
Closed Sat. (except dinner twice a month), Sun., 3 wks. in Aug. & Christmas. Open until 10:30 p.m. Private room: 10. Air cond.

The roaring success of his bistro annex has not distracted Jacques Cagna from the business of pleasing the moneyed, cosmopolitan gourmets who prefer to dine at the "old original". The witty, charming Cagna spends most of his time presiding over the prettiest tavern in old Paris, with its ancient oak beams and woodwork, its Flemish still lifes and discreet lighting. The atmosphere is so elegant you might think twice before raising a fork. Happily, this is not a museum. Food, drink, and—measured—merriment are right at home.

Jacques Cagna's guardian angel is his sister Anny, who glides among the tables dispensing smiles and good counsel. She will not, however, toss angel-dust in your eyes: there is nothing Jacques Cagna likes less than foolery (except, perhaps, fusty cooking). He is at once a Left-Bank sophisticate and a peasant, attached to the solid, lusty fare of his native Normandy. We used to think his classic training had bred in him a secret preference for dark, murky sauces—but we see that in fact his "jus" are wonderfully clean, light and sapid. Take for example the deeply flavorful rabbit essence he drizzles over a sea bass meunière with puréed celery and fried celery leaves, or the polished-but-rustic oyster-stuffed brill bathed in a reduction of watercress, or a sensational consommé simmered slowly with a divinely tender veal shin and perfumed with foie gras. And what happy harmony Sauternes and honey bring to the Brittany pigeon with carrots and sweet onions! Or the sauce of shallots, bone marrow, and limpid meat juices that enhances an incomparable Angus rib steak, aged for a full three wks. and served up with a satisfying side dish of puréed potatoes. Finish with the delightful baba au kirsch topped with whipped cream and cherries, and your palate will have known an hour of unalloyed bliss... To drink? of course there are ruinously expensive bottles of Côte-Rôtie, Hermitage, Burgundy or Bordeaux. On the other hand, one need not smash one's piggy bank to feast on Cagna's astonishingly good fixed-price lunch menu.
A la carte: 600-900 F. Menus: 260 F (weekdays lunch only).

12/20 Le Caméléon

6, rue de Chevreuse
43 20 63 43
Closed Sun., Mon. & Aug. Open until 10:30 p.m.

An archetypal Montparnasse bistro dripping with memories and bustling with lively patrons, Le Caméléon serves uncomplicated, homey fare (braised veal with fresh pasta, codfish Provençal, pear clafoutis). Charming service and an excellent list of growers' wines.
A la carte: 160-230 F.

 Aux Charpentiers

10, rue Mabillon
43 26 30 05,
fax 46 33 07 98
Closed Sun. & holidays. Open until 11:30 p.m. Terrace dining.

Pierre Bardèche has opened a new fish restaurant across the street (L'Ecaille de PCB) but continues to serve his

renowned home-style cuisine in this former carpenters' guild hall. The menu revolves around full-flavored daily specials such as codfish aïoli, stuffed cabbage and veal sauté, accompanied by pleasant little wines.
A la carte: 180-260 F.

 Le Chat Grippé
87, rue d'Assas
43 54 70 00
Closed Sat. lunch & Mon. Open until 10:30 p.m. Air cond.
Chef Eric Thore, trained at Taillevent, cooks in a classic vein to which he lends many a judicious personal touch. Seafood is his strong suit—witness the delicious fresh codfish minestrone, casserole of shellfish, oysters and crustaceans with ginger. But this establishment's roots in the Quercy region are commemorated with warm foie gras with celery and apples, honeyed roast pigeon with spices, cabécous goat cheese and a magnificent gratin aux poires. The robust red wines of Cahors hold a place of honor on the wine list.
A la carte: 320-450 F. Menus: 180 F (weekdays lunch only), 325 F (dinner, except holidays).

12/20 Dominique
19, rue Bréa
43 27 08 80
Closed July 17-Aug. 16. Open until 10:30 p.m. Private room: 40. Air cond.
This famed Montparnasse Russian troika—take-out shop/bar/restaurant—steadfastly refuses perestroika when it comes to cuisine and decor: purple-and-gold walls, steaming samovars, and goulash Tolstoi. Delicious smoked salmon, bortsch, and blinis. And vodka, of course, both Russian or Polish.
A la carte: 240-310 F. Menu: 154 F.

11/20 Drugstore Saint-Germain
149, bd St-Germain
42 22 92 50
Open daily until 1:30 a.m. Air cond.
The reliable, unpretentious cuisine (salads, grilled sausage, hamburgers) is served in a handsome, comfortable setting designed—wouldn't you know it—by Slavik.
A la carte: 200 F. Menu: 78 F.

 L'Ecaille de PCB
Pierre et Colette Bardèche
5, rue Mabillon
43 26 73 70,
fax 46 33 07 98
Closed Sat. lunch & Sun. Open until 11 p.m. Private room: 10. Air cond. Valet parking.
Pierre Bardèche, owner of the renowned Aux Charpentiers across the way, recently bought this old Basque *auberge* and transformed it into one of the city's better fish restaurants. Simple dishes, fresh ingredients and an oft-changing menu spell success. Try the oysters, the baked fish assortment, or the fine fish soup, as well as Brittany lobsters offered here at very low prices. Short but shrewdly chosen wine list.
A la carte: 300-350 F. Menu: 125 F.

11/20 Guy
6, rue Mabillon
43 54 87 61
Dinner only (and lunch Sat.). Closed Sun. & Aug. 8-31. Open until 12:45 a.m. Air cond.
This is a Brazilian dinner club with a festive decor and atmosphere (guitars, killer batidas, bossa-nova...). The cuisine is modest, but portions are generous.
A la carte: 220-320 F. Menus: 97 F (Tues.-Thurs. dinner only), 188 F (Sat.lunch).

12/20 Chez Henri
16, rue Princesse
46 33 51 12
Closed Sun. Open until 11:30 p.m.
Regulars flock here for the sure-value bistro cooking by chef Henri Poulat: calf's liver with creamed onions, farmbred chicken in vinegar, roast lamb, apple clafoutis.
A la carte: 100 F. Menu: 160 F.

11/20 La Hulotte
29, rue Dauphine
46 33 75 92
Closed Sun., Mon. & Aug. Open until 10:15 p.m.
The proof is in the pudding: Bernard Güys is mad about desserts, especially chocolate mousse (he makes it in six delicious variations). Start your meal with tasty grilled meats, coq au vin and other traditional dishes, made with love and generously apportioned.
A la carte: 180 F. Menu: 150 F (wine incl.).

12/20 Joséphine
Chez Dumonet
117, rue du Cherche-Midi
45 48 52 40,
fax 42 84 06 83
Closed Sat., Sun., July 3-31 & Dec. 18-27. Open until 10:30 p.m.
Joséphine is a right honorable early 1900s bistro frequented by prominent jurists, journalists and an intellectual theater crowd. The chummy atmosphere is animated by owner Jean Dumonet and fueled by the perennially popular cuisine, a heady mix of bourgeois and Southwestern fare. Humble herrings with warm potatoes at 59 francs flank truffle feuilleté at 530 F; leg of lamb with beans, or leeks in vinaigrette vie with truffled andouillette in flaky pastry for one's attention. Appropriately, the wine cellar abounds in

Bordeaux, both modest and mighty.
A la carte: 300-400 F. Menu: 170 F (lunch only, wine incl.).

Lapérouse

51, quai des Grands-Augustins
43 26 68 04,
fax 43 26 99 39
Closed Sun., Sat. & Mon. lunch, Aug. Open until 10:30 p.m. Private room: 50. Air cond.
For years we felt a pinch at our heartstrings each time we strolled along the Left-Bank quais past Lapérouse. A landmark restaurant, founded in 1766, it long numbered among the best eating places in Paris. Here Belle Epoque *cocottes* flirted—and more—in ravishing little private salons (and used the diamonds they earned with their naughtiness to scratch their names in the mirrors). But the once-noted cuisine slipped badly in the 1970s, and gourmets abandoned Lapérouse.
What a delight, then, to learn that new owners have restored the decor to its former luster, and put a brilliant young chef in the kitchen. Gabriel Biscaye, late of the Royal Monceau, has a rare gift for combining tastes and textures in unusual but utterly satisfying ways. A glance at the new *carte* reveals a host of surprising, appetising dishes like tête de veau caramélisée aux huîtres, assiette de poissons à l'encre de seiche, rognon de veau rôti à la moutarde de violette, and a rich array of desserts. Lapérouse is once again an enchanting choice for a romantic dinner by the Seine.
A la carte: 400-600 F. Menus: 250 F (lunch only), 370 F, 480 F.

> *The prices in this guide reflect what establishments were charging at press time.*

12/20 Lipp

151, bd St-Germain
45 48 53 91,
fax 45 44 33 20
Open daily until 1 a.m. Air cond.
The interregnum is over: Lipp has lost both the legendary Roger Cazes and his heir-apparent, Michel Cazes. The new *patron* is an interior architect named Perrichon. Despite the often disappointing food (choucroute, bœuf gros sel) and the cruel whims of fashion, this glossy turn-of-the-century brasserie still manages to serve some 400 to 500 clients a day. Of course, the clientele is not what it was, though one still catches sight of a powerful politico or a beauty queen ensconced at a ground-floor table, admiring the gorgeous decor.
A la carte: 270-320 F.

11/20 La Lozère

4, rue Hautefeuille
43 54 26 64
Closed Sun., Mon., Aug. & 1 wk. at Christmas. Open until 10:30 p.m.
You can taste bracing air of the rural Lozère region in the warm winter soups, herbed sausages, and pâtés served in this charming old-Paris establishment, a combination regional tourist-office, crafts shop and restaurant.
A la carte: 150 F. Menus: 82 F (lunch only, wine incl.), 106 F, 129 F.

La Marlotte

55, rue du Cherche-Midi
45 48 86 79
Closed Sat., Sun. & Aug. Open until 11 p.m. Private room: 9. Terrace dining. Air cond.
This old timbered restaurant's pleasant rustic setting is softened by madras upholstery and candlelight in the evening. The cuisine runs to hearty country flavors meticulously prepared. Try the homemade terrines, the veal

kidney with mustard sauce and the delectable chocolate gâteau. Crowded both at lunch and dinner, often with the smart set.
A la carte: 220-280 F.

Le Muniche

22, rue G.-Apollinaire
46 33 62 09
Open daily until 1:30 a.m. Terrace dining. Air cond.
In its new location (just around the corner from its former site) across from the Church of Saint-Germain-des-Prés, the Muniche remains the liveliest, most feverishly overcrowded of Parisian brasseries. The Layrac brothers and their attentive, smiling staff will regale you with oysters, choucroute garnished with veal knuckle, thick-sliced calf's liver and grilled pigs' ears, washed down with perfect little *pots* of red, white and rosé.
A la carte: 210-260 F. Menu: 140 F.

11/20 Le Parc aux Cerfs

50, rue Vavin
43 54 87 83
Closed Aug. Open daily until 11 p.m. Air cond.
This was one of the Montparnasse neighbourhood's first "neo-bistros"—with revisited Lyonnais specialties served in a jovial, youthful atmosphere. Inexpensive lunch menu, and good Rhône wines (by the bottle or carafe).
A la carte: 180-200 F. Menus: 92 F, 120 F.

Le Paris

Hôtel Lutétia
45, bd Raspail
49 54 46 90,
fax 49 54 46 64
Closed Sat., Sun. & Aug. Open until 10 p.m. Air cond. Valet parking.
Philippe Renard, the young chef, still can't decide whether his style should be classic or inventive, but delicious dishes like the glorious crab and

green cabbage ravioli attest to his progress and have won back the two toques he earned at the Hôtel Scribe. If only the decor wasn't so dreary and the wine list so depressingly expensive, this restaurant would enjoy the popularity the food and pleasant service deserve.

A la carte: 450-550 F. Menus: 295 F (lunch only), 395 F (dinner only).

10/20 Le Petit Mabillon

6, rue Mabillon
43 54 08 41

Closed Sun., Mon. lunch & 1 wk. at Christmas. Open daily until 11 p.m. Terrace dining.

The good Italian home cooking features two daily pasta choices (fusilli, lasagne). Picturesque bistro decor, garden court.

A la carte: 180-200 F. Menu: 72 F.

10/20 Le Petit Saint-Benoît

4, rue St-Benoît
42 60 27 92

Closed Sat. & Sun. Open daily until 10 p.m. Terrace dining.

An unfading coachman's eating-house whose crowded pavement terrace is a refuge for fashionable fast-food haters in search of cheap eats: hachis Parmentier, streaky bacon with lentils.

A la carte: 100 F.

Le Petit Zinc

11, rue St-Benoît
46 33 51 66

Open daily until 1 a.m. Terrace dining. Air cond.

Le Petit Zinc shares the same kitchen and country cooking as the equally popular Le Muniche next door, but with an emphasis on Southwestern specialties: oysters, shellfish, poule au pot, thick-sliced calf's liver, duck thighs with apples. In summer the animated terrace spreads its fluttering tablecloths across the side-

walk.

A la carte: 210-260 F. Menu: 140 F.

La Petite Cour

8, rue Mabillon
43 26 52 26

Open daily until 11:30 p.m. Garden dining.

Owners and chefs may come and go, but the discreet charm of this old restaurant with its garden-court and splashing fountain remains. The dining room's Napoleon III decor is equally appealing and the cuisine, though not terribly ambitious, is fresh and generous: skate with cabbage, beef stew with carrots. Tasty, low-priced Saumur and Valençay wines.

A la carte: 270-370 F. Menus: 160 F (lunch only), 180 F (dinner only).

11/20 Polidor

41, rue Monsieur-le-Prince
43 26 95 34

Open daily until 12:30 a.m. (except Sun. 11 p.m.).

Authentic country fare (boudin with mashed potatoes, rabbit in mustard) and attractive little wines are served in a dining room that has not changed an iota in a hundred years.

A la carte: 100 F. Menus: 50 F (weekdays lunch only), 100 F.

Princesse

Castel
15, rue Princesse
43 26 90 22

Dinner only. Closed Sun. & Aug. Open until 5 a.m. Private room: 40. Air cond.

In 1992 owners Jean and Yolande Castel celebrated 30 years of undisputed success for their exclusive club-restaurant. Unfortunately, if you aren't a member you probably won't get in, and will therefore have to settle for imagining the Belle Epoque decor and chef

Didier Aupetit's succulent home-style cuisine, which features the likes of skate with cabbage and boned saddle of rabbit aux fines herbes.

A la carte: 500-800 F (at Le Foyer: 250-350 F).

11/20 Le Procope

13, rue de l'Ancienne-Comédie
43 26 99 20

Open daily until 1 a.m. Private room: 80. Terrace dining.

The capital's oldest café was recently restored to its original seventeenth-century splendor and now serves good, simple brasserie fare to a clientele in which tourists predominate. Try the oysters (reasonably priced), merlan Colbert, and calf's head.

A la carte: 200-350 F. Menus: 98 F (lunch only), 289 F (wine incl.).

Relais Louis XIII

8, rue des Grands-Augustins
43 26 75 96,
fax 44 07 07 80

Closed Mon. lunch, Sun. & July 24-Aug. 24. Open until 10:15 p.m. Private room: 22. Air cond.

Louis XIII was proclaimed King of France in this luxurious seventeenth-century tavern whose beams, polished paneling, and time-worn stones groan with history. The cuisine may not be inspired, but it is reliably rich and classic: lobster fricassée, sole and prawns with coriander, and truffled filet de bœuf. In addition to the stupendous and shockingly expensive 1934 Latour (8,750 francs) or 1921 Quarts de Chaume (2,000 francs), the wine cellar also boasts a few accessibly priced bottlings.

A la carte: 400-500 F. Menu: 240 F (lunch only).

The prices in this guide reflect what establishments were charging at press time.

La Rôtisserie d'en Face

2, rue Christine
43 26 40 98
Closed Sun. Open until 11 p.m. (Mon-Thurs.), 11:30 p.m. (Fri-Sat). Air cond.

Jacques Cagna's spiffy annex with its single-price menu (160 francs) encountered immediate success with Parisians hungry for rousing bistro fare at clement prices. Start off a satisfying meal with crisp, deep-fried smelts or ravioli stuffed with escargots, then segue into a savory civet of hog jowls and carrots or farm-raised Challans chicken with mashed potatoes, and finish up with an Alsatian apple tart. Whatever you choose, you'll find a frisky, inexpensive wine to accompany it from among the twenty or so on offer. Rumor has it that another Rôtisserie is in the planning stages for the seventeenth arrondissement.
Menu: 180 F.

12/20 La Rotonde

105, bd Montparnasse
43 26 68 84
Open daily until 1 a.m. Terrace dining. Air cond.

Along with La Coupole, Le Dôme, and Le Select, La Rotonde belongs to the pantheon of Montparnasse brasseries. No earthshaking food, but the scallop salad with coriander dressing is delicate and fresh, the steak "Prince Albert" (with wine sauce and potato cake) delicious, and the Berthillon sorbets splendid, of course.
A la carte: 250-330 F. Menu: 165 F.

11/20 Chez Claude Sainlouis

Le Golfe Juan
27, rue du Dragon
45 48 29 68
Closed Sat. dinner, Sun., Aug., 2 wks at Easter & 2 wks at Christmas. Open daily until 11 p.m. Air cond.

Reliable salads and steaks are served here in an amusing, theatrical decor.
Menu: 200 F (wine and dessert incl.).

12/20 La Table de Fès

5, rue Sainte-Beuve
45 48 07 22
Dinner only. Closed Sun. & Aug. 10-26. Open until 12:15 a.m.

The owners have changed, the chef has not: Zohra continues to turn out authentic pastillas, couscous, and tajines as she has for the past 25 years. Fès can get crowded and close in the evening.
A la carte: 200-250 F.

 ## Yugaraj

14, rue Dauphine
43 26 44 91
Closed Mon. lunch. Open until 11 p.m. Private room: 18. Air cond.

Yugaraj's out-of-the-ordinary Indian cuisine is served in a pleasant, spotless setting reminiscent of a native temple. The generous and warming specialties such as tandoori lamb are flanked by rather disappointing samosas and pastries. Well-chosen wine list. Interesting game dishes in season.
A la carte: 260-300 F. Menus: 130 F (lunch only), 180 F, 220 F.

7th arrondissement

12/20 Chez les Anges

54, bd de Latour-Maubourg
47 05 89 86,
fax 45 56 03 84
Closed Sun. dinner. Open until 10:30 p.m. Private room: 15. Air cond.

Former owner Armand Monassier, a winegrower, continues to supply this comfortable Burgundian restaurant with barrels of his delicious Rully. To accompany them ever-reliable chef Bernard Labrosse trots out his predictable roster of classic ham in parsley aspic, coq au vin, and rosy, thick-sliced calf's liver. The atmosphere and setting are refined. Splendid Burgundy wine list, regular clientele studded with senators and deputies.
A la carte: 400-500 F. Menus: 320 F (wine incl.), 230 F.

 ## Antoine et Antoinette

16, av. Rapp
45 51 75 61
Closed Sat. & Sun. Annual closings not available. Open until 10 p.m. Terrace dining.

Chef Jean-Claude Pernot has no quarrel with classic cuisine, and in the best tradition offers a winter menu and a summer menu. The dependable quality of his cooking accounts for the success of his cushy little restaurant, which sparkles with fine silver, crystal, and lovely linens. We recommend the calmars en escabèche, the honeyed roast pigeon, the fish tartare, and kidneys with mustard. Modest bottlings available for around 80 francs.
A la carte: 220-320 F. Menu: 160 F.

 ## Arpège

Alain Passard
84, rue de Varenne
45 51 47 33,
fax 44 18 98 39
Closed Sun. lunch & Sat. Open until 10:30 p.m. Private room: 14. Air cond.

The 220-franc lunch menu is so outstanding that the waiters seem to want to keep it all to themselves. You must ask for it specifically or wind up ordering à la carte—not a bad thing really, as Arpège's stellar young chef Alain Passard has earned his four toques for far more than a fine prix-fixe meal. Allow us to harp on for a moment: Passard began his career in Reims under Gérard Boyer, then worked as an assistant to Senderens at this same address when it housed L'Archestrate. After proving himself at the Duc d'Enghien, and later at the Carlton in Brussels, he returned here as owner.

At age 38, Passard is a virtuoso. Light though his touch may be, you will never catch him indulging in legerdemain. His inventiveness and imagination are always precisely controlled. Passard's compositions, whether variations on well-known themes (sweetbreads with chestnuts and truffles; saddle of hare with walnuts and cèpes), or new symphonies of tastes (crab with mustard butter and cabbage; scallops with leeks and garlic oil), are uniformly harmonious. We single out the John Dory baked with bay leaves inserted under the skin: a masterpiece. How to sum up the secret of Passard's success in a word or two? He is blessed with the touch of the master which pares away superfluities to reveal flavors in all their brilliant clarity. And now, in addition to his fine wine cellar, proven staff, and adoring public (he ministers to many in the neighborhood's ministries), Passard finally possesses decent kitchens and a sleek, sophisticated setting in tune with his symphonic cuisine!

A la carte: 550-900 F. Menus: 260 F (weekdays lunch and holidays), 350 F (lunch only), 590 F, 690 F.

 Bellecour
22, rue Surcouf
45 51 46 93
Closed Sat. (except dinner Oct.-May), Sun. & Aug. 10-30. Open until 10:30 p.m. Terrace dining. Air cond.

A new chef has stepped into the shoes of Stéphane Pruvot,

the star pupil of Lorain at Joigny, now off to seek his fortune in the Marquesas. Denis Croset will henceforth oversee the preparation of the traditional *cuisine lyonnaise* that has made Gérald Goutagny's establishment—a vintage bistro with a vaguely colonial setting—a perennial favorite with the well-heeled locals. The ethereal desserts are the handiwork of Gérald Goutagny himself (a former pastry chef), and are among the best to be found in Paris.

A la carte: 330-480 F. Menus: 180 F (lunch only), 380 F.

11/20 Le Bistrot de Breteuil
3, pl. de Breteuil
45 67 07 27
Open daily until 10:30 p.m. Terrace dining.

An old corner café converted into an up-to-date bistro, the Breteuil serves traditional offerings such as foie gras, smoked salmon, and escargots aux noisettes. The fixed-price menu is a remarkably good deal (it includes an apéritif and coffee as well as wine). Pleasant terrace.

Menu: 165 F (wine and coffe incl.).

 La Boule d'Or
13, bd de Latour-Maubourg
47 05 50 18
Closed Sat. lunch & Mon. Open until 10 p.m. Private room: 25. Air cond.

Prim and proper provincial decor, a steady clientele, and a charming proprietor: the Boule rolls on. François Le Quillec, the new chef, complicates some dishes unduly, but we have only praise for his truffled young guinea fowl. Stiffish prices.

A la carte: 300-400 F. Menus: 195 F, 360 F.

 Le Bourdonnais
113, av. de La Bourdonnais
47 05 47 96,
fax 45 51 09 29
Open daily until 11:30 p.m. Private room: 25. Air cond.

Owner Micheline Coat earns this year's "Warmest Welcome" award. Never before has her cheerfully redecorated restaurant been so crowded with the chic and powerful. Success has been borne on a south wind, for the keen flavors of Provence pervade chef Philippe Bardau's short but appetizing menu. A disciple of Outhier and Maximin, Bardou excels with his tuna gazpacho with grilled artichokes, his sea bass and fennel with a touch of tomato, a pigeon sandwich with celery and Parmesan, a rabbit fillet with cabbage and bacon, and a lush fig gratin with almond cream. The fixed-price offerings at lunch (220 francs) and dinner (280 francs) are outstanding values.

A la carte: 350-500 F. Menus: 220 F (lunch only, wine incl.), 280 F (dinner only), 380 F.

 Clémentine
62, av. Bosquet
45 51 41 16
Closed Sat. lunch, Sun. & Aug. 15-30, Christmas & Dec.31-Jan. 1. Open until 10:30 p.m. Private room: 25. Terrace dining. Air cond.

Michèle and Bernard Przybyl (you're right, that's Polish) pay homage to the cuisine of their respective/adopted homes: Languedoc (duck cassoulet) and Brittany (skate with capers, lobster à la nage). The rosy decor is dandy, but the tables are still a bit too close for comfort. Pretty people, modest prices and an ever-expanding wine cellar.

A la carte: 230-300 F. Menu: 168 F.

UNE HEURE ET DEMIE PASSÉE DANS VOTRE ÉTABLISSEMENT EST LE PREMIER DES PRIVILEGES. LE SECOND EST D'Y BOIRE DE L'EAU D'EVIAN.

EVIAN. L'EAU MINERALE DES MEILLEURES TABLES DU MONDE.

CHÂTEAU CHEVAL BLANC

PREMIER GRAND CRU CLASSÉ "A"
SAINT-ÉMILION

Aux Délices de Szechuen

40, av. Duquesne
43 06 22 55
Closed Mon., Aug. 2-22 & Dec. 24-28. Open until 10:30 p.m. Terrace dining. Air cond.
Fresh and tasty Chinese specialties are served here with flair. The chef has a ten-year track record of proven reliability. Try the Peking duck (in three courses), the grilled won tons served with a ginger-scented sauce, and the beef fillet with orange peel. Elegant decor, excellent service.
A la carte: 180 F. Menu: 96 F (weekdays and Sat.).

Duquesnoy

6, av. Bosquet
47 05 96 78,
fax 44 18 90 57
Closed Sat. lunch, Sun. & Aug. Open until 10:30 p.m. Air cond.
The Best and the Brightest (in business and TV) flock to Jean-Paul Duquesnoy's comfortable, posh little restaurant, filling both lunch and dinner sittings year round. The light touch extends from the decor and service (directed by the discreet and charming Françoise Duquesnoy) to the cuisine. Jean-Paul steers a skillful course between classicism and novelty, pleasing his elegant patrons with turbot and bacon bathed in a rich veal jus, Bresse chicken in a sauce enlivened with sherry vinegar, or sardines accompanied by lasagne layered with black-olive purée. Luscious desserts include honey-nougat ice cream, walnut crème brûlée, and an assortment of milk and bitter chocolates. Exquisite wines from the Loire, Burgundy and Côtes-du-Rhône swell the rather stiff à la carte prices. Excellent prix-fixe lunch menu.
A la carte: 500-650 F. Menu: 250 F (weekdays lunch only).

Ecaille et Plume

25, rue Duvivier
45 55 06 72
Closed Sat. lunch & Sun. Open until 10:30 p.m. (upon reservation). Private room: 10. Air cond.
A master matchmaker, Marie Naël puts heart and soul into her innovative cuisine. Seasonal game specialties and seafood are her strong points: try the briny salade océane, or foie gras en terrine with potatoes, or, in its short season, Scottish grouse flambéed with single-malt whisky. The decor is cozy, the wines well chosen but oh-so-expensive!
A la carte: 280-400 F.

La Ferme Saint-Simon

6, rue Saint-Simon
45 48 35 74,
fax 40 49 07 31
Closed Sat. lunch, Sun. & 1st 3 wks. of Aug. Open until 10:15 pm. Private room: 20. Air cond.
Parliamentarians, publishing magnates and food-loving CEOs savor succulent specialties in the intimate little dining rooms of "the farm" (rustic only in name). Owner Francis Vandenhende dashes like the proverbial chicken from La Ferme to his other, equally renowned restaurant, Le Manoir de Paris in the seventeenth arrondissement. The cuisine here is generous and traditional, but with a modern touch: homemade duck foie gras, brill with veal jus, a hearty tourte filled with oxtail and beef jowls, caramelized almond pastry, and bitter-chocolate tart. Big and little appetites—and thin and thick wallets—will be equally satisfied.

A la carte: 300-400 F. Menu: 170 F (lunch only).

11/20 Aux Fins Gourmets

213, bd St-Germain
42 22 06 57
Closed Sun., Mon. lunch & 1 wk. at Christmas. Open until 10 p.m. Terrace dining.
Hearty Basque/Béarnaise cuisine served in a lively family-run bistro frequented by a smart old-Paris crowd. The charcuteries and confits are good, but skip the desserts. Nice choice of wines from the Southwest.
A la carte: 180 F.

12/20 La Flamberge

12, av. Rapp
47 05 91 37,
fax 47 23 60 98
Closed Sat. lunch, Sun., Dec. 22-31 & Aug. 10-20. Open until 10:30 p.m. Private room: 24. Air cond. Valet parking.
The prices are so steep in this pretty little establishment swathed in rosy chintz that soon only millionaires and big-spending senators will be able to afford them. Perfect oysters, grilled sea bass with fennel (250 francs, if you please!), baked sea bream. Well-chosen bottlings in a wide range of prices.
A la carte: 350-500 F. Menu: 230 F.

11/20 La Fontaine de Mars

129, rue St-Dominique
47 05 46 44
Closed Sun., Dec. 25 & Jan. 1. Open daily until 11 p.m. Terrace dining.
Checked tablecloths, low prices and hearty country fare are the perennial attractions of

---

The A la carte restaurant prices given are for a complete three-course meal for one, including a half-bottle of modest wine and service. Menu prices are for a complete fixed-price meal for one, excluding wine (unless otherwise noted).

this modest neighborhood eating-house (andouillette, duck fricassée, Cahors at around 50 francs a bottle).

A la carte: 200 F (wine incl.). Menu: 85 F (lunch only).

12/20 Chez Françoise
Aérogare des Invalides
47 05 49 03
Closed Sun. & May 1. Open until midnight. Terrace dining. Valet parking.

Chez Françoise is an immense subterranean hall decorated in a pseudo-tropical style that has somehow retained its charm, despite 30 years of wear and tear. This is a favorite haunt of hungry Parliamentarians. They blithely ignore the good fixed-price offering and opt instead for the pricier, terribly conservative à la carte fish dishes, grilled lamb and foie gras.

A la carte: 250-300 F. Menu: 160 F.

Les Glénan
54, rue de Bourgogne
45 51 61 09
Closed w.-e. (except Sun. dinner) & Aug. Open until 10:30 p.m. Private room: 20. Air cond.

Fresh seafood is the Glénan's strongest suit: John Dory with garlic cream sauce or red mullet with mascarpone. The new owner has revamped the decor, and put capable Thierry Bourdonnais (who earned 15/20 at his last post) in the kitchen.

A la carte: 300-350 F. Menus: 150 F (lunch only, wine incl.), 240 F (dinner only), 350 F.

Le Divellec
107, rue de l'Université
45 51 91 96,
fax 45 51 31 75
Closed Sun., Mon., Dec. 24-Jan. 4 & Aug. Open until 10 p.m. Air cond. No pets. Valet parking.

France's *Présidents de la République*—past and present—honor Jacques Le

Divellec with their presence, as do press moguls, TV icons and other high-toned patrons who fill this "yacht-club" dining room noon and night. But let's be frank: it's not the big-wigs that make this establishment great: it's the fish! We think Jacques Le Divellec is now at the top of his form: he bowled us over on a recent visit with his sublime shrimp in walnut oil with truffle bâtonnets, his flavourful smoked whiting lavished with herbs, and his delectable braised sole napped in a sensational fish-fumet-based hollandaise enhanced with Pouilly-Fuissé and fresh cream. The desserts (vacherin à l'orange, strawberry chaud-froid) are better than ever. Pangloss would be proud: the service is efficient, the wine steward shrewd, and the hostess smiling. In short, all is for the best at Le Divellec.

A la carte: 650-950 F. Menus: 270 F and 370 F (lunch only).

Chez Marius
5, rue de Bourgogne
45 51 79 42
Closed Sat., Sun. Dec. 24-Jan. 2 & Aug. 5-30. Open until 10:30 p.m. Air cond.

Restaurant pro Michel Perrodo took over this long-lived establishment a few years back, and has no intention of fiddling with a successful formula. Still present on the menu are the famed "bouillabaisse Marius", succulent shellfish dishes and tasty standbys like grilled red mullet or roast saddle of lamb. Mixed crowd, with a sprinkling of Parliamentarians. Superb wine cellar.

A la carte: 370-520 F. Menu: 180 F.

Red toques signify modern cuisine; white toques signify traditional cuisine.

12/20 L'Œillade
10, rue St-Simon
42 22 01 60
Closed Sat. lunch & Sun. Open until 11 p.m. Air cond.

Things are looking up: the dynamic duo of Huclin and Molto, late of Chez Toutoune, have recently taken over this charming bistro. The prices are as reasonable as ever, the food hearty and unpretentious: mackerel with mustard, calf's liver with gratin dauphinois. Selected wines are available by the glass.

Menu: 145 F (except holidays).

Le Petit Laurent
38, rue de Varenne
45 48 79 64,
fax 42 66 68 59
Closed Sat. lunch, Sun. & 15 days in Aug. Open until 10:30 p.m. Private room: 16.

Hearty cuisine is served here in an ultraclassic, comfortable Louis XVI decor. Try the terrine of sweetbreads, the skate in truffled butter, or the roast sea bream with mango: you'll appreciate, as we do, their precise, clearly defined flavors. The cheerful M. Pommier is making an admirable effort to keep prices in line. In fact, his appetizing 175-franc menu is one of the best deals on the Left Bank! A perfectly decent Entre-Deux-Mers sells for just 98 francs.

A la carte: 250-300 F. Menu: 175 F (except holidays).

11/20 La Petite Chaise
36, rue de Grenelle
42 22 13 35
Open daily until 11 p.m.

This charming little eating-house has been in service since the days of Louis XIV (1680). Sit elbow-to-elbow with university students and publishing people and tuck into the hearty fixed-price menu (Baltic herrings, tripe baked with onions and white

wine, and so on).
Menu: 170 F (wine incl.).

10/20 Au Pied de Fouet
45, rue de Babylone
47 05 12 27
*Closed Sat. dinner, Sun., Aug. &
Dec. 24-Jan. 3. Open until 9 p.m.*
In an ancient and authentic
coachman's bistro, enjoy such
simple classics as nicely
seasoned lentil salad, blanquette de veau, poule au pot and
clafoutis.
A la carte: 100 F.

Le Récamier
4, rue Récamier
45 48 86 58,
fax 42 22 84 76
*Closed Sun. Open until
10:30 p.m. Private room: 15.
Garden dining. Air cond.*
Martin Cantegrit, the courtly
owner of this elegant Empire-
style establishment, has been
cheek by jowl with chef
Robert Chassat for over fifteen
years, a most felicitous union.
Burgundian classics (game
pâtés, jambon persillé, beef
bourguignon with fresh
tagliatelle) flank subtly lightened dishes (tiny scallops with
mushrooms, pan-fried tuna
with pesto sauce) and yummy
desserts. Cantegrit's farm
supplies the fresh produce. Le
Récamier's clientele—
politicos, publishers, and
media moguls—also enjoy
tapping the 100,000-bottle
cellar, surely one of the city's
best. In summer the
restaurant's lovely terrace
spills across a sheltered
pedestrian zone (for fume-free
outdoor dining).
A la carte: 500-600 F.

Chez Ribe
15, av. de Suffren
45 66 53 79
*Closed Sun., Dec. 24-Jan. 2 &
Aug. 8-30. Open until
10:30 p.m. Private room: 30.
Terrace dining.*
You can still eat here for not
much more than 200 francs,

including a Bordeaux *primeur*
or a tasty little white Saumur.
Granted, a 178-franc prix-fixe
meal is not—yet—any trick to
offer even in Paris, but chef
Pérès's oft-changing menu is
always delicious, well prepared and generously
apportioned. Our last visit
yielded a delicate shellfish
sauté, sautéed veal kidneys
with fresh pasta and a luscious
puff-pastry tart, all graciously
served in comfortable 1900-
style surroundings.
Menu: 178 F.

Tan Dinh
60, rue de Verneuil
45 44 04 84
*Closed Sun. & Aug. Open until
11 p.m. Private room: 30. Air
cond. No cards.*
Tan Dinh's huge wine list
(best Pomerols in Paris) has
few peers, even among the
city's top restaurants—some
say it outclasses the menu!
One almost suspects that for
the Vifian brothers, cuisine is
an afterthought, though it was
they who twenty years ago introduced Paris to the newest,
most refined and creative
Vietnamese fare. Though that
early thrill is gone, Robert Vifian acquits himself admirably
of such delicious dishes as a
fondant of steamed scallops,
langoustines with eggplant,
and subtle shrimp sautéed
with scallop coral. If one resists
the pricier temptations of the
wine list, a dinner here amid
the select and stylish Left-Bank
crowd need not lead to finan-
cial disaster.
A la carte: 300-400 F.

11/20 Thoumieux
79, rue St-Dominique
47 05 49 75
*Open daily until 0:30 a.m. Air
cond.*
A busy, successful bistro
where you can tuck into the
hearty classics of Auvergne
and the Southwest: terrines,
cassoulets, pigs' trotters, etc.

Don't overlook the fine calf's
head, or the cheap-and-cheer-
ful wine list. The dinner crowd
is surprisingly glossy.
A la carte: 180-200 F. Menu:
62 F.

Jules Verne
Tour Eiffel, 2nd floor
45 55 61 44,
fax 47 05 94 40
*Open daily until 10:30 p.m. Air
cond. No pets. Valet parking.*
Flash! As we go to press, we
learn that Alain Bariteau is flying off to the kitchens of
Maxim's at Roissy. Taking over
here is Alain Rex (a two-toque
chef from Strasbourg), whose
new menu will feature foie
gras de canard studded with
slivers of mild garlic, smoked
salmon wrapped in a layer of
crisp pastry, apple strudel escorted by a scoop of
gingerbread ice cream, and
cold dessert soup of fresh figs
and citrus fruit with dried-fig
ice cream. We can't wait to dig
in!
A la carte: 600-800 F.

Vin sur Vin
20, rue de Monttessuy
47 05 14 20
*Closed Sat. lunch, Sun. &
Mon., Aug. 15-Sep. 1 & Dec. 23-
Jan. 2. Open until 10 p.m.*
Former sommelier Patrice
Vidal has assembled a first-rate
cellar made up exclusively of
growers' wines, from which he
selects a few each week to sell
by the glass. The same infec-
tious enthusiasm inspires his
brother Marc to concoct inventive dishes that complement the wines: rabbit
sausage studded with
peanuts, monkfish brochette,
and scallops with citrus fruits.
Too bad the prices are high
and climbing, with no prix-fixe
relief in sight.
A la carte: 300-350 F.

> *Monday, like Sunday, is a day of
> rest for many shopkeepers.*

8th arrondissement

12/20 Al Ajami
58, rue François-Ier
42 25 38 44
Open daily until midnight. Terrace dining. Air cond. Valet parking.
Fortunately the menu's perfunctory French offerings are outnumbered by authentic dishes from the Lebanese highlands—assorted mezes, chawarma, keftedes and deliciously sticky pastries. The wines contribute a dash of local color to the refined, gray-and-blue dining room.
A la carte: 200-300 F. Menus: 99 F and 109 F (weekdays only), 119 F.

12/20 L'Alsace
39, av. des Champs-Elysées
43 59 44 24,
fax 42 89 06 62
Open daily 24 hours. Terrace dining. Air cond.
Since this lively brasserie never closes, one can go there any time at all to enjoy perfect oysters, delicious sauerkraut and the fresh white wines of Alsace.
A la carte: 250-300 F.

Les Ambassadeurs
Hôtel de Crillon
10, pl. de la Concorde
44 71 16 16,
fax 44 71 15 02
Open daily until 10:30 p.m. Private room: 120. Air cond. No pets. Valet parking.
The magnificent and intimidating dining room, rich in gold, marble and history, seems more fitting for an ambassadors' banquet than an intimate dinner or a joyous feast. Customers eat with their voice kept low and their elbows off the table, terrified someone will drop a fork. At least you'll enjoy the cooking

of Christian Constant, who after a tentative start is now giving full rein to his talent and personality. His dishes have a reassuringly rural feel that contrasts with the coolly formal setting: wild mushrooms in a bordelaise sauce, duck and spinach sausage, turbot barded with bacon, oxtail and bone marrow, and a braised Bresse chicken with baby onions. Just two small criticisms—we'd like to see rather less formal service and more flattering lighting in the evenings. The excellent wine list can make an already stiffish bill still harder to swallow, but sommelier Jean-Claude Maître is always willing to recommend some more affordable selections.Menus: 320 F (weekdays lunch only), 570 F.

11/20 Aux Amis du Beaujolais
28, rue d'Artois
45 63 92 21
Closed Sat. dinner & Sun. Open until 9 p.m.
The full gamut of French home-style and bistro fare is represented here—poule au riz, rabbit in mustard sauce, calf's head, roast beef and french fries—washed down with one of the ten tasty *crus* of Beaujolais, which the jolly owner bottles himself. Friendly prices, full plates, forgettable decor.
A la carte: 150-180 F.

12/20 Baumann Marbeuf
15, rue Marbeuf
47 20 11 11,
fax 47 23 69 65
Closed 2 wks. in Aug. Open until 1 a.m. Private room: 22. Air cond.
Patrons perch on stools at the bar, or sit at convivial round tables amid the splendid marbles and mirrors of designer Slavik's decor, to feast on briny shellfish,

baroque choucroutes (not all equally successful), and nicely aged meats from Scotland and southwestern France. We like the chocolate cake, too, and the thirst-quenching Alsatian wines.
A la carte: 260-350 F.

12/20 Bice
6, rue Balzac
42 89 86 34
Closed Sat. lunch, Sun., Dec. 23-Jan. 4 & Aug. 3-17. Open until 11:30 p.m. Private room: 48. Air cond. Valet parking.
Amiable Italian (or Italian-style) waiters leap and dash among the young, moneyed clientele (Saint-Tropez, *prêt-à-porter*, the Levant) that forgathers in this refined, blond-wood version of Harry's Bar. The food used to be pretty good; that is no longer the case: we were disappointed with the insipid roasted peppers, overcooked lamb and lamentably inauthentic tiramisù. What's more, it's a pricey *pasto*, friends, and the Italian wines are expensive too. The dining room gets terribly crowded after 10 p.m.
A la carte: 340-420 F.

Le Bistrot du Sommelier
97, bd Haussmann
42 65 24 85
Closed Sat. dinner, Sun. & Aug. 1-29. Open until 10:30 p.m. Private room: 25. Air cond.
Thanks to a new chef, the cuisine is now on par with this bistro's fabled wine cellar: we can recommend the fresh tuna steak with mild garlic, young rabbit with tiny onions and Chablis, and rib steak with red wine (a robust Syrah, in this case). Owner Philippe Faure-Brac, one of the city's most worthy wine wallahs, was crowned "World's Best Sommelier" in 1992.
A la carte: 280-400 F. Menu: 350 F (weekdays dinner only, wine incl.).

**12/20 Le Bœuf
sur le Toit**

34, rue du Colisée
43 59 83 80
Open daily until 2 a.m. Air cond.
From a seat on the mezzanine watch the dazzling swirl of diners and waiters reflected a hundredfold in this mirrored, flower-filled room. But don't get so distracted that you can't enjoy the faultless seafood, copious brasserie fare or the fruity young wines served in *pichets.*
A la carte: 230-280 F.

 Chez Bosc

7, rue Richepanse
42 60 10 27
Closed Sat. lunch, Sun. & Aug. 1-15. Open until 10:30 p.m.
Yves Labrousse transferred his restaurant last year from the Left Bank to this new, elegant, streamlined setting. Happily, he brought along his penchant for moderate prices (the prix-fixe lunch hasn't inflated in three years). Unfortunately, our last visit left us wondering if he hadn't lost some of his formerly flawless technique. Alongside a flavorful, perfectly cooked dish of sweetbreads and morels, we sampled a tasteless sole soufflée and a severely oversalted mussel feuilleté. The staff, cut to the bare bones, does what it can—but the service is not so gracious as once it was.
A la carte: 350-400 F. Menu: 190 F.

 Le Bristol

Hôtel Bristol
112, rue du Faubourg-St-Honoré
42 66 91 45,
fax 42 66 68 68
Open daily until 10:30 p.m. Private room: 60. Air cond. No pets. Heated pool. Garage parking.
The ambience and prices are what you might expect in this heavily guarded hotel near the French President's residence

and surrounded by embassies and high-class shops. Seated in the sumptuous dining room lined with Regency wood paneling or outside on the patio with its potted orange trees, you'll find no jarring notes from the dishes prepared by Emile Tabourdiau. Impeccably trained staff will serve you langoustine salad, crab and avocado ragoût, brill with spinach, or saddle of rabbit in a delectable crust of sliced potatoes. The desserts are equally tempting and the cellar boasts a breathtaking array of expensive vintages.
A la carte: 700-800 F. Menus: 440 F and 590 F.

 Le Carpaccio

Hôtel Royal Monceau
35-39, av. Hoche
45 62 76 87,
fax 45 63 04 03
Closed Aug. Open until 10:30 p.m. Air cond. No pets. Heated pool. Valet parking.
A warm Italian atmosphere awaits you beneath the Carpaccio's chandeliers, where you can sample the sunny cuisine of Italy at its best. Start off with the eponymous carpaccio, paper-thin raw beef further glorified with aged Parmesan, olive oil and a spritz of lemon juice. Save room for the fresh pasta with pesto sauce and veal escalopes stuffed with eggplant and herbs, and wash down these delightful dishes with a slightly chilled Valpolicella.
A la carte: 450-650 F. Menus: 280 F (lunch only, wine incl.), 340 F (dinner only, wine incl.).

12/20 Caviar Kaspia

17, pl. de la Madeleine
42 65 33 32
Closed Sun. Open until 12:30 a.m. Private room: 25. Air cond.
The fine-feathered folk who frequent this dark but charming upper room opposite the

Madeleine come to nibble (caviars, salmon roe, smoked sturgeon) rather than feast (smoked fish assortments, bortsch, etc.). But all the offerings, large and small, are quite good and are courteously served.
A la carte: 300-350 F (without caviar).

 Chiberta

3, rue A.-Houssaye
45 63 77 90,
fax 45 62 85 08
Closed Sat., Sun., Dec. 24-Jan. 3 & Aug. 1-29. Open until 11 p.m. Air cond.
Along with Fouquet's, Chiberta is the only haunt of *le Tout-Paris* left on the Champs-Elysées. Nabobs from the worlds of finance and television forgather here at lunch, relayed by the *beau monde* in the evening. The dining room's discreet, modern decor is aging gracefully, the floral displays are as sumptuous as ever and—the big news—the food has never been better. Chef Philippe Da Silva was number two here for ten years, but since his recent promotion, he has surpassed himself (and his predecessor!) in the execution of a menu that highlights sublime sauces and a sophisticated use of herbs and seasonings. Examples? Cold crayfish consommé with a crème au caviar; lobster cannelloni with a truffled shellfish fumet; fresh cod sautéed with a coulis of wild mushrooms and Belgian endive; red mullet in a curried Sauternes sauce; veal kidney cooked whole in its juices with horseradish and capers. All these dishes attest to Da Silva's finesse and good taste. Proprietor Louis-Noël Richard's passion for red Burgundies is communicative (but ruinous for the wallet). Remarkable desserts.
A la carte: 500 F and up.

Clovis

Pullman Windsor
4, av. Bertie-Albrecht
45 61 15 32
Closed Sat., Sun. & holidays. Open until 10:30 p.m. Air cond. Valet parking.
The chef, a former assistant to Michel Rostang, is a master of culinary technique. And we are pleased to announce that he seems to have developed an appealing style all his own. Gone are the heavy hand and the *tours de force*; instead, there are bright-tasting dishes such as terrine de jarret de veau à l'orange, pork fillet garnished with a carrot galette and a sprightly salad of squid and baby artichokes. Clever, tasty desserts, and an interesting wine list. Service is flawless in the pretty pink-and-beige dining room.
A la carte: 400-500 F. Menus: 175 F (dinner only), 190 F, 345 F.

 Copenhague

142, av. des Champs-Elysées
43 59 20 41,
fax 42 25 83 10
Closed Sun., holidays, 1st wk. of Jan. & Aug. 2-29. Open until 10:30 p.m. Air cond.
Salmon—smoked, pickled, marinated or grilled—and delicious tender herring prepared in every imaginable way, are the stars of this limited menu. The other dishes are dull and terribly expensive. If the weather is fine, ask to be seated on the patio behind the Flora Danica.
A la carte: 350-550 F.

 La Couronne

Hôtel Warwick
5, rue de Berri
45 63 14 11,
fax 45 63 75 81
Closed holidays & Aug. Open until 10:30 p.m. Private room: 120. Air cond.
Covered with international cooking awards, chef Van

Gessel has hit his stride once more. The delicious prix-fixe lunch (a bargain compared to the costly à la carte offerings) might, on a given day, consist of warm salad of lotte and duck liver, sole matelote with onion confit, excellent cheeses and a yummy apple macaroon. The newly redone dining room will not win any awards for interior decoration, and it is unfortunately stuck into a corner of the Hotel Warwick lobby. Van Gessel's fine work deserves a larger audience than just the hotel guests and business people at lunch.
A la carte: 420-500 F. Menu: 220 F (weekdays lunch only), 270 F (weekdays & Sat. dinner), 390 F (weekdays dinner & Sat., wine incl.).

12/20 Diep

55, rue P.-Charron
45 63 52 76
22, rue de Ponthieu
42 56 23 96
Open daily until 11:45 p.m. Air cond.
This is the flagship of the Diep family's three-restaurant fleet. The decor is Bangkok swank, and the food is Asian eclectic; the grilled chicken with lemon grass and the gar-

lic pork are successful, but the shrimp and rice crêpes and the heavy fish fritters are not. Desserts are worth a try (we like the sticky-rice cake with coconut), but the wines are too expensive. Other address: 28, rue Louis-le-Grand in the second arrondissement.
A la carte: 240-310 F.

11/20 Drugstore des Champs-Elysées

133, av. des Champs-Elysées
47 23 54 34
Open daily until 1:30 a.m. Terrace dining. Air cond.
Believe it or not, the food at this landmark of 1960s chic is not bad at all. The 78-franc two-course meal is more than acceptable, and the meal-in-one salads, the grills and the crisp pommes frites go very well with the vibrant, bustling atmosphere.
A la carte: 150-200 F. Menu: 78 F.

 Chez Edgard

4, rue Marbeuf
47 20 51 15
Closed Sun. & Aug. 1-23. Open until 12:30 a.m. Private room: 35. Terrace dining.
Just because it has often been said that the *gratin* of

The milk of Sacré-Cœur

An evergreen favorite with amateur artists and the most popular subject of Parisian postcards, the Sacré-Cœur owes its dazzling whiteness to a stone that secretes a milky substance when it rains. Whether you love or loathe its striking Byzantine architecture, it's hard to escape the basilica, which stands atop the highest point of Montmartre. It took more than 40 years to build and since its consecration in 1919 a continuous succession of faithful volunteers have been praying round the clock to atone for the sins of humanity. Climb up to the dome for a sweeping view that takes in Montmartre cemetery and a patchwork of private walled gardens.

French politics eats here, don't expect to see Michel Rocard or Laurent Fabius seated across from you. "Monsieur Paul" serves four to five hundred meals here each day, and in any case the Parisian powers-that-be are always whisked off to the quiet private rooms upstairs. Downstairs, amid the typically Gallic brouhaha, the rest of us may enjoy an eclectic cuisine that runs from fresh thon à la basquaise to onglet à l'échalote, all prepared with care and skill.
A la carte: 300-400 F.

 ### Elysée-Lenôtre
10, av. des Champs-Elysées
42 65 85 10,
fax 42 65 76 23
Closed Sat. lunch & Sun. Open until 10:30 p.m. Private room: 150. Terrace dining. Air cond. Valet parking.
Business was so bad in this Belle Epoque pavilion, once dear to the hearts of Edward VII and Alphonse XIII that the proprietors were rumored to be on the verge of throwing in the towel. But things began to look up, and now tables are much in demand. It's hard to imagine a better spot for a restaurant: in the middle of gardens in the middle of the city, just over the wall from Mitterrand's flower beds. The 340-franc prix-fixe luncheon has been a great success with a select clientele, who choose from among ten first courses (mallard terrine with juniper berries, for example) and ten main dishes (an excellent breast of Loire chicken with endive is popular). There are cheeses to finish, along with desserts in the grand tradition (we applaud the caramelized pears with licorice flan). If you order à la carte, be prepared to pay much (much) more.
A la carte: 500-800 F.

Menus: 340 F (lunch only), 580 F (dinner only).

 ### Les Elysées du Vernet
Hôtel Vernet
25, rue Vernet
47 23 43 10
Closed Sat., Sun & Aug. Open until 10 p.m. Air cond. No pets. Valet parking.
Which way is the Riviera please? We'd suggest this elegant address just off the Champs Elysées. You won't have a view of the Mediterranean, but Bruno Cirino's cuisine brings all the perfumes and flavors of Provence right into the glass-roofed dining room. This talented chef often flies home to Nice at weekends to fetch the vegetables, herbs and other specialties he finds it hard to cook without. You might like to whet your appetite with a dish of tiny fish (red mullet, fresh anchovies, squid and langoustines) with garlic mayonnaise before moving on to lobster with smoked bacon or a roast farmhouse duckling scented with mushrooms and olives and so tasty you'd swear it was a wild bird. Bruno Cirino's desserts are still improving too: try the warm bitter chocolate tart or the aromatic coffee ice-cream. Let's hope his honeymoon at Les Elysées du Vernet lasts and that the prices stop their ever-upward spiral.
A la carte: 400-500 F.
Menus: 270 F (lunch only), 420 F (dinner only).

11/20 Elysées Mandarin
23, rue Washington
42 25 71 20
Closed Sun. & Aug. 6-15. Open until 11:30 p.m. Air cond.
Book a table in the front room (which is fridge-and-microwave-free, unlike the rear dining room), and enjoy the good Thai food: grilled ravioli, shrimp salad, Szechuan

shrimp and shellfish soup scented with lemon grass.
A la carte: 190-240 F.
Menus: 80 F, 85 F, 129 F.

 ### Fakhr el Dine
3, rue Q.-Bauchart
47 23 74 24
Open daily until 12:30 a.m. Air cond. Valet parking.
Ignore the insipid decor, and focus instead on the delicious Lebanese mezes, which dazzle the eye as they delight the palate: bone-marrow salad, brains in lemon sauce, spinach fritters, fried lamb's sweetbreads, etc. These tidbits are offered in servings of 8, 10, 15 or 20, depending on the size of the company and your appetite.
A la carte: 220-300 F.
Menus: 210 F, 230 F.

 ### La Fermette Marbeuf 1900
5, rue Marbeuf
47 20 63 53,
fax 40 70 02 11
Open daily until 11:30 p.m. Terrace dining. Air cond.
Jean Laurent wisely decided not to send prices skyward after a genuine Belle Epoque decor—now listed by the Beaux-Arts—was discovered during renovations some years ago. Reasonable prices still prevail at the Fermette for superb andouillette, saddle of lamb, and hearty stewed pig's jowls with a hint of ginger, and there is a delicious 160-franc prix-fixe dinner, too. Moderation, quality, and affability are the rule here. As a result, customers quickly become regulars, and the staff remains the same—two good signs.
A la carte: 280-300 F. Menu: 160 F.

> *Remember to call ahead to reserve your table, and please, if you cannot honor your reservation, be courteous and let the restaurant know.*

Fouquet's
99, av. des Champs-
Elysées
47 23 70 60,
fax 47 20 08 69
Open daily until 12:30 a.m. Private room: 200. Terrace dining. Valet parking.
Aesthetically speaking, Fouquet's decor is no great shakes, but in the end the only way to save this nerve center of Parisian high life was to have it listed. At the same time the management has attracted some of the younger bloods of the film and advertising world, so the tone of the place is lively once more. The menu can be a bit of a minefield, but you won't go far wrong if you order the perennially perfect merlan Colbert, the daube of beef with carrots, or the charcoal-grilled steak. Paradoxically, the food is considerably better at the two new Fouquet's restaurants (at the Bastille and La Défense) than here at the old original.
A la carte: 300-600 F. Menu: 250 F.

Chez Francis
7, pl. de l'Alma
47 20 86 83,
fax 45 56 98 42
Open daily until 1 a.m. Private room: 70. Terrace dining. Air cond.
The smart patrons are reflected and multiplied by rows of engraved mirrors—so much the better for them, since they obviously take more pleasure in who they're seeing than in what they're eating (though the canard en daube au gratin de macaroni is quite good, as are the shellfish).
A la carte: 300 F. Menu: 180 F (wine incl.).

Some establishments change their closing times without warning. It is always wise to check in advance.

 Les Géorgiques
36, av. George-V
40 70 10 49
Closed Sat. lunch & Sun. Open until 10:30 p.m. Private room: 18. Air cond.
Twenty years' training with the masters of the old school (Rostang, etc.) have left Katsumaro Ishimaru forever stranded in a culinary time warp, amid tournedos Rossini, turbot stuffed with foie gras in Madeira and similiar dinosaurs. Too bad that his fine technique is chained to so banal a repertoire. The decor is downright funereal; prices are chilling.
A la carte: 350-600 F. Menus: 180 F (lunch only), 360 F.

11/20 Germain
19, rue Jean-Mermoz
43 59 29 24
Closed Sat., Sun., Aug. & holidays. Open until 9:30 p.m.
One of the last bastions of French home cooking anywhere near the Champs-Elysées, this 30-seat restaurant offers beef bourguignon, coq au vin, etc. at popular prices.
A la carte: 150-180 F.

 Le Grenadin
44-46, rue de Naples
45 63 28 92
Closed Sat., Sun., wk. of July 14 & wk. of Aug. 15. Open until 10:30 p.m. Private room: 16. Air cond.
A lovely dining room of little nooks and levels, enlarged with mirrors, is a very pleasant setting for Patrick Cirotte's flavorful, adventurous cooking. Ingredients are the key here—they are uniformly first-rate and handled with respect and simplicity, from the foie gras sautéed without a speck of fat and served with a lentil salad, to the delicious sea bass fillet baked in a salt crust. Desserts are far above average.

A la carte: 350-400 F. Menus: 200 F, 320 F, 370 F.

 Au Jardin du Printemps
32, rue de Penthièvre
43 59 32 91
Closed Sun. & Aug. Open until 11:30 p.m. Private room: 30. Air cond.
The three Tan brothers tend to fawn over the political and social celebrities who over the years have come to regard their restaurant as an unofficial clubhouse. Alongside some decent Chinese standards, Tan Le-Huy prepares some very good Vietnamese specialties, many of which are given an appealing personal twist. Try the pho soup, peppery grilled beef fillet, and spareribs in black bean sauce. Elegant lacquered decor.
A la carte: 200-350 F.

 Le Jardin du Royal Monceau
Hôtel Royal Monceau
35, av. Hoche
45 62 96 02,
fax 45 63 04 03
Open daily until 10:30 p.m. Garden dining. Air cond. Heated pool. Valet parking.
You step into another world when you enter the bright dining room, its french windows opening onto manicured lawns and immaculate flower beds. Surrounded by buildings, this garden seems to have been brought to central Paris by the wave of a magic wand. The same spell operates in the kitchen, where Bernard Guilhaudin conjures up delectable food with no unnecessary embellishments, each dish the object of infinite care. The ox cheek cooked in celery stock or cabbage stuffed with veal and shellfish are as tasty as they are unpretentious. This talented chef handles desserts with similar passion: try the blancmange or

the banana and mango millefeuille. The service is impeccable and the young sommelier provides excellent advice on a well-chosen wine list.

A la carte: 400-550 F. Menus: 280 F (weekdays lunch and holidays), 420 F (dinner except Sun., wine incl.).

Lasserre
17, av. F.-Roosevelt
43 59 53 43,
fax 45 63 72 23
Closed Mon. lunch, Sun. & Aug. Open until 10:30 p.m. Private room: 55. Air cond. Valet parking.

One of the few surviving examples of *le grand restaurant à la française*, this grandiose establishment merits your attention for the ethnological interest it presents. Nowhere else is the service so minutely choreographed, the atmosphere so festive yet well-bred (piano music, soft lights, glowing silver, silken carpets...). Don't forget to look up as Lasserre's retractable roof brings you (weather and visibility permitting) the stars. As you look back down you'll notice that the menu is a rich Texas rancher's dream of French cuisine: duck à l'orange, tournedos béarnaise and crêpes flambées. Look more closely and you'll find some lighter, more interesting options like freshwater perch with crabs, precisely cooked scallops with asparagus, Bresse chicken en papillote... But no matter how hard you squint at the wine list, you won't find a bottle of wine for less than 300 francs!

A la carte: 600-800 F.

Remember to call ahead to reserve your table, and please, if you cannot honor your reservation, be courteous and let the restaurant know.

Laurent
41, av. Gabriel
42 25 00 39,
fax 45 62 45 21
Closed Sat. lunch, Sun. & holidays. Open until 11 p.m. Private room: 84. Terrace dining. Air cond. Valet parking.

Parisians are talking about Laurent's new decor: has Jimmy Goldsmith opened his Scotsman's purse wide enough to restore a gastronomic pleasure dome on the opulent order of Ledoyen and Elysée-Lenôtre? The debate is still open. Joining a team that includes an intelligent manager, a virtuoso maître d'hôtel, and one of the best sommeliers on the planet has been added a talented young chef from Robuchon's stable, Philippe Braun. His food is not flashy, but it is based on ingredients that are absolutely prime: pearly turbot with fresh pasta and morels, kid with thyme and mild garlic, sea bream with baby onions and asparagus all evince clean-cut, clearly focused flavors. The desserts, by comparison with the rest of the menu (or the fabulous wine list!), seem lackluster.

A la carte: 800 F and up. Menus: 380 F (lunch only), 880 F.

Ledoyen
Carré des Champs-Elysées
47 42 23 23,
fax 47 42 55 01
Closed Sun. Open until 10:30 p.m. Private room: 250. Air cond. Valet parking.

Régine has ended her association with this gilt-edged eatery, and chef Philippe Dorange followed right on her heels. Sous-chef François Lemercier is now in charge of Le Carré (the establishment's elegant grill) and—here's the kicker—Ghislaine Arabian, the toast of Lille, has been tapped to head the prestigious *restaur-*

ant gastronomique on the first floor. A three-toque (18/20) winner at her last establishment, Mme Arabian plans to seduce the Parisian dining public with her signature dishes based on Northern ingredients: smoked mussel soup, turbot poached in beer, vanilla cream with ginger bread... As soon as she's settled in, we'll sample her menu and will report straight back to you—watch this space!

Menus: 350 F (lunch only), 600 F (dinner only).

Lucas-Carton
9, pl. de la Madeleine
42 65 22 90,
fax 42 65 06 23
19.5
Closed Sat. lunch, Sun., 3 1st wks. of Aug. Open until 10:30 p.m. Private room: 14. Air cond. Valet parking.

Will Alain Senderens be inducted into the Pantheon one day as the inventor of ravioli de pétoncles? It is easy to have fun at the expense of this culinary wizard, as his cultural significance (and pretensions?) continue to grow. His meteoric rise from apprentice to legendary chef has not stopped at the kitchen door; just as Bocuse cast off his apron to become a roving "ambassador of French cuisine", Senderens bids fair to become the philosopher of Gallic gastronomy.

A literate chef was once as astonishing a rarity as Dr. Johnson's woman preacher, but with more and more young *cuisiniers* entering the kitchen from university, the craft of cookery has acquired a cultural dimension. Having said that, however, anyone with normally tuned tastebuds is sufficiently equipped to savor Senderens's extraordinary inventions. So, as the French say: à table.

Eventhia Senderens's skills as a hostess have greatly improved, so that the ambience in this stunning Belle Epoque dining room, paneled in glowing blond wood, has warmed up considerably, making the food seem more wonderful still. And at its best, Senderens's cooking is wonderful beyond words. Yet as some disgruntled readers have not failed to point out, when one pays more than 300 francs for roast lamb, or 480 francs for the famed homard à la vanille, one is not disposed to countenance anything but sheer perfection. And when flaws do occur, it is natural to blame Senderens for straying from his kitchen. In all fairness, though, one ought not to confuse his role with that of his head chef. For even in the master's absence the thoroughly drilled staff, led by Bertrand Guéneron and Philippe Peudenier, delivers pluperfect versions of such Senderens creations as a sublime confit of foie gras with tiny artichokes, or prawns sautéed in tarragon butter served with a heavenly bouillon, or cod cooked in its skin to retain all its juices, accompanied by fragrantly herbal "crumbled" potatoes, or lapin Isidoria (the saddle roasted with mustard, the hind legs shredded and tossed with foie gras). Not every dish is above criticism: a perfectly cooked sea bream with a bracing touch of vinegar sported a fussy, purely "decorative" garnish of almonds and cuttlefish ravioli. And pink peppercorns—that plague of nouvelle cuisine—added nothing to a savory pigeon cressonnière. But our pleasure in his gâteau au chocolat croustillant, or the aumonière au coulis d'abricots, or the sublime vanilla ice cream hasn't diminished a whit. And Lucas-Carton is surely the place where today's most thrilling marriages of food and wine are arranged (Dominique Derozier presides over the unparalleled cellar).

Menus: 420 F (lunch only), 990 F (wine incl.) 750 F.

12/20 Le Manoir Normand

77, bd de Courcelles
42 27 38 97
Closed Sun. & July 10-18, wk. of Aug. 15. Open until 10:30 p.m. Terrace dining. Parking.

In France, a restaurateur named Pommerai (roughly equivalent to "apple orchard"), can hardly do otherwise than give his restaurant a Norman accent. But apart from some fish in cream-based sauces and a fine apple tart, the menu is agreeably free from regional chauvinism. Delicious *plats du jour*, and excellent meats grilled in the big fireplace. Glass-enclosed terrace.

A la carte: 280-350 F. Menus: 100 F (except holidays), 145 F.

 ### La Marée

1, rue Daru
43 80 20 00,
fax 48 88 04 04
Closed Sat., Sun. & Aug. Open until 10:30 p.m. Air cond. Valet parking.

At a restaurant named for the tide—La Marée—you would naturally expect to eat fish. But the best meal we've ever had here was a juicy saddle of rabbit served whole with small onions, chanterelles and courgettes. The old-fashioned pâté en croûte is still among the best in Paris and the once-famous pastry selection has regained its former glorious heights.
The best news, however, is that the fish are no longer drowned in creamy sauces or cooked to the point of no flavor-return. After an exquisite skate terrine with an herbed vinaigrette or a luxurious lobster carpaccio, one can move on to the bracingly briny sea bream with its unusual accompaniment of Swiss chard stewed in meat essence. These and other dishes are served, as always, by a courteous, even benevolent staff. Take your time over the wine list, which features some exceptional bargains (like the '85 white Burgundy Les Perrières from Simon Bize, priced at 140 francs).

A la carte: 550 F and up.

 ### Maxim's

3, rue Royale
42 65 27 94,
fax 40 17 02 91
Open daily (except Sun. in July-Aug). Open until 11:30 p.m. Private room: 90. Air cond. Valet parking.

Now that Maxim's once-frightful prices are common currency at many another less glamorous establishment, is this glorious Belle Epoque monument doomed to become just another restaurant? Heaven forfend! The trouble is, times have changed. The chic, sleek Parisians who made Maxim's a legend now keep their jewels locked up in the family safe, and leave revelry to the young and the hoi polloi; the day of the dapper *boulevardier* is long over. But Maxim's remains, its marvelous mahogany, bronzes and glass sparkle and glow—it's become a mausoleum for an era whose passing it refuses to acknowledge. The ghost of Maxim's former gaiety occasionally returns at lunch, when an urbane crowd fills the place with sophisticated chatter as they pick at their food. Speaking of the food, chef Michel Menant does a bang-up job, considering the hundreds of meals he is obliged to serve each day. We were enchanted, on a recent visit, by the prawns en gelée, delectable fried baby red mullet and delicious bœuf mode.

A tip of the hat to him, (and the invariably stylish, civilized service).

A la carte: 500-700 F (lunch only), 900 F and up (dinner only).

 Daniel Metery

4, rue de l'Arcade
42 65 53 13
Closed Sat. lunch, Sun. & 1st wk. of Aug. Open until 10:15 p.m.
Metery, a dedicated and hard-working disciple of the renowned Michel Guérard, not long ago took over this pretty pink-and-beige restaurant above the Passage du Madeleine. Though he has yet to realize his full potential, we are delighted with his pigeon salad, his exotically flavored lamb with vegetable ravioli and a luscious honey-apricot pastry. The cellar is expanding, and some good wines are offered by the glass.

A la carte: 340-400 F. Menus: 230 (dinner only), 175 F.

11/20 Mollard

113, rue St-Lazare
43 87 50 22
Open daily until 1 a.m. Private room: 100.
An extraordinary turn-of-the-century ceramic mural depicts destinations reached by the trains that depart from the Gare Saint-Lazare across the street. The food is not nearly so enchanting. Safe bets include the shellfish platter, the chateaubriand and the omelette surprise, but skip the sandre à la vanille. Courteous welcome, discreet service.

A la carte: 220-280 F. Menu: 178 F.

Gault Millau's ratings are based solely on the restaurants' cuisine. We do not take into account the atmosphere, decor, service and so on; these are commented upon within the review.

 Napoléon

Hôtel Napoléon
38, av. de Friedland
42 27 99 50,
fax 47 66 82 33
Closed Sat., Sun. & Aug. Open until 10:30 p.m. Private room: 20. Air cond.
Better known as the sauerkraut king, Guy-Pierre Baumann is now branching out into seafood. He has opened for business with a brand-new decor and a Senderens-trained chef. So far, however, the results aren't entirely convincing. The food is delicate and imaginative, yes, but also fussy and complicated. Nicely garnished with Jerusalem artichokes and snow peas, the skate was more than a shade overcooked; a commendable sea bream baked in a salt crust was needlessly encumbered with vegetable chips. Desserts are quite good, and the cellar is stocked with some wonderful white wines. Stay tuned.

A la carte: 400-500 F. Menu: 240 F.

12/20 L'Obélisque

Hôtel de Crillon
10, pl. de la Concorde
44 71 15 15,
fax 44 71 15 02
Closed holidays & Aug. Open until 10:30 p.m. Air cond. Valet parking.
To eat at the Hôtel Crillon without breaking the bank, try its other, less formal restaurant. You'll still benefit from top-notch service and a menu supervised by Christian Constant, chef of Les Ambassadeurs (see above). The food is classic and filling: pig's trotter sausage with potato purée, tongue and foie gras wrapped in flaky pastry, fresh rhubarb tart.

A la carte: 250-350 F. Menu: 230 F.

 Au Petit Montmorency

26, rue J.-Mermoz
42 25 11 19
Closed Sat., Sun. & Aug. Open until 10:30 p.m. Private room: 20. Air cond.
Twenty years ago we discovered Daniel Bouché at Le Petit Montmorency, in the Marais district of Paris, and enthralled by the aromas that emanated from his closet-sized kitchen, we predicted a great future for this bold, inventive chef. We later tracked him down to the rue Rabelais, where Au Petit Montmorency was surrounded by barricades and soldiers assigned to protect the nearby Israeli embassy. But luck smiled down on Bouché, who recently acquired the shop next door to his restaurant, giving him a new address and an unimpeded entrance.

Inside, the restaurant is pleasantly old-fashioned, with an eclectic decor of culinary prints and bric-a-brac. Eclectic too are Bouché's tastes, but he has successfully struggled to tame his more outlandish fantasies, and now gives disciplined expression to his culinary imagination. The result is a pure, luminous cuisine that fully deserves three toques.

Bouché dazzled us not long ago with sublime fresh truffles veiled in a diaphanous crust and heightened by a lightly creamy, boldly spiced truffle jus; afterwards came a sumptuous turbot steak (he fetches the fish himself, in Normandy) simply baked with tomatoes and olive oil. Meatlovers will go for the rosy, peppery veal kidney, or the beef entrecôte en pot-au-feu, the stuffed rabbit with wild rice, or a sweet-and-sour duck with turnips. Finish with cheese, if you like—you'll rarely encounter a better Livarot or a more expertly aged Cantal—but you

really should save room for the marvelous souffléed lemon crêpes, or a coupe of caramelized honey ice cream with gingerbread croûtons. Nicole Bouché tends the splendid cellar, and greets customers with disarming warmth. Lulled by this deliciousness, your shock may be all the greater when the waiter presents the bill!
A la carte: 450-900 F.

Le Pichet
68, rue P.-Charron
43 59 50 34
Closed Sat., Sun., Dec. 19-Jan. 3 & Aug. 10-30. Open until midnight. Air cond.
New owners have scrubbed and polished this old Pichet, which is currently enjoying considerable success with its excellent shellfish assortments, *plats du jour* and some creditable fish dishes (skate in warm vinaigrette; cod à l'unilatérale). These and other simple dishes play to a sporty but urbane crowd, which sometimes includes François Mitterrand.
A la carte: 350-400 F.

Le Prince de Galles
Marriott Prince de Galles
33, av. George-V
47 23 55 11
Open daily until 10:30 p.m. Private room: 180. Garden dining. Air cond. Valet parking.
The Prince of Wales beats King George (see below) hands down in the culinary arena. Ex-Robuchon disciple (and former chef to the Rothschilds), Dominique Cécillon has emerged from a dry spell and is now back in peak form, preparing a cuisine laudably free of hotel-dining-room pomposity, but which maintains a suitably high tone. Warm prawns with chanterelles, turbot à la nage, lobster in Sauternes cream,

and pot-au-feu of beef fillet are very nearly as delicious as they are expensive. In contrast, the set menus are incredible bargains, especially considering the luxurious setting and service. But please, chef Cécillon, do chuck the fussy, precious menu appellations that make your wonderful dishes sound ridiculous!
A la carte: 400-700 F. Menus: 250 F (Sun. lunch only, wine incl.), 235 F.

Les Princes
George-V
31, av. George-V
47 23 54 00
Open until 10:30 p.m. Private room: 54. Terrace dining. Air cond. Valet parking.
This dog-eared hotel dining room is undergoing renovations at last. But the facelift alone won't lure back the public–chef Pierre Larapidie should consider revamping his menu, which could also do with some grace and style. In fine weather, book a table on the beautiful flower-decked patio. And when the winter winds blow, give the Princes a cold shoulder and head instead for the Grill George-V, a convivial venue where prices are more clement and Larapidie's repertoire shows flashes of its former verve.
A la carte: 600-750 F. Menus: 350 F (weekdays lunch only, wine incl.), 450 F (except weekdays lunch and holidays).

15 Montaigne
La Maison Blanche
15, av. Montaigne
47 23 55 99
Closed Sat. lunch & Sun. Open until midnight. Private room: 40. Terrace dining. Air cond. Valet parking.
José Martinez now presides over the dazzling, ultra-modern kitchens built for his brother-in-law, the late,

lamented José Lampreia. Lampreia's inventive, very personal style still marks the menu: cod with lemon tajine, pigeon with dates, potato galette with salt cod and aïoli are all fresh and appealing, if skimpily apportioned. The juvenile serving staff is far more competent than at the restaurant's debut, and the welcome has warmed up a few degrees as well.
A la carte: 500-600 F.

Régence-Plaza
Plaza Athénée
25, av. Montaigne
47 23 78 33
Open daily until 10:30 p.m. Private room: 110. Garden dining. Air cond. Valet parking.
The new chef, Gérard Sallé from Deauville, has brought a breath of fresh air to what had been a rather stuffy menu. Lobster soufflé and seafood mixed grill have made way for scallops simmered with coriander, delicate veal sweetbreads perfumed with sage and braised crab brimful of natural flavor. Gérard Sallé will probably find it harder to modify the menu at the hotel's grill restaurant, *Le Relais*. Opulent flowers, old-world service, musical luncheons *et tout le tralala*.
A la carte: 500-600 F. Menu: 330 F (lunch except weekdays).

Le Relais Vermeer
Hôtel Golden Tulip
218, rue du Faubourg-St-Honoré
49 53 03 03
Closings not available. Open until 10 p.m. Private room: 190. Air cond. Heated pool. Valet parking.
A luxurious restaurant for a luxurious hotel, owned by the Dutch Golden Tulip chain. In a restful gray-blue-and-pink dining room, sample Scandinavian fare full of piquant contrasts between sweet

and salty flavors: reindeer fillet with an onion and orange confit, smoked eels in puff pastry and salmon in every possible permutation. Good hot cheese dishes. Chilly service. Steven Spurrier designed the wine list, don't you know.
A la carte: 300-500 F. Menu: 195 F.

12/20 Le Saint-Germain
74, av. des Champs-Elysées
45 63 55 45
Closed w.-e. Open until 9:30 p.m. Air cond.
Buried beneath the Claridge's shopping arcade, this pleasant establishment boasts a new chef, who offers careful, thoughtful cooking: seafood ragoût with fresh pasta, roast lamb au jus with fresh mint, etc. Appealing pastries, and good set menus.
Menus: 65 F, 98 F, 165 F, 280 F.

Saint-Moritz
33, av. de Friedland
45 61 02 74
Closed Sat. & Sun. Open until 10:15 p.m. Terrace dining. Air cond.
Chef Alain Raichon hails from the Jura, and his cooking too is rooted in that hearty mountain region. Sample his Morteau sausage with warm potato salad, fresh morels and asparagus tips in puff pastry, or sole fillets cooked in Arbois white wine. Fresh seasonal specialties (dilled red-mullet terrine; fig and citrus soup) are featured on the single-price menu, which makes this elegant, wainscoted dining room a popular choice for business luncheons.
Menu: 185 F.

12/20 Savy
23, rue Bayard
47 23 46 98
Closed Aug. Open until 11 p.m.
Cramped, ill-lit, with ancient imitation-leather banquettes

and an even more ancient ceiling fan, Savy has a hard-to-fathom charm that keeps customers (including some of the capital's most noted radio personalities) coming back for robust country cooking: stuffed cabbage, Auvergne-style calf's liver, tripe, and so on.
A la carte: 220-300 F.

12/20 Sébillon Elysées
66, rue Pierre-Charron
43 59 28 15
Open daily until midnight. Air cond.
As in the sister establishment in Neuilly (see Suburbs), excellent but expensive shellfish platters are followed here by Sébillon's famous leg of lamb, cooked to rosy tenderness and carved before one's eyes. Elegant decor, energetic service.
A la carte: 300-350 F.

Stresa
7, rue de Chambiges
47 23 51 62
Closed Sat. dinner, Sun., Dec. 20-Jan. 3 & Aug. 3-31. Open until 10:30 p.m. Private room: 12. Terrace dining. Air cond.
This tacky but somehow soothing dining room is always jammed full of press, fashion and theatre folk who love the antipasti drizzled with fruity Tuscan olive oil, the toothsome osso buco and the unctuous tiramisù prepared by Marco Faiola. Claudio and Toni seat their guests with a sure social sense of who's up, who's down, who's in, who's out.
A la carte: 350-450 F.

Plan to travel? Look for Gault Millau's other Best of guides to Chicago, Florida, France, Hawaii, Hong Kong, Germany, Italy, London, Los Angeles, New England, New Orleans, New York, San Francisco, Thailand, Toronto and Washington, D.C.

Taillevent
15, rue Lamennais
45 63 39 94,
fax 42 25 95 18
Closed Sat., Sun., Feb. 13-21 & July 24-Aug. 22. Open until 10:30 p.m. Private room: 32. Air cond. Valet parking.
Having narrowly escaped expropriation, Taillevent's proprietor, Jean-Claude Vrinat, can now concentrate on other pressing matters, like enlarging the restaurant's antediluvian kitchens and, even more critically, reaching a new equilibrium now that chef Claude Deligne has retired after more than 30 years of brilliant service.
His successor, Philippe Legendre, a Robuchon disciple was formerly number two at Taillevent, and is behind the recent shift toward a more creative, perhaps more subtle menu featuring dishes like a delicious cold cream of rock lobster dotted with minuscule diced vegetables, roasted crayfish tails napped with a divine, lightly spiced cream sauce, tiny red mullet with basil in a delicate wine sauce, or suprême de pigeon with its giblets in Médoc wine.
The future, it is safe to say, of this noble institution will be guided by Vrinat's policy of grounding the kitchen's innovations in the classics and altering the menu prudently, to suit evolving tastes. It will be interesting to observe how Legendre's talent accommodates itself to the Taillevent tradition. In short, the good life, the hushed business luncheons, the quiet cosmopolitan soirées will certainly continue here in a setting of rich hangings, wood paneling, and old pictures (we wouldn't shed a tear, however, should the drab blue velvet and the bibelot cabinets suddenly disappear). Didier Bordas guides guests through Taillevent's justly vaunted

cellars, and the service functions at the highest level of efficiency and discretion. A la carte: 700-900 F.

 Chez Tante Louise

41, rue Boissy-d'Anglas
42 65 06 85,
fax 42 65 28 19
Closed w.-e. & Aug. Open until 10:30 p.m. Private room: 14. Air cond.
A regular clientele loves being pampered in this snug little restaurant. The Lhiabastres (from Aveyron) know how to make their guests comfortable, feeding them very good Southwestern cooking that features (slightly) lightened versions of foie gras, snail fricassée, duck à l'orange and crêpes Suzette. A la carte: 300-400 F. Menu: 200 F.

 Le Trente

Fauchon
30, pl. de La Madeleine
47 42 56 58,
fax 47 42 28 71
Closed Sun. Open until 10:30 p.m. Garden dining. Air cond. Valet parking.
Whoever dreamed up the name (Le Trente—30—is the building's address) of Fauchon's new restaurant won't win any prizes for creativity, but the decorator might, for his "Roman fantasy" interior complete with atrium, columns and trompe-l'œil paintings. Bruno Deligne, son of Taillevent's Claude Deligne, has yet to affirm a clear personality in the kitchen. The menu is too timid by half, particularly since Fauchon is (with Hédiard) the city's temple of rare and exotic foodstuffs. The cuisine is skillful, however, and based on superior ingredients. Desserts are superb, and the wine list is surprisingly affordable. A la carte: 400-500 F.

12/20 Le Val d'Or

28, av. F.-Roosevelt
43 59 95 81
Open for lunch only. Closed w.-e.
Mme. Rongier holds firmly to the traditions of French home-cooking, pleasing her patrons with beef in bone-marrow sauce and lapin à la moutarde, escorted by well-chosen wines at reasonable "bistro" prices. The ground-floor bar stays open at night, serving wine by the glass, charcuterie and sandwiches. A la carte: 200-300 F.

12/20 Chez Vong

 27, rue du Colisée
43 59 77 12,
fax 43 59 59 27
Closed Sun. Open until 9:30 (midnight on Sat.). Private room: 60. Air cond. Valet parking.
Here's everyone's dream of a Chinese restaurant: embroidered silk, furniture inlaid with mother-of-pearl, lots of little nooks, an air of mystery and dishes named "dancing eels", or "plate of the five happinesses". The cooking is generally well done. Oddly enough, the cellar is rich in fine claret. A la carte: 290-360 F.

 Yvan

1 bis, rue J.-Mermoz
43 59 18 40,
fax 45 63 78 69
Closed Sat. lunch & Sun. Open until midnight. Air cond. Valet parking.
Yvan Zaplatilek spells it out for his customers on the restaurant's sign: "Yvan - Cuisine Française". The food is indeed primarily French, and quite creditably done, with an occasional Belgian touch here and there (sea scallops accompanied by a mousseline flavored with Gueuze beer; pheasant garnished with endive). Yvan also has a penchant for exotic seasonings, and

turns out an excellent lotte with ginger, and veal kidneys spiced with cumin. Not the least of this establishment's virtues are the affordable tariffs, unmatched in this upscale neighborhood. A la carte: 250-350 F. Menus: 168 F, 228 F and 278 F (dinner only), 188 F.

9th arrondissement

11/20 Anarkali

4, pl. G.-Toudouze
48 78 39 84
Open daily until 12:30 a.m. Terrace dining.
One of the first Indian restaurants in Paris, this little spot on a quiet, shady square is still one of the best. The tandooris and chicken tikka are good, authentic, and inexpensive. A la carte: 150 F. Menu: 61 F.

Auberge Landaise

23, rue Clauzel
48 78 74 40,
fax 48 78 20 96
Closed Sun. & Aug. 3-25. Open until 10 p.m. Private room: 35. Parking.
In a rustic atmosphere conducive to a hearty tuck-in, Dominique Morin treats his customers to the best cassoulet in town (served piping hot in an individual earthenware pot), pipérade landaise, braised duck with wild mushrooms, foie gras and an array of sturdy Southwestern wines. Do not overlook the collection of Armagnacs, a perfect way to end a meal in this friendly, relaxed restaurant. A la carte: 250-350 F.

Find the address you are looking for, quickly and easily, in the index.

Le Bistrot Blanc
52, rue Blanche
42 85 05 30
Closed Sat., Sun., Aug. 1-Sep. 6. Open until 10 p.m.
Bruno Borni, a Marseille native who held the rank of sauce chef at La Tour d'Argent (indeed, his sauces are excellent, well concentrated, light and fragrant), deserves its first toque. Recommended are his flavorful ravioli stuffed with fresh sheep's cheese, pigeon roasted in a salt crust and, to finish, the citrus fruit "marvel". The ambience of this soft-pink dining room manages to be charming, despite the stand-offish service. Limited cellar.
A la carte: 250-300 F. Menu: 79 F.

12/20 **La Champagne**
10 bis, pl. de Clichy
48 74 44 78,
fax 42 80 63 10
Open daily until 3 a.m. Private room: 30. Air cond.
Until the small hours you can join the carefree, festive crowd that pays high prices for homard flambé, onion soup, oysters and sauerkraut at this effervescent restaurant. Clever, cheerful staff.
A la carte: 300-400 F.

 Charlot
Roi des Coquillages
81, bd de Clichy (pl. de Clichy)
48 74 49 64,
fax 40 16 11 00
Open daily until 1 a.m. Air cond.
A fine view of the Place de Clichy, a warm welcome, and attentive service will take your mind off the overbearing Art Deco interior. Sparkling fresh oysters, spectacular shellfish assortments, generous bouillabaisse à la marseillaise and lobsters prepared every possible way are the staples here.
A la carte: 330-430 F. Menu: 250 F (lunch only, wine incl.).

10/20 **Chartier**
7, rue du Faubourg-Montmartre
47 70 86 29
Open daily until 9:30 p.m.
Nothing has changed since 1896 at this rigorously preserved bistro, including the classics (roast chicken, calf's head) offered at obstinately philanthropic prices.
A la carte: 70-100 F. Menu: 82 F (wine incl.).

11/20 **L'Echiquier**
48, rue St-Georges
48 78 46 09
Closed Sun. & Mon. Open until 10 p.m. (11 p.m. w.-e.).
This is a good spot for after-theater suppers, so long as your tastes run to simple dishes like terrines, duck breast, confits and fruit tarts.
A la carte: 180-350 F. Menu: 95 F (until 9:30 p.m.).

12/20 **Le Grand Café Capucines**
4, bd des Capucines
47 42 19 00
Open daily 24 hours. Terrace dining. Air cond.
The waiter won't pull a face if you order just one course—a shellfish assortment, for example, or a grilled pig's trotter. The extravagant decor is a replica of a Belle Epoque *café boulevardier.*
A la carte: 240-310 F. Menus: 195 F, 256 F, 370 F.

 Les Muses
Hôtel Scribe
1, rue Scribe
44 71 24 26,
fax 42 65 39 97
Closed w.-e., holidays & Aug. Open until 10:30 p.m. Private room: 70. Air cond. Valet parking.
The muse of interior design was off-duty the day this basement-level restaurant was designed. On the other hand, chef Patrice Guibert seems privy to a regular fount of inspiration judging from his technically rigorous, beautifully presented cuisine. He earned a second toque for dishes that bear an appealing personal stamp, like a picture-perfect saumon glacé au vin, a peppery lamb fillet given an extra jolt of coffee flavor, osso buco of monkfish with crab, and ethereal pastries (tarte Tatin, sour-cherry clafoutis, caramelized apple mille-feuille). The wine list is notable for balance rather than length.
A la carte: 400-500 F. Menus: 210 F (lunch only), 350 F (dinner only).

 Opéra Restaurant
Café de la Paix
3, pl. de l'Opéra
40 07 32 32,
fax 42 66 12 51
Closed w.-e. Open until 11 p.m. Air cond.
How lucky that the untold sums spent restoring, regilding, re-marbling and reappointing this vast temple of Second Empire opulence did not render it solemn, stuffy and boring. *Au contraire* the ambience is exuberant, animated by whirling waiters who juggle the Baccarat crystal, fine china, and gilded silver with aplomb. But chef Jacky Fréon, lured away from the kitchens of the Hôtel Lutétia, has yet to hit his stride here. We can't believe that this award-winning *cuisinier* cannot do better than the over-cooked John Dory with scallops that disappointed us the other day; or the gummy mashed potatoes that ruined an otherwise delicious truffled boudin blanc. We're taking back the second toque until Fréon gets his bearings back again.
A la carte: 500-600 F.

Red toques signify modern cuisine; white toques signify traditional cuisine.

12/20 Au Petit Riche

25, rue Le Peletier
47 70 68 68,
fax 48 24 10 79
*Closed Sun. Open until
12:15 a.m. Private room: 45.*
The brass trim, mirrors and
woodwork of this nostalgic
bistro are sparkling once
again. This is everyone's preferred after-theater spot (an excellent all-in fee procures an
orchestra seat in one of eight
surrounding theaters, plus dinner), for top-notch chicken
liver mousse, pan-roasted cod
with cabbage, andouillette
simmered in Vouvray and delicious wines from the Touraine
region.
A la carte: 250-300 F. Menu:
180 F (wine incl.).

12/20 Chez Roger

52, rue de Douai
48 74 77 19
*Closed Sun. dinner, Mon., July-
Aug. & Christmas wk. Open until
10:30 p.m. Air cond.*
The jovial host, Roger
Sebban, chats up and jokes
with his guests, telling improbable stories of colonial life in
North Africa. The couscous is
decent, the paella fragrant and
good, and the pastries are imported from Dalloyau.
A la carte: 220-280 F.

12/20 Le Saintongeais

62, rue du Faubourg-
Montmartre
42 80 39 92
*Closed Sat., Sun., Dec. 25-31
& Aug. 9-29. Open until
9:30 p.m. Private room: 10.*
The decor is a study in brown
(walls, imitation-leather upholstery...); the menu is rather
more cheerful, with good
mouclade, chowder and other
specialties from the French
Atlantic seaboard. Attractive
little selection of wines from
the Loire.
A la carte: 230-300 F. Menu:
135 F (weekdays dinner only).

La Table d'Anvers

2, pl. d'Anvers
48 78 35 21,
fax 45 26 66 67
*Closed Sat. lunch, Sun. & Aug.
Open until 11:30 p.m. Private
room: 35. Air cond.*
Cooking, as he does, at a
remove from the city's more
fashionable districts, Christian
Conticini perhaps feels freer to
flout culinary trends. As ever,
his knack for creating novel
flavor combinations is nothing
short of staggering. But we
now find that his technique is
more finely honed, and his
cuisine is a marvel of balance
and character.
So put aside your prejudices,
and prepare for a real gastronomic adventure: try
Conticini's gâteau of oysters
and bone marrow heightened
with smooth balsamic vinegar;
or his tart filled with snails,
tomato, chanterelles and
spinach, seasoned with a saffron vinaigrette; or a fricassée
that brings together morels,
tiny peas, asparagus tips, baby
broad beans, carrots and
turnips in tarragon and
chicken juices (an ode to
springtime!). Complicated,
you say? Trust us: what looks
like a litany of disparate ingredients will burst into a harmony of delicate nuances on
the palate.
Conticini is equally adept at
bringing out the best of a single, perfect ingredient, witness
his roasted foie gras "steak",
well-seared on the outside,
very rare within; or the lightly
cooked skate, all moist and
pearly under a crust of mace-
scented hazelnuts.
We could go on about all
these exciting new ideas, but
we must leave room to mention the fabulous cheeses, and
the astonishing desserts
crafted by Christian's brother,
Philippe Conticini. Don't be
put off by the latter's imposing
waistline: his chocolate-ban-
ana-coffee "combo", his

macaron au fromage frais, lait
d'amande et griotte, or
mango-rhubarb puff pastry
with a hint of cinnamon are all
light as a summer breeze...
Now that the dismal service
has been overhauled by top
professional Serge Calvez, it
only remains to revamp the
unattractive decor (clumsily
camouflaged under an
avalanche of plants). While tariffs are well below what this
sort of food would command
in a more upscale
neighborhood, the cellar
tends to be overpriced.
A la carte: 500-700 F.
Menus: 190 F (lunch only),
240 F, 290 F and 320 F (dinner only).

12/20 Taverne Kronenbourg

L'Ambassade d'Alsace
24, bd des Italiens
47 70 16 64
*Open daily. Open until 3 a.m.
Private room: 100. Terrace dining. Air cond.*
The last of the *cafés-concerts*
on the Grands Boulevards (orchestra nightly) serves robust,
unpretentious brasserie fare:
shellfish, pork knuckle with
cabbage, sauerkraut and fine
Alsatian wines.
A la carte: 190-260 F.

10th arrondissement

12/20 Brasserie Flo

7, cour des Petites-
Ecuries
47 70 13 59
*Open daily until 1:30 a.m. Air
cond. Valet parking.*
The archetypal Alsatian
brasserie, Flo is a jewel: nowhere else will you find the
atmosphere, the superb
decor, the lively patrons, delicious sauerkraut washed
down with carafes of frisky
Riesling.... Note the "night
owl" supper, offered after
11 p.m.: a main dish, dessert

and wine cost only 99 francs. A la carte: 200-300 F. Menu: 99 F (weekdays lunch only, wine incl.).

 Au Chateaubriant
23, rue de Chabrol
48 24 58 94
Closed Sun., Mon., 1 wk. in winter & Aug. Open until 10:15 p.m. Air cond.
A very cozy, elegant little restaurant decorated with prints by modern masters (Picasso, Foujita, Chagall...). The menu offers opulent, no-nonsense Italian cuisine: scampi fritti with tartar sauce, ravioli stuffed with foie gras and truffles, delicious pasta and fine desserts (zabaglione al Marsala). Lately chef-proprietor Guy Bürkli has been experimenting most successfully in a Mediterranean vein, with dishes that give starring roles to fruits and vegetables, for example skate with fresh figs in raspberry butter, or young rabbit in aspic with fennel and artichokes.
A la carte: 350-500 F. Menu: 150 F (weekdays only).

12/20 **Les Deux Canards**
Chez Catherine
8, rue du Faubourg-Poissonnière
47 70 03 23
Closed Sat. lunch & Sun. Open until 10 p.m. Air cond.
The naïve charm of this dining room crammed with bric-a-brac close to the Grands Boulevards will surely win you over. The voluble owner (a former dentist) does not allow smoking—*nous aimons les fumeurs, pas la fumée*—so diners may enjoy the delicious duck terrine, sardines with pesto, Barbary duck à l'orange, and Provençal mussels in an unpolluted atmosphere. Admirable cellar.
A la carte: 250-400 F.

12/20 **Julien**
16, rue du Fg-St-Denis
47 70 12 06
Closed Dec. 24 dinner. Open until 1:30 a.m. Air cond. Valet parking.
If only for the pleasure of dining in these exuberant, wildly charming surroundings (vintage 1880), we are willing to put up with mediocre food; frankly, the kitchen turns out more than its share of botched dishes. But if you stick to the oysters, the cassoulet or eggs poached in red wine, you are likely to come away with a pleasant memory.
A la carte: 210-310 F. Menus: 99 F (weekdays lunch only, wine incl.), 143 F (w.-e. lunch and holidays).

 Le Louis XIV
8, bd St-Denis
42 08 56 56
Closed June 1-Aug. 31. Open until 1 a.m. Valet parking.
The decor is more Louis XV (Pompadour period!) than Louis XIV, but no one seems to mind. The festive, dressy crowd that dines here is too busy tucking into succulent roast duck, roast lamb, roast pigeon or juicy ribs of beef—preceded, ideally, by a sparkling assortment of fresh shellfish. Other seafood dishes are systematically overcooked. Jolly atmosphere.
A la carte: 300-550 F.

 Chez Michel
10, rue de Belzunce
48 78 44 14
Closed Sat. & Sun. (summer). Open until 10:30 p.m. Private room: 40. Air cond. Parking.
Sauces seem to be the chef's strong suit, witness the rich beurre blanc that accompanies chive-steamed turbot, or the sauce diable that adorns grilled Bresse chicken. We were also impressed by the suave salad of foie gras and artichoke bottoms and a lush lobster omelette. Prices are

outlandish, but the faithful habitués do not appear to notice or care.
A la carte: 400-450 F. Menus: 175 F (weekdays lunch and Sat.), 250 F (weekdays dinner and Sat.).

11/20 **Da Mimmo**
39, bd de Magenta
42 06 44 47
Closed Sun. & Aug. Open until midnight. Terrace dining.
Neapolitan Domenico (Mimmo) Sommella serves terrific spaghetti seasoned with hot-pepper oil and topped with tender clams. Delicious Italian cold meats, wonderful pizzas and good tiramisù round out the list of specialties, which the regulars wash down with carafes of tasty Apulian wine.
A la carte: 180-230 F. Menu: 90 F (wine incl.).

 La P'tite Tonkinoise
56, rue du Faubourg-Poissonnière
42 46 85 98
Closed Sun., Mon., Dec. 22-Jan. 4 & July 26-Sep. 7. Open until 10 p.m.
Old Indochina hands come regularly for a whiff of the exotic nostalgia that is practically palpable in this quiet establishment. The Costas, who ran a restaurant in Haiphong, have put their son Michel in charge of the kitchen, where he prepares an authentic repertoire of spring rolls, ginger-sautéed crab and mi-xao with seven vegetables in a crispy rice galette.
A la carte: 200-250 F.

12/20 **Terminus Nord**
23, rue de Dunkerque
42 85 05 15
Closed Dec. 24 dinner. Open until 12:30 a.m. Private room: 10.
Now part of the brasserie group of which Flo (see above) is the flagship, the Ter-

minus serves exactly the same food as the rest of the fleet. Enjoy the lively atmosphere, the gay 1925 decor, and look no farther than the sauerkraut, the briny oysters and the steak with chips. Nimble service.

A la carte: 250-350 F. Menu: 108 F (after 11 p.m. only).

11th arrondissement

 ### L'Aiguière

37 bis, rue de Montreuil
43 72 42 32
Closed Sat. lunch & Sun. Open until 10:30 p.m. Private room: 45. Air cond.
Elegant down to the last meticulous detail, this little restaurant serves romantic dinners with candlelight and piano music. The chef spurns simplicity, but his first-rate ingredients are prepared with care: try the prawn ravioli with sweet peppers, or tournedos with sweetbreads and truffles, then finish with a feuillantine de poires en chaud-froid. Excellent set menus.

A la carte: 350 F. Menus: 115 F (weekdays lunch only), 175 F.

 ### Astier

44, rue J.-P.-Timbaud
43 57 16 35
Closed Sat., Sun., Dec. 18-Jan. 4 & July 30-Sep. 6. Open until 10:30 p.m. Air cond.
For 130 francs, choose from a dozen first courses, another dozen main dishes (including several seafood offerings), a huge array of cheeses and at least six excellent desserts. This is French home-style cooking at its seasonal, market-fresh best: red mullet pan-roasted in olive oil, magret au cidre, skate with capers, rabbit in mustard sauce, yellow-plum clafoutis, and so on. The atmosphere is good-humored and noisy. Intelli-

gent, far-ranging cellar.
Menu: 130 F.

 ### La Belle Epoque

Holiday Inn
10, pl. de la République
43 55 44 34
Closed Sat. lunch, Sun. & Aug 1-29. Open until 10:30 p.m. Air cond.
Chef Patrice Trincali's subtle, sure, personal cuisine comes as something of a surprise in the hotel dining room of a Holiday Inn. The recent renovation of the premises will, we hope, attract the larger, more attentive public that this valiant young *cuisinier* deserves. You'll echo our praise after a taste of his delicate prawn salad with potatoes and cream, lobster in an aromatic broth with Thai-spiced ravioli or the delectable salmon roasted with honey and spices. Remarkable service; serious cellar.

A la carte: 350-450 F. Menus: 245 F (lunch only), 305 F and 405 F (dinner only).

 ### Cartet

62, rue de Malte
48 05 17 65
Closed Sat., Sun. & Aug. Open until 9 p.m.
The half-dozen tables and faded furnishings are a throwback to the days of the Front Populaire. The cooking is equally nostalgic, with no concessions made to modern-day calorie-counters: sheep's trotters in sauce poulette, tripe à la lyonnaise flambée, quenelles, croûte aux morilles and delicious sugar-dusted bugnes (fritters) that go down wonderfully with the wines of Bugey.

A la carte: 250-320 F.

> *Remember to call ahead to reserve your table, and please, if you cannot honor your reservation, be courteous and let the restaurant know.*

 ### Chardenoux

1, rue J.-Vallès
43 71 49 52
Closed Sat. lunch, Sun. & Aug. Open until 10:30 p.m. Parking.
In the heart of the old cabinet-makers' district, this graceful (listed) corner bistro displays its charms of marble, moldings and etched glass. Chef Dominique Mazelin blends country and bourgeois cooking in a most appealing manner: there's a novel salad of boudin and sour cherries, braised leg of lamb Auvergne-style, perfect aligot (garlicky mashed potatoes with cheese) and a wonderfully flaky apple tart. Connoisseur's cellar.

A la carte: 200-270 F.

 ### Chez Fernand

17, rue de la Fontaine-au-Roi
43 57 46 25
Closed Sun., Mon. & 3 wks. in Aug. Open until 11 p.m. Air cond.
This simple little storefront bistro celebrates the culinary glories of Normandy, with (in particular) an astonishing array of Camemberts, lovingly matured by the owner (who also makes his own bread and butter!). An enthusiastic corps of regulars is regaled with tasty terrines, a salad of marinated sardines with crisp vegetables, numerous duck dishes and an apple tart flamed with Calvados. Good wines from the Southwest and the Loire, at nice prices. (You'll spend even less at the restaurant's annex, Les Fernandises, two doors down the street.)

A la carte: 200-270 F. Menu: 130 F (weekdays lunch only).

11/20 Nïoullaville

32-34, rue de l'Orillon
43 38 30 44
Open daily until 12:30 a.m. Parking.
Most of the hundreds of dishes served to thousands of customers in this huge Chin-

ese food factory are quite good. Dim sum and roast meats are dispensed from trolleys rolled along by rude, glowering waiters. But never mind. The ambience is noisy and effervescent, and there is a dizzying selection of set menus (don't expect much help or advice from the aforementioned waiters).
A la carte: 180-250 F.

 Chez Philippe
Auberge Pyrénées-Cévennes
106, rue de la Folie-Méricourt
43 57 33 78
Closed w.-e., holidays & Aug. Open until 10:30 p.m. Air cond. Parking.
The menu written in purple ink is nothing if not eclectic: herrings Bismarck, grilled lobster, a monumental cassoulet, paella (the best in Paris), York ham with macaroni au gratin, beef bourguignon, turbot Dugléré, rock lobster in port and an old-fashioned braised hare. Believe it or not, it's all delicious and satisfying. Best of all, these earthy delights are served in the most convivial atmosphere imaginable, complete with a jovial host. Great Burgundies at giveaway prices only add to the gaiety.
A la carte: 300-400 F.

 Le Repaire de Cartouche
99, rue Amelot or 8, bd des Filles-du-Calvaire
47 00 25 86
Closed Sat. lunch, Sun. & Aug. 1-25. Open until 10:30 p.m.
Emmmanuel Salabert, a young chef with a brilliant resumé, presides over this shrine of Southwestern cooking. The prices and repertoire have so far remained stable, but the execution suffers occasional lapses—as does the slowcoach service. Try the warm foie gras wrapped in cabbage leaves, the lotte

stewed in Madiran wine or the Landais pie laced with Armagnac.
A la carte: 230-300 F. Menus: 220 F (Sat. dinner only), 150 F, 350 F.

 12th arrondissement

12/20 La Connivence
1, rue de Cotte
46 28 46 17
Open daily until 11 p.m. Private room: 50.
The endearingly low prices make the short, seasonal *carte* all that much more appealing: lentil salad with stuffed pig's tail, sautéed mussels with parsley, and a potée of guinea hen, cabbage and Lyonnais sausage with a spark of cumin are enjoyed by a trendy, slightly bohemian Bastille crowd.
A la carte: 140-200 F. Menu: 120 F.

12/20 Fouquet's Bastille
130, rue de Lyon
43 42 18 18
Closed Sat. lunch & Sun. Open until midnight. Air cond.
Sign of the (economic) times: Fouquet's Bastille has downscaled its "gastronomic" image for a much-simplified, lower-priced menu. Instead of tabs reaching 400 francs and more, patrons now shell out about half that sum for curried seafood salad, veal kidneys béarnaise, millefeuilles, all served with style and a smile. But culinarily speaking, the creative current has been cut. We'll follow the situation and report back later... watch this space!
A la carte: 200-250F. Menu: 165 F.

> *Some establishments change their closing times without warning. It is always wise to check in advance.*

 La Frégate
30, av. Ledru-Rollin
43 43 90 32
Closed Sat., Sun. & Aug. Open until 10 p.m. Air cond.
The huge menu of this friendly haven for bons vivants is dedicated to seafood. In addition there is an ample list of fresh, bountiful *plats du jour*, marred only by an occasional lapse in execution. We like the prawns served in the shell, the sea bass in Bouzy wine and the tasty marmite du pêcheur.
A la carte: 350-450 F. Menus: 200 F, 300 F.

 La Gourmandise
271, av. Daumesnil
43 43 94 41
Closed Sun., Mon., May 1-8 & Aug. 8-28. Open until 10:30 p.m. Parking.
Gourmand or gourmet, you'll be tempted to indulge in Alain Denoual's creative cuisine, served in a new, terribly chic decor of beige and blue. We were bowled over by the sheer inventiveness of his steamed sea bream cleverly heightened by black olives in vinaigrette, the duo of foie gras and magret backed up by a potato gratin, and the timbale de lapin aux choux. Cinnamon ice cream with an apple sablé is a dreamy dessert. The cellar (and the prices!) are progressing slowly but surely.
A la carte: 360-510 F. Menus: 190 F, 340 F.

 Le Mange Tout
24, bd de la Bastille
43 43 95 15
Closed Sun. & Aug. 15-30. Open until 11:30 p.m. Private room: 18. Terrace dining.
A refugee from the Latin Quarter, the Mange Tout has transferred its kitchens to the new Eldorado of the Bastille. The move didn't harm Michel Simon's tasty Southwestern repertoire, which he has extended to include some credit-

able fish dishes (rascasse à l'orange, grilled salmon béarnaise). Note the good regional wines (Gaillac, Cahors) and the irresistible prix-fixe menus. Well worth a toque.

A la carte: 200-250 F. Menus: 98 F, 380 F (for 2, wine incl.).

12/20 Chez Marcel

Restaurant Antoine
7, rue St-Nicolas
43 43 49 40
Closed Sat., Sun., Aug. & holidays. Open daily until 9:30 p.m.

Neither Marcel—nor Antoine, for that matter—mans the kitchen here any more. Jean-Claude Trottet gets the credit for the classic pig's trotters (served by the pair, if you please!), tripe, charcuterie and good baby lamb with beans. The decor is tumbledown, but the atmosphere wins one over with its friendly warmth. A wonderful spot!

A la carte: 200 F and up. Menu: 150 F.

 Au Pressoir

257, av. Daumesnil
43 44 38 21,
fax 43 43 81 77
Closed Sat., Sun., 1st wk. Feb. school holidays & Aug. Open until 10:30 p.m. Private room: 35. Air cond. Valet parking.

Forgotten by most Parisians since the Colonial Exposition closed 60 years ago, the Porte Dorée district is home to a covey of fine restaurants of which Le Pressoir is no doubt the best. Henri Séguin is a chef unmoved by trends who pursues his search for exciting flavors wherever it may lead him. We quiver with pleasure at the memory of a savory cassolette of Swiss chard, Jerusalem artichokes and truffles; of a crusty salmon with vegetable marmalade; of lotte with split peas and

bacon; of veal kidneys à l'orange with mushroom mousse; and of capon roasted with asparagus. Nor are we likely to forget such unprecedented desserts as pan-roasted quince with nougat or chocolate soup with warm brioche. The decor, which was progressing from dog-eared to dilapidated, recently underwent a facelift.

A la carte: 450-600 F. Menu: 360 F.

 Le Quincy

28, av. Ledru-Rollin
46 28 46 76
Closed w.-e., Mon. & Aug. 8-Sep. 10. Open until 10 p.m. No cards.

Here is a small, friendly, countrified restaurant that features hearty, simple dishes from rural France, washed down with Loire and Rhône Valley wines.

A la carte: 250-400 F.

 Sipario

69, rue de Charenton
43 45 70 26
Closed Sat. lunch & Sun. Open until midnight.

Not your corner pizzeria, Sipario has pretensions both aesthetic (the cool, airy dining room decorated with giant-vegetable frescoes is most attractive) and culinary. Regional Italian dishes, so hard to find in Paris, are proposed by a chef who claims that they are absolutely authentic versions. But though we salivate as we peruse the menu, we are sometimes disappointed by the reality (an insipid bollito misto, for example, and a guinea fowl that tasted distinctly of reheating). Yet the crostino al prosciutto is gooey and good, the involtini di vitello are plump and tender, and the tiramisù, for those who like it, is probably the best version around. The Italian wine list is wonderful.

A la carte: 230-330 F. Menu:

220 F (weekdays and Sun. dinner).

 La Sologne

164, av. Daumesnil
43 07 68 97
Closed Sat. lunch, Sun. & holidays. Open until 10:30 p.m. Parking. Air cond.

Koji Kaeriyama, the Japanese chef who purchased this neighborhood eating house not long ago, shows touching dedication to tradition: he maintains not only the house repertoire of game dishes offered in autumn and winter, but the restaurant's dated hunting-motif decor as well. The original, oft-renewed menu lists a delicious half-cooked, half-smoked duck with horseradish, galette de langoustines, and a filet de pigeon with truffle essence (the sauce is admirably light). Reasonable prices—particularly for the enticing set menus—and deft, professional service.

A la carte: 350-400 F. Menus: 175 F, 250 F.

 Le Temps des Cerises

216, rue du Faubourg-St-Antoine
43 67 52 08
Open daily until 10:30 p.m. Private room: 20. Terrace dining. Air cond.

A toque for Bernard Bergounioux's sagaciously seasonal cooking, which pays fragrant homage to the Southwest. Order the generously served and brightly seasoned terrine of young rabbit and prunes, the duck fillet sprinkled with sesame or a light navarin of lamb with young vegetables, and finish up with the delectable crème brûlée flavored with roasted chicory. The set menu is a bargain.

A la carte: 200-280 F. Menus: 95 F, 200 F.

Le Train Bleu

Gare de Lyon, 1st floor
20, bd Diderot
43 43 09 06,
fax 443 43 97 96
Open daily until 10:30 p.m. Private room: 100.

The extravagant, colossal, delirious, dazzling decor of Le Train Bleu has always been more than adequate compensation for the boring, "standard French" cooking (veal chop Foyot, quenelles, coquelet Val-de-Saône...) served here. But the advent of Michel Comby, a talented (though conservative) veteran chef, is bound to bring the menu in line with the glorious surroundings. Stay tuned!
A la carte: 330 F. Menu: 195 F.

12/20 Le Traversière

40, rue Traversière
43 44 02 10
Closed Sun. dinner, holidays & Aug. Open until 10 p.m.

Here is the neighborhood French restaurant of your dreams: a peaceful, provincial oasis where charming hosts are happy to serve you their hearty, delicious cooking. Don't miss the duck terrine, the leek gratin with lardons, or the young boar with wine-stewed pears. The cellar features wonderful Chinons. A la carte: 230-280 F. Menu: 150 F.

 ### Au Trou Gascon

40, rue Taine
43 44 34 26,
fax 43 07 80 55
Closed Sat., Sun., Aug. & Christmas wk. Open until 10 p.m. Air cond.

As chef Alain Dutournier tells it, a boyhood spent roaming the Gascon countryside inspired his deep-rooted devotion to the region's fresh produce. Though he now spends most of his time at his three-toque restaurant, Le Carré des Feuillants (see first arrondissement), Dutournier oversees the menu of the Trou Gascon, and develops new dishes which are prepared on a daily basis by the talented Jacques Faussat, who trained with the eminent Michel Guérard. Even Dutournier's oldest and most faithful fans would be hard put to say whether he or Faussat is behind the toothsome medley of asparagus and broad beans with aged ham, the warm pâté of cèpes with a parsley sauce, the pan-roasted foie gras, the calf's brains with morels, the rich duck and pork cassoulet. Game dishes are also close to Dutournier's heart (his spiced saddle of hare is pure magic), and they are best washed down, as is all this robust fare, by the cellar's marvelous Madirans and Jurançons. The lunch-hour set menu (the price hasn't budged for three years) is a delicious bargain.
A la carte: 380-550 F. Menus: 200 F (lunch only), 450 F.

 ## 13th arrondissement

12/20 Bœuf Bistrot

4, pl. des Alpes
45 82 08 09
Closed Sat. lunch, Sun., Christmas, 2 wks. in March & Aug. Open until 10:30 p.m. Private room: 50. Terrace dining.

Attention carnivores! A prime selection of pan-fried, boiled, grilled and roasted beef awaits you here in this oxblood-colored bistro. Between salad and dessert, admire the enviable collection of prints and drawings by Szafran, Giacometti, Van Velde and others displayed on the walls. Though the atmosphere is agreeably relaxed and casual, the prices are quite stiff.
A la carte: 290-360 F. Menus: 120 F (weekdays lunch only), 155 F (except holidays lunch).

 ### Les Marronniers

53 bis, bd Arago
47 07 58 57,
fax 43 36 03 80
Closed Sun. & July 27-Sep. 9. Open until 11 p.m. Terrace dining. Air cond. Valet parking.

In fine weather one may choose between a table in the pretty pink interior or one on a pleasant patio under the eponymous chestnut trees. The day's special dishes are usually the best part of chef Lorenzati's reliably appealing menu. Look for a good cassolette of wild mushrooms and shallots, Auvergne-style turbot, or succulent rabbit à la piémontaise.
A la carte: 280-350 F. Menu: 200 F.

Le Petit Marguery

9, bd de Port-Royal
43 31 58 59
Closed Sun., Mon., Dec. 23-Jan. 2 & July 27-Sep. 3. Open until 10:15 p.m. Private room: 15. No cards.

Michel and Jacques Cousin cook in a virile vein (game, offal, fresh fish, regional dishes) for an appreciative and very faithful public. Their bright, old-fashioned bistro is a most convivial spot; Alain Cousin directs fleet-footed waiters who deliver generous platefuls of pan-roasted wild mushrooms, gratin of fresh cod with oysters and asparagus, or partridge purée with juniper berries, as well as robust bourgeois classics like tête de veau ménagère and salt-cured duck à la poitevine. Delicious wines, improved desserts. Prices are still on the rise.
A la carte: 350-450 F. Menus: 160 F (lunch only), 320 F, 450 F.

Les Vieux Métiers de France
13, bd A.-Blanqui
45 88 90 03
Closed Sun. & Mon. Open until 10:30 p.m. Private room: 16. Air cond.

Onto an austere modern building, chef Michel Moisan (with considerable help from his friends) has grafted the most amazing medieval decor of sculpted wood, stained glass, ancient beams and antique paintings. What saves all this quaintness from tipping over into kitsch is Moisan's flavorful, personalized cuisine: pig's ear with prawns, seafood minestrone, spiced shoulder of lamb with barley meal and an array of luscious desserts. The cellar is an oenophile's dream.
A la carte: 350-400 F. Menus: 165 F, 290 F.

14th arrondissement

 L'Amuse Bouche
186, rue du Château
43 35 31 61
Closed Sat. lunch, Sun. & wk. of Aug. 15. Open until 10:30 p.m.

A former bouillabaisse joint has been transformed into an elegant apricot-colored dining room, where well-heeled patrons enjoy light dishes with clear, focused flavors. We suggest you sample the delicate warm artichokes with vegetables in vinaigrette, freshwater perch bathed in a fragrant prawn coulis, or meltingly tender young pigeon with a Provençal garnish of baby broad beans and tomatoes, then finish with the superb gâteau mousseux au chocolat amer. Succinct, well-designed wine list.
A la carte: 280-340 F. Menu: 145 F (lunch only).

 Les Armes de Bretagne
108, av. du Maine
43 20 29 50
Closed Sun. dinner, Mon. & Aug. Open until 11 p.m. Private room: 40. Air cond. Valet parking.

Here is an establishment that proudly upholds old-fashioned traditions of hospitality, service and French culinary showmanship in a luxurious Second Empire dining room. Top-quality seafood from Brittany stars in William Dhenin's best dishes: fresh oysters, sea bass en croûte with beurre blanc, abalone fricassée and grilled lobsters.
A la carte: 300-500 F. Menu: 200 F (weekdays only).

 L'Assiette
181, rue du Château
43 22 64 86
Closed Mon., Tues., Aug. & 2 wks. in Dec. Open until 10:30 p.m.

Lucette Rousseau ("Lulu"), the temperamental proprietress of this pretty, very Parisian spot, is first and foremost an A-1 cook. Behind the bantering charm she applies to her celebrated customers (Françoise Sagan, Karl Lagerfeld...) lies the dedicated soul of an inspired chef. We adore her generous, polished versions of Southwestern country classics: the salad of duck breast and foie gras, the braised vegetable medley with fresh truffles, the sweetbreads with meadow mushrooms, or the fine Pyrenees lamb. Prices are terrifying, but that is only to be expected when a potato and truffle salad contains nearly equal rations of both tubers!
A la carte: 400-500 F.

12/20 **Le Bar à Huîtres**
112, bd du Mont-parnasse
43 20 71 01
Open daily until 2 a.m. Private room: 15. Terrace dining. Air cond.

Everything's improving, even the service, at this popular oyster bar where, if you wish, you can order and eat just one oyster—but that would be a shame. Six or a dozen belons, fines, or spéciales would surely be more satisfying. Or book a table in the dining room and sample, in addition to the excellent shellfish, some good salt cod with aïoli or salmon with broccoli. Interesting cellar of white wines.
A la carte: 220-350 F.

 La Cagouille
In front of
23 rue d'Ouest,
12, pl. C.-Brancusi
43 22 09 01
Closed April 13, April 25-May 3, June 1, Aug. 8-30 & Nov. 2. Open until 10:30 p.m. Terrace dining.

Gérard Allemandou has a rare talent for drawing hordes of seafood lovers to the most improbable locations. Three years ago, even Parisian taxi drivers had never heard of the place Brancusi. Now the address is noted in every restaurant guide in the city, thanks to La Cagouille. The decor is a little cool (and awfully noisy), the welcome is lukewarm and the service often clumsy, but then this is not a grand restaurant—it is a *bistro du port*, where dishes made from the very freshest fish and shellfish (delivered direct from Atlantic ports) are chalked on a blackboard: depending on the day's catch, offerings might include tiny black scallops from Brest, fresh fried anchovies, red mul-

---

The A la carte restaurant prices given are for a complete three-course meal for one, including a half-bottle of modest wine and service. Menu prices are for a complete fixed-price meal for one, excluding wine (unless otherwise noted).

let with sea salt, cod and cabbage, divinely plump whiting with mustard sauce, steamed gilthead, or thick, juicy sole. If you are content to drink a modest Aligoté or Quincy, your bill will not rise much above 350 francs. But beware if you succumb to the temptations of the finest Cognac collection in Paris (or maybe the world)!
A la carte: 350-500 F.

 ### La Chaumière des Gourmets
22, place Denfert-Rochereau
43 21 22 59
Closed Sat. lunch, Sun., Aug. & 1st wk. of March. Open until 10:30 p.m. Private room: 12. Terrace dining.
The new owners, Jean-Paul and Nicole Huc, have not altered the cozy provincial decor, but the menu has been instilled with welcome new vigor: tuna carpaccio with fresh truffles, a very successful salad of sweetbreads and turnips, refreshing jellied bouillabaisse with garlic mayonnaise, and a good thin apple tart with bilberry coulis. Attractive list of white wines.
A la carte: 340-440 F. Menus: 165 F, 240 F.

12/20 La Coupole
102, bd du Montparnasse
43 20 14 20,
fax 43 35 46 14
Closed Dec. 24 dinner. Open until 2 a.m. Air cond.
This Montparnasse landmark has survived the takeover by the Flo brasserie group with its mystique intact; indeed, improved after a most successful facelift (layers of grime were removed from the famous murals). La Coupole's traditional lamb curry, fried whiting with tartar sauce, and cassoulet à l'oie are still on offer (and nicely prepared to boot), as are the exemplary shellfish

platters. Carafes of sprightly house Riesling delivered by swift, efficient waiters add to the charm.
A la carte: 230-280 F. Menu: 109 F (after 11 p.m. only, wine incl.).

11/20 La Créole
122, bd du Montparnasse
43 20 62 12
Open daily until 10:30 p.m. Air cond.
Tropical delights spill out onto the pavement from the plant-filled veranda. A warm, smiling staff serves forth rum punches and codfish fritters as preludes to zesty Creole specialties like stuffed sea urchin, octopus fricassée and more. Prices are on the rise.
A la carte: 220-250 F. Menu: 120 F.

 ### Le Dôme
108, bd du Montparnasse
43 35 25 81,
fax 42 79 01 19
Closed Mon. Open until 12:45 a.m. Private room: 10. Air cond.
A second toque for Le Dôme, in recognition of chef Franck Graux's wonderful *carte*, which now extends well beyond the traditional house specialties of bouillabaisse and lobster. His prawns wrapped in paper-thin pastry and served with a sapid shellfish bouillon are brilliant; bracing is the word that comes to mind for his tonic tartare of sea bream and salmon with watercress; fresh cod with vegetables and garlicky aïoli is superb. Desserts are worth saving room for: we loved the warm citrus baba napped with custard sauce. Service, of late, is more precise and cheerful, and the cellar is filled with bottles that beg one to splurge.
A la carte: 400-500 F.

 ### Le Duc
243, bd Raspail
43 20 96 30
Closed Sat., Sun., Mon., Dec. 21-Jan. 4 & wk. of Aug. 15. Open until 10:30 p.m. Air cond. No cards.
Jean Minchelli is no more, but his brother Paul (*"le génie du poisson"*) has returned from a lengthy sabbatical, and is running Le Duc's kitchen in person. It was he who taught Parisians to love raw fish; today, with his faithful disciple—Tonio—he continues to prepare raw sea bass fillets rubbed with shallots, cloves and Cognac, "petals" of coquilles Saint-Jacques, tiny clams sautéed with thyme, red mullet with pesto, and steamed turbot according to the Minchelli method. The classiest crowd in town still graces Le Duc's dining room, where the service is artfully orchestrated by Dominique Turpin. The cellar is a treasure trove of fabulous white wines, from Meursault-Les Charmes to the more modest (but excellent) Muscadet-sur-lie. Did we mention that prices are very high? Or that the chocolate cake is the only decent dessert? In parting, we must warn you that while all of our experiences at Le Duc have been memorable, some readers and colleagues have not always been so lucky...
A la carte: 500-850 F.

11/20 Au Feu Follet
5, rue R.-Losserand
43 22 65 72
Closed Sat. lunch, Sun., Aug. 9-25. Open until 10:15 p.m.
The chef-proprietor knows his traditional bistro repertoire inside out. The duck confit and the tarte Tatin will never disappoint, nor will the wines or hospitality offered at this modest but attractive little spot.
A la carte: 180-230 F. Menu: 72 F (weekdays only).

11/20 **Giovanna**

22, rue E.-Jacques
43 22 32 09
*Closed Sat. lunch, Sun. & Aug.
24-Jan. 2. Open until 10:30 p.m.*
You, your companion and
sixteen other diners can tuck
into perfectly wrought fresh
pasta and other tasty Italian
dishes in this minute *trattoria*.
Don't miss the osso buco.
A la carte: 120-160 F. Menu:
65 F (lunch only).

 Aux Iles Marquises

15, rue de la Gaîté
43 20 93 58
*Closed Sat. lunch, Sun. & Aug.
1-17. Open until midnight. Private room: 15.*
Once a favorite haunt of
Edith Piaf and her chums, the
Iles Marquises is now decked
out with a fresh nautical decor
(shrimp-colored walls with
seascape frescoes) which has
effectively erased any raffish
air that still hung about the
place. Chef-proprietor
Mathias Théry, a "disciple", so
he claims, of the Troisgros
brothers, ought to put a bit
more of his own personality
into such technically flawless
dishes as delicious pan-
roasted prawns and zucchini,
or the suave biscuit of
sweetbreads and morels, or
the tender young pigeon
roasted with garlic. Dessert
brings an outstanding sabayon
of pears and citrus fruits. The
cellar is rich in fine white
wines.
A la carte: 350-400 F.
Menus: 130 F and 150 F (except holidays).

12/20 **Justine**

Le Méridien Paris-
Montparnasse
19, rue du Comman-
dent-Mouchotte
43 20 15 51
*Open daily until 11 p.m. Air
cond. Valet parking.*
A gracious winter conservatory facing a green lawn is the

backdrop for Raoul Caïga's
dandy buffet lunch, which
counts as one of Paris's best in
the value-for-money league.
For 185 francs you can help
yourself to any amount of
soup, crudités, mixed salads,
terrines, fish, oyster and crab
dishes, not to mention three
hot dishes, cheese, pastries
and desserts.
A la carte: 250-300 F. Menu:
185 F (except Sun. lunch).

 Lous Landés

157, av. du Maine
45 43 08 04
*Closed Sat. lunch, Sun. & Aug.
1-29. Open until 10:30 p.m. Private room: 14. Terrace dining. Air
cond.*
Hervé Rumen's South-
western specialties range from
the frankly robust to more
refined versions of country
cooking: salad of quail and
smoked duck breasts in truffle
juice, superb sautéed wild
mushrooms, a cassoulet
which would be exceptional
with less mealy beans, and
delicious quail's legs grilled
with foie gras (oddly garnished
with raspberries and as-
paragus tips). Desserts are all
you would expect from a former colleague of Christian
Constant. A good cellar with a
notably excellent Cahors and
Madirans. Pretty green decor,
a lovely hostess and attentive
service.
A la carte: 330-430 F. Menu:
290 F.

 Le Moniage Guillaume

88, rue de la Tombe-
Issoire
43 22 96 15
*Closed Sun. & Aug. Open until
10:30 p.m. Private room: 25.
Terrace dining. Valet parking.
Hôtel: 5 rms, 240-320 F.*
A good address for fish. Prices are steep and the rustic-inn
look is not wildly attractive
(though the fireside tables and
the terrace are quite pleasant),

but Nelly Garanger's welcome
is wonderful and the dishes
prepared by her husband
Michel are always top quality.
Only good surprises can be
had from the fresh shellfish
(available year-round), roast
turbot, seasonal game and fine
apple tart. Far-ranging cellar.
A la carte: 330-600 F.
Menus: 195 F (weekdays
lunch only, wine incl.), 260 F,
420 F.

 Montparnasse 25

Le Méridien Paris-
Montparnasse
19, rue Cdt-Mouchotte
44 36 44 25,
fax 44 36 49 01
*Closed Sat., Sun. & Aug. Open
until 10:30 p.m. Private
room: 15. Air cond. Valet parking.*
The Art Deco interior opens
onto a tiny garden, bringing a
note of idyllic charm to the
surrounding concrete jungle.
Chef Jean-Yves Guého, im-
ported from the chain's Hong
Kong hotel, entices appetites
with turbot with wild
mushrooms, succulent duck
stew with potato gnocchi, and
one of the most remarkable
cheese boards in Paris. Delicate desserts round off an elegant and memorable meal. The
young sommelier is happy to
offer an excellent choice of
wines by the glass.
A la carte: 400-500 F.
Menus: 230 F (lunch only),
290 F and 380 F (dinner only).

12/20 **L'Olivier-Ouzerie**

9, rue Vandamme
43 21 57 58
*Closed Sun. & Aug. Open until
11:30 p.m.*
A small patio off a quaint
stone-and-tile interior is the
scene for an authentic
repertoire of Greek dishes:
squid à la grecque, moussaka,
spala and so on.
A la carte: 120-180 F.
Menus: 59 F (weekdays lunch
only, wine incl.), 89 F.

Pavillon Montsouris

20, rue Gazan
45 88 38 52,
fax 45 88 63 40
Open daily until 10:30 p.m. Private room: 40. Garden dining. Valet parking.

A walk across the Parc Montsouris at sunset will help you work up an appetite for a fine feast in this turn-of-the-century greenhouse overlooking the park, once a favorite rendezvous of the beautiful spy, Mata Hari. Stéphane Ruel's 255-franc menu adds allure to this Parisian charm spot, bringing hordes of people clamoring for his basil-scented bouillon of langoustines, or a deluxe hachis Parmentier made with duck, truffles and foie gras—every bit as good as Michel Guérard's. The honey-spiced duck served in two courses is a truly great dish, and for dessert, try the triple-chocolate concoction; our only cavil is that the vanilla-pod ice cream with candied oranges tastes very little of vanilla. Yvan Courault, who used to manage the Grand Véfour, excels in the art of warmly greeting and treating his clients.
Menu: 255 F.

 ## Les Petites Sorcières

12, rue Liancourt
43 21 95 68
Closed Sat. lunch & Sun. Open until 10:30 p.m. Terrace dining.
Christian Teule is a talented chef of the Robuchon school. Helped by his wife Carole, he has worked up a remarkable repertoire of simple and hearty dishes in his modest bistro: moules marinière, duck consommé with ravioli, or filet de rascasse au pistou. Good wines are available by the carafe.

A la carte: 180-230 F. Menu: 110 F (lunch only).

11/20 Aux Petits Chandeliers

62, rue Daguerre
43 20 25 87
Open daily until 11:30 p.m. Private room: 50.
A Creole decor around a flowered patio where you can drink a mean rum punch and eat sunny dishes like duck curry, enhanced with the spicy island sauces known as rougails.
A la carte: 150-250 F.

11/20 Rendez-Vous des Camionneurs

34, rue des Plantes
45 40 43 36
Closed Sat., Sun., Aug. & 1 wk. Feb. school holidays. Open until 9:30 p.m. Air cond.
We've never actually spotted a truck driver here, but all sorts of people crowd this friendly bistro where a big-hearted *patron* serves up toothsome pâté de campagne followed by a rack of lamb or flank steak with tasty white beans. Carafes of plonk are bargain-priced at 5 francs.
A la carte: 100 F. Menu: 58 F.

11/20 Le Restaurant Bleu

46, rue Didot
45 43 70 56
Closed Sat., Sun., July & Aug. Open until 10 p.m.
Hearty and generous fare—pork rillettes, mutton tripe, confits, and omelette with cèpes—are served forth here in a dining room all decked out in blue.
A la carte: 200-220 F. Menu: 80 F.

 ## Vassanti

3, rue Larochelle
43 21 97 43
Closed Tues. lunch & Mon. Open until 11 p.m. Air cond.
Tucked away in a cul-de-sac, this vintage Indian eatery has just inaugurated a good-looking Mogul-style decor. Mother presides at the stove, producing admirably light vegetable samosas, a creditably moist chicken tikka and some superb rice dishes. All would be perfect if the spicing were just a pinch more bold...
A la carte: 200-250 F. Menus: 99 F and 130 F (lunch only).

 ## Les Vendanges

40, rue Friant
45 39 59 98
Closed Sat. lunch, Sun. & Aug. Open until 10 p.m.
Here is a newcomer to the Southwestern scene. The enchaud en gelée (pork terrine) merits a recommendation, as does the filet de saumon au lard et aux cèpes, the magret with apples and potatoes and the prunes poached in tea. The Madiran wines are good (but not cheap), and the old-fashioned decor is not without charm.
A la carte: 270-370 F. Menu: 155 F.

12/20 Le Vin des Rues

21, rue Boulard
43 22 19 78
Lunch only (and dinner Wed. & Fri. upon reservation). Closed Sun., Mon., Feb.14-21 & Aug. Terrace dining. No cards.
Ex-baker Jean Chanrion's noisy, cramped bistro offers an exemplary Lyonnais repertoire, ranging from pot-au-feu to coq au Beaujolais and salt cod à la lyonnaise. The Beaujolais and Mâconnais wines are sold by the *pichet*, of course.
A la carte: 100-150 F.

15th arrondissement

 L'Aubergade
53, av. de La Motte-
Picquet
47 83 23 85
*Closed Sun. dinner, Mon., Dec.
27-Jan. 5, April 12-22 & Aug.
Open until 10:30 p.m. Private
room: 15. Terrace dining.*
Pierre and Rosanna Moisson
have shuffled off their mourn-
ful decor for a fresh new one.
Jean-Claude Poulnais is a
gifted chef who aims straight
for the taste buds with his
salmon with tomato compote,
andouillette de Troyes au
Chablis and a delicate apple
tart. The remarkable all-in business menu includes kir, wine
and coffee.
A la carte: 330 F. Menu:
150 F (lunch only).

Le Barrail
17, rue Falguière
43 22 42 61
*Closed Sat. & Sun. Open until
10 p.m. Private room: 15. Air
cond.*
An attractive spot done up in
soft pink tones. The cooking is
polished but low-key, and the
prices won't cause a heart
attack. Alain Magna's superb
langoustines au foie gras and
canard confit aux haricots retain the succulent savors of the
Southwest. Unbeatable prices
for lobster and even for such
luxurious dishes as rémoulade
de truffes aux girolles au foie
gras cru. Ho-hum cellar.
A la carte: 240 F. Menus:
100 F (lunch only), 150 F,
198 F.

 Bistro 121
121, rue de la Conven-
tion
45 57 52 90,
fax 45 58 07 59
*Open daily until midnight. Air
cond. Valet parking.*
This 30-year-old bistro,
founded by Jean Moussié and

decorated by Slavik, faithfully
serves the sort of classic,
sauce-heavy fare that will always be considered by some
to be "real" French cooking.
Hare à la royale and poached
stuffed chicken are two hold-
overs from the Bistro's early
days, but current chef André
Jalbert now concentrates on a
repertoire of rich, seasonal,
mainly seafood dishes: bay
scallops with three sauces,
panaché de sole au homard et
langoustines, roast baby lamb
with a (pedestrian) gratin
dauphinois. While à la carte
prices are steep, the two set
menus offer terrific value.
A la carte: 300-400 F.
Menus: 150 F and 200 F (wine
incl.).

 Le Bivio
101, rue de la Croix-
Nivert
48 28 31 88
*Open daily until 11 p.m. Private
room: 60. Terrace dining.*
A broad glass front opens
onto a coldly modern interior,
but conviviality reigns in this
lively Italian restaurant run by
the jovial Ermanno Chioda.
Wonderful hams, pappardelle
ai porcini and sage-scented
saltimbocca are just a few of
the appetizing transalpine
offerings. To help them on
their way, choose from an extensive selection of fine Italian
wines.
A la carte: 160-250 F. Menu:
120 F.

12/20 **Casa Alcalde**
117, bd de Grenelle
47 83 39 71
*Closed Mon. lunch & Dec. 20-
Jan. 6. Open until 10:45 p.m.
Private room: 40. Terrace dining.
Air cond.*
A folksy, rustic tavern where
one eats at blue-tiled tables in
a resolutely Spanish decor.
Tasty, straightforward fare
with strong Hispano-Basque
overtones: delicious chistorras
(grilled sausages with pep-

pers), confit de canard à
l'eskualduna (with ratatouille),
paella, and salt cod à la
luzienne. Judiciously selected
Spanish wines.
A la carte: 200-300 F.

 Les Célébrités
Hôtel Nikko
61, quai de Grenelle
40 58 20 00,
fax 45 75 42 35
*Open daily until 10 p.m. Private
room: 22. Air cond. Heated
pool. Valet parking.*
The Roman emperors who
stare down at the perpetual
parade of roast lobster and
stuffed pigs' trotters passing
under their plaster noses don't
seem as bored as we now are
with them—and with the rest of
this pompous, passé decor.
Still, there is the view of the
Seine beyond the bay
window, the comfort of well-
spaced tables, soft seating, the
attentive, well-trained staff and
above all, the artful cuisine of
Jacques Sénéchal. This former
Tour d'Argent chef has adroitly stepped into the shoes of
Joël Robuchon, the Nikko's
old star. His repertoire may be
a bit static, but we always welcome an opportunity to sample Sénéchal's virtuoso
cooking. Prices are steep here,
but that's to be expected these
days. What counts is the
food's irreproachable quality.
We cannot speak highly enough of the risotto with
prawns, turbot, and a sprightly
touch of tomato and basil; or
the monumental volaille de
Bresse aux morilles et à la
crème; or lush sweets like the
bright-tasting raspberry
clafoutis or unctuous tiramisù.
Surprisingly, the superb cellar
is less pricey than one might
fear. Impeccable service. Note
the worthwhile prix-fixe lunch:
it's the only bargain in sight.
A la carte: 700-800 F.
Menus: 250 F (lunch only),
610 F, 710 F.

Le Clos Morillons
50, rue des Morillons
48 28 04 37
Closed Sat. lunch, Sun., Feb. 22-28 & Aug. 8-24. Open until 10:15 p.m. Air cond.
Since he took over this quiet neighborhood bistro from Pierre Vedel some years ago, Philippe Delacourcelle has served consistently good food at reasonable prices. His menus, including the more expensive one which includes fine Loire wines (Pierre and his brother Marc are great connoisseurs) offer a selection of clever dishes that combine innovation and tradition in a most satisfying synthesis. To wit: terrine pressée de pommes de terre et foie gras au gros sel, roast salt cod with bacon and a smoky-flavored purée, young pigeon with sesame seeds. The many delectable desserts (Delacourcelle was once a pâtissier at Fauchon) provide instants of pure bliss in a light, charming new decor.
A la carte: 275-375 F. Menus: 150 F (dinner only), 220 F, 285 F.

 L'Entre-Siècle
49, av. Lowendal
47 83 51 22
Closed Sat. lunch, Sun. & Aug. Open until 10:30 p.m. Air cond.
Olivier Simon is a young Belgian chef out to conquer Paris with a repertoire that mixes Belgian dishes such as carbonnade à la flamande and waterzoï de volaille à la gantoise with more exotically inspired dishes such as a "beggar's purse" (crêpe) filled with Tunisian-spiced duck, or salmon with leeks and a hint of curry. Desserts are interesting too (just taste the spice-steamed pear with orange sauce). A small, eclectic wine list includes Belgian teas and beers.
A la carte: 280-350 F.

Menus: 160 F (lunch only), 210 F and 240 F (dinner only).

11/20 L'Epopée
89, av. E.-Zola
45 77 71 37
Closed Sat. lunch, Sun. dinner & Dec. 24-Jan. 3. Open until 10:30 p.m. Terrace dining.
An earnest little restaurant, recommended for its hospitality, fine cuisine and value for money. Appetizers (seafood salad, vegetable terrine with tomato purée) are often priced under 50 francs, while main dishes (calf's head ravigote, pané de bœuf grillé sauce marchand de vin) run from 80 to 100 francs. Suggestions change daily. To drink, order up a tasty Coteaux-du-Tricastin red from the Domaine de Grangeneuve—at 90 francs, you could hardly do better!
A la carte: 230-280 F. Menus: 145 F, 175 F, 225 F.

 Erawan
76, rue de la Fédération
47 83 55 67,
fax 47 34 85 98
Closed Sun. & Aug. 2-Sep. 2. Open until 10:30 p.m. Air cond.
A noisy clientele crowds into the little dining rooms of this appealing Thai bistro. The food is exciting and exotic, some of the best of its kind in Paris. Try the bite-sized shrimps, the pork and corn, fish steamed in a banana leaf, and beef with basil and green peppercorns.
A la carte: 180-380 F. Menus: from 132 F to 175 F.

12/20 La Farigoule
104, rue Balard
45 54 35 41
Closed Mon. dinner, Sun. & Aug. 14-30. Open until 10 p.m.
At nearly 60, Jean Gras is a colorful character if ever there was one. He has gone back to concocting the fragrant bouillabaisses and bourrides that made his former restaur-

ant, Aux Senteurs de Provence, a fixture in the fifteenth arrondissement. This is the best place in town for authentic sheep's tripe and trotters à la marseillaise.
A la carte: 250-300 F.

 Jacques Hébert
38, rue S.-Mercier
45 57 77 88
Closed Sun., Mon. & Aug. 1-20. Open until 10 p.m. Private room: 18.
Once the bulldozers have finished tearing up this arrondissement and the high-rise blocks of flats are finally built, a number of excellent bistros will come to light, courageously peeking out of the rubble. Jacques Hébert is already on the scene, patiently waiting for success. After working under Robuchon and having been the chef at the Sofitel-Invalides hotel for six years, Hébert decided to strike out on his own, in a small restaurant that is a little jewel of homey simplicity and taste. Try his saddle of rabbit with tarragon, or the calf's head with baby vegetables. The country wines are astutely chosen.
A la carte: 350-450 F. Menu: 260 F (dinner only).

 Kim-Anh
15, rue de l'Eglise
45 79 40 96
Dinner only. Open until 11:30 p.m. Air cond.
Charming Kim-Anh runs this tidy, flower-filled little Vietnamese restaurant while his wife Caroline practices her culinary craft in a lilliputian kitchen made for contortionists. She prepares her dishes with fresh herbs, delectable leaves and shoots, subtle spices and light sauces. Try the shredded beef pan-fried with peanuts and vinegar, steamed snails Tonkin, caramelized prawns and the best spring rolls in Paris. Quite a good

wine selection and some surprisingly yummy desserts.
A la carte: 250-330 F.

 Morot-Gaudry

8, rue de la Cavalerie
45 67 06 85,
fax 45 67 55 72
*Closed Sat. & Sun. Open until
10:30 p.m. Private room: 20.
Terrace dining. Air cond.*
It would be hard to find a
more ample or appetizing
lunch for 200 francs, a price
unchanged for years and
served by Jean-Pierre Morot-
Gaudry on the roof of this
1930's building. He offers a
choice of five first courses,
such as a very good house-
smoked salmon or soft-boiled
eggs with prawn coulis. Five
main dishes include a fabulous
tête de veau and a chervil-
scented lamb blanquette.
Cheese is followed by a lovely
selection of desserts: buckwheat crêpes filled with fruit
and spices, or an excellent
crème brûlée. A charming little wine—Coteaux-du-
Lyonnais, Gaillac, or
Haut-Poitou—is included.
Danièle Morot-Gaudry's welcome is wonderful, and from
the verdant terrace you can
glimpse a corner of the Eiffel
Tower.
But Morot-Gaudry doesn't
stop there. His à la carte menu
is a subtle marriage of classic,
rustic and contemporary
dishes such as lasagne de
petits-gris (small snails) with
morels, a ragoût of salmon and
perch with fennel and rosemary, or mouthwatering aged
beef sauce béarnaise.
Some impressive and costly
wines are available such as a
Montrachet "Marquis de
Laguiche" or a Gruaud-Larose
'28. But what thrills us at
Morot-Gaudry is the selection
of Jurançons, Chinon Vieilles
Vignes, Savennières and
Vouvrays which give enormous pleasure without breaking
the bank.

A la carte: 400-550 F.
Menus: 200 F (lunch only,
wine incl.), 520 F (wine incl.),
370 F.

 L'Oie Cendrée

51, rue Labrouste
45 31 91 91
*Closed Sat. lunch, Sun., holidays
& July 14-Aug. 15. Open until
10 p.m. Private room: 15.*
The two rooms could do
with a dash of gaiety and less
constricting tables. The new
chef's cuisine is a faithful interpretation of Southwestern
specialties, based on top-quality ingredients: slightly bland
goose quenelles with spinach,
foie gras, cassoulet and prunes
in Armagnac. A tiny cellar of
regional wines.
A la carte: 170-250 F.
Menus: 95 F, 125 F.

 Olympe

8, rue N.-Charlet
47 34 86 08,
fax 44 49 05 04
*Closed Mon., Sat. lunch & Sun.,
Aug. 14-17 & Dec. 23-25. Open
until 11 p.m. Air cond.*
Now that she is working on
other projects, notably at the
Virgin Megastore on the
Champs-Elysées (a resounding
success, we might add),
Dominique Nahmias no lon-
ger rules over Olympe. But Albert Nahmias is still on hand,
and has relaunched the
restaurant as a fashionable
bistro, serving food that is
rather more clever and robust
than sophisticated. The now-
famous sautéed crayfish are
still available, but there is also
a 200-franc menu (served at
lunch and dinner) which offers
calf's-brains fritters with
capers, roast rabbit with
artichoke pesto, duck ravioli
au jus, and for dessert, a Paris-
Brest or crémet à l'orange. In
the same spirit, Albert hunts
up good little wines at pleasing
prices. The à la carte menu
retains the distinctive house
style, prepared (successfully,

so far) by a well-trained team.
The Orient-Express decor
could do with a facelift but the
largely Parisian and Californian clientele isn't complaining.
A la carte: 300 F. Menus:
200 F (lunch only, wine incl.),
160 F (lunch only), 285 F.

**11/20 Le Patio
Montparnasse**

30-32, bd de Vaugirard
43 22 30 25
*Closed Sat. lunch, Sun. & 2 wks.
in Aug. Open until 10:30 p.m.
Terrace dining.*
Not a bad decor and a good
little set menu: curried
fricassée of cockles and
mussels, pan-fried kidneys and
brains, frozen nougat with caramelised almonds. Interesting
little cellar, too.
Menus: 110 F (lunch only),
125 F (dinner only).

12/20 Le Petit Mâchon

123, rue de la Conven-
tion
45 54 08 62
*Closed Sun. & July 20-Aug. 20.
Open until 11 p.m. Terrace dining.*
This is Slavik's re-creation of
an old-fashioned bistro and it's
devoted to the rib-sticking
cuisine of Lyon: first-rate
charcuterie, caviar lyonnais
(hot lentils with shallots), pigs'
trotters, and tripe. Ice cream
from Berthillon for dessert.
A la carte: 130-190 F.

 **La Petite
Bretonnière**

2, rue de Cadix
48 28 34 39
*Closed Sat. lunch, Sun. & Aug.
Open until 10 p.m. Parking.*
In eight years, Alain Lamaison and his wife Georgia have
perked up this little restaurant
with a modest, charming
decor worthy of the splendid,
essentially Southwestern cuisine. Lamaison's dishes are
lively and daring, particularly
in their treatment of vegetables and fruit. Prices are no

longer what they were, but the food is worth the money: pigeon roasted in spiced wine, served with a date purée; warm foie gras with a pear-and-celeriac gratin; and a crisp honey-sweet pastry with dried fruits and nuts. Very good cellar, rich in Bordeaux.

A la carte: 400-450 F. Menu: 240 F (lunch only).

12/20 Chez Pierre

117, rue de Vaugirard
47 34 96 12
Closed Sun., Sat. lunch, Mon. & Aug. Open until 10:15 p.m. Air cond. Parking.

Some good country dishes such as bœuf bourguignon aux pâtes fraîches, cassoulet, and confit de canard in an exemplary neighbourhood restaurant.

A la carte: 250 F. Menus: 120 F (lunch only), 175 F.

Raajmahal

192, rue de la Convention
45 33 29 39
Open daily until 10:45 p.m. Air cond.

You can still feast your eyes on the lavish Hindu decor of this temple of North Indian cuisine, and you won't tire of the wonderful selection of breads. The famous lamb curry, the meat samosas, the boti tandoori aren't quite as irresistibly scrumptious as they once were, but the food is more than respectable, and generously apportioned to boot. Perfect service. The economical prix-fixe lunch includes one appetizer plus a main dish for just 59 francs.

A la carte: 230-300 F. Menu: 59 F (lunch only).

Le Relais de Sèvres

Hôtel Sofitel Paris
8-12, rue L.-Armand
40 60 30 30
Closed Sat., Sun., Aug. & Dec. 23-Jan. 1. Open until 10 p.m.

Private room: 15. Air cond. Heated pool. Valet parking.

Roland Durand is off on his own now. He has passed on his apron to his former second-in-command, 33-year-old Martial Enguehard. In order to encourage the latter's efforts, the Sofitel at last gave the dining room a long-overdue facelift. The pale-blue walls and Champagne-colored tablecloths may not be stunning, but they are fresh and inviting. The cuisine retains Durand's inimitable touch: sample the crab with foie gras and broccoli, ravioles d'escargot en gelée, turbot with mustard, or veal kidneys with a bright garnish of sorrel and caramelised tomatoes, before choosing one of the superb desserts: creamy soupe de semoule aux mangues, or gingery nougat glacé. The question is: will Enguehard develop his own style, or continue to serve Durand's repertoire? This year will undoubtedly tell the story. An excellent, reasonably priced cellar; exceptionally varied set lunch.

Menus: 290 F and 430 F (dinner only), 320 F (lunch only).

Aux Senteurs de Provence

295, rue Lecourbe
45 57 11 98,
45 58 66 84
Closed Sun., Mon., Aug. 2-24 & 1 wk. in winter. Open until 10 p.m.

The owner is Tuscan and his new chef is a native of Burgundy, but they remain faithful to the Provençal repertoire long prepared here by former owner Jean Gras. Every Wednesday in the long, narrow dining room with cork-covered walls and jaunty nautical prints, the *plat du jour* is a wonderful aïoli complete with garlicky rouille and fat sea snails. Bouillabaisse and

daube d'agneau provençale can be had any day of the week. To drink, order one of the good wines from the Coteaux-d'Aix.

A la carte: 250-350 F. Menus: from 195 F to 225 F.

Uri

5, rue Humblot
45 77 37 11
Closed Sun. & Aug. Open until 10:30 p.m. Air cond.

Paris boasts few good Korean restaurants, so it's not difficult to understand why you can hardly get through the door of this one. It's always packed with homesick exiles in search of kimchee, raw skate salad, and any number of fiercely salted and vinegary native dishes. Expect a cordial welcome from the Cho family.

A la carte: 170-270 F.

Pierre Vedel

19, rue Duranton
45 58 43 17,
fax 45 58 42 65
Closed Sat. & Sun. Annual closings not available. Open until 10:15 p.m.

Be sure to book your table in advance, because Pierre Vedel's warm and wonderful Parisian bistro is invariably jam-packed. Little wonder the place is popular, with offerings like shellfish ravioli, chicken-liver mold with lobster coulis and sweetbreads en blanquette with wild mushrooms on the menu. True to his Southern roots, Vedel also prepares an admirably authentic bourride de lotte à la sétoise (a garlicky monkfish soup), and a satisfying nougat glacé studded with candied fruit. If you order one of the more modest growers' wines from the interesting list, you can rest assured that the bill won't be too bad—Vedel's clients are friends, and he means to keep them!

A la carte: 300-350 F.

12/20 Le Volant

13, rue B.-Dussane
45 75 27 67
*Closed Sat. lunch, Sun. & Aug.
1-15. Open until 11 p.m.*
Georges Houel is an ex-racing champion who wears his four-score years very lightly. He's a champ in the kitchen too, where he turns out superb red meats, top-flight ris de veau and succulent veal kidneys. All washed down with Georges Dubœuf's fruity Beaujolais.
A la carte: 180-250 F.

12/20 Le Western

Hilton
18, av. de Suffren
42 73 92 00
Open daily until 11 p.m.
Serving staff in jeans and check shirts welcome you to the Hilton's American-style restaurant, Le Western, which overlooks the garden with its cacti and Indian statuary. Chef Alain Bertrand prepares Tex-Mex favorites and Stateside specialties such as spareribs, mixed grill and jumbo shrimp with peppercorn sauce. Starters include guacamole and crab fritters, and there's cheesecake, brownies and apple and pecan pie for dessert. On weekdays the "Pony Express" menu —starter, choice of two main courses, dessert and coffee—lets you lunch in 45 minutes flat.
A la carte: 250-300 F. Menu: 150 F.

16th arrondissement

Amazigh

2, rue La Pérouse
47 20 90 38
Closed Sat. lunch, Sun. & Aug. Open until 11 p.m. Air cond.
Antiques and Oriental knick-knacks against a brick-colored background make up the decor of this elegant dining room. You can expect attentive and courteous service, and highly refined North African cuisine: try the unusual stuffed sardines, the seafood briouat, tajines of fresh broad beans or lamb and eggplant, or a good couscous royal (the vegetables and broth could do with bolder seasoning). A few African wines are on hand, as well as a wider selection of French bottlings (the latter fetch fearsome prices).
A la carte: 300-350 F.

10/20 Auberge du Bonheur

Bois de Boulogne
Allée de Longchamp
42 24 10 17
Closed Fri. & Sat. (Nov.-April). Open until 11 p.m. Garden dining. Valet parking.
Happy indeed are the patrons seated in sun-dappled comfort under broad parasols and venerable plane trees at this delightful Bois de Boulogne venue. Charming service (quite a feat, considering the crowds) and simple, unpretentious food: salads, grilled meats, good desserts.
A la carte: 200-270 F.

La Baie d'Ha Long

164, av. de Versailles
45 24 60 62
Closed Sun. & Aug. Open until 10:15 p.m. Air cond.
Roger, the proprietor of this small Vietnamese spot, is far more interested in his collection of birds and exotic fish than in food. It is his wife Nathalie who works away in the kitchen producing delicious, exotically flavorful dishes from her native Vietnam: spicy soups, brochettes made with extraordinary fresh herbs, duck grilled with ginger. Generous portions. The cellar holds some surprisingly good wines.
A la carte: 200-240 F. Menu: 95 F (lunch only).

12/20 Bellini

28, rue Le Sueur
45 00 54 20
Closed Sat. lunch, Sun. & Aug. 3-29. Open until 11 p.m. Air cond.
Comfy banquettes, smoked mirrors, gray marble and peach-toned walls create a cozy setting for Bellini's somewhat Frenchified Italian fare. Sample the risotto with white truffles (or black truffles, when the short season for tartufi bianchi ends), spaghetti alla bottarga (with mullet eggs), fresh vegetables in olive oil and a smooth tiramisù, all washed down with appealing wines from Friulia, Tuscany and the Veneto. The set lunch is good value.
A la carte: 250-350 F. Menus: 150 F (lunch only), 200 F (dinner only).

Paul Chène

123, rue Lauriston
47 27 63 17
Closed w.-e., July 31-Sep. 1 & Dec. 23-Jan. 3. Open until 10:30 p.m. Private room: 30. Air cond. Parking.
Paul Chène has turned over his popular restaurant to new owners, but the spirit of his provincial, home-style cuisine is carried on by his chef André Ravigneau. Some improvements have been made, and now the food evinces a lighter touch and more vigorous flavors. All the more reason, then, to rediscover the marvelous fresh mackerel in Muscadet, flawless breast of duckling with foie gras in a light jelly, or daube de bœuf à l'ancienne. For dessert, there are dainty apple fritters with redcurrant jelly. The cellar boasts a far-ranging, judicious selection, but the tasty house Bordeaux is not to be neglected.
A la carte: 350-450 F. Menu: 250 F.

Conti

72, rue Lauriston
47 27 74 67
Closed 3 wks. in Aug. Open until 10:30 p.m. Air cond.

Slavik has refurbished Conti's rather Luciferian decor of mirrors with black and gold highlights. Chef Michel Ranvier took the cue, and has revamped his repertoire of provincial Italian dishes, giving them a vigorous, modern— French!—zest. His puff-pastry tart of fennel and fresh anchovies is the lightest, most ethereal "pizza" you are likely to encounter; appetizing too are the Gorgonzola flan with Marsala butter, sea scallops bristling with rosemary leaves, and a poached chicken breast with anchovies and truffles. The best tiramisù in Paris is to be found right here, along with a superb Italian cellar, excellent service and a chic, well-bred clientele.
A la carte: 400-500 F. Menu: 265 F (weekdays lunch only, wine incl.).

 L'Estournel

Hôtel Baltimore
1, rue L.-Delibes
44 34 54 34,
fax 44 34 54 44
Closed Sat., Sun., Aug. 1-29. Open until 10 p.m. Private room: 80. Air cond. Parking.

The new decor features admirably executed frescoes, but their charm is virtually canceled out by the bland furnishings. Oh well, at least the room is spacious and comfortable, and the elegant staff warms up the atmosphere nicely. Chef Daniel Le Quéré works in a classic mode, with considerable success. Despite a flawed dish or two (the prawn and basil salad lacked character, we thought) we enjoyed a recent meal that included a flavorful chartreuse of red mullet and an exceptional tarte Tatin. Encyclopedic cellar; high prices.

A la carte: 400-500 F. Menu: 250 F (weekdays only).

 Fakhr el Dine

30, rue de Longchamp
47 27 90 00
See 8th arrondissement.

 Faugeron

52, rue de Longchamp
47 04 24 53,
fax 47 55 62 90
Closed Sat. (except dinner Oct.-April), Sun., Dec. 23-Jan. 3 & Aug. Open until 10 p.m. Private room: 14. Air cond. Valet parking.

Golden oak paneling now enhances Faugeron's large blue-and-saffron dining room, a decor that some find rather chi-chi, but which everyone finds comfortable. Under the smiling supervision of hostess Guerlinde Faugeron, prize-winning sommelier Jean-Claude Jambon and a whole squadron of courteous (but never obsequious) waiters tend to the patrons, while chef-proprietor Henri Faugeron runs the kitchen. Although he is not obsessed by novelty, Faugeron renews his menu often enough to keep our mouths watering and our curiosity alive. Surely one never tires of such classics as soft-boiled eggs with truffle purée, admirable house-smoked salmon, wild mushrooms with foie gras, Challans duckling with turnips, or tender fillet of beef with bone marrow; yet one is delighted to discover new dishes like prawns in a spiced vinaigrette with fried celery, salmon steak with muscat butter and a tonic touch of mint, or a truly memorable combination of young rabbit and potatoes perfumed with fresh dill.
A pear millefeuille with honey cream sauce, or pistachio-caramel ice cream are a final thrill to be savored along with the last drops of a great Bordeaux,

a voluptuous Burgundy, or a more modest Chinon or Sancerre. The calm, unruffled ambience attracts a classy clientele; the impressive four-course set lunch has numerous fans.
A la carte: 650-850 F. Menus: 320 F (lunch only), 550 F (dinner only, wine incl.), 780 F (truffles in seas.), 500 F.

 Jean-Claude Ferrero

38, rue Vital
45 04 42 42,
fax 45 04 67 71
Closed Sat. (lunch in winter), Sun., holidays, May 1-18 & Aug. 10-Sep. 5. Open until 10:30 p.m. Private room: 35. Valet parking.

If you're looking for a winter treat, book a table here when Jean-Claude Ferrero is serving his famous "all-truffle" menu. Throughout the winter months, this Second Empire *hôtel particulier* welcomes a faithful, very Parisian crowd avid to sample those irresistible, earthy delights. Less expensive and just as lustily flavorful are Ferrero's aïoli with salt cod, blanquette de veau à l'ancienne, and bœuf aux carottes, dishes which are regularly featured in the prix-fixe lunch. But Ferrero earned his third toque last year for more spirited, often ingenious creations that make dining here an adventure. We're thinking of the fragrant old prawns "Monsieur le Préfet", or truffled calf's foot and sweetbreads, or the wonderful langoustes aux huiles douces, or a garlic-studded leg of Pauillac lamb served with a creamy gratin dauphinois. But there are plenty of other marvellous offerings to choose from (bouillabaisse raphaëloise, sea bass à la porquerollaise...). Our sole quibble is that desserts do not always live up to the standards set by the rest.
A la carte: 450-800 F.

Menus: 220 F (lunch only), 350 F.

12/20 Les Filaos

5, rue Guy-de-Maupassant
45 04 94 53
Closed Sun. & 2 wks. in Aug. Open daily until 10:30. Air cond.
The dining room is tidy and neat, the cuisine straight from the island of Mauritius—its spicy Creole fare (deliciously fiery rougails) with a strong Indian influence (Madras-style curry). The savory pork curry with red beans will put tropical sunshine in your veins and fire in your belly!
A la carte: 200 F. Menu: 82 F (lunch only).

La Fontaine d'Auteuil

35 bis, rue La Fontaine
42 88 04 47
Closed Sat. lunch, Sun., Feb. 21-28 & Aug. Open until 10:15 p.m. Private room: 12.
Shy, modest Xavier Grégoire, late of the Hilton's Toit de Paris, has spread his wings since he came to this flower-decked establishment next to the Maison de la Radio. Try his marinated sardines—rollmop style—his pan-fried coquilles Saint-Jacques sprinkled with chopped nuts and garlic, his luscious vanilla ice cream, and an airy millefeuille. A la carte prices are too high, but the set menu served at lunch is a very good deal indeed. Attractive little cellar.
A la carte: 380-450 F. Menu: 170 F (lunch only).

Chez Géraud

31, rue Vital
45 20 33 00
Closed off-season Sat. lunch, Sun. & Aug. Open until 10 p.m. Air cond.
Right across the street from Jean-Claude Ferrero, Gérard Rongier has converted a former bakery into a small neighborhood restaurant complete with banquettes, Sarreguemines tiles, immaculate napery and attentive service. Géraud packs in an appreciative audience with a menu that features sole aux morilles, raie à la moutarde à l'ancienne, roast rabbit with garlic and succulent roast Bresse chicken. And the patrons just keep coming back for more. Fans of Côtes-du-Rhône, Savigny-lès-Beaune or Pineau des Charentes (the latter a golden nectar to sip as an apéritif) will love the wine list. Desserts, though improved, still need work.
A la carte: 250-330 F.

Le Grand Chinois

6, av. de New-York
47 23 98 21
Closed Mon. & Aug. Open until 11 p.m. Private room: 30.
The Peking duck is still golden and crisp, but the other disheus we've tried here recently seem to indicate that the chef is losing his touch. How else can we explain the unpleasantly sticky, greasy sautéed shrimp and vegetables? Or the bland, uninteresting sautéed turbot? Owner Colette Tan's warm smile and greeting didn't allay our disappointment—nor do they lessen the sting of the bill! Sorry, but we're knocking two points off the rating this year.
A la carte: 220-300 F.

La Grande Cascade

Bois de Boulogne
Near the race-track
45 27 33 51,
fax 42 88 99 06
Closed Dec. 20-Jan. 20. Open until 10:30 p.m. Private room: 50. Garden dining. Valet parking.
In springtime everyone (it seems) heads to the half-moon terrace of Napoléon III's former pleasure pavilion, shaded by a graceful glass-and-iron marquee. This stylish Belle Epoque establishment offers the reassuring culinary repertoire of Jean Sabine, an enlightened classicist who doesn't mistake tradition for stuffiness. Try his scallop salad sprinkled with walnut oil, salmon with bits of bacon and curly Savoy cabbage, sautéed veal kidneys, or rack of lamb with wild thyme. The cellar houses 80,000 bottles, service is formal, and though à la carte prices are anything but rustic, the set lunch is relatively economical.
A la carte: 600-800 F. Menu: 270 F (weekdays lunch only).

Marius

82, bd Murat
46 51 67 80
Closed Sat. lunch, Sun. & Aug. Open until 10:30 p.m. Terrace dining.
Come summer, the bright little dining room is enlarged by a terrace, nicely shaded by a row of spindle trees. New owners have brought a youthful, energetic tone to this old bouillabaisse institution, and have bucked up the quality considerably (the prices remain reasonable, we are glad to report). Try the wonderfully bracing crab salad, or the simple, satisfying smoked haddock with butter sauce. Delicious desserts. Smiling (but often slow) service.
A la carte: 250-320 F.

11/20 Mexico Café

1, pl. de Mexico
47 27 96 98
Open daily until 11 p.m. (Sat. & Sun. until midnight). Terrace dining.
An amusing retro decor, attentive service and a pro in the kitchen: fresh pasta salad, andouillette, magret de canard. Cheerful spot, beloved of young trendies.

Verre Harcourt, créé en 1825.

SUR LES AILES DU TEMPS UN BACCARAT S'ENVOLE.

A la carte: 200-250 F. Menu: 135 F (lunch only).

Al Mounia

16, rue de Magdebourg
47 27 57 28
Closed Sun. & mid-July-Aug. Open until 11 p.m. Air cond.
The owner, his chef, and the sous-chef all hail from Casablanca. They produce some fine tajines and a delectable lamb couscous served in a seductive Moorish setting. A tiny cellar offers the usual Moroccan wines.
A la carte: 300 F.

Passy-Mandarin

6, rue Bois-le-Vent
42 88 12 18
Closed 2 wks. in Aug. Open until 11:15 p.m. Air cond.
Lots of local color in the three bright, spacious dining rooms. Dashing white-coated waiters serve forth dishes prepared by a chef at the top of his form. Highly original stews (cocks' combs, fish...), lotte with soy beans, and excellent stuffed frogs' legs keep the Mandarin's toque firmly in place. Cheerful service.
A la carte: 160-320 F.

Le Pergolèse

40, rue Pergolèse
45 00 21 40,
fax 45 00 81 31
Closed Sat., Sun. & Aug. Open until 10:30 p.m. Private room: 25.
The pastel-pink decor of this stylish establishment is as classy as the service. A well-bred, well-heeled clientele converses in hushed tones while chef Albert Corre pampers them with scallops with thyme blossoms, scrambled eggs with snails and chanterelles, braised sweetbreads with cèpes and other less complicated but clever dishes. Delectable desserts, good regional wines.
A la carte: 440-500 F.
Menus: 230 F, 300 F.

Le Petit Bedon

38, rue Pergolèse
45 00 23 66,
fax 45 01 96 29
Closed Sat. (except Sep. 15-April 15), Sun. & July 31-Aug. 29. Open until 10 p.m. Air cond.
Chef Pierre Marchesseau is known for his television appearances and as a cookbook author. He won over the chic clientele of Le Petit Bedon's little dining room (the decor is straight out of *House and Garden*) with spirited renditions of culinary classics (now more often prepared, as Marchesseau admits, by his associate chef, Bernard Troullier). Try the filets de rouget à la fondue de foie gras et d'oignon, duck with lentils, rack of lamb with gratin dauphinois, or the lush poularde au vin jaune. The desserts—profiteroles au chocolat, honey-caramel-pistachio ice cream, cherry fondue—will titillate even the most jaded palate. A fine cellar, professional service, dizzying prices.
A la carte: 500-600 F. Menus: 185 F (lunch only), 250 F, 350 F.

Le Port Alma

10, av. de New-York
47 23 75 11
Closed Sun. & Aug. Open until 10:30 p.m. Private room: 15. Air cond.
"Scandalous", we wrote a while back, having noticed all the empty seats in one of the finest fish restaurants in town. Luckily, a lot of Parisian seafood aficionados took our protest to heart, for things are definitely looking up in this bright (too bright? maybe even loud?) dining room. Madame Canal's welcome is lovely and warm, and the astonishingly fresh crustaceans and fish are prepared with a light touch by the Dôme's former chef. Sample the wonderful hot oysters with cockles, a fillet of turbot

scented with thyme and escorted by a delicate ragoût of fresh broad beans, or the engaging fricassée of sole with foie gras; for dessert, choose a walnut crème brûlée or a thin apple tart. Wash it all down with a bottle of Roger Neveu's Sancerre or an Hermitage from Guigal, and you'll know the meaning of bliss. Paul Canal is one chef who doesn't skimp on quality ingredients, or mask their flavors with superfluous sauces. For committed carnivores the menu lists just one meat dish, but it is a côte de bœuf de Salers: a rib of some of the finest beef in France.
A la carte: 400-600 F. Menu: 200 F (lunch only).

Le Pré Catelan

Bois de Boulogne
Rte de Suresnes
45 24 55 58,
fax 45 24 43 25
Closed Sun. dinner, Mon. & Feb. school holidays. Open until 10 p.m. Private room: 30. Garden dining. Valet parking.
Colette Lenôtre has retired to her vineyard in Bordeaux, leaving this Second Empire landmark in the capable hands of Roland Durand. Working in brand-new kitchens, this talented chef has thoroughly revamped the house repertoire, marking it with his personal stamp and style. Judging by diners' reactions, Durand's menu is a rousing success. They—and we—applaud the rich gratin de macaroni au foie gras, the truffled rabbit terrine, scallops given a boost with a dash of cinnamon, which underscores their natural sweetness, and the rib of prime Bavarian beef bathed in a sapid parsley and marrow jus.
A la carte tariffs continue to spiral skyward; we recommend that you take a close look at the appealing "menu-carte" (a fixed-price

65

formula which offers a wider choice than the traditional set menu) that Durand has just designed. The cellar is large, with manageable prices. But don't fool yourself–depending on how recklessly you order, the bill may add up to more than you can swallow!

A la carte: 700-1,000 F. Menus: 550 F, 650 F.

Quach

47, av. R.-Poincaré
47 27 98 40
Closed Sat. lunch. Open until 11 p.m.
Aquariums decorate this elegant dining room where Mr. Quach serves some delectable little Cantonese and Vietnamese dishes: shrimp grilled with lemon grass, squid with red peppers, and five-flavor grilled lamb. But it's the Peking duck that keeps the upscale patrons coming back for more. Served, as it should be, in three separate courses, the duck is indeed a delight. Prices are quite reasonable–for the neighborhood.

A la carte: 220-280 F. Menus: 92 F (weekdays lunch only), 109 F.

Le Relais d'Auteuil

Patrick Pignol
31, bd Murat
46 51 09 54,
fax 40 71 05 03
Closed Sat. lunch, Sun. Annual closings not available. Open until 10:15 p.m. Air cond. Valet parking.
Patrick Pignol is a young chef in a hurry, eager to earn recognition for his inventive, resolutely contemporary cuisine. His dishes often combine flavors in provocative, unexpected ways that can perk up the most jaded appetite. Examples? How about delicate bay scallops served in their shells with a thyme-scented broth, or a plump, juicy pigeon cooked en cocotte with Chin-

ese truffles, or, for dessert, a buttery madeleine with the haunting taste of heather honey? All the dishes are most attractively presented, with painstaking attention to detail. Interesting cellar; charming welcome.

A la carte: 400-500 F. Menus: 200 F (lunch only), 410 F.

12/20 Le Relais du Bois

Bois de Boulogne,
Croix-Catelan
Rte de Suresnes
42 88 08 43,
fax 45 25 95 56
Closed Sun. dinner. Open until 10 p.m. Private room: 250. Terrace dining.
This rustic rendezvous–a Second Empire hunting pavilion where naughty ladies and gents once engaged in rather outrageous behavior–is now the backdrop for tame family parties and corporate banquets. The comfortable dining room has its charms, but the huge summer garden is truly delightful. Good–if unexciting– food: fish soup, grilled andouillette, confit de canard.

A la carte: 150-250 F.

Robuchon

32, rue de Longchamp
47 27 12 27
Closed Sat., Sun. & July 5-31. Open until 10:15 p.m. Private room: 14. Air cond. Valet parking.
We would love to think it was just a joke, but knowing Joël as we do, we're pretty sure he means it: on his fiftieth birthday–in 1995–Robuchon will doff his toque and hang up his apron to write *the* cookbook, become a much-sought-after restaurant consultant and manage the soon-to-open restaurant/château he and his associates have built in Tokyo. All the more reason, then, to hurry and put your name on the

interminable waiting-list presided over by manager Jean-Jacques Caimant. Do not pretend to be a personal friend of François Mitterrand, or Jacques Chirac's long-lost cousin–it won't get you a table. There's nothing for it but to wait patiently until the day when you too can be one of the 45 privileged people seated in the celadon-colored dining room or in the charming first-floor private salon that seats fifteen.

We've said everything there is to say about Robuchon's brilliant talent, we've praised his technique, his taste for perfection and the passion for detail which he dins into his disciples like a drill sergeant. But what stuns us still is this fantastic artisan's (he's too modest to call himself an artist) powers to thrill and surprise us at every visit.

The first time one tastes his crab perfumed with thyme, saffron and curry, or the sesame sole, or a poulet de Bresse au jus à l'ancienne et aux truffes, one might understandably think that one has reached the summit–but then next time Robuchon astounds one again with his soupe chaude à la gelée de poule, which the intense tastes of truffle and black pepper push to a paroxysm of flavors. Each mouthful of his creamy fennel and sea-urchin soup, spaghetti tossed with prawns and white truffles, his roast milk-fed kid with a persillade of green garlic, or his farm-bred guinea hen set atop a slice of roast foie gras will make you groan with delight.

Frankly, we would love to catch him out just once–but no luck. Neither the cristalline de chou aux ris de veau with its garnish of grilled morels and asparagus, nor the extraordinary lamb steak with baby broad beans and tiny artichokes, nor the much-touted mashed potatoes (often imitated, never duplicated!) is open to the slightest criticism, any more than desserts like the turban de pommes à la cannelle, the frozen feuillantine made with almond milk and diaphanous apple slices, Robuchon's peerless crème brûlée, or the wines chosen with unmatched flair by sommelier Antoine Hernandez.

Gone, however, is the legendary 160-franc set lunch. Today's soaring prices may well appall you, but this degree of perfection is necessarily costly. And remember, to serve 45 diners, Joël Robuchon employs a staff of 35.

A la carte: 750-1,500 F. Menu: 890 F.

 ## Sous l'Olivier

15, rue Goethe
47 20 84 81
Closed Sat., Sun. & holidays. Open until 10:30 p.m. Terrace dining.

We aren't wild about the Nile-green decor or the harsh lighting that does little for patrons' complexions, but summer lunches on the terrace are engagingly lively. The food is uneven, seasonings in particular lack gusto; but the crab pâté with braised leeks, the herring fillets with warm potatoes and bacon and the chocolate feuillantine are creditable enough.

A la carte: 300-350 F.

 ## Le Sully d'Auteuil

78, rue d'Auteuil
46 51 71 18,
fax 46 51 70 60
Closed Sat. lunch & Sun., Aug. 10-30 & Dec. 25-Jan. 1. Open until 10:30 p.m. Private room: 70. Terrace dining. Air cond.

The exaggeratedly precious nomenclature of the overlong menu has been toned down a bit, but Gil Bourgeois remains

faithful to the spirit of a sauce-rich — t e c h n i c a l l y accomplished—cuisine. The rich note blends in perfectly with the emphatically elegant decor set in place by Michel Brunetière in this idyllic pavilion attached to the Auteuil railway station. There's an attractive summer terrace, and a large clientele which is not put off by staggering bills for pan-roasted foie gras with quail eggs and bacon, sole soufflée with shellfish, or calf's head sauce tortue with essence of sherry. Luscious desserts and a tempting array of old brandies.

A la carte: 450-500 F.

 ## Le Toit de Passy

94, av. Paul-Doumer
45 24 55 37,
fax 45 20 94 57
Closed Sat. lunch, Sun. & Dec. 22-Jan. 4. Open until 10:30 p.m. Private room: 25. Terrace dining. Air cond. Parking.

Check your bank balance before you book a table at Yannick Jacquot's rooftop restaurant. If you're feeling flush, go ahead and treat yourself to a meal in this pleasant, plant-filled dining room, with its broad terrace overlooking Paris, and retractable roof for dining (weather permitting) under the stars. Jacquot is not an innovator, but he has a nearly infallible knack for combining flavors in utterly convincing ways. Try his exquisite consommé de langoustines en gelée de petits légumes en croustillant of frogs' legs with garlic cream sauce, or the gently spiced aiguillettes of Challans duck breast, or his perfect chocolate millefeuille layered with praline cream and napped with a chicory-flavored sauce. The cellar holds 45,000 bottles, so the wine list will take some perusing. Good cigars, too.

A la carte: 500-600 F.

Menus: 275 F and 295 F (lunch only), 485 F.

 ## Villa Vinci

23, rue Paul-Valéry
45 01 68 18
Closed Sat., Sun. & Aug. Open until 10:30 p.m. Air cond.

A business crowd at lunch and an up-market local clientele in the evening frequent this comfortable, luxurious restaurant. Though the pasta is still remarkable, the hors-d'œuvres are ordinary, and the Venetian calf's liver bland and pedestrian. Desserts (like tiramisù) save the day, along with the rich and varied Italian cellar.

A la carte: 350-450 F. Menu: 170 F (lunch only).

 ## Vivarois

192, av. V.-Hugo
45 04 04 31,
fax 45 03 09 84
Closed Sat., Sun. & Aug. Open until 10 p.m. Private room: 10. Air cond. Parking.

If we'd known how happy and serene a fourth toque would make chef Claude Peyrot, we would have awarded it sooner. His life has changed, his restaurant is full, and he's no longer talking of retiring to his native Ardèche or of opening a bistro at the North Pole. This marvelously versatile chef sticks faithfully to a concise repertoire enriched daily with a half-dozen dishes created on the spur of the moment. On a given day the maître d'hotel might announce the presence of a fondant of vegetables with a lusty black-olive purée, a fabulous dartois de sole that combines ethereal puff pastry and succulent layers of fish, or pigeon sauce au vin, or, in season, a stupendous hare à la royale garnished with quince that takes one's taste buds to the limits of lusciousness. Neither classic nor modern, this cuisine is uniquely

Peyrot's. An unrivaled technician, he also possesses a sensitivity and grace all his own. To add to the pleasure, there are wines, magnificent and modest, discovered by wine steward extraordinaire Jean-Claude Vinadier, and served under the benevolent but vigilant eye of Jacqueline Peyrot. We are relieved to report that the much-criticized decor is due for a change. Here's hoping that the cold, contemporary furnishings will be replaced by something more sprightly and warm... Stay tuned.

A la carte: 600-800 F. Menu: 385 F (lunch only).

17th arrondissement

12/20 Alexandros

18, rue St-Ferdinand
45 74 75 11
Closed Sun. & Aug. 1-23. Open until 10 p.m.
Plain, lusty food—the sort that Greeks thrive upon, but which is so hard to find outside those blessed isles. Try the good pikilias (assorted hors-d'œuvres), the brochette of suckling pig with two vegetables, or the appealing salt cod with olives. Interesting and inexpensive Greek wines. A la carte: 120 F.

Amphyclès

78, av. des Ternes
40 68 01 01,
fax 40 68 91 88
Closed Sat. lunch, Sun. & July 10-31. Open until 10:30 p.m. Air cond. Parking.
Chef Philippe Groult's cuisine resembles its author: strong, full of character, absolutely unaffected and often diabolically subtle. His deft way with herbs and spices lends extra spark to daring liaisons of textures and tastes. But the couplings are never gratuitous, witness the well-matched ravioli of pigeon and crayfish, admirable dish-fellows though one wonders why they're blanketed with a dull veal-based sauce. Groult injects a velouté of langoustines with a jolt of extra flavor from cumin and marjoram. Divine. And true bliss is assured with the very first forkful of his mitonnée de porcelet aux condiments, or the exemplary canard de Challans au coriandre. Cheeses are something special here, and desserts are over-the-moon: caramelized apples with almonds, soufflé chaud au chocolat, simple yet sublime vanilla ice cream. The cellar is still young but interesting, overseen by a shrewd young sommelier who trained with Robuchon, Guérard and Lameloise. A final tip: Groult's set lunch, which features an appetizer, a hearty main dish (casseroled veal with lentils, joues de bœuf braisées aux carottes confites...), cheeses and dessert, is surely one of the best deals in town.

A la carte: 500-800 F. Menus: 220 F (lunch only), 580 F, 680 F.

Apicius

122, av. de Villiers
43 80 19 66
Closed Christmas wk. & Aug. Open until 10 p.m. Air cond. Valet parking.
Jean-Pierre Vigato is film-star handsome, but this shy *cuisinier* has eschewed "stardom", preferring to keep hard at work in his kitchen. Vigato is a master of two distinct but complementary culinary styles: an imaginative, modern, highly refined register, and a heartier, more rustic mode steeped in the traditions of the French countryside. They coexist in harmony, and both bear Vigato's unmistakable stamp, whether it's the robust tête de veau en ravigote or the delicate bouillon of lobster with bone marrow brightened with piquant Thai herbs, the light and engaging steamed skate garnished with fruit and capers, or a succulent filet de bœuf napped with a beefy sauce. For our money, Vigato's cooking is better than ever—a recent fabulous meal (lamb carpaccio with Parmesan on a salad of fresh herbs; plump prawns flash-fried in a diaphanous batter of spices, Japanese flour and egg white; spiced steamed cod; crisp morsels of sweetbreads en brochette with a light coating of crumbs, parsley, tarragon and chervil) convinced us of that. In the dessert league, Vigato's incredible chocolate-based creations—gâteaux, mousses, shells, sorbets—take top honors. Apicius is usually packed with the Paris carriage trade, who know a good thing when they taste it. Madeleine Vigato supervises the two warmly decorated dining rooms with smiling courtesy. A la carte: 500-850 F.

Augusta

98, rue de Tocqueville
47 63 39 97
Closed Sat. lunch, Sun., Aug. 7-23. Open until 10 p.m. Air cond.
Scrupulously seasonal, rigorously precise, based on sumptuous, sparkling seafood: Lionel Maître's cuisine is all this and more. Desserts, somewhat neglected in the past, have vastly improved; and the langoustines à la vanille on a salad of lamb's lettuce, the saffron-tinctured red mullet and zucchini, the turbot roasted with honey and lemon, and pan-roasted scallops on a bed of bean sprouts perfumed with basil have hoisted Augusta high into the ranks of the best fish restaurants in Paris. Lionel Maître is still young, yet his technique is astonishingly mature. And he is quite a taskmas-

ter too, judging from the choleric commands that resound in the kitchen (and sometimes carry into the slightly fusty blue dining room). The cellar boasts a superb collection of white wines.

A la carte: 450-500 F.

La Barrière de Clichy

1, rue de Paris
92110 Clichy
47 37 05 18
Closed Sat. lunch, Sun. & 15 days in Aug. Open until 10 p.m. Private room: 15. Air cond.
Superchefs Guy Savoy and Bernard Loiseau cut their baby-teeth here. Now in charge of the Barrière's kitchen is 34-year-old Gilles Le Gallès, who trained with Loiseau... The establishment suffers from being cut off by the beltway that slices Paris off from Clichy. Confronted with that concrete problem, Gilles Le Gallès's preferred weapons are patience—and his talent to surprise. His light, inventive cuisine (he prefers cooking juices to sauces) is marked by interesting marriages: tiny squid stuffed with chicken livers on a bed of zucchini fondue, escargots paired with ris de veau, fillets of young rabbit matched with Camembert, or goat cheese with lamb. Most chefs couldn't pull it off, but Le Gallès does—beautifully. The menu lists a few classics too: warm oysters wrapped in spinach leaves and dressed with shallot vinaigrette, salmon steak with sea salt and pigeonneau aux choux. To finish, bold and conservative tastes alike cast their votes for the tarte fine Verger aux pommes. The cellar leans heavily toward fine Bordeaux.

A la carte: 350-450 F. Menus: 220 F (weekdays only), 270 F (weekdays lunch only, wine incl.), 370 F.

Les Béatilles

127, rue Cardinet
42 27 95 64
Closed Sat. & Sun. Open until 10:15 p.m.
A light, easily digestible, nearly irreproachable cuisine that aims for simplicity. Join the well-heeled neighborhood crowd that forgathers around pretty tables in the intimate white dining rooms for foie gras aux lentilles, red-mullet lasagne, a winy lamb daube with fresh pasta, or a rich and flaky duck tourte dressed with a meat-juice vinaigrette. Come time for dessert, a gingery charlotte aux épices will make you happy you came.

A la carte: 300 F. Menus: 130 F (lunch only), 180 F and 290 F (dinner only).

Billy Gourmand

20, rue de Tocqueville
42 27 03 71
Closed Sat. lunch, Sun. & 3 wks. in Aug. Open until 10 p.m. Private room: 14. Air cond.
Philippe Billy, a young pupil of Jacques Chibois and Claude Deligne, has managed to elbow his way into an already restaurant-saturated *quartier*. Against a backdrop of mirrors and large potted plants you

can choose from a classic yet personalized menu: a fragrant ragoût of baby scallops and mushrooms with fresh herbs, turbot piccata with mussels, fillet of Angus beef and some pleasing traditional desserts. Good wines by the glass.

A la carte: 280-380 F. Menu: 150 F (dinner, except holidays).

Le Bistrot d'à Côté

10, rue G.-Flaubert
42 67 05 81,
fax 47 63 82 75
Closed Sat. lunch & Aug. 1-15. Open until 11:30 p.m. Terrace dining. Valet parking.
All you want from a bistro: hustle, bustle and cheeky waiters. After a slight falling

---

New Bridge is old

Despite its name, the *Pont-Neuf* ("new bridge") is the oldest bridge in Paris. Completed in 1604, it was the first in Paris to be built without houses blocking the view of the river. It even had sidewalks—quite a novelty at the time—and a series of semicircular bays whose stone benches still make an ideal stopping place during a romantic stroll. In its early days, the bridge buzzed with a gaudy population of charlatans, traders and troubadours (who satirized unpopular politicians or the king's latest mistress). The Pont-Neuf's most recent claim to fame came in 1985 when the American sculptor Christo wrapped it lovingly in bridal white to fashion a two-week work of art.

---

off, this cheery eatery has bounced back to become a perfect Lyonnais-style *bouchon* with a few unexpected dishes—lamb curry mauricienne—thrown in for good measure. The hearty warm lentil salad with cervelas sausage, the corn and salmon galette, and the smooth crème brûlée have won over a faithful corps of repeat customers. The wines, however, are too expensive for this sort of establishment. Another Bistrot d'à Côté is located at 16, avenue de Villiers, 47 63 25 61.

A la carte: 260-320 F.

 ### Le Bistrot de l'Etoile-Niel

75, av. Niel
42 27 88 44
Closed Sun. Open until midnight. Terrace dining. Air cond. Valet parking.

Guy Savoy has gone into partnership with his former pupil, Bruno Gensdarmes, to assure the success of this bistro, now as popular as the one on rue Troyon (see below). Try the museau ravigote au chou craquant, the gratin d'épaule d'agneau aux aubergines, and round things out with one of the irresistible desserts. The house wine, a Merlot, is served "en pot", Lyonnais-fashion; other choices from the limited cellar are rather pricey.

A la carte: 200-260 F.

 ### Le Bistrot de l'Etoile-Troyon

13, rue Troyon
42 67 25 95
Closed Sat. lunch & Sun. Open until midnight. Air cond.

Wonderfully old-fashioned bistro cuisine is here given a youthful touch by William Ledeuil, who spent three years with Guy Savoy. The latter oversees this successful and busy bistro from his own establishment across the street. Specialties include cuisse de canard aux haricots rouges, pan-roasted tuna and a pudding aux griottes. Drink the tasty house Merlot served in carafes.

A la carte: 220-300 F.

Some establishments change their closing times without warning. It is always wise to check in advance.

12/20 Le Cadre Noir

4, rue Gounod
40 54 02 29
Closed Sat. lunch & Sun. Open until 10:30 p.m.

It would be hard to find a more clever or varied menu— 95 francs for a starter and a main dish—than the one on offer in this discreetly elegant little restaurant. Too bad the tiny wine list doesn't follow suit. Delectable crab terrine spiced with saffron, and a good noisette de veal with an artichoke galette.

Menus: 95 F, 169 F (dinner only, wine incl.).

 ### Charly de Bab-el-Oued

95, bd Gouvion-St-Cyr
45 74 34 62,
fax 45 74 35 36
Open daily until 11:30 p.m. Air cond.

An inviting place to dream of the *Arabian Nights'* amidst colorful tiles, cedarwood and palm trees. Feast here on excellent couscous, pastillas and tajines, followed up by sweet Eastern pastries that are made on the spot. Perfect service.

A la carte: 200-300 F.

 ### Clos Longchamp

Le Méridien Paris-Etoile
81, bd Gouvion-St-Cyr
40 68 30 40
Closed Sat., Sun. & Aug. 14-22. Open until 10:30 p.m. Private room: 20. Air cond. Valet parking.

Chef Jean-Marie Meulien is at the top of his form this year. Not content with being a master craftsman, he combines the flavors of the Mediterranean with the spices of South-East Asia to produce tempting dishes in which the influence of his mentor, Louis Outhier, still lingers. This year we especially enjoyed the steamed crevettes perfumed with Champagne vinegar, sea bream and young leeks, red mullet on a bed of crisp eggpl-

ant, ginger-scented lobster, crawfish with Thai herbs, and spicy duck steak. Not to mention fillet of lamb coated in an astonishing but delicious coffee sauce and tender veal chops sprinkled with pollen and topped by a sauce delicately flavored with honey. Hot chocolate tart and candied chestnut charlotte are among the delightful deserts and award-winning sommelier Didier Bureau is sure to recommend just the right wine to round out the meal. The exuberant central garden has flourished so well you would think you were in sunnier climes, and almost makes you forget the strange, banana-shaped dining room that surrounds it.

A la carte: 550-800 F. Menus: 250 F (lunch, except holidays), 450 F (dinner, except holidays).

12/20 Le Congrès

80, av. de la Grande-Armée
45 74 17 24
Open daily, 24 hours. Air cond.

A huge barracks-like brasserie, open all day and all night, vigilant about the consistent quality of its battle horses: shellfish (sparkling fresh year round) and large slabs of charcoal-grilled meats: beef fillets, T-bone steaks, and huge ribs of beef. A good tarte Tatin rounds things off nicely. The decent selection of inexpensive house wines will not empty your wallet.

A la carte: 200-250 F.

 ### La Coquille

6, rue du Débarcadère
45 72 10 73
Closed Sun., Mon., Dec. 23-Jan. 3 & July 27-Sep. 2. Open until 10:30 p.m. Air cond.

There aren't many restaurants like this well-bred bistro where today's patrons may order exactly the same dishes (just as overcooked and heavily sauced) as their parents and grandparents before them. To wit: the eponymous coquilles Saint-Jacques au naturel, sea bass Escoffier, jugged hare, boudin grillé aux pommes and the seemingly immortal hazelnut soufflé. Exceptional cellar.

A la carte: 330-430 F.

 Le Cougar
10, rue des Acacias
47 66 74 14
Closed Sat. lunch & Sun. Open until 10:30 p.m. Air cond.

Taïra Kurihara, a brilliant star in the galaxy of Japanese practitioners of French cuisine, is engaged like many of his colleagues in turning out Gallic dishes influenced by master chefs (in this case, Robuchon, Cagna, Besson). Kurihara's technique has gained authority, and he has developed a knack for creating subtle flavors and vibrant seasonings. In view of all these assets, we shall overlook a few debits (a salad of terribly overcooked prawns), and encourage you to sample the perfect John Dory with rice vinegar and sesame oil, or fresh cod with seaweed and olive oil. The menu is deliberately short on meat dishes. Fine cellar, improved decor.

A la carte: 330-430 F. Menu: 320 F (dinner only).

 L'Ecrin d'Or
35, rue Legendre
47 63 83 08
Closed Sat. lunch, Mon. & Aug. 4-25. Open until 11 p.m. Private room: 16. Air cond. Parking.

Huge mirrors, moldings, Venetian chandeliers and great swathes of velvet hangings make this a supremely comfortable restaurant, and the cuisine of the young chef, Gilles Cendres, is a pleasant discovery indeed. Sample his precise, personal interpretations of rockfish with bell-pepper

coulis, salade de jarret de veau, duckling à l'orange and bitter-chocolate fondant. Judicious cellar.

A la carte: 260-330 F. Menus: 95 F, 155 F.

 Epicure 108
108, rue Cardinet
47 63 50 91
Closed Sat. lunch & Sun. Open until 10:30 p.m.

Here's a quiet little restaurant with a pretty, well-lit interior and a decidedly up-market tone. The oft-changing menu attracts a good lunchtime turnout with consistent, palatable dishes (sometimes a bit shy on seasonings) by chef Tetsu Goya. The 170-franc set lunch features an exquisite shellfish and zucchini galette, delicious sea bream roasted with herbs and a dessert (the desserts need work). Good cellar, and the reception has warmed up lately by several degrees.

Menus: 230 F (for 2), 170 F.

 L'Etoile d'Or
Hôtel Concorde-
La Fayette
3, pl. du Gal-Kœnig
40 58 50 68
Closed Sat. lunch & Sun. Open until 10:30 p.m. Private room: 40. Air cond. Valet parking.

Jean-Claude Lhonneur, formerly of Le Grand Véfour and La Tour d'Argent, produces precise, tasty cuisine that lacks only a hint of boldness. An attractive seafood platter and lamb noisettes with juniper berries are among the highlights. Classy, comfortable setting, fine cellar with some affordable bottles, and irreproachable service.

A la carte: 500-600 F. Menu: 250 F.

 Faucher
123, av. de Wagram
42 27 61 50,
fax 46 22 25 72
Closed Sat. lunch, Sun. & wk. of Aug. 15. Open until 10:30 p.m. Terrace dining. Valet parking.

Gérard and Nicole Faucher have embraced the *beaux quartiers*: they are the proud proprietors of a very handsome dining room embellished with paintings, sumptuous bouquets and elegant table settings. Nicole welcomes patrons while a bevy of nimble young waiters serve Gérard's clever, exciting cuisine. We gobbled up his light, fresh and very inventive millefeuille of thin-sliced raw beef and spinach leaves, his remarkable galette which incorporates potatoes and cod (the latter in its fresh and salted forms) bathed in meat juices, a flavorful osso buco with a "minestrone" of vegetables and homey braised short ribs ennobled with a beurre aux truffes. Desserts are equally gorgeous. The cellar is a bit too expensive, but the summer terrace is irresistible.

A la carte: 350-500 F. Menus: 180 F (lunch only), 390 F.

11/20 Chez Fred
190 bis, bd Pereire
45 74 20 48
Closed Sun. & 2 wks. in Aug. Open daily until 11 p.m.

An influx of trendies has not spoiled the service, the simplicity of the setting, or the heartwarming sincerity of Fred's cuisine: streaky bacon with lentils, pot-au-feu and blanquette de veau. No-nonsense wines sold by the *pichet*.

A la carte: 200-220 F. Menu: 145 F (lunch only, wine incl.).

The A la carte restaurant prices given are for a complete three-course meal for one, including a half-bottle of modest wine and service. Menu prices are for a complete fixed-price meal for one, excluding wine (unless otherwise noted).

La Gazelle

9, rue Rennequin
42 67 64 18
*Closed Sun. Open until
11:30 p.m.*
The prettiest, most distinguished and exotic African restaurant in Paris, La Gazelle boasts a surprising range of intensely flavorful dishes prepared by the *patronne*, who hails from Cameroon: n'dolé of dried salt cod with chopped bitter spinach, tender and delicious shrimp in a spicy sauce, marinated kid en papillote with African corn. Slow-paced service.
A la carte: 200-250 F. Menu: 48 F (weekdays lunch only), 95 F, 130 F.

Chez Georges

273, bd Pereire
45 74 31 00,
fax 45 74 02 56
*Closed Aug. Open until
11:30 p.m. Private room: 30.
Terrace dining.*
The quintessential brasserie-bistro with all its little flaws—some dishes are a bit too expensive, a few appetizers lack zest, the upstairs dining room has all the warmth and charm of Siberia—and its immense virtues: an appealingly worn decor (downstairs, of course), an effervescent clientele (tourists, TV personalities, celebrities) and swift, professional waiters who set before one platefuls of picture-perfect bistro fare: heavenly saucisson chaud, juicy roast beef with gratin dauphinois, tête de veau, rare roast lamb with tender beans.
A la carte: 280-350 F.

Graindorge

15, rue de l'Arc-de-Triomphe
47 54 00 28
Closed Sat. lunch & Sun. Open until 10:30 p.m.
Bernard Broux, for six years the chef at Alain Dutournier's Trou Gascon, has lit out on his

own. What's more, he has forsaken the Southwest and its earthy savors in favor of the cuisine of his native Flanders. Broux's inaugural menu features unpretentious ingredients handled in clever, original ways: there's a salad of potatoes and sardine "rollmops" (that is, pickled like herring in spiced vinegar), pork braised in a sauce spiked with gin, and caramelized brioche "French toast". The wine list merits your attention, but beer-lovers will be knocked out by the superb selection of rare brews.
A la carte: 200-250 F. Menus: 160 F (lunch only), 180 F (dinner only).

12/20 Goldenberg

69, av. de Wagram
42 27 34 79
Open daily until midnight.
Patrick Goldenberg creates a typically Yiddish ambience of good humor and nostalgia, Jewish jokes and anecdotes in which to enjoy delicious pastrami, corned beef, veal sausage and other Central European classics. There's an amusing take-out delicatessen and a sunny terrace for fine weather...
A la carte: 200-250 F. Menu: 98 F (wine incl.).

Guyvonne

14, rue de Thann
42 27 25 43
Closed Sat., Sun., Dec. 24-Jan. 3 & Aug. 6-30. Open until 10 p.m. Private room: 11. Terrace dining.
Guy Cros is a droll and charming chap, a great upholder of the French culinary tradition. With renewed vigor, he has lately applied his skill to country dishes, updated classics, and "market-basket" cuisine. A large and faithful clientele flocks to Cros's (rather dreary) beige-and-blue dining room and to the terrace a stone's throw from the Parc Monceau, for Guyvonne is

justly considered one of the best seafood restaurants in Paris. No argument from us: we love the prawns with chanterelles and artichokes, the crayfish with chervil root, and the oysters with Chinese truffles (tasty little violet potatoes). Desserts are guaranteed diet-busters, and the cellar is stocked with first-rate Bordeaux.
A la carte: 350-400 F. Menu: 230 F.

L'Impatient

14, passage Geffroy-Didelot
43 87 28 10
Closed Sat., Sun., 15 days Easter & Aug. 15-Sep. 10. Open until 10 p.m. Air cond.
The new owners are a hard-working pair: they do everything themselves, from picking flowers to adorn their three comely Art Deco dining rooms, to gathering fresh fruits and vegetables, and then preparing them in novel, amusing ways: warm sardine terrine with apples, rabbit croustade, potato crêpes studded with corn kernels. Good prix-fixe menus, attentive service.
A la carte: 200-280 F. Menus: 98 F (lunch only), 280 F (dinner only), 145 F.

Chez Laudrin

154, bd Pereire
43 80 87 40
Closed Sat. lunch, Sun. & May 1-9. Open until 10:30 p.m. Air cond.
Age settles gently but graciously over Jacques Billaud's "yacht-club" dining room, his regional repertoire and the mustachioed smile with which he has greeted customers for thirty-odd years. Wines are served by the magnum and tariffed by "the centimeter" (that is, you pay for what you actually consume). Some of the best tripe dishes in Paris are made in this kitchen, as well as fresh cod

with aïoli, grilled stuffed bay scallops, goujonnettes de sole and a hearty monkfish bourride (fish soup). The obligatory dessert here is the house baba au rhum.

A la carte: 320-420 F. Menu: 250 F.

Chez Lee

13, rue Rennequin
43 80 91 48,
fax 42 27 72 46
Closed Sun. & Aug. 1-26. Open until 11 p.m. Air cond.
For highly original, light and flavorful Chinese cooking, come to see Mr Lee (and his associate, Mr Lo). Treat yourself to the unusual steamed dumplings, the shrimp with savory salt, Szechuan duck, and pork in a spicy sauce served by slightly furtive black-garbed waiters in an elegant dining room dotted with silk screens.

A la carte: 150-250 F. Menus: 78 F (weekdays lunch only), 99 F.

12/20 Chez Léon

32, rue Legendre
42 27 06 82
Closed w.-e., Aug. & 1 wk. in Feb. Open until 9:45 p.m. Private room: 20.
A traditional bistro with the usual robust fare—terrines, tête de veau, and cassoulets. But our old friend Léon had better stop serving tough haricot beans with his gigot d'agneau, and pull the ears of the cook responsible for our unevenly baked apple tart! Service is pleasant, and so are the Beaujolais wines.

A la carte: 210-290 F. Menu: 160 F.

Le Madigan

22, rue de la Terrasse
42 27 31 51
Closed Sat. lunch, Sun. & holidays. Open until 9:30 p.m. Terrace dining. Air cond.
The owner is a music buff and his chef a fervent disciple of Escoffier. They have combined their talents to launch a perilous enterprise: the musical supper, a rarity in this city. At liqueur time, Le Madigan's sober yet sumptuous dining room is transformed into a concert hall. Hopeful young talents and international prize-winners take their place at the Steinway grand for what are often remarkable recitals. The bearded young chef ably turns out lush, nineteenth-century dishes: poached eggs Rossini, lobster Cardinal and sweetbreads à la Demidoff. Top-notch ingredients and subtle preparation ensure a harmonious evening on every scale.

A la carte: 310-475 F. Menus: 150 F and 250 F (lunch only), 180 F and 280 F (dinner only).

Le Manoir de Paris

6, rue P.-Demours
45 72 25 25,
fax 45 74 80 98
Closed Sat. lunch & Sun. Open until 10:30 p.m. Private room: 50. Air cond. Valet parking.
When Philippe Groult left the Manoir to open his own Amphyclès just down the road, Francis Vandenhende and Denise Fabre (the latter a native Niçoise whose heart belongs to the South) encouraged their new chef, Gilles Méry, to give the menu a Mediterranean slant. And now the Manoir's lavish dining room with its Tiffany-style skylight, mirrored pilasters, intricately carved woodwork, abundant flowers and greenery, is drenched in Provençal sunshine thanks to a menu studded with Southern flavors: langoustines rôties aux blettes et fumet de truffe, herb and mushroom cannelloni napped with a mouthwatering roast veal gravy, an ambrosial pumpkin soup with tiny chinese gnocchi and crisp lardons, roasted lotte with caramelized tomatoes and braised fennel, and pigonneau en cocotte à la polenta with a wild-mushroom sauce.

Desserts include an unctuous tiramisù, and a warm hazelnut-cocoa gâteau accompanied by a glass of Beaumes-de-Venise Domaine de Coyeux from sommelier Remy Aspect's impressive —and costly—cellar.

A la carte: 620-800 F. Menus: 290 F (lunch only), 380 F, 460 F.

La Niçoise

4, rue Pierre-Demours
45 74 42 41,
fax 45 74 80 98
Closed Sat. lunch & Sun. Open until 11 p.m. Private room: 50. Air cond. Valet parking.
Honest, simple Niçois specialties. The fresh, flowery decor is reminiscent of Nice at holiday-time, or of a stage set for a turn-of-the-century operetta. An inexplicably tense staff serves robust, full-flavored ravioli de daube, stuffed sardines, pasta with pistou and for dessert a pinenut tart, all dishes which deserve a round of applause—and a toque. Perfect Provençal cellar.

A la carte: 200-280 F. Menu: 145 F (lunch only).

Le Petit Colombier

42, rue des Acacias
43 80 28 54,
fax 44 40 04 29
Closed Sun. lunch, Sat. & July 21-Aug. 17. Open until 10:30 p.m. Private room: 30. Air cond. Parking.
Bernard Fournier is a wise restaurateur. When one is lucky enough to inherit a delightful "provincial" *auberge* from one's father, the sort of place they stopped making in the nineteenth century, one doesn't go messing it up with trendy lacquered ceilings,

salmon-colored fabric and halogen lighting. In fact, the patrons of Le Petit Colombier (which has just celebrated 60 years of family management) wouldn't stand for it. They come here to tuck a napkin under their chins, make themselves comfortable in the glow of burnished copper and wrought-iron, and discover anew the reassuring flavors of classic French food, a repertoire that will never grow stale in the capable hands of chef Bernard Fournier. For Le Petit Colombier is not a fusty sanctuary of dyspeptic pre-war cuisine. New dishes often slip onto the menu, and a bit of seaweed mixed with pâtes fraîches or a hint of dill in a seafood pot-au-feu doesn't create a ripple among the clientele. But Bernard Fournier's brigade can also instill fresh spirit and zest into a traditional salad of potatoes with fresh truffles, or a gratin de homard à la Newburg, or roast to rosy perfection a young partridge which actually tastes like a partridge and not a chicken raised on fishmeal. And respect for tradition doesn't mean one can't keep up-to-date; air-conditioning, a "smoking" area, a bilingual staff, and a computer are all part of the mod cons here—as is a business menu which is one of the best (and least known) bargains in the city. And to toast all these delights, there is a fabulous cellar with some 50,000 bottles...

A la carte: 400-550 F. Menu: 200 F (lunch only).

12/20 **Le Petit Salé**

99, av. des Ternes
45 74 10 57
Open daily until 11 p.m. Terrace dining.

The boyish young chef has changed nothing in the generous house repertoire of petit salé aux lentilles, confits and

tarte Tatin which has made the reputation of this solid old bistro. The dining room has been renovated, however: with the bar removed, twice as many diners can contribute to the always-jolly ambience.

A la carte: 180-230 F.

13 **La Petite Auberge**

38, rue Laugier
47 63 85 51
Closed Sun. dinner, Mon. & Aug. Open until 10:30 p.m. Private room: 14.

Veteran chef Léo Harbonnier has handed over his chef's whites to Joël Ducloux, a pupil of Paul Bocuse. The dining room and the menu have both been spruced up a bit. Fine, fresh ingredients are the basis for succulent foie gras with shallot purée, snail ravioli with Roquefort butter, fish assortment with cockle-flavored butter, and Grand Marnier soufflé. Cheerful welcome, good cellar.

A la carte: 270-400 F. Menu: 160 F.

12/20 Petrus

12, pl. du Maréchal-Juin
43 80 15 95
Open daily until 11 p.m. Private room: 22. Terrace dining. Air cond. Valet parking.

Petrus has ridden the waves of change through new chefs, new owners, new managers; the excellence and variety of the seafood have remained constant in this luxurious restaurant, with its spacious dining room and terrace. But we are obliged to revise our rating, for our most recent meal here certainly did not deserve two toques. A turbot with the texture of cotton, a mediocre shellfish platter and an assortment of fish sauced with an insipid Armoricaine are inexcusable in a restaurant famed for its seafood. So it's no toque at all, we're afraid, until the kitchen comes out of its current careless slump!

A la carte: 450-500 F. Menu: 250 F.

 Michel Rostang

19 20, rue Rennequin
47 63 40 77,
fax 47 63 82 75
Closed Sat. lunch (& dinner May-Sep.), Sun. & Aug. 1-15. Open until 10:15 p.m. Private room: 25. Air cond. Valet parking.

Though his serene demeanor doesn't betray the fact, Michel Rostang is a busy man, what with his triumphant New York restaurant, his Bistrots d'à Côte, the luxury hotel in the Caribbean, La Bonne Auberge in Antibes overseen by his brother, Philippe, and the restaurant that bears his name and occupies most of his time. Nevertheless this youthful 45-year-old manages to keep his composure, even while putting his kitchen brigade through its paces like a veritable ringmaster.

To call a chef "industrious" may sound like a back-handed sort of compliment. Yet Michel Rostang works hard at his craft, like the skilled artisan he is. And he knows how to improvise too, creating a subtly nuanced, colorful, intensely pleasing cuisine. A menu of ten appetizers and a dozen fish and meat dishes always offers a core of tried-and-true classics (oven-roasted Sisteron lamb flanked by pan-roasted lamb sweetbreads and a compotée of lamb's trotter with salsify; Bresse duck with a wine sauce enriched by a foie-gras liaison) along with a bouquet of personal creations, like asparagus tips "breaded" with a cèpe duxelles, a superlative terrine de langoustines in a vigorously seasoned shellfish gelée, a delectable Provençal-inspired sea bass with olives and fennel purée, or curried saddle of young rabbit cleverly garnished with a purée of spinach and pears. Though Michel's gratin dauphinois is perhaps a hair less lush than his father's—the benchmark of the genre—his poularde à la crème aux morilles is a monument.

For dessert choose a grilled pear with tea sauce, or prune "bonbons" coated in rosemary-flavored sugar accompanied by an astonishing pepper sorbet, or tarte chaude au chocolat for a taste of pure ecstasy. Alain Ronzatti administers the select, high-priced wine cellar.

A la carte: 650-950 F. Menus: 285 F (lunch only), 495 F, 660 F (except holidays).

Guy Savoy

18, rue Troyon
43 80 40 61,
fax 46 22 43 09
Closed Sat. lunch (& dinner Easter-Sep.) & Sun. Open until 10:30 p.m. Private room: 35. Air cond. Valet parking.

If a client requested it, we're certain that the ever-so-affable Guy Savoy would provide a chauffeur-driven car to drive him home—free of charge. But who would ever want to leave this beautiful, welcoming establishment, a haven of charm and grace? How marvelous to be a "regular" *chez* Savoy, with one's special table reserved in the spacious green-and-rosy-beige dining room dotted with contemporary prints and paintings—an original, elegant setting, surely one of the most attractive in the city.

For bearded, eternally youthful Guy Savoy life is beautiful—his dining room is full and diners' happy faces bespeak their delight. Routine never casts its pall over Savoy's kitchen—every day he fashions new, exquisite, unexpected flavors into fascinating meals. If we had to pin it down with a single adjective, we would

call Savoy's cuisine "intelligent". Textures and aromas are brought together with astonishing skill; they are never masked by superfluous sauces, but highlighted by the judicious use of jus, coulis, essences and spice blends that give each dish its singular style and cachet. Beyond Savoy's technical vigor lies his acute perceptions of taste, those of a true country lad who has never forgotten the savor of fresh garden vegetables, farmyard poultry or the good smells of country cooking.

Guy Savoy is not out to dazzle his patrons. He pleases himself first, and if others like the results, so much the better. But frankly who wouldn't like his ragoût of sea urchins and Chinese artichokes? or fat, tender frogs' legs pan-roasted and served with a garlicky green-bean jus? or saddle of wild rabbit stuffed with foie gras and casseroled to juicy perfection? or John Dory poked through with basil leaves, presented on a bed of sautéed dandelion greens?

We'll stop there. Savoy's imagination works at lightning speed, and we leave it to you to discover the latest marvels on a constantly changing menu (if, when you visit, the risotto with mascarpone, shellfish and a touch of arugula is still on offer—order it! Same goes for the breast of veal, slowly stewed in goose fat, then pan-roasted to a crispy turn). Desserts are voluptuous (grapefruit terrine with a tea-scented sauce, vanilla millefeuille in a ruby pool of berry coulis) and the wines, delicate or full-bodied, as you prefer, are overseen by Eric Mancio, a sommelier with the soul of a poet.

A la carte: 650-1,000 F.
Menu: 650 F.

Sormani

4, rue du Général-Lanzerac
43 80 13 91
Closed Sat. & holidays. Open until 10:30 p.m. Private room: 18. Terrace dining. Air cond. Valet parking.

Indisputably the best Italian restaurant in Paris, Sormani is the first non-French establishment to win three Gault Millau toques. Pascal Fayet hails from Savoie, so he is not, strictly speaking, a "foreign" chef. He owes his passion for Italian cuisine to his Piedmontese grandmother. Fayet's *cucina italiana* is indisputably Frenchified; for him, the Italian repertoire is more a source of inspiration than a model to be followed to the letter.

This sensitive artist works with flavors and ingredients from Florence, Genoa and Tuscany but he is never shy about adding his personal signature to a dish. A trickle of truffled oil on the carpaccio and scallop salad, and suddenly a classic dish is reborn. Lasagne layered with foie gras and truffles, or zesty squid sautéed with hot peppers and bits of salt pork arranged on a bed of potatoes, or a hot soufflé of brandade de morue (puréed salt cod), or a thin slice of veal wrapped around a fat black truffle and your taste buds snap to delighted attention. Fayet's vegetables are uniformly delicious, for he oven-roasts them à l'italienne instead of blanching them in the more usual French style. Thoroughly Italian too is his sensual tiramisù, a poem of mascarpone, chocolate and caramel ice cream. Among the treasures in the cellar are a marvelous Venetian Pinot Grigio, a Peppoli Antinori '86, and other superb Italian wines that the chauvinistic French too often neglect. Aspects of his "go-for-baroque" decor are in dubious taste, but the overall effect of

75

the frescoes and *faux-marbre* is amusing and fun.

A la carte: 400-650 F. Menus: 300 F, 400 F, 450 F.

La Soupière

154, av. de Wagram
42 27 00 73
Closed Sat. lunch, Sun. & Aug. 9-22. Open until 10:30 p.m. Terrace dining. Air cond.

The pretty decor is *trompe-l'œil*, but chef Christian Thuillart's cuisine definitely isn't. His straightforward menu shows a distinctive personality at work, as in the lobster salad, salmon à l'unilatéral or roast Pauillac lamb. A passionate connoisseur of rare and expensive mushrooms, he has built special menus around truffles and morels, served when their season is at its height.

A la carte: 250-350 F. Menus: 160 F (weekdays only), 185 F (Sat. only), 240 F.

Le Timgad

21, rue Brunel
45 74 23 70
Open daily until 11 p.m. Private room: 15. Air cond. Parking.

With its molded-plaster arabesques and enameled tiles, this extravagant palatial decor is one of the most successful of its kind in Paris. On his good days, Ahmed Laasri's couscous is perhaps the best in town. But don't neglect his admirable pastilla, the lamb's-brain tajine with pickled lemons, and the out-of-this-world spit-roasted lamb. A very comprehensive cellar of North African wines, curiously all priced the same. Remember to book in advance for a table at this understandably popular restaurant.

A la carte: 300-350 F.

The prices in this guide reflect what establishments were charging at press time.

La Toque

16, rue de Tocqueville
42 27 97 75
Closed Sat., Sun., Dec. 24-Jan. 2 & July 23-Aug. 22. Open until 9:30 p.m. Air cond.

Jacky Joubert's cuisine is light, refined, seasonal, and highly inventive—though never "precious" (a failing not infrequent among certain of Michel Guérard's disciples). Laudably low prices add to the pleasure one derives from a terrine de joue de bœuf with tiny vegetables, filets de rougets pan-fried with smoked-salmon butter, and the unusual, powerfully flavorful hot game pie with apricots. Prepare to bash elbows with your neighbors in this tiny dining room swathed in yellow crushed velvet.

A la carte: 280-330 F. Menus: 160 F, 210 F.

18th arrondissement

A. Beauvilliers

52, rue Lamarck
42 54 54 42,
fax 42 62 70 30
Closed Mon. lunch, Sun. & Aug. 30-Sep. 13. Open until 10:45 p.m. Garden dining. Air cond.

If ever there was a restaurant designed for *fêtes* and celebrations, it is surely Beauvilliers. Owner Edouard Carlier has lovingly fitted out three irresistible dining rooms with Louis-Philippe-era paintings, old prints, damask napery and fanciful flower displays; and then there's the adorable little "newlywed" salon with its soft lighting and collection of wedding garlands worn by country brides of yore, pinned like butterflies in glass vitrines; and now, there are even three outdoor terraces with wonderful views of Montmartre.

Michel Deygat, who officiated

in the kitchen for the last five years, has been replaced by his former chef-saucier, Gilles Renault. Yet the change is barely perceptible, for the menu was conceived by Carlier (himself a trained chef) and bears his inimitable stamp. Refinement, classicism and rustic touches blend beautifully in dishes like boned rabbit with chopped parsley aspic, or a salad of haricots verts topped with tiny fried squid, or a guinea fowl rubbed with spices then roasted and served with a parmentier of potatoes and mushrooms, a "gigot" of monkfish, a baby pigeon with young peas and lettuce, or a lordly loin of veal presented complete with the kidneys, napped in a fragrant truffle jus. Only a heavy, dizzyingly rich tourte filled with sweetbreads, foie gras and lobster strikes a false note. To accompany this splendid fare there is a huge selection of rare Champagnes, old port and some glorious wines.

We are always surprised when others criticize the welcome as "cold" not to say "glacial". His plumpness King Edouard is the cream of hosts. But perhaps he has too many chums to greet, and thus ignores some first-time visitors...?

A la carte: 600-900 F. Menus: 185 F (weekdays lunch only), 300 F (lunch only, wine incl.).

Charlot Ier

Les Merveilles des Mers
128 bis, bd de Clichy
45 22 47 08,
fax 44 70 07 50
Closed Mon. (July-Aug.). Open until 1 a.m. Air cond. Parking.

An able new chef is handling the traditional house repertoire of no-nonsense seafood classics (bouillabaisse, braised skate, red mullet in aromatic broth). More meat-based and seasonal dishes have appeared on the menu, but the best bets here are and remain the simplest preparations, starting with the extraordinary assortments of raw shellfish.

A la carte: 350-500 F. Menus: 150 F (dinner, except holidays), 200 F (weekdays lunch and Sat.).

 Clodenis

57, rue Caulaincourt
46 06 20 26
Closed Sun. dinner, Mon. & Jan. 10-31. Open until 11 p.m.
Some genuine sun-kissed Provençal specialties distinguish this charming little restaurant set in a highly touristic area of Montmartre. Prices are as steep as the Butte, but the food is first-rate and the brandade de morue, the lapin au thym, or the stuffed zucchini blossoms won't disappoint. Wine prices are climbing up there too.
A la carte: 250-370 F. Menu: 200 F (lunch only).

 Le Cottage Marcadet

151 bis, rue Marcadet
42 57 71 22
Closed Sun., April 30-May 16 & Aug. 14-31. Open until 10 p.m. Air cond.
The location is not exactly a Montmartre charm spot but the Cottage itself is appealing. Even more so is the appetizing *carte* with its mussel galette with apples, cockle ravioli with a chicken-based cream sauce, and honey-roasted spareribs. As for the wine list, it is short, but perfectly relevant to the food at hand (nice prices, too). The set menu, served at noon and at night, is good news— and good value!
A la carte: 260-400 F. Menu: 200 F (wine incl.).

12/20 Chez Frézet

181, rue Ordener
46 06 64 20,
fax 46 06 10 79
Closed Sat. lunch, Sun. & Aug. Open until 10:45 p.m. Garden dining. Valet parking.
Christian Marie is the proud owner of this freshly decorated neighbourhood restaurant which gives onto a minuscule back garden. In the evening, people come for the carefully prepared *plat du jour* (turbot hollandaise, leg of lamb in a flaky crust) and the rest of the time for generous portions of decent smoked haddock with cabbage, kidneys with mustard sauce, or grilled duck breast.
A la carte: 200-400 F. Menu: 150 F (weekdays and Sat. dinner).

 Grandgousier

17, av. Rachel
43 87 66 12
Closed Sat. lunch & Sun. Open until 10 p.m. Parking.
Léon Marzynski and his wife, Renée, have overcome the doldrums of their sleepy corner of Montmartre, right near the entrance to the famous cemetery. The new decor is a rousing success with its gay, bright, and flower-filled dining room and large, well-spaced tables. The cooking is up to par too. Léon prepares a scrumptious salad of boned quail with foie gras, an original fillet of sole with Belgian endive and black currants, salmon with capers and cranberry butter and a fine guinea fowl roasted with basil in a Beaujolais-based sauce. The set menu hasn't gone up a single *centime* in five years.
A la carte: 280-320 F. Menu: 145 F.

 Langevin

Au Poulbot Gourmet
39, rue Lamarck
46 06 86 00
Closed Sun. Open until 10:30 p.m. Private room: 34. Air cond.
This small establishment delivers high quality, but few surprises. Run by Normandy native Jean-Paul Langevin, the cuisine is based on top-notch seasonal ingredients, with a few discreet nods to traditional country cooking. Try the "tournedos" of salmon with boletus mushrooms, roast saddle of hare, and the oh-so-yummy frozen charlotte aux deux chocolats. Tables are a bit crowded, the background music a little too loud, but the typically Montmartrois decor complete with terrace is sure to delight you.
A la carte: 240-300 F

11/20 Chez Marie-Louise

52, rue Championnet
46 06 86 55
Closed Sun. lunch, July-beg. Sept. & holidays. Open until 10 p.m.
Kidneys with Madeira, coq au vin du patron, clafoutis of seasonal fruits—here's honest bistro cooking, unchanged for 30 years, served amid copper saucepans and prints of carousing monks.
A la carte: 180-200 F. Menu: 120 F.

12/20 Aux Négociants

27, rue Lambert
46 06 15 11
Closed Sat., Sun., Mon. & Wed. dinner & Aug. Open until 10:30 p.m. No cards. Parking.
Jean Navier, a winner of the *Meilleur Pot* ("best glass of wine award"), has recently spruced up his bistro, where he serves a wonderful selection of modest but tasty growers' wines, with an emphasis on the Loire. Wine buffs should sample a

Plan to travel? Look for Gault Millau's other Best of guides to Chicago, Florida, France, Hawaii, Hong Kong, Germany, Italy, London, Los Angeles, New England, New Orleans, New York, San Francisco, Thailand, Toronto and Washington, D.C.

Jasnières or a Bourgeuil at the bar, but the Rhône wines are velvet on the tongue when married to the hearty home-style offerings simmered by *la patronne*. Forget frills like tablecloths and concentrate instead on robust rillettes, farm-reared veal en cocotte, and cassoulet.
A la carte: 150-200 F.

11/20 Palais de Kashmir
77, rue du Poteau
42 59 40 86
Open daily until 11:30 p.m. Air cond.
Exoticism abounds here with fountains, glass, carved wood and other Kashmiri delights but the Indo-Pakistani cuisine lacks similar brilliance: try a modest butter chicken, rice biryani with 25 spices, Indian hot breads and refreshing salted lassi.
A la carte: 180-200 F. Menu: 119 F.

 Le Restaurant
32, rue Véron
42 23 06 22
Closed Mon. lunch & Sun. Open until 11 p.m.
Yves Peladeau worked his way up from busboy to owner-chef of his dream-place at the foot of the Butte. His Restaurant is as modern, bright and appetizing as the imaginative dishes he concocts, for example the pan-roasted squid with spicy chorizo sausage, bell peppers, leeks and shellfish jus, or a crystalline salad of fresh artichokes, mango, cockles and lobster punched up with piquant chutney, or a savory veal steak with meat juices and (yes!) vanilla-scented carrots. Desserts include a seductive warm chocolate tart. The wine list is short but to the point.
A la carte: 240 F. Menu: 148 F (except Sat. dinner and holidays).

12/20 Wepler
14, pl. Clichy
45 22 53 24
Open daily until 1 a.m. Air cond.
A deluxe brasserie with a well-conceived menu and good service. The shellfish is some of the freshest in Paris; other interesting options are the hearty (and truly delicious) headcheese, oxtail stew and a copious choucroute garnie. Fine bouillabaisse, too.
A la carte: 200-400 F. Menu: 150 F.

19th arrondissement

 Au Cochon d'Or
192, av. Jean-Jaurès
42 45 46 46
Open daily until 10:30 p.m. Private room: 40. Air cond. Valet parking.
Times have changed since the Ayral family set up shop here in 1924. The nearby slaughterhouses are now defunct; butchers and meat-packers have given way to the cultured, worldly crowd disgorged by the Cité des Sciences at La Villette. In short, the restaurant has evolved along with its clientele. Under René Ayral's management, and with 30 years experience, chef François Médina continues to grill, roast and pan-fry the choicest morsels of beef: filet mignons, prime ribs and shell steaks. Earthier choices include pigs' trotters served with sauce Choron, boudin and apples, or calf's-head salad. Let's cut the bull: this is the best bet for red meat in town! A crack sommelier oversees the wine cellar.
A la carte: 300-450 F. Menu: 240 F.

Red toques signify modern cuisine; white toques signify traditional cuisine.

12/20 Dagorno
190, av. J.-Jaurès
40 40 09 39
Open daily until 12:15 a.m. Air cond. Valet parking.
Here's a comfortable deluxe brasserie that serves perfectly honorable, uncomplicated food. You won't be disappointed by the oysters, the calf's head with lentils, or the enormous côte de bœuf sauce bordelaise. Some original desserts, and an unbeatable set menu.
A la carte: 300-400 F. Menu: 168 F (wine incl.).

11/20 Ly-Ya
5, rue du Hainaut
42 08 34 98
Closed Mon. Open until 10:30 p.m.
A benevolent Buddha, arms upraised, presides over the dining room. In terms of value for money this tasty, fresh, mainly Vietnamese cuisine wins hands down. Try the fritot de crevettes, spicy shrimp soup, stuffed crab and chicken with lemongrass and ginger.
A la carte: 100-120 F. Menus: 45 F and 65 F (weekdays lunch only, wine incl.).

 Le Pavillon Puebla
Christian Vergès
Parc des Buttes-Chaumont
42 08 92 62
Closed Sun., Mon. & 2 wks. in Aug. Open until 10 p.m. Private room: 80. Garden dining. Valet parking.
This stylish Napoléon III hunting lodge, nestled in greenery at the foot of the Buttes Chaumont park is a joy for all seasons. When the weather is clement, you can sit under leafy trees and parasols on the terrace (the interior decor suffers from a heavy hand). Christian Vergès has been in residence here for five

years, always touched by the Catalan spirit that inspires his rich, varied and vigorous cuisine. Mediterranean flavors and strong colors bring a singular charm to his red mullet and John Dory perfumed with basil, his terrine of tomatoes and smoked salmon, the poached salt cod with lentils, or the gently spiced galette of potatoes and sweetbreads. One of the city's best crème brûlées is made right here and some splendid Banyuls can be found on the extensive wine list.

A la carte: 380-530 F. Menu: 230 F.

12/20 Le Sancerre
13, av. Corentin-Cariou
40 36 80 44
Closed Sat. & Sun. Annual closings not available. Open until 10:30 p.m.
The new management hasn't changed the nostalgic ambience of this vestige of the old abattoir district of La Villette. But the chef has been ill-advised to introduce a number of Americanized salads. His talent seems surer in traditional dishes such as lamb stew, braised short ribs of beef and juicy double lamb chops. As for wines, look no further than the wonderful Morgon and Sancerre sold by the centimeter (you pay only for what you drink from the bottle placed on the table). It is wise to book ahead for lunch.

A la carte: 250-300 F. Menus: 169 F (wine incl.), 110 F.

 20th arrondissement

 ### Aux Becs Fins
44, bd de Ménilmontant
47 97 51 52
Closed Sun. & Sep. 5-21. Open until 9:30 p.m.
This winsome little bistro runs alongside the Père Lacha-

ise cemetery. The colorful owner (Edith Lefebvre) relies on a faithful clientele of regulars who no longer notice the hideous decor (the centerpiece of which is a ghastly old fridge!). The cuisine sometimes backfires, but the pied et tête de veau sauce gribiche and the terrines and cassoulet "mère Edith" keep the toque in place... for now.

A la carte: 220-400 F. Menus: 240 F (except Sun., wine incl.), 180 F.

11/20 Le Courtil
15, rue St-Blaise
43 70 09 32
Closed Sun., Mon., Feb. school holidays & Aug. 3-31. Open until 9:45 p.m. Private room: 25. Terrace dining. Air cond.
The sunny dining room gives onto a flowered garden in the rear. On Tuesday evenings a jazz duo enlivens the simple but robust menu, which includes seafood choucroute, and for dessert a deeply chocolaty ganache à la fève de Guanaja.

A la carte: 200-250 F.

THE SUBURBS

ARGENTEUIL
95100 Argenteuil – (Val-d'Oise)
Paris 14 · Pontoise 20 · St-Germain-en-L. 15

 ### La Closerie Périgourdine
85, bd J.-Allemane
39 80 01 28
Closed Sat. lunch & Sun. dinner. Open until 10 p.m. Private room: 30.
Despite the fussy decor—stone walls, velvet-covered beams and corner fireplace, the menu offers a promising list of regionally rooted specialties: chanterelles en feuilleté, duck confit, escargots aux cèpes, lotte with mustard and thyme, and walnut cake. The wine list in-

cludes a good selection of Cahors, Bordeaux and fine Burgundies.

A la carte: 280-400 F. Menus: 159 F and 198 F (wine incl.), 135 F.

ASNIÈRES
92600 Asnières – (Hauts/Seine)
Paris 9 · Argenteuil 6 · Saint-Denis 8

 ### L'Ecurie
4 bis, Grande-Rue-Ch.-de-Gaulle
47 90 91 30
Closed Sat. lunch, Sun. & Aug. 2-29. Open until 10 p.m. Private room: 15.
An intelligent and generous prix-fixe menu is offered during the week at lunch and dinner (98 francs for a starter plus main course, such as a delicious blue-cheese tart followed by a mildly spiced chicken fricassée). One of the good desserts, like the walnut soufflé, will cost extra but won't break the bank. The charming *patron*, André Fontaine, also makes excellent sole fritters, quick-cooked turbot with citrus fruits and rognons de veau au Margaux. His desserts are remarkable, and so is the fresh new pastel decor.

A la carte: 200-300 F.

 ### Le Van Gogh
2, quai Aulagnier
47 91 05 10,
fax 47 93 00 93
Closed w.-e., Dec. 18-Jan. 6 & Aug. 13-24. Open until 10 p.m. Private room: 12. Terrace dining. Air cond. Valet parking.
Robert and Pierrette Daubian have dropped anchor in this ultramodern establishment on Robinson island. The dining room resembles the interior of a luxury liner, with portholes and bay windows offering views of the Seine. The cuisine looks out to sea, with dishes like lobster and

prawn feuilleté, and filet de bar royal cooked with the freshest produce. Desserts are superb (try the delicious berry gratin with Champagne), and there are fine Bordeaux to wash it all down.

A la carte: 400-500 F.

BLANC-MESNIL (LE)
93150 Blanc-Mesnil (Le) – (Seine-St-D.)
Paris 12 - Bobigny 6 - Aulnay 3

12/20 **La Vallière**

8, av. Paul-Vaillant-Couturier
48 69 52 01
Closed Sat. lunch, Sun. & Aug. 7-30. Open until 9:30 p.m. Private room: 30.
This small, provincial restaurant stands in dreary surroundings but the food, honest and simple (and improving, we note) is carefully prepared: crêpes filled with basil-scented escargots, andouillette sausage, salmon with citrus fruit, and banana bavarois with apricot coulis. The chocolate mousse is excellent, and we appreciate the detailed (even didactic) wine list.

A la carte: 230-280 F. Menu: 90 F.

BOULOGNE-BILLANCOURT
92100 Boulogne-Billancourt – (Hauts/Seine)
Versailles 11

---

 14 **L'Auberge**

86, av. J.-B.-Clément
46 05 22 35,
fax 46 05 23 16
Closed Sat., Sun., holidays & July 31-Aug. 29. Open until 10 p.m. Terrace dining. Air cond.
Both the decor and the cooking have undergone a radical change of style in this restaurant once devoted to the regional fare of Franche-Comté, but the owners and chefs are still the same. Cancoillotte, a soft, pungent cheese spread, and mountain sausages have

disappeared from the menu to be replaced by cabbage stuffed with pigeon and foie gras, stuffed mussels with basil butter, and nougat glacé au Grand Marnier (a bit too sweet but nice and creamy). The traditional duck terrine is still available however, and there are Jura wines in the excellent cellar.

A la carte: 350-400 F. Menus: 150 F (dinner only), 190 F.

---

 13 **La Bretonnière**

120, av. J.-B.-Clément
46 05 73 56
Closed Sat. & Sun. Open until 9:45 p.m.
A former head waiter, René Rossignol, has switched to cooking and brought this restaurant back up to standard. Taste the wonderful marinated sardines, Angus beef with mashed potatoes, and yummy, uncomplicated desserts like chocolate mousse with orange sauce. Excellent Loire wines.

A la carte: 300-350 F. Menus: 150 F (dinner only), 200 F (lunch only).

---

 16 **Au Comte de Gascogne**

89, av. J.-B.-Clément
46 03 47 27,
fax 46 04 55 70
Closed Sat. lunch & Sun. Open until 10:30 p.m. Private room: 15. Garden dining. Air cond. Valet parking.
Three palm trees, a fountain and lots of flowers make it feel like spring time all year round in the delightful courtyard garden. Business lunches actually become enjoyable, while dinner in the suburbs turns into an exotic outing. Gérard Vérane, the jovial Gascon who created this tropical greenhouse with its sliding roof, has handed over the kitchen to Henri Charvet, who once served the best meals in Aix-en-Provence.

The Gascon flavor lingers on in the seven or eight variations on foie gras, including the wonderful smoked duck foie gras with cucumber and bacon, and in the world-class collection of Armagnacs. But it was the sun-kissed Provençal dishes that really captured our attention: smoked salmon with fennel confit, lobster soup with ravioli filled with green-tomato "jam", red mullet pan-roasted in a basil jus flanked by delicious stuffed vegetables, and steamed cod drizzled with Maussane olive oil. The young sommelier, Patrice Marchand, will help you choose from among the 10,000 wines in his cellar.

A la carte: 500-700 F.

12/20 **Le Poivre Vert**

1, pl. B.-Palissy
46 03 01 63,
fax 47 12 08 27
Closed dinner Dec. 24, 25 & 31. Open until 11 p.m. Air cond.
Book early for a top-value meal in this modern, plant-filled setting: the 99.50-franc formula (a starter and main course) is understandably much in demand. Try the seafood bouchée, the crisp roast leg of rabbit, and the flaky feuillantine of caramelized pears. Well-chosen wines. The waiters are very efficient, but there just aren't enough of them.

A la carte: 170 F.

BUC
78530 Buc – (Yvelines)
Paris 22 - Versailles 5 - Sceaux 8

---

 14 **Relais de Courlande**

2, rue Collin-Mamet
39 56 24 29,
fax 39 56 03 92
Closed Sun. dinner, Mon. & Aug. 1-23. Open until 10 p.m. Private

room: 35. *Garden dining. Hotel: 12 rms 250-360 F. Parking.*

The pretty garden and terrace of this former coaching inn are becoming popular for business lunches. Besides its central location, the restaurant's success can be attributed to Ivan Vautier's lively cooking. He makes a mean salad of prawns dressed with mango mayonnaise, a lush pigeon roasted with

The toque, circa 1700

Have you ever wondered about the origin of that towering, billowy (and slightly ridiculous) white hat worn by chefs all over the world? Chefs have played an important role in society since the fifth century B.C., but the hats didn't begin to appear in kitchens until around the eighteenth century A.D. The toque is said to be of Greek origin: many famous Greek cooks, to escape persecution, sought refuge in monasteries and continued to practice their art. The chefs donned the tall hats traditionally worn by Orthodox priests but to distinguish themselves from their fellows, they wore white hats instead of black. The custom eventually was adopted by chefs from Paris to Peking.

cinnamon honey and an interesting lamb dish with walnuts and tomatoes enhanced by caraway seeds and dragon grass. All are served by a professional, smiling staff.

A la carte: 400-460 F. Menus: 130 F, 240 F, 380 F.

CELLE-SAINT-CLOUD (LA)
78170 Celle-Saint-Cloud (La) — (Yvelines)
Paris 16 - Saint-Cloud 5 - Bougival 2

 Au Petit Chez Soi
Pl. de l'Eglise
39 69 69 51
Closed Sun. dinner off-season. Open until 10 p.m. Private room: 60. Terrace dining.

Just outside Paris, on an authentic village square complete with fountain, this adorable *auberge* offers wonderfully modern, flavorful food prepared by Louis Lavandier. Follow our lead and order the lemon-marinated salmon, a flawlessly cooked roast lotte in a creamy sauce, or a succulent filet de bœuf—Great stuff! The wine list is short but very much to the point (we appreciate the obvious effort made to keep prices down). Expect a charming welcome from the cheerful *patronne.*

A la carte: 220-320 F. Menu: 155 F.

CHÂTEAUFORT
78117 Châteaufort — (Yvelines)
Paris 28 - Versailles 10 - Orsay 11

 La Belle Epoque
10, pl. de la Mairie
39 56 21 66
Closed Sun. dinner & Mon. Open until 10 p.m. Private room: 6. Terrace dining.

From the terrace shaded by lime trees just twenty minutes out of Paris, you can enjoy a splendid view of the Mérantaise Valley. Inside, Alain Rayé (expropriated from his restaurant near the

Champs-Elysées) has just taken over from Michel Peignaud. In fact, since our deadline coincided with his opening, we visited La Belle Epoque the day after Rayé moved in! He and his staff were still getting their bearings (hence, we suppose, the excess salt in one dish; the insipid gelée that marred another), but they managed to turn out a beautifully refreshing vegetable starter featuring zucchini "marmalade", green-bean salad and cauliflower with cumin, an enormous sole brightened with the sunny tastes of lemon and rosemary, a superb chop of farm-raised veal perfumed with sage, and several luscious old-fashioned desserts (blancmange, waffles with rhubarb compote). Expect a vivacious welcome from Brigitte Rayé.

A la carte: 350-400 F. Menu: 350 F.

CHAVILLE
92370 Chaville — (Hauts/Seine)
Paris 13 - Versailles 9 - Meudon 1 - Boulogne 2

 La Tonnelle
29, rue Lamennais
47 50 42 77
Closed Mon., Feb. school holidays & Aug. 5-25. Open until 10:30 p.m. Private room: 15. Terrace dining. Air cond.

Pretty pink-and-blue curtains and new wallpaper make for an elegant interior, while the garden-terrace with its old wine press is a winner on sunny days. Guy Tardif's cooking is scrupulously classic and ever more skillful: fine pan-fried foie gras set atop an artichoke bottom, perfectly cooked red mullet, pigeon with citrus fruits and a scrumptious vanilla millefeuille. Smiling staff; plenty of attractive half-bottles on the wine list.

Menus: 240 F (except holidays), 180 F (except dinner holidays).

CHENNEVIÈRES-SUR-MARNE
94430 Chennevières-sur-Marne – (Val/Marne)
Paris 17 - Lagny 20 - Coulommiers 51

12/20 L'Ecu de France
31, rue de Champigny
45 76 00 03
Closed Aug. 30-Sep. 6. Open until 9:30 p.m. Private room: 50. Terrace dining. Valet parking.
Lots of people were vying for tables the last time we visited this exceptionally situated restaurant on the banks of the River Marne. But truth to tell, we ended up wondering why: after listening to the hostess argue with the headwaiter, after learning that our reservation had been lost (not that anyone one seemed to care), after refusing the outrageously expensive wine that the sommelier brought us instead of the bottle we had ordered, after searching in vain for the sweetbreads in our champignons farcis aux ris de veau, and after paying crippling prices for those and for a dried out curried sole. Sorry, folks, no toque this year!
A la carte: 400-600 F.

Au Vieux Clodoche
18, rue de Champigny
45 76 09 39
Open daily until 10 p.m. Garden dining. Parking.
On the riverside terrace in summer or near the fireplace in winter, Brigitte Huerta's cooking will capture your attention—not only because of the high prices it commands. The delicate duck foie gras au torchon, marvelous turbot in a spice crust, the tender seven-hour leg of lamb, rich sweetbreads en feuilleté, and lively ginger soufflé are very nicely handled indeed, but we repeat: they are too costly by half!
A la carte: 400-500 F.

CHESNAY (LE)
See Versailles

CLICHY
92110 Clichy – (Hauts/Seine)
Paris 7 - Saint-Germain-en-Laye 17

La Barrière de Clichy
1, rue de Paris
47 37 05 18
See *Paris 17th arr. page 69.*

La Bonne Table
119, bd J.-Jaurès
47 37 38 79
Closed Sat. lunch, Sun. & Aug. 4-Sep. 2. Open until 10 p.m. Air cond.
Gisèle Berger is a culinary pillar in Clichy: a true *cordon bleu*, respected for her talent and adherence to tradition. We find her prices a bit high for the suburbs, but there's the recent redecoration to pay for as well as the top-quality seafood Gisèle demands for her dishes. You'll enjoy her warm oysters with salmon, lobster lasagne, brandade en aïoli, bouillabaisse and the refreshing white wines selected by René, the *patron*.
A la carte: 350-450 F.

COURBEVOIE
92400 Courbevoie – (Hauts/Seine)
Paris 11 - St.-Germain-en-Laye 13 - Levallois 4

Les Feuillantines
23, pl. de Seine
La Défense 1
47 73 88 80,
fax 40 90 96 03
Closed dinner & w.-e. (except upon reservation). Terrace dining. Air cond. Parking.
A largely business clientele enjoys a view of the Seine and the Ile de la Jatte from the third-floor terrace. The menu is rather long and expensive, but proposes carefully cooked dishes like a ragoût of snails and artichokes, scallops with Belgian endive, pintade aux choux

and luscious lemon-filled crêpes. The "diet" menu keeps your calorie consumption down to just 1,000...
A la carte: 320-450 F. Menu: 220 F.

Le Monarque
pl. des Reflets
La Défense 2 - 48, espl. du Gal-de-Gaulle
47 78 84 59
Closed w.-e., holidays & Aug. 1-23. Open until 9:45 p.m. Private room: 25. Terrace dining. Air cond. Parking.
The pretentious decor was probably intended for important tête-à-têtes and VIP luncheons. But if you go past the velvet-covered armchairs and Oriental carpets, you'll find a splendid outdoor terrace shaded by young plane trees and looking toward the Arc de Triomphe through the Arche de La Défense. Whichever setting you choose, you can expect the same faultless service from waiters dressed in wing collars and striped jackets. The cooking of Antoine Gayet is delicate, innovative and expensive. But tell yourself that luxury doesn't come cheap, and savor the baked scallops in their shells, red mullet paired with foie gras, roast pigeon with a shirred egg and to finish, a kirsch-flavored peach gratin. Search the wine list and you may find a bottle for under 200 F...
A la carte: 380-530 F. Menus: 220 F and 250 F and 300 F and 320 F (wine incl.).

La Safranée sur Mer
12, pl. des Reflets
La Défense 2
47 78 75 50
Closed Sat., Sun., Dec. 24-Jan. 2. & Aug. Open until 10:30 p.m. Private room: 30. Terrace dining. Air cond. Valet parking.
With its luxurious wood-paneled decor and fine

service, this seafood restaurant is a favorite lunch venue for business people with important clients to impress. The chef purchases premium ingredients, but a bit more care could be taken in their preparation (our sole fillets were slightly undercooked). Other more successful dishes include warm red-mullet salad, pan-roasted scallops with oyster jus and fricassée de lotte.

A la carte: 400-500 F. Menus: 220 F (dinner only), 300 F, 350 F, 370 F.

 Les Trois Marmites
215, bd St-Denis
43 33 25 35
Closed Sat., Sun. & Aug. 1-27. Open until 10 p.m. Private room: 16. Air cond.
This comfortable, elegant restaurant has maintained a traditional bistro decor set off by indirect lighting. Marc Faucheux's honest, seasonal dishes include cockle salad with beurre blanc sauce, filet de turbot au cidre, roast pigeon with pommes boulangère and freshwater perch with leeks. The regional wines are good, but just as pricey as the rest.

A la carte: 280-400 F. Menu: 200 F.

CRÉTEIL
94000 Créteil — (Val/Marne)
Paris 12 · Evry 20 · Melun 35 · Bobigny 17

 Le Cristolien
29, av. P.-Brossolette
48 98 12 01
Closed Sat. lunch & Sun. Open until 10 p.m. Terrace dining. Air cond. Parking.
It's no surprise that every senior executive and managing director in Créteil comes here to eat; it's the best spot in this huge, modern suburb. Alain Donnard, who opened here a few years ago, delights his customers with carefully

prepared classic dishes like tuna carpaccio rémoulade, salt-cured duck with a suave orange sauce, turbot in an aromatic broth and a lush chocolate-and-caramel millefeuille. The business lunch is a terrific deal. Pleasant but frankly amateurish service.

A la carte: 250-320 F. Menu: 180 F.

CROISSY-BEAUBOURG
77183 Croissy-Beaubourg — (Seine/Marne)
Paris 29 · Melun 34 · Meaux 30

 L'Aigle d'Or
8, rue de Paris
60 05 31 33,
fax 64 62 09 39
Closed Sun. dinner & Mon. Open until 9 p.m. Private room: 30. Garden dining. Parking.
The Gilliams brothers have created a discreet and elegant decor in pink and white, with a huge fireplace and mezzanine. Hervé Gilliams carefully tends to his long repertoire of regional dishes: sweetbreads with chestnuts and almonds, salmon on a bacon-studded biscuit, truffled boudin blanc with warm duck foie gras, and a scrumptious fruit cake with plum liqueur. Jean-Louis Gilliams oversees the attentive service. Alas, prices are high and rising.

A la carte: 450-550 F. Menus: 250 F (except holidays), 450 F.

ENGHIEN
95880 Enghien — (Val-d'Oise)
Paris 18 · Argenteuil 16 · Chantilly 32

 Duc d'Enghien
3, av. de Ceinture
34 12 90 00
Closed Sun. dinner, Mon., Jan. 4-13 & Aug. 2-Sep. 1. Open until 10:30 p.m. Terrace dining.
The nicest spot is outdoors on the lakeside terrace with its geranium beds. In the recently

decorated dining room, huge bouquets of flowers do their best to cheer up the ugly airport-style ceiling. Michel Kéréver confirms his triple-toque rating with a menu that, under a fairly classical guise, offers dishes of rare astuteness and acute flavors. Yes, the food is expensive, but paying the bill is sure to be less painful than losing a similar sum in the casino next door! Here the choices are all winners, as you'll agree after tasting the red mullet in a saffron broth, or lobster with tiny légumes à la grecque, or the thin tomato tart keenly perfumed with pesto, or the regal fillet of lamb with its liver, sweetbreads and kidney. Desserts are better than ever; our special favorite is a peach roasted in its juices served with a scoop of delicate verbena ice cream. And now the wine list proposes a few modest bottles and half-bottles alongside the *grands crus* of Bordeaux. Graceful service, directed by Michel Santier.

A la carte: 600-700 F. Menus: 325 F (weekdays lunch and Sat., wine incl.), 340 F (weekdays dinner only), 460 F.

EURO DISNEY
See Marne-la-Vallée

FONTENAY-SOUS-BOIS
94120 Fontenay-sous-Bois — (Val/Marne)
Paris 7 · Saint-Mandé 2 · Nogent-sur-Marne 3

 La Musardière
61, av. du Mal-Joffre
48 73 96 13
Closed Sun., Mon. & Tues. dinner, & Aug. Open until 9:45 p.m. Air cond.
This bright, comfortable restaurant lies in the heart of a huge new administrative and shopping center largely composed of glass and ceramic. The *patron*, formerly of the

Savoy Hotel in London, is an attentive host, and his chef, Christian Landier, produces handsome classic dishes with a light touch: saumon au gros sel, smoked haddock and lentils, and kidney with mustard sauce. The excellent fish dishes vary with the market and the set menu is good value. Attractive cellar. A la carte: 250-350 F. Menu: 140 F.

GARENNE-COLOMBES (LA)
92250 Garenne-Colombes (La)– (Hauts/Seine)
Paris 12 · Courbevoie 2 · Asnières 4

 ## Auberge du 14-Juillet
9, bd de la République
42 42 21 79
Closed w.-e., holidays & 2 wks. in May. Open until 9:30 p.m.
Regular customers are happy to see that this family-run restaurant has a new decor. In contrast to the nearby concrete structures of La Défense, it is a charming, intimate place offering several excellent duck specialties and sumptuous seafood dishes, prepared with increasing confidence by Jean-Pierre Baillon. His son Laurent helps out with the day's catch to make dishes like freshwater perch with Loire wine and bacon, bass quenelles perfumed with lemongrass, and salmon sprinkled with fragrant olive oil. Charming welcome. A la carte: 300-450 F. Menu: 220 F.

 ## Aux Gourmets Landais
Hôtel de Paris
5, av. Joffre
42 42 22 86
Closed Sun. dinner & Mon. Open until 10:45 p.m. Private room: 35. Garden dining. Hotel: 12 rms 180-250 F.
Josette Velazco's Southwestern hospitality routine

contributes to the success of this excellent establishment, which now boasts a small garden with sliding roof. Her husband Alain adds the same regional flavor to his much-improved cuisine, which features salade landaise rich with foie gras and fatted duck breast, beautifully cooked suprême of sea bass with aromatic vegetables, and light, tender tourtière (apple pie) laced with Armagnac. Tempting selection of affordable regional wines. A la carte: 300-400 F. Menus: 120 F, 200 F.

12/20 ## Rose
10, pl. J.-Baillet
42 42 22 07
Closed Mon., Feb. 15-22 & Aug. 1-22. Open until 9 p.m. Private room: 50. Garden dining.
Cozy and full of flowers, this increasingly charming restaurant has recently added tables outside in the courtyard. The patron's rich, intricate dishes would gain from a little lightening, but they are well prepared and full of flavor: millefeuille of celery root and salmon, chateaubriand flavored with a quartet of spices, confit de canard with baby broad beans, all served in a pretty dining room where everything—even the bill—is pink. A la carte: 320-480 F. Menu: 180 F (except Sun. dinner).

ISSY-LES-MOULINEAUX
92130 Issy-les-Moulineaux – (Hauts/Seine)
Boulogne-Billancourt 1

 ## La Manufacture
20, espl. de la Manufacture
40 93 08 98
Closed Sat. lunch, Sun. & 2 wks. in Aug. Open until 10:30 p.m. Terrace dining. Air cond.
Jean-Pierre Vigato, who also runs the three-toque Apicius in Paris, hasn't opened a second restaurant just to make more

money; he sees it as an outlet for another aspect of his personality. Unlike Apicius, Manufacture is a hip, bright, spacious restaurant converted from an old tobacco factory. Vigato's former number two, David Van Laer, is the chef, putting his all into making this an exciting, original counterpart to Apicius. All the dishes are appetizing, but the execution occasionally falls off. After a delicious feuille à feuille d'escargots, we were disappointed by a rather bland casserole of pork and root vegetables; the chocolate cake is rich and yummy, but we didn't see the point of the accompanying coffee coulis. Short but pertinent wine list; cheerful yet scatter-brained service. A la carte: 260-330 F. Menu: 190 F (weekdays lunch only).

JOUY-EN-JOSAS
78350 Jouy-en-Josas – (Yvelines)
Paris 21 · Versailles 4 · Rambouillet 35

 ## Fondation Cartier
Restaurant du Château
3, rue de la Manufacture
39 56 46 46
Closed Mon., Tues. & Wed. dinner, Sat. lunch, Dec. 19-Jan. 3 & July 20-Aug. 16. Open until 10 p.m. Private room: 80. Garden dining. Air cond. Parking.
It's probably because he counts cooking as one of the fine arts that Alain-Dominique Perrin called on master chef Gérard Vié to oversee the kitchens of this restaurant filled with prestigious works of modern art by César, Garouste, Arman and others. All Vié has to do in practice is to let the capable chef, Christian Aubertin, turn out the very good lamb terrine with figs, steamed sole roulades in a gingery broth, and tulipe au chocolat with orange sauce. The ideas are all fine, but the execution occasionally lags.

Top Bordeaux and Cahors (of which Perrin is himself a producer) round out the meals taken in this elegant black-white-and-gray decor. A la carte: 350-400 F. Menus: 230 F (weekdays lunch only), 280 F (weekdays dinner and Sat., Sun. lunch & holidays), 380 F (except Sun. dinner).

LEVALLOIS-PERRET
92300 Levallois-Perret – (Hauts/Seine)
Neuilly 4

 Gauvain
11, rue L.-Rouquier
47 58 51 09
Closed Sat., Sun. & Aug. Open until 10 p.m. Air cond.
A commendable establishment, driven by the talent of a creative young chef whose personal, oft-renewed repertoire fully merits a toque. The single-price menu might, on a given day, suggest thread-fin with baby green peppercorns, sea bream with shallots stewed in red wine, followed by floating island in a pool of chestnut coulis. The wine list needs filling out (though the selection of Loire bottlings is adequate), and the staff needs training in the service of wine: a bottle should never be brought to the table already opened!
A la carte: 250-280 F. Menu: 190 F.

12/20 **Le Jardin**
9, pl. J.-Zay
47 39 54 02
Closed Sat. lunch, Sun. & wk. of Aug. 15. Open until 10 p.m. Terrace dining. Parking.
Just off the beltway, a relaxing country atmosphere has been created here. The patron, who is not above leaving the kitchen to chat with his customers, prepares rich, generous dishes such as terrine de confit de canard with fresh foie gras, and sole in

trout mousse.
A la carte: 300-350 F. Menu: 155 F.

12/20 **Le Petit Poste**
39, rue Rivay
47 37 34 46
Closed Sat. lunch & Sun. Open until 10:15 p.m.
Fifteen tables crowded around the bar–this is exactly the type of bistro Brassens used to write about in his songs. Now it is a favorite with Levallois office workers, who come to enjoy the cooking of Pierre Leboucher, formerly of Lucas-Carton and La Marée: rissole d'artichaut au foie gras, navarin of sole à la vanille, lamb sweetbreads sauce diable, and a delicious pineapple terrine. Wash these good dishes down with one of the fine Loire wines.
A la carte: 230-280 F.

 Pointaire
46, rue de Villiers
47 57 44 77,
fax 43 34 98 17
Closed w.-e. & Aug. 1-23. Open until 9:30 p.m.
Père Pointaire remains a legend within the prettily renovated walls of this rustic bistro, through the dishes which were his glory: fresh-water perch in butter sauce and beuchelle tourangelle (a regional specialty involving cocks' combs and kidneys). But the current chef has some nicely prepared offerings of his own to suggest: sea urchin flan, pheasant in Champagne with chanterelles, and a darkly delicious chocolate marquise. We would love to see a better selection of wines to complement the good food.
Menu: 180 F.

Remember to call ahead to reserve your table, and please, if you cannot honor your reservation, be courteous and let the restaurant know.

LINAS
91310 Linas – (Essonne)
Paris 25 - Etampes 23 - Orsay 13 - Montlhéry 2

 L'Escargot de Linas
136, rue de la Division-Leclerc
69 01 00 30
Closed Sun., Mon. lunch & Aug. 9-31. Open until 9:30 p.m. Terrace dining. Parking.
Those who love the good old-fashioned style of careful cooking will delight in this elegant, mannered Louis XVI restaurant, offering omelette Curnonsky, fricassée périgourdine, and tournedos à la bordelaise with fresh marrow. But Maurice Comte is capable of more adventurous fare, using seasonal produce from nearby Rungis market to produce a wide selection of handsome dishes such as gratin of shellfish with saffron, asparagus flan flavored with chervil, and breast of pheasant with juniper berries and buttery cabbage. If the prices hadn't got so steep, we would come here every night in summer to dine on the flowery terrace.
A la carte: 300-400 F. Menu: 200 F (weekdays and Sat.).

LIVRY-GARGAN
93190 Livry-Gargan – (Seine-St-D.)
Paris 17 - Senlis 42 - Aubervilliers 13

 Auberge Saint-Quentinoise
23, bd de la République
43 81 13 08
Closed Sun. dinner & Mon. (except holidays). Open until 10 p.m. Private room: 15.
The courtyard terrace with ivy-covered walls is clearly the star attraction, although the elegant, newly renovated dining room has now come into its own. The classic dishes skillfully prepared by Michel Nicoleau come as a real surpr-

ise in this glum suburb: méli-mélo de sole au citron vert, lobster in an anise-scented broth with mild garlic, tender lamb cooked to perfection (no need for the sauce), and a rich chocolate-truffle cake. Satisfactory service and a good wine list, rich in Bordeaux. A la carte: 280-450 F. Menu: 180 F.

LOUVECIENNES
78430 Louveciennes – (Yvelines)
Paris 24 - Versailles 7 - St-Germain-en-Laye 6

 Aux Chandelles

12, pl. de l'Eglise
39 69 08 40
Closed Sat. lunch, Wed., & Aug. 15-31. Open until 10 p.m. Private room: 20. Terrace dining.
The upstairs dining room offers a view of the enclosed garden. The young owner-chef, Stéphane Dohollon, who studied with Gérard Besson, produces dishes that are so delicate you could almost accuse him of pretension. The set meals are excellent value, particularly the 260-franc menu which includes wine and features saffron-flavored perch, and a winy civet de joues de cochon. Perfect service in a setting ideal for romantic dinners.
A la carte: 300-370 F. Menus: 160 F (weekdays lunch only), 260 F (except weekdays lunch, wine incl.).

MAISONS-LAFFITTE
78600 Maisons-Laffitte – (Yvelines)
Paris 21 - Pontoise 18 - St-Germain-en-L. 8

 Le Laffitte

5, av. de Saint-Germain
39 62 01 53
Closed Sun. dinner, Mon., Feb. 7-14 & Aug. Open until 10 p.m.
Offering good seafood, classic cooking and a long list of carefully prepared dishes, André Laurier's restaurant is an address worth noting and

just the place for hearty appetites. Sample the escargots in crisp pastry accented with pistou, lotte au curry, skate with cabbage, veal tenderloin en persillade, and dark-chocolate fondant.
A la carte: 280-440 F. Menus: 220 F, 320 F.

Le Tastevin

9, av. Eglé
39 62 11 67
Closed Mon. dinner, Tues. Open until 10 p.m. Terrace dining.
The wine list is still out of this world, but we found our last meal here terribly disappointing, despite the handsome presentation of the food. The gazpacho with prawns was notable only for its lack of flavor, an oyster mold was napped with a boring curry sauce, and a beautiful piece of roast turbot was ruined by an excess of salt. Things started looking up, however, with the pigeon en confit flanked by foie-gras croquettes and a wonderful little fried potato basket. Superb chocolate mousses were counterbalanced, alas, by an alarmingly bad crème brûlée. We wonder too why the *plats du jour* listed on the menu had nothing to do with the dishes actually available; and why the tasting menu was described to us with every detail except the price! The only course we can take, this year, is to suspend the rating, in hopes that Le Tastevin will reconquer its two toques next time.
A la carte: 470 F. Menu: 230 F.

 La Vieille Fontaine

8, av. Grétry
39 62 01 78,
fax 39 62 13 43
Closed Sun., Mon. & Aug. Open until 10 p.m. Garden dining.
Manon Letourneur and François Clerc treat all their customers with the same con-

sideration as the many celebrities (like Catherine Deneuve) who dine here. Even with a thriving catering business to take care of, François Clerc is always on duty in the kitchen when the restaurant is open. We just wish he would add some new dishes to his repertoire, to vary the pleasures procured by his classic braised lobster with baby vegetables, pigeon stuffed with four kinds of cabbage, calf's kidney accented with a touch of licorice, and saddle of rabbit with mustard meringue. The menu available at both lunch and dinner offers excellent value: you might choose mixed salad with rosy cold roast beef, tarragon-flavored chicken ham, thyme-scented hot goat cheese, and pain perdu aux fruits. We're sure you'll love the romantic setting, too, and the gracious hospitality of Manon Letourneur.
A la carte: 550-900 F. Menus: 230 F (dinner only), 250 F (lunch only, wine incl.).

MARNE-LA-VALLÉE
77206 Marne-la-Vallée – (Seine/Marne)
Paris 28 - Meaux 28 - Melun 40

In nearby Euro Disney
(Access by A4)
77206 Marne-la-Vallée – (Seine/Marne)

 Blue Lagoon

In the Park,
Adventureland
64 74 20 74
Open daily until 11 p.m.
Palm trees and a tropical lagoon are the setting for agreeably spicy fare: grilled swordfish and shrimp, chicken curry, Jamaican nougat and coconut ice cream. Right nearby are the boats that ferry passengers into the exciting *Pirates of the Caribbean*, one of the resort's most popular attractions.
Menu: 125 F.

California Grill

Outside the Park
60 45 65 00,
fax 60 45 65 33
Private room: 80. Air cond. Valet parking.
The "gastronomic" restaurant of the Disneyland Hotel offers inventive dishes based on premium American-style ingredients. In his superb, ultra-modern kitchens, the (French) chef and his team prepare a delicious warm goat-cheese tart, beef carpaccio strewn with basil and anointed with drops of fruity olive oil, salmon with a maple-syrup glaze, a thick veal chop with black olives and polenta, and for dessert, an ethereal honey-walnut millefeuille. Impeccable service; crippling prices.
A la carte: 450-550 F.

12/20 Cape Cod

Disney Festival
60 45 55 93
Open daily until 11 p.m.
To allay pre-dinner hunger pangs, servers dressed in sailor suits bring appetizers of hot garlic bread drizzled with olive oil to every table. But be sure to leave room for the good things that follow, like generous portions of coquilles Saint-Jacques with bacon or swordfish grilled with fresh herbs. One can also dine at the (pricier: 350 francs) Yacht Club, on crabcakes, shellfish, lobster and such.
Menus: 180 F (dinner only), 280 F (lunch only).

Key West Seafood

Disney Festival
60 45 70 61
Open daily until 11 p.m.
Overlooking the (artificial) lake is a huge space decked out to resemble an unpretentious Florida fish house. Would real Florida fishermen pay these prices, we wonder, for garlicky blue crab, spicy giant shrimp, seafood stew (195 francs) and Key Lime pie?

The wine cellar is Californian.
A la carte: 250-350 F.

12/20 Los Angeles Bar

Disney Festival
60 45 71 14
Open daily until 11 p.m.
Also lakeside is this bright, airy and modern dining room where you can enjoy gazpacho with a well-seasoned crab croûton, a grilled vegetable platter with goat cheese and caramelized garlic, grain-fed chicken with tomatilla sauce and other clever, nicely executed dishes. Pizza and light snacks on tap upstairs.
Menu: 225 F.

Manhattan Club

Outside the Park,
near the lake
60 45 73 50,
fax 60 45 73 55
Open daily until 11 p.m.
At 7 p.m. sharp, an orchestra in evening clothes (tails, no less!) strikes up a cha-cha to kick off the soirée. Waiters in equally formal togs skim over the thick carpet, bearing caviar, smoked salmon, foie gras, lobster Thermidor, tournedos Rossini and other rich and famous dishes concealed under silver serving bells. The scene is perfect—everyone feels like movie stars! Until that is, the check comes and you are actually required to pay...
A la carte: 500-700 F.

12/20 Park Side

Outside the Park
60 45 75 13
Open daily until 11 p.m.
Good, simple American culinary food prepared while you watch: chicken-noodle soup, grilled salmon with bacon, veal loaf with mushroom gravy and celery-root purée. Served forth in a big, bustling New York–style setting.
Menu: 195 F.

10/20 Silver Spur Steakhouse

In the Park, Frontierland
60 45 70 50
Open daily until 11 p.m.
Hearty appetites meet their match here, with huge portions of barbecued chicken wings and prime ribs of beef, served in a reconstituted Wild West saloon (just don't ask for a whiskey: no alcohol is permitted in the Park!).
A la carte: 250-300 F.

10/20 Walt's An American Restaurant

In the Park, Main Street
64 74 24 08
Open daily until 11 p.m.
A stairway decorated with photographs of Walt Disney leads to a series of charming little dining rooms; one is less taken by the food, however, which is only mildly interesting (good orange and shrimp salad, overcooked meats, boring desserts).
Menu: 145 F.

MARNES-LA-COQUETTE
92430 Marnes-la-Coquette — (Hauts-de-Seine)
Paris 15 - Versailles 4 - Vaucresson 1

11/20 Les Hirondelles

18, rue G.-et-X.-Schlumberger
47 41 00 20
Closed Sun. dinner, Wed., Aug. & Dec. 23-Jan. 2. Open until 9:30 p.m.
Home-style cooking prevails at this friendly little bistro, but sometimes the chef decides to surprise his customers with a deftly grilled salmon and cèpes à la provençale.
A la carte: 150-250 F.

The prices in this guide reflect what establishments were charging at press time.

13 La Tête Noire

6, pl. Mairie
47 41 06 28
*Closed Sun. dinner & Mon.
Open until 9:30 p.m.*
A pretty view of leafy little square and the minuscule church just opposite add to the charm of this establishment, which is popular with the local gentry. Christian Lièvre's cooking is characterized by straightforward flavors and a judicious dose of invention. We can recommend his tourte of frogs' legs and spinach, a rich sculpin fillet souffléed with lobster sauce, and the luscious coffee-and-chocolate entremets. The wine cellar is small but well composed.
A la carte: 240-340 F.

MEUDON
92190 Meudon – (Hauts/Seine)
Paris 12 · Versailles 10 · Boulogne 3

15 Relais des Gardes

42, av. du Général Gallieni
45 34 11 79
Closed Sat. lunch, Sun. dinner & Aug. 6-Sep. 6. Open until 10 p.m. Private room: 70. Terrace dining.
Jean-Claude Cahagnet is in command of the kitchens of this handsome brick restaurant where a classical repertoire and style reign supreme. The atmosphere in the formal beige dining room is certainly quite serious and the maître d'hotel positively solemn, but the cooking is well done with no redundant frills: tricolor vegetable terrine, oxtail vinaigrette with a robustly flavored aspic, poularde braisée en paupiette and a fantastic baba au rhum, rivaled only by the délice aux abricots confits. The wine list is superb, prices are high, and hostess Mme. Oudina is smilingly omnipresent.
A la carte: 300-400 F.

Menus: 290 F (wine incl.), 190 F.

MONTMORENCY
95160 Montmorency – (Val-d'Oise)
Paris 18 · Pontoise 20 · Enghien 3 · St-Denis 8

12/20 Au Cœur de la Forêt

Av. du Repos-de-Diane
39 64 99 19
Open daily until 9:30 p.m. Private room: 25. Terrace dining. Parking.
Next time you go walking in the Montmorency forest, ferret around until you find this large establishment hidden in the trees. You'll enjoy the family atmosphere and the nicely crafted, seasonal cuisine, for example a delicate turbot with herbed aspic, sole with mussel butter, a bright-tasting duck with apricots, and a good warm banana-rum tart.
A la carte: 260-370 F.
Menus: 125 F, 185 F.

NANTERRE
92000 Nanterre – (Hauts/Seine)
Paris 13 · Neuilly 5 · St-Germain 8 · Boulogne 7

12/20 L'Ile de France

83, av. du Mal-Joffre
47 24 10 44
Closed Sun. & Aug. Open until 9:30 p.m. Terrace dining. Parking.
Don't be put off by appearances! This is not a disused warehouse but a comfortable and serious reataurant that caters to business people. It's peaceful and bright, swathed from stem to stern in brown carpeting and dotted with large, well-spaced tables where one can enjoy a generous set menu of seafood salad, a flavorful beef sauté spiced up with green peppercorns, and a yummy gâteau filled with chocolate and raspberry mousses. Service is adequate, no more.

A la carte: 280-330 F. Menu: 155 F (except holidays).

NEUILLY-SUR-SEINE
92200 Neuilly-sur-Seine – (Hauts/Seine)
Argenteuil 9 · Versailles 16

13 Le Bistrot d'à Côté

4, rue Boutard
47 45 34 55
See Paris 17th arr.

12/20 Brasserie des Arts

2, rue des Huissiers
46 24 56 17
Closed Sun. Open until 11 p.m.
A simple and unpretentious address often filled with celebrities from this chic neighborhood. They come for the brioche with bone marrow, chicken-liver terrine, smoky finnan haddie napped in a suave beurre blanc sauce, good grilled meats and crème brûlée. Prices geared to local incomes.
A la carte: 180-250 F.

12/20 Café de la Jatte

60, bd Vital-Bouhot
47 45 04 20,
fax 47 45 19 32
Open daily until midnight. Private room: 250. Terrace dining. Air cond. Valet parking.
The decor revolves around the giant skeleton of a pterodactyl surrounded by a jungle of plants. Wicker furniture, gay colors, and lots of space and light make up the rest. Young waiters zoom around serving plentiful, fresh, and surprisingly well-presented dishes to tables of tanned people "in advertising": raw tuna with sesame seed, pot-au-feu of beef and veal, noisettes of lamb with fresh vegetables. The cellar could be a little more inventive.
A la carte: 260-350 F.

Carpe Diem

10, rue de l'Eglise
46 24 95 01
Closed Sat. lunch, Sun., Dec. 24-Jan. 4 & Aug. 1-28. Open until 9:30 p.m. Air cond.
The high prices fully warrant the exigencies of this little bistro's clientele who are obviously drawn to the warm, simple decor, the *patronne's* gentle attentions and the diligent service. Serge Coquoin's soigné menu features a thin asparagus tart with calf's liver and kidneys, roasted tuna with celery and scampi, and delicate chocolate and praline beignets. Portions could be larger.
A la carte: 300-400 F. Menu: 180 F (dinner only except holidays).

 ## Jacqueline Fénix

42, av. Charles-de-Gaulle
46 24 42 61,
fax 46 40 19 91
Closed Sat., Sun., Aug. & Dec. 25-Jan. 2. Open until 10 p.m. Air cond.
Jacqueline Fénix is now actively involved in getting a new restaurant off the ground, so she has delegated her authority to Patrick Rozeau, who greets and seats patrons with admirable distinction, with well-spaced, beautifully set tables. A new chef, Patrick Juhel, makes the most of the premium ingredients he's given to work with, creating elegant, harmonious dishes that display a pleasing personal touch: we're thinking of the cold oyster soup with winkles, brill roasted in a black-olive "crust", and silken crêpes filled with pineapple and swathed in an apricot coulis. A solid toque, then, for the restaurant's promising new departure.
A la carte: 450-550 F. Menu: 330 F.

 ## Les Feuilles Libres

34, rue Perronet
46 24 41 41,
fax 46 40 77 61
Closed Sat., Sun. & Aug. 1-23. Open until 10 p.m. Private room: 6. Terrace dining. Air cond.
Every second Tuesday of the month, a harpsichord concert adds a tinkling accompaniment to dinners served in this charming, peaceful dining room. Patrick Hardy prepares a repertoire that sparkles with lightness and personality, as well as an occasional touch of bold invention. We enjoyed the clever presentation of a "coupelle", or cup of cauliflower and veal, as well as the earthy hog-jowl daube flanked by molded apples. A good cellar also keeps the local clientele happy.
A la carte: 350-450 F. Menus: 160 F (weekdays lunch only), 255 F (wine incl.).

 ## Focly

79, av. Charles-de-Gaulle
46 24 43 36
Open daily until 11 p.m. Private room: 22. Air cond.
This elegant dining room is a pleasant change from the bogus exoticism of many Asian restaurants. The talented chef proposes a repertoire of appealing Chinese, Vietnamese, Cambodian and Thai dishes somewhat confusingly presented on an interminable menu. Among the best bets are the smoked shrimp with bananas, spareribs cooked with Champagne and spiny lobster prepared with Chinese wine. Delightful welcome.
A la carte: 200-250 F. Menus: 105 F and 125 F (weekdays lunch only).

 ## La Guinguette de Neuilly

Ile de la Jatte
12, bd de Levallois
46 24 25 04
Closed at Christmas. Open until 11 p.m. Garden dining.
Trendy artists are drawn to this old barge and its handful of tables for a cuisine that we think merits a toque: leeks with fresh shrimp, salmon en papillote with green vegetables and a long-simmered pot-au-feu made with no fewer than five kinds of meat. In fine weather, try to nab a table on the terrace by the Seine.
A la carte: 200-260 F.

12/20 ## Chez Livio

6, rue de Longchamp
46 24 81 32
Closed Sat. & Sun. in Aug., May 1, Dec. 24 & Dec. 31. Open until 10:45 p.m. Private room: 18. Garden dining. Air cond.
A real Italian trattoria in the heart of Neuilly, manned by the Innocenti clan. Here is generous and simple cuisine, which features ravioli al magro, gnocchi with basil, pizzas, osso buco and *tutti quanti*. The roof of the dining room rolls back so that you can dine under a canopy of blue sky or stars. Reservations (sometimes hard to come by) are a must.
A la carte: 170-250 F.

 ## San Valero

209 ter, av. Charles-de-Gaulle
46 24 07 87
Closed Sat. lunch, Sun. & Dec. 24-Jan. 1. Open until 10:30 p.m.
Come for a fiesta and a feast at Valero's Spanish restaurant: the menu offers paella of course, but also more authentic offerings, like squid and sole with julienne vegetables, scallops in a garlicky sauce with bits of dried tuna, and baby lamb marinated in herbs, a specialty of the Rioja region. The wine list is worthy

of close perusal: you'll find some terrific bottles from beyond the Pyrenees.

A la carte: 250-300 F. Menus: 150 F (weekdays only), 190 F (except holidays).

 Sébillon

Paris-Bar
20, av. Ch.-de-Gaulle
46 24 71 31
Open daily until midnight. Air cond. Valet parking.

The chefs come and go, the menu stays the same. The pride of the house is its famous Sébillon roast lamb and the giant éclair. Add to that the magnificent rib of beef and the tarte Tatin "à l'ancienne," as well as some good fresh seafood and a thick salmon steak grilled with fennel. Nice Loire wines at affordable prices.

A la carte: 300-350 F.

12/20 La Tonnelle Saintongeaise

32, bd Vital-Bouhot
46 24 43 15
Closed Sat., Sun., Aug. 2-22, Dec. 24-Jan. 6. Open until 10 p.m.

In summer crowds tend to gather under the trees and parasols of this Ile de la Jatte terrace. The cuisine is pleasant enough, without being challenging. There are poached eggs bordelaise to start, followed by (for example) calf's liver with raisins and bits of salt pork or mouclade. The cellar leans markedly toward Bordeaux.

A la carte: 220-320 F.

ORLY
94396 Orly – (Val/Marne)
Paris 16 - Corbeil 17 - Villeneuve-St-Georges 12

 Maxim's

Aérogare d'Orly-Ouest
46 87 16 16
Closed Sat., Sun., holidays & Aug. Open until 10 p.m. Air cond.

A complete overhaul has resurrected Maxim's Orly,

even giving it a bit of the cachet of the illustrious mother house. Gil Jouanin, a talented *cuisinier* formerly of the Café de la Paix, is in command of the kitchen. His new job seems to have inspired him to reach for new culinary heights, for he makes the most of the excellent ingredients he is provided with in subtle dishes like a juniper-scented grouse terrine with foie gras, red-mullet fillets set atop tomato fondue with a lively citrus butter, and a remarkably tender veal en casserole. Succulent figs baked in port round out a thoroughly successful meal. The 30,000-bottle cellar holds wines in every price range, from modest to outrageous. Next door, the Grill serves a quality set menu including wine and coffee, for 250 francs.

A la carte: 500-600 F. Menu: 250 F (wine & coffee incl., at the Grill).

ORSAY
91400 Orsay – (Essonne)
Paris 27 - Versailles 20 - Evry 24

 Le Boudin Sauvage

6, rue de Versailles
69 28 42 93
Closed Sat. & Sun. Open until 10 p.m. Private room: 20. Garden dining.

Anne-Marie de Gennes is turning away customers these days; we wonder if it has to do with the popularity of her spicy boudin sauvage which gives this establishment its name (but is served only in

winter) or the fact that her husband, Pierre-Gilles just won the Nobel Prize for physics! We're inclined to think that the cooking is what draws people here. Anne-Marie works with top-quality ingredients to produce her prawns with coriander-scented tomato fondue, noisettes of lamb roasted in sea salt, and unctuous crème brûlée. The charming decor looks out on an old garden where you can sit in fine weather.

A la carte: 400-500 F. Menu: 260 F (lunch only).

OZOIR-LA-FERRIÈRE
77330 Ozoir-la-Ferrière – (Seine/Marne)
Paris 34 - Melun 27 - Lagny-sur-Marne 21

12/20 La Gueulardière

66, av. du Gal-de-Gaulle
60 02 94 56,
fax 60 02 98 51
Closed Sat. lunch, Sun., winter school holidays & Aug. Open until 9:30 p.m. Garden dining.

It gets better every year. Double glazing has made Alain Bureau's intimate and rustic decor an even quieter and more charming a spot in which to savor his rich, classic cuisine: foie gras, marinated scallops and salmon, sole meunière and veal tournedos with Parma ham. The cellar is improving, but prices are on the increase. All the more reason to be thankful for the attractive set meals.

A la carte: 350-400 F. Menus: 140 F (except holidays), 210 F.

We're always happy to hear about your discoveries and receive your comments on ours. We want to give your letters the attention they deserve, so when you write to Gault Millau, please state clearly what you liked or disliked. Be concise but convincing, and take the time to argue your point.

90

PERREUX (LE)
94170 Perreux (Le) – (Val/Marne)
Paris 15 · Créteil 11 · Vincennes 6 · Lagny 17

 Les Magnolias
48, av. de Bry
48 72 47 43
*Closed Aug. 1-15. Open until
10 p.m. Air cond.*
Gérard Royant simply won't
let the sorry sight of the surrounding suburbs get to him.
Each year he does something
to improve his cozy decor of
oak paneling, red velvet
curtains, deep-pile carpeting
and well-spaced tables. But his
cuisine seemed less interesting to us this year, less carefully prepared and refined.
The prawn ravioli with shellfish
butter were disappointing, the
pan-roasted abalone with garlic and parsley lacked defined
flavors. A pear and almond
feuillantine saved the day, and
then there is always the
remarkable cellar, with its
treasure trove of vintage
Champagnes.
A la carte: 400-500 F. Menu:
280 F (lunch only).

PONTAULT-COMBAULT
77340 Pontault-Combault – (Seine/Marne)
Paris 26 · Melun 29 · Coulommiers 41

 Le Canadel
Aire des Berchères
64 43 45 47,
fax 64 40 52 43
*Closed Sat., Sun. & Aug. Open
until 10 p.m. Private room: 10.
Air cond. Parking.*
Jean-Pierre Piovan's cooking
is rich and admirably classical:
grilled red mullet with a lemony sabayon, sweetbreads
with creamed spinach,
chicken pot-au-feu, cold
chocolate soufflé. The decor is
luscious too: chandeliers,
murals, stucco columns, comfortable chairs and well-
spaced tables. Stylish service;
top-notch cellar.

A la carte: 300-400 F.
Menus: 175 F, 245 F.

PONTOISE
95300 Pontoise – (Val-d'Oise)
Paris 34 · Beauvais 55 · Rouen 91 · Mantes 39

 In nearby Méry-sur-Oise

(5 km E on N 322)
95540 Pontoise – (Val-d'Oise)

Le Chiquito
La Bonneville
30 36 40 23
*Closed Sat. lunch, Sun., Dec. 23-
Jan. 1 & Aug. Open until
9:30 p.m. Private room: 14. Air
cond. Parking.*
A pleasant decor topped
with painted beams opens out
onto a flowered courtyard.
Chef Alain Mihura has
definitely paid his dues; at 30
years of age he has already put
together an impressive
résumé (he's worked with
Savoy and Kéréver among
others) and is currently
developing a personal style.
Capable execution marks his
braised salmon and veg-
etables cooked in parchment,
his marinière of fish in a
delicately flavored cockle
sauce, and the noisettes and
paupiettes of lamb with thyme
served with a savory vegetable
marmalade. Papa Mihura and
his children provide the aff-
able welcome and service.
A la carte: 400-450 F. Menu:
240 F.

PORT-MARLY (LE)
78560 Port-Marly (Le) – (Yvelines)
Paris 21 · Versailles 10 · Louveciennes 3

 **Auberge
du Relais Breton**
27, rue de Paris
39 58 64 33
*Closed Sun. dinner, Mon.,
& Aug. Open until 10 p.m. Private room: 35. Garden dining.*
Here is an attractive place for
a winter meal when a fire is
roaring in the immense fire-

place, but not to be overlooked in summer when you
can sit in the lovely garden and
be serenaded by little birds
while enjoying rather staid, but
fresh and handily executed
cuisine. We liked the fricassée
of lobster with tiny vegetables,
steamed turbot and a fragrant
cassolette de lotte. Desserts
are ho-hum, but the cellar is
judiciously stocked. Very nice
set menus.
A la carte: 250-300 F.
Menus: 209 F (wine incl.),
159 F.

12/20 **Les Danaïdes**
1, rue Jean-Jaurès
39 16 44 88
*Closed Sat. lunch & Sun. dinner.
Open until 10:30 p.m. Garden
dining.*
The old Port-Marly post
office has a lovely country
look thanks to its delightful terrace and ravishing garden. But
success has taken a toll on
Alain Houdayer's cooking: the
ingredients seem to be of
lesser quality, and the portions
have shrunk noticeably!
Seafood salad dressed with
truffle vinaigrette was stingily
served indeed, and the prawns
sautéed with chanterelles
were microscopic (though
nicely cooked). Despite a very
good tarte aux pommes, we're
obliged to shave a point off the
rating.
A la carte: 220-300 F.
Menus: 128 F, 155 F.

PRÉ-SAINT-GERVAIS (LE)
93310 Pré-Saint-Gervais (Le) – (Seine-St-D.)
Lagny 27 · Meaux 38

 Le Pouilly-Reuilly
68, rue A.-Joineau
48 45 14 59
*Closed Sun., holidays & end July-
Sep. 6. Open until 10 p.m. Private room: 25.*
Jovial Jean Thibaut has been
at the helm of this authentic
and popular suburban bistro-
inn for a quarter of a century.

You pass through the kitchen full of nose-tingling aromas to reach the dining room with its yellow tables and zinc-topped bar. Lately, though, the traditional bistro dishes appear to have lost some of their former zip. A point less, this year, for the meager portion of fried smelts and the bland chicken jambonnette with morels, followed by a decent tarte Tatin. An imprecise wine list doesn't do full justice to the cellar, rich in fine Bordeaux.
A la carte: 230-350 F.

PUTEAUX
92800 Puteaux — (Hauts/Seine)
Paris 10 - Versailles 14 - St-Germain-en-Laye 11

 Les Communautés

Paris-La-Défense, in the CNIT
2, pl. de la Défense
46 92 10 10,
fax 46 92 10 30
Closed Sat. & Sun. Open until 10 p.m. Air cond. Valet parking.
Pierre Miécaze has definitely hit his stride here at the Sofitel hotel restaurant at La Défense. He works tirelessly with premium ingredients, searching for bold, new flavor harmonies; he keeps a close eye on the what his colleagues are cooking up too, and he doesn't hesitate to try out a rare condiment or spice. In a word, Miécaze works from the principle that cooking is a constantly evolving art. The results of his research are often dazzling, even astonishing: take, for example, his crispy tart of wild mushrooms and hazelnuts; or the red mullet with braised lettuce, shallots and strips of pig's ear; or roasted duck breast in a bewitching sweet-and-sour sauce; or a brioche topped with poached green apples and acacia honey—so much talent and brio are fully deserving of two toques.

What's more, this interesting cuisine is well served by the elegant surroundings of the Sofitel dining room, the superb cellar and the stylish staff.
A la carte: 350-450 F. Menus: 200 F and 400 F (dinner only, wine incl.).

 Les Deux Arcs

34, cours Michelet
La Défense 10
47 76 44 43,
fax 47 73 72 74
Closed Sat. & Sun. lunch. Open until 10:30 p.m. Private room: 100. Terrace dining. Air cond. Valet parking.
This is the elder of the two Sofitel hotels at La Défense. The cooking is serious, executed by a shy young chef who lacks the boldness of his colleague at the CNIT (see above). Yet some delicious meals are served here, composed of (say) crab ravioli with crab sauce, salmon grilled à l'unilatéral, sea bass with artichoke fricassée, with a crisp, bright-tasting raspberry croustillant for dessert. The cellar, we are happy to report, is growing and service has improved.
A la carte: 350-400 F. Menu: 180 F (dinner only).

 Fouquet's Europe

CNIT, Paris-La Défense
46 92 28 04,
fax 46 92 28 16
Closed Sat. & Sun. Open until 10:30 p.m.. Terrace dining. Air cond. Valet parking.
The stark and austere CNIT tower at La Défense is surely the last place one would expect to find modern French cooking that pays homage to its regional roots. But that is just the sort of satisfying fare that 28-year-old Alexandre Faix is regaling his patrons with at Fouquet's Europe. An exceptionally bright pupil of the great Robuchon, Faix cooks with imagination, enthusiasm

and—this is his secret—a rare sense of split-second timing. His dishes are never under- or over-, they're perfectly cooked. You'll see we aren't exaggerating a bit when you fork into the suckling pig stuffed with foie gras, the gurnard fillet spiced with coriander, a succulent grain-fed Loué chicken or a meltingly buttery shortbread topped with apples and rhubarb. Opulent cellar; top-drawer service.
A la carte: 450-500 F.

11/20 Le Vercanaille

6, bd R.-Wallace
45 06 05 24
Closed Sat. lunch. Open daily until 11 p.m. Private room: 25. Valet parking.
A wine bar where you can drink tasty little wines and enjoy simple but nicely prepared dishes like vegetable terrine, calf's liver with lime, or herring with potato salad. There's a 100-franc lunch formula (starter plus main course) and a take-out shop as well.
A la carte: 230-250 F. Menus: 100 F, 150 F and 200 F (weekdays dinner and Sat.).

ROISSY-EN-FRANCE
95700 Roissy-en-France — (Val/d'Oise)
Paris 26 - Meaux 36 - Senlis 28 - Chantilly 28

Maxim's

Aéroport
Charles-de-Gaulle
48 62 16 16,
fax 48 62 45 96
Open daily. Lunch only. Air cond.
Just as we're on deadline, we discover that double-toque *cuisinier* Alain Bariteau of the Jules Verne in Paris (two-toques) is scheduled to pilot the kitchen here... We wish him a happy landing, and will report back to you soon!
A la carte: 350-600 F.

ROMAINVILLE
93230 Romainville – (Seine-St-D.)
Paris 10 - Livry-Gargan 9 - Aulnay-sous-Bois 9

 Chez Henri
72, rte de Noisy
48 45 26 65,
fax 48 91 16 74
Closed Sat. lunch, Mon. dinner, Sun., holidays & Aug. 7-24. Open until 9:30 p.m. Private room: 18. Air cond. Parking.
Parkings and warehouses are not the ideal environment for a fine restaurant. But Henri Bourgin takes it in his stride, as does his clientele of regulars, who know that behind the sombre, unobtrusive façade lies a comfortable dining room where an instinctive, expert chef is at work. You'll soon forget the charmless surroundings when you tuck into a superb salad of skate with asparagus and orange vinaigrette, or pan-roasted lobster with coriander-scented baby vegetables, suprême de pintade en tapenade, or veal en gelée with black and green olives, followed by a luscious walnut, hazelnut and almond craquelin topped with Sauternes sabayon. A keen-flavored, appetizing style of cooking. Fine cellar, diligent service.
A la carte: 300-400 F.
Menus: 145 F, 200 F.

RUEIL-MALMAISON
92500 Rueil-Malmaison – (Hauts/Seine)
Paris 15 - Versailles 11 - Argenteuil 12

12/20 El Chiquito
126, av. P.-Doumer
47 51 00 53,
fax 47 49 19 61
Closed Sat., Sun. & 15 days in Aug. Open until 9:45 p.m. Garden dining. Air cond. Valet parking.
Chefs come and go here; the latest is perhaps not the most gifted of the lot. His cooking, while respectable, surely doesn't justify the stiffish tabs:

a decent salade gourmande segued into a marinated red mullet sauce aigrelette with oddly undefined flavors, followed by a tasty crème à la vanille served with over-baked madeleines. On the plus side, there's a good cellar and out back is a wonderful garden which blots out the traffic.
A la carte: 400-600 F. Menu: 250 F (dinner except holidays).

12/20 Relais de Saint-Cucufa
114, rue du Gal-de-Miribel
47 49 79 05
Closed Sun. dinner, Mon. & Aug. 15-30. Open until 9 p.m. Garden dining.
A terrace and garden enlarge the rustic dining room in fine weather. The Breton *patron* welcomes guests warmly, and sings the praises of his Italian wife's cooking. Indeed, she chooses her ingredients with care, and turns them into generous, delicious dishes. Try her turbot with prawns, the escalope of sweetbreads with morels, and finish up with a bright fruit charlotte. Small but choice cellar, reasonably priced.
A la carte: 350-400 F.

RUNGIS
94150 Rungis – (Val/Marne)
Paris 13 - Corbeil 26 - Longjumeau 1

 La Rungisserie
20, av. Ch.-Lindbergh
46 87 36 36,
fax 46 87 08 48
Open daily until 11 p.m. Private room: 60. Garden dining. Air cond. Valet parking.
A huge and happy hotel restaurant with a soothing, modern decor. The good lunch menu (prix-fixe, with wine included) and the large hors-d'œuvre buffet attract a faithful clientele from the Rungis market. The à la carte

menu includes some solid offerings such as sparkling-fresh scallops in buttery pastry, aiguillettes de canard and appealing, delicious desserts. The far-ranging wine cellar (with bottles from California, Chile, Spain...) is over-priced.
A la carte: 300-500 F.
Menus: 185 F (weekdays only, wine incl.), 210 F.

SAINT-CLOUD
92210 Saint-Cloud – (Hauts/Seine)
Paris 12 - Boulogne 3 - Versailles 10

12/20 La Désirade
2, bd de la République
47 71 22 33,
fax 46 02 75 64
Open daily until 10 p.m. Garden dining. Air cond. Parking.
Colorful fabrics make for a gay, charming decor, but the chef needs rousing, we think. Our last experience here (duo de saumons with crisp-cooked cabbage, fillet of salt cod with julienne vegetables, apricot parfait) left an impression of imprecise cooking and blurry flavors. And the service still lacks zip.
Menu: 150 F.

11/20 Vanida
6, rue Dailly
47 71 31 05
Closed Sat. lunch, Sun. & Aug. 1-23. Open until 11 p.m. Private room: 50.
A benevolent Buddha beams out over the fresh, white decor of this establishment which is going off a bit, alas. On our last visit the Thai fish fritters were doughy and the rice sautéed with shrimp definitely lacked its usual flavor.
A la carte: 150-200 F. Menus: 85 F (weekdays lunch only), 112 F, 145 F.

> *Red toques signify modern cuisine; white toques signify traditional cuisine.*

SAINT-DENIS
93200 Saint-Denis – (Seine-St-D.)
Paris 10 · Argenteuil 10 · Chantilly 30

 La Saumonière

1, rue Lanne
48 20 25 56
Closed Sat. lunch, Sun. & Aug. Open until 10 p.m. Air cond.
You'd be wise to follow the maître d's suggestions, for he is well-versed in the talented new chef's repertoire of specialties, which includes a wonderfully fresh scallop and lobster salad, numerous dishes based on foie gras, an admirably seasoned turbot aux pommes de terre and a very fine tarte Tatin. In fact, the food is so good that we would happily dine in this spacious, slightly overstuffed decor—were it not for the ever-rising prices!
A la carte: 250-550 F. Menu: 180 F.

SAINT-GERMAIN-EN-LAYE
78100 Saint-Germain-en-Laye – (Yvelines)
Paris 21 · Chartres 81 · Dreux 70 · Beauvais 69

 Cazaudehore

1, av. du Président-Kennedy
34 51 93 80
Closed Mon. (except holidays). Open until 10 p.m. Private room: 140. Garden dining. Parking.
On the edge of the forest in a wonderful setting of greenery and flowers, sits this ravishing establishment elegantly and luxuriously decorated with old prints and English chintzes; for summer dining, there's a huge terrace that looks out on the trees. It is at this point that the superb and unshakeable "Cazau" sometimes goes off track, its luxurious cuisine suffering under the pressure of numbers. Still, irregularities are not the rule and you are sure to enjoy dishes like an elegant veal terrine; but we found the calf's head

vinaigrette unnecessarily complicated, and the truffled freshwater perch was overcooked. Superb cellar, stylish service.
A la carte: 350-500 F. Menu: 240 F (weekdays lunch only).

12/20 La Feuillantine

10, rue des Louviers
34 51 04 24,
fax 39 21 07 70
Annual closings not available. Open until 10 p.m. Air cond.
Full (and very delicious!) meals at 130 francs don't grow on trees in affluent Saint-Germain. That is why La Feuillantine's dining room is so crowded these days: taste the pan-roasted salmon with tender Belgian endive, a scrumptious chicken blanquette with basmati rice and morels, and a rich fondant au chocolat. The service remains cheerful, even amid the crush—our only complaint is that portions have grown noticeably smaller!
Menu: 130 F.

12/20 Les Nuits des Thés

17bis, rue des Coches
34 51 65 64
Open noon-7 p.m. Closed Mon., Aug. & holidays.
The decor is rich: white lacquer, pink upholstery, mercury mirrors, damask tablecloths, antique furniture and watercolors on the walls. The welcome may be cool if you aren't a regular, but the clientele is noticeably at ease, chatting about such weighty topics as dog pedigrees, boating and the latest literary successes. They nibble on salads and main-dish pies and tarts of all sorts, but truth to tell, only the desserts are really exceptional (we're thinking of the caramelized cream cheese tart and the raspberry macaroons). You'll spend something over 100 Francs for lunch, half that for tea and a

pastry.
A la carte: 100 F.

 Le Pavillon Henri-IV

21, rue Thiers
34 51 62 62,
fax 39 73 93 73
Open daily until 10:30 p.m. Private room: 350. Terrace dining. Air cond. Parking.
Lively it's not (neither the staff nor the patrons appear to be having much fun), but the cuisine fully merits a gourmet's attention. It encompasses dishes so classic as to have nearly disappeared from most modern menus, all (not so incidentally) adroitly prepared. As a result, a meal here resembles nothing so much as a trip to some gastronomic museum; the attractive wine list is a plus.
A la carte: 350-400 F. Menu: 240 F (weekday lunch only).

SAINT-OUEN
93400 Saint-Ouen – (Seine-St-D.)
Paris 7 · Saint-Denis 4 · Chantilly 34

 Le Coq de la Maison Blanche

37, bd J.-Jaurès
40 11 01 23
Closed Sun. & Aug. 1-15. Open until 10 p.m. Private room: 120. Terrace dining.
The long and lovely menu is handwritten daily to entice diners with jambon persillé, coq au vin or grilled kidneys. Seasonal dishes also take pride of place and are prepared in grand bistro tradition with a touch of youthful exuberance. The salad of Breton crab's claws, the saddle of lamb with white beans, or the eel sautéed in white wine with spinach and broccoli perfectly suit the convivial atmosphere of this likeable establishment run by a sensational *patron*, Alain François.
A la carte: 300-400 F.

Chez Serge

7, bd J.-Jaurès
40 11 06 42
Lunch only (& dinner Thurs.).
Open until 9 p.m. Air cond.
Short, simple and sweet—
that sums up the menu chez
Serge Cancé. And that policy
has brought enviable success
to this bistro set in a bleak
banlieue north of Paris. Chef
Fabrice Gay's cooking is more
notable for its generosity than
for its finesse: a copious portion of the house terrine was
disappointingly bland on our
last visit, and so was the lotte
au safran. But the pork knuckle
with lentils could not have
been better, and it was
followed by an exceptional
chocolate cake. The cellar, we
regret to note, is unworthy of
a bistro with a reputation for
serving well-chosen wines! A
point less this year.
A la carte: 220-320 F.

SCEAUX
92330 Sceaux – (Hauts/Seine)
Paris 12 - Versailles 16 - Antony 3 - Bagneux 3

12/20 L'Orangerie

13, rue M.-Charaire
43 50 83 00
Closed Sun. dinner, Mon. & Aug.
Open until 9 p.m.
The cooking is generally consistent, the service pleasant
and comfort is assured in this
peaceful spot situated in a
pedestrian zone. But muddled
flavors mar some of Jean-
Pierre Baudoin's dishes, and
the quality of certain ingredients could be improved
(witness the gizzards and foie
gras in a very mediocre salade
périgourdine). Though a copious portion of grilled fish
was overcooked, the roast
rack of lamb we tried was irreproachable. All in all, it
didn't add up to a toque this
year.
A la carte: 300-390 F.

SÈVRES
92310 Sèvres – (Hauts/Seine)
Paris 12 - Boulogne 3 - Versailles 8

11/20 Phileas Fogg

5, pl. Pierre-Brossolette
46 26 48 80
Closed Sun. dinner & Mon.
Open until 10:30 p.m. Terrace
dining.
Travel no farther than to the
Sèvres railway station to go
around the world in eighty
dishes. The cooking is nicely
handled by (get this) the wife
of an ex-script writer for the
defunct (but often rerun)
television series *The Avengers:*
try her tasty jambalaya, fish pie
or lamb with apricots. A simple
decor and a smiling welcome.
Superb whiskies.
A la carte: 170-200 F.

VARENNE-ST-HILAIRE (LA)
94210 Varenne-St-Hilaire (La) – (Val/Marne)
Paris 16 - t-Maur 3 - Chennevières 2

La Bretèche

171, quai de Bonneuil
48 83 38 73,
fax 42 83 63 19
Closed Sun. dinner, Mon. & Feb.
school holidays. Open until
10 p.m. Private room: 18. Gar-
den dining.
Chef Philippe Regnault has
lots of bright ideas, but the
flavors of his fine ingredients
cry out for more definition.
Creamy scrambled eggs with
fresh truffles suffered from just
a bit too much salt; a
beautifully cooked sea bream
with potatoes and bay leaves
was insufficiently seasoned;
the prune-studded chocolate
ganache, however, hit the
bull's eye with its focused intensity. The cellar is well
stocked with bottles in a wide
range of prices. And the sunny
decor is seductive indeed. Still,
when the weather is fine we
opt for the terrace, where the
eye wanders over the
soothingly verdant banks of
the Marne.

A la carte: 270-370 F. Menu:
150 F.

Le Pavillon Bleu

66, prom. des Anglais
48 83 10 56,
fax 43 97 21 21
Open daily until 11 p.m. Private
room: 80. Terrace dining.
Once a former suburban
dance-café, Le Pavillon Bleu is
now a luxurious—and expensive—riverside restaurant.
Though prices are high and
rising, the cuisine is on a definite downswing. Readers echo
our disappointment with
botched dishes (like the soft-
boiled egg with caviar served
with a severely undercooked
potato) and lackluster flavors
(if there were any pistachios in
our crème brûlée à la pistache,
they were imperceptible).
Owing to a perfectly prepared
cod with garlic purée we'll
leave the toque in place, but
we're subtracting a point just
the same. If the dining room's
thick carpet and heavy
curtains don't thrill you, try the
leafy terrace on the water's
edge.
A la carte: 350-450 F.
Menus: 200 F (weekdays
lunch and Sat.), 300 F
(weekdays dinner and Sat.
lunch).

VARENNES-JARCY
91480 Varennes-Jarcy – (Essonne)
Paris 29 - Corbeil-Essonnes 14 - Melun 20

12/20 Hostellerie de Varennes

14, rue de Mandres
69 00 97 03
Closed Tues. dinner, Wed. &
Aug. 2-27. Open until 9:30 p.m.
Private room: 85. Terrace dining.
Parking.
Francis Gautier's charming
establishment is graced with a
delightful garden full of
flowers. The cuisine strikes a
pleasing balance between
simple (young rabbit terrine,
grilled andouillette, and duck

confit) and rich dishes (scallops in chervil cream sauce; lush desserts).
A la carte: 250-380 F. Menu: 195 F.

VERSAILLES
78000 Versailles – (Yvelines)
Paris 23 - Mantes 44 - Rambouillet 31

11/20 Brasserie du Théâtre
15, rue des Réservoirs
39 50 03 21
Open daily until 12:30 a.m.
Classic brasserie food (head cheese, pepper steak, sauerkraut, steak tartare), served in a supremely Gallic decor with great mirrors, glowing woodwork and leather banquettes.
A la carte: 160-260 F.

12/20 Au Chapeau Gris
7, rue Hoche
39 50 10 81,
fax 39 02 77 46
Closed Tues. dinner, Wed. & July. Open until 10 p.m. Private room: 80.
As the ancient exposed beams attest, this is the oldest restaurant in Versailles, and it attracts an extremely well-heeled crowd. The cuisine is honest enough, though not always precise. Traditional dishes are the house specialty: eggs scrambled with fresh truffles, soufflé of turbot with saffron sauce, nougat glacé with black currants. Exceptional wine list. Classic, thoroughly professional service.
A la carte: 300-400 F. Menu: 155 F.

11/20 La Flotille
in the Château
de Versailles park
39 51 41 58
Open for lunch only. Parking.
Set on the edge of the château's Grand Canal, with a marvelous view of Le Nôtre's gardens, the unpretentious

cuisine served here is tasty indeed (rabbit cooked with mustard, pan-roasted salmon with pasta, duck confit). Delightful summer terrace.
A la carte: 160-260 F. Menu: 125 F.

12/20 Le Lac Hong
18, rue des Frères-Caudron, D 91
30 44 03 71
Closed Wed. Open until 9:30 p.m.
Fine Chinese-Vietnamese cuisine at low prices (caramelized fresh tuna, quail rubbed with five-spice powder, grilled crab). Exceptionally affordable wines, charming welcome.
A la carte: 130-200 F. Menu: 120 F (except holidays).

12/20 Le Pot-au-Feu
22, rue de Satory
39 50 57 43
Closed Sat. lunch, Sun. & Aug. 10-17. Open until 10 p.m. Private room: 12.
Pot-au-feu in its classic or seafood versions get top billing, but the chef's repertoire also extends to mussels à la sétoise, plaice poached in hard cider and veal confit à l'indienne. Attractive set meals.
A la carte: 220-280 F. Menus: 115 F, 175 F.

 Le Potager du Roy
1, rue du Mal-Joffre
39 50 35 34,
fax 30 21 69 30
Open daily until 10:30 p.m. Air cond.
Alas and alack! Gérard Vié's former "Trois Marches" has lost the magic of yore! Though chef Philippe Letourneur, Vié's one-time associate, started out here creditably enough, our recent experiences here have been (not to put too fine a point on it) unfortunate. Even were we not to consider the inexistent welcome, the fearsomely expensive cellar,

the flustered service, we cannot in conscience bestow a two-toque rating on cuisine that has lost its creativity and finesse. Did success come too quickly? Is it too late to hope for a turnaround? Stay tuned!
A la carte: 300-400 F. Menus: 120 F (weekdays and Sat.), 165 F (weekdays, Sat. and holidays).

12/20 Le Quai n°1
1, av. de St-Cloud
39 50 42 26
Closed Sun. dinner & Mon. Open until 11 p.m. Terrace dining. Air cond.
A dependable address for fine shellfish and skillfully prepared seafood dishes at reasonable prices. Try the exemplary 115-franc menu: mussels marinière, tuna provençale, Roquefort with figs and walnuts and dessert. Amusing nautical decor.
A la carte: 220-370 F. Menus: 115 F, 160 F.

 Rescatore
27, av. de St-Cloud
39 50 23 60,
fax 30 21 96 57
Closed Sat. lunch & Sun. Open until 10 p.m. Air cond.
Jacques Bagot is a native of the Norman port of Granville; his specialty is vibrantly fresh fish and seafood prepared in refined, imaginative ways. Try the sea bass in a bosky morel fumet, the unusual combination of oysters and duck breast called rôti d'huîtres au magret, or a keen-flavored ballotine of prawns with ratatouille. Fine cellar.
A la carte: 380-480 F. Menus: 200 F (weekdays lunch only), 375 F.

Les Trois Marches
1, bd de la Reine
39 50 13 21,
fax 39 51 66 55
Closed Sun., Mon. & Aug. Open until 10 p.m. Private room: 20.

Quality Inn
Paris
Rive Gauche

Your right choice in the heart of Paris

LOCATION
In the heart of the left bank, walking distance of
St-Germain des Prés, Jardin du Luxembourg and Montparnasse.

ACCOMODATION
134 rooms including 6 Junior Suites, all fully air conditionned
with bath, shower, hairdryer, digital safe, mini-bar, radio,
local and satellite TV including C.N.N. international
direct dial telephone. No smoking rooms.

FACILITIES
Piano-bar GREGORY'S, meeting room for 15 people.
Buffet breakfast in Café des Fontaines.
Change service, theatre bookings, car rental, excursions,
laundry/dry cleaning, in house parking.

RATES
Single rooms from 600 FF. Double rooms from 670 FF.
Junior Suite from 930 FF.
(Taxes and services included).
All major credit card accepted.

CHOICE HOTELS
INTERNATIONAL

Sleep Comfort Quality Clarion

92, rue de Vaugirard - 75006 PARIS
Tél. : (1) 42 22 00 56 - Fax : (1) 42 22 05 39

Terrace dining. Air cond. Valet parking.

Gérard Vié and his brigade have moved en masse to the Trianon Palace, where they now benefit from the most technically sophisticated equipment imaginable. But despite the high-tech surroundings, Vié remains loyal to his country roots.

Vié's cuisine has what it takes to thrill and captivate. Witness the warm belon oysters with foie gras, duck liver with strong rancio wine, rabbit gelée with leeks, fillets of sole marinated—almost conserved—in olive oil, roast lobster with thyme, turbot with onions and pommes Anna, braised young pigeon with spices and apricots, and duck with turnips and truffles, simmered for four hours. Even his simple country-style dishes are delicious and full of provincial goodness (beef braised with carrots, cassoulet with Couïza sausages).

The formidable cellar's grand wines push the bill skyward, but prices are not out of line given the quality. There are many fine bottlings at around 100 francs, and the fixed-price lunch menu is a marvel.

A la carte: 600-800 F. Menus: 260 F (weekdays lunch only), 395 F.

In nearby Le Chesnay

(NE)
78150 Versailles – (Yvelines)

 ## Le Chesnoy

24, rue Pottier
39 54 01 01

Closed Sun. dinner, Mon. & Aug. 4-25. Open until 10 p.m. Garden dining. Air cond.

Bustling and brimming over with *bon vivants*, Le Chesnoy is a welcome oasis in a sea of cement. The sunny dining room opens onto a summer terrace. Late of Les Glénan and Marius et Janette, chef Georges Torrès excels with fish dishes, for instance a lightly smoked sea bass with leek sabayon, and a crispy salmon cooked in its skin within a salt crust. There are also several fine meat dishes on the menu (veal sweetbreads cooked with rum and nutmeg). Monsieur Baratin, the owner, will guide you expertly through his cellar.

A la carte: 250-320 F.

 ## Le Connemara

41, rte de Rueil
39 55 63 07

Closed Sun. (except lunch 1st & 2nd Sun. of the month), Mon. & Aug. 1-20. Open until 9:30 p.m. Private room: 15.

Ireland features only modestly on the Connemara's menu: succulent smoked salmon, Aran scallop soup, and a dizzying choice of whiskeys. The rest of chef Pascal Eynard-Machet's repertoire plays variations on classic themes, which are tunefully updated with fruit (sole and salmon served with grapefruit) or vegetables (lamb mignon with fresh white beans, small turbot with a turnip and apple gratin). The handsome decor is done in salmon hues, and the restaurant is set in a swath of greenery.

A la carte: 250-360 F. Menu: 145 F.

 ## L'Etoile de Mer

17, rue des Deux-Frères
39 54 62 70

Closed Sun. dinner, Mon. & Aug. Open until 10 p.m. Air cond. Parking.

L'Etoile de Mer's intimate, modern dining room opens onto the town marketplace. The view features a crowded lobster tank, and beyond it, the fishmonger's shop attached to the restaurant. Whence chef Yann Cadiou plucks the freshest, best fish and shellfish, and transforms them into spectacular assortments and cooked dishes: superb lightly grilled scampi, magnificent sea bass, and fresh summer soup made with large prawns. Charming welcome. Negligible wine cellar.

A la carte: 250-450 F. Menus: 90 F (weekdays lunch only). 155 F.

VILLEBON-SUR-YVETTE
91120 Villebon-sur-Yvette – (Essonne)
Paris 23 - Versailles 21 - Evry 22 - Etampes 31

 ## La Morvandelle

86, av. du Général-de-Gaulle
60 10 29 61

Open daily until 10 p.m. Private room: 40. Garden dining. Parking.

Yvon Blandin has a knack for preparing seafood, and lots of innovative ideas, witness his tasty little ragoût of lobster and escargots, or the firm and flavorful turbot aux épices. To finish, you could do worse than order the outstanding tarte Tatin made with figs instead of apples. Decent cellar. Sunny, elegant decor, pleasant summer terrace.

A la carte: 300-450 F. Menus: 165 F, 360 F.

VILLENEUVE-LA-GARENNE
92390 Villeneuve-la-Garenne — (Hauts/Seine)
Paris 11 - St-Denis 2 · St-Germain 18

 ## Les Chanteraines

Av. 8-Mai-1945
47 99 31 31

Closed Sat., Sun. dinner & Aug. 15-31. Open until 10 p.m. Terrace dining. Parking.

This smart new restaurant is lost in the leaden suburbs north of Paris. The decor has a 1930s feel, and the dining room looks out on the municipal park and pond. Though more modern and less

---

Find the address you are looking for, quickly and easily, in the index.

Burgundian, the food here is not unlike that of the Coq de la Maison Blanche (see above, Saint-Ouen), which is run by the proprietor's husband. Try classic asparagus sauce mousseline, scallops set on a bed of lamb's lettuce, finnan haddie with green lentils, or the comforting leg of lamb with gratin dauphinois. Great chocolate cake; interesting wine cellar.

A la carte: 300-360 F. Menu: 170 F.

VILLIERS-LE-BÂCLE
91190 Villiers-le-Bâcle – (Essonne)
Paris 24 - Trappes 15 - Chevreuse 11

 La Petite Forge
1, rte de Gif
60 19 03 88
Closed Sat., Sun., Aug. 2-16, Dec. 24-Feb. Open until 9:30 p.m.
This charming little stopover at the mouth of the Chevreuse Valley boasts an intimate, roughcast decor with exposed beams. Alas, the frightfully high prices keep all but the wealthiest away. Chef and proprietor Kleber Ernimo nonetheless does his utmost to justify the cost. His cuisine is based on top-quality ingredients and prepared with loving care. The fish are fabulous and fresh, the game delicious, and the farmhouse cheeses remarkable. The cellar is home to many excellent Bordeaux.

A la carte: 330-430 F.

HOTELS

INTRODUCTION

Paris hotel rooms come in every possible style, size and price range. But whatever the category of the room you seek, remember to book well in advance to get exactly what you want. Our selection ranges from sumptuous suites to far humbler lodgings, but note that certain hoteliers put as high a price on charm or modern facilities as others do on pure luxury, so don't assume that "charming" means "cheap". The prices quoted include taxes and service.
Hotels are classified as follows: Luxury, First Class, Classical, Charming, Practical, Airport and The Suburbs.

RESERVATION SERVICE

Les Hôtesses de Paris can arrange a same-day reservation in any hotel in Paris or the rest of France. The service costs 18 to 55 francs, depending on the hotel. These friendly hostesses also provide tourist information for Paris and France. All you need to do is drop in (don't telephone) at one of the locations listed in *Basics* under Tourist Information.

NO ROOM AT THE INN?

If your every attempt to find a hotel room has failed, you needn't panic. Here are two companies that can track down a room for you or even rent you a high-class studio or apartment. The latter come with every guarantee of home comforts, security and such options as maid, laundry and repair services. Prices range from 450 to 2,500 francs and up, depending on the size and accommodations. Townhouses and houseboats are available as well!
Just contact: *Paris-Séjour-Réservation*, 90, avenue des Champs-Elysées, Paris 8th arr., tel. 42 56 30 00, Monday through Friday 9 a.m.-7 p.m., Saturday 10 a.m.- 6 p.m.; or *Paris Bienvenue*, 10, avenue de Villars, Paris 7th arr., tel. 47 53 80 81, Monday through Friday 8:30 a.m.-7:30 p.m., Saturday 10 a.m.-5 p.m.

APARTMENT HOTELS

At the apartment hotels listed below, you'll enjoy the same service you would find in a hotel, for a lower price. Rates start at about 600 francs per night for a studio for two.
• *Carré d'Or*, 46, av. George-V, 8th arr., 40 70 05 05, fax 47 23 30 90. 23 stes 3,950-17,350 F. No pets. Parking.

• *Les Citadines-Austerlitz,* 27, rue Esquirol, 13th arr., 44 23 51 51, fax 45 86 59 76. 2 apts 870 F. 49 studios 490-610 F. Bkfst 38 F. Parking.
• *Les Citadines-Bercy,* 14-18, rue de Chaligny, 12th arr., 40 01 15 15, fax 40 01 15 20. 97 apts 540-870 F. Bkfst 38 F. Parking 35 F / day.
• *Les Citadines-Montparnasse,* 67, av. du Maine, 14th arr., 40 47 41 41, fax 43 27 29 94. 72 studios 550-950 F. Garage parking.
• *Les Citadines-Trocadéro,* 29 bis, rue Saint-Didier, 16th arr., 44 34 73 73, fax 47 04 50 07. 6 apts 920-1,150 F. 66 studios 464-660 F. No pets. Garage parking.
• *Flatotel,* 14, rue du Théâtre, 15th arr., 45 75 62 20, fax 45 79 73 30. 247 rms & apts 490-3,900 F. Bkfst 45 F. Parking.
• *Flatotel,* 52, rue d'Oradour-sur-Glane, 15th arr., 45 54 93 45, fax 45 54 93 07. 179 rms & apts 600-1,950 F. Bkfst 45 F. Parking.
• *Flatotel Porte de Versailles,* 52, rue d'Oradour-sur-Glane, 15th arrondissement, 45 54 93 45.
• *Métropole Opéra,* 2, rue de Gramont, 2nd arr., 42 96 91 03, fax 42 96 22 46. 6 apts 950-1,300 F. 27 studios 600-1,200 F. Bkfst 50 F.
• *Orion Les Halles,* 4, rue des Innocents, 1st arr., 45 08 00 33, fax 45 08 40 65. 55 apts 960-1,050 F. 134 studios 620-700 F. 1 appt for disabled.
• *Orion La Défense,* 8, bd de Neuilly, La Défense 1, 92400 Courbevoie, 47 62 55 55. 130 apts 740 F. 104 studios 480 F.
• *Résidence du Roy,* 8, rue François-Ier, 8th arr., 42 89 59 59, fax 40 74 07 92. 31 apts & 51 rms 1,140-2,950 F. Bkfst 65 F. Parking.

SYMBOLS & ABBREVIATIONS

Our opinion of the comfort level and appeal of each hotel is expressed in the following ranking system:

🏰	Very luxurious
🏰	Luxurious
🏠	Very comfortable
🏠	Comfortable
🌲	Very quiet

Symbols in red denote charm.
Rms: rooms.
Stes: suites.
Air cond.: Air conditioning.
Half-board: rate per person for room, breakfast and one other meal (lunch or dinner).
No cards: no credit cards accepted.

LUXURY

 Beverly Hills
8th arr. - 35, rue de Berri
43 59 55 55,
fax 42 56 52 75
*Open year-round. 14 stes 2,500-
9,900 F. Parking.*
The extravagant decor of
marble, mirrors and precious
woods literally reeks of
money: this apartment-hotel is
designed for millionaires,
emirs and merchant princes
who want to wallow in over-
the-top luxury. Security is provided for with total electronic
surveillance. The huge suites
offer every imaginable amenity, from dining rooms to wide-
screen. Piano bar and
restaurant.

 Le Bristol
8th arr. - 112, rue du
Faubourg-Saint-Honoré
42 66 91 45,
fax 42 66 68 68
*Open year-round. 45 stes
6,250 F and up. 152 rms 2,450-
4,150 F. Bkfst 140 F. Restaurant.
Air cond. No pets. Heated pool.
Valet parking.*
The elegance of its decor
(genuine period furniture, as
well as lovely reproductions),
the comfort of its rooms, the
luxury of its suites and the prestige of its clientele make Le
Bristol one of the rare authentic luxury hotels in Paris
(as well as one of the most
expensive). The Bristol's two
distinct wings comprise 35
newer, modern suites housed
in a former Carmelite convent,
and 150 more traditionally
decorated rooms and suites.
Among the innumerable
amenties and facilities are
video surveillance, ultramodern conference rooms, a
heated swimming pool, a
superb laundry service and a
hair salon. An extraordinary
restaurant (Le Bristol) opens
onto the lawn and flowers of a
formal French garden, see

Restaurants. The staff is both
cordial and impressively
trained.

 Hôtel de Crillon
8th arr. - 10, pl. de la
Concorde
42 65 24 24,
fax 44 71 15 02
*Open year-round. 33 stes 4,600-
52,000 F. 130 rms 2,350-
3,800 F. Bkfst 130 F. Restaurants.
Air cond. Valet parking.*
The Crillon, originally an
eighteenth-century palace, is
the last of the Parisian luxury
hotels to have remained authentically French: with its
inner courtyards; terraces
overlooking the place de la
Concorde; extravagantly
sumptuous public rooms;
guest rooms that, though not
always immense or well
soundproofed, are exquisitely
decorated; and the most
splendid suites one could
hope for. Let's not forget the
well-trained staff. Yes, the
Hôtel de Crillon has
reestablished its link with the
elegant, magnificent ambience of years past (Louis
XVIth–style furniture, silk
draperies, pastel walls and
woodwork ornamented with
gold leaf, cleverly concealed
minibars). Relais et Châteaux.
Restaurants: Les Ambas-
sadeurs and L'Obélisque, see
Restaurants.

 George-V
8th arr. - 31, avenue
George-V
47 23 54 00,
fax 47 20 40 00
*Open year-round. 53 stes 6,500-
14,500 F. 298 rms 2,300-
5,500 F. Bkfst 115 F. Restaurants.
Air cond. Valet parking.*
The new management has
made a Herculean attempt to
instill new life and spirit into
this "monument in decline."
The bar and the restaurant (Les
Princes, see *Restaurants*; both
open onto a delightful patio)
have been redecorated, a Grill
has been added, and many of

the rooms have been
renovated, with as much concern for elegance as for modernity (electronic panels
located at the head of the beds
allow guests to close the
venetian shutters, control both
the television and the air conditioning, call room service
and so on). The Galerie de la
Paix (recently converted into
an ultrachic tea room, see *Tea
Rooms*), as well as the pictures, rare ornaments and
lovely furniture in the public
rooms still radiate the legendary George V charm. But alas!
such surroundings cry out for
absolutely first-rate maintenance and service, neither of
which is provided here. How
distressing for guests to feel
that they are disturbing the
personnel when they make a
request...

 Le Grand Hôtel
9th arr. - 2, rue Scribe
40 07 32 32,
fax 42 66 12 51
*Open year-round. 16 stes 4,000-
15,000 F. 482 rms 1,750-
2,500 F. Bkfst 150 F. Air cond.
Valet parking.*
The renovation of this grand
hotel, built in 1862, is now
complete. In the past ten
years, this monumental
Second Empire structure has
recovered all the splendor it
displayed when Empress
Eugénie inaugurated it. The
huge central lobby, topped
with a glittering glass dome, is
a wonder to behold. Guest
rooms provide everything the
international traveler could
require in the way of amenities, as well as the most contemporary business
equipment available, a health
club and much more. Excellent bar, see *Cocktail Bars.*

> *Remember to call ahead to
> reserve your room, and please,
> il you cannot honor your
> reservation, be courteous and
> let the hotel know.*

Inter-Continental
1st arr. - 3, rue de
Castiglione
44 77 11 11,
fax 44 77 14 60
Open year-round. 70 stes 2,800-
12,000 F. 380 rms 1,650-
2,450 F. Bkfst 100 F. Restaurants.
Air cond.
Garnier, the architect of the
Opéra, designed this vast
hotel; three out of its seven
immense and spectacular
salons are ranked for their high
standards. With its remarkably
equipped conference rooms,
it answers perfectly to the business world's needs; and as for
charm and comfort, you'll find
them both in the lovely patio
filled with flowers, in the decor
and the incomparable loveli-
ness of many of the rooms
(though some are tiny and
dark), as well as in the small
singles located in the attic,
from which there is a fine view
of the Tuileries. Bathrooms are
often out-dated and on the
small side. The suites (with
Jacuzzi) are luxurious. Three
restaurants: La Rôtisserie
Rivoli, Le Café Tuileries and La
Terrasse Fleurie, see
Restaurants; and a bar.

 Hôtel Lotti
1st arr. - 7, rue de
Castiglione
42 60 37 34,
fax 40 15 93 56
Open year-round. 7 stes 4,500-
6,000 F. 133 rms 1,320-3,000 F.
Bkfst 120 F. Restaurant. Air cond.
Pets 50 F. Valet parking.
This elegant hotel is very
popular with members of the
European aristocracy. Each of
the spacious rooms, whose
comfort is worthy of their
clientele, is uniquely
decorated and offers excellent
facilities. The restaurant, the
lobby and all the rooms were
recently renovated. The staff's
standards are not so high as
once they were: the con-
cierges and receptionists are
occasionally careless. The

charming attic rooms are
reserved for non-smokers.

 Marriott
Prince de Galles
8th arr. - 33, avenue
George-V
47 23 55 11,
fax 47 20 96 92
Open year-round. 30 stes 2,500-
8,000 F. 140 rms 1,700-2,400 F.
Bkfst 95 F. Restaurant. Air cond.
Valet parking.
The open-roofed patio en-
circled by columns is a delightful place to have lunch on a
warm day; the paneled Regency Bar is another pleasant
spot, distinguished by excellent service. But upstairs in the
guest rooms, the facilities
show their age, a fact which,
given the price policy
practiced here, we find more
than difficult to swallow. Yet
for many travelers, those very
flaws are part of this
establishment's "Old World"
charm. The service can be off-
hand. Restaurant: Le Prince de
Galles, see *Restaurants*.

 Meurice
1st arr. - 228, rue de
Rivoli
44 58 10 10,
fax 44 58 10 15
Open year-round. 36 stes 5,000-
15,000 F. 143 rms 2,200-
3,500 F. Bkfst 130 F. Restaurant.
Air cond. in 125 rms. Valet park-
ing.
The Meurice has undergone
substantial renovation in the
past few years, to restore its
glamour and prestige. Most
recently, the admirable salons
on the main floor were
refurbished; the guest rooms
and suites (which offer a view
of the Tuileries) were equipped with air conditioning and
tastefully redecorated; and the
pink-marble bathrooms are
now ultramodern and superb.
The Meurice has regained its
place as one of the best and
most elegant grand hotels in
Paris. The newly designed
restaurant, Le Meurice, is now

lodged in the salon des Tuileries, which gives onto the gardens. Tea and cocktails are
served to the sound of discreet
piano music in the salon
Pompadour, see *Cocktail Bars*.
Free secretarial service is available, and hotel guests are
given free use of the hotel's
box at the Longchamp race
track during the season.

 Plaza Athénée
8th arr. - 25, av.
Montaigne
47 23 78 33,
47 20 20 70
Open year-round. 42 stes 6,000-
9,390 F. 210 rms 2,630-5,520 F.
Bkfst 110 F. Restaurants. Air
cond. Valet parking.
At the Plaza, one finds nothing but discretion, efficiency
and friendly courtesy. The
rooms and suites are bright,
generous in size and outfitted
with every available hotel
amenity. The rooms overlooking avenue Montaigne are perfectly soundproofed. At about
11 a.m., guests gather in the
bar (Plaza-Bar Anglais, where
Mata Hari was arrested), see
Cocktail Bars; and, from 4 p.m.
to 7 p.m. in particular, you'll
see them in the gallery (of
which Marlene Dietrich was
particularly fond). Two
restaurants, Le Relais and Le
Régence-Plaza, are located
just across from the wonderful
patio, where tables are set in
the summer among cascades
of geraniums and ampelopsis
vines, see *Restaurants*. Dry-
cleaning services are provided, as well as a beauty
salon, Dow Jones agency and
so on.

 Raphaël
16th arr. - 17, av. Kléber
44 28 00 28,
fax 45 01 21 50
Open year-round. 35 stes 2,800-
6,500 F. 52 rms 1,700-2,300 F.
Bkfst 100 F. Restaurant. Air cond.
in 40 rms. Valet parking
Built during those wild years
between the two World Wars,

the Raphaël has maintained an atmosphere of refinement and elegance. The Oriental rugs strewn upon the marble floors, the fine woodwork, old paintings and period furniture make Le Raphaël a luxurious place to stay, preferred by a wealthy, well-bred clientele. The spacious rooms (all with two beds) are richly furnished in various styles; the wardrobes and bathrooms are immense. Top-drawer reception and service. Bar, see *Cocktail Bars.*

 Résidence Maxim's de Paris
8th arr. - 42, av. Gabriel
45 61 96 33,
fax 42 89 06 07
Open year-round. 37 stes 3,000-22,000 F. 4 rms 2,250 F. Bkfst 110 F. Restaurant. Air cond. Valet parking.

Pierre Cardin himself designed the hotel of his dreams, a small but palatial establishment that may well be the world's most luxurious. The landings of each floor are decorated like elegant salons, with beautiful and unusual antique pieces and paintings. Polished stone and sumptuous murals adorn the bathrooms. The suites must be seen to be believed, particularly those on the top floor, which are lacquered in vivid colors and furnished with pieces designed by Cardin. Obviously, such accommodations are well beyond the bank balances of most ordinary mortals.

 Ritz
1st arr. - 15, place Vendôme
42 60 38 30,
fax 42 60 23 71
Open year-round. 45 stes 3,900-49,000 F. 142 rms 2,100-3,500 F. Bkfst 160 F. Restaurant. Air cond. No pets. Heated pool. Valet parking.

The most famous hotel in the world is poised to enter the twenty-first century with state-of-the-art facilities, but without having in the least betrayed the distinctive character that won the Ritz its reputation. In other words, even if nowadays you can change the video program or make a phone call without leaving your bed or marble tub (Charles Ritz was the first hotel owner to provide private bathrooms for his clients), nothing has altered the pleasure of stretching out on a wide brass bed surrounded by authentic antique furniture. Add to that a full view of one of the city's most spectacular squares, in an atmosphere of old-fashioned luxury so distinguished that a new word ("ritzy") had to be coined for it. The liveried staff knows the difference between courtesy and obsequiousness. Recent improvements include an eighteen-meter swimming pool, a squash court, a sumptuous health club built to resemble a thermal spa of antiquity, and a roof-top heliport. The restaurant, L'Espadon, see *Restaurant*, boasts its own garden. Additional entertainment possibilities include a nightclub and several bars.

 Royal Monceau
8th arr. - 37, av. Hoche
45 61 98 00,
fax 42 56 90 03
Open year-round. 40 stes 4,200-11,000 F. 179 rms 1,950-2,950 F. Bkfst 130 F. Restaurants. Air cond. No pets. Heated pool and beauty center. Valet parking.

This large, luxurious and discreet hotel attracts politicians, foreign business people and entertainers with spacious rooms, magnificent marble bathrooms and all the usual ingredients of hotel comfort (including excellent room service). Extras include a fashionable piano bar, a spacious health club (with sauna, Jacuzzi, swimming pool and a massage service), outstanding ultramodern conference rooms and a well-equipped "business club." The rooms overlooking the charming flowered patio are the most sought-after by the hotel's habitués. Restaurants: Le Carpaccio see Restaurants and Le Jardin.

 Saint-James et Albany
1st arr. - 202, rue de Rivoli
42 60 31 60,
fax 40 15 92 21
Open year-round. 56 stes 1,400-2,500 F. 155 rms 850-1,050 F. Bkfst 65 F. Restaurant. Garage parking.

The new management is working hard to make this hotel worthy of its four-star rating, and its exceptional location facing the Tuileries Gardens. For reasonable prices, the Saint-James et Albany provides studios, two-room apartments, suites and duplexes equipped with kitchenettes; the rooms overlook a courtyard or an inner garden, and are perfectly quiet. Other amenities include a sauna, a cozy bar with background music (see *Cocktail Bars*) and a restaurant, Le Noailles.

 Scribe
9th arr. - 1, rue Scribe
44 71 24 24,
fax 42 65 39 97
Open year-round. 11 stes 2,800-5,400 F. 206 rms 1,450-2,100 F. Bkfst 130 F. Restaurant. Air cond. Valet parking.

Behind the Scribe's Napoléon III façade stands a prime example of the French hotelier's art. All the rooms, suites and duplexes (the latter are composed of a mezzanine bedroom, a living room that also serves as a dining room/office, a bathroom, dressing room and two entrances) are comfortably furnished in classic style, and boast huge bathrooms. Streetside rooms have double windows and either contemporary or Louis XVIth–style furniture; those overlooking the courtyard are furnished with Louis-Philippe–style pieces and are perfectly quiet. Nineteen TV channels are available, as well as 24-hour room service. Restaurant: Les Muses, see *Restaurants*; and a bar, see *Cocktail Bars*.

 Westminster
2nd arr. - 13, rue de la Paix
42 61 57 46,
fax 42 60 30 66
Open year-round. 17 stes 2,700-4,300 F. 84 rms 1,650-2,450 F. Half-board 2,060 F. Bkfst 95 F. Restaurant. Air cond. in 73 rms. Valet parking, 120 F/day.
Recent and extensive renovation has completely transformed this charming mid-size luxury hotel advantageously situated between the Opéra and the place Vendôme. The pink-and-beige-marble lobby is splendid and luxurious; the bar (with piano) is more than comfortable, see *Cocktail Bars*; the conference rooms are superbly equipped; and the elegant air conditioning rooms are handsomely decorated with attractive fabrics, chandeliers and Louis XV–style furnishings and are fitted with minibars, safes and satellite Restaurant: Le Céladon, see *Restaurants*.

FIRST CLASS

 Ambassador-Concorde
9th arr. - 16, bd Haussman
42 46 92 63,
fax 40 22 08 74
Open year-round. 2 stes 3,000-3,500 F. 296 rms 1,300-2,000 F. Bkfst 100 F. Restaurant. Air cond. Valet parking.
A fine traditional hotel, proud of its luxurious fittings. The relatively spacious guest rooms have been modernized

in excellent taste with sumptuous fabrics, thick carpeting and Art Deco furniture. The lobby and public rooms are imposing indeed: pink marble columns are topped with gilded Corinthian capitals; floors are marble too, and Aubusson tapestries hang on the walls. The penthouse suites look out over Sacré-Cœur. Bar.

 Astor Madeleine L'Horset
8th arr. - 11, rue d'Astorg
42 66 56 56,
fax 42 65 18 37
Open year-round. 128 rms 860-920 F. Bkfst 70 F. Restaurant.
Marble, dark-oak woodwork, inviting leather sofas and huge vases of flowers can be found year-round in the lobby, with its English-style bar. Guest rooms are handsomely decorated in excellent taste. A major renovation is planned for 1993. Restaurant: La Table de l'Astor.

 Baltimore
16th arr. - 88 bis, av. Kléber
44 34 54 54,
fax 44 34 54 44
Open year-round. 1 ste 3,200 F. 104 rms 1,600-2,500 F. Bkfst 95 F. Restaurant. Air cond. Parking.
Six fully equipped meeting rooms are located in the basement; the largest and most luxurious is the former vault room of the Banque Nationale de Paris. The comfortable guest rooms are decorated with understated elegance, in keeping with the neighborhood and the tastes of the clientele. Restaurant: L'Estournel, see *Restaurants*.

 Hôtel Balzac
8th arr. - 6, rue Balzac
45 61 97 22,
fax 42 25 24 82
Open year-round. 14 stes 3,000-6,000 F. 56 rms 1,380-2,100 F.

Bkfst 90 F. Restaurant. Air cond. No pets. Valet parking.
A discreet and luxurious establishment near the place de l'Etoile, frequented by celebrities and jet-setters. The huge rooms are decorated in delicate tones, with lovely furniture, beautiful chintzes and thick carpeting. Most have king-size beds, all have superb modern bathrooms. Unobtrusive yet attentive staff. Restaurant: Bice, see *Restaurants*.

 California
8th arr. - 16, rue de Berri
43 59 93 00,
fax 45 61 03 62
Open year-round. 16 stes 3,300-8,000 F. 156 rms 1,100-1,900 F.

Hidden treasures in the Marais

Since 1960, many of the aristocratic homes in the Marais district (which started out life as a swamp) have been restored to their former glory. Just thirty years ago, the splendid hôtels particuliers—townhouses—were practically invisible, lurking behind blackened and weather-beaten façades. Nowadays, one may spend a marvelous afternoon taking in such architectural treasures as the Hôtel Carnavalet at 23 rue de Sévigné, the Roman-inspired Hôtel d'Hallwyll at 28 rue Michel-le-Comte and the imposing Hôtel de Soubise at 60 rue des Francs-Bourgeois.

Restaurant. Half-board 1,350-2,150 F. Bkfst 100 F. Air cond. Valet parking. Fitness club.

Nothing to remind one here of California, but there is a light-filled lobby, and a sunny lounge, as well as cheerful, adequately sized rooms decorated with chintzes and neo-eighteenth-century furniture, spacious marble bathrooms and extremely pleasant service. Accomodations that overlook the courtyard are amazingly quiet, despite the proximity of the Champs-Elysées. Restaurant on the premises.

 Castille
1st arr. - 37, rue Cambon
42 61 55 20 (will change)
Open year-round. 15 stes 3,000 F. 73 rms 1,300-1,600 F. Restaurant. Air cond. No pets.
After a thoroughgoing renovation, this hotel nextdoor to Chanel and just opposite the Ritz, will reopen in January '93 soon with even more luxurious amenities.

 Château Frontenac
8th arr. - 54, rue Pierre-Charron
47 23 55 85,
fax 47 23 03 32
Open year-round. 4 stes 1,480 F. 102 rms 850-1,300 F. Bkfst 75 F. Restaurant. Air cond. in 20 rms.
A reasonably priced hotel (given the location), with variously sized rooms done in vaguely Louis XV style. Superb marble bathrooms. The soundproofing is effective, but the rooms overlooking the rue Cérisole are still the quietest. Restaurant: Le Pavillon Russe.

 Chateaubriand
8th arr. - 6, rue Chateaubriand

40 76 00 50,
fax 40 76 09 22
Open year-round. 28 rms 1,400-1,700 F. Bkfst 65 F. Air cond. No pets.
Built in 1991, this luxury hotel tucked away behind the Champs-Elysées is still fresh and pristine, but has yet to develop a personality, an atmosphere.

 Claridge-Bellman
8th arr. - 37, rue François-Ier
47 23 54 42,
fax 47 23 08 84
Open year-round. 42 rms 1,100-1,300 F. Bkfst 70 F. Air cond. No pets. Restaurant.
A small, unpretentious hotel with rooms of reasonable size, each of which boasts a special feature, be it a crystal chandelier, antique furniture, a fine print or painting, or a marble fireplace. Friendly, stylish service.

 Concorde-La Fayette
17th arr. - 3, pl. du Général-Koenig
40 68 50 68,
fax 40 68 50 43
Open year-round. 28 stes 3,000-8,000 F. 970 rms 1,350-2,100 F. Bkfst 95 F. Restaurants. Air cond. Parking.
The Concorde–La Fayette is immense: a huge oval tower that houses the Palais des Congrès and its 4,500 seats; banquet rooms that can accommodate 2,000; scores of boutiques; four movie theaters; nightclubs; and 1,500 parking places. The hotel's 1,000 rooms are neither spacious nor luxurious, but they offer all the modern amenities one has come to expect: magnetic locks, color TV, adjustable air conditioning, soundproofing, minibars and clock radios. Airport shuttles can be relied upon to stop here. The hotel's upper floors lodge the Top Club, whose members benefit from luxur-

ious rooms and personalized service. Panoramic bar, three restaurants, including L'Etoile d'Or, see *Restaurants*.

 Concorde Saint-Lazare
8th arr. - 108, rue Saint-Lazare
40 08 44 44,
fax 42 93 01 20
Open year-round. 6 stes 1,950-3,500 F. 300 rms 1,150-1,950 F. Restaurant. Bkfst 90 F. Air cond. in 150 rms. Valet parking.
An enormous hotel, built in 1889 by Gustave Eiffel. The rooms have been thoroughly renovated with pink or beige fabric, attractive lamps and English-style mahogany furniture. Streetside rooms offer the most spacious accommodation. Though large, the bathrooms are a bit old-fashioned. The hotel's most arresting feature is the lobby, a listed architectural landmark, that soars three stories up to coffered ceilings aglitter with gilt, marble and crystal chandeliers. A magnificent billiard room on the main floor is open to the public, as are the cocktail lounge and brasserie.

 Elysées Star
8th arr. - 19, rue Vernet
47 20 41 73,
fax 47 23 32 15
Open year-round. 4 stes 2,400-3,000 F. 38 rms 1,410-2,400 F. Bkfst 80 F. Restaurant. Air cond. Valet parking.
Different decorative styles—from Louis XV to Art Deco—distinguish the various floors of this prestigious hotel near the Champs-Elysées, a veritable paradise for business people. Superb facilities.

 Golden Tulip
8th arr. - 218-220, rue du Fg-St-Honoré
49 53 03 03,
fax 40 75 02 00
Open year-round. 20 stes 2,300-3,700 F. 52 rms 1,550-1,750 F. Bkfst 95 F. Restaurant. Half-

board 1,840 F. Air cond. Pool. Garage parking.

Owned by a Dutch chain, this comfortable hotel is decorated in modern style using traditional materials (marble, wood, quality fabrics, trompe-l'œil paintings). The spacious rooms offer every amenity; all are air conditioning, with splendid marble bathrooms. Restaurant: see Le Relais Vermeer.

Hilton
15th arr. - 18, av. de Suffren
42 73 92 00,
fax 47 83 62 66
Open year-round. 35 stes 3,500-12,000 F. 456 rms 1,500-2,300 F. Bkfst 130 F. Restaurants. Air cond. Valet parking.

The city's first postwar luxury hotel is still living up to Hilton's high standards. Rooms are airy and spacious, service is courteous and deft, and children—of any age!—can share their parents' room for free. Closed-circuit TV shows recent films. Ten stories up are the two "Executive Floors", with their particularly fine rooms (spectacular views of the Seine) and special services. The Hilton houses two restaurants, La Terrasse and Le Western (see Restaurants), and three bars, (Lobby Bar, Bar Suffren and Bar du Toit de Paris, see Cocktail Bars), as well as a hair salon and prestigious boutiques. 24 hours room-service.

Lancaster
8th arr. - 7, rue de Berri
43 59 90 43,
fax 42 89 22 71
Open year-round. 10 stes 3,500-7,200 F. 50 rms 1,590-2,500 F. Bkfst 110 F. Restaurant. Air cond. in 30 rms. Valet parking.

Once you recover from the immense, breathtaking bouquet of flowers in the lobby, you'll be able to admire the general setting—furniture, draperies, paintings, or-naments—of this refined and luxurious hotel. The ravishing indoor garden, with its flowers, fountains and statues (meals are served there on sunny days), lends an unexpected rural touch to this hotel located only a few steps from the Champs-Elysées. The rooms and suites all have period furniture and double windows; their comfort is much appreciated by the aristocrats, statesmen and business tycoons who frequent the Lancaster. Excellent reception; attentive and punctual service. The small conference rooms have fine equipment.

Littré
6th arr. - 9, rue Littré
45 44 38 68,
fax 45 44 88 13
Open year-round. 4 stes 1,280 F. 96 rms 660-875 F. Bkfst 50 F. Air cond. No pets.

The style and decor of this four-star hotel are out of tune with the times, but the Littré's many habitués find the old-fashioned comfort and service entirely satisfactory. In the spacious rooms you'll find high, comfortable beds, ponderous furniture, wonderfully large closets and huge bathrooms. English bar.

Hôtel du Louvre
1st arr. - Pl. André-Malraux
44 58 38 38,
fax 44 58 38 01
Open year-round. 22 stes 3,500-5,000 F. 178 rms 1,300-2,500 F. Restaurant. Bkfst 90 F. Air cond. Valet parking.

From the door of this comfortable, classic hotel, one can see the Gardens of the Palais-Royal, the Louvre and the Tuileries. While most of the guest rooms are spacious and high-ceilinged, offering the decor and all the conveniences one has come to expect from this chain, others are on the small and gloomy side—so be forewarned. Brasserie, piano bar.

Lutétia
6th arr. - 45, bd Raspail
49 54 46 46,
fax 49 54 46 00
Open year-round. 27 stes 3,000-4,000 F. 276 rms 1,100-2,200 F. Bkfst 115 F. Restaurants. Air cond. in 190 rms. Valet parking.

A Left-Bank landmark, the Lutétia is a noteworthy example of Art Deco furnishing. Marble, gilt and red velvet grace the stately public areas where government big-wigs, elected officials, captains of industry and well-heeled travelers come and go. Leading off the imposing entrance are the lounge, a bar, a brasserie, a restaurant, (Brasserie Lutétia and Le Paris, see Restaurants) and conference rooms. The large and expensive suites are done up in pink, with understated furniture and elegant bathrooms—the overall look is very 1930s. As for the service, though occasionally impersonal, it is dependably efficient and precise.

Le Méridien Paris-Etoile
17th arr. - 81, bd Gouvion-Saint-Cyr
40 68 34 34,
fax 40 68 31 31
Open year-round. 17 stes 3,800-7,500 F. 989 rms 1,400-1,950 F. Bkfst 85 F. Restaurants. Air cond. Valet parking. 3 rms for disabled.

The Méridien is the largest hotel in Western Europe, and one of the busiest in Paris. The rooms are small but remarkably well equipped. A variety of boutiques, a nightclub, the Hurlingham Polo Bar (see Cocktail Bars) and four restaurants (Le Café Arlequin; La Maison Beaujolaise; the Yamato; and the excellent Clos Longchamp, see Restaurants) liven things up, as does the popular cocktail lounge where top jazz musicians play, (Club Lionel Hampton, see *Live Music*). Other services include Le Café Arlequin, vast conference rooms, a sauna and travel agencies.

Le Méridien Paris-Montparnasse

14th arr. - 19, rue du Cdt-Mouchotte
44 36 44 36,
fax 44 36 49 00
Open year-round. 15 stes 4,000-6,000 F. 950 rms 1,200-1,800 F. 3 rms for disabled. Bkfst 78 F. Restaurants. Air cond. Valet parking.

Luxurious, soigné and comfortable—that's the Méridien in a nutshell. Try to reserve one of the newer rooms, which are particularly bright and spacious. Or the Presidential Suite, if your means permit. Certain accommodations are for non-smokers only; all rooms afford fine views of the city. Three restaurants: Café Atlantique; Justine and Montparnasse 25, see *Restaurants*; bar, Le Platinium; boutiques.

Montalembert

7th arr. - 3, rue de Montalembert
45 48 68 11,
fax 42 22 58 19
Open year-round. 5 stes 2,400-3,000 F. 51 rms 1,450-1,850 F. Bkfst 90 F. Restaurant. Air cond. No pets. Valet parking.

The new management has been unstinting in its efforts to restore this 1926 hotel to its former splendor with luxurious materials (marble, ebony, sycamore, leather), designer fabrics and linens. Guests love the huge bath towels, cozy dressing gowns and premium toiletries they find in the rooms. Restaurant open at lunch only; breakfast buffet. The hotel bar is a favorite rendezvous of writers and publishers.

A red hotel ranking denotes a place with charm.

Pergolèse

16th arr. - 3, rue Pergolèse
40 67 96 77,
fax 45 00 12 11
Open year-round. 40 rms 850-1,500 F. Bkfst 70 F. No pets.

A spanking-new deluxe hotel, the Pergolèse provides a classy address as well as first-rate service and amenities for what are still (relatively) reasonable prices.

Pont-Royal

7th arr. - 7, rue de Montalembert
45 44 38 27,
fax 45 44 92 07
Open year-round. 75 rms 850-1,550 F. No pets.

Business types and movie actors have taken over the fairly spacious, traditionally furnished rooms where writers—from Faulkner to Sagan—have sojourned. On the ninth floor, three rooms have terraces with views of all of Paris. Bar: Pont-Royal, see *Cocktail Bars*; restaurant.

Régina

1st arr. - 2, place des Pyramides
42 60 31 10,
fax 40 15 95 16
Open year-round. 10 stes 2,200-3,200 F. 120 rms 900-2,000 F. Restaurant. Half-board 890-1,240 F. Bkfst 80 F. Air cond. in 7 rms. Valet parking.

Opposite the Tuileries is one of the city's most venerable luxury hotels, with immense rooms, precious furnishings (Louis XVI, Directoire, Empire) and—a practical addition—double-glazed windows. The grandiose lobby is graced with handsome old clocks that give the time of all the great European metropolises. A quiet bar and a little restaurant that opens onto an indoor garden are pleasant places to idle away an hour.

Saint James Paris

16th arr. - 5, pl. du Chancelier-Adenauer
47 04 29 29
Open year-round. 31 stes 2,200-3,500 F. 17 rms 1,350-1,900 F. Bkfst 120 F. Restaurant. Air cond. in 48 rms. Valet parking.

Since its purchase by a hotel group, the hotel part of this private club has been open to the public. A staff of 100 looks after the 48 rooms and suites—a luxury level of attention with prices fixed accordingly. The sizeable rooms are decorated in an austere 1930s style, with flowers, plants, and a basket of fruit adding warmth. Marble bathrooms.

San Régis

8th arr. - 12, rue Jean-Goujon
43 59 41 90,
fax 45 61 05 48
Open year-round. 10 stes 2,800-4,000 F. 34 rms 1,325-2,525 F. Bkfst 100 F. Restaurant. Air cond. in 35 rms. Valet parking.

This jewel of a hotel, much appreciated by celebrities from the worlds of show business and *haute couture*, provides a successful mix of traditional comfort and the latest technology. Beautifully kept rooms boast splendid period furniture and paintings, sumptuous bathrooms and lots of space, light and character. The staff is irreproachable.

La Trémoille

8th arr. - 14, rue de La Trémoille
47 23 34 20,
fax 40 70 01 08
Open year-round. 14 stes 2,750-5,100 F. 96 rms 1,600-2,900 F. Bkfst 100 F. Restaurant. Air cond. Valet parking.

Cozy comfort, antique furniture, balconies with window-box filled with bright flowers and service worthy of a grand hotel. Several duplexes are brand new and remarkably comfortable; all of the rooms have terrific bathrooms. The delightful dining room/salon is warmed by a crackling fire in winter. Restaurant: Le Louis d'Or.

Hôtel Vernet
8th arr. - 25, rue Vernet
47 23 43 10,
fax 40 70 10 14
Open year-round. 3 stes 3,200 F. 54 rms 1,400-1,950 F. Bkfst 100 F. Restaurant. Air cond. Valet parking.

This is one of the city's finest hotels, combining the best of modern and traditional comforts. The rooms and suites are handsomely decorated with genuine Louis XVI, Directoire or Empire furniture, and walls are hung with sumptuous blue or green fabric. Jacuzzi in all the bathrooms; guests are granted free access to the luxurious Thermes du Royal Monceau health spa. Restaurant: Les Elysées du Vernet, see *Restaurants*.

La Villa Saint-Germain
6th arr. - 29, rue Jacob
43 26 60 00,
fax 46 34 63 63
Open year-round. 4 stes 1,600-1,950 F. 30 rms 800-1,250 F.

A laser beam projects room numbers onto the doors; the bathroom sinks are crafted of chrome and sanded glass; orange, violet, green and red leather furniture stand out vividly from the subdued gray walls: Marie-Christine Dorner has created a high-tech environment for this new hotel, which attracts a trendy, moneyed clientele. Jazz club on the lower level (La Villa, see *Live Music*), with name acts.

Warwick
8th arr. - 5, rue de Berri
45 63 14 11,
fax 45 63 75 81
Open year-round. 5 stes 3,160-8,100 F. 141 rms 1,620-2,420 F. Bkfst 105 F. Restaurant. Air cond. Valet parking.

Luxurious and modern, just off the Champs-Elysées, this hotel offers bright, spacious

rooms done up in pastel colors and chintz—they are designed more for relaxing and living in than for a quick stopover. Efficient soundproofing and air conditioning. There is an attractive bar with piano music in the evening and pleasant rooftop terraces. Room service is on tap 24 hours a day. Restaurant: La Couronne, see *Restaurants*.

CLASSICAL

Agora Saint-Germain
5th arr. - 42, rue des Bernardins
46 34 13 00,
fax 46 34 75 05
Open year-round. 39 rms 530-640 F. Bkfst 40 F. No pets.

A very well-kept establishment which was completely renovated in 1987. Bright rooms with comfortable beds, minibar, radio and television. Bathrooms with such welcome amenities as hairdryers.

Alexander
16th arr. - 102, av. Victor-Hugo
45 53 64 65,
fax 45 53 12 51
Open year-round. 3 stes 1,950 F. 59 rms 830-1,370 F. Bkfst 65 F. Air cond. in 7 rms. No pets.

Stylish comfort and impeccable maintenance distinguish this peaceful establishment. Rooms are decorated with slightly outmoded elegance (leaf-patterned wallpaper, gray carpeting). Nice big bathrooms with all the modern fixtures. The reception is most courteous. No restaurant.

Aramis Saint-Germain
6th arr. - 124, rue de Rennes

45 48 03 75,
fax 45 44 99 29
Open year-round. 41 rms 500-750 F. Bkfst 45 F.

These new, well-soundproofed and attractively decorated rooms have soft lighting, modern equipment and perfect bathrooms. The service is especially attentive. Piano bar; no restaurant.

Bastille Speria
4th arr. - 1, rue de la Bastille
42 72 04 01,
fax 42 72 56 38
Open year-round. 42 rms 460-690 F. Bkfst 35 F. No pets.

The interior was renovated in a restrained modern style in 1988. The rooms, though not large, are perfectly quiet thanks to double windows. Very pleasant reception and service.

Bradford
8th arr. - 10, rue Saint-Philippe-du-Roule
43 59 24 20,
fax 45 63 20 07
Open year-round. 2 stes 1,100 F. 46 rms 700-950 F. Bkfst 30 F. No Air cond. No pets.

A traditional hotel, where elegant simplicity combines with exemplary service to give guests true comfort. Decorated in a predominantly Louis XVI style, the rooms are slightly old-fashioned, but spacious and soothing. Good singles; rooms ending with the numbers 6 and 7 are the largest. No restaurant.

Hôtel de la Bretonnerie
4th arr. - 22, rue Ste-Croix-Bretonnerie
48 87 77 63,
fax 42 77 26 78
Closed Aug. 2-29. 1 ste 800-900 F. 30 rms 530-750 F. Bkfst 40 F. No pets.

A seventeenth-century townhouse, tastefully renovated and redecorated. Spacious rooms with beams and antique furniture; modern bathrooms. The pink-and-white suite is much in demand.

Britannique

1st arr. - 20, av. Victoria
42 33 74 59
Open year-round. 40 rms 490-680 F. Bkfst 40 F. No pets.
A warm welcome and good service characterize this family-run hotel. The rooms are tastefully decorated with pale walls, dark carpeting, minibar and modern comfortable furniture. Satellite television.

Cayré

7th arr. - 4, bd Raspail
45 44 38 88,
fax 45 44 98 13
Open year-round. 126 rms 900-1,300 F. Bkfst 50 F.
A pink-and-gray marble floor, glass pillars and red-leather furniture lend an air of luxury to the lobby. The rooms, modern and thoroughly soundproofed, are completely impersonal. Marble bathrooms.

Claret

12th arr. - 44, bd de Bercy
46 28 41 31,
fax 49 28 09 29
Open year-round. 52 rms 320-490 F. Bkfst 40 F. Restaurant. Half-board 420-590 F.
This neat, modernized hotel with a family atmosphere features a wine bar in the basement.

Colisée

8th arr. - 6, rue du Colisée
43 59 95 25,
fax 45 63 26 54
Open year-round. 44 rms 580-850 F. Air cond. in 19 rms.
Rooms are on the small side (those whose numbers end with an 8 are more spacious), but quite comfortable, with a floral decor and tiled baths. The four attic rooms have wood-beamed ceilings and considerable charm. There is a bar and lounge, but no restaurant.

Commodore

9th arr. - 12, bd Haussman
42 46 72 82,
fax 47 70 23 81
Open year-round. 11 stes 2,150-3,500 F. 151 rms 1,000-1,800 F. Bkfst 80 F. Restaurant. Valet parking.
This commendable traditional hotel is located a few steps away from the new Drouot auction house and its parking lot. Some of the rooms have just been fully renovated in a bright, elegant style. As for the others, well... All, however, are spacious; newlyweds should request the honeymoon suite, which must be seen to be believed.

Courcelles

17th arr. - 184, rue de Courcelles
47 63 65 30,
fax 46 22 49 44
Open year-round. 42 rms 530-670 F. Bkfst 40 F.
All the rooms here are equipped with remote-control color TVs, direct phone lines, clock-radios and minibars. Walls are covered with pink or green fabric that coordinates with the bedspreads and curtains; the furniture is of the modern, lacquered variety. Very pleasant reception and service.

Duminy-Vendôme

1st arr. - 3, rue du Mont-Thabor
42 60 32 80,
fax 42 96 07 83
Open year-round. 79 rms 590-850 F. Bkfst 22 F.
Duminy-Vendôme's rooms have impeccable bathrooms and 1920s–style furnishings. Rooms on the sixth and seventh floors have slightly sloping ceilings, and those with numbers ending in 10 are larger than the rest. A small summer patio is located on the main floor, as is the rather amazing bar, swathed in red velvet.

Edouard VII

2nd arr. - 39, av. de l'Opéra
42 61 56 90,
fax 42 61 47 73
Open year-round. 4 stes 1,800 F. 70 rms 750-1,080 F. Bkfst 50 F. Restaurant. Half-board 948 F. Air cond. in 33 rms.
A certain style of 1960s luxury characterizes this hotel near the Opéra. Half the rooms have been redecorated this year. Well-equipped bathrooms. Restaurant: Le Delmonico, see *Restaurants*.

Elysa

5th arr. - 6, rue Gay-Lussac
43 25 31 74
Open year-round. 30 rms 450-660 F. Bkfst 35 F. No pets.
In the heart of the Latin Quarter, near the Luxembourg Gardens. The pretty pink or blue rooms with white-lacquered furniture are soundproofed. Buffet breakfast.

Elysées-Maubourg

7th arr. - 35, bd de Latour-Maubourg
45 56 10 78,
fax 47 05 65 08
Open year-round. 2 stes 800-1,200 F. 28 rms 520-690 F. Bkfst 40 F. Air cond.
The 30 rooms of this Best Western hotel are decorated without much originality in green, blue or beige tones, but they are superbly equipped and very comfortable. There is a Finnish sauna in the basement, a bar and a flower-filled patio. No restaurant.

Frantour Suffren

15th arr. - 20, rue Jean-Rey
45 78 50 00,
fax 45 78 91 42
Open year-round. 11 stes 1,900-3,400 F. 396 rms 810-990 F. Bkfst 70 F. Restaurant. Air cond. Garage parking.
The Frantour Suffren is a large, modern hotel located next to the Seine and the

Champ-de-Mars. The simple rooms are regularly refurbished and offer excellent equipment. There is an attractive, plant-filled restaurant (Le Champ de Mars), and a garden where meals are served in summer.

Holiday Inn (République)
11th arr. - 10, pl. de la République
43 55 44 34,
fax 47 00 32 34
Open year-round. 4 stes 2,200-3,200 F. 314 rms 1,190-1,990 F. Bkfst incl. Restaurant. Air cond.
The architect Davioud, who designed the Châtelet, built this former Modern Palace in 1867. Today it belongs to the largest hotel chain in the world, which completely restored and modernized it. The rooms and suites are functional, pleasant and well soundproofed; the most attractive ones overlook the flower-filled indoor court. Restaurant: La Belle Epoque, see *Restaurants*.

Le Jardin de Cluny
5th arr. - 9, rue du Sommerard
43 54 22 66
Open year-round. 40 rms 525-695 F. Bkfst 45 F. No pets.
A perfectly functional hotel, with comfortable rooms and modern bathrooms.

Kléber
16th arr. - 7, rue de Belloy
47 23 80 22,
fax 49 52 07 20
Open year-round. 1 ste 950-1,250 F. 21 rms 670-780 F. Bkfst 45 F. Parking.
A family-run hotel managed in a thoroughly professional way, this impeccable little establishment has about twenty rooms spread over six floors. All are equipped with double-glazed windows and pretty bathrooms. The decor is mod-

ern but warm. Bar, no restaurant.

Latitudes Saint-Germain
6th arr. - 7-11, rue Saint-Benoît
42 61 53 53,
fax 49 27 09 33
Open year-round. 117 rms 610-890 F. Bkfst 58 F. Air cond.
This large, modern hotel, opened in 1988, is located in the heart of Saint-Germain-des-Prés; it used to be a printing shop, and its gracious turn-of-the-century façade has been preserved. The spacious rooms are well equipped, attractively decorated in pastel shades. A cellar jazz club provides hot and cool live music every night but Sunday, from 10:30 p.m.

Lenox
14th arr. - 15, rue Delambre
43 35 34 50,
fax 43 20 46 64
Open year-round. 6 stes 890 F. 46 rms 490-610 F. Bkfst 45 F.
The lobby is cold rather than inviting, but the penthouse suites are attractive indeed. Rooms vary in size, yet are uniformly comfortable and well kept. Light meals are served at the bar until 2 a.m. (there is no restaurant).

Madison
6th arr. - 143, bd St-Germain
43 29 72 50,
fax 40 51 60 01
Open year-round. 55 rms 680-1,220 F. Bkfst 60 F. Air cond.
A comfortable hotel with some antique furniture, and pretty Provençal tiles in the bathrooms. Very well equipped: double- glazing, air conditioning, minibar, satellite television, hairdryer. Smiling service and a generous buffet for breakfast.

Mercure Paris-Bercy
13th arr. - 6, bd V.-Auriol
45 82 48 00,
fax 45 82 19 16
Open year-round. 89 rms 540-800 F. Restaurant. Air cond.
A modern hotel near the Bercy sports complex and the Gare d'Austerlitz, the Mercure offers easy access from the *péripherique* (the expressway that encircles Paris). Well suited to the needs of business people, the rooms are soundproofed and have a large work surface. Some rooms have a terrace.

Mercure Paris Montparnasse
14th arr. - 20, rue de la Gaïté
43 35 28 28
Open year-round. 7 stes 1,100 F. 178 rms 590-900 F. Bkfst 35 F. Restaurant. Air cond. Garage parking.
The comfortable rooms are just big enough, with double-glazing, minibar, direct telephone and ten television channels. Functional bathrooms; generous breakfast buffet.

Mercure Paris-Vaugirard
15th arr. - 69, bd Victor
45 33 74 63,
fax 48 28 22 11
Open year-round. 91 rms 680-1,500 F. Restaurant. Air cond. Garage parking.
The well-designed, air conditioning (with individual controls) and soundproofed rooms all offer modern amenities; the remarkable bathrooms are equipped with radios, hairdryers and magnifying mirrors. Perfect for business people (the Exhibition Grounds are close at hand).

Remember to call ahead to reserve your room, and please, il you cannot honor your reservation, be courteous and let the hotel know.

Modern Hôtel Lyon

12th arr. - 3, rue Parrot
43 43 41 52
Open year-round. 1 ste 770-875 F. 47 rms 510-660 F. Bkfst 36 F. No pets.

The location is most convenient (near the Gare de Lyon). Rooms are comfortable, unpretentious and equipped with minibars. Thoughtful service.

Montana Tuileries

1st arr. - 12, rue St-Roch
42 60 35 10
Open year-round. 25 rms 580-1,050 F. Bkfst 50 F.

This very chic little hotel doesn't actually overlook the Tuileries Gardens, but they are only a stone's throw away. All double rooms, well equipped. Numbers 50 and 52 have balconies.

Napoléon

8th arr. - 40, av. de Friedland
47 66 02 02,
fax 47 66 82 33
Open year-round. 36 stes 1,550-4,500 F. 66 rms 800-1,950 F. Bkfst 75 F. Restaurant. Air cond. in 6 rms. Valet parking.

Admirably situated, this fine hotel provides top-flight service along with excellent equipment and amenities. The spacious rooms have a classic (though not very cheery) decor. The pleasant banquet rooms (L'Etoile, for example) are much in demand for receptions and conferences. Restaurant: Le Napoléon, see *Restaurants.*

Hôtel des Nations

5th arr. - 54, rue Monge
43 26 45 24,
fax 46 34 00 13
Open year-round. 38 rms 550-580 F. Bkfst 50 F.

At this well-kept, functional hotel the curtains and bedcovers match the paper or fabric wallcoverings. Tiled bathrooms, double-glazing.

Some rooms look out over a garden that in summer is abloom with flowers.

Nikko de Paris

15th arr. - 61, quai de Grenelle
40 58 20 00,
fax 45 75 42 35
Open year-round. 9 stes 3,140-7,680 F. 772 rms 1,260-1,880 F. Restaurants. Half-board 1,555 F. Bkfst 75 F. Air cond. Heated pool. Valet parking.

Thirty-one floors piled up to resemble an immense beehive. You can opt either for vaguely Japanese-style or modern, ultrafunctional rooms; the large porthole windows overlook the Seine and the Pont Mirabeau. The six upper floors are reserved for luxury rooms with personalized service. Boutiques, conference rooms, a heated swimming pool with sauna, fitness club and a massage service are just some of the Nikko's most attractive features. You'll also find an excellent bar, restaurants (Les Célébrités, see *Restaurants*) and a brasserie within the complex.

Parc Victor-Hugo

16th arr. - 55-57, av. R.-Poincaré
44 05 66 66,
fax 44 05 66 00
Open year-round. 117 rms 1,900-2,500 F. Bkfst 115 F. Restaurants. Air cond. Valet parking.

The management is just now putting the finishing touches on a full refurbishment of this sumptuous hotel, opened in 1987. You can expect to find perfectly comfortable, impeccably equipped rooms and a glorious large indoor garden.

Pavillon de la Reine

3rd arr. - 28, pl. des Vosges
42 77 96 40,
fax 42 77 63 06
Open year-round. 22 stes 1,800-3,200 F. 33 rms 1,400-1,600 F. Bkfst 90 F. Air cond. Valet parking.

The air conditioning rooms, duplexes and suites, all equipped with marble bathrooms, are tastefully decorated; they artfully blend authentic antiques with lovely reproductions. They overlook either the place des Vosges and its garden or a quiet inner patio filled with flowers. No restaurant.

Pullman Saint-Honoré

8th arr. - 15, rue Boissy d'Anglas
42 66 93 62,
fax 42 66 14 98
Open year-round. 7 stes 1,580 F. 112 rms 750-995 F. Bkfst 85 F. No pets.

Comfortable and functional, favored by business travelers and visitors to the nearby American Embassy, this well-renovated hotel consists of seven stories of identically furnished, pleasant, modern rooms with impeccable bathrooms. The bar, open from 10 a.m. to 2 a.m., is decorated with marquetry from the trains of the *Compagnie Internationale des Wagons Lits.* Ten duplexes are located on the seventh floor; there is one suite on the eighth floor. No restaurant, but light meals are available around the clock from room service, and the breakfast buffet is open until 10:30 a.m.

This symbol signifies hotels that offer an exceptional degree of peace and quiet.

HÔTEL
PLAZA ATHÉNÉE

25, Avenue Montaigne, 75008 Paris

Téléphone : (1) 47.23.78.33 ★ Téléfax : (1) 47.20.20.70 ★ Télex 650092 Plaza Paris

FORTE

Pullman Saint-Jacques

14th arr. - 17, bd Saint-Jacques
40 78 79 80,
fax 45 88 43 93
Open year-round. 14 stes 1,825-2,000 F. 797 rms 1,095-1,360 F. Bkfst 90 F. Restaurant. Air cond. Valet parking.

The Pullman Saint-Jacques is conveniently close to Orly airport. It offers good-sized rooms with comfortable bathrooms, air conditioning and blackout blinds that allow guests to sleep off their jet lag. For entertainment, there are two bars and four restaurants; or you could ask one of the staff to show you the "Deluxe" suite, which has often served as a setting for films.

 Pullman Windsor

8th arr. - 14, rue Beaujon
45 63 04 04,
fax 42 25 36 81
Open year-round. 5 stes 1,900-2,700 F. 130 rms 1,250-1,900 F. Bkfst 90 F. Restaurant. Air cond. Valet parking.

This solid, austere building (built in 1925) houses a comfortable if charmless hotel, whose facilities (ultramodern equipment for the business clientele) are constantly being updated. The largish, bright rooms are decorated with understated, functional furniture (minibars, color TVs and video programming). Room service. Restaurant: Le Clovis, see *Restaurants*.

 Quality Inn Paris-Rive Gauche

6th arr. - 92, rue de Vaugirard
42 22 00 56,
fax 42 22 05 39
Open year-round. 6 stes 960-1,025 F. 128 rms 600-890 F. Bkfst 60 F. Air cond. Garage parking. Rms equipped for disabled.

Part of an American chain with about 1,000 hotels worldwide, this is a quiet, elegant

establishment. Well-equipped rooms with mini-bar and satellite TV, some furnished in cruise-liner style. Piano bar filled with plants. Substantial breakfasts are served until 11 a.m. Impeccable service.

 Le Relais de Lyon

12th arr. - 64, rue Crozatier
43 44 22 50
Open year-round. 34 rms 400-498 F. Bkfst 35 F. No pets. Garage parking.

This pleasant hotel provides bright, comfortable, well-equipped rooms which are absolutely quiet (double windows, blinds). Most overlook a little patch of garden, and those on the fifth floor have a terrace. Friendly reception.

 Résidence Bassano

16th arr. - 15, rue de Bassano
47 23 78 23,
fax 47 20 41 22
Open year-round. 3 stes 1,600-1,950 F. 27 rms 750-1,150 F. Bkfst 65 F. Air cond. No pets. Parking.

Housed in a building of Haussmann vintage, these high-class accommodations offer impeccable, thoughtfully designed and equipped guest rooms, enhanced with Art Deco–style furniture. Among the amenities are a sauna, Jacuzzi and 24-hour room service.

 Résidence Monceau

8th arr. - 85, rue du Rocher
45 22 75 11,
fax 45 22 30 88
Open year-round. 1 ste 820 F. 50 rms 615 F. Bkfst 42 F.

Though it lacks atmosphere, the Résidence Monceau is functional and well kept, and employs a courteous staff. All the rooms have private

bathrooms, color TVs, minibars and automatic alarm clocks. Good privacy; breakfast is served on a patio. No restaurant.

 Résidence Saint-Honoré

8th arr. - 214, rue du Faubourg-St-Honoré
42 25 26 27,
fax 45 63 30 67
Open year-round. 91 rms 630-1,000 F. Bkfst 40 F. Air cond. in 70 rms.

A surprising range of styles has been used in the gradual renovation of the spacious rooms, which are more comfortable than luxurious. Dynamic management, uncommonly courteous staff. The Saint-Honoré auction house is situated on the hotel's lower level.

 Rond-Point de Longchamp

16th arr. - 86, rue de Longchamp
45 05 13 63,
fax 47 55 12 80
Open year-round. 57 rms 590-1,200 F. Bkfst 45 F. Restaurant. Air cond.

The sizeable, comfortable rooms are nicely fitted and prettily decorated (gray carpeting, burled-walnut furniture), and offer marble bathrooms. There is an elegant restaurant with a fireplace, as well as a billiards room.

 Saint-Ferdinand

17th arr. - 36, rue St-Ferdinand
45 72 66 66,
fax 45 74 12 92
Open year-round. 42 rms 630-820 F. Bkfst 40 F. Air cond. in 27 rms.

This small, functional hotel opened in 1985. The rooms are tiny (the bathrooms even more so), but they are well equipped with television, minibar, safe and hairdryer. Soothing decor.

Saxe-Résidence

7th arr. - 9, villa de Saxe
47 83 98 28,
fax 47 83 85 47
*Open year-round. 4 stes 760 F.
48 rms 545-710 F. Bkfst 55 F.
Parking. No pets.*
Situated between two convents and a bouquet of secret gardens, this hotel is miraculously quiet. The rooms are constantly updated, and there is a 1950s-style bar. Even the singles are of decent size. Courteous reception.

Hôtel de Sévigné

16th arr. - 6, rue de Belloy
47 20 88 90,
fax 40 70 98 73
Open year-round. 30 rms 630-760 F. Bkfst 42 F. Garage parking.
A classic hotel. The modern, comfortable rooms have white walls, flowered curtains and tiled bathrooms. Expect friendly service and reception.

Splendid Etoile

17th arr. - 1 bis, av. Carnot
45 72 72 00,
fax 45 72 72 01
*Open year-round. 7 stes 1,450 F.
50 rms 880-1,150 F. Bkfst 70 F.
Restaurant. Air cond. in 30 rms.
No pets.*
The Splendid Etoile features 50 well-maintained, comfortably furnished, good-size rooms, all with double windows (some afford views of the Arc de Triomphe). Attractive English-style bar. Restaurant: Le Pré Carré.

Sofitel Paris

15th arr. - 8, rue Louis-Armand
40 60 30 30,
fax 45 57 04 22
Open year-round. 2 stes & 11 junior stes 1,900-2,250 F. 622 rms 950 F. Bkfst 80 F. Restaurants. Air cond. Heated pool. Valet parking.
Thirty-seven meeting and conference rooms (with simultaneous translation avail-able in five languages) are connected to a central administration office. The hotel also features recreational facilities (exercise room, sauna and a heated swimming pool with sliding roof on the 23rd floor) and a panoramic bar. The rooms, all equipped with magnetic closing systems, were recently renovated. Restaurant: Le Relais de Sèvres, see *Restaurants.*

Terrass Hôtel

18th arr. - 12, rue Joseph-de-Maistre
46 06 72 85,
fax 42 52 29 11
Open year-round. 13 stes 1,330-1,780 F. 88 rms 800-950 F. Bkfst 60 F. Restaurant. Half-board 735-1,000 F. Air cond in 6 rms. Garage parking.
A just-completed renovation has spruced up this excellent hotel. Located at the foot of the Butte Montmartre hill, the Terrass offers a majestic, unsurpassable view of almost all of Paris. Rooms are comfortable and nicely outfitted, with some attractive furniture and Italian-tile bathrooms. Up on the seventh floor, the panoramic terrace doubles as a bar in summer. Restaurant: Le Guerlande.

Victoria Palace

6th arr. - 6, rue Blaise-Desgoffe
45 44 38 16,
fax 45 49 23 75
Open year-round. 110 rms 780-1,320 F. Bkfst 50 F. No pets. Garage parking.
Still a reliable establishment, despite a slightly tired decor (currently undergoing renovation). The rooms are sizeable and comfortable, with really spacious closets and good bathrooms. Bar and restaurant.

Vieux Paris

6th arr. - 9, rue Gît-le-Cœur
43 54 41 66,
fax 43 26 00 15.
Open year-round. 7 stes 1,370-1,470 F. 13 rms 1,070-1,270 F. Bkfst 90 F. No pets.
Here's a hotel that wears its name well, for it was built in the fifteenth century. An overhaul in 1991 turned the Vieux Paris into a luxurious stopover, whose comfort and first-rate amenities fully justify the high rates. Rooms are handsomely furnished and perfectly quiet, with Jacuzzis in every bathroom. Warm reception.

Vigny

8th arr. - 9, rue Balzac
40 75 04 39,
fax 40 75 05 81
Open year-round. 12 stes 2,600-5,000 F. 25 rms 1,700-2,200 F. Bkfst 90 F. Restaurant. Air cond. Valet parking.
A handsome and brand-new hotel, the Vigny offers English mahogany furniture, comfortable beds, and fine marble bathrooms: the virtues of another age simplified and brought up to date. The suites provide all-out luxury. Excellent service. Lunch and light suppers are served at the bar (Le Baretto) designed by Adam Tihany.

Yllen

15th arr. - 196, rue de Vaugirard
45 67 67 67,
fax 45 67 74 37
Open year-round. 1 ste 950-1,070 F. 39 rms 490-710 F. Bkfst 40 F.
Yllen's modern, functional rooms have an understated decor and are well soundproofed—but they are very small. Corner rooms (those with numbers ending in 4) on the upper floors are the best. Energetic management, friendly reception.

> *Remember to call ahead to reserve your room, and please, il you cannot honor your reservation, be courteous and let the hotel know.*

CHARMING

 ## Abbaye Saint-Germain
6th arr. - 10, rue Cassette
45 44 38 11,
fax 45 48 07 86
Open year-round. 4 stes 1,660-1,900 F. 44 rms 800-1,400 F. Air cond. in 7 rms. No pets. No cards.

Set back from the street, this serene eighteenth-century residence located between a courtyard and a garden offers well-kept, elegantly decorated rooms which are not, however, particularly spacious; the most delightful accommodations are on the same level as the garden (number 4 even has a terrace). No restaurant.

 ## Agora
1st arr. - 7, rue de la Cossonnerie
42 33 46 02,
fax 42 33 80 99
Open year-round. 29 rms 315-580 F. Bkfst 30 F.

In the heart of the pedestrian district of Les Halles, these rooms are exquisitely decorated and well soundproofed. Lovely pieces of period furniture and engravings are everywhere; the cleanliness is impressive. Cheerful reception. No restaurant.

 ## Angleterre
6th arr. - 44, rue Jacob
42 60 34 72,
fax 42 60 16 93
Open year-round. 3 stes 1,100-1,300 F. 26 rms 700-900 F. Bkfst 40 F.

Hemingway once lived in this former British Embassy, built around a flower-filled patio. The impeccable rooms have been completely renovated; some are quite spacious, with high wood-beamed ceilings. Large, comfortable beds; luxurious bathrooms. Downstairs, there is a bar and lounge with a piano.

 ## Atala
8th arr. - 10, rue Chateaubriand
45 62 01 62,
fax 42 25 66 38
Open year-round. 1 ste 1,400 F. 48 rms 750-1,300 F. Bkfst 50 F. Restaurant. Air cond. in 30 rms.

On a quiet street near the Champs-Elysées, this hotel provides cheerfully decorated rooms that open onto a verdant garden. Balconies and terraces come with rooms on the sixth and eighth floors. L'Atalante, the hotel's bar and restaurant, offers garden dining in fine weather. Excellent service.

 ## Banville
17th arr. - 166, bd Berthier
42 67 70 16,
fax 44 40 42 77
Open year-round. 39 rms 550-650 F. Bkfst 40 F.

A fine small hotel, with flowers at the windows (some of which open to panoramic views of Paris) and bright, cheerful rooms, well soundproofed thanks to thick carpeting. Marble or tile bathrooms. Excellent English breakfasts; no restaurant.

Belle Epoque
12th arr. - 66, rue de Charenton
43 44 06 66,
fax 43 44 10 25
Open year-round. 3 stes 800 F. 30 rms 500-740 F. Bkfst 50 F.

Not far from the Gare de Lyon, this well-kept hotel is furnished and decorated in 1930s style. Comfortable beds, modern bathrooms and double-glazing throughout.

 ## Bersoly's Saint-Germain
7th arr. - 28, rue de Lille
42 60 73 79,
fax 49 27 05 55
Closed Aug. 2-30. 16 rms 550-650 F. Bkfst 50 F.

The hotel's furniture is largely provided by the nearby "golden triangle" of antiques dealers; reproduction paintings adorn the walls. Breakfast is served in the attractive vaulted basement. Faultless reception.

Brighton
1st arr. - 218, rue de Rivoli
42 60 30 03,
fax 42 60 41 78
Open year-round. 1 ste 1,000 F. 69 rms 360-780 F. Restaurant. No pets.

A dream setting opposite the Tuileries gardens, near the Louvre, is offered at very reasonable prices. The large rooms on the rue de Rivoli have wonderful views, high molded ceilings, huge brass beds, nineteenth-century furniture and good-sized bathrooms. The little attic rooms are especially good value.

 ## Centre Ville Etoile
17th arr. - 6, rue des Acacias
43 80 56 18,
fax 47 54 93 43
Open year-round. 20 rms 650-900 F. Bkfst 50 F. Air cond. Restaurant.

A quiet building, tastefully refurbished. The attractive, contemporary rooms boast minitels (electronic telephone directories), satellite TV and spotless bathrooms. Restaurant: Le Cougar, see *Restaurants.*

We're always happy to hear about your discoveries and receive your comments on ours. We want to give your letters the attention they deserve, so when you write to Gault Millau, please state clearly what you liked or disliked. Be concise but convincing, and take the time to argue your point.

Crystal Hôtel

6th arr. - 24, rue St-
Benoît
45 48 85 14,
fax 45 49 16 45
*Open year-round. 1 ste 1,000-
1,200 F. 25 rms 480-700 F. Bkfst
38 F.*
A charming small hotel with
a friendly atmosphere, favored
by artists and writers. The
rooms are simply decorated
with some antique furniture,
and thoughtfully equipped
bathrooms.

Danemark

6th arr. - 21, rue Vavin
43 26 93 78,
fax 46 34 66 06
*Open year-round. 15 rms 540-
720 F. Bkfst 40 F. Air cond.*
This small hotel was carefully
renovated in a 1930s style.
Rooms are not very large, but
elegant, with pleasant lighting,
mahogany, ash or oak furniture and gray-marble
bathrooms (number 10 boasts
a Jacuzzi). No restaurant.

Les Deux Iles

4th arr. - 59, rue Saint-
Louis-en-l'Ile
43 26 13 35,
fax 43 29 60 25
*Open year-round. 17 rms 620-
750 F. Bkfst 39 F. No cards.*
This particularly welcoming
hotel, like many buildings on
the Ile-Saint-Louis, is a lovely
seventeenth-century house.
You'll sleep close to the Seine
in small, pretty rooms
decorated with bright fabrics
and painted furniture. No
restaurant.

Duc
de Saint-Simon

7th arr. - 14, rue Saint-
Simon
45 48 35 66,
fax 45 48 68 25
*Open year-round. 5 stes 1,500-
1,900 F. 29 rms 1,000-1,500 F.
Bkfst 70 F. Air cond. in 8 rms. No
cards.*
Set back from the street
between two gardens, this
quiet, elegant nineteenth-cen-

tury building houses a most
appealing hotel. Fully
renovated by its Swedish
owners, it provides discreet
luxury and comfort, with antiques, fine paintings and objets
d'art, good lighting and an enchanting decor. The four
rooms on the second floor
have terraces that overlook
the garden. There is a bar, but
no restaurant.

Ducs d'Anjou

1st arr. - 1, rue Saint-Op-
portune
42 36 92 24,
fax 42 36 16 63
*Open year-round. 38 rms 390-
840 F. Bkfst 42 F.*
Located on the delightful
small place Sainte-Opportune,
this ancient building has been
restored from top to bottom.
The rooms are small (as are the
bathrooms) but quiet; rooms
61 and 62 are larger, and can
comfortably accommodate
three people. Rooms over-
looking the courtyard are a bit
gloomy. No restaurant.

Elysée

8th arr. - 12, rue des
Saussaies
42 65 29 25,
fax 42 64 64 28
*Open year-round. 2 stes 1,250-
1,450 F. 30 rms 540-950 F. Bkfst
60 F. Air cond. in 2 rms. No pets.*
An intimate, tastefully
renovated hotel where you
will receive a most pleasant
welcome. All the rooms are
different; the two suites under
the eaves are particularly in
demand.

Ermitage Hôtel

18th arr. - 24, rue
Lamarck
42 64 79 22,
fax 42 64 10 33
*Open year-round. 12 rms 320-
420 F. No pets. No cards.*
This charming hotel oc-
cupies a little white building
behind the Sacré-Cœur. Personalized decor in each room;
pretty little bathrooms. There
is a garden and terrace for

relaxing after a busy day.
Friendly reception.

Etoile Park Hôtel

17th arr. - 10, av. Mac-
Mahon
42 67 69 63,
fax 43 80 18 99
*Open year-round. 28 rms 455-
710 F. Bkfst 49 F.*
Modern decorated in un-
derstated good taste, this hotel
offers refined but somehow
cold guest rooms. Well-
designed bathrooms. Ex-
tremely good-humored
reception.

Etoile-Pereire 🌲🌶

17th arr. - 146, bd
Pereire
42 67 60 00,
fax 42 67 02 90
*Open year-round. 5 stes 900 F.
21 rooms 500-700 F. Bkfst 50 F.
No pets.*
Attention to detail is a prior-
ity at this welcoming hotel.
Located at the back of a quiet
courtyard, the spacious rooms
are most attractive. More than
twenty different varieties of
delicious jams are served at
breakfast. Both the
atmosphere and service are
charming and cheerful. No
restaurant.

Ferrandi 🌲🌶

6th arr. - 92, rue du
Cherche-Midi
42 22 97 40,
fax 45 44 89 97
*Open year-round. 1 ste 850-
1,250 F. 41 rms 440-950 F. Bkfst
60 F. Parking.*
In a quiet street near
Montparnasse, with a reception area that matches the
charm of the rooms. Some of
the guest rooms have four-
poster beds, others a fireplace.
All have good bathrooms
(hairdryer) and double-glazing. Delightful reception.

Garden Elysée

16th arr. - 12, rue Saint-
Didier

47 55 01 11,
fax 47 27 79 24
Open year-round. 48 rms 800-1,600 F. Restaurant. Half-board 800-1,560 F. Bkfst 80 F. Air cond. No pets. Parking.
Located in a new building set back from the street are elegant, unusually spacious rooms that overlook a bucolic garden (where breakfast is served on warm days). The 1930s decor is fresh and appealing, and the equipment is particularly fine (satellite television, individual safes, Jacuzzi).

 ### Hameau de Passy

16th arr. - 48, rue de Passy
42 88 47 55,
fax 42 30 83 72
Open year-round. 32 rms 480-560 F. Bkfst 25 F.
Tucked away in a flower-filled cul-de-sac, this exceptionally quiet hotel was modernized in 1990. Plain, comfortable rooms, some connecting, all overlook the garden. Smiling service and reception.

L'Hôtel

6th arr. - 13, rue des Beaux-Arts
43 25 27 22,
fax 43 25 64 81
Open year-round. 3 stes 2,700-3,500 F. 24 rms 900-2,100 F. Bkfst 90 F. Restaurant. Air cond.
The little effort given to renovation explains the slightly faded character of the rooms in this delightful Directoire-style building—whether it's number 16, the room once occupied by Oscar Wilde, the Imperial room (decorated in a neo-Egyptian style), the Cardinale room (swathed in purple) or number 36, which contains the Art Deco furniture from the home of music-hall star Mistinguett. The seventh floor houses two lovely suites. Despite the dog-eared decor, the atmosphere here reproduces that of a private home and is truly unlike

what one usually finds in a hotel. Restaurant: Le Bélier, see *Restaurants*, and piano bar on the premises.

 ### Hôtel du Jeu de Paume

4th arr. - 54, rue Saint-Louis-en-l'Ile
43 26 14 18,
fax 40 46 02 76
Open year-round. 32 rms 770-1,200 F. Bkfst 70 F. No pets.
This is a seventeenth-century building with a splendid wood-and-stone interior, featuring a glass elevator that ferries guests to their bright, quiet rooms. There is a sunny little garden, too.

 ### Hôtel Left Bank

6th arr. - 9, rue de l'Ancienne-Comédie
43 54 01 70,
fax 43 26 17 14
Open year-round. 1 ste 1,100 F. 30 rms 850-950 F. Bkfst 25 F. Air cond.
An eighteenth-century building, with loads of charm. The tasteful but rather repetitive decor features custom-made walnut furniture in Louis XIII style, lace bedcovers, brass lamps and marble bathrooms.

 ### Hôtel du Léman

9th arr. - 20, rue de Trévise
42 46 50 66,
fax 48 24 27 59
Open year-round. 24 rms 370-710 F. Bkfst 40 F.
This charming, out-of-the-ordinary small hotel has been tastefully modernized. Tuscany marble inlays enhance the modern decor in the lobby. The rooms are pleasantly decorated with attractive bedside lamps and original drawings and watercolors. Some have king-size beds. Generous buffet breakfast served in the vaulted basement.

 ### Lenox

7th arr. - 9, rue de l'Université

42 96 10 95,
fax 42 61 52 83
Open year-round. 2 stes 840 F. 32 rms 510-710 F. Bkfst 45 F. No pets.
These petite but most attractive rooms were recently renovated with elegant wallpaper and stylish furniture; numbers 22, 32 and 42 are the most enchanting. On the top floor are two duplexes with exposed beams and flower-filled balconies. No restaurant, but cold meals may be served in the rooms.

 ### Hôtel Lido

8th arr. - 4, pass. de la Madeleine
42 66 27 37,
fax 42 66 61 23
Open year-round. 32 rms 730-830 F.
A laudable establishment, situated between the Madeleine and the place de la Concorde. The lobby is most elegant, with Oriental rugs on the floor and tapestries on the stone walls. The guest rooms, decorated in pink, blue or cream, have comfortable beds with white lace covers, modern bathrooms and double-glazed windows. The staff is thoughtful and courteous.

 ### Lutèce

4th arr. - 65, rue Saint-Louis-en-l'Ile
43 26 23 52,
fax 43 29 60 25
Open year-round. 23 rms 590-740 F. Bkfst 42 F. No pets. No cards.
A tasteful, small hotel for people who love Paris, this handsome old house has some twenty rooms (there are two charming mansards on the upper floor), with whitewashed walls and wooden ceiling beams, decorated with bright, cheerful fabrics. The bathrooms are small but modern and impeccable. The lobby features lavish bouquets and a stone fireplace which is often used in winter. No restaurant.

Hôtel Moulin

9th arr. - 39, rue Fontaine
42 81 93 25,
fax 40 16 09 90
Open year-round. 2 stes 940 F. 48 rms 520-690 F. Bkfst 50 F. No pets.

A hotel full of charm and surprises near the place Pigalle, with its appealing Pompeiian-style lobby and rooms of varying sizes (some are extended by a small terrace overlooking the inner courtyards). An excellent buffet-style breakfast is served until noon. No restaurant.

Majestic

16th arr. - 29, rue Dumont-d'Urville
45 00 83 70,
fax 45 01 21 50
Open year-round. 3 stes 1,600 F-1,800 F. 27 rms 1,000-1,300 F. Bkfst 55 F. Air cond. in 14 rms.

Some rooms are awaiting redecoration, but all boast comfortable beds, thick carpeting and on the top floor, a lovely penthouse features a small balcony filled with flowers. Old-World atmosphere. No restaurant.

Les Marronniers

6th arr. - 21, rue Jacob
43 25 30 60,
fax 40 46 83 56
Open year-round. 37 rms 440-690 F. Bkfst 45 F. No pets. No cards.

Set back a bit from the rue Jacob, this delightful hotel boasts a small garden where breakfast is served. Chose a room just above this garden, or one of the rather bizarre but absolutely adorable (and bright) attic rooms on the seventh floor, which have views of the belfry of Saint-Germain-des-Prés. No television, no radio: your tranquillity is assured!

Notre-Dame Hôtel

5th arr. - 1, quai St-Michel
43 54 20 43,
fax 43 26 61 75
Open year-round. 3 stes 1,030 F. 26 rms 570-770 F. Bkfst 35F.

Situated in a noisy area, but the hotel is protected by efficient double-glazing. The sixth floor houses three split-level attic rooms with red carpeting, rustic furniture and a mezzanine that affords superb views over Notre-Dame and the Seine.

Panthéon

5th arr. - 19, pl. du Panthéon
43 54 32 95,
fax 43 26 64 65
Open year-round. 34 rms 500-700 F. Bkfst 35 F. No pets.

A clever use of mirrors makes the entrance and lounge seem bigger. The elegant rooms are quite spacious, decorated in Louis XVI or Louis-Philippe style, with fabric wallcoverings in pastel colors. Room 33 has a four-poster bed; all rooms are equipped with minibars and cable television.

Regent's Garden Hôtel

17th arr. - 6, rue Pierre-Demours
45 74 07 30,
fax 40 55 01 42
Open year-round. 39 rms 620-900 F. Bkfst 36 F. Parking.

This handsome Second Empire building, just a stone's throw from the place de l'Etoile, offers large, nicely proportioned rooms with high, ornate ceilings. Comfortable and well kept, the hotel also boasts a gorgeous flower garden. No restaurant.

Relais Christine

6th arr. - 3, rue Christine
43 26 71 80,
fax 43 26 89 38
Open year-round. 17 stes 1,950-2,500 F. 34 rms 1,300-1,450 F. Bkfst 80 F. Air cond. No pets. Valet parking.

This sixteenth-century cloister was transformed into a luxury hotel in the early 1980s. While it has retained some of the peace of its earlier vocation, the hotel now boasts all the comfort and elegance of the present age, from double-glazing to perfect service. The rooms are all decorated in individual styles, with Provençal prints and pink Portuguese marble baths. The best rooms are the duplexes and the ground-floor room with private terrace, but all are spacious, comfortable, quiet and air conditioning, with marble bathrooms. Courteous reception. No restaurant.

Relais Saint-Germain

6th arr. - 9, carrefour de l'Odéon
43 29 12 05,
fax 46 33 45 30
Open year-round. 1 ste 1,790 F. 10 rms 1,190-1,380 F. Bkfst incl. Air cond.

About ten large rooms, all different from one another, are marvelously decorated in a refined and luxurious manner, with superb furniture, lovely fabrics, exquisite lighting and beautiful, perfectly equipped marble bathrooms. The tall, double-glazed windows open onto the lively Odéon intersection. You will surely fall in love with Paris staying at this tiny jewel of an establishment. No restaurant.

Saint-Grégoire

6th arr. - 43, rue de l'Abbé-Grégoire
45 48 23 23,
fax 45 48 33 95
Open year-round. 1 ste 1,000-1,200 F. 19 rms 720-1,200 F. Bkfst 60 F. Air cond. in 2 rms. No pets.

The cozy lounge has a fireplace and there's also a small garden. The rooms are painted in attractive shades of yellow and pink, with matching chintz curtains, white damask bedspreads and some fine antique furniture. Double-glazing and modern bathrooms. Perfect breakfasts.

Saint-Louis

4th arr. - 75, rue Saint-Louis-en-l'Ile
46 34 04 80,
fax 46 34 02 13
Open year-round. 21 rms 620-720 F. Bkfst 42 F. No cards.
Elegant simplicity characterizes this appealing hotel, where attention to detail is evident in the gorgeous flower arrangements

---

For whom the clock tolls

The first public clock in Paris, dating from 1370, is still ticking away on a turret of the *Conciergerie* (a medieval fortress on the Ile de la Cité). The clock's darkest hour was during the Revolution, when its chimes told thousands of unfortunate inmates of this palace-turned-prison that their time was up. Prisoners condemned at the courthouse next door spent their last night at the Conciergerie before heading to the guillotine at dawn. Among the famous victims were Queen Marie-Antoinette and the revolutionary leaders Danton and Robespierre.

---

and polished antiques. Small, perfectly soundproof rooms offer comfortable beds and thick carpeting underfoot. Modern bathrooms, but no elevator. No restaurant.

Saint-Louis Marais

4th arr. - 1, rue Charles-V
48 87 87 04,
fax 48 87 33 26
Open year-round. 16 rms 490-690 F. Bkfst 37 F. No pets. No pets.
Reasonable prices and a delightful reception at this former convent annex in the heart of historic Paris. Each room is different, but all are charming and comfortable.

Saint-Merry

4th arr. - 78, rue de la Verrerie
42 78 14 15,
fax 40 29 06 82
Open year-round. 12 rms 400-1,000 F. Bkfst 40 F. No pets. No cards.
A former presbytery, this seventeenth-century building is home to an original collection of Gothic furniture, which the owner has been buying at auctions for over 30 years. Unusually large rooms with bathrooms not much bigger than closets, and no television. But the charm of the place is such that you have to book well in advance during the summer. Renovation work is currently being done.

Hôtel des Saints-Pères

6th arr. - 65, rue des Saints-Pères
45 44 50 00,
fax 45 44 90 83
Open year-round. 3 stes 1,600 F. 37 rms 400-1,200 F. Bkfst 50 F. Air cond. No pets.
Situated in two buildings, with all the elegantly furnished rooms overlooking a garden. Suite 205 is particularly attractive. Professional service.

Sainte-Beuve

6th arr. - 9, rue Sainte-Beuve
45 48 20 07,
fax 45 48 67 52
Open year-round. 1 ste 1,600 F. 22 rms 600-1,250 F. Bkfst 80 F. No pets.
The Sainte-Beuve is a tasteful, harmonious example of the neo-Palladian style of decoration promoted, most notably, by David Hicks. In the guest rooms tender colors, chintzes and the odd antique create a soothing atmosphere. Most attractive too are the marble-and-tile bathrooms, and the elegant lobby with its comfortable sofas arranged around the fireplace. No restaurant.

Select Hôtel

5th arr. - 1, pl. de la Sorbonne
46 34 14 80,
fax 46 34 51 79
Open year-round. 1 ste 980-1,300 F. 67 rms 490-860 F. Bkfst 30 F. Air cond. in 45 rms.
A glass-roofed atrium with a plethora of plants has been built at the heart of this hotel next door to the Sorbonne. The pleasant, spacious rooms are functionally furnished. Generous buffet breakfast.

Solférino

7th arr. - 91, rue de Lille
47 05 85 54,
fax 45 55 51 16
Closed Dec. 23-Jan. 3. 32 rms 245-598 F. Bkfst 35 F. Air cond. No pets.
Almost opposite the Musée d'Orsay, here are simple rooms done in fresh colors, with bath or shower. There is a charming little lounge, a sky-lit breakfast room and charming ornaments everywhere: The Solférino is both relaxing and pleasantly antiquated. Friendly reception. No restaurant.

Suède
7th arr. - 31, rue Vaneau
47 05 18 65,
fax 47 05 69 27
Open year-round. 1 ste 1,050 F.
40 rms 540-850 F. Bkfst 50 F. No
pets.
Done in tones of gray in a refined but rather austere Empire style, the guest rooms are quiet and nicely equipped. From the third floor and up you'll have a view of the foliage and the parties given in the Matignon gardens. No restaurant. Bar and snack service from 6:30 a.m. to 10 p.m.

Tamise
1st arr. - 4, rue d'Alger
42 60 51 54,
fax 42 86 89 97
Open year-round. 19 rms 450-650 F. No pets.
Designed by the architect Visconti and situated just 20 yards from the Tuileries Gardens, this tiny establishment offers authentic luxury (note the pretty English furniture—in keeping with the hotel's name which is French for "Thames") at astonishingly low rates.

Université
7th arr. - 22, rue de l'Université
42 61 09 39,
fax 42 60 40 84
Open year-round. 27 rms 600-1,400 F. Bkfst 50 F. No pets. No cards.
Comfortable beds and modern bathrooms are featured in an intelligently renovated seventeenth-century residence that is ever so appealing with its beams, half-timbering and period furniture.

Varenne
7th arr. - 44, rue de Bourgogne
45 51 45 55,
fax 45 51 86 63
Open year-round. 24 rms 470-630 F. Bkfst 37 F.
A cheerful reception is always to be had at this small hotel whose provincial air is

underscored by a courtyard filled with flowers and trees (where breakfast is served on sunny days). Street-side rooms have double windows. No restaurant.

La Villa Maillot
16th arr. - 143, av. de Malakoff
45 01 25 22,
fax 45 00 60 61
Open year-round. 3 stes 2,200-2,400 F. 39 rms 1,680-1,800 F. Bkfst 100 F. Restaurant. Air cond. Valet parking.
Formerly an embassy, this recent conversion is sophisticated and modern: an exemplary establishment. The very comfortable rooms, equipped with kitchenettes, have a gray and beige color scheme that gives them an Art Deco feel. Pink-marble bathrooms; wonderful breakfast buffet served in an indoor garden.

PRACTICAL

Alison
8th arr. - 21, rue de Surène
42 65 54 00,
fax 42 65 08 17
Open year-round. 35 rms 420-690 F. Bkfst 45 F. No pets.
The 35 modern, functional rooms are bright and cheerful, with tidy, tiled bathrooms. Bar and lounge on the ground floor. Two mansard rooms on the top floor can be combined to form a suite. No restaurant.

Ambassade
16th arr. - 79, rue Lauriston
45 53 41 15,
fax 45 53 30 80
Closed Aug. 38 rms 440-550 F. Bkfst 35 F.
The rooms behind a lovely façade are decorated with printed wallpaper and lacquered cane furniture. Small gray-marble bathrooms. Ask for a room overlooking

the courtyard and you'll think you're in the country. No restaurant.

Aurore Montmartre
9th arr. - 76, rue de Clichy
48 74 85 56,
fax 42 81 09 54
Open year-round. 24 rms 370-420 F. Bkfst 35 F.
A simple hotel offering smallish rooms, soundproofed and perfectly kept. Minibar. Friendly reception.

Beaugrenelle St-Charles
15th arr. - 82, rue St-Charles
45 78 61 63,
fax 45 49 04 38
Open year-round. 51 rms 350-440 F. Bkfst 32 F.
Near the Beaugrenelle shopping complex, this friendly hotel provides modern, well-equipped rooms decorated in restful colors. Breakfast is served in the rooms upon request. Good value.

Bergère
9th arr. - 34, rue Bergère
47 70 34 34,
fax 47 70 36 36
Open year-round. 134 rms 490-890 F. Bkfst 45 F.
All the quiet rooms (most of which overlook a courtyard garden) have been freshened up and modernized, including the bathrooms. The setting is modern and simple, with country-style furniture. Fine equipment.

Le Bois
16th arr. - 11, rue du Dôme
45 00 31 96,
fax 45 00 90 05
Open year-round. 41 rms 395-58 F. Bkfst 40 F.
This simple hotel offers excellent value. In addition to a warm welcome, guests find small, well-kept rooms, which were attractively redecorated

in 1990 with Laura Ashley fabrics and wallpaper.

 ### Hôtel des Chevaliers

3rd arr. - 30, rue de Turenne
42 72 73 47,
fax 42 72 54 10
Open year-round. 24 rms 530-580 F. Bkfst 40 F. Parking.
In the heart of the Marais, a small hotel frequented by film people. The rooms are bright and pleasantly furnished; some are perfectly quiet. Warm reception.

 ### Hôtel du Collège de France

5th arr. - 7, rue Thénard
43 26 78 36,
fax 46 34 58 29
Open year-round. 29 rms 480-530 F. Bkfst 30 F. Air cond. No pets.
The simple rooms of Hôtel du Collège de France, located on a quiet little street, are tidy and comfortable. Most charming are the garret rooms, with their wooden beams and a view of the towers of Notre-Dame. No restaurant.

 ### Eber Monceau-Courcelles

17th arr. - 18, rue Léon-Jost
46 22 60 70,
fax 47 63 01 01
Open year-round. 5 stes 995-1,260 F. 13 rms 580-630 F. Bkfst 50 F. No pets.
This former bordello has been totally renovated, and "adopted," so to speak, by people in fashion, photo and film. Rooms are on the small side, but they're tastefully decorated and furnished, with good bathrooms. A large duplex on the top floor has a lovely terrace. Breakfast is served on the patio in summer. No restaurant.

 ### Etoile

17th arr. - 3, rue de l'Etoile
43 80 36 94,
fax 44 40 49 19
Open year-round. 25 rms 820-920 F. Bkfst 50 F.
L'Etoile is strategically located between the place de l'Etoile and the place des Ternes. Rooms are clean, modern and functional (renovated in 1991). A little expensive for the level of comfort and service. No restaurant. Courteous reception.

 ### Favart

2nd arr. - 5, rue de Marivaux
42 97 59 83
Open year-round. 37 rms 495-600 F. Bkfst incl.
Goya stayed here when he fled to Paris in 1824. Set on a quiet square opposite the Opéra Comique, this hotel exudes a certain faded charm. Reasonable rates.

 ### Hôtel Flora

10th arr. - 1-3, cour de la Ferme-St-Lazare
48 24 84 84,
fax 48 00 91 03
Open year-round. 45 rms 525-610 F. Bkfst 40 F.
Near the Gare du Nord and the Gare de l'Est, the Flora offers pleasant, well-equipped modern rooms decorated in pastel shades.

 ### Folkestone

8th arr. - 9, rue Castellane
42 65 73 09,
fax 42 65 64 09
Open year-round. 50 rms 680-950 F. Bkfst 45 F.
The beamed rooms, decorated with fabric wallcovering or Japanese wallpaper, have Art Deco armchairs and comfortable beds. Generous buffet breakfasts, with sweet rolls and pastries baked on the premises. Gracious reception.

 ### Fondary

15th arr. - 30, rue Fondary
45 75 14 75,
fax 45 75 84 42
Open year-round. 20 rms 365-405 F. Bkfst 38 F. Air cond.
A neat and tidy hotel with a pretty pastel decor. Service is warm and efficient. No restaurant.

 ### Grands Hommes

5th arr. - 17, pl. du Panthéon
46 34 19 60,
fax 43 26 67 32
Open year-round. 32 rms 500-700 F. Bkfst 35 F. No pets.
Opposite the Panthéon. The fairly spacious rooms are decorated with pink, cream or floral fabric wallcoverings. Room 22 has a four-poster bed, 60 and 61 boast balconies and terrific views. Cable television, minibar. The staff is pleasant and efficient.

 ### Ibis Jemmapes

10th arr. - 12, rue Louis-Blanc
42 01 21 21,
fax 42 08 21 40
Open year-round. 1 ste 1,000-1,200 F. 50 rms 370-445 F. Bkfst 35 F. Garage parking.
Near the Canal Saint-Martin, this well-designed business hotel is perfectly tailored for a busy clientele attending conventions and seminars. The rooms (which we found to be on the chilly side) are spacious, modern and fully equipped. Generous breakfast buffet. No restaurant.

 ### Ibis Paris-Bercy

12th arr. - 77, rue de Bercy
43 42 91 91,
fax 43 42 34 79
Open year-round. 368 rms 455 F. Bkfst 35 F. Restaurant. Half-board 640 F. Parking.
This very professional establishment, surely one of the best in the chain, boasts a superb marble lobby. Guest rooms have a blue-and-white decor and dark carpeting. One room on each floor is

reserved for the disabled. Plain, well-kept bathrooms.

Istria

14th arr. - 29, rue Campagne-Première
43 20 91 82,
fax 43 22 48 45
Open year-round. 26 rms 440-540 F. Bkfst 40 F.
Elm furniture and pastel colors grace the rooms and bathrooms of this well-kept hotel, where Mayakovski, Man Ray and Marcel Duchamp have slept. The building was fully modernized in 1988.

Le Jardin des Plantes

5th arr. - 5, rue Linné
47 07 06 20,
fax 47 07 62 74
Open year-round. 33 rms 390-640 F. Bkfst 40 F. Restaurant. Air cond.
This hotel, set in a quiet street behind the Botanical Gardens, has appealing, delightfully decorated rooms—flowers and floral motifs abound. On the sixth floor, there is a terrace with a lovely view; in the basement, there is a sauna and an ironing room. Restaurant-tea room on the ground floor.

Les Jardins d'Eiffel

7th arr. - 8, rue Amélie
47 05 46 21,
fax 45 55 28 08
Open year-round. 44 rms 530-850 F. Air cond. in 20 rms. Garage parking.
Some rooms are awaiting renovation, but 44 have already been redecorated in attractive colors and re-equipped with double-glazing, minibars, hairdryers and trouser presses. The upper floors overlook the Eiffel Tower. Sauna, many services, charming reception. No restaurant.

> *A red hotel ranking denotes a place with charm.*

Le Laumière

19th arr. - 4, rue Petit
42 06 10 77,
fax 42 06 72 50
Open year-round. 54 rms 230-350 F. Bkfst 30 F. Parking.
This meticulously kept small hotel is located a few steps away from the Buttes-Chaumont park, in a district where modern hotels are not exactly plentiful. Convenient to the La Villette exhibition center. Rooms are well soundproofed and moderately priced. No restaurant.

Longchamp

16th arr. - 68, rue de Longchamp
47 27 13 48,
fax 47 55 68 26
Open year-round. 23 rms 580-750 F. Bkfst 50 F.
The quiet, comfortable rooms are equipped with minibar, direct telephone and television with two channels in English. Intimate atmosphere, charming reception.

La Louisiane

6th arr. - 60, rue de Seine
43 29 59 30,
fax 46 34 23 87
Open year-round. 1 ste 600 F. 77 rms 300-600 F. Bkfst 25 F. No pets.
An artistic clientele (writers, dancers, models, musicians) frequents this large Art Deco hotel that stands smack in the middle of the Buci street market. Regulars know they will find a warm reception, and rooms that are simple and comfortable, either painted or hung with Japanese wallpaper.

Luxembourg

6th arr. - 4, rue de Vaugirard
43 25 35 90,
fax 43 26 60 84
Open year-round. 34 rms 450-685 F. Bkfst 40 F. Air cond.
Near the Luxembourg Gardens, in the heart of the Latin Quarter. The pleasant rooms

have minibar, hairdryer, and individual safe; small bathrooms. Gracious reception by the charming owner.

Magellan

17th arr. - 17, rue Jean-Baptiste-Dumas
45 72 44 51,
fax 40 68 90 36
Open year-round. 75 rms 390-515 F. Bkfst 35 F. No pets. Parking.
Business people will appreciate the quiet and comfort of the rooms (more functional than luxurious) in this creditable hotel, known for the regularity and quality of its service. Attractive garden. No restaurant.

Marais

3rd arr. - 2 bis, rue de Commines
48 87 78 27,
fax 48 87 09 01
Open year-round. 39 rms 320-480 F. Bkfst 30 F.
A simple, neat hotel between Bastille and République offers small, bright, modern rooms. Connecting rooms on the first, second and fifth floors are ideal for families.

Hôtel de Neuville

17th arr. - 3, place Verniquet
43 80 26 30,
fax 43 80 38 55
Open year-round. 28 rms 610-680 F. Bkfst 40 F. Air cond. Restaurant.
This pleasing lovely hotel on a quiet square offers simple rooms, tastefully decorated with lovely floral fabrics and equipped with fine bathrooms. Pleasant salon/winter garden and basement restaurant, Les Tartines.

Nouvel Hôtel

12th arr. - 24, av. du Bel-Air
43 43 01 81,
fax 43 44 64 13
Open year-round. 28 rms 275-490 F. Bkfst 40 F. No pets.
The rooms of the Nouvel Hôtel are peaceful and attrac-

tive, though rather eclectically furnished (the prettiest is number 9, on the same level as the garden). Good bathrooms; hospitable reception. No restaurant.

Novanox

6th arr. - 155, bd du Montparnasse
46 33 63 60,
fax 43 26 61 72
Open year-round. 27 rms 540-660 F. Bkfst 45 F. No pets.
The owner of this hotel, opened in 1989, has made a judicious mixture of 1920s, 1930s and 1950s styles for the decor. On the ground floor, a large, cheerful room serves as lounge, bar and breakfast room.

Novotel Bercy

12th arr. - 85, rue de Bercy
43 42 30 00,
fax 43 45 30 60
Open year-round. 1 ste 1,170-1,300 F. 128 rms 690-730 F. Bkfst 55 F. Restaurant. Air cond.
An ultramodern steel-and-glass structure, right next door to the Bercy sports complex. The accommodations are furnished and equipped to the chain's standards, with minibars, direct telephones and room service from 6 a.m. to midnight. In addition to meeting rooms and business facilities, there is a large terrace, used for receptions in fine weather.

Novotel Paris Les Halles

1st arr. - 8 pl. Marguerite-de-Navarre
42 21 31 31,
fax 40 26 05 79
Open year-round. 5 stes 1,500 F. 280 rms 790-860 F. Bkfst 55 F. Restaurant. Air cond.
This ultramodern building constructed of stone, glass and zinc is located in the heart of the former market district, near the Pompidou Center and the Forum des Halles. The huge rooms offer perfect com-

fort, but their air conditioning (alas!) prevents one from opening the windows. The restaurant is open from 6 a.m. to midnight, and there is a bar on a terrace. The conference rooms can be tailored to size by means of movable partitions. Other services include a travel agency and a duty-free shop.

Odéon Hôtel

6th arr. - 3, rue de l'Odéon
43 25 90 67,
fax 43 25 55 98
Open year-round. 34 rms 650-1,000 F. Bkfst 50 F. Air cond. No pets.
The 34 smallish but pleasant and beautifully furnished rooms in this listed building have recently been redecorated. The hotel is located on a strategic street between the Odéon theater and the square of the same name. No restaurant.

Orléans Palace Hôtel

14th arr. - 185, bd Brune
45 39 68 50,
fax 45 43 65 64
Open year-round. 92 rms 470-520 F. Bkfst 45 F.
A quiet and comfortable traditional hotel that offers good value. The well-equipped and soundproofed rooms are in need of redecoration. Indoor garden.

Ouest Hôtel

17th arr. - 165, rue de Rome
42 27 50 29,
fax 42 27 27 40
Open year-round. 50 rms 300-380 F. Bkfst 30 F.
This cozy establishment has thick carpeting, efficient double windows and modest, modern rooms that are well maintained. No restaurant.

Parc Montsouris

14th arr. - 4, rue du Parc-Montsouris

45 89 09 72,
fax 45 80 92 72
Open year-round. 7 stes 470 F. 35 rms 310-480 F. Bkfst 35 F. Air cond.
This small, quiet hotel, recently modernized, features plainly furnished white rooms with bright, new bathrooms. The lovely Parc Montsouris is just steps away.

Passy Eiffel

16th arr. - 10, rue de Passy
45 25 55 66,
fax 42 88 89 88
Open year-round. 50 rms 500-620 F. Bkfst 30 F.
Five stories of spotless, comfortable rooms (though not all equally attractive); four are large enough to suit families. A pleasant breakfast room faces a tiny, glassed-enclosed indoor garden. No restaurant.

Perreyve

6th arr. - 63, rue Madame
45 48 35 01,
fax 42 84 03 30
Open year-round. 30 rms 415-500 F. Bkfst 35 F. No pets.
Near the lovely, leafy Luxembourg Gardens, the Perreyve's 30 comfortable rooms have small but faultless bathrooms. There is a small salon on the main floor with mahogany furniture and inviting armchairs. No restaurant.

Hôtel de la Place du Louvre

1st arr. - 21, rue Prêtres-St-Germain-Auxerrois
42 33 78 68,
fax 42 33 09 95
Open year-round. 20 rms 480-800 F. No pets.
This totally renovated hotel is decorated with paintings and sculptures throughout. Fairly large rooms, all comfortably furnished and with good bathrooms. Breakfast is served in a vaulted cellar that dates from the sixteenth century. The owner gives a warm welcome.

Hôtel du Pré

9th arr. - 10, rue P.-Sémard
42 81 37 11,
fax 40 23 98 28
Open year-round. 41 rms 395-490 F. Bkfst 35 F.
Actually two hotels, comfortable and close to the Gare du Nord and the Gare de l'Est. Downstairs, guests have the use of a bar, a bright lounge and a pleasant breakfast room. The guest rooms sport painted wood paneling or Japanese wallpaper, paired with cane and bamboo furniture. Good bathrooms.

Queen's Hôtel

16th arr. - 4, rue Bastien-Lepage
42 88 89 85,
fax 40 50 67 52
Open year-round. 23 rms 290-510 F. Bkfst 40 F. No pets.
For an "English" atmosphere and rather petite but delightful modern rooms, try this modest little hotel with a lovely white façade and flower-filled balconies. Excellent reception. No restaurant.

Regyn's Montmartre

18th arr. - 18, pl. des Abbesses
42 54 45 21,
fax 42 54 45 21
Open year-round. 22 rms 360-440 F. Bkfst 38 F.
Each of the rooms in this excellent renovated hotel has a direct telephone line, radio, color TV and bathroom; the decor is simple but pleasant. Charming reception. No restaurant.

Le Relais du Louvre

1st arr. - 19, rue Prêtres-St-Germain-Auxerrois
40 41 96 42,
fax 40 41 96 42
Open year-round. 2 stes 1,100-1,400 F. 18 rms 570-880 F. Bkfst 50 F.
The original façade of this historic building opposite the

Tuileries Gardens has been preserved, but the interior is fully modernized. The rooms, decorated by Constance de Castelbajac, overflow with charm. Those with numbers ending in 1 are slightly smaller than the rest. Wonderfully hospitable reception.

Résidence des Gobelins

13th arr. - 9, rue des Gobelins
47 07 26 90,
fax 43 31 44 05
Open year-round. 32 rms 350-450 F. Bkfst 35 F. No pets.
A delightful small hotel not far from the Latin Quarter and Montparnasse. The warm welcome of the young owners merits a detour. Rooms are decorated in blue, green or orange, a different color for each floor.

Résidence Saint-Lambert

15th arr. - 5, rue E.-Gibez
48 28 63 14,
fax 45 33 45 50
Open year-round. 48 rms 380-550 F. Bkfst 38 F.
This pleasant, quiet hotel near the exhibition center at Porte de Versailles has tidy, smallish but nicely outfitted rooms, some overlooking the garden. A laundry and bar are on the premises.

Résidence Trousseau

11th arr. - 13, rue Trousseau
48 05 55 55,
fax 48 05 83 97
Open year-round. 9 stes 780-1,300 F. 57 rms 354-510 F. Garage parking.
Completed in 1989, this self-service hotel is situated in a quiet side street. Pleasant, modern decor and all mod cons: sink, refrigerator, electric hotplates, dishes, coffee machine and microwave oven.

Riboutté-Lafayette

9th arr. - 5, rue Riboutté
47 70 62 36,
fax 48 00 91 50
Open year-round. 24 rms 360-450 F. Bkfst 28 F.
This small and charming hotel faces rue La Fayette and is located within walking distance of the Opéra, the Bourse and the *grands boulevards.* Its quiet rooms are small and attractive. Very hospitable management.

Royal Médoc

9th arr. - 14, rue Geoffroy-Marie
47 70 37 33,
fax 47 70 34 88
Open year-round. 41 rms 550-680 F. Bkfst incl. No pets.
Ten minutes away from the Opéra and close to the main boulevards, this modern, functional hotel (with tidy rooms, direct telephone lines and a helpful, multilingual staff) near the Bourse (Stock Exchange) is perfect for international business travelers. No restaurant.

Saint-Dominique

7th arr. - 62, rue Saint-Dominique
47 05 51 44,
fax 47 05 81 28
Open year-round. 34 rms 450-690 F. Bkfst 40 F. Air cond.
This most modest of the three "Centre Ville" hotels is also the most charming, and the location is excellent. The delightful little rooms are homey and comfortable. No restaurant.

Hôtel de Saint-Germain

6th arr. - 50, rue du Four
45 48 91 64,
fax 45 48 46 22
Open year-round. 30 rms 500-690 F. Bkfst 50 F. Air cond. in 5 rms. Parking.
This small hotel with its delightful decor and English furniture offers round-the-clock room service, babysit-

ting and various tours of Paris (by helicopter, minibus or on foot).

Saint-Romain
1st arr. - 5-7, rue St-Roch
42 60 31 70,
fax 42 60 10 69
Open year-round. 1 ste 900-1,020 F. 33 rms 470-760 F. Bkfst 40 F. Air cond. No pets.
Recently renovated, this small hotel offers business services that many of its classier cousins do not, such as typing, photocopying, fax and telex. Simple, comfortable rooms decorated in pretty colors, and marble baths.

Sénateur
6th arr. - 10, rue de Vaugirard
43 26 08 83,
fax 46 34 04 66
Open year-round. 42 rms 550-1,080 F. Bkfst 40 F.
A comfortable, modern hotel with a huge mural and plenty of greenery brightening up the ground floor. The rooms, decorated in gray or beige, are rather impersonal. Fine views from the top floor.

Hôtel du 7e Art
4th arr. - 20, rue St-Paul
42 77 04 03,
fax 42 77 69 10
Open year-round. 22 rms 260-600 F. Bkfst 35 F.
Posters and photographs evoking the movies—known in France as the seventh art—paper the walls. Small, comfortable rooms with tiny, well-equipped bathrooms. No room service, but there is a restaurant (City Light).

La Tour d'Auvergne

9th arr. - 10, rue de La Tour d'Auvergne
48 78 61 60,
fax 49 95 99 00
Open year-round. 25 rms 550-650 F. Bkfst 45 F. Air cond. No pets.
A competently run, no-nonsense hotel. Each room has a decor from a different period;

all rooms are furnished with four-poster beds and double-glazed windows. A fine little establishment, ideal for business travelers.

Trocadéro
16th arr. - 21, rue Saint-Didier
45 53 01 82,
fax 45 53 59 56
Open year-round. 23 rms 495-595 F. Bkfst 35 F.
The smallish rooms are done up in soothing pale tones, and the bathrooms are well outfitted. The management and staff are unfailingly cheerful. Note the relatively low prices (considering the neighborhood). No restaurant.

Tim'hôtel Montmartre
18th arr. - 11, rue Ravignan
42 55 74 79,
fax 42 55 71 01
Open year-round. 63 rms 312-430 F. Brkfst 39 F.
On an adorable little square near the Bateau-Lavoir (where Picasso painted the *Demoiselles d'Avignon* this hotel gives guests a taste of Montmartre's "village" life. Book a room on the upper floors for the best views.

Utrillo
18th arr. - 7, rue A.-Bruant
42 58 13 44,
fax 42 23 93 88
Open year-round. 30 rms 280-410 F. Bkfst 35 F. No pets.
Located behind the rue Lepic in a still-typical Montmartre neighborhood, this former boarding house has been totally renovated. The new rooms feature freshly whitewashed walls, and the upholstery and bedding are done in cheerful fabrics. Clean and hospitable. No restaurant.

Vieux Marais
4th arr. - 8, rue du Plâtre
42 78 47 22,
fax 42 78 34 32
Open year-round. 30 rms 350-550 F. Bkfst 30 F. No pets.
Small, friendly hotel in a quiet street. The rooms are simply decorated and well equipped.

Villa des Artistes
6th arr. - 9, rue Grandre-Chaumière
43 26 60 86,
fax 43 54 73 70
Open year-round. 59 rms 480-780 F. Air cond. No pets.
An oasis of calm amid the urban noise and hustle. Luxury, quiet and comfort are assured in this hotel, built around a garden patio in the heart of Montparnasse. Excellent value for this neighborhood.

Wallace
15th arr. - 89, rue Fondary
45 78 83 30,
fax 40 58 19 43
Open year-round. 35 rms 530-570 F. Bkfst 40 F.
This hotel exudes old-fashioned charm. Most of its small but cheerful rooms overlook a quiet garden.

Welcome Hôtel
6th arr. - 66, rue de Seine
46 34 24 80,
fax 40 46 81 59
Open year-round. 30 rms 300-475 F. No pets. No cards.
You can almost forget the busy intersection of the nearby boulevard Saint-Germain behind the quiet-enhancing double windows in these small, cozy, tidy rooms. And if you want a taste of the bohemian life, you'll find it on the sixth floor (you can take the elevator!) where you will discover a quaint wooden-beamed attic. No restaurant.

🌲
This symbol signifies hotels that offer an exceptional degree of peace and quiet.

AIRPORT

ORLY
94396 Orly – (Val/Marne)
Paris 16 · Corbeil 17 · Villeneuve-St-Georges 12

Altea Paris-Orly

Orly-Ouest
94547 Orly-Aérogare
46 87 23 37,
fax 46 87 71 92
Open daily. 1 ste 900-1,100 F. 193 rms 600-930 F. Restaurant. Air cond. Parking.
The hotel has been recently renovated, and provides soundproof rooms decorated in lively, bright colors. Bathrooms are terrific. Rooms can be rented for the day only (10h-18h) for 220 francs. Minigolf and airport shuttle bus.

Hilton International Orly

Aérogare Orly-Sud
46 87 33 88,
fax 49 78 06 75
Open daily. 359 rms 880-1,180 F. Air cond.
Functional, comfortable rooms near the airport with a free shuttle service. Excellent facilities for conferences or seminars. Round-the-clock room service. Bar and shops.

ROISSY-EN-FRANCE
95700 Roissy-en-France – (Val/d'Oise)
Paris 26 · Meaux 36 · Senlis 28 · Chantilly 28

Holiday Inn

1, allée du Verger
34 29 30 00,
fax 34 29 90 52
Open daily. 245 rms 800-1,030 F. Restaurant. Half-board 980-1,200 F. Air cond. Heated pool. Parking.
It is situated in the old village of Roissy. Rooms are large, bright and functional. There's a health club for use by hotel guests (sauna, gym, Jacuzzi, etc). Free shuttle to the terminals and the exhibition grounds at Villepinte.

Sofitel

Aéroport
Charles-de-Gaulle
48 62 23 23,
fax 48 62 78 49
Open daily. 8 stes 1,500 F. 344 rms 850-950 F. Restaurant. Air cond. Heated pool. Tennis. Valet parking.
A comfortable airport hotel with a discothèque, sauna and coffee shop. Round-the-clock room service and a free shuttle to the airport. There are two restaurants, one with a panoramic view.

THE SUBURBS

AULNAY-SOUS-BOIS
93600 Aulnay-sous-Bois – (Seine-St-D.)
Paris 16 · Senlis 38 · Meaux 30 · St-Denis 13

Novotel

4 km NW on N 370,
carrefour de l'Europe
48 66 22 97,
fax 48 66 99 39
Open daily. 138 rms 450-490 F. Restaurant. Half-board 630-850 F. Air cond. Heated pool. Parking.
This handsome modern hotel is located near the Villepinte exhibition center. Surrounded by gardens, it is especially suitable for families. Good conference facilities.

Les Relais Bleus

Rue L.-de-Vinci
48 66 99 46,
fax 48 66 99 21
Open daily. 117 rms 260-310 F. Restaurant.
A stone's throw from the exhibition center and only minutes from Charles de Gaulle airport, this small hotel has pleasant, convenient rooms.

Hôtel de Strasbourg

43, bd de Strasbourg
48 66 60 38,
fax 48 66 15 71
Open daily. 1 ste 300-340 F. 23 rms 225-280 F. Air cond.
This small suburban hotel offers conventional rooms that are charming, comfortable and now soundproofed as well. Bar.

BAGNOLET
93170 Bagnolet – (Seine-St-D.)
Paris 6 · Meaux 41 · Lagny 27

Novotel Paris-Bagnolet

1, av. de la République
49 93 63 00,
fax 43 60 83 95
Open daily. 9 stes 950 F. 602 rms 615-660 F. Restaurant. Air cond. Heated pool. Parking.
Just outside Paris, this is a good address for seminars and conferences. The rooms are modern, functional and well soundproofed. Piano bar.

BLANC-MESNIL (LE)
93150 Blanc-Mesnil (Le) – (Seine-St-D.)
Paris 12 · Bobigny 6 · Aulnay 3

Novotel Paris-Le Bourget

2, rue J.-Perrin
48 67 48 88,
fax 45 91 08 27
Open daily. 143 rms 450-490 F. Restaurant. Half-board 580 F. Air cond. Heated pool. Parking.
Eight kilometers from the permanent science exhibition at La Villette and close to the Aeronautics and Space Museum. The rooms are bright and functional.

BOULOGNE-BILLANCOURT
92100 Boulogne-Billancourt – (Hauts/Seine)
Versailles 11

 ### Hôtel Adagio
20-22, rue des Abondances
48 25 80 80,
fax 48 25 33 13
Open daily. 75 rms 695-790 F.
Restaurant. Parking.
This modern, glass-and-concrete hotel has bright, spacious rooms fitted with every convenience and pleasantly furnished. The basement houses a vast complex of conference rooms. Brunch served on Sundays until 3 p.m.

CERGY
95000 Cergy – (Val-d'Oise)
Paris 30 - Conflans-Sainte-Honorine 7

 ### Novotel
3, av. du Parc
30 30 39 47,
fax 30 30 90 46
Open daily. 191 rms 450-490 F.
Restaurant. Air cond. Heated pool. Parking.
Twenty minutes from Paris and Versailles, this newly renovated hotel has quiet rooms and activities such as table tennis and French billiards. Special weekend rates.

CRÉTEIL
94000 Créteil – (Val/Marne)
Paris 12 - Evry 20 - Melun 35 - Lagny 26

 ### Climat
Rue des Archives
49 80 08 00,
fax 49 80 15 99
Open daily. 51 rms 320 F.
Restaurant. Parking.
This well-kept hotel offers simple but cozy rooms three minutes from the métro.

 ## Novotel Créteil-le-Lac
N 186, rue J. Gabin
42 07 91 02,
fax 48 99 03 48
Open daily. 110 rms 470-520 F.
Restaurant. Air cond. Heated pool. Parking.
The rooms in this lakeside hotel have recently been modernized. Sports complex with windsurfing nearby.

ENGHIEN
95880 Enghien – (Val-d'Oise)
Paris 18 - Argenteuil 16 - Chantilly 32

 ### Le Grand Hôtel
85, rue du Gal-de-Gaulle
34 12 80 00,
fax 34 12 73 81
Open daily. 3 stes 1,400-2,680 F.
48 rms 690-1,100 F. Restaurant.
Half-board 1,260-1,680 F. Air cond. Valet parking.
This bleak building stands in lovely grounds next to the spa. The spacious, comfortable rooms are decorated with period furniture.

EURO DISNEY
See Marne-la-Vallée

KREMLIN-BICÊTRE (LE)
94270 Kremlin-Bicêtre (Le) – (Val/Marne)
Paris 8 - Boulogne-Billancourt 10 - Versailles 22

 ### Les Relais Bleus
6, rue Voltaire
46 70 15 35,
fax 46 70 58 10
Open daily. 152 rms 340 F.
Restaurant. Half-board 450-550 F. Parking.
This hotel is a stone's throw from the Paris beltway and the Porte d'Italie. The rooms are welcoming and well equipped.

We're always happy to hear about your discoveries and receive your comments on ours. We want to give your letters the attention they deserve, so when you write to Gault Millau, please state clearly what you liked or disliked. Be concise but convincing, and take the time to argue your point.

MARNE-LA-VALLÉE
77206 Marne-la-Vallée – (Seine/Marne)
Paris 28 - Meaux 28 - Melun 40

In nearby Euro Disney
(Access by A4)
77206 Marne-la-Vallée – (Seine/Marne)

 ### Disneyland Hotel
Outside the Park
60 45 65 00,
fax 60 45 65 33
Open daily. 21 stes 3,100-8,750 F. 479 rms 1,950-2,500 F.
Air cond. Pool. Restaurant.
This enormous candy-pink Victorian pastiche is the *nec plus ultra* of Euro Disney hotels. Sumptuous suites, first-class service; but the pseudo setting and stiff atmosphere are surely not everyone's cup of tea, and the prices are simply staggering. Restaurant: California Grill, see *Restaurants*.

 ### Cheyenne Hotel
Desperado Road
60 45 62 00,
fax 49 30 71 00
Open daily. 1,000 rms 550-750 F. Restaurant.
Perhaps the most fun of all the Euro Disney hotels: fourteen separate structures recall the frontier towns of the Far West. One almost expects John Wayne to saunter down the street. Luxurious it isn't, but the rooms are tidy and spacious. Tequila and country music at the saloon, restaurant, playground for the young 'uns.

 ### New York Hotel
Outside the Park, near the lake
60 45 73 50,
fax 60 45 73 55
Open daily. 26 stes 1,600-2,750 F. 574 rms 1,100-1,600 F.
Restaurant. Pool. Tennis.
Manhattan in the 1930s is the theme, complete with skyscrapers, Wall Street and Rockefeller Center. The Art Deco guest rooms feature mahogany furniture, king-size beds and well-equipped baths.

Among the many amenities are a beauty salon, an athletic club and a conference center. Restaurant: Manhattan Club, see *Restaurants.*

 Newport Bay Club
Disney Festival
60 45 55 00,
fax 49 30 71 00
Open daily. 21 stes 1,150-2,000 F. 1,098 rms 750-1,100 F. Restaurant. Pool.
Were it not five times the size of any real New England inn, the Newport Bay Club would be an almost-convincing facsimile of an East Coast summer resort. Perhaps it is to polish up the details and make the place even more lifelike that Disney officials have decided to close the hotel (just months after the official opening) until sometime in the spring of 1993... Restaurant: Cape Cod, see *Restaurants.*

 Santa Fe Hotel
In the Park, near the Pueblos Indian village
60 45 78 00,
fax 49 30 71 00
Open daily. 1,000 rms 550-750 F. Restaurant.
Forty-two "pueblos" make up an ersatz Indian village, dotted with giant cacti; the parking lot is built to look like a drive-in movie theater. Game rooms for the children.

 Sequoia Lodge
In the Park, near Buena Vista lake
60 45 51 00,
fax 49 30 71 00
Open daily. 1,011 apts 750-1,100 F. Restaurant. Pool.
Bare stone and rough-hewn wood evoke a Rocky Mountain lodge. The sequoias have yet to reach their majestic maturity (nor will they any time soon...) but guests will find plenty of entertainment at the hotel's restaurants, shops, piano bar, or exercise room.

A red hotel ranking denotes a place with charm.

NEUILLY-SUR-SEINE
92200 Neuilly-sur-Seine – (Hauts/Seine)
Argenteuil 9 - Versailles 16

 Hôtel International de Paris
58, bd V.-Hugo
47 58 11 00,
fax 47 58 75 52
Open daily. 3 stes 1,850-3,900 F. 327 rms 850-1,300 F. Restaurant. Air cond. Parking.
A large, contemporary hotel surrounded by lawns and gardens, which has just undergone a luxurious renovation. Elegant, utterly comfortable rooms with every amenity. Sumptuous breakfast buffet.

 Neuilly Park Hôtel
23, rue M.-Michelis
46 40 11 15,
fax 46 40 14 78
Open daily. 30 rms 650-770 F. Restaurant.
One of the more recent additions Neuilly's clique of fine hotels. This is a luxurious and refined establishment with perfectly appointed rooms, an understated, soothing decor and some super bathrooms.

 Hôtel du Parc
4, bd du Parc
46 24 32 62
Open daily. 71 rms 295-450 F.
Between the Porte de Champerret and the Défense, on the Ile de la Jatte facing the Seine, is this small 1930s hotel with well-equipped, regularly renovated rooms.

NOGENT-SUR-MARNE
94130 Nogent-sur-Marne – (Val/Marne)
Paris 11 - Créteil 7 - Lagny 17 - Montreuil 5

 Nogentel
8, rue du Port
48 72 70 00,
fax 48 72 86 19
Open daily. 60 rms 540-580 F. Restaurant. Parking.
This is a modern hotel in the Nogent marina, well equipped for receptions and seminars

(250-seat auditorium). Panoramic restaurant and grill.

PONTAULT-COMBAULT
77340 Pontault-Combault – (Seine/Marne)
Paris 26 - Melun 29 - Coulommiers 41

 Saphir Hôtel
Aire des Berchères
64 43 45 47,
fax 64 40 52 43
Open daily. 21 stes 895 F. 159 rms 495-535 F. Air cond. Heated pool. Tennis. Restaurant.
A brand new hotel next to Euro-Disneyland Park. Rooms are airy, pleasant and well equipped. Facilities include conference rooms, sauna and a superb covered swimming pool. Grill. Restaurant: Le Canadel, see *Restaurants.*

PUTEAUX
92800 Puteaux – (Hauts/Seine)
Paris 10 - Versailles 14 - St-Germain-en-Laye 11

 Les Communautés
Paris-la-Défense,
in the CNIT
2, pl. de la Défense
46 92 10 10,
fax 46 92 10 50
Open daily. 6 stes 2,500-3,200 F. 141 rms 1,300 F. Air cond. Restaurant.
The hotel targets a business clientele with its huge rooms (some boast a view of the Grande Arche), luxurious bathrooms, and 24-hour room service. Restaurant: Les Communautés, see *Restaurants.*

 Dauphin
45, rue J.-Jaurès
47 73 71 63,
fax 47 75 25 20
Open daily. 30 rms 450 F. Tennis. Valet parking.
The Dauphin stands opposite the Princesse Isabelle, and is run by the same family. Generous buffet breakfasts are set up in the sitting room; guestrooms are comfortable and pretty, with cable televi-

THE LEGEND OF PARIS

The heart of Paris. Seintillating and alive. Legendary. The magic of the Etoile and of the Champs Elysées. The chic of the Faubourg Saint Honoré and the most exclusive shops in the world. □ An encounter between history and modernity... the calm elegance of the Hotel Royal Monceau. A hotel that combines the traditional refinement of Parisian architecture and furnishings with modern facilities and a quality of service which is second to none. □ Savour the superb French haute cuisine of "Le Jardin," and feast on the finest Italian fare served in the sumptuous "Ristorante Carpaccio." □ Jog in the Monceau Park nearby, have a game of squash in the hotel court, then relax in a spa, in the ancient Roman tradition, "Les Thermes." The best equipped water therapy and fitness centre you could ever imagine. □ Whether you are on business or for pleasure, the excitement of Paris is right on your doorstep, when you stay at the Hotel Royal Monceau.

ROYAL MONCEAU HOTEL

SERVICE AND ELEGANCE OF A TRADITIONAL PARISIAN PALACE COMBINED WITH THE "THERMES"
SOPHISTICATED HEALTH AND FITNESS FACILITIES IN THE ANCIENT ROMAN TRADITION
See Luxury Hotels — Hotel Royal Monceau and Hotel Vernet.
See Restaurants Eight Arrondissement — Le Jardin, Il Carpaccio, Les Elysées.

GROUPE   ROYAL   MONCEAU   *RM*   THE   ART   OF   TRADITION

HOTEL ROYAL MONCEAU, 37 AVENUE HOCHE, 75008 PARIS. TEL: (33) 1 45 61 98 00. FAX: (33) 1 42 56 90 03
For Reservations: Contact the Hotel directly, your Travel Agent or our Sales Offices: USA/Canada: 1 800 832 27 91 — Japan: (03) 5434 8060 — United Kingdom: 081 392 99 93
Italy: Cogeta PalaceHotels Associated Hotels: 1678 21057 — Germany: (0) 130 81 79 21 — Belgium: (0) 78 11 95 79 — Switzerland: (0) 155 04 11 or Utell International

francesco smalto

BOUTIQUES : 44 rue François 1ᵉʳ. 75008 Paris / 5 place Victor Hugo. 75016 Paris

sion. Some rooms are kept for non-smokers. Free shuttle to the RER station.

 Sofitel Paris La Défense
34, cours Michelet
La Défense 10
47 76 44 43,
fax 47 73 72 74
Open daily. 1 ste 2,500 F. 149 rms 1,200 F. Air cond. Restaurant.
A new link in the chain, warmly decorated with gilt mirrors and pale marble. Rooms are quiet with superb pink-marble bathrooms. Service is top-notch and breakfasts are delicious. Good facilities for conferences. Restaurant: Les Deux Arcs, see *Restaurants*.

 Hôtel de Dion-Bouton
19, quai de Dion-Bouton
42 04 35 54,
fax 45 06 39 51
Open daily. 33 rms 450-520 F.
On the Seine with pleasant, English-style rooms. Pretty bathrooms and an indoor patio.

 Princesse Isabelle
72, rue J.-Jaurès
47 78 80 06,
fax 47 75 25 20
Open daily. 1 ste 850 F. 29 rms 620 F. Tennis. Air cond in 4 rms. Valet parking.
The rooms of this hotel near La Défense are prettily decorated, and boast Jacuzzi bathtubs or multi-jet showers. Some give directly onto the flowered patio. There's a free chauffeur service to the RER and the Pont de Neuilly métro station.

> *Remember to call ahead to reserve your room, and please, il you cannot honor your reservation, be courteous and let the hotel know.*

 Syjac Hôtel
20, quai de Dion-Bouton
42 04 03 04
Open daily. 7 stes 850-1,500 F. 29 rms 550-800 F. Parking.
A recently built hotel which has managed to shun the concrete solidity of nearby La Défense. Rooms are very pleasing, large and well appointed. There are some nice duplexes overlooking the Seine (with fireplace) and a pretty flowered patio. Free sauna. Meals on trays.

 Le Victoria
85, rue R.-Wallace
45 06 55 51,
fax 40 99 05 97
Open daily. 32 rms 390-540 F.
Not far from the Arche de La Défense, this recently opened hotel offers comfortable, well-equipped rooms.

RUNGIS
94150 Rungis – (Val/Marne)
Paris 13 - Corbeil 26 - Longjumeau 10

 Holiday Inn
4, av. Ch.-Lindbergh
46 87 26 66,
fax 45 60 91 25
Open daily. 168 rms 795-995 F. Half-board 985-1,185 F. Air cond. Parking.
Comfortable and well-kept rooms near Orly airport (free shuttle). A view of the Rungis halles (the Paris wholesale food market). Shops.

 Pullman Paris-Orly
20, av. Ch.-Lindbergh
46 87 36 36,
fax 46 87 08 48
Open daily. 2 stes 1,400 F. 196 rms 600-750 F. Air cond. Heated pool. Restaurant.
A reliable, comfortable chain hotel with excellent soundproofing, air conditioning, color television and direct telephone lines. Among the amenities on offer are a non-stop shuttle to and from the airports, a panoramic bar, a

sauna, shops and a swimming pool. There are deluxe rooms ("Privilège") and several lounges. Restaurant: La Rungisserie, see *Restaurants*.

SACLAY
91400 Saclay – (Essonne)
Paris 21 - Versailles 11 - Palaiseau 8

 Novotel Saclay
Rue Ch.-Thomassin
69 35 66 00,
fax 69 41 01 77
Open daily. 136 rms 450-490 F. Restaurant. Half-board 685 F. Air cond. Heated pool. Tennis. Parking.
Part of the Novotel chain with functional, comfortable rooms, recently renovated and air conditioning. Minigolf, bar. Summer barbecues.

SAINT-CLOUD
92210 Saint-Cloud – (Hauts/Seine)
Paris 12 - Boulogne 3 - Versailles 10

 Hôtel Quorum
2, bd de la République
47 71 22 33,
fax 46 02 75 64
Open daily. 58 rms 440-550 F. Restaurant.
A bright new hotel with quietly elegant, modern public rooms, and spacious guestrooms with grey marble baths. The best are on the upper floors with a view over the Parc de Saint-Cloud. The race track and Saint-Cloud golf club are nearby. Restaurant: La Désirade, see *Restaurants*.

 Villa Henri IV
43, bd de la République
46 02 59 30,
fax 49 11 11 02
Open daily. 36 rms 420-500 F. Restaurant. Parking.
A pleasant address off the boulevard. Rooms are decorated in Louis XVI, Louis-Philippe or Norman style and are huge, bright and well equipped.

129

SAINT-GERMAIN-EN-LAYE
78100 Saint-Germain-en-Laye – (Yvelines)
Paris 21 - Chartres 81 - Dreux 70 - Beauvais 69

 ### La Forestière
1, av. du Président-Kennedy
39 73 36 60
Open daily. 6 stes 1,000-1,300 F. 24 rms 680-850 F. Restaurant.
Thirty rooms and suites have been recently renovated and pleasantly furnished in an old-fashioned style with fresh, spring-like fabrics. The hotel sits on extensive, flower-filled grounds at the edge of the forest. Relais et Châteaux. Restaurant: Cazaudehore, see *Restaurants.*

 ### Le Pavillon Henri-IV
21, rue Thiers
34 51 62 62,
fax 39 73 93 73
Open daily. 3 stes 1,900 F. 39 rms 400-1,300 F. Half-board 660-1,010 F. Restaurant.
This is where Louis XIV was born, Alexandre Dumas wrote *The Three Musketeers,* and Offenbach composed a number of operettas. Total comfort inhabits the 45 huge rooms and suites. The public rooms are magnificent and there's a splendid view over the immense park. Restaurant: Le Pavillon Henri-IV, see *Restaurants.*

SURVILLIERS
95470 Survilliers – (Val-d'Oise)
Paris 30 - Chantilly 14 - Senlis 18 - Lagny 32

 ### Novotel Paris-Survilliers
A 1 then D 16
34 68 69 80,
fax 34 68 64 94
Open daily. 79 rms 470-520 F. Restaurant. Air cond. Heated pool. Parking.
This rather nice modern hotel is set in the middle of a park just five kilometers from the Chantilly forest. Meeting and conference rooms. Bar and grill open from 6 a.m. to midnight.

VÉLIZY
78140 Vélizy – (Yvelines)
Paris 15 - Versailles 7 - Jouy-en-Josas 4

 ### Holiday Inn
22, av. de l'Europe
39 46 96 98,
fax 34 65 95 21
Open daily. 182 rms 725-965 F. Restaurant. Air cond. Heated pool. Parking.
Situated near a shopping center, the Holiday Inn offers functional rooms and excellent facilities. Free shuttle to the Pont-de-Sèvres métro station.

VERSAILLES
78000 Versailles – (Yvelines)
Paris 23 - Mantes 44 - Rambouillet 31

 ### Bellevue Hôtel
12, av. de Sceaux
39 50 13 41,
fax 39 02 05 67
Open daily. 24 rms 380-520 F.
The Bellevue's Louis XV/XVI-style rooms are soundproofed and well equipped (new beds) but rather worn, despite a recent remodeling. Located near the château and conference center.

 ### Eden Hôtel
2, rue Ph.-de-Dangeau
39 50 68 06,
fax 39 51 35 23
Open daily. 25 rms 210-340 F.
Eden lies between the railway station and the château, in a quiet street near the police station. The rooms are regularly refurbished and updated.

 ### Home Saint-Louis
28, rue St-Louis
39 50 23 55,
fax 39 21 62 45
Open daily. 27 rms 160-315 F.
This family-style hotel is located in the quiet Saint-Louis neighborhood.

 ### Pullman
2 bis, av. Paris
39 53 30 31
6 stes 1,300 F. 146 rms 690 F. Restaurant. Air cond. in 75 rms. Valet parking.
Exceptionally well situated near the place d'Armes and the château but set back from the street, this Pullman offers spacious, modern rooms and prestigious amenities. Excellent reception. Piano bar.

 ### Richaud
16, rue Richaud
39 50 10 42,
fax 39 53 43 36
Open daily. 39 rms 250-390 F. Parking.
A small, quiet hotel in the center of the shopping district. Recently remodeled rooms.

 ### Trianon Palace
1, bd de la Reine
30 84 38 00,
fax 39 51 66 55
Open daily. 32 stes 2,200-7,500 F. 62 rms 1,300-2,000 F. Restaurants. Heated pool. Tennis. Parking.
After sprucing up the place to the tune of $60 million, owner Yusake Miyama has thrown open the gilded gates of his stupendously lavish hotel. From videoconference equipment to a medically supervised spa, it is the last word in luxury. Restaurant: Les Trois Marches, see *Restaurants.*

 ### Le Versailles
7, rue Ste-Anne
39 50 64 65,
fax 39 02 37 85
Open daily. 48 rms 370-480 F. Parking.
Conveniently situated near the entrance of the château and facing the convention center, Le Versailles's modern rooms boast recently refitted bathrooms. Direct elevator access to parking. Garden and patio.

CAFES

& QUICK BITES

CAFES

Café Beaubourg
4th arr. - 43, rue Saint-Merri - 48 87 63 96
Open 8 a.m.-1 a.m. (Sat. & Sun. 8 a.m.-2 a.m.).

The vast central space is punctuated by eight columns. To your left, as you enter, a section is reserved for reading French and foreign newspapers. Relatively private spots can be found on the upper level, where the efforts of budding artists are displayed. And virtually every seat affords a view of the esplanade of the Centre Pompidou, with its buskers, fire-eaters and mad poets. Though the coffee, salads and croque-monsieurs are A-OK, the sandwiches are not up to scratch.

Café Costes
1st arr. - 4-6, rue Berger, Place des Innocents - 45 08 54 39
Open 8 a.m.-2 a.m. (Dec. 24 until 8 p.m.).

Designer Philippe Starck may be justly proud of his glass-and-steel temple of postmodern leisure. Paris hadn't seen a café of this caliber open in a good fifty years. Starck's metal café chairs turn out to be more comfortable than they look, perfect for observing the action on the place des Innocents. The spiffy waiters serve good coffee (16 francs) and tasty croque-monsieurs.

Café de Flore
6th arr. - 172, bd Saint-Germain 45 48 55 26
Open daily 7 a.m.-1:30 a.m.

Guillaume Apollinaire and Jean-Paul Sartre are gone, but writers with less illustrious reps still frequent the Flore, as do a few actors, many locals and a plethora of tourists. The café's upper room is no longer an exclusively homosexual haunt; it is now a quiet spot where one may read or write in peace while sipping the house tipple (Pouilly-Fumé from Ladoucette) or forking into the good Welsh rarebit.

Café Mouffetard
5th arr. - 116, rue Mouffetard 43 31 42 50
Open 7 a.m.-9 p.m. Closed Sun. p.m. & Mon.

Overbrimming with the charm of *vieux Paris*—and with patrons, especially on weekend mornings—this café is an obligatory stop for anyone visiting the picturesque open-air market on the rue Mouffetard. The croissants are tops.

Café des Musées
3rd arr. - 49, rue de Turenne - 42 72 96 17
Open 7 a.m.-8 p.m. (Sat. & Sun. 7 a.m.-10:30 p.m.).

What looks like a typical French café is in fact a special spot where the boss pampers clients with excellent expresso, sandwiches made with choice charcuteries and cheeses, abundant salads and remarkable hot *plats du jour*. What's more, this tiny but exemplary establishment is within a stone's throw of the Musée Carnavalet, the place des Vosges and the Musée Picasso.

Café de la Paix
9th arr. - 12, bd des Capucines 40 07 30 20
Open daily 10 a.m.-1:30 a.m.

Is it just us, or have the waiters at this Parisian landmark grown terribly blasé? Too much notoriety, too many tourists seem to have taken a fatal toll on this once-glorious café. Sneak inside for a peek at the Second-Empire restrooms (on the first floor), but avoid the crowded, noisy tables. In all fairness we must say that the coffee (six varieties) is pretty good.

La Coupole
14th arr. - 102, bd du Montparnasse - 43 20 14 20
Open daily 7:30 a.m.-2 a.m. Closed Dec. 24 evening.

Back in 1988, the Coupole's new owners promised not to alter this hallowed monument to the creative energy of Montparnasse, its writers, artists and hangers-on; on the whole, they kept their word. The terrace of the restored and refurbished Coupole is a fine place to sit with a beer or a coffee and watch Parisian life whiz by.

Les Deux Magots
6th arr. - 170, bd Saint-Germain 45 48 55 25
Open 7:30 a.m.-1:30 a.m. Closed Jan. 18-24.

Over there, a group of Japanese tourists is sipping the famous "old-fashioned chocolate"—made from chocolate bars melted in rich milk, and whipped to creamy lightness. Beneath the eponymous Magots (the twin bronze figures perched at ceiling level), a German couple sips the house Muscadet. Out on the newly remodeled terrace, Americans try out their French on the weary waiters, while nattily dressed locals gossip over jugs of coffee. The legendary habitués of the post-war era have long since vanished, but an air of excitement still floats about this archetypal Parisian café.

Aux Deux Saules
2nd arr. - 91, rue Saint-Denis - 42 36 46 57
Open 11 a.m.-midnight. Closed Tues.

For nearly a century this appealing café has served up mussels and french fries, as well as the usual drinks and snacks, to famished denizens of Les Halles. The clientele changed considerably as the district was transformed from the city's market basket to an art/fashion center, but the gracious wood, tile and enamel decor conserves the charm of yore.

Le Fouquet's

8th arr. - 99, av. des Champs-Elysées - 47 23 70 60
Open daily 7 a.m.-2 a.m.

Historically, this is *the* café on the Champs-Elysées, with its sprawling terrace on the "good" side of the avenue. True, some TV and film celebs can be spotted here, but mainly one sees tourists and other ordinary folks (who are willing, that is, to spend 25 francs for a cup of coffee) soaking up the morning sun or the evening neon.

La Palette

6th arr. - 43, rue de Seine - 43 26 68 15
Open 8 a.m.-2 a.m. Closed Sun., Aug. & 1 wk. Feb. school holidays. No cards.

Painters, gallery owners, antiques dealers and art students are the pillars of this venerable café, an unofficial annex of the nearby Beaux-Arts school. When the weather is clement, it's fun to grab one of the sidewalk tables that stretch half-way up the rue Jacques-Callot, order up a beer and a *guillotine* (a ham sandwich made with chewy Poilâne bread), and take in all the details of this delightful Left-Bank scene.

Au Roi du Café

15th arr. - 59, rue Lecourbe - 47 34 48 50
Open 7 a.m.-11 p.m. (Sun. 8 a.m.-4 p.m.).

Here is that rare find, a café for coffee buffs! We mean people who know and care about the differences between beans grown in Costa Rica and Brazil, Colombia or New Guinea. Good *plats du jour* are on offer at lunch; service is helpful and jolly.

Le Sancerre

18th arr. - 35, rue des Abbesses 42 58 08 20
Open daily 7 a.m.-1:30 a.m.

As you enter, look up and admire the mermaid painted on the ceiling. This is a café with character, hard by the scenic and very lively place des Abbesses. The patrons are a colorful mix of local trades-men, workers, rockers and Bohemians, artists and the odd tourist. For your refreshment, the menu offers good wines by the glass, sandwiches and salads.

Le Select

6th arr. - 99, bd du Montpar-nasse - 45 48 38 24
Open daily 8 a.m.-2 a.m. (w.-e. until 4 a.m.).

A more select class of eccentric prefers this café to other, flashier Montparnasse venues. A funky place to rendezvous before a seafood dinner at Le Dôme or Le Duc.

Le Train Bleu

12th arr. - 20, bd Diderot - 43 43 09 06
Open daily 9 a.m.-10 p.m.

Many people know that Le Train Bleu restaurant in the Gare de Lyon boasts a stunning interior; but not everyone is aware that this stunning Belle Epoque gem is also a bar and café. Why waste time in the lugubrious buffets and bistros on the station level, when a beautiful, comfortable (though admittedly more expensive) place of refreshment awaits up one flight of stairs?

QUICK BITES

Al Diwan

8th arr. - 30, av. George-V - 47 20 84 98
Open daily 8 a.m.-11:30 p.m.

The carry-out shop of the Al Diwan restaurant stocks all the fixings for an impromptu Lebanese picnic: choose chawarma (marinated beef), labneh (fresh cheese), makanek (spicy sausages) or felafel sandwiches on the bread of your choice, round out your basket with some baklava and walnut cakes, pick a bottle of Lebanese wine (don't forget the corkscrew!), and you're set!

Bastille Corner

12th arr. - 47, rue de Charenton 43 47 12 17
Open noon-3 p.m. & 7:30 p.m.-12:30 a.m. Closed Sun., Aug., at Christmas & New Year's.

Hankering for an enchilada? Head over to this Mexican-American hangout, where you can also grab a spicy lunch or late supper of nachos and chili con carne followed by a cool-ing ice-cream sundae.

La Boutique à Sandwichs

8th arr. - 12, rue du Colisée - 43 59 56 69
Open 11:45 a.m.-1 a.m. Closed Sun. & Aug.

On the second floor of this restaurant, you might see a few famous faces seated together around raclette, veg-etable soup and other modest but tasty dishes. For our part, we remain loyal to the ground floor, where some of the best sandwiches in Paris are put together, featuring shrimp, chicken and smoked ham. The excellent corned beef, served hot or cold with horseradish, pickles and Poilâne bread (pickelfleisch), bears compari-son to a good New York deli version. A great spot for a quick lunch on the cheap.

Café de Mars

7th arr. - 11, rue Augereau - 47 05 05 91
Open noon-2:30 p.m. & 8 p.m.-11:30 p.m. (Sat. 8 p.m.-11:30 p.m.; Sun. noon-4 p.m. & 8 p.m.-11:30 p.m.). Closed 10 days in Aug.

An American menu, a jovial atmosphere and a cos-mopolitan crowd account for the Café's swift rise to success.

Brunch-style dishes are served up any day, any time, but the staff goes all out to produce a traditional brunch on Sunday.

Café des Lettres

7th arr. - 53, rue de Verneuil - 42 22 52 17
Open noon-3 p.m. & 7 p.m.-11 p.m. Closed Sun. & last 2 wks. of Dec.

This annex to the very serious Maison des Ecrivains (a writers' center) eschews French food in favor of Italian and Scandinavian dishes. Herring, shrimp and composed salads dominate the lunch offerings, along with a few lunch daily specials. After 3 p.m. tea, cakes, Swedish waffles and assorted light refreshments are served.

Coffee-Parisien

7th arr. - 5, rue Perronet - 45 44 92 93
Open daily 11 a.m.-7 p.m. (Fri. until midnight). Closed Aug. No cards.

For a mile-high, deli-style sandwich (hot pastrami or roast beef, tuna or chicken salad, from 30 to 70 francs) hop on a stool at this likeable little eatery. If you like, the sandwiches can be packed to go... how about a picnic in the Luxembourg?

Cosi

6th arr. - 54, rue de Seine - 46 33 35 36
Open daily noon-11 p.m. No cards.

Don't let the long line discourage you—just listen to the

A precarious perch

The column that towers over the *Place Vendôme* seems to be equipped with an ejector seat. More than one famous figure has experienced the precarity of that particular perch since the first version was erected in 1686. The statue of the Sun King, Louis XIV, destroyed during the Revolution, was followed by Napoléon in a number of guises, briefly interrupted by King Henri IV when the monarchy was restored in 1814. Henri, who reigned in the late sixteenth and early seventeenth centuries, was the father of the Duke of Vendôme who gave his name to this magnificent square. The present Napoléon—dressed, like the original, in Roman garb—watches over the jewelers, couturiers and furriers of this opulent neighborhood.

Cafétéria du Musée Picasso

3rd arr. - 5, rue Thorigny - 42 71 25 21
Open 9:15 a.m.-5:15 p.m. Closed Tues.

Even if you aren't a Picasso fan, you can still duck into his museum, housed in the noble Hôtel Salé, for a bite in the cafeteria—a ticket isn't required. Salads, quiches, savory tarts and pastries compose the list of light offerings.

music, and study the sandwich components listed on the blackboard: fresh goat cheese, cucumber, smoked Italian ham, prosciutto, salmon and more can be stuffed in any combination into an oven-fresh pita pocket (35 to 45 francs). Wash your sandwich down with a glass of good Italian wine, then follow up with a Yankee-style dessert: a brownie, fruit crumble or a dip of Häagen-Dazs. These goodies may be consumed

upstairs (one of the two rooms is reserved for nonsmokers), at a communal board or a table for one, as you wish.

Cuisine Gourmande

4th arr. - 63, rue Saint-Louis-en-l'Ile - 46 33 33 33
Open daily 11 a.m.-11 p.m.

A jolly crew of regulars keeps the ambience lively at this "island" hangout. Granted, the dishes on the menu are pre-cooked but look who did the cooking: top French chefs Morot-Gaudry, Dutournier, Faugeron, Fournier, who specialize in hearty Southwestern cuisine. Petrossian, no less, supplies the salmon and the cheeses come from Androuet. To irrigate all these goodies, there is of course an appropriate range of wines.

Danny Rose

15th arr. - 41, bd Pasteur - 45 66 82 82
Open daily 11 a.m.-9:30 p.m. Closed at Christmas & New Year's.

Here's fast food with variety—and it's excellent value to boot! In addition to the usual hamburgers, you'll find chili, Texas meatballs and beef kebabs on menus that range from 24 to 37 francs. For dessert, try one of Cynthia's peerless brownies, or a gooey ice-cream sundae.

Eggstra

10th arr. - 66, rue du Faubourg-Poissonnière & 31, rue de Paradis
48 00 01 80
Open 11:30 a.m.-4 p.m. Closed Sun.

Inventive, high-quality fast food does exist in Paris, and it's prepared by an American chef! Her delicious pita sandwiches (15 to 20 francs), fresh salads, light french fries and tongue-tingling chili are winning new converts to the American way of lunch. Even if you finish with a brownie, cheesecake or pecan tart, you won't spend over 50 francs. American beer, fresh fruit juices and California wines will wash these treats down.

Fauchon

8th arr. - 30, place de la Madeleine - 47 42 60 11
Open 9:40 a.m.-7 p.m. Closed Sun.

The MO for getting through this place would drive anyone (but a Frenchman!) bonkers. First you line up to choose your main dish, dessert and coffee, then you take your ticket to the cash register (another line), line up again to retrieve your meal, and finally set off in search of a place to consume it (don't hope for a table). The up side? Well, the food is very good indeed—and so is the coffee. Figure on spending 100 to 140 francs for a full meal, 12 to 35 francs for a pastry and coffee.

Flora Danica

8th arr. - 142, av. des Champs-Elysées - 43 59 20 41
Open daily noon-2:30 p.m. & 7:15 p.m.-11 p.m. Closed Dec. 24 evening.

This Danish outpost at the top of the Champs-Elysées is as popular as ever. After a movie, come here for a platter of Baltic herring (smoked or with cream) and potato salad, or gravlax or smoked salmon, along with a frosty Tuborg beer and perhaps a danish pastry.

Fructidor

9th arr. - 46, rue Saint-Georges 49 95 02 10
Open 11 a.m.-3 p.m. Closed Sat. & Sun.
9th arr. - 67, rue de Provence 48 74 53 46
Open 11 a.m.-3 p.m. Closed Sun.

Anti-stress dishes are accompanied by vitamin-packed fruit and vegetable cocktails. Fortunately, there is as much flavor as nutrition in the onion tourte, the salade paysanne and the leek quiche.

Both establishments feature identical food, but the rue Saint-Georges address is more pleasant.

Lina's

2nd arr. - 50, rue Etienne-Marcel 42 21 16 14
Open 10 a.m.-6 p.m. (Sat. 10 a.m.-6:30 p.m.). Closed Sun. & holidays.
8th arr. - 8, rue Marbeuf - 47 23 92 33
Open 10:30 a.m.-5 p.m. (Sat. 10 a.m.-6:30 p.m.). Closed Sun.

The friendly, swift staff works as you watch, building delicious, obviously fresh sandwiches. Shrimp, cucumber, bacon and pastrami are but a few of the many options which you can take out, or munch on a stool behind the broad glass shopfront. With a dessert (brownies, pecan pie, ice cream...) and a glass of Bordeaux, you'll spend 50 to 60 francs.

Lord Sandwich

1st arr. - 15, rue Duphot - 42 60 55 94
8th arr. - 134, rue du Faubourg Saint-Honoré - 42 56 41 68
Open 11 a.m.-5 p.m. Closed Sat. & Sun.

By now, no doubt everyone is familiar with the tale of John Montagu, Lord Sandwich, who had a passion for all-night card games and who accidentally invented the sandwich one night toward dawn, when he ordered his butler to bring him a slice of ham between two slices of bread to avoid getting the cards greasy. This Lord Sandwich offers some of the best-tasting such creations in Paris, along with the greatest selection. These range from simple BLTs to far more sophisticated compilations. Vegetarians and weight-watchers have an array of salads to choose from. The cafeteria format is reminiscent of a fast-food outfit, but on the second floor there is a garden-style dining room.

Marais Plus

3rd arr. - 20, rue des Francs-Bourgeois - 48 87 01 40
Open daily 10 a.m.-7:30 p.m.

Though the decor does not amount to much, and the food is no more than decent, this is a handy address to know if you're in the Marais, dying of hunger, and unwilling to spend a bundle for your late breakfast, lunch, tea or Sunday brunch.

Le Melrose

3rd arr. - 8, rue du Pas-de-la-Mule 40 29 90 50
Open noon-4 p.m. & 7 p.m.-11 p.m. (Sat. noon-11 p.m. & Sun. noon-7 p.m.).

Revel in the splendid view of the place des Vosges and discover what French "fast food" is all about: *tartines* (open-faced sandwiches) of goat cheese, country ham or smoked duck breast, platters of carpaccio or satisfying quiches and tarts may be followed by gooey chocolate cake, or a simple and refreshing fruit cocktail. This sumptuous snack will run you approximately 80 francs.

Le Mexico

16th arr. - 1, place de Mexico 47 27 96 98
Open noon-3 p.m. & 7:30 p.m.-11 p.m. (Sat. & Sun. noon-midnight).

In choosing Le Mexico as their *cantina*, the neighborhood's gilded youth have shown that their good taste extends beyond their signed and logo'd togs. Follow their lead and try the good fresh pasta, shrimp in sherry, platters of smoked salmon or duck breast and the cool, inventive salads. But for dessert, sneak off to Angélina, across the street.

Some establishments change their closing times without warning. It is always wise to check in advance.

Midi Trente

14th arr. - 56, rue Daguerre - 43
20 49 82
*Open 11 a.m.-6 p.m. Closed
Sun.*

Actresses and cover girls
congregate in this refined and
very feminine lunch spot. Your
hostesses will advise you on
whether to choose their rich
chicken liver terrine, or the
refreshing zucchini terrine
with a zippy tomato and pepper coulis, then guide you on
to pick a hot *plat du jour* or a
smoked salmon platter. Even
with a lemon tart or fragrant
orange fondant for dessert,
you're sure to spend under
100 francs.

Pain, Salade et Fantaisie

5th arr.- 22, rue Gay-Lussac - 40
51 05 01
*Open 9 a.m.-8 p.m. Closed Sun.
& holidays.*

An irresistible fragrance of
fresh-baked bread wafts forth
from this appealing sandwich
shop, situated just a stone's
throw from the Luxembourg
Gardens. Impeccably fresh
fillings—goat cheese, salmon,
braised or country ham,
mortadella and more—are
stuffed into whole-wheat pita
pockets, or piled onto chewy
Poilâne bread (9 to 23 francs).
Shrimp or chicken salads,
brownies and great raspberry
muffins round out the bill of
fare. The unfailingly cheerful
proprietors of this family-
owned shop promise that the
menu will soon be expanded
to include chili, strudel,
cheesecake and teas from
Mariage Frères.

Pastavino

1st arr. - Forum des Halles,
9, Grande-Galerie - 40 26 54 62
*Open 9 a.m.-7:30 p.m. Closed
Sun.*

If you've descended into the
Forum des Halles for a non-
stop shopping spree, you
needn't resurface for lunch.
Perch on a stool at Pastavino's

black-marble counter and
savor a re-energizing bowl of
fresh pasta or a refreshing platter (tomatoes, mozzarella,
Parma ham), followed by a serious dessert (tiramisù, Italian
pastries) and excellent expresso. Or you can snack
while you shop, with a take-
out sandwich made on crusty
Italian bread (18 to 28 francs).

Au Plaisir des Pains

6th arr. - 62, rue de Vaugirard
45 48 40 45
*Open 10 a.m.-8 p.m. Closed
Sun.*

What this sandwich shop
lacks in warmth it makes up for
in the freshness of the food on
offer: we recommend the hot
pita sandwiches filled with
grilled peppers, or herbed
ham, eggplant caviar or
tomatoes and mozzarella (20
to 25 francs), as well as the
delicious tomato tart, the
Roquefort turnover, and the
"special" salad, which includes peppers, eggplant,
herbs and fromage blanc. A
10-franc surcharge is added if
you consume your purchase
in the shop, but why not save
money and take your goodies
over to the nearby Lux-
embourg Gardens?

Au Régal

16th arr. - 4, rue Nicolo - 42 88
49 15
*Open 9 a.m.-11 p.m. (Sun.
10 a.m.-3 p.m. & 6 p.m.-
11 p.m.). Closed 2 wks. wk. of
Aug. 15.*

A sudden craving for caviar
can be satisfied (for a price!) at
this traditional Russian grocery-cum-restaurant. More
modestly tariffed and perfectly
delicious are the salmon eggs,
zakuski, herring any way you
like it, borscht and pirozkis,
and the wonderful vatrouchka
(Russian cheesecake). We
hear that Brigitte Bardot occasionally comes in to feast on
blinis and smoked salmon.

Seine Rive Gauche

13th arr. - 3, rue Louise-Weiss
44 23 80 02
*Open 8 a.m.-7 p.m. Closed Sun.
& holidays.*

The savvy, demanding
clientele that the new Finance
Ministry and the future
Bibliothèque de France are
bringing into the
neighborhood, is delighted to
discover this elegant,
resolutely modern tea room. A
well-designed menu features
inventive cold platters
(smoked salmon, avocado
and grapefruit), generous
salads, warming gratins and
savory tarts, all made with top-
quality ingredients chosen
fresh every morning at the
market. Breakfast and teatime
specials include treats like
homemade jams and chocol-
ate prepared the old-
fashioned way, which patrons
may enjoy while perusing the
newspapers and magazines
thoughtfully left at their dis-
posal by the friendly, efficient
staff.

Sydney Health Food

2nd arr. - 46, passage Choiseul
49 26 01 71
*Open 9:30 a.m.- 6 p.m. Closed
Sat. & Sun.*

Low-fat, low-salt and low-
cost, Sydney's health food
specialties are nevertheless
high in flavor. The fresh-fruit
juices, soups, savory tarts,
salads and sandwiches on
gutsy whole-wheat bread are
uniformly delicious, and
generously apportioned. Eat-
in facilities are barely functional (a tiny counter downstairs,
a small dining room up a
rickety flight of stairs), but the
foods will be packed in sturdy
take-out containers at your
request.

Virgin Café

8th arr. - 56, av. des Champs-
Elysées - 42 89 46 81
*Open 10 a.m.-11:30 p.m. (Sat. &
Sun. 10 a.m.-12:30 a.m.).*

The gallery-restaurant that
crowns the Virgin Megastore

is a surprisingly pleasant and comfortable spot for lunch, tea or light refreshments any time of day. Celebrity chef Dominique Nahmias ("Olympe" to her friends) has concocted a simple, appetizing menu based on fresh ingredients: sautéed shellfish scented with thyme, garlicky brandade of sole, scrambled eggs on polenta... The Virgin Afternoon Tea offers the tea of your choice accompanied by little sandwiches, scones with jam and the pastry du jour, all for just 55 francs.

West Side Café

17th arr. - 34, rue Saint-Ferdinand - 40 68 75 05
Open 10 a.m.-6 p.m. Closed Sun. & holidays.

This American-style diner looks like something Edward Hopper might have painted. At noontime, customers cluster around the counter for tasty turkey, lox, shrimp or guacamole sandwiches (25 to 45 francs), or the chicken and West Side salads. It's fun to munch on a brownie or some cookies and contemplate this very Parisian take-off on an old Yankee tradition.

Xavier Gourmet

8th arr. - 89, bd de Courcelles
43 80 78 22
*Open daily noon-3:30 p.m. &
7 p.m.-11:30 p.m.*
9th arr. - 19, rue Notre-Dame-de-Lorette - 45 26 38 46
*Open daily 9 a.m.-4 p.m. &
6 p.m.-11:30 p.m. (Sat., Sun. &
holidays noon-11:30 p.m.).*

For a quick bite before or after the play, this pleasing little eatery in the heart of the theater district proposes sandwiches made with Poilâne's wonderful sourdough bread filled with smoked salmon, tarama or tomatoes and mozzarella drizzled with fruity olive oil, as well as salads and an all-in grill menu (meat, salad and sautéed potatoes for 59 francs). If you want to end

with a sweet, steer clear of the mediocre pastries, and go for the Häagen-Dazs ice cream instead.

TEA ROOMS

A Priori-Thé

2nd arr. - 35-37, galerie Vivienne
42 97 48 75
*Open noon-7 p.m. (Sun.
12:30 p.m.-6 p.m.). Closed Dec.
25 & Jan. 1.*

We would be hard pressed to come up with a prettier or more charming spot in Paris than the passage Vivienne. You slip beneath a glass roof supported by bas-relief carved goddesses and horns of plenty, to reach this honey-colored room (the scrap of a terrace out front is marked by rattan armchairs). From noon until 3 p.m. fashion mavens, journalists and intellectuals lunch on interesting cold platters, tempting *plats du jour* (try the welsh rarebit) and such homey desserts as fruit crumble and pecan pie. Come teatime, you'll find a nice selection of teas served with scones, muffins and jam. Main dishes run between 70 and 100 francs; Sunday brunch is tariffed at 145 francs.

Angélina

1st arr. - 226, rue de Rivoli - 42 60 82 00
*Open 9:30 a.m.-7 p.m. (Sat. &
Sun. 9:30 a.m.-7:30 p.m.).
Closed Aug.*
16th arr. - 10, place de Mexico -
47 04 89 42
Open daily 8:30 a.m.-8 p.m.
17th arr. - Palais des Congrès,
Porte Maillot - 40 68 22 51
Open daily 9 a.m.-8 p.m.

This is it, the high-water mark of posh Paris society—or at least it used to be. Angélina still appears to be *the* elegant tea room in town, a kingdom of elderly grande dames in green hats. But has it really maintained its once-lofty social position? Not according to the aforementioned grande

dames, who sniff at the increasingly common clientele—rich young bourgeois in leather jackets and young ladies just out of convent schools, smoking and squealing. And perhaps these newcomers *are* out of place in this room, with its bronzed moldings, cream-of-tomato-colored pilasters and faded Côte d'Azur frescoes.

But for those with a soft spot for this sort of place, there's still plenty of charm in the heavy curtains, the wealth of gilt molding and the motherly waitresses bustling about with silver trays. And there are plenty of calories in the notorious Mont-Blanc (sweet chestnut purée in a meringue shell, heaped with whipped cream) and the legendary thick hot chocolate.

L'Arbre à Cannelle

2nd arr. - 57, passage des Panoramas - 45 08 55 87
Open 11 a.m.-6 p.m. Closed Sun. & holidays.

You'll find this charming Second Empire tea room sheltered in the newly refurbished, wonderfully luminous passage des Panoramas. Stockbrokers and people in advertising drop by here for lunch; they are joined, at teatime, by a cadre of elegant elderly ladies. We're particularly fond of the homemade apple crumble and the excellent walnut tart, perfect with one of the many fine teas.

L'Auberge du Bonheur

16th arr. - Bois de Boulogne, av. de Longchamp (behind Grande Cascade restaurant)
42 24 10 17
Open daily May.-Oct. noon-10:30 p.m. Closed evenings & Fri. & Sat. in winter, & 3 wks. in Feb.

This little country inn in the heart of the Bois de Boulogne has the special attraction of a lovely terrace for long summer evenings. But the Auberge is a treat in winter, too, when you can squeeze into a comfortable banquette after a stroll in the Bois de Boulogne. These former stables have been done over prettily: exposed beams, red-and-white-checked curtains, lots of plants and a smartly turned-out service staff. In this utterly cozy little spot, grandmas catch up with their little darlings over a cup of tea and a treat, perhaps a tart or ice cream. At noon, people who work near the Bois show up for the 135-franc prix-fixe lunch (the children's menu is priced at 55 francs).

Boissier

16th arr. - 184, av. Victor-Hugo
45 04 87 88
Open 9 a.m.-7:30 p.m. (Sun. 10 a.m.-7 p.m.).

This elegant, traditional tea room gives onto the square Lamartine. Inside, little girls in kilts and white ankle socks devour such house specialties as enormous chocolate candies and delicately flaky apple tarts. Their mothers, no doubt more concerned with their figures, order mushroom salads or the superb *Marceau* platter of Parma ham, mozzarella, tomatoes and raw mushrooms, along with a glass of Château de Lussac. Among the pastries, our vote goes to the Breda (a rich coffee mousse), and the filbert-based Noisettine. And on a blustery afternoon, nothing comforts like Boissier's divine hot chocolate, which comes in five different flavors. Tea or chocolate and a pastry will cost about 50 francs.

Brocco

3rd arr. - 180, rue du Temple 42 72 19 81
Open daily 6:30 a.m.-7:30 p.m.

Piping hot bittersweet chocolate, a creamy rhubard Chiboust with a touch of lemon and a crunch of caramel, a Royal rich with pral-

ine—these are just a few of the superior sweets on offer at Brocco, an unassuming, old-fashioned pastry shop near the place de la République.

La Bûcherie

5th arr. - 41, rue de la Bûcherie
43 54 24 52
Open daily 3 p.m.-6 p.m.

There are surely better ways to spend blustery afternoons than before the Bûcherie's crackling fire, with a cup of fine tea, a slice of tart lemon meringue pie, a view of Notre-Dame and a book from Shakespeare & Co. (right next door)—trouble is, we can't think of a single one.

Cador

1st arr. - 2, rue de l'Amiral-Coligny - 45 08 19 18
Open 9 a.m.-6:30 p.m. Closed Mon. & Aug. 15-Sept. 15.

Utterly worthy of its prestigious setting just opposite the Louvre, Cador is a regal little pastry shop with a gilt decor fit for a king. Seated at pink and taupe marble tea tables, tourists and locals alike make short work of the dainty cakes that make such a mouthwatering display in the window. The Petits Cadors (chocolate and orange peel on a short-pastry base) and the mousseline, a recent creation that is accompanied by a luscious Grand Marnier custard sauce, attract their fair share of customers.

Carette

16th arr. - 4, pl. du Trocadéro 47 27 88 56
Open 8 a.m.-7 p.m. Closed Tues. & Aug.

Carette is famous for its macaroons—chocolate, vanilla, lemon—and its coffee. The wealthy heirs and heiresses of the avenue Mozart have long come here to chat over tea. But now the younger generation is moving in; if their racket is not to your liking, just remember that Car-

ette is also a pastry shop and caterer: you can stop by, pick up some macaroons and go home to eat them in peace.

Casta Diva

8th arr. - 27, rue Cambacérès
42 66 46 53
Open 11:30 a.m.-6:30 p.m. Closed Sun., holidays, Sat. in June & in July & in Aug. No cards.

These two quite chic white rooms under the arcades, with their spacious alcoves and heavy pistachio-colored curtains, shelter a posh, well-shopped-for clientele. The furniture, all in mahogany, is richly evocative of the Empire. Even the salads and savory tarts are rich. Desserts uphold the house standards very well, (try the apple délice with Calvados or the chocolate mousse cake). The tea list features rare selections from Mariage Frères, and Verlet supplies the coffee. Either beverage and a pastry will set you back about 60 francs.

La Charlotte de l'Isle

4th arr. - 24, rue Saint-Louis-en-l'Isle - 43 54 25 83
Open 2:30 p.m.-4 p.m. (Wed. 2 p.m.-8 p.m.). Closed Mon. & Tues.

Tea tins piled everywhere, posters, paintings, old mirrors, hats, bouquets of dried flowers and, yes, even a piano: such are the elements of this wonderful, artistically disordered decor. Fruit tarts sit nicely with any of the 30 teas (we like the spice tea), served with dignity on small etched trays, in antique teapots and cups, with silver carafes for the hot water. Hot-chocolate lovers will be more than happy with the old-fashioned version offered here, which carefully preserves the aroma of the chocolate.

Find the address you are looking for, quickly and easily, in the index.

La Chocolatière
6th arr. - 5, rue Stanislas - 45 49 13 06
Open 9 a.m.-7 p.m. Closed Sun.
At lunch and teatime, people from the nearby TV station, high schoolers (Lycée Stanislas is next door) and Luxembourg Garden strollers all gather in this cozy spot. At noon, order a quick lunch of a salad, tourte and dessert for 59 francs. We recommend you skip the tabouli, but the gratins are tasty and warming. For afternoon snacks, there is caramel tea, lovely with dark-chocolate cake, or old-fashioned hot chocolate, served in a china chocolate pot, with crème fraîche and a glass of ice water on the side (30 francs). This goes nicely with the hot apple and almond fondant (26 francs) or light pound cake—homemade, of course.

Concertea
7th arr. - 3, rue Paul- Louis-Courier - 45 49 27 59
Open 11:30 a.m.-7 p.m. (Mon. 11:30 a.m.-4 p.m.). Closed Sun.
If you like Mozart with your chocolate tart, Verdi with your lemon meringue pie, or Bach with your vegetable quiche, this charming spot will suit you to a... tea. Check out the menu (written on a musical staff), then enjoy the concert while sipping smoky Lapsang Souchong from Mariage Frères or nibbling on one of

the fresh and delicious homemade gâteaux (30 francs).

Coquelin Aîné
16th arr. - 67, rue de Passy - 45 24 44 00
Open 9 a.m.-7:30 p.m. Closed Sun.

Heroic taxpayers

After the architectural free-for-all of the Middle Ages, the development of the *place des Vosges* in the early seventeenth century heralded an era of elegance and symmetry with its arcades, stone-and-brick façades and steep slate roofs. Despite various renovations, the 36 houses have retained their homogeneous aspect. The place des Vosges was given its present name in 1800 in honor of the first French department to pay its taxes after the Revolution.

Coquelin Aîné—what a truly Parisian treat. Yes, my dear, we know exactly where we are the moment we enter this tea room and see Hermès scarves in the necks of Burberry raincoats. Sweet, snobby little things from the local private school come in for tea and a tart, éclair, meringue or Coquelin's famed macaroon. In warm weather, we like to lunch on the terrace (135 francs) and savor the view of the pretty place de Passy.

A la Cour de Rohan
6th arr. - 59-61, rue Saint-André-des-Arts
43 25 79 67
Open noon-7:30 p.m. Closed Mon., Aug., Dec. 25 & Jan. 1. No cards.
Tucked away in a little passage off the boulevard Saint Germain is this cozy tea room that's as comfortable as a private home: dishes designed by Cocteau, Louis XVI furniture and old Limoges china. Patrons seated at chintz-skirted tables murmur quietly over lunch (good chicken-liver salad) or teatime treats

(yummy rhubarb crumble), while the charming hostess attends to their comfort. The delicious homemade jams and scones are available for take-out.

Dalloyau
2nd. - 25, bd des Capucines - 47 03 47 00
Open 8:30 a.m.-7:30 p.m. (Sat. 9 a.m.-7:30 p.m.). Closed Sun.
6th arr. - 2, pl. Edmond-Rostand 43 29 31 10
Open daily 9 a.m.-6:45 p.m.
8th arr. - 99-101, rue du Faubourg-Saint-Honoré 43 59 18 10
Open daily 8:30 a.m.-9 p.m.
15th arr. - 69, rue de la Convention - 45 77 84 27
Open daily 9:30 a.m.-7:30 p.m. (Sun. 9 a.m.-19 p.m.)
Dalloyau will always be Dalloyau. Nothing changes: grandmothers from the sixth arrondissement still chat together or bring their grandchildren in for a treat, schoolgirls still sit telling each other schoolgirl stories, and the young couples still smile timidly at each other after a walk around the Luxembourg Gardens across the street. A conscientious staff serves a substantial choice of teas, fruit juices, good hot chocolate, delicate pastries and sumptuous ice cream concoctions. The lunchtime crowd favors fresh salads and tasty *plats du jour* that don't cost the earth.

Aux Délices de Scott
17th arr. - 39, av. de Villiers - 47 63 71 36
Open 8:30 a.m.-8 p.m. Closed Sun. & holidays.
Aux Délices is nothing short of an institution. The grand chandelier is hung so high up in the vault of the ceiling that it looks small. The huge room, tiled in blue and sienna with ivory woodwork and endless mirrors, was once graced by the likes of Sarah Bernhardt and Sacha Guitry. Tea is served with all due ceremony, and may be accompanied by

ethereal macaroons or a nougat parisien, among other excellent pastries.

Les Deux Abeilles

7th arr. - 189, rue de l'Université
45 55 64 04
Open 9 a.m.-7 p.m. Closed Sun. & Aug. No cards.

The classically elegant decor reflects the well-bred, well-heeled clientele that swarms to Les Deux Abeilles for breakfast, lunch and tea. The place buzzes most busily at noontime, when inventive salads, smoked salmon feuilleté and an uncommonly good tomato tart appear on the menu (a full lunch runs 80 to 100 francs). Later in the afternoon pastries are featured, including an unusual chestnut cake; and for those who don't fancy tea, may we suggest the lemony ginger drink that is a specialty of the house.

Djarling

15th arr. - 45-47, rue Cronstadt
45 32 47 17
Open noon-6 p.m. (Fri. & Sat. noon-8 p.m.).

Come teatime, the pretty cups on the pink paisley tablecloths sit patiently waiting to be filled with one of fifteen premium teas (the classics plus rare blends, including sturdy brews from Kenya) that the house offers. All the appropriate accompaniments are on hand: pound cake, scones, crêpes and wonderful ice creams. Sunday brunch is served from noon to 6 p.m.

Les Enfants Gâtés

4th arr. - 43, rue des Francs-Bourgeois - 42 77 07 63
Open daily 12:30 p.m.-8 p.m. (Sat. & Sun. noon-7 p.m.). Closed 3 wks. in Aug.

The ambience is soft, the lighting is subdued, and the round tables and deep armchairs are arranged between tall ivory-painted columns beneath whirling ceiling fans. An ideal place for tea (or even better, hot chocolate) and conversation. If your sweet tooth demands indulgence, order the brownie (the waitress may try to convince you to order the *tarte du jour,* but stand your ground!). Stiffish prices.

La Fourmi Ailée

5th arr. - 8, rue du Fouarre - 43 29 40 99
Open noon-7 p.m. Closed Tues., Dec. 25 & Jan. 1.

From the outside, La Fourmi Ailée looks like a bookstore. Inside, why, it is a bookstore, but one that artfully conceals a tea room—a blissfully intimate, casual tea room. Awaiting you on a rustic sideboard sit a fresh, fragrant spice cake, a Norman tart and scones served with two kinds of jam. Wisps of steam rise from the spouts of a mixed assortment of teapots set on the tables (sixteen types of tea are offered). One could easily while away the better part of an afternoon in so inviting a spot, with a newly purchased volume of, say, Virginia Woolf (most of the books are by women authors, and the selection is international).

Les Fous de l'Ile

4th arr. - 33, rue des Deux-Ponts
43 25 76 67
Open noon-11:30 p.m. (Sat. 3 p.m.-11:30 p.m., Sun. 11 p.m.-6 p.m.). Closed Mon.

The upper levels above this large, windowed room are lined with books, china is displayed in glass cases, and here and there black-and-white photographs hang. It's a busy place, very relaxed and pleasant, with a student atmosphere. The clientele is young, cosmopolitan and at ease, and the waiters officiate in T-shirts and jeans. A variety of teas are offered, including Sakura (green tea flavored with cherry) and Caraibes (Indian, Ceylon and Caribbean flowers), all of which go well with the creamy house cheesecake. The popular Sunday brunch (100 to 160 francs) is served from 11 a.m.

Galerie Gourmande

3rd arr. - 38, rue de Sévigné - 42 74 48 40
Open noon-7 p.m. Closed Mon.

The scrumptious orange fondant, pound cake, clafoutis and fruit cake are baked according to old family recipes, and then daintily served on immaculate napery along with a steaming cup of tea. What could be more restorative after a visit to the Musée Carnavalet or a tour of the Marais's townhouses? The Galerie Gourmande can also set you up with fresh, delicate salads at lunchtime, and the house hot chocolate is a creamy, fragrant masterpiece.

Galerie de la Paix

Hôtel George-V
8th arr. - 31, avenue George-V
47 23 54 00
Open daily 9 a.m.-7 p.m.

The power tea, it seems, has replaced the power breakfast as an occasion for wheeling and dealing. The best place in Paris to perform this new ritual of ambition is the stately *salon de thé* recently inaugurated in the Hôtel George V. Cement an alliance, plan a merger or acquire an adversary's assets over a cup of Japanese Matcha Uji or Russian Czar Alexander tea (prepared according to the "five essential laws of tea brewing") from Mariage Frères, and a plate of miniature French pastries or sandwiches. These delicacies are served beneath the benevolent gaze of Peace and Abundance, allegorical figures who star in an immense tapestry that is the Galerie's most prominent feature. And an abundance of money is what you'll need when the bill comes: 35 to 50 francs for coffee, tea or chocolate,

50 francs for fruit juice and for pastries or sandwiches (note, however, that a club sandwich will set you back 130 francs).

L'Heure Gourmande
6th arr. - 22, passage Dauphine
46 34 00 40
Open 11:30 a.m.-7 p.m. Closed Sun., 3 1st wks. of Aug., 1 wk. at Christmas-New Year's & 1 wk. at May 1.

Sheltered in the picturesque passage Dauphine is a pluperfect little tea room that offers handsome surroundings, a hospitable welcome, fabulous cheesecake and the peace necessary to enjoy it all—stay an hour, or two hours if you like. For tea and cake, you'll pay about 65 francs; a light lunch runs about 100 francs.

L'Heure des Thés
9th arr. - 1, rue Chaptal - 45 26 85 94
Open 11 a.m.-7:30 p.m. Closed Sat., Sun. Aug. & holidays.

Yellow rattan chairs, pine furniture and cheerful flowered tablecloths make an ideal setting in which to dream of country life. Let a pot of smoky Chinese tea soothe away the urban blues, and indulge in a slice of lemon tart or chocolate fondant. Luncheon dishes (tarte provençale and the like) are priced between 37 and 49 francs; the relaxing atmosphere carries no extra charge.

Ladurée
8th arr. - 16, rue Royale - 42 60 21 79
Open 8:30 a.m.-7 p.m. Closed Sun., Aug. & holidays.

Cherubs on faded frescoes, plush red carpet, oaken woodwork and round tables in veined black marble are all part of the charm of this tiny institution, which is always full as a tick. Especially Saturdays, when lovely ladies from the best neighborhoods put down their Hermès shopping bags for a few minutes to enjoy tea

with a macaroon or two (they are the best in Paris, you know). Lunchtime is surprisingly lively: choices run to the likes of omelets, chicken, such daily specials as cassoulet, or minuscule crab and salmon sandwiches that will empty your wallet long before they fill your stomach.

Le Loir dans la Théière
4th arr. - 3, rue des Rosiers - 42 72 90 61
Open noon-7 p.m. (Sun. 11 a.m.-7 p.m.). Closed 3 1st wks. of Aug., Dec. 25 & Jan. 1. No cards.

Young women as graceful as nymphs ferry bulbous teapots among the low sofas. A faint feeling of nostalgia, a faded carpet, old armoires from Normandy, soft lights, frescoes on the walls—these elements always make us feel like we're back in Auntie's parlor out in the provinces. The atmosphere is quaint and a tad intellectual. The place is run on a kind of cooperative basis, and since the waiters and cooks are constantly changing, it is impossible to recommend specific dishes. The clientele, which is more bourgeois and conventional than the place itself, tends to favor the straightforward pastries and the hazelnut cake called Alice's Secret (though we've found it to be rather heavy). The service, although a little too whirly, is friendly and engaging. Expect to spend 60 francs for tea and a pastry, and about 80 francs for lunch.

Maison du Chocolat
8th arr. - 52, rue François-ler - 47 23 38 25
Open 9:30 a.m.-7 p.m. Closed Sun. & holidays.

Both haven and heaven for the truly devout—chocoholic, that is—can be found here. Maison du Chocolat is a tea room that lives up to its name by serving neither tea nor coffee, just hot chocolate. And the house drink has but one

fault: it's too small. Poured from a hot chocolate pot into Limoges china cups, the divine stuff comes in five incarnations: Guayaquil, a classic and elegant brew; Caracas, bitter, full-bodied, recommended for true lovers of chocolate; Brésilien, lightly flavored with coffee; Seville, spiced with a bit of cinnamon; and Bacchus, which leaves you dreaming of the Antilles. All come accompanied with whipped cream on the side. You can also try the worthy chocolate frappé, with either ice cream or sorbet. If you're still not sated, try one of the pastries, perhaps the Gounod with bits of orange peel or the Mokambo with its fresh raspberry flavor, or an assortment of fifteen chocolates lovingly dreamed up by Robert Linxe, the tutelary genius of the place.

Mariage Frères
4th arr. - 30, rue du Bourg-Tibourg - 42 72 28 11
Open daily noon-7 p.m.
6th arr. - 30, rue des Grands Augustins - 40 51 82 50
Open daily noon-7 p.m.

A jungle of teas, teapots, teacups, tea balls—Mariage Frères is, in short, a tea-ocracy. For more than a century it has sold tea, 350 kinds of it, from the strongest Imperial Slavic blends to the most delicately perfumed varieties. Nonsmokers may station themselves at a table on the ground floor beneath the exotic palms and the ceiling fans. Those dedicated to tobacco as well as tea leaves climb, at their own risk, the steep stairs to a place in which they will be welcomed. Everybody is kept happy here. The teas, prepared with filtered water, are served at the appropriate temperatures in insulated infusion-style teapots, and the waiters respect the ritual of tea. Watching them wheel between the tables, impecca-

141

bly garbed in something vaguely Indian, one wonders when they have time to read their Kipling. Delicate house pastries valiantly accompany these sublime teas. A grand number of brunch items are served on Sunday.

La Mosquée de Paris

5th arr. - 39, rue Geoffroy-Saint-Hilaire - 43 31 18 14
Open daily 11 a.m.-9 p.m. Closed July 27-Sept. 10. No cards.
When you emerge—skin softened, hair shining and scented—from the hammam that is part of the Paris Mosque complex, prolong your sense of well-being with a stop at the Mosque's tea room. In a cool, dim atmosphere, with music playing in the background, sample North African and Middle Eastern pastries accompanied by strong, sweet mint tea, Turkish coffee or barley water.

Muscade

1st arr. - 36, rue de Montpensier & 67, galerie de Montpensier, Jardin du Palais Royal
42 97 51 36
Open daily 3 p.m.-6 p.m. Closed 1 wk. at Christmas-New Year's.
A wall of mirror and another of window give the actors (from the nearby Comédie Française) and government officials who frequent this chic little tea room a many-angled view of the Palais-Royal gardens. In fine weather, take a cue from the regulars: lay claim to a table outside, then go inside to inspect the pastries and make your choice.

Les Nuits des Thés

7th arr. - 22, rue de Beaune - 47 03 92 07
Open noon-7 p.m. Closed Sun., Aug. & holidays.
The decor is rich: white lacquer, pink upholstery, mercury mirrors, damask tablecloths, antique furniture and watercolors on the walls. The welcome may be cool if

you aren't a regular, but the clientele is noticeably at ease, chatting about such weighty topics as dog pedigrees, boating and the latest literary successes. They nibble on salads and main-dish pies and tarts of all sorts, but truth to tell, only the desserts are really exceptional (we're thinking of the caramelized cream cheese tart and the raspberry macaroons). You'll spend something over 100 francs for lunch, half that for tea and a pastry.

Pandora

2nd arr. - 24, passage Choiseul 42 97 56 01
Open 11:30 a.m.-7 p.m. Closed Sat., Sun. & Aug.
Take a good look at the pastry selection as you cross the front room, then proceed to the chocolate-colored salon in the back, where daylight pours down from the glass ceiling. At lunchtime, crisp toasted bread and fresh butter are already set out on the well-spaced round tables; the menu offers zucchini flan, a remarkable chicken salad and other light dishes. Late afternoon is a quieter time, perfect for indulging in Pandora's chocolate-chestnut cake, or the rhubarb or coffee tarts. Reasonable prices. It is advisable to book in advance for lunch.

La Pâtisserie Viennoise

6th arr. - 8, rue de l'Ecole-de-Médecine - 43 26 60 48
Open 9 a.m.-7:15 p.m. Closed Sat., Sun., mid July-end Aug. & holidays.
Medical and literature students are among the enlightened crowd who fill up the seats of this citadel of the Latin Quarter, its seats worn smooth and shiny by generations of devotion. La Pâtisserie Viennoise opened in 1928, and the youthful ambience remains as tasteful as the cakes are tasty—the strudel and the poppy-seed

cake (called the *flanni*) are among our favorites. The teas are perfect and the Viennese hot chocolate is a dream; they all marry beautifully with a croissant or a raisin brioche. Everything is made on the premises and everything is good. There's only one drawback: the place is always packed. But so what—just pile on in or find a stool at the bar. It's worth it! You'll think you've been transported from Paris to a *Konditorei* in Vienna.

Le Ritz

Hôtel Ritz
1st arr. - 15, place Vendôme - 42 60 38 30
Open daily 4 p.m.-6 p.m.
A harpist adds a magical note to this enchanted garden where classical busts, plane trees and elegant patrons create an otherworldly haven. A discreet, attentive staff serves decent tea; for our money (130 francs, to be precise) only the millefeuille rises above the ordinary. But the atmosphere is worth the price of admission.

Rose Thé

1st arr. - 91, rue Saint-Honoré 42 36 97 18
Open noon-6:30 p.m. Closed Sun. No cards.
Your grandmother from Philadelphia would love it here: tasteful paintings, subdued lighting, antiques, plants and a sideboard displaying some luscious-looking cakes. Tea lovers will certainly fall for the rose-thé, an exquisite blend of Bulgarian rose with a touch of jasmine and lotus. Devotees of something more solid will find no fault with the old-fashioned rich chocolate cake made from real chocolate bars. And the hot chocolate is not to be missed. Between noon and 2 in the afternoon, the regulars, including the antiques dealers of the neighborhood, come to nibble on gratins, quiches and the

famous meat pie. In summer a sheltered terrace provides a spot of calm in the madding heart of Paris.

Le Salon du Chocolat

8th arr. - 11, bd de Courcelles 45 22 07 27
Open 2:30 p.m.-6:30 p.m. Closed Sun., Aug. 15, Easter & 4 wks. at Christmas.

Not content to offer just wonderfully intense chocolates (try the palets made with cocoas from Java, Ghana and Colombia), the Salon now proposes rich pastries, too. Lunch brings an appealing selection of hot dishes, but the place really comes into its own at teatime, with a wide choice of brews from China and India, and a sublime version of hot chocolate, served in a Limoges chocolate pot. The triple-chocolate cake, we might add, is in a class by itself. Plan to spend 50 francs for a beverage and pastry.

Le Stübli

17th arr. - 11, rue Poncelet - 42 27 81 86
Open 10:30 a.m.-6:30 p.m. (Sun. 10:30 a.m.-1 p.m.).

In the ground-floor shop you can choose from among the best German and Viennese pastries in Paris— Linzertorte, Sachertorte, Black Forest cake and, of course, apple strudel (about 25 francs). On the second floor, in the warm atmosphere of an Austrian chalet, all of these pastries and more can be tasted along with a hot chocolate or a cup of Viennese coffee. It's *Stüblime!* And in case you're really hungry, don't worry—there's Bavarian salad, Swabian onion tart (38 francs), a Baltic platter and the Stübli, a plate of hot beef sausage and potato salad.

The prices in this guide reflect what establishments were charging at press time.

Tarterie

11th arr. - 10, rue Saint-Sébastien - 43 55 27 31
Open 11:30 a.m.-15:30 p.m. Closed Sat. & Sun. No cards.

What sets this former dairy shop apart from the common run of tea rooms is the menu's South American (Colombian, to be specific) accent. Alongside the leek and mushroom quiche, you'll find corn cakes with meat and a rousing chili sauce. Traditional sweets like dark-chocolate cake and fruit crumble appear at teatime. You'll spend about 60 francs at lunch, 40 francs for tea and a pastry.

The Tea Caddy

5th arr. - 14, rue Saint-Julien-le-Pauvre - 43 54 15 56
Open noon-7 p.m. (Sun. 11:30 a.m.-7 p.m.). Closed Tues., Wed. & 3 wks. in Aug. No cards.

This place has a medieval feel about it, with exposed ceiling beams and stained-glass windows. It's famous for a warm atmosphere and reasonable prices, and its clientele tends to be young and international (we overheard Swedes discussing with Parisians in English the relative merits of Australian cinema). The pastry list has an English and Austrian accent: chocolate Sachertorte, Linzertorte with cinnamon and raspberries, fruit pies with cream, scones and muffins are complemented by six or seven types of tea. Unfortunately, the quality is uneven.

Tea Follies

9th arr. - 6, pl. Gustave-Toudouze - 42 80 08 44
Open 9 a.m.-9 p.m. (Sun. 9 a.m.-7 p.m.). No cards.

The refurbishment did away with the '30s-style facade. Those who used to hide behind the green carved shutters must now wear sunglasses, for a big window is all that separates Tea Follies from the shady little square outside.

Another change, an air-filtering device, allows one to breathe more easily in the smokers' dining room (another area is reserved for non-smokers). The white walls are enlivened with watercolors, and the friendly service remains professional to the hilt. At lunch, the savory tarts, the famous chicken pie or a refreshing tuna tartare with apples get to the table in record time. Afternoons are more leisurely: young ladies murmur demurely over tea, scones and jam.

Tea and Tattered Pages

6th arr. - 24, rue Mayet - 40 65 94 35
Open 11 a.m.-7 p.m. Closed Sun., Dec. 25 & Jan. 1.

Why do we feel like putting on bell bottoms and a flowered vest when we come here? Must be the atmosphere redolent of hippiedom that floats among these used English-language books, and over the tea tables laden with brownies, muffins, scones and delicious cheesecake. The Americans, Canadians and Brits who gather here chat and joke noisily in their native tongue(s). Tea and a cake will cost you about 50 francs.

Thé Cool

16th arr. - 10, rue Jean-Bologne 42 24 69 13
Open noon-7 p.m. (Sun. 11 a.m.-6 p.m.). Closed wk. of Aug. 15.

Thé Cool exudes the charm of an airy English garden—it's a haven of calm in the middle of a busy neighborhood. At lunch, enjoy the view of the pretty square opposite while tucking into an attractive platter of, say, mozzarella, salmon, or air-dried beef. Those who live for teatime will rejoice at the selection of 30 rare and wonderful brews, which may be accompanied by a mouthwatering range of sweets (chocolate marquise with crème anglaise, fruit tarts, apple crumble...).

Thé au Fil
2nd arr. - 80, rue Montmartre
42 36 95 49
Open noon-5 p.m. Closed Sat., Sun., Aug. & holidays.

From the apricot walls plastered with posters, the newspapers and magazines neatly arranged on poles, and the paisley tablecloths, we knew immediately we were in a tea room. But the liveliness of the place is closer in feel to a neighborhood bistro at happy hour. Be that as it may, the tea list is exceptional, the atmosphere convivial, and the appetizing luncheon salads are reasonably priced. Teatime treats include poppyseed strudel and Russian-style cheesecake.

La Théière
14th arr. - 118, bd du Montparnasse - 43 27 22 00
Open 10:30 a.m.-7:45 p.m. Closed Sun. & holidays.

At this mecca for tea buffs, you will also find excellent coffees, jams, chocolates and appealing breads, fudgy brownies, an exceptionally good pear tart, and a tea cake imported especially from England. Simple but delicious hot dishes appear at lunchtime (salmon en papillote, salads and such).

Toraya
1st arr. - 10, rue Saint-Florentin
42 60 13 00
Open 10 a.m.-7 p.m. Closed Sun.

Westerners may be disconcerted by the taste of green tea, which the courteous staff serves forth on a tray that is itself a work of art. Or by the pastries with their transcendant, poetic names: In spring you'll be offered the toyamazakura (*the cherry trees on the far mountain*), in summer the semi no ogawa (*he red fish*) and in winter the matso no yuki (snow-covered pines). Each of these exotic delights bears a resemblance to its name. Strange, very strange, is the colorless agar-agar (gelatin substitute) topped with an aduki bean paste. The staff will probably tell you that Japanese pastry has something for all five senses: the pleasure of the sound of the name, the treat for the eyes, the pleasant contact of the red-bean paste with the tongue and teeth, and the pleasing sound of the rice crunching. There remains then only to define the pleasure of the taste. Well, it must be delicious—after all, Toraya has been purveyor to the Emperor of Japan since 1789.

Verlet
1st arr. - 256, rue Saint-Honoré
42 60 67 39
Open noon-6:30 p.m. Closed Sun. & Mon., Easter Sat. & Sun., Oct. 1, Aug., Dec. 25, Jan. 1 & May 1.

At Verlet, it isn't Champagne or the proximity of your beloved that goes to your head, but rather the delicious aromas of tea and coffee. Once inside the door and in the presence of sacks and sacks of both of these earthly delights, we lose all desires except to be served a steaming cup of *something*. This is one of the best places in Paris for either tea or coffee. Seated on the rickety chairs (which, by the way, are few in number and hotly fought over at lunchtime), in an all-wood decor dating from 1880, coffee devotees sip Jamaican, an excellent Moka or the house blend, Grand Pavois. For tea drinkers, there are more than 30 varieties, including a nicely perfumed Chinese tea called White Flowers and, of course, the famous Darjeeling, which seems particularly soft and subtle here. If you want a snack, there is silky Viennese strudel.

WINE BARS

L'Ange-Vin
11th arr. - 24, rue Richard-Lenoir
43 48 20 20
Open 11 a.m.-8:30 p.m. (Tues. & Thurs. 11 a.m.-2 a.m.). Closed Sat., Sun., July & holidays.

The luscious dessert wines for which Anjou is famous—Montlouis, Coteaux-de-l'Aubance, Vourvray and Coteaux-de-Layon—here get the star billing they deserve. The '89 and '90 harvests yielded some stellar examples, which owner Jean-Pierre Robinot would be only to happy to pour for you (16 to 24 francs a glass).

Les Bacchantes
9th arr. - 21, rue Caumartin - 42 65 25 35
Open 11:30 a.m.-5:30 a.m. (Sun. 11:30 a.m.-10 p.m.).

We're happy to report that service has greatly improved at this all-night wine bar, where judiciously chosen charcuteries, superb cheeses and tasty daily specials provide ideal company for the Minervois, Béarn rouge, Pacherenc de Vic Bilh and other unusual bottlings selected by boss man Raymond Pocous.

Bar du Caveau
1st arr. - 17, pl. Dauphine - 43 54 45 95
Open 8:30 a.m.-8 p.m. Closed Sat., Sun. & last 2 wks. of Dec.

Lawyers, it seems, will always be lawyers. And lawyers can always be found at the Bar du Caveau, pleading their cases over glasses of Bordeaux. In winter, when the interior of this well-heeled establishment gets a bit cramped, their verbal antics can wax tiresome. You may prefer sitting quietly with a Parisian daily, presented in the old reading-room style on a thin pole, or simply to enjoy a salad, an open-faced sandwich and a glass of one of the excellent Bordeaux selected by the management, which also runs the restaurant next door. In summer the tiny sidewalk terrace on the place Dauphine is a treat.

Le Baron Rouge
12th arr. - 1, rue Théophile-Roussel - 43 43 14 32
Open 10 a.m.-2 p.m. & 5 p.m.-9:30 p.m. (Sat. 10 a.m.-8 p.m.; Sun. 10 a.m.-2 p.m.). Closed Mon. & holidays.

New owners have laid in a new selection of wines and have spruced up the dining room. The same colorful clientele of trendies, old-time Parisians, artisans and artists drops in for a plate of charcuterie and incredibly low-cost wines (Côtes-du-Rhône goes for 22 francs a liter).

Beaujolais Saint-Honoré
1st arr. - 24, rue du Louvre - 42 60 89 79
Open daily 6 a.m.-2 a.m.

Ever since the Pyramide du Louvre became one of the planet's top tourist attractions, this venerable bistro (one-time winner of the "Best Jug of Wine" award) has won a new lease on life. Though the decor remains somewhat sad and weary, you can rely on the quality of the Beaujolais, the charcuteries and the perfectly ripened cheeses.

La Bergerie
16th arr. - 21, rue de Galilée - 47 20 48 63
Open 8 a.m.-8 p.m. Closed Sat., Sun., Aug. & holidays.

Another award-winning wine bar, notable not only for its Beaujolais, but also for a deliciously fruity Bourgueil. The hearty *plats du jour* bring in an enthusiastic crowd at lunchtime.

The prices in this guide reflect what establishments were charging at press time.

Bistrot des Augustins
6th arr. - 39, quai des Grands-Augustins - 43 54 41 65
Open daily 11 a.m.-2 a.m.

Down at the bottom of the boulevard Saint-Michel, amid the fast-food chains and greasy spoons, stands this honest-to-god bistro, unflagging in its devotion to French culinary tradition. Robust homemade terrine, a satisfying cheese assortment, delicious omelettes are solidly supported by a range of proprietors' wines: Muscadet, Cérons (a honeyed dessert wine), Sinard's Côtes-du-Rhône sell for 12 to 18 francs a glass.

Le Bistrot du Sommelier
8th arr. - 97, bd Haussmann - 42 65 24 85
Open noon-2:30 p.m. & 7:30 p.m.-10:30 p.m. Closed Sat. eve., Sun. & July 24-Aug. 24.

Despite the name, this is hardly a bistro; it's more like a classic-style restaurant. But there's certainly a sommelier: Philippe Faure-Brac, elected World's Best Sommelier in 1992. His own predilection is for wines from the Rhône valley, of which he is a native, and *Bordeaux from the other side of the river* (Saint-Emilion, Pomerol). An excellent address for people who wish to learn more about wine and about matching wines with food. No concessions are made to accessibility or easy drinking: here you'll find neither Sancerre nor Beaujolais nor Muscadet. Prices are high.

Aux Bons Crus
1st arr. - 7, rue des Petits-Champs - 42 60 06 45
Open noon-10 p.m (Sat. 10 a.m.-5:30 p.m.). Closed Sun. & Aug. 15.

After a thorough-going facelift, this ultra-Parisian institution is now a wine bar that manages to be both rustic and elegant—perfectly in tune with

its location near the fashionable place des Victoires. The food still runs to bistro dishes with a Lyonnais accent, accompanied by a wide and clever range of wines from the Loire Valley, Beaujolais and Bordeaux.

Le Bouchon du Marais
4th arr. - 15, rue François-Miron - 48 87 44 13
Open noon-3 p.m. & 6 p.m.-2 a.m. Closed Sun. & at Christmas.

Just opened in 1992, this bar is already a classic. In a convivial atmosphere, you can down some choice Loire Valley vintages (the proprietor himself owns a vineyard in Chinon), along with the usual selection of sandwiches, grilled andouillette or, for a change of pace, the potato-and-cheese dish from Savoie known as raclette.

Ma Bourgogne
8th arr. - 133, bd Haussmann 45 63 50 61
Open 7 a.m.-8:30 p.m. Closed Sat. & Sun.

Nothing ever seems to change at this temple to Beaujolais, a friendly place where a faithful lunchtime crowd returns religiously for coq au Juliénas, boeuf bourguignon and parsleyed ham terrine. The owner, Burgundy-born Louis Prin, continues to purchase his wines direct from the producers, as he has done for the past 30 years. His Hautes-Côtes-de-Beaune possesses a rare finesse.

La Cave Drouot
9th arr. - 8, rue Drouot - 47 70 83 38
Open 7:30 a.m.-9:30 p.m. Closed Sun. & July-Sept.

This long-lived establishment across from the Drouot auction house is at once a wine bar, a brasserie and a restaurant. The choice of edibles thus ranges from open-faced sandwiches to full-

145

fledged *cuisine gastronomique.* Antiques dealers, auctioneers and collectors rely on Jean-Pierre Cachau to select the perfect wine to accompany their meal: perhaps the Ladoix from Burgundy, which he bottles himself; or a slightly sweet Pacherenc de Vic Bilh, from his native Béarn.

Caves Bailly

5th arr. - 174, rue Saint-Jacques 43 26 80 74
Open 6 p.m.-midnight. Closed Sun. & Mon.

What pleasanter place for a plate of cheese or cold meats and a glass of Bordeaux than this ancient wine shop in the heart of the Latin Quarter? We would surely make it a more frequent stop on our itinerary were the prices a bit more reasonable: 37 francs for a glass of Ermitage de Chasse-Spleen '88 is a few francs too much.

Les Caves Petrissans

17th arr. - 30 bis, av. Niel - 42 27 83 84
Open noon-10:15 p.m. Closed Sat., Sun., holidays & 3 wks. in Aug.

This wine shop, one of the most prestigious in Paris, will soon be 100 years old. Down through the years, a cavalcade of literati and bon vivants have drunk the good wines and Champagnes of Martin Petrissan and his descendants. Currently, Christine, the great-granddaughter, and her husband, a former lawyer who left the bar (so to speak), run the establishment. Now it includes a full-fledged (and quite elegant) restaurant which offers splendid regional menus with wines to match. For 170 francs one may dine on soup, poulet au vinaigre de cidre, cheese and crème brûlée; attractive accompaniments would be Dauvissat's Chablis (210

francs) or a Beaujolais from Jean-Charles Pivot (95 francs).

Les Caves Solignac

14th arr. - 9, rue Decrès - 45 45 58 59
Open noon-2 p.m. & 7:30 p.m.-10 p.m. Closed Sat., Sun., 2 wks. at Christmas & holidays.

With a vaguely Italian decor highlighted by lots of old posters and a curious collection of antique siphons, this well-run *bistrot à vin* balances on the cusp of the fashionable. Owner Jean-François Banéat takes great pains to serve only the freshest fare (the house foie gras is a marvel) backed up by a tantalizing roster of wines. Nor does he hesitate to transfer any wine that needs it into a (lovely) decanter—a laudable practice we don't often encounter in the city's wine bars.

La Cloche des Halles

1st arr. - 28, rue Coquillière - 42 36 93 89
Open 8 a.m.-10 p.m. (Sat. 10 a.m.-6 p.m.). Closed Sun.

The wooden clock is still there, a small replica of the bronze one that used to ring to signal the closing of the huge central markets. The bistro itself has gracefully survived the great changes in the area. Serge Lesage, who recently took over the reins, is scrupulously maintaining tradition. There are always several special dishes in addition to the excellent open-faced sandwiches, quiches and good wines bottled on the premises. At lunchtime, a bit of patience is in order; people stand three-deep around the bar, a friendly mix of hipsters elbow-to-elbow with police inspectors, notaries and shopkeepers. Fully refreshed, you'll have spent a few dozen francs at most.

> Monday, like Sunday, is a day of rest for many shopkeepers.

Clown Bar

11th arr. - 114, rue Amelot - 43 55 87 35
Open noon-3:30 p.m. & 6:30 p.m.-1 a.m. (Sat. 6 p.m.-1 a.m.). Closed Sun. & Aug. No cards.

Countless drawings, figurines and posters of clowns, clowns, clowns fill this historic establishment. While the 1919 decor alone is worth the trip, why neglect the marvelous wines and good food served here? Tables are few and hotly contested, so remember to book ahead.

La Côte

2nd arr. - 77, rue de Richelieu 42 97 40 68
Open 7:30 a.m.-8:30 p.m. Closed Sat. & Sun.

The fleet-footed Fabre brothers are famed for their victories in waiters' races around the world (the object of these contests is to run to a distant finish line while holding a tray with two full glasses and a bottle of wine). Both also run Paris wine bars: this one is a simple bistro that offers good and hearty daily specials (rabbit in mustard sauce, boeuf bourguignon), excellent cheeses and a varied choice of wines from the Loire Valley and Beaujolais. A large, eclectic clientele moves in at lunchtime, and the service sometimes suffers from the crush.

Les Coteaux

15th arr. - 26, bd Garibaldi - 47 34 83 48
Open 10 a.m.-10 p.m. (Mon. 10 a.m.-7:30 p.m.). Closed Sat., Sun., Aug. & holidays.

This attractive newcomer looks like a winner to us. In the bright little dining room a cheerful staff serves generous charcuteries (the house terrine is plunked down on the table, so you can serve yourself!), warming *plats du jour* (we liked the sage-scented veal stew on a bed of fresh pasta) and nicely matured cheeses.

The owners, who formerly ran a wine shop in Montmartre, have put together an intelligent wine list that includes an ample choice of offerings by the glass.

Le Coude-Fou

4th arr. - 12, rue du Bourg-Tibourg - 42 77 15 16
Open daily noon-4 p.m. & 7 p.m.-2 a.m. (Sun. 7 p.m.-2 a.m.).
This place doesn't empty out until late, mostly because the customers feel so at home. Conversations flow freely among the big and little tables. The cooking is simple and straightforward (boudin, poultry dishes and the like). If you prefer the bar to a table, the wines by the glass and the charcuterie platters will keep you happy and speed you on your promenade through the Marais. The house usually offers about 30 wines, half of them by the glass. The Côtes-du-Rhône wines and those from the Loire are well chosen, and there are some nice little wines from Savoie. Honesty obliges us to note, however, that we have on occasion encountered a few oxydized examples.

La Courtille

20th arr. - 1, rue des Envierges 46 36 51 59
Open daily noon-11 p.m.
Atop the picturesque heights of Belleville, a working-class district where Edith Piaf and Maurice Chevalier frolicked as kids, two noted wine wallahs, François Morel of the neighboring Cave des Envierges (see below) and his associate, Bernard Pontonnier, preside over La Courtille, a spiffy new wine bar-cum-brasserie. From before noon till nearly midnight you can feast here on such earthy delights as oxtail salad, boudin with caramelized apples or blanquette de veau, all perfect foils for the astutely chosen growers' wines (we like Foillard's manly Morgon). Photos by Willy Ronis of Belleville in the 1950s punctuate the airy, ivory and pine-green decor.

L'Ecluse Bastille

11th arr. - 13, rue de la Roquette 48 05 19 12
Open noon-1:30 a.m. (Thurs., Fri. & Sat. until dawn). Closed at Christmas & New Year's.
The latest link in the Ecluse chain boasts the chic atmosphere, trendy clientele, stylish staff and huge range of Bordeaux that are the company's time-honored trademarks. For a festive apéritif, sample the bubbly Lassime Crémant de Bordeaux (17 francs), then move on to steak tartare (75 francs) with a glass of Ségur de Cabanac '87, followed by warm apple tourte laced with Armagnac (a glass of Sauternes—perhaps a Château Coutet'84—would be ideal at this juncture). To wind up the evening, a smooth Calvados: Lemorton '55 (25 francs), would be just the ticket.

L'Ecluse François-ler

8th arr. - 64, rue François-ler - 47 20 77 09
Open daily noon-1:30 a.m.
  See *text above.*

L'Ecluse Les Halles

1st arr. - 5, rue Mondétour - 40 41 08 73
Open noon-1:30 a.m. Closed Sun., Dec. 25 & Jan. 1.
A high-class operation like L'Ecluse is rare in these parts, where tourist traps and grungy cafés abound. You'll spot the familiar facade at the end of the rue Rambuteau, tucked behind the Forum des Halles. Inside, a comfortable room and a hospitable welcome await you, along with some good—though expensive—dishes (carpaccio, foie gras, smoked goose breast...) and a wide-ranging selection of red, white and even sparkling Bordeaux. L'Ecluse makes extensive use of the recent inert-gas replacement devices that allow an opened wine to be maintained in a perfect state for up to ten days. This allows for a top château by the glass (for 60 francs and up) to be offered each week.

L'Ecluse Madeleine

8th arr. - 15, pl. de la Madeleine 42 65 34 69
Open daily noon-1:30 a.m.
  See *L'Ecluse Bastille.*

L'Ecluse Saint-Michel

6tht arr. - 15, quai des Grands-Augustins - 46 33 58 74
Open daily noon-1:30 a.m. Closed Sun., Christmas & New Year's.
  See *L'Ecluse Bastille.*

L'Enoteca

4th arr. - 25, rue Charles-V - 42 78 91 44
Open noon-2 a.m. Closed Dec. 24-Jan. 2.
Should you be seized by an irresistible urge for a bottle of Brunello di Montalcino, of Sassicaia or of a lush Malvasia dei Lipari, head over to the Marais and L'Enoteca, the city's first Italian wine bar. Already a hit with journalists and people in politics, this engaging trattoria features succulent pasta dishes, authentic Italian snacks and a mind-boggling, 100 per cent Italian wine list. We can't think of a better place for a Sunday-night supper (neither can a lot of other folks—remember to book your table in advance).

L'Entre-Deux-Verres

2nd arr. - 48, rue Saint-Anne - 42 96 42 26
Open noon-3 p.m. Closed Sat., Sun., Aug. & holidays.
The food, the wines, the owners: every element of this charming establishment, lodged in an ancient coaching inn, hails from Bordeaux! Lampreys from the Gironde River are a fixture on the

menu, as are wines from the family vineyards in Entre-Deux-Mers and Fronsac.

Les Envierges

20th arr. - 11, rue des Envierges
46 36 47 84
Open noon-2 a.m. (Sat. & Sun. noon-8 p.m.). Closed Mon. & Tues.

Renaissance man (he holds diplomas in philosophy and art history) and wine meister François Morel is the proud proprietor of one of the city's most successful *bars à vins*, where customers may hoist a glass or buy a bottle to take home. Loire Valley bottlings occupy the place of honor, but Morel is not averse to promoting his finds from Roussillon or the Jura. Keeping good company with these choice wines is Nadine's generous, warming bistro cooking.

L'Espace Hérault

5th arr. - 8, rue de la Harpe - 46 33 00 56
Open noon-2 p.m. & 7:30 p.m.-10:30 p.m. Closed Sun. & Aug.

Fragrant wines and down-home dishes from the Languedoc-Roussillon region cop top billing at this jovial bistro, an annex to Patrick Pagès's popular restaurant of the same name next door.

Au Franc Pinot

4th arr. - 1, quai de Bourbon - 43 29 46 98
Open 11:30 a.m.-3 p.m. & 7 p.m.-midnight. Closed Sun. & Mon. lunch.

Another annex to a well-known restaurant; the Franc Pinot is one of the oldest taverns on the banks of the Seine, and you couldn't ask for a more picturesque spot. The lower levels (the cellars purportedly descend to river-bottom level) are reserved for dining, but the ground-floor entry, with its centuries-old walls, is a comfortable wine bar. Loire and Burgundy wines made from the Pinot grape figure prominently on the list.

Le Griffonnier

8th arr. - 8, rue des Saussaies 42 65 17 17
Open 8 a.m.-9 p.m. Closed Sat., Sun., July & holidays.

Listening to the witty exchanges between the boss and his waiter is a great way to hone your repertoire of snappy comebacks in French—if, that is, you can cut through the *patron*'s Auvergnat accent! Robert Savoye's bistro is a favorite with couturiers and gallery owners, who "ooh" and "aah" over the perfectly ripened Fourme d'Ambert (a buttery blue cheese from Auvergne), the collection of Beaujolais and the remarkable Mâcon-Chaintré.

Juvenile's

1st arr. - 47, rue de Richelieu - 42 97 46 49
Open 10 a.m.-midnight. Closed Sun.

Juvenile's is new and improved: and the overhaul, by owner Tim Johnston's account, is not over yet—just wait till the air-conditioning is installed! But with or without added creature comforts, we've always felt perfectly at ease in this hybrid wine-and-tapas bar, where the Queen's English is spoken and American is understood. The rare sherries that headline the wine list are ideal companions to the Spanish-style bar snacks (chicken wings, marinated fish, country ham and such) that are the house specialty. But the vineyards of southern Burgundy, the Rhône and Bordeaux are not neglected; and the menu even sounds a British note with a roast beef sandwich and nursery desserts.

Jacques Mélac

11th arr. - 42, rue Léon-Frot - 43 70 59 27
Open 9 a.m.-midnight. (Mon. 9 a.m.-6 p.m.). Closed Sat., Sun.,
Aug. & 1 wk. at Christmas-New Year's.

The proud father of a southern vineyard, Jacques Mélac is brimming with joy. Just thinking about the latest vintage on three-year-old property in Lirac is enough to set his mustache quivering and his ever-present suspenders snapping. Over the years he has kept in training by vinifying the harvest from his Parisian vines, making the Château Charonne which he sells at auction for the price of Lafite. In his bistro, one of the most successful ones around, you can choose between Chinon, Cahors, Chignin or Coteaux-du-Layon. You'll do well to avoid the Chinon white, rare but overrated, and the Saint-Joseph, which the staff has a tendency to push. Yes, it's a little crowded and rambunctious, but the simple, authentic fare is worth it: try the blue-cheese omelette, the tripe from Aveyron or the plate of charcuterie from remote Rouergue. Reservations are not accepted, so either come early or come prepared to wait.

Le Millésime

6th arr. - 7, rue Lobineau - 46 34 22 15
Open daily 11 a.m.-1 a.m.

No fewer than 32 wines are offered by the glass, priced from 8 to 32 francs. Now, that's a lot of open bottles, and since we must confess that we haven't tasted them all, we can't swear that none of them is oxidized. But we like the bar (the back room is well insulated from street noise), the generous open-faced sandwiches, the charcuterie platter (49 francs), some of the *plats du jour* and the cheerful, friendly staff.

Find the address you are looking for, quickly and easily, in the index.

Le Moulin à Vins

18th arr. - 6, rue Burq
42 52 81 27
Open 11 a.m.-2 a.m. Closed
Sun., Mon. & 2 wks. in Aug.

Charming Danièle Denis-Bertin presides over this convivial wine bar perched on the flank of the Butte Montmartre. Let her help you choose from among her attractive bottlings, a selection that has won the hearts and minds of the neighborhood's finicky wine buffs. The quality of the *plats du jour* has risen noticeably; so why not order a generous plate of boeuf mode along with a glass (or three) of Guerbois's Gamay de Touraine (13 francs a glass), then finish up with a delicious sweet Jurançon? Don't be surprised if the regulars decide to strike up a song, and someone brings out an accordion—it's a great way to spend an evening in Montmartre.

Aux Négociants

18th arr. - 27, rue Lambert - 46 06 15 11
Open noon-10:30 p.m. (Mon. & Wed. noon-8 p.m.). Closed Sat., Sun., holidays & Aug.

A Montmartre landmark; one of the pillars of this wine bar is a man dressed up like Aristide Bruand, complete with a jaunty red muffler tossed over his shoulder. But this is no self-consciously picturesque tourist attraction—no, Aux Négociants is a place for serious drinking, as you will observe from the mouthwatering multi-regional wine list that features (among others) bottles from Jasnières and Gaillac. And serious chowing down: the food is robust, all homemade and perfectly delicious (check out the rillettes de canard and the other excellent poultry dishes).

> Don't plan to do much shopping in Paris in August—a great many stores are closed for the entire vacation month.

La Nuit des Rois

11th arr. - 3, rue du Pasteur-Wagner - 48 07 15 22
Open 7 p.m.-5 a.m. Closed Sun.

Since this Champagne bar is now in the hands of a new owner, we'll have to reserve judgment on the quality of the food. But we can vouch for the attractive selection of Champagnes from large firms and small growers.

L'Œnothèque

9th arr. - 20, rue Saint-Lazare - 48 78 08 76
Open noon-10:30 p.m. Closed Sat., Sun., 2 wks. Feb. school holidays, May 1-9 & last 3 wks. of Aug.

Not so much a bar as a *restaurant à vin* (and one of the best in the city, at that), Daniel Hallée's Oenothèque offers simple yet refined cuisine that perfectly complements his fabulous wine collection. If only the welcome were as warm as the attractive decor!

Le Pain et le Vin

16th arr. - 1, rue d'Armaillé - 47 63 88 29
Open 11:30 a.m.-3 p.m. and 7 p.m.-12:30 a.m. Closed Sun., evening of Dec. 24 & 31, Dec. 25 & Jan. 1.

Improved service and fresher, more appealing cuisine have brought us back to this wine bar, created by four enterprising chefs (Dutournier, Morot-Gaudry, Fournier and Faugeron). The food is hearty and simple (steak tartare, tête de veau), but the main attraction is the wine list: 120 different bottlings, chosen by the chefs themselves, of which no fewer than 40 are available by the glass.

Bernard Péret

14th arr. - 6, rue Daguerre - 43 22 57 05
Open 9:30 a.m.-8 p.m. Closed Sun., Mon., Aug. & holidays.

With all the little food shops along this street, we always work up quite a hunger and thirst. But Bernard Péret is here

to remedy that, as were his father and grandfather, with mountain sausage and a fine glass of Morgon. The wine cellar is immense—the shop side sells wine right out onto the sidewalk—but the bistro is tiny, six tables and a *zinc* (bar counter), offering about fifteen wines by the glass. English connoisseurs in Paris, who consider Péret's Chénas and the Beaujolais nouveau the best available, can often be found here toward the end of the business day, elbow-to-elbow with the butcher and the baker.

Les Pipos

5th arr. - 2, rue de l'Ecole-Polytechnique - 43 54 11 40
Open 8 a.m.-8:30 p.m. (Sat. 8 a.m.-2 a.m.). Closed Sun. & Aug.

Christine and Jean-Michel Delhoume are a couple of pros in the wine dodge, and their long experience serves their patrons well. This establishment across from the old Ecole Polytechnique (whose alumni are known as *Pipos*) smells of aged wood and polished metal. It makes for a warm and convivial atmosphere in which to partake of Guerbois's excellent Gamay (13 francs) or René Sinard's fine Côtes-du-Rhône. Inspired by the 1910 phonograph, patrons occasionally burst into song, much to the enjoyment of the owners who indeed seem in perfect harmony with themselves, their work and their customers.

Le Relais Chablisien

1st arr. - 4, rue Bertin-Poirée - 45 08 53 73
Open 8 a.m.-11 p.m. Closed Sat., Sun. & last 3 wks. of Aug.

As its name suggests, this inviting bistro promotes the wines of northern Burgundy: Aligoté (10 francs a glass at the bar), Servin's crisp Chablis (14 francs), a delicious Irancy and a Givry from Parize

149

(88 francs a bottle). But Christian Faure is no jingoist—his wine list features fine bottles from all over France. Copious *plats du jour* at 80 francs can be savored near the bar, or under the ancient beams of the tiny mezzanine. Reservations are recommended.

Le Relais du Vin

1st arr. - 85, rue Saint-Denis - 45 08 41 08
Open 10 a.m.-1:30 a.m. Closed Sun. & 1st wk. of Aug.

The rue Saint-Denis is famed for appealing to appetites somewhere south of the taste buds, but at this Relais, only your palate will be titillated with the likes of Henri Clerc's Burgundy, a green-tinged Saint-Véran or Guiton's Ladoix Premier Cru. Solid bistro chow is also served here, in an atmosphere reminiscent of the now-vanished Halles.

Le Repaire de Bacchus

6th arr. - 13, rue du Cherche-Midi - 45 44 01 07
Open 10:30 a.m.-8:30 p.m. Closed Sun., Mon. & holidays.

The best butcher in town and some eminent wine writers frequent this wine shop-cum-bistro, where the "discoveries of the month" are always worth a look and a taste (recent examples have included a suave Montlouis and a floral Crozes-Hermitage blanc). A well-turned-out neighborhood crowd stops in around 1 p.m. for a glass of something good and a plate of charcuterie.

Le Réveil du Xe

10th arr. - 35, rue du Château-d'Eau - 42 41 77 59
Open 7 a.m.-8 p.m. (Tues. 7 a.m.-11:30 p.m.). Closed Sat., Sun. & holidays.

Every first Tuesday of the month, Marie-Catherine Vidalenc cooks up a huge pot of aligot (garlicky mashed potatoes with cheese) that brings a tear of nostalgia to the

eye of every native-born Auvergnat who tastes it. Her potato pâté, stuffed cabbage, tripe and down-home charcuteries have a similar effect. Meanwhile, Daniel Vidalenc, son and grandson of bistro proprietors, serves forth the wines he chooses, purchases and bottles himself (the Chénas and Morgon go for 15 francs a glass), as well as excellent growers' wines like Amirault's stunning Bourgueil and Delubac's Cairanne from the Côtes-du-Rhône.

Le Rouge-Gorge

4th arr. - 8, rue Saint-Paul - 48 04 75 89
Open 9 a.m.-2 a.m. Closed Sun., holidays & Aug. 16-25.

After a stroll among the antiques dealers (one of whom boasts an enviable collection of corkscrews), why not stop in here and see what good bottles the "theme of the week" has brought forth? Every two weeks, in fact, a different region of France is highlighted. Recently the Jura was featured; we sampled Rolet's sherry-like vin jaune, and his sturdy red Poulsard. Hot dishes are served at lunchtime (and in the evening, if the noontime crowd hasn't gobbled everything up!).

Le Rubis

1st arr. - 10, rue du Marché-Saint-Honoré - 42 61 03 34
Open 7 a.m.-10 p.m. (Sat. 9 a.m.-4 p.m.). Closed Sun. & 2 wks. in Aug.

Ages ago, at this very spot, old Léon Gouin first raised the banner for good wine and excellent charcuterie. In his honor, the regulars, from firemen to fashion plates, continue to call the place by its former name, Chez Léon. After all, the menu has never veered off course, and the selection of wines is still pretty good, though there are some who say they notice some weaknesses in the Beaujolais. The food includes a daily hot

special in addition to the customary array of open-faced sandwiches and cheese and cold meat platters. The real problem of the place is its size; it's just too small to handle all its devotees! In the summer, after having done elbow-to-elbow combat to get a glass of wine and some food from the bar, you can carry your conquest out to the sidewalk, where upended wine casks serve honorably as tables.

Le Sancerre

7th arr. - 22, av. Rapp 45 51 75 91
Open 7:30 a.m.-8:30 p.m. (Sat. 7:30 a.m.-4 p.m.). Closed Sun., holidays & wk. of Aug. 15.

Reserve a table if you want to eat lunch here; in a fancy neighborhood where good bistros are rare, this one fills up fast. And it doesn't lack for personality, especially that of the owners, the Mellot family. They also own the Domaine de la Moussière vineyard in Sancerre, and they sell their wine here direct from their cellars. Omelettes, andouillette (sausage) and crottin de Chavignol (small, round goat cheeses) are the rule here, but then they always have been, even before that sort of thing was in style. And don't be put off by the slick window dressing out front—Le Sancerre is very comfortable.

Au Sauvignon

7th arr. - 80, rue des Saints-Pères 45 48 48 02
Open 8:30 a.m.-10 p.m. Closed Sun., Aug., 2 wks. Feb. school holidays & holidays.

The changing of the guard (now the "youngsters" have taken over) and the extension of the terrace have fortunately done nothing to alter the style and tone of this excellent bistro. The formula for success is simple: a few good wines (oh! that Quincy!) and some appetizing *tartines* of tangy goat cheese and premium charcuterie (on neighbor

Lionel Poilâne's bread, of course!).

Au Soleil d'Austerlitz

5th arr. - 18, bd de l'Hôpital - 43 31 22 38
Open 6 a.m.-9 p.m. (Sat. 7 a.m.-6 p.m.). Closed Sun. & Aug.

An immutable institution, without which the neighborhood wouldn't be the same. Where to go after meeting a friend at the train station? Or after a meander through the nearby Jardin des Plantes? Come here, for a fruity Régnié (the most recently proclaimed cru of Beaujolais) or boss André Calvet's latest discovery. As for solid sustenance, you can count on earthy charcuterie from Aveyron and warming daily specials (try the boeuf bourguignon).

Tabac de l'Institut

6th arr. - 21, rue de Seine - 43 26 98 75
Open 8:30 a.m.-8 p.m. Closed Sun. & Aug.

From the outside, it's just another news-and-tobacco shop with a long row of tables in the back. But upon entering, you find yourself in a dark, wood-paneled, quiet bar, where you can taste some excellent wines: Mâcon-Viré, various Beaujolais and Sauvignons and so forth. This is a surprising address—right in the middle of the School of Fine Arts neighborhood—for an intimate conversation.

La Tartine

4th arr. - 24, rue de Rivoli - 42 72 76 85
Open 8:30 a.m.-10 p.m. (Wed. noon-10 p.m.). Closed Tues. & Aug. 1-20.

It's easy to picture Trotsky here, seated at the tables in the back or with his elbows up on the big marble bar, in a debate with his cronies over a glass of red wine. His followers, and his opponents, still come to listen for his echoes and to mix with the varied crowd on this end of the rue de Rivoli in the

---

Art on the wall

Paris is officially encouraging the revival of a forgotten art form —the painted wall. The first *mural advertisements* that emerged in the nineteenth century had some artistic merit, but as the suburbs and the Métro spread they lost their impact in a morass of mediocre slogans. In 1943 a law was passed limiting the size of such dubious decoration to a measly fifty square feet. However the work of some talented fly-by-nighters during the '60s and '70s put mural art back on the Paris map, and in 1979 companies were once again allowed to tout their wares on walls. Since 1976 the city authorities have financed the decoration of between five and seven walls a year. Artists are invited to submit designs and a jury selects which ones will give a facelift to some of the city's bleaker buildings. The best way to appreciate a wall painting is probably to come across one by chance, but here are some starters: Philippe Rebuffet's firemen at 45 rue Saint-Fargeau in the twentieth arrondissement; "trompe-l'œil" workmen putting up a sign at 52 rue de Belleville, also in the twentieth; Cueco's little girl playing in the passage Gatbois, in the twelfth; "Shadow of a tree", a reflection of reality at 47 boulevard de Strasbourg in the tenth arrondissement.

Marais. The complete range of Beaujolais, from generic to Villages all the way through the ten crus is on hand, and at noon you'll find a daily hot special. And of course, open-faced sandwiches (*tartines*) are served at any time.

Taverne Henri-IV

1st arr. - 13, pl. du Pont-Neuf 43 54 27 90
Open noon-10 p.m. (Sat. noon-4 p.m.). Closed Sun. & 3 wks. in Aug.

For more than 30 years the fruits of Beaujolais, Montlouis and the greater and lesser Bordeaux vineyards have been flowing through this old so-called bistro. It continues to fill with advertising types, travel agents, publishers, journalists, lawyers and so forth, not to mention tourists fresh from excursions on the Seine. Behind the counter—or seated with one of the regulars—you'll

find the owner, Robert Cointepas, loud and ruddy-faced, and his wife, a vintner's daughter. Cointepas knows how to buy wine even better than he knows how to sell it. He travels to the vineyards to select his wines in October, then offers them in peak condition all year, including the Beaujolais in its traditional pint *pot*. The standard open-faced sandwiches are of good quality, and fine charcuterie and wines are available for takeout.

Le Val d'Or

8th arr. - 28, av. Franklin-Roosevelt - 43 59 95 81
Open 8 a.m.-9 p.m. (Sat. 8 a.m.-5 p.m.). Closed Sun., at Christmas, New Year's & holidays.

Géraud (not Gérard, thank you) Rongier, who hails from deep in the Auvergne, is one of the grand masters of the wine profession. He trains good wine stewards and some excellent colleagues, such as Serge Lesage, who now runs Rongier's former establishment, La Cloche des Halles. Several years ago Rongier took over this unknown little bistro near Saint-Philippe-du-Roule, and with his personal renown, it has attracted a wide following. At midday, it's filled with advertising execs, civil servants from the Ministry of the Interior, fashion-industry women and television folk from the nearby TV business centers. One of the old Gallic guard of the wine profession, Rongier has harsh words for many of the upstarts who are invading it. And it's hard to argue with him when you taste his selection from the Loire, his Côte-de-Brouilly, his Mâcon-Clessé, his Bordeaux or his Aloxe-Corton. All of these are offered at highly competitive prices. As for more solid sustenance, Rongier himself prepares ham cooked on the bone, rillettes and cheeses that he ages himself.

Au Vin des Rues

14th arr. - 21, rue Boulard - 43 22 19 78
Open 10 a.m.-8 p.m. (Wed. & Fri. dinner at 9 p.m.). Closed Sun., Mon., Aug. & holidays. No cards.

Jean Chanrion sold his Moulin de la Boulange to open this place. Combined with the recent takeover of the nearby Cagouille by another fine specialist, and the established presence of Bernard Péret, the opening virtually transforms the neighborhood into a wine-lover's crossroads. The atmosphere of this Everyman's bistro is only bolstered by the qualities we expect of Chanrion: the excellent choice of Beaujolais and Mâcons and the daily specials made from the best ingredients. Ah, the baked andouillette with a little white wine...

Willi's Wine Bar

1st arr. - 13, rue des Petits-Champs - 42 61 05 09
Open 11 a.m.-11 p.m. Closed Sun.

The Englishmen who founded this establishment are probably the best connoisseurs in Paris (among the English, that is) of wines from the Côtes-du-Rhône, which figure prominently on their wine list both in quality and number. We never grow weary of trying new ones, red and white. At the bar, Williamson and Johnston have a habit of offering discoveries from other regions, such as Australian novelties, a wonderful Vouvray, wines from Madeira or sweet wines from all over. The marble and blond-wood dining room is comfortable and frequented by an unobjectionable crowd: bankers and art buffs at noon, tony regulars at night. You can figure on spending 300 francs for dinner (by the way, we think the food gets better here all the time).

NIGHTLIFE

BEER BARS

L'Académie de la Bière
5th arr. - 88 bis, bd de Port-Royal
43 54 66 65
Open noon-2 a.m. (Sun. noon-midnight).

As the name suggests, those dedicated to the immortal delights of Gambrinus (the mythical king/inventor of beer) gather here to clink mugs into the night. University types from the neighborhood sit alone resting their eyes on the collections of bottles and labels that adorn the walls. The wooden benches are a bit hard, and at busy times elbows get pressed pretty close together, but these quibbles are small beer compared to the tasty house brew, drawn perfectly under the practiced eye of a true artist of the tap, Pierre Marion.

Bar Belge
17th arr. - 75, av. de Saint-Ouen
46 27 41 01
Open daily 11 a.m.-3 a.m.

Two of the many lusty beers on tap at this authentically Flemish watering hole are a Lindermans kriek and a Lambic Vieux Bruges; the superb list of bottled beer is topped by Belgium's famous Judas-sur-Lie. Like the other jolly habitués who gather here, we always order a plate of the excellent jambon d'Ardenne to accompany our brew.

Bedford Arms
6th arr. - 17, rue Princesse - 46 33 25 60
Open 10 p.m.-dawn. Closed Sun.

Whether or not you gain admittance to this classy pub will depend on your demeanor (smile!) and your possession of a valid passport. Once inside, you can order up a cool lager, a pint of ale or a fine malt whisky, in the company of actors, TV personalities and other urbane night hawks (the ultra-exclusive Castel's is just next door).

Le Café de la Plage
11th arr. - 59, rue de Charonne
47 00 91 60
Bar: open 8 p.m.-2 a.m. Downstairs: open from 11 p.m. Closed Sun. & Mon.

A trendy, eclectic nightspot featuring live music (downstairs in the cave: jazz, salsa, blues or fusion), and a cosmopolitan young crowd. Beer—particularly Smithwicks—is the tipple of choice.

Finnegan's Wake
5th arr. - 9, rue des Boulangers
46 34 23 65
Open 10 p.m.-midnight (Sat. & Sun. 4 p.m.-midnight. Closed 1 wk. at Christmas.

Though it is a recent addition to the Latin Quarter scene, Finnegan's Wake is already a popular student haunt (they work up a powerful thirst poring over dusty tomes in the library around the corner!). English is spoken in this friendly Irish pub, where the draft beer is drawn as it should be: slow and easy.

Flann O'Brien
1st arr. - 6, rue Bailleul
42 60 13 58
Open daily 4 p.m.-2 a.m. Closed Dec. 25 & Jan. 1.

The most authentically Irish of the city's pubs. James, the owner, makes sure that the Guinness is served just as it would be in Dublin or Cork: rich, smooth, with virtually no gas bubbles.

Le Général La Fayette
9th arr. - 52, rue La Fayette - 47 70 59 08
Open 10 a.m.-3 a.m. (Sat. 3 p.m.-3 a.m.). Closed Sun.

Join the jolly jostlers around the convivial bar for a cool pint of Guinness or a Belgian brew, or else choose a table inside or on the terrace for a light meal (salads, charcuterie, herrings, cheese...). The service is simpatico, and so is the cosmopolitan clientele.

Gobelet d'Argent
1st arr. - 11, rue du Cygne - 42 33 29 82
Open daily 4 p.m.-1 a.m.

This is the place in town for Guinness and loads of Irish ambience.

La Gueuze
5th arr. - 19, rue Soufflot - 43 54 63 00
Open noon-2 a.m. Closed Sun.

One is surprised by the size of this immense but discreet establishment located halfway between the Pantheon and the Luxembourg Gardens. From the nearby Sorbonne, teachers and students alike flock here at noon and in the evening. The classic array of Belgian beers is sufficiently inclusive to satisfy any lover of fine suds. Of the bountiful food offered here, we prefer the herbed white cheese, which you spread on slices of hearty bread and wash down with a solid Duvel beer.

Irish Pub
2nd arr. - 55, rue Montmartre
42 33 91 33
Open daily 4 p.m.-12:30 a.m. Closed 2 days at Christmas.

The convivial Irish atmosphere is accented by ditties and ballads direct from the Emerald Isle, and Guinness stout served at precisely the right temperature, topped with the correct amount of foam.

James Joyce
1st arr. - 5, rue du Jour - 45 08 17 04
Open daily noon-1 a.m.

The great Irish writer, who liked to take a drop himself now and again, is the presiding spirit at this immense beer hall. Film director John Ford might well have dreamed up the decor, which evokes a Hibernian port town.

Kitty O'Shea's
2nd arr. - 10, rue des Capucines
40 15 00 30
*Open noon-1:30 a.m. (Fri. & Sat.
until 2 a.m.). Closed Dec. 25.*
Kitty doesn't have any culinary ambitions; one comes here to put down a few Smithwicks and Guinnesses, served on tap at ideal temperature and pressure—like in Dublin. The smoked salmon, the chicken pie and the Irish coffee never fail to be everything the regulars expect them to be. The decor, which is half-bar, half-dining room, has its charm. But you can't be in too much of a hurry or too picky about the selection.

La Marine
6th arr. - 59, bd du Montparnasse - 45 48 27 70
*Open daily 6:30 a.m.-2:30 a.m.
(Fri. & Sat. until 3:30 a.m.).*
Thankfully, the sanitizing and bleaching of the once-colorful Montparnasse area has not yet reached La Marine; it still retains its folkloric charm—even if little except the varnished tables and copper portholes remains of the nautical motif. A big sign (which we've translated for you) announces Our job is to serve a good beer, so leave us the choice and have no fear, thereby setting the tone: beer is queen here. Dark, light or amber, it is accompanied at any hour by Nuremburg sausages or weisswurst (or a combination plus apples and fries), or mussels in beer sauce.

Mayflower
5th arr. 49, rue Descartes - 43 54 56 47
Open daily 10:30 a.m.-4 a.m.
While we wouldn't call it puritanical, this classy British-style pub in the heart of the Latin Quarter stands apart from the more down-and-dirty establishments that surround it. By day, weary pilgrims wander in for a quiet drink and a

snack, but at nightfall a livelier crew takes over.

La Micro-Brasserie
2nd arr. - 106, rue de Richelieu
42 96 55 31
Open 8 a.m.-2 a.m. Closed Sun.
Yes, the house beers are actually brewed on the premises, in huge copper vats that make up a big part of the interior decor. To accompany the delicious amber brew (far better than the house lager), try some of the surprisingly light fare that incorporates hops and malt: prime rib *marchand de bière*, filets of rockfish cooked in pale beer and so forth. Some excellent cheeses from the north and east of France can be found here as well. Too bad that the salmon-and-black postmodern decor is so cold and noisy, for overall this is a very successful experiment.

L'Oiseau de Feu
11th arr. - 12, place de la Bastille
40 19 07 52
Open daily 9 a.m-5 a.m.
An off-shoot of the popular Général Lafayette tavern (see above), this spiffing establishment offers a fine selection of draft beers and a short menu of home-style dishes. The view of the new Opera house is a plus—or a minus, depending on your tastes in architecture.

Sous-Bock Tavern
1st arr. - 49, rue Saint-Honoré
40 26 46 61
*Open 11 a.m.-5 a.m. (Sun.
3 p.m.-5 a.m.).*
No fewer than 400 beers and 180 whiskies are on offer at this bustling bar, a recent but very welcome addition to the Paris pub scene. The concise but appealing menu features classic brasserie fare (we can recommend the excellent rillettes and civet de sanglier).

La Taverne de Nesle
6th arr. - 32, rue Dauphine - 43 26 38 36
Open daily 8 p.m.-dawn.
Hundreds of beers and seventeen krieks (a Belgian brew) are served in this tavern, where you can while away a pleasant evening, if you don't mind the noise of the last-round revelers who drift in after energetic soirées in the area. The video entertainment does its best to thwart all conversation. We prefer to come here around 8 p.m. for an apéritif, such as the good draft beer, and a relaxed chat or a glance at a video number.

CABARETS

Crazy Horse
8th arr. - 12, av. George-V - 47 23 32 32
For two score years now, saloon-keeper Alain Bernardin has entertained convoys of tourists with his bevy of buxom beauties. Clad only (and only briefly!) in leather wasp-waisters, these *femmes fatales, the most sophisticated in the universe,* (so states the program) cavort and form—presumedly—erotic tableaux. But for our money, the most exciting aspect of the show is the astonishingly inventive lighting, which clothes Lova Moor, Betty Buttocks and their cohorts with laser beams. Herculean bouncers stationed at the doors make sure that the atmosphere doesn't turn too steamy. The show is stylish and professional, yes; but is it sexy...?

Folies Bergère
9th arr. - 32, rue Richer - 42 46 77 11
The Folies-Bergères are (conceivably) worth a visit to get a peek at the fabulous interior decor of the Great Hall. But sadly, the much-touted floor show is only a pale copy of what it used to

155

be. The Folies Bergère, the doyenne of Parisian music halls where Josephine Baker used to strut her stuff, now serves up fare that even grannies in Peoria would consider ho-hum.

Le Lido
8th arr. - 116 bis, av. des Champs-Elysées - 40 76 56 10
Closer in spirit to an athletic event than a cabaret performance, this fast-moving show features grandiose stage sets, magnificently costumed dancers (including the 60 leggy, toothy, busty Blue Bell Girls) and a host of occasionally breathtaking novelty acts. Need we mention that most Parisians have never—would never—set foot in the place? "Who cares?" reply the wide-eyed tourists for whom a night at Le Lido is a dream come true.

Le Moulin Rouge
18th arr. - 82, bd de Clichy - 46 06 00 19
You've all seen the movie; now you can see the genuine article—in the flesh! Tradition is everything here, and the famous Doriss Girls scrupulously respect it: twice a night, seven nights a week, they prance on stage and cancan their cans off.

Le Paradis Latin
5th arr. - 28, rue du Cardinal-Lemoine - 43 25 28 28
What can be said about a cloyingly sweet floor show led by dancers who look like a nice bunch of sorority sisters decked out in feathers and rhinestones? *Viva Paradis*, a revue in 24 tableaux, delivers all the obligatory numbers— French cancan, erotic tango and so on. Yet a few stars manage to shine through: Chicagoan Ursuline Kairson, with her warm, thrilling voice; the energetic Lucien who puts the troupe through their paces; and Mister Sergio, the

house emcee, who could liven up a funeral. Nevertheless, this magnificent Belle-Epoque theater designed by Gustave Eiffel deserves a kinder fate.

Les Trottoirs de Buenos Aires
1st arr. - 37, rue des Lombards 40 26 28 58
Open 10:30 p.m. (Sun. 4 p.m.; Tues. 9 p.m.). Closed Mon.
Nostalgic expatriates meet at this concert-café to drink and listen to the passionate, plaintive strains of *el nuevo tango*. Argentine jazz-fusion bands are scheduled as well, and they play for a switched-on, appreciative audience. The atmosphere varies nightly: Tuesdays, Wednesdays and Sundays are tango nights, when couples can demonstrate their technique on the dance floor (novices can take lessons on Sunday afternoons).

COCKTAIL BARS

Banana Café
1st arr. - 13, rue de la Ferronnerie 42 33 35 31
Open 4:30 p.m.-5 a.m. (Fri. & Sat. 4:30 p.m.-6 a.m.).
A trendy venue with a tropical twist for a young, clean-cut crowd. Sip cocktails or wines-by-the-glass at the bar, or lend an ear to the improvised jazz and pop concerts staged downstairs.

Le Bélier
L'Hôtel
6th arr. - 13, rue des Beaux-Arts 43 25 27 22
Open daily noon-2 a.m.
A half-dozen tables, a few stools, the gentle sound of a fountain, warm colors, a cheeky bartender... and the cocktails—such as the Bélier (vodka, Curaçao, grenadine, fruit juices)—are good, too. This is an ideal spot to wind up an evening.

Birdland
6th arr. - 8, rue Guisarde - 43 26 97 59
Open 8 p.m.-dawn. (Sun. 10 p.m.-dawn). Closed at Christmas & New Year's.
The owners recently refurbished this cozy nest for jazz-loving night owls, situated in the heart of Saint-Germain-des-Prés. Sip a cocktail (a few non-alcholic offerings are available) and lend an ear to what is surely one of the finest collections of jazz recordings in town.

La Casbah
11th arr. - 18-20, rue de la Forge-Royale - 43 71 71 89
Open daily 9 p.m.-5 a.m.
A neo-Moorish nightspot with a fascinating "pre-worn" decor, La Casbah draws a hip, handsome crowd with its exotic cocktails and feverish atmosphere. You can join these trendy revelers if (and only if) the surly doorman/bouncer likes your looks.

Chapman
2nd arr. - 25, rue Louis-le-Grand 47 42 98 19
Open 5 p.m.-2 a.m. Closed Sun. & holidays.
Just a short putt away from the Opéra, this wood-paneled bar festooned with golfers' paraphernalia plays the "English club" card to the hilt. Bernard, the owner and chief mixologist, is an alumnus of the famed Harry's Bar. He welcomes a clean-cut crew of habitués (stockbrokers and such) with cleverly concocted cocktails and a soothing ambience.

Le China Club
12th arr. - 50, rue de Charenton 43 43 82 02
Open 7 p.m.-1:30 a.m. Closed at Christmas & New Year's.
The chic denizens of the Bastille nightlife district like to forgather at this glamorous, multilevel club: either at the long ground-floor cocktail bar, upstairs in the smoky *fumoir*

where choice Cognacs and Armagnacs are poured, or downstairs in the new jazz club dubbed "Le Sing Song," where live music can be heard from Tuesday through Saturday from 11 p.m.

Closerie des Lilas

6th arr. - 171, bd du Montparnasse - 43 26 70 50
Open daily 10:30 a.m.-2 a.m.

Sure, this place once served the likes of Hemingway and Gide, though now only Jean-Edern Hallier (who?) holds court at his table by the door. But there is still a superb decor, particularly inviting in warm weather with the laurel-enclosed terrace, the high-class, polished service and the excellent cocktails. Snobby and expensive? You bet. But remember, you're not out for a beer at the neighborhood tavern.

Le Comptoir

1st arr. - 14, rue Vauvilliers - 40 26 26 66
Open noon-2 a.m. (Fri. & Sat. until 4 a.m.).

Here's a splendid place to mingle with a very Parisian throng, and down a selection of delicious tapas accompanied by an appealing choice of spirited libations. On Friday and Saturday nights, the presence of a DJ keeps the joint jumping, but effectively thwarts any effort at conversation.

Le Dépanneur

9th arr. - 27, rue Fontaine - 40 16 40 20
Open daily 24 hours.

"Tequila, tequila, arriba!" Here comes Miss Tequila, packing icy bottles of Jalisco in her holsters, a cartridge belt loaded with shot glasses slung across her chest, ready to serve a "rapido" to her hard-drinking customers. Strategically located within shootin' distance of the big guns on the Pigalle nightlife circuit, this

neo-postmodern watering hole is open 24 hours a day.

Le Forum

8th arr. - 4, bd Malesherbes - 42 65 37 86
Open 11:30 a.m.-2 a.m. (Sat. & Sun. 5:30 p.m.-2 a.m.). Closed holidays.

This is the archetypal French cocktail bar, with flawless service, a lovely decor (even the cocktail shakers are a work of art) and an iron-clad policy of discretion. At about seven in the evening, couples (legit and less so) drift in for an intimate chat before heading home. The 150 cocktails and the selection (one of the best in Paris) of scotch whiskies are accompanied by olives and peanuts. The armchairs are comfortable, and the touch of nostalgia in the atmosphere is quite soothing.

George-V

Hôtel George-V
8th arr. - 31, av. George-V - 47 23 54 00
Open daily 11 a.m.-1:30 a.m.

The clientele comes from top-drawer conferences, seminars and other such gatherings. Where are the movie stars you'd expect to see? The atmosphere is a little chilly in this otherwise comfortable bar, which opens onto a series of intimate salons where you can engage in quiet conversation while nursing a whisky selected by Monsieur Jacques, who is fluently conversant on the subject.

Le Grand Hôtel

Le Grand Hôtel
9th arr. - 2, rue Scribe - 40 07 32 32
Open daily 11 a.m.-2 a.m.

Come cocktail time, dandies, loafers and other elegant fauna gather beneath the Grand Hôtel's immense glass-and-steel dome to see and be seen. Intimate it's not, but the scene is a hoot, and the ex-

pertly mixed drinks are served with style.

Harry's Bar

2nd arr. - 5, rue Daunou - 42 61 71 14
Open daily 10:30 a.m.-4 a.m. Closed at Christmas.

Time weighs lightly on this Parisian landmark, which looks much the same today as it did at the Liberation. The main bar is a bustling, convivial place where sports fans (particularly rugby rooters) discuss their favorite teams; the downstairs piano bar is more conducive to quiet conversation.

Hurlingham Polo Bar

Le Méridien Paris-Etoile
17th arr. - 81, bd Gouvion-Saint-Cyr - 40 68 34 34
Open daily 11:30 a.m.-2 a.m.

A pleasant place to hoist a "wee dram" in good company. Georges and his staff will initiate you into the lore of rare old whiskies amid improbably British surroundings—leather armchairs, tartan fabrics, a gas-log fire... Champagnes and judiciously chosen wines are also on offer.

Meurice

Hôtel Meurice
1st arr. - 228, rue de Rivoli - 44 58 10 60
Open daily 10 a.m.-2 a.m.

One visits this bar chiefly to sip tea or nibble on a toast au caviar (365 francs) in a sumptuous "Pompadour" decor (Madame herself would have loved it). But if the need for stronger stimulation arises, the waiter can provide a classy selection of whiskies and Armagnacs.

Le Moloko

9th arr. - 26, rue Fontaine - 48 74 70 76
Open daily 8 p.m.-dawn.

White-hot nights go down at Serge Krüger's happening nightspot, a *bar de nuit* where the chic and eccentric feed the

157

juke box and commune over cocktails in a wildly eclectic, vaguely Russian decor. Though this is not a private club, first-time patrons should expect to get a cool once-over at the door.

Le Normandy

1st arr. - 7, rue de l'Echelle - 42 60 30 21
Open daily 11 a.m.-1 a.m. (Sat. & Sun. 11 a.m.-1 p.m. & 6 p.m.-1 a.m.).

The Normandy's comfy Chesterfield armchairs don't attract the preen-and-be-seen set, but you may hear the confidential murmurings of journalists and others enjoying a pre–Comédie Française drink. This is a bar where women alone can feel at ease, and the cocktails shaken up by Serge, Jean and Xavier are as fine as every other feature of this mellow hotel bar. There is a fine choice of brandies, featuring Cognacs from Delamain and a superb Armagnac 1957, Cuvées Normandie.

La Perla

4th arr. - 26, rue François-Miron 42 77 59 40
Open daily noon-2 a.m.

La Perla was a pioneer in the wave of Mexican bars that hit Paris a few years back. The corner premises on a charming street in Le Marais give patrons a wide-angle view of the passing scene, which they may contemplate while enjoying a Dos Equis, a shot of tequila, or an exotic cocktail. A short menu proposes decent tortillas, enchiladas and chili con carne.

Plaza Bar Anglais

Plaza Athénée
8th arr. - 25, av. Montaigne - 47 23 78 33
11 a.m.-1:30 a.m.

Classier than this, there isn't. Here is a bar where you can talk business or speak of love, safe in the knowledge that you will be neither interrupted nor

importuned. Service is impeccable and discreet; in the evening, a piano provides unobtrusive background music.

Pont-Royal

Hôtel Pont-Royal
7th arr. - 7, rue de Montalembert 45 44 38 27
Open noon-midnight (Sat. noon-10 p.m.). Closed Sun. & Aug.

Publishers, writers and agents regularly meet for apéritifs and literary chit-chat at this dark, wood-paneled bar. At off hours, the leather club chairs are just as inviting, and the ambience far more calm: perfect for correcting the manuscript of one's memoirs, or for making sentimental conversation.

Raphaël

Hôtel Raphaël
16th arr. - 17, av. Kléber - 44 28 00 28
Open daily 11 a.m.-midnight.

The bar of the Hotel Raphaël is opulent and refined, with bronze sculptures, carved wood, plush carpets and expertly mixed cocktails. Exclusive and very expensive, this bar is a favorite watering hole for stars seeking a respite from their admiring throngs.

Le Rosebud

14th arr. - 11 bis, rue Delambre 43 35 38 54
Open 7 p.m.-2 a.m. Closed Aug.

With each passing decade, a new generation of appreciative fans is introduced to this Montparnasse landmark, where intellectuals and other observers of the urban scene exchange ideas over a drink and a bowl of the bar's famous chili.

The Ile Saint-Louis opens up

Instead of huddling behind high walls as was usual for many of the capital's finest residences, the townhouses here were built facing the Seine to give their occupants the benefit of a view and fresh air. King Louis XIII acquired the two separate islands that today constitute the Ile Saint-Louis in 1611, had them joined with two stone bridges and started 50 years of building work under the supervision of architect Louis Le Vau. The result is a harmonious architectural whole best enjoyed during a leisurely stroll. The Church of Saint Louis-en-l'Ile, with its original ironwork clock and wooden sculptures, is the only monument on the island open to the public.

Saint-James & Albany

Hôtel Saint-James & Albany
1st arr. - 6, rue du 29-Juillet - 42 60 31 60
Open daily 10 a.m.-1 a.m. (dawn).

In fine weather, the doors open onto a pretty garden—a plus that few hotel bars can boast. On the other hand, the list of cocktails offers slim pickings, and the service does not always live up to the grandeur of the setting.

Le Scribe

Hôtel Scribe
9th arr. - 1, rue Scribe 44 71 24 24
Open daily 9 a.m.-2 a.m.

Along with the rest of the hotel, Le Scribe's bar got a much-needed facelift which transformed it into a pluperfect hotel bar, where guests and visitors may enjoy excellent cocktails, soft piano music and private conversation in newly luxurious surroundings.

Choiseul et Montgolfier

Hôtel Sofitel Paris
15th arr. - 8, rue Louis-Armand
40 60 30 30
Open daily 8:30 a.m.-1 a.m. (Choiseul); open daily 6 p.m.-2 a.m. (Montgolfier).

The Choiseul and Montgolfier bars (the latter famous for nightly jazz) are the only more-or-less quiet (or appropriately lively) spots in this neighborhood surrounding the huge exhibition complex known as the Salons of the Porte de Versailles. They are good meeting spots, where you needn't fear being overwhelmed by a tidal wave of show visitors and exhibitors.

Le Suffren et Le Toit de Paris

Hôtel Hilton
15th arr. - 18, av. de Suffren - 42 73 92 00
Le Suffren: open 7 a.m.-11 p.m. (Sun. until 2 a.m.). Le Toit de Paris: 6 p.m.-2 a.m., closed Sun.

Le Suffren manages to maintain a relaxed, friendly atmosphere—no mean feat in this sort of place. Big-business types from nearby offices meet here to discreetly settle deals. Meanwhile, up on the tenth floor, wealthy foreign visitors unwind in the Toit de Paris bar, sipping cocktails made by Christian Viel, mixmaster extraordinaire, and enjoying a splendid view of the Eiffel Tower. On Sundays Le Toit de Paris gives you a glass of Champagne when you take brunch, a hearty spread featuring roast rib of beef and daily specials like lobster or salmon alongside eggs prepared to order and a choice of desserts.

Le Vigny

Hôtel Vigny
8th arr. - 9-11, rue Balzac - 40 75 04 39
Open daily 7 a.m.-2 a.m.

A beautiful bar in an equally beautiful hotel, just off the Champs-Elysées. Polished wood, mellow leather and soft lights create a luxurious setting that is dependably quiet and discreet—unless, of course, a gaggle of groupies awaiting the appearance of their idol has taken over the turf! A glass of premium whisky will set you back about 80 francs.

Le Westminster

Hôtel Westminter
2nd arr. - 13, rue de la Paix - 42 61 57 46
Open daily 9 a.m.-midnight.

Ensconced in a tony hotel between the Opéra and the place Vendôme, this posh, polished bar is a convenient spot for a pre-prandial drink. In our estimation, though, the atmosphere is not conducive to leisurely conversation.

LIVE MUSIC

Le Baiser Salé

1st arr. - 58, rue des Lombards 42 33 37 71

For jazz fans eager to discover talented musicians destined for fame (if not fortune, the jazz life being what it is); years from now, you'll be able to say "I saw them play in Paris before anybody had heard of them..."

Caveau de la Huchette

5th arr. - 5, rue de la Huchette 43 26 65 05

This is a shrine to good old-fashioned swing and Dixieland, situated in a cellar in the Latin Quarter. You'll feel you've been transported back to the 1950s: there's a live orchestra, clouds of smoke, romantic young tourists, graduate students who never will, and some veteran dancers with a real sense of rhythm for the jitterbug and bebop.

Club Lionel Hampton

Le Méridien Paris-Etoile
17th arr. - 81, bd Gouvion-Saint-Cyr - 40 68 34 34

A Who's Who of jazz and blues greats have played in this plush, comfortable lounge, located in one of the city's finest hotels. We can recall spending memorable evenings here with Fats Domino, Monty Alexander, John Hendrix, the Count Basie orchestra, Screamin' Jay Hawkins and many more.

Au Duc des Lombards

1st arr. - 42, rue des Lombards 42 33 22 88

A popular jazz venue somehow reminiscent of an English pub, where prices are comparatively low (the first drink is tariffed at 65 francs). Though the audience doesn't listen in religious silence, but musicians like to play here anyway because the acoustics are just right. Relaxed atmosphere, quality bands. Jam sessions on Tuesdays.

L'Eustache

1st arr. - 37, rue Berger - 40 26 23 20

Lots of people, lots of noise: L'Eustache is one big party, night after night. The more solemn sort of jazz buff spurns it absolutely, but L'Eustache does not pretend to be a concert hall. The acoustics are so-so, yet we've heard some terrific hard-bop horn blowing here.

Le New Morning

10th arr. - 7-9, rue des Petites-Ecuries - 45 23 51 41

Unquestionably the city's premier jazz club, the scene of unforgettable evenings with the late Chet Baker and Stan Getz, Gary Burton, Betty Carter, Oscar Peterson, Archie

Shepp... The New Morning's 400-seat auditorium boasts surprisingly comfortable seating and superb acoustics. You can purchase tickets at the door an hour before the gig.

Opus Café

10th arr. - 167, quai de Valmy 40 38 09 57

Now for something completely different. The Opus Café is a former British officers' mess from World War I which has been transformed into a classical music venue. Why should the background music be cocktails for two be loud and strident? Here, by the Canal Saint-Martin, you can sip a highball while you listen to a Mozart string quartet or a Schumann sonata—Cheers!

Le Petit Journal Montparnasse

14th arr. - 13, rue du Commandant-Mouchotte - 43 21 56 70

Le Petit Journal Montparnasse features first-rate jazz musicians in a room with good sight lines, good acoustics and a long, comfortable bar. A good time is guaranteed. Its sister establishment at 71, boulevard Saint-Michel, leans to swing and Dixieland bands, but the Claude Bolling trio plays there with some regularity, as does saxophonist Benny Waters and plenty more. Both clubs offer a constantly rotating roster of musicians for a solid selection of contemporary and classical jazz.

Le Petit Opportun

2nd arr. - 15, rue des Lavandières Sainte-Opportune - 42 36 01 36

An evening at the Petit Op' is musically rewarding, but physically resembles a descent into hell. A dark, cramped, smoky cellar is the scene of remarkable concerts by the distinguished likes of Steve Lacy and Steve Potts, Barney Wilen and hosts of lesser-

Opera in Paris

There's no opera at the Opéra any more: the richly ornamented Palais Garnier, for over one hundred years the city's temple of lyric art, is now the scene of ballet and other dance performances, as well as the occasional concert. The Opéra Bastille, one of President Mitterrand's most controversial contributions to Parisian architecture, now hosts the official lyric season. Lately, however, some of the most acclaimed opera productions in Paris have been staged at the Théâtre de la Ville. Other venues that regularly present operatic performances are the Théâtre des Champs-Elysées and the Opéra Comique. For information about specific productions, check *Le Monde* or *Le Figaro's* magazine supplement on **Wednesdays**, or *Pariscope* or *L'Officiel des Spectacles*, which also appear on Wednesdays.
Opéra Palais Garnier, **place de l'Opéra, 9th arr. Reservation: 47 42 53 71.**
Opéra de Paris Bastille, **20 rue de Lyon, 12th arr. Reservations: 44 73 13 00.**
Théâtre de la Ville, **2 place du Châtelet, 4th arr. Reservations: 42 74 22 77.**
Théâtre des Champs-Elysées, **15 avenue Montaigne, 8th arr. Reservations: 49 52 50 50.**
Opéra Comique (Salle Favart), **5 rue Favart, 2nd arr. Reservations: 42 86 88 83.**

known but always exceptional jazz musicians.

Le Sunset

2nd arr. - 60, rue des Lombards 40 26 46 60

Improbably neat and ship-shape, this jazz cellar presents an unusual program of modern, expressive, sometimes over-the-top music. An offbeat spot for a nightcap (cover and first drink, 120 francs), where you can catch a whiff of things to come in the world of jazz.

Utopia

14th arr. - 9, rue Champollion 43 26 84 65

No way you can feel bad when the music is so good and the atmosphere so laid-back and friendly. Nearly every night brings a rock or blues concert (sometimes several!) to this hip Montparnasse nightery.

La Villa

Hôtel La Villa Saint-Germain 6th arr. - 29, rue Jacob - 43 26 60 00

Top jazz personalites from Europe and the U.S. are charmed by this intimate club, hidden away on the lower level of a Saint-Germain hotel. Here is where the great drummer Billy Hart chose to play when he came through town a few months back (cover and first drink, 120 francs).

NIGHTCLUBS

Les Bains

3rd arr. - 7, rue du Bourg-l'Abbé 48 87 01 80
Open daily 11:30 p.m.-dawn. Restaurant: open daily 9 p.m.-4 a.m.

Stars, dandies and young beauties who live to preen and be seen haunt this exclusive venue, where they rub shoul-

PERNOD

SPIRITUEUX — ANISÉ

PARIS

Enjoy it long with 5 parts of water, orange juice, tonic...

Le Bristol
Paris

112, rue du Faubourg Saint Honoré - 75008 Paris
Tél.: 33 (1) 42 66 91 45 - Fax: 33 (1) 42 66 68 68 - Télex: 280961

ders (and more!) with poohbahs from the worlds of show biz, advertising and fashion. Mike Tyson has been seen here; so have Madonna, Jean-Paul Gaultier, Roman Polanski, Linda Evangelista and Jack Nicholson. In order to get through the door, jealously guarded by Marilyn, it helps to be insanely chic, madly elegant or wildly notorious. Otherwise, it's advisable to be (or be with) an habitué. At 3 a.m. *El Divino*, the private club-within-a-club, opens its doors to a select group. How do you rate your chances of getting in?

Le Balajo

11th arr. - 9, rue de Lappe - 47 00 07 87
Open 3 p.m.-6:30 p.m. & 11:30 p.m.-5 a.m. (Thurs. 11:30 p.m.-5 a.m. & Sun. 3 p.m.-6:30 p.m.). Closed Tues.

In the 1980s mega-DJs Serge and Albert made Le Balajo a byword among night owls from Manhattan to Tokyo, Copenhagen and Buenos Aires. Alas, the two have parted company, and now Albert makes only occasional appearances. The end of an era? Perhaps, but a new generation is poised to take over, dancing to newly popular mambo and rumba rhythms under the benevolent gaze of the burly bouncers whose bored faces say, "This trend, too, shall pass."

Castel-Princesse

6th arr. - 15, rue Princesse - 43 26 90 22
Open 11:30 p.m.-dawn. Restaurant: 9 p.m. Closed Sun.

But for the rare exception, this club is strictly members-only. The Castel gang numbers 3,000 and constitutes a private community of honored members: uppercrust Parisians, show biz personalities, literary celebrities, and affiliated members who belong to other exclusive clubs. They sup (very well),

drink and dance and gossip together, far from the night's vulgar rabble. To join this late-night coterie, you need two sponsors, a file on your life history, and several thousand francs to cover application and fees. Only 50 new members are admitted per year. Now, if you are still interested, good luck!

La Chapelle des Lombards

11th arr. - 19, rue de Lappe - 43 57 24 24
Open 8 p.m-dawn. Closed Sun.

This is the land of rum punch, Afro-Cuban music, the samba and the tropics. It is here that sunshine breaks through gray Paris skies. The beat is hot, real hot. Come mingle with the reggae crowd—they're on to a good thing, and they know it.

Keur Samba

8th arr. - 79, rue de La Boétie 43 59 03 10
Open daily midnight-dawn.

Le Keur starts to samba when other clubs are winding down. Even a slow night goes on until 7 or 8 in the morning, but some nights go on until 11... tomorrow. The African jet set, fashion models, diplomats, wealthy business people and carefree youth party here, overseen by N'Diaye Kane: he keeps the dancers happy with an unending wave of West-Indian, Brazilian and Afro-Cuban rhythms. If this sounds like your idea of a good time, don your smartest togs, put on a smile and forget "attitude": the man at the door likes easy-going elegance.

La Locomotive

18th arr. - 90, bd de Clichy - 42 57 37 37
Open 11 p.m.-6 a.m.. Closed Mon.

Young night hawks adore the Locomotive. It's so big you can get lost in it, and it draws the rockers like moths to a

flame. The menu is unchanged since the great days of rock 'n' roll... in the '60s this was the land of the Who, the Rolling Stones and the Kinks. Today the Locomotive claims to be at the cutting edge of rock (well, that's what the bouncer told us, anyway). Dress in your best sneakers, Levi's and a clean T-shirt and you'll fit right in with the dancing, flirting, youthful mob.

Le Niel's

17th arr. - 27, av. des Ternes - 47 66 45 00
Open daily 12:30 a.m.-dawn. Restaurant: open daily 9:30 p.m.- 12:30 a.m.

No noise, no glare, no uncouth behavior disturb the well-mannered revels at this posh, wood-paneled club, a new stopover on the Paris night circuit. Le Niel's (the name is supposed to remind you of a New York venue... Guess which one?) is semi-private, so the odds of your getting in are slim unless you come with a regular, or have an introduction—the concierge of your high-class hotel could perhaps arrange for one.

Olivia Valère

8th arr. - 40, rue du Colisée - 42 25 11 68
Open daily 23:30 pm-dawn. Restaurant: open daily 9:30 p.m.-2 a.m.

Thanks to lots of panache and sleepless nights, Olivia Valère has pushed her club up into the lofty ranks of hot Parisian nightspots. There is a piano bar for intimacy, a discreet and comfy restaurant and a dance floor for the young and energetic. The question now: is Olivia Valère or Régine the reigning queen of the night? It's not an easy choice. Nightclubbers are quite demanding, after all. What is essential is to be seen... and Olivia's club, where the Middle East meets Deauville and

161

Saint-Tropez, is an excellent showcase.

La Poste

9th arr. - 34, rue Duperré - 42 80 66 16

Open 11 p.m.-2 a.m. Closed Sun. & Mon.

Near the seamy, steamy place Pigalle, the town house where Bizet composed *Carmen* and which in later incarnations became a bordello and a post office, is now an exuberantly ornate supper club. A dressy, young crowd comes here to dine, drink and dance before moving off to the area's more down-and-dirty nocturnal attractions.

Régine's

8th arr. - 49, rue de Ponthieu 43 59 21 13

Open 11:30 p.m.-dawn. Restaurant: open 9 p.m.-11 p.m. Closed Sun.

The envious (those who get turned away at the door) badmouth it. Régine's flamboyant friends, the silk-tie-and-satin-knickers brigade, ignore the critics and continue to spend large sums of money with total insouciance. But one unmistakable sign of the club's vitality is the fact that a younger crowd comes to dance here now: the children of film stars and the scions of wealthy families all seem to have membership cards in their pockets. They sail in the door, no questions asked. But for the common run of mortals, Régine's door is still irrevocably shut.

Rex Club

2nd arr. - 5, bd Poissonnière - 42 36 10 96

Open 11 p.m.-dawn (Wed. 11:30 p.m.-dawn). Closed Sun. & Aug.

Dance to a different beat every night of the week (but never on Sunday) at the Rex Club's wild and woolly theme parties. Midweek is your best bet: Tuesday is *New Jack Swing* time; Wednesday brings *Metallic Jungle Rock*; and on Thursday, DJ Laurent Garnier hosts *Wake Up, Paris,* a soirée of garage, disco and techno-house sounds.

Le Shéhérazade

9th arr. - 3, rue de Liège - 48 74 41 68

Openings vary.

Bewitching, beguiling Shéhérazade! *The* place to dance and party with a cosmopolitan crowd, in an extravagant setting straight out of the *Arabian Nights.* Raï, jazz-rap and English house music keep the incredibly pumped-up dancers shaking their booty far into the night. A cozy downstairs bar offers a respite from the frenetic action.

Slow Club

1st arr. - 130, rue de Rivoli - 42 33 84 30

Closed Sun. & Mon.

A jitterbugging couple flashes on the neon sign outside: the retro mood is set. When you hear the swing and big-band sounds inside, you may think you've walked into a 1940s time warp. The middle-aged dancers are sure

they've recaptured their youth. But this is no old folks' home: there's great music on tap, performed by first-rate (mostly French) dance and Dixieland bands who have plenty of youthful fans. For a cheap and cheerful night on the town (admission is only 65 francs on weekends) you couldn't do better!

Le Tango

3rd arr. - 13, rue au Maire - 42 72 17 78

Open Tues. 1:30 p.m.-6:30 p.m., Thurs. 10 p.m.-4 a.m., Fri. & Sat. 11 p.m.-5 a.m., Sat. 2 p.m.-6:30 p.m., Sun 2 p.m.-8 p.m. & 10 p.m.-4 a.m. Closed Mon.

Thanks to Serge Krüger, Afro-Latin music is back, alive and well, on Wednesday to Friday in this old dance hall. Black and white members of the Paris African scene flock here to warm their hearts (and shake the rest) to the beat of the beguine, the calypso and the salsa. If you're the type who hates nightclubs, fashion and Top 40 hits, but likes chance encounters and cha-cha, head over here for one last tango in Paris.

Le Timmy's

6th arr. - 76, rue de Rennes - 45 44 22 84

Open 11:30 p.m.-6 a.m. (Sun. 5 p.m.-midnight). Closed Mon.

This upscale address near Saint-Germain swings to an Afro-Creole beat and caters to black jet-setters. To fit in with this dressy crowd, only your smartest clothes will do.

Kiosques

Two popular addresses with folk who decide to go to the *theater* at the last minute. You're likely to get a good seat because this is where *tickets* that originally went to booking agencies wind up when they're not sold and they're half price. But you'll probably have to stand in line.

1st arr. - Metro station: Châtelet-les-Halles, open 12:30 p.m.-7:30 p.m., closed Sun. & Mon. 8th arr. - Place de la Madeleine, open 12:30 p.m.-8 p.m. (Sun. noon-4 p.m.), closed Mon.

SHOPS

ANTIQUES

■ ANTIQUES CENTERS

La Cour aux Antiquaires
8th arr. - 54, rue du Faubourg-Saint-Honoré - 42 66 96 63
Open 10:30 a.m.-6:30 p.m. Closed Sun., Mon. & July 20-Sept. 5.
Aspects of the art and antiques market are brought together in these little, highly polished boutiques. Eighteen shops combine to offer inlaid furniture of the seventeenth through nineteenth centuries, paintings, engravings, ceramics, jewelry and quality *bibelots* for a refined clientele.

Le Louvre des Antiquaires
1st arr. - 2, pl. du Palais-Royal 42 97 27 00
Open 11 a.m.-7 p.m. Closed Mon. (Sun. & Mon. in July & Aug.). No cards.
Le Louvre des Antiquaires, a marketplace for objets d'art, is the greatest success of its kind in France and probably the world. The former Magasins du Louvre department store has been beautifully redone and now houses some 250 dealers on three levels. These merchants are the most select, professional and scrupulous in the trade, if not the most famous. There isn't a single piece offered for sale whose authenticity and quality is not absolutely assured. Of course, the prices reflect this. Thirty specialties are represented—from archaeological artifacts to eighteenth-century furniture, from nineteenth-century minor masters to Art Deco ornaments, from old porcelain to rare stamps and from animal bronzes to lead soldiers and ship models, fans, rare books and fabulous jewels. In addition, Le Louvre des Anti-

quaires provides a delivery service, a club, exhibition halls and bars. Its annual exhibitions are mounted around selected themes on the second floor.

Village Saint-Paul
4th arr. - 23-27 rue St-Paul
Closed Tues. & Wed. No cards.
A new area of antiques dealers was inaugurated between the rue Saint-Paul and the rue Charlemagne about fifteen years ago. Encompassing some 70 stores, the Village is a good source for jewelry, pictures, glass and crystal, country furniture and decorative objects from the 1900–1930 period.

Le Village Suisse
15th arr. - 78, av. de Suffren and 54, av. de la Motte-Piquet
Open Thurs.-Sun. 10:30 a.m.-7 p.m.
With 150 dealers offering everything from "junque" to rare and precious pieces, this "Village" is a popular attraction for dedicated antiques hounds and Sunday strollers alike. Among the top merchants are Maud and René Garcia, for African art; Michel d'Istria, for sixteenth- and seventeenth-century wooden furniture from France, Spain, Italy and England; Jeannine Kugel, for animal bronzes; and Antonin Rispal,

Le Marché aux Puces

Each weekend some 150,000 visitors trek out to Saint-Ouen, a northern suburb just beyond the eighteenth arrondissement, to the world's largest antiques market. From dawn on Friday through Monday afternoon, dealers sell everything from used kitchen utensils to vintage jeans, from Art Deco clocks and bibelots to signed eighteenth-century secretaries. The Marché Biron boasts the classiest merchandise—crystal chandeliers, rare silver and such; the Marché Serpette draws clients from the fashion and entertainment fields with trendy retro and Art Deco pieces; the open-air Marché Paul-Bert is an eclectic treasure trove where early birds can unearth some terrific finds; the Marché Vernaison, the heart of the flea market, numbers 400 stands hawking vintage linens, crockery, stamps and miscellaneous collectibles; the tiny, tidy shops of the Marché Malassis present cleaned-up, restored merchandise in a modern, high-tech setting; the newest arrival, the Marché Dauphine, is still seeking to carve out its own niche.
93400 Saint-Ouen
Marché Biron: **85, rue des Rosiers;**
Marché Serpette: **110, rue des Rosiers;**
Marché Paul Bert: **104, rue des Rosiers & 18, rue Paul Bert;**
Marché Vernaison: **99, rue des Rosiers & 136, rue Michelet;**
Marché Malassis: **142, rue des Rosiers;**
Marché Dauphine: **138, rue des Rosiers.**

for Art Nouveau glass by Daum, Gallé, Carabin and Majorelle.

■ FRENCH ANTIQUES

ART NOUVEAU, ART DECO & 1930s

Maria de Beyrie
6th arr. - 23, rue de Seine - 43 25 76 15
Open 11 a.m.-1 p.m. & 2 p.m.-7 p.m. (Mon. 2 p.m.-7 p.m.). Closed Sun., Aug. & holidays. No cards.

Lovely antiques from the turn of the century can be found in this shop, as well as pieces by the great designers from the years 1925–1930: Legrain, Rousseau, Printz, Ruhlmann and others. And that is not to mention the architect-designed furniture, particularly pieces crafted in metal, from 1925 to 1950. You will also find the creations of the Union des artistes modernes, run by René Herbst with Le Corbusier, Chareau, Mallet-Stevens, Charlotte Periand, Eileen Gray and others.

Jean-Jacques Dutko
6th arr. - 13, rue Bonaparte, corner rue des Beaux-Arts - 43 26 96 13
Open 10:30 a.m.-12:30 p.m. & 2:30 p.m.-7 p.m. Closed Sun., Mon. & Aug.

Dutko was one of the early promoters of Art Deco, particularly at the Paris Biennale. Clustered all around him are the top designers of the period (Gray, Ruhlmann, Printz, Dunand). Modern art, Dutko's second love, is represented by paintings and sculptures by Fautrier, Bourdelle and Poliakoff, Léger, as well as by paintings and drawings by André Masson (whose prices he has driven considerably higher).

Félix Marcilhac
6th arr. - 8, rue Bonaparte - 43 26 47 36
Open 10 a.m.-noon & 2:30 p.m.-7 p.m. Closed Sat., Sun., Aug. & holidays. No cards.

Félix Marcilhac is one of the big boys in Art Deco, recognized far and wide for his expertise in other areas as well. He sells to the grandest museums in the world, and his top-quality objects attract a rich-and-famous clientele.

Le Roi Fou
8th arr. - 182, rue du Faubourg-Saint-Honoré - 45 63 58 91
Open 10:30 a.m.-7 p.m. Closed Sun., Mon., Aug. & holidays.

Alexandre Mai has accumulated a considerable pile of all sorts of objects from 1880 through 1930: furniture, bronzes, ivories, porcelain, clocks, jardinières (flower stands) and Art Deco chandeliers. If you are willing to rummage a bit, your efforts will often be rewarded.

DIRECTOIRE, EMPIRE, RESTORATION & CHARLES X

Au Directoire
7th arr. - 12, bd Raspail - 42 22 67 09
Open 10:30 a.m.-noon & 2:30 p.m.-7 p.m. (Mon. 2:30 p.m.-7 p.m.). Closed Sun. & Aug. No cards.

In 1982 Thierry Winsall opened this store on the boulevard Raspail, where the Dubreuil family once sold Empire furniture. He maintained his own specialty from his former store on the rue de Grenelle: the end of the eighteenth century through the beginning of the nineteenth, featuring desks, bookcases, commodes, bronzes, lamps and, his special interest, chairs. There is lots of mahogany, and the prices are sufficiently reasonable to attract other, mostly foreign, dealers.

Raoul Guiraud Brugidou-Malnati
7th arr. - 90, rue de Grenelle - 42 22 61 04
Open 10:30 a.m.-12:30 p.m. & 2:30 p.m.-7 p.m. Closed Sun., Aug. & holidays. No cards.

A shop that celebrates the pleasure of objects that combine beauty and utility, such as scientific instruments, marine objects, curiosities, and seascapes from the nineteenth and twentieth centuries.

Mancel-Coti
7th arr. - 42, rue du Bac - 45 48 04 34
Open 10 a.m.-1 p.m. & 2 p.m.-7 p.m. (Mon. 2:30 p.m.-7 p.m.). Closed Sun., (Sat. in summer), Aug. & holidays. No cards.

This is a venerable establishment reputed for its furniture, clocks and porcelain of the Directoire, Consulate and Empire periods. Its clients are eminent connoisseurs, and have included Prince Murat and the Legion of Honor museum.

Renoncourt
6th arr. - 1-3, rue des Saints-Pères - 42 60 75 87
Open 10 a.m.-12:30 & 2 p.m.-7 p.m. Closed Sun. No cards.

A far-ranging selection of mahogany and fruitwood furniture from the Empire, Restoration and Charles X periods. The objects are of the highest quality, and the Renoncourts are generous in sharing their charm and their extensive knowledge.

LOUIS-PHILIPPE, NAPOLEON III & LATE NINETEENTH CENTURY

Calvet
9th arr. - 10, rue Chauchat - 42 46 12 36
Open 9:30 a.m.-12:30 p.m. & 2:30 p.m.-6:30 p.m. (Sat. by

appt.). Closed Sun., Aug. & holidays. No cards.

Calvet is the third generation of specialists in furniture built during the Second Empire in the manner of the great eighteenth-century masters; in fact, the best cabinetmakers of the period were those who worked in that classic style, perfected in the Age of Enlightenment.

Madeleine Castaing
6th arr. - 21, rue Bonaparte - 43 54 91 71
Open 10 a.m.-1 p.m. & 3 p.m.-7 p.m. Closed Sun., Mon. & holidays. No cards.

Madeleine Castaing, a renowned decorator, friend to painters, patron of Soutine, was one of the very first to rediscover these dainty little furniture pieces and decorative objects of the Second Empire, which she sells at imperial prices. She also carries a substantial selection of carpeting and fabrics she designed herself.

MEDIEVAL & RENAISSANCE

Jacqueline Boccador
7th arr. - 1, quai Voltaire - 42 60 75 79
Open 10 a.m.-7 p.m. (Mon. 2 p.m.-7 p.m.). Closed Sun., Aug. & holidays. No cards.

Often called to act as expert witness for the French Customs Service, Jacqueline Boccador (the "High Priestess of Medieval Sculpture") combines her remarkable familiarity with medieval antiques with an equally profound knowledge of Renaissance pieces. She is the author of several superb scholarly works, and is endowed with the ability to communicate her passion for furniture, statues and tapestries to her customers. She recently vacated her shop on the rue du Bac for new, more impressive premises on the quai Voltaire.

Edouard et Gabriel Bresset
7th arr. - 5, quai Voltaire - 42 60 78 13
Open 10 a.m.-12:30 p.m. & 2:30 p.m.-7 p.m. Closed Sun., Aug. & holidays. No cards.

No one will dispute the fact that the Bressets are the world's top specialists in medieval statuary, whether in wood or stone, unpainted or polychrome. They also sell Gothic tapestries to major museums, as well as paintings, furniture and carved wood—wonderful cabinets encrusted with tortoiseshell or ebony—and bronze, ivory and enameled sculpture from the Middle Ages and Renaissance. When you visit, be sure to explore the superb vaulted cellars on the quai Voltaire.

Jean-Claude Edrei
7th arr. - 44, rue de Lille - 42 61 28 08
Open 10 a.m.-7 p.m. (Mon. from 2 p.m.). Closed Sun., Aug. & holidays.

Here is a huge, beautiful store dedicated in part to the medieval period, and in particular to china and pewterware, for which Edrei is well known as a top-quality dealer. You can also find tapestries here, which enhance some massive furniture pieces the seventeenth and eighteenth centuries.

Antony Embden
7th arr. - 15, quai Voltaire - 42 61 04 06
Open 10:30 a.m.-12:30 p.m. & 2:30 p.m.-7 p.m. Closed Sun., Mon., Aug. & holidays. No cards.

Here is a rich source of Renaissance sculpture in bronze, marble and ivory, as well as some exquisite old faïence and a wide selection of high-quality objects from the sixteenth and seventeenth centuries.

Don't plan to shop on Sundays, the vast majority of Paris stores are closed.

Perpitch
7th arr. - 240, bd Saint-Germain 45 48 37 67
Open 9 a.m.-12:30 p.m. & 2 p.m.-6:30 p.m. Closed Sun., Aug. & holidays. No cards.

With 50 years of experience, Antoine Perpitch is a renowned expert on the Flemish and Italian Renaissance, as well as on French Gothic and medieval statuary. Louis XIII chairs, credenzas and tables, including some enormous monastery pieces, and tapestries of the sixteenth and seventeenth centuries are on display in his spacious shop, advantageously situated on the corner of the rue du Bac.

SEVENTEETH & EIGHTEENTH CENTURIES

Didier Aaron
8th arr. - 118, rue du Faubourg-Saint-Honoré - 47 42 47 34
Open 10 a.m.-12:30 p.m. & 2:30 p.m.-6:30 p.m. (Sat. from 11 a.m.). Closed Sun., Aug. & holidays. No cards.

In London, New York and Paris, Didier Aaron enjoys a brilliant reputation for his prestigious collection of eighteenth-century inlaid furniture and objets d'art. He has extended his interests to the purchase and sale of fine paintings and the art of interior decoration: his firm now includes a design office headed by celebrity decorator, Jacques Grange.

Antiquités de Beaune
7th arr. - 14, rue de Beaune - 42 61 25 42
Open 11 a.m.-12:30 p.m. & 2:30 p.m.-7 p.m. (Mon. 2:30 p.m.-7 p.m.). Closed Sun., Aug. & holidays. No cards.

A noted specialist in French eighteenth-century country furniture crafted in cherry, maple, sycamore and walnut, Mr. Horowitz also possesses a large selection of porcelain from the eighteenth and early nineteenth centuries.

Aveline

8th arr. - 20, rue du Cirque - 42
66 60 29
*Open 9:30 a.m.-7 p.m. Closed
Sun., Aug. & holidays. No cards.*

Here is a respected establishment whose eighteenth-century "museum quality" furniture and painting are indeed often purchased by major museums (the Louvre, the Getty, the Musée de Compiègne, to name but a few). Jean-Marie Rossi is also known for his collection of outstanding curiosities that are always both beautiful and strikingly original. Naturally, all of these treasures fetch stratospheric prices.

Bernard
Baruch Steinitz

9th arr. - 75, rue du Faubourg-
Saint-Honoré - 47 42 31 94
*Open 10 a.m.-7 p.m. Closed
Sun., 1 wk. in Aug. & holidays.
No cards.*

An inveterate traveler in search of unusual objects, Steinitz has left his former shop near the Drouot auction house for a spiffy showplace on the Faubourg, opposite Le Bristol. The quality of his mainly eighteenth- and nineteenth-century furniture and ornaments is beyond question, and the pieces reflect Steinitz's eclectic tastes. In his workshops, 30 select artisans maintain the highest tradition of restoration. The prices, oh my, the prices. Let's just say they're in the highest tradition also. But one may visit simply for the visual pleasure.

Etienne Lévy
La Cour de Varenne

7th arr. - 42, rue de Varenne - 45
44 65 50
*Open 10 a.m.-1 p.m. & 2 p.m.-
7 p.m. (Sat. until 6 p.m.). Closed
Sun., Aug. & holidays. No cards.*

This lovely shop opens not only onto the street but also onto a beautiful inner courtyard, around which stand the outbuildings of the former residence of Madame de Staël. Claude Lévy has accumulated some real treasures: seventeenth- and eighteenth-century clocks and furniture with secret compartments. Despite astronomical prices, these peerless pieces find buyers in the four corners of the globe. On the ground floor, a gallery displays a wonderful collection of mostly nineteenth-century paintings.

Fabius Frères

8th arr. - 152, bd Haussmann
45 62 39 18
*Open 9:30 a.m.-noon &
2:30 p.m.-6 p.m. Closed Sat. (except appt.), Sun., Aug. &
holidays. No cards.*

Since 1867 the Fabius family has been antiques dealers in Paris—the business handed down from father to son (except when a son named Laurent chose the political scene instead). The firm's clients are museums and the high and mighty who appreciate the choice collection of seventeenth- and eighteenth-century furniture and objects. Also on view are impressive holdings of Empire pieces, as well as nineteenth-century paintings and animal bronzes by Barye and Carpeaux.

Galerie
Camoin-Demachy

7th arr. - 9, quai Voltaire - 42 61
82 06
*Open 10 a.m.-7 p.m. Closed
Sun. & Aug. No cards.*

This is perhaps the most beautiful antiques store in Paris, with magnificent pieces magnificently presented. Decorator Alain Demachy has done things just right, and his plan is ambitious: to bring together rare and lovely furniture of the eighteenth and nineteenth centuries, including Russian, Italian and Austrian creations, with objets d'art and decorative ornaments

from diverse periods and styles. The result is strikingly luxurious and more than a little intimidating.

Galerie Perrin

7th arr. - 3, quai Voltaire - 42 60
27 20
8th arr. - 98, rue du Faubourg-
Saint-Honoré - 42 65 01 38
*Open 10 a.m.-1 p.m. & 2 p.m.-
7 p.m. (Mon. 2 p.m.-7 p.m.).
Closed Sun. & Aug. No cards.*

Perrin can be counted among the major players in the antiques business. In a flamboyant decor of lacquer and black aluminum, Patrick and Philippe Perrin stage a presentation of some spectacular pieces from the seventeenth and eighteenth centuries: Boulle commodes, Mazarin desks and other signed masterpieces of the period.

Gismondi

8th arr. - 20, rue Royale - 42 60
73 89
*Open 10 a.m.-7 p.m. Closed
Sun., Mon., 1 wk. at Christmas-
New Year's, Aug. & holidays. No
cards.*

Already well known among collectors for his Antibes shop, Gismondi now also occupies a prestigious address on the rue Royale, which he placed under the supervision of his daughter, Sabrina. With a pronounced predilection for spectacular baroque pieces, such as sumptuous German and Italian cabinets, gilded bronzes and desks by Boulle overlaid with copper and tortoiseshell, she also presents a magnificent variety of decorative objets d'art and paintings, from the seventeenth and eighteenth centuries. And the posh, theatrical ambience with a distinctly Italian feel is itself something to behold.

---

*Some establishments change
their closing times without warning. It is always wise to check in
advance.*

Kraemer

8th arr. - 43, rue de Monceau 45 63 24 46

Open 9 a.m.-7 p.m. Closed Sun., Aug. & holidays (except appt.). No cards.

Evidently it is possible to be one of the world's top experts on the French seventeenth and eighteenth centuries, to sell to museums and top-flight collectors a range of furniture, chairs, bronzes and objets d'art and yet to remain charmingly modest. For such are the accomplishments of Philippe Kraemer, who now works in collaboration with his son. Their mind-boggling gallery is itself as fascinating as a world-class museum.

Jean de Laminne

8th arr. - 148, bd Haussmann 45 62 08 15

Open 10 a.m.-12:30 p.m. & 2 p.m.-6 p.m. Closed Sat., Sun., Aug. & holidays. No cards.

Since 1937, in his 2,000-square-foot shop, Jean de Laminne (now working in tandem with his son) has displayed stunning pieces of furniture from the eighteenth century. Devotees of Regency furniture crafted in ebony or black wood with copper finework won't go wrong with purchases of Laminne's superb commodes and mirrors, which still bear their original patina.

Michel Meyer

8th arr. - 24, av. Matignon - 42 66 62 95

Open 10 a.m.-1 p.m. & 2 p.m.-7 p.m. (Mon. 2 p.m.-7 p.m.). Closed Sun., Aug. & holidays. No cards.

Meyer grew up in a veritable palace crammed with antiques, and it shows. The ever-replenished stock of furniture and objects from the eighteenth century reflects a fondness for chiseled bronzes and mounted objects. With his excellent reputation, Meyer is an influential figure in the Paris biennial shows.

Maurice Segoura

8th arr. - 20, rue du Faubourg-Saint-Honoré - 42 65 11 03

Open 9 a.m.-6:30 p.m. (Sat. 9 a.m.-12:30 p.m. & 2 p.m.-6 p.m.; Mon. 9 a.m.-6 p.m.). Closed Sun. & holidays. No cards.

Segoura is another big name among Parisian antiques dealers. Three floors of furniture, objets d'art and spectacular decorative arts are destined for an international clientele and for prestigious private collections. He has also developed a reputation for buying and selling works by such French painters as Greuze, Watteau, Fragonard, whose canvases are scattered here and there in the shop, enhancing even further the stunningly beautiful furniture.

■ FOREIGN ANTIQUES

AFRICAN, OCEANIC & PRE-COLUMBIAN

Arts des Amériques

6th arr. - 42, rue de Seine - 46 33 18 31

Open 10:30 a.m.-7:30 p.m. (Mon. from 3 p.m.). Closed Sun. & holidays.

Within this friendly little shop is an enormous selection of primarily pre-Columbian art, from Mexico, Costa Rica and Colombia. The statues, stones and terracotta objects are all sold with a photograph and a certificate of authenticity.

Galerie Carrefour

6th arr. - 141, bd Raspail - 43 26 58 03

Open 9 a.m.-noon & 2 p.m.-6:30 p.m. Closed Sun., Aug. & holidays. No cards.

Monsieur Vérité (Truth! That's his real name) has assembled here a huge, diverse but well-selected wealth of mostly African objects: Ibéji, Yoruba and Dan masks, Ibo statues, Ashanti bronzes, Senufo doors, Akan jewelry, Baoulé statuettes and so forth. The range of prices is as wide as the turnover is high. In addition, there's a department of Mediterranean Basin antiques (displaying about 300 objects).

Galerie Mermoz

8th arr. - 9, rue du Cirque - 42 25 84 80

Open 10 a.m.-12:30 p.m. & 2 p.m.-7 p.m. Closed Sun., Aug. & holidays. No cards.

This is a highly specialized store of the finest sort. It is well known at all the Paris shows on account of its rigorously selected array of pre-Columbian works. Prices to match.

BRITISH

British Import

92200 Neuilly - 23, bd du Parc, Ile-de-la-Jatte - 46 37 27 75

Open 11 a.m.-7 p.m. (Sun. by appt.). Closed Aug.

1st arr. - 4, allée Topino, Louvre des Antiquaires - 42 60 19 13

Open 11 a.m.-7 p.m. Closed Mon. & Aug.

15th arr. 78, av. de Suffren, Swiss Village - Sous-Sol, n° 3 - 45 67 87 61

Open 11 a.m.-12:30 p.m. & 3 p.m.-7 p.m. Closed Tues., Wed. & Aug.

This establishment has just one specialty: English furniture of the eighteenth and nineteenth centuries, primarily in mahogany. At the Ile de la Jatte (a popular subject of Seurat) location, there's a restoration workshop for repairs and French polishing. Approximately 100 pieces arrive every few months.

Andrée Higgins

7th arr. - 54, rue de l'Université 45 48 75 28

Open 9:30 a.m.-1 p.m. & 2 p.m.-5 p.m. Closed Sun., Mon., Aug. & holidays. No cards.

She was one of the first to introduce Paris to the taste for things English, just after World War II. She chooses her furniture from the eighteenth and nineteenth centuries with the utmost care. The renewed popularity of the colonial style has led her to collect lovely Chinese lacquer-panel tables and secretaries, which were fashionable in England at the turn of the century. On our last visit, we also spotted some superb French furniture from the seventeenth and eighteenth centuries. The stock is always changing, and presentations can be made in customers' homes.

Aliette Massenet

16th arr. - 169, av. Victor-Hugo
47 27 24 05
Open 10 a.m.-6:30 p.m. Closed Sun., Aug. & holidays. No cards.

Every month the charming owner, Aliette, takes delivery of British specialties such as furniture and nineteenth-century objects, tea services, table settings for fish courses, porcelains, sporting prints, silver and bronze frames, pipe holders and costume jewelry.

FAR EASTERN

Beurdeley

7th arr. - 200, bd Saint-Germain
45 48 97 86
Open 10 a.m.-12:30 p.m. & 2:30 p.m.-7 p.m. Closed Sun., Mon., Aug. & holidays. No cards.

An expert if ever there was one, Jean-Michel Beurdeley is recognized as one of the great specialists in Far Eastern art. He supplies the big museums, and though you'll rarely see him in Paris—he travels extensively—his gallery continues to bring together some of the best work from China and Japan.

La Boutique du Marais

4th arr. - 16, rue de Sévigné - 42
74 03 65
Open 10:30 a.m.-1 p.m. & 2 p.m.-7 p.m. Closed Sun., Mon., 3 1st wks. of Aug. & holidays.

From opium pipes to Japanese cupboards (Tansu), Marie-

Anne Baron specializes in works from India, China and Japan. Recently, though, the artisanship of India is giving way more and more to the antique furnishings of China and Japan. A second shop displays Far Eastern graphic arts: screens, miniatures, paintings and kakemonos.

Bernard Captier

7th arr. - 25, rue de Verneuil - 42
61 00 57
Open 10:30 a.m.-7 p.m. (Mon. from 2:30 p.m.). Closed Sun. & Aug. No cards.

This specialist in Japanese antiques is known to give excellent value for the money his clients invest. Perhaps it's because he is one of the few Paris dealers to travel to Japan several times a year in search of nineteenth-century objects and furniture (chests, commodes), which he restores in Paris for his wife to sell. (Note: He will also buy them back at the selling price plus inflation.) China and Korea are also represented, and on our last visit, we noticed some very handsome screens.

Compagnie de la Chine et des Indes

8th arr. - 39, av. de Friedland - 42
89 05 45
Open 9:30 a.m.-noon & 2 p.m.-6:30 p.m. Closed Sun., Aug. & holidays. No cards.

Ah, to discover the entire Far East under one roof. A top-notch selection of Chinese porcelain, pottery, furniture, Indian and Khmer sculpture, paintings and screens is displayed on three floors. Some of the objects are truly museum quality, and the head of the shop, Jean-Pierre Rousset, can be counted on for wise counsel.

Gérard Lévy

7th arr. - 17, rue de Beaune - 42
61 26 55
Open 10 a.m.-1 p.m. & 2 p.m.-6 p.m. (& 2 Sun. in Dec.). Closed Sun. & Aug.

Lévy is a most reliable guide to the art of China, Cambodia, Japan, Korea and Thailand, and in his pretty shop we've encountered some ardent collectors. He sells important pieces to museums, but there are always more accessible items

---

March on the Arch

When Napoléon Bonaparte had the *Arc de Triomphe* built to celebrate his battlefield victories, it stood on the outer edge of Paris and the view took in the surrounding countryside. Nowadays you look out over the ultrachic eighth and sixteenth arrondissements while to the northwest the Arch's modern cousin, the *Grande Arche de la Défense*, guards the city's newest business district. Twelve broad avenues compose the "star" that radiates from the *place de l'Etoile*, former name of the place Charles-de-Gaulle. The best way to appreciate this urban galaxy is to climb (or take the elevator) to the top of the Arc de Triomphe. At the foot of Napoléon's monument an eternal flame burns over the *Tomb of the Unknown Soldier*, chosen among the many unidentified victims of the tragedy that was World War I. The eternal flame symbolizes the nation's enduring sorrow and pity.

as well—always of a refined and high quality. Lévy is also an antique photograph buff, and is an official expert on the subject.

Jan et Hélène Lühl

6th arr. - 19, quai Malaquais - 42 60 76 97
Open 2 p.m.-7 p.m. Closed Sun., Mon., Aug. & holidays. No cards.
These knowledgeable collectors of engravings will sweep you up in their enthusiasm. Their shop is located in what was once the gallery of famed collector Ernest Le Veél (whose prints and engravings were dispersed in three historic auctions at the Hôtel Drouot). They have examples from all fields—we found some fascinating culinary etchings from Japan.

Yvonne Moreau-Gobard

6th arr. - 5, rue des Saints-Pères 42 60 88 25
Open 10 a.m.-12:30 p.m. & 2 p.m.-7 p.m. Closed Sun. & Aug. No cards.
The wife of the noted appraiser Jean-Claude Moreau-Gobard, Yvonne offers a comprehensive array of archaeological objects from China, India and Cambodia. The number of pieces displayed here is as impressive as their quality.

Orient-Occident

6th arr. - 5, rue des Saints-Pères 42 60 77 65
Open 10 a.m.-12:30 p.m. & 2 p.m.-7 p.m. Closed Sun. & Aug. No cards.
As unassuming and media-shy as possible, Jean-Loup Despras, who reads hieroglyphs like we read the funnies, is an ace specialist in Egyptian antiques. He shares the premises with Yvonne Moreau-Gobard (see above), a first-rate expert on Indian and Far Eastern arts. Gobard's bronzes, pottery and ceramics are on display.

Janette Ostier

3rd arr. - 26, pl. des Vosges - 48 87 28 57
Open by appointment only. No cards.
This charming little boutique is primarily devoted to Japanese art; included are drawings, etchings, pictures, painted screens, masks, and lacquered boxes. Janette Ostier gives each client her full attention, since she now receives them by appointment only.

ISLAMIC

Arts de l'Orient

6th arr. - 21, quai Malaquais 42 60 72 91, fax 42 61 01 52
Open 10:30 a.m.-12:30 p.m. & 2:30 p.m.-7 p.m. Closed Sun., Aug. & holidays. No cards.
Annie Kevorkian is one of France's top specialists in Middle Eastern art. She has a magnificent collection of Islamic ceramics, in addition to miniatures, antique glass and terracotta objects and some exquisite bronzes.

Philippe et Claude Magloire

4th arr. - 13, pl. des Vosges - 42 74 40 67
Open 1 p.m.-6 p.m. Closed Mon.
Claude and Philippe Magloire, who are geologists and collectors as well as expert appraisers attached to the French Court of Appeals, spent ten years in Iran. In 1981, they opened a gallery on the place des Vosges to introduce and promote Iranian art, a refined but little-understood tradition in the West. Treasures such as bronzes from Luristan, Islamic ceramics (from Nishapur) and antique rugs form a good collection of Asian art and archaeology.

Jean Soustiel

1st arr. - 146, bd Haussmann - 45 62 27 76
Open 9:30 a.m.-1 p.m. & 2 p.m.-7 p.m. Closed Sat., Sun., Aug. & holidays. No cards.
Nineteen eighty three marked the 100th anniversary of this gallery; four generations of the family have promoted Islamic art here. Jean Soustiel, a highly regarded expert among his colleagues, runs one of the most famous and reputable galleries in the world. He is also the author of an exhaustive study of Islamic ceramics, which has become the collector's bible. His associate, Marie-Christine David, specializes in Indian ceramics.

MEDITERRANEAN

Nina Borowski

7th arr. - 40, rue du Bac - 45 48 61 60
Open 10:30 a.m.-12:30 p.m. & 2 p.m.-7 p.m. (Mon. 2:30 p.m.-7 p.m.). Closed Sun., Aug. & holidays. No cards.
Daughter of the great Borowski of Basel, the erudite and charming Nina Borowski displays a significant collection of pottery, vases, bronzes and marbles of Greek, Roman and Etruscan origin. Each year, she organizes an exhibit of archaeological artifacts. It's possible here to find small Greek terracotta pieces at reasonable prices.

Mythes et Légendes

4th arr. - 18, pl. des Vosges - 42 72 63 26
Open 10 a.m.-12:30 p.m. & 2 p.m.-7 p.m. Closed Sun. & 2 wks. in Aug.
Gilles Cohen has assembled a major collection of antiquities from Egypt, Rome, the Far East and pre-Columbian America. Pieces on display include Egyptian amulets as well as some rare and important Cambodian finds. He offers a certificate of expertise and a mail-order catalog.

170

A la Reine Margot

6th arr. - 7, quai de Conti - 43 26 62 50

Open 10:30 a.m.-1 p.m. & 2 p.m.-7 p.m. Closed Sun. & holidays.

This is the oldest gallery of its kind in Paris. These days more and more space is being devoted to archaeology. Michel Cohen (father of Gilles, see above), the proprietor, mounts excellent exhibits each year and publishes fascinating catalogs. There are, as always, medieval, Renaissance and seventeenth-century pieces on display, to admire or buy.

RUSSIAN

Artel

6th arr. - 25, rue Bonaparte - 43 54 93 77

Open 10:30 a.m.-12:30 p.m. & 3 p.m.-7 p.m. Closed Sun., Mon., Aug. & holidays. No cards.

Though the supply of objets d'art from czarist Russia is increasingly rare, the demand remains high. Keeper of Russian and Greek icons ranging in origin from the fifteenth to the nineteenth century, Martine Cuttat also sees to the restoration of these fragile pieces.

A la Vieille Cité

1st arr. - 350, rue Saint-Honoré 42 60 67 16

Open 10:30 a.m.-6:30 p.m. Closed Sat., Sun., July 14-Sept. 1. & holidays.

This very Louis Philippe-style decor showcases a treasury of hammered silver, beautiful icons, Fabergé pieces, porcelain, Russian painting and a collection of delicately worked stone Easter eggs, over which presides collector and expert appraiser Alexandre Djanchieff.

We're always happy to hear about your discoveries and receive your comments on ours. We want to give your letters the attention they deserve, so when you write to Gault Millau, please state clearly what you liked or disliked. Be concise but convincing, and take the time to argue your point.

▉ SPECIALISTS

BANKING, STAMPS & STOCKS

Le Marché aux Timbres

8th arr. - av. des Champs-Elysées, Carré Marigny

Open Thurs., Sat., Sun. & holidays 10 a.m.-6 p.m. No cards.

On the right side of the Champs-Elysées near the corner of the avenues Marigny and Gabriel, 70 licensed sellers set up booths along the sidewalk and the alleyways. They are there almost all day buying, selling and exchanging.

Numistoria

2nd arr. - 49, rue Vivienne - 42 33 93 45

Open 11 a.m.-7 p.m. (Sat. by appt.). Closed Sun. & July 14-Aug. 31. No cards.

This huge and constantly changing presentation of all kinds of bank notes and certificates offers everything from stocks and bonds to coins and old deeds. There's no place like it this side of Ali Baba's cave.

BRONZES

Moatti

6th arr. - 77, rue des Saints-Pères 42 22 91 04

Open 10 a.m.-13 p.m. & 2 p.m.-7 p.m. Closed Sun. & Aug. No cards.

In his townhouse on the rue des Saints-Pères, this dealer shows almost exclusively by appointment. This collection of bronzes and rare pieces presents what connoisseurs consider to be the world's most judiciously selected Renaissance bronzes. Here prices are whispered in a way that suggests that art is beyond any valuation. Every piece must first pass a three-part scrutiny verifying its authenticity, quality and rarity. An artwork purchased from Moatti bears the additional value of the firm's worldwide renown.

COINS & MEDALS

Emile et Sabine Bourgey

9th arr. - 7, rue Drouot - 47 70 35 18

Open 9:15 a.m.-noon & 2 p.m.-6:15 p.m. (Sat. 9 a.m.-noon). Closed Sun. & Aug. No cards.

Located in a Belle Epoque apartment opposite the sales room of the famous Drouot auction house, Emile Bourgey's offices have maintained the plush, discreet ambience of an earlier age. For over 30 years, everything here has been dedicated to coin collecting: the exquisite display cases, the library of several thousand titles on the subject and the attention that Bourgey and/or his daughter provide to initiate clients into the realm of numismatics.

Numismatique et Change de Paris

2nd arr. - 3, rue de la Bourse - 42 97 46 85

Open 9 a.m.-5:30 p.m. Closed Sat. (except in summer 9:30 a.m.-12:30 p.m.), Sun., Aug. & holidays. No cards.

While he reserves the trade in collectors' pieces for his boutique, at this address Jean Vinchon leaves his daughter Annette in charge of buying and selling gold coins, ingots, tokens, old bills and bank notes. Gold pieces are sealed into transparent plastic sachets in the presence of the buyer, a unique procedure that provides a valuable guarantee. If you are interested in selling gold here, you should know that there is a 10 percent commission.

Jean Vinchon

2nd arr. - 77, rue de Richelieu
42 97 50 00
Open 9 a.m.-6 p.m. Closed Sat.,
Sun., Aug. & holidays. No cards.

Jean Vinchon is not only one of the world's foremost coin experts, he was also among the first to recognize that coin collecting is more than a hobby or an esoteric specialty. He has worked diligently for its acceptance as an art. In the hushed atmosphere of his shop, great collectors argue the merits of individual coins each worth a fortune, while Vinchon advises those interested in less exalted pieces with the same careful attention.

CRYSTAL & GLASS

L'Arlequin

4th arr. - 19, rue de Turenne - 42 78 77 00
Open 2:30 p.m.-7 p.m. Closed
Sun., Mon. & Aug. No cards.

This is the kind of shop whose address gets handed around from family to family when the little one has broken an heirloom wineglass or the stopper to the carafe has mysteriously vanished. L'Arlequin stocks hundreds of styles from every period (the house specialty is nineteenth century), and at a wide range of prices.

La Brocante de Marie-Jeanne

17th arr. - 14, rue Saussier-Leroy
47 66 59 31
Open 11 a.m.-7 p.m. Closed
Sun., Mon. & Aug. No cards.

Among all the glasses and crystal, sold in sets or individually, and the liqueur decanters and the toiletry accessories, it would be surprising if Marie-Jeanne Schuhmann couldn't find that out-of-the-ordinary tiny carafe you've been hunting for. But if she can't, you can console yourself with a beautiful Art Deco vases, or perhaps a lamp or lovely bedside carafe.

Galerie Altero

7th arr. - 21, quai Voltaire - 42 61 19 90
Open 10:30 a.m.-12:30 p.m. &
2:30 p.m.-7 p.m. (Mon.
2:30 p.m.-7 p.m.). Closed Sun.,
Aug. & holidays. No cards.

This is another one of those places worth seeing even if you are not a devotee; seventeenth-century furniture and eighteenth-century glass cases function as the decor for the display of glasses and carafes from all periods from Louis XIV to Napoléon III.

CURIOS & UNUSUAL OBJECTS

Air de Chasse

7th arr. - 8, rue des Saints-Pères
42 60 25 98
Open 11 a.m.-1 p.m. &
2:30 p.m.-7 p.m. Closed Sun.,
Aug. & holidays. No cards.

Here in Jeanine Gerhard's shop is everything you can imagine that in some way or other is connected with hunting or shooting: eighteenth, nineteenth- and twentieth-century prints, decorative objects, bronze animal statuettes, duck decoys, birds in terracotta.

Aux Fontaines de Niepce et de Daguerre

18th arr. - 20, rue André-del-Sarte - 42 54 27 13
Open 10:30 a.m.-5 p.m. Closed
Sun., Mon., Aug. & holidays.

This superb store, with its Second Empire decor, is home to the best-known antique-photographic-equipment specialist in Paris. Within the walls of this vast shop/museum, Mr. Bomet has amassed a fine collection of seemingly every sort of apparatus. Bomet's crown jewels include the eighteenth-century grandfather to all cameras, the *camera oscura*, the first Eastman from 1885 and a rare Sigrist stereoscope. In all there are close to 500 pieces, displayed with the daguerrotypes and

ambrotypes also collected by Bomet.

Brocante Store

6th arr. - 31, rue Jacob - 42 60 24 80
Open 10:30 a.m.-7 p.m. Closed
Sun. & Mon. No cards.

Amid the pretty English antiques lurk innumerable charming objects, including little chests, instruments and lamps.

Galerie 13

6th arr. - 13, rue Jacob - 43 26 99 89
Open 2:30 p.m.-7 p.m. Closed
Sun. No cards.

Once a specialist in antique games, Martine Jeannin is now more interested in charming decorative objects and curiosities. She carries wood carvings from the eighteenth century, overmantels and folding screens alongside whimsical and strange items, such as bird cages, romantic baubles, embroidery, expensive turned-wood objects from Florence, as well as naive artworks.

Nicole Kraemer

1st arr. - 5, allée Desmalter, Louvre des Antiquaires - 42 61 57 95
Open 11 a.m.-1 p.m. & 2 p.m.-
7 p.m. Closed Mon. (Sun. &
Mon. in July & Aug.).

This pretty shop to an enthusiastic connoisseur of decorative objects and curios. Small eighteenth-century French pill boxes and fans are her specialty, but Nicole Kraemer's tastes are quite catholic, extending even (for example) to surgical instruments.

Magnolia

7th arr. - 78, rue du Bac - 42 22 31 79
Open 10 a.m.-7 p.m. Closed
Sun.

This congenial assemblage of bric-a-brac is crowned by a display of turn-of-the-century bridal bouquets preserved under glass. In addition, we've also come across chromo-lithographs, busts in plaster or bronze, pill boxes, powder boxes, engraved flasks, antique jewelry, baptismal medals and several beautiful Art Deco lamps.

Emmanuel Thiriot
Bernard Escher
16th arr. - 29, rue de la Tour - 45 04 46 54
Open 10:30 a.m.-7:30 p.m. (Sat. & Mon. 2 p.m.-7:30 p.m.). Closed Sun. No cards.
Original, top-quality decorative pieces collected with unfailing but highly eclectic tastes. On our last visit we came upon a beautiful piece of furniture from the 1950s next to a lovely Chinese cabinet, a ship model from the turn of the century beneath a large decorative lacquered panel signed by Jouve. Don't come here looking for something practical; everything is devoted to the decorative arts, and everything has loads of flair. Do stop by frequently—you won't be disappointed.

FABRICS

Aux Fils
du Temps
7th arr. - 33, rue de Grenelle - 45 48 14 68
Open 2 p.m.-7 p.m. Closed Sat., Sun., Mon., Aug. & holidays. No cards.
In an early-nineteenth-century decor, Marie-Noëlle Sudre sits pretty amid her treasures: bolts and bolts of antique fabric from all over the planet. These representatives are piled up like the crates of an explorer back from a long voyage through time and space—in Sudre's case, it is from the eighteenth century to the 1950s. If you're looking for something specific, you should call ahead, and Sudre will have things ready when you arrive.

Les Indiennes
4th arr. - 10, rue St-Paul - 42 72 35 34
Open 2:30 p.m.-7:30 p.m. (morning & Aug. by appointment only). Closed Sun.
The Silk Road passes through the rue Saint-Paul: here is a wonderland of shimmering brocades, damasks and satins, many from the eighteenth century. Many exotic and colorful samples of silken fabrics from the East are on view here, fairly calling out to be fashioned into cushions, curtains or fashion accessories.

FANS

Georges Antiquités
1st arr. 26, rue de Richelieu - 42 61 32 57
Open 12:30 a.m.-6:30 p.m. (Sat. by appt.). Closed Sun., Aug. & holidays. No cards.
A most refined presentation of ivory objects and various collectibles. From every period from Louis XIV to Louis-Philippe comes a display of fans made of tortoiseshell, lace, feathers, mother-of-pearl, tulle with sequins, finely worked bone, painted parchment, ostrich plumes and more. Prices vary drastically.

FIREPLACES

Michel Elbaz
(S.C.A.D.)
10th arr. - 29 bis, rue de Rocroy 45 26 40 00
Open 9:30 a.m.-6:30 p.m. (Sat. until 12:30 p.m.). Closed Sun. & Aug. No cards.
Elbaz's selection of fireplaces from the seventeenth century through 1900 come mainly in marble, and prices start at around 2,000 francs. Also through this savvy dealer, you can obtain older examples in stone or wood. A wide range of attractive prices.

Fernandez-Blanchard
11th arr. - 36, rue Sedaine - 47 00 67 59
Open 10 a.m.-5 p.m. Closed Sat., Sun. & Aug. No cards.
The selection is enormous, and the fireplaces are all beautiful old specimens in marble, wood and often Burgundian stone. There are also some garden fountains, and restoration service is provided.

Jean Lapierre
3rd arr. - 58, rue Vieille-du-Temple - 42 74 07 70
Open 11 a.m.-7:30 p.m. Closed Sun., Mon. & Aug. No cards.
Oak doors, parquet floors, stairs and other antique architectural elements are sold either "as is" or nicely restored. But the chief attraction is the stonework from (primarily) the Mâcon area: fireplaces in their entirety or in separate pieces, mostly eighteenth century, as well as some interesting carved well copings. In short, this is the place to go if you're looking for any manner of stone objects and sculpture from the eighteenth century, even (the occasional) terracotta tiles.

Pierre Madel
6th arr. - 4, rue Jacob 43 26 90 89
Open 3 p.m.-7 p.m. Closed Sun., Mon. & mid July-beg. Sept. No cards.
The impressive array of wrought-iron articles from the seventeenth century to 1900 includes fireplace tools, pokers, ash pans, mechanical roasting spits and so forth.

FOLK ART

Georges Bernard
8th arr. - 1, rue d'Anjou - 46 65 23 83
Open 10:30 a.m.-6:30 p.m. Closed Sun. & holidays. No cards.
Here you'll find original objects and documents in the domains of science, industry

and commerce. Mr. Bernard is an ardent student and collector of implements, especially antique tools, and anything that pertains to the history of cooking. From a Gallo-Roman cooking pot to an old-fashioned cake pan, there's a panoply of antique objects and rare documentary literature on such subjects as wine making. Yet another specialty is scale models of machinery.

Galerie d'Art Populaire
7th arr. - 10, rue de Beaune - 42 61 27 87
Open 2:30 p.m.-7 p.m. Closed Sun., Aug. & holidays.

This gallery, located on the site of the barracks of Dumas' Musketeers, is permeated with a nice smell of furniture polish. It is filled with beautiful old country furniture, wrought-iron and folk-art objects, such as butter molds, salt boxes and sheep collars.

L'Herminette
1st arr. - 4, allée Germain, Louvre des Antiquaires - 42 61 57 81
Open 11 a.m.-7 p.m. Closed Mon. (Sun. & Mon. in July & Aug.).

A fine, highly specialized establishment that features the art of ironwork, locks and old tools. Prices range from a few hundred to several thousand francs.

JEWELRY

Gillet
4th arr. - 19, rue d'Arcole - 43 54 00 83
Open 11 a.m.-6 p.m. Closed Sun., Mon. & Aug.

Hidden away among the souvenir shops that surround Notre-Dame, this charming boutique stands out with its eighteenth-century decor and its covetable selection of romantic jewelry: you'll find authentic antique pieces as well as fashionable ornaments from the 1940s.

Jacqueline Subra
6th arr. - 51, rue de Seine - 43 54 57 65
Open 11:30 a.m.-12:30 p.m. & 2 p.m.-6:30 p.m. Closed Sun., Mon., Aug. & holidays.

Whether from the end of the nineteenth century, Art Nouveau, Art Deco or the 1950s, the jewelry sold by Jacqueline Subra is always of the best quality, in both materials and design.

Garland
2nd arr. - 13, rue de la Paix - 42 61 17 95
Open 9:30 a.m.-1 p.m. & 2 p.m.-6:30 p.m. (Sat. from 10 a.m.). Closed Sun. & 10 days in Aug.

Minouche Messager never sells one of her rare and antique jewels without a twinge of regret. She is the queen of antique jewelry in Paris; some of the pieces that have passed through her shop are such treasures as the bracelet offered to Sarah Bernhardt by the czar, and a superb nineteenth-century necklace that belonged to King Farouk. Recently her husband, Bernard Messager, a former craftsman at Cartier, has joined her and makes fine contemporary jewelry that is sold in the shop.

C. Gustave
8th arr. - Carré d'Or, 46, av. George-V - 47 23 03 03
Open 11 a.m.-7 p.m. Closed Sun., Mon., Aug. & holidays.

Founded in 1874, this long-established firm was the first in Europe to import cultured pearls. Here you'll find some lovely antique ornaments, stones of a quality you do not see anymore and pieces signed by Van Cleef and Boucheron.

Remember that if you spend 2,000 francs or more in a store, you are entitled to a full refund of the value-added tax (VAT). See Basics *for details.*

MINERALS, GEMS & SHELLS

Claude Boullé
6th arr. - 28, rue Jacob - 46 33 01 38
Open 10:30 a.m.-12:30 p.m. & 2 p.m.-7 p.m. (Mon. 2 p.m.- 7 p.m.). Closed Sun. No cards.

Boullé is a top specialist in the field with a taste for rare and unique minerals. Among the famous collectors of "pretty stones" who have frequented this shop are André Breton, Roger Caillois and Vieira da Silva. Beautiful limestone bowls from Tuscany, marble from Bristol, jasper from Oregon, sandstone from Utah... the list seems endless.

Michel Cachoux
6th arr. - 16, rue Guénégaud - 43 54 52 15
Open 11 a.m.-2:30 p.m. & 2:30 p.m.-7:30 p.m. Closed Sun., Mon. & Aug. (except by appointment).

Several times a year Michel Cachoux travels to Brazil, the United States, Madagascar or simply down to the Alps, to track down dazzling minerals. We still remember the one-ton amethyst geode he exhibited in his shop window several years ago. These days he is also going in for fossils and objects in hard stone, such as boxes and jewelry. And his prices are, if anything, falling. His themed exhibits are invariably fascinating.

Deyrolle
7th arr. - 46, rue du Bac - 42 22 30 07
Open 9 a.m.-12:30 p.m. & 2 p.m.-6:15 p.m. (Sat. until 5 p.m.). Closed Sun. No cards.

A fabulous shop, this sumptuous mansion houses an astonishing array of minerals of every size and description. In addition, there are displays of shells, fossils, butterflies, botanical specimens and stuffed animals—from partridges to polar bears. Kids love it!

Sciences, Art et Nature
5th arr. - 87, rue Monge - 47 07 53 70
Open 10 a.m.-6:30 p.m. Closed Sun. & Mon. No cards.
Inheritor of the famous house of Boubee, founded in 1846 but now defunct, Françoise Morival still deals in the treasures of the natural world: among her teeming collections are minerals, fossils, shells, rare insects and other delights of taxidermy. Each piece sold is accompanied by an identification card that verifies its unique-object status.

MIRRORS & FRAMES

Georges Bac
6th arr. - 37, rue Bonaparte - 43 26 82 67
Open 10 a.m.-noon & 2 p.m.-6:30 p.m. Closed Sun., Aug. & holidays. No cards.
Museums and major art dealers have long known of the impressive inventory of gilded wood frames, consoles and mirrors from the seventeenth and eighteenth centuries housed in this gallery, which enjoys the highest reputation.

Marguerite Fondeur
7th arr. - 24, rue de Beaune - 42 61 25 78
Open 2 p.m.-6:30 p.m. Closed Sun., Aug. & holidays. No cards.
There is no risk of getting stuck with a tricked-up phony cherub from the Italian or Spanish trade here in this fine old establishment founded by Mme. Fondeur's parents. But the acquisition of a lovely gilded-wood piece or a mirror from the eighteenth century, with full proof of authenticity, involves a significant investment. There are also lovely, if not gilded, furniture, chairs and objects of the period.

Lebrun
8th arr. 155, rue du Faubourg-Saint-Honoré - 45 61 14 66
Open 2:30 p.m.-7 p.m. Closed Sat., Sun. & Aug. No cards.
Mirrors, consoles, barometers and sculpted wood all can be found here in addition to some magnificent frames from the fifteenth to the nineteenth century that constitute one of the largest collections in Paris. Annick Lebrun is the fifth generation of her family to run this establishment, founded in 1847. The restoration work is top-notch.

Navarro
6th arr. - 15, rue Saint-Sulpice 46 33 61 51
Open 2:30 p.m.-7 p.m. Closed Sun., Mon., Aug. & holidays. No cards.
Colette Navarro is mad for gilt and gold leaf. Her mirrors, barometers and gilded wood from the seventeenth, eighteenth and nineteenth centuries are graciously lent out for "home trial" before purchasing. Certificates of authenticity, as well as an inventory that covers price ranges (and attracts an international clientele), are available upon request.

MUSICAL INSTRUMENTS

André Bissonnet
3rd arr. - 6, rue du Pas-de-la-Mule 48 87 20 15
Open 2 p.m.-7 p.m. Closed Sun., Aug. & holidays. No cards.
Brother of the noted Parisian butcher Jean Bissonnet, André—himself a butcher for years—one day turned in his cleaver and apron, exchanging them for the antique musical instruments he loves—and can play very well. He transformed his butcher shop (the decor is still virtually intact) into a shrine to the ancient muses of harmony and music; it is surely one of the more amusing and astonishing boutiques in all of Paris.

PORCELAIN & CHINA

Dominique Paramythiotis
1st arr. - 170-172, galerie de Valois - 42 96 04 24
Open 1 p.m.-7 p.m. (Sat. from 2 p.m.). Closed Sun. & holidays. No cards.
Displayed here are various styles of china service from the beginning of the nineteenth century through the 1930s: Limoges, Gien, Sarreguemines, Creil, as well as various Paris manufacturers—in every conceivable shape, color and price range (except, of course, cheap!).

Hélène Fournier-Guérin
6th arr. - 25, rue des Saints-Pères 42 60 21 81
Open 11 a.m.-1 p.m. & 3 p.m.-7 p.m. (Mon. 3 p.m.-7 p.m.). Closed Sun., Aug. & holidays.
Here is a tasteful selection of mostly eighteenth-century porcelain and faïence primarily from the houses of Moustiers and La Compagnie des Indes. Also: painted faïence from Marseille, Strasbourg, Rouen and Nevers. This show is run by certified experts.

L'Imprévu
6th arr. - 21, rue Guénégaud - 43 54 65 09
Open 2:30 p.m.-7 p.m. Closed Sun., Aug. & holidays. No cards.
Under the sign of the unexpected, you'll discover poured ceramic ware, brightly colored and fashioned in relief, such as those pieces that flourished in the last 30 years or so of the nineteenth century: dessert plates, asparagus plates, oyster plates, plates from Salins, Sarreguemines, Clement, Longchamp and plates created by Delphin Massier at Vallauris. Then there's the stock of nineteenth-century printed plates from such manufacturers as Creil-Montereau, Choisy-le-Roi and Sarregue-

mines. And finally, the house's little specialty, *trompe-l'oeil* platters adorned with fish or reptiles in the style known as "Bernard Palissy." Recently L'Imprévu has begun to deal in Second Empire objects and furniture.

Lefebvre et Fils
7th arr. - 24, rue du Bac - 42 61 18 40
Open 10 a.m.-12:30 p.m. & 2 p.m.-7 p.m. Closed Sun. & Aug.
Parisian society heads here to purchase their faïence, porcelain and sculpture from the sixteenth to the eighteenth century. This respected establishment is run by the city's leading expert in antique ceramic ware and celebrated its centennial in 1980. Lefebvre proudly lists among its former clients Victor Hugo and Marcel Proust.

Nicolier
7th arr. - 7, quai Voltaire - 42 60 78 63
Open 10:30 a.m.-noon & 2:30 p.m.-6:30 p.m. Closed Sun., Mon., Aug. & holidays. No cards.
For three generations, this establishment has presented an astounding collection of faïence from the ninth to the nineteenth century: Iranian pieces, seventeenth-century china, decorated ceramic ware from the Italian Renaissance (Urbino, Gubbio), vases, platters and statuettes in faïance and porcelain from all over Europe, including Delft, Sèvres, Saxony, Rouens, Moustiers, Nevers and Chantilly. Of course, all of it is of the best quality and in perfect condition. All sales are accompanied by a certified guarantee.

Trésors du Passé
8th arr. - 131, rue du Faubourg-Saint-Honoré - 42 25 05 39
Open 10 a.m.-1 p.m. & 2:30 p.m.-7 p.m. (Mon. & Sat.

3 p.m.-7 p.m.). Closed Sun., Aug. & holidays. No cards.
Stunning pieces of antique faïence from the seventeenth and eighteenth centuries are displayed for purchase here, including Sèvres porcelain and high-quality china. The walls are adorned with a number of eighteenth-century prints in black and white and in color, as well as drawings, all of which are also for sale.

Vandermeersch
7th arr. - 27, quai Voltaire - 42 61 23 10
Open 10 a.m.-12:30 p.m. & 2 p.m.-6:30 p.m. Closed Sun., Mon., Aug. & holidays.
One of the founders of the Paris biennial shows, Pierre Vandermeersch was a major figure in the world of antiques. His son, Michel, carries on the business in a new store on the ground floor of the Villette mansion (where Voltaire died). The stock is small but very select: this is a prestigious address for porcelain and faïence.

RUGS & TAPESTRIES

Berdj Achdjian
8th arr. - 10, rue de Miromesnil - 42 65 89 48
Open 10 a.m.-12:30 p.m. & 2 p.m.-6:30 p.m. (Sat. 2 p.m.-6:30 p.m.). Closed Sun., Aug. & holidays.
Berdj Achdjian receives by appointment collectors looking for old and rare rugs. Here, for excellent prices, you can find every manner of old Oriental rug: Caucasian, Armenian, Chinese and Turkish. Competent specialists, Achdjian has some rare gems in its collection, dating back to the sixteenth century, to complement the modern and highly decorative rugs.

Benadava
8th arr. - 28, rue de la Boétie - 43 59 12 21
Open 9:30 a.m.-1 p.m. & 2 p.m.-6:30 p.m. Closed Sun., Aug. & holidays. No cards.
Benadava is a specialist in the restoration, appraisal and cataloging of rare rugs from the Far East. In addition, the shop carries tapestries from Flanders and Aubusson, even from the Gobelins, as well as a sizeable collection of European rugs from Spain, France and Portugal.

Jacqueline Boccara
8th arr. - 184, rue du Faubourg-Saint-Honoré - 43 59 84 63
Open 10:30 a.m.-1 p.m. & 2:30 p.m.-6:30 p.m. Closed Sun., Mon. & Aug. No cards.
No need to look any further for that tapestry you have been wanting to hang in your *salon*. From the Middle Ages, the Renaissance, the Baroque era or the Age of Enlightenment, Jacqueline Boccara has them. She supplies tapestries to the big European sales and auctions as well as to museums. If there is something she doesn't have, she will find it for you. And she also displays an array of collector's items and old drawings that she sells for reasonable (considering...) prices.

Chevalier
7th arr. - 15, quai Voltaire - 42 60 72 68
Open 10 a.m.-1 p.m. & 2 p.m.-7 p.m. (Sat. 11 a.m.-6:30 p.m., Mon. 2 p.m.-7 p.m.). Closed Sun., Aug. & holidays.
You'll think you're in a gracious private home, with glowing woodwork and soft lighting. This firm opened in 1917, and today two of the founder's grandsons carry on the restoration work of the rugs and tapestries. Certified experts, the Chevalier team sells pieces of the highest quality, be they Oriental or European. The rugs are complemented by a fine selec-

tion of very beautiful and decorative cushions (ask to see them).

Lefortier

8th arr. - 54, rue du Faubourg-Saint-Honoré - 42 65 43 74
Open 10 a.m.-12:30 p.m. & 2 p.m.-6:30 p.m. Closed Sat., Sun. & Aug.

When a firm of this quality turns 100, it may safely be regarded as an institution. Heads of state come to Lefortier from all over the world for gifts of state, and for appraisals of old rugs. Mme. Potignon-Lefortier, who runs the establishment, is an official expert on rugs for the Customs department and for the Court of Appeals of Paris.

Robert Mikaeloff

8th arr. - 23, rue de la Boétie - 42 65 24 55
Open 9 a.m.-noon & 2 p.m.-7 p.m. Closed Sun., Aug. & holidays. No cards.

To get the full effect of Robert Mikaeloff and his passion for his silk rugs from Tabriz, or his rarest Keshans, you must see him in action. It is more accurate to say that he *stages* his rugs rather than exhibits them. For the convenience of his clients, he maintains a restoration service.

SCIENTIFIC & NAUTICAL INSTRUMENTS

Arts et Marine

8th arr. - 8, rue de Miromesnil 42 65 27 85
Open 11 a.m.-7 p.m. (Sat. 2 p.m.-6 p.m.). Closed Sun., Aug. & holidays.

Jean-Noël Marchand-Saurel is the sort of expert who knows about everything from shipbuilders' large-scale ship models to miniature vessels in ivory. All those afflicted with nostalgia for things marine come here to fish for dioramas, sperm-whale teeth, eighteenth- and nineteenth-century hourglasses, and anti-

que ships in a bottle (1,500 francs and up). Restoration services are provided.

Balmès-Richelieu

3rd arr. - 21, pl. des Vosges - 48 87 20 45
Open 10 a.m.-noon & 2 p.m.-7 p.m. (Mon. 2 p.m.-7 p.m.). Closed Aug. & holidays. No cards.

Here are some of the most beautiful marine articles in Paris. Nevertheless, Mr. Balmès's great specialty remains clocks and scientific instruments from the sixteenth to the nineteenth century.

Alain Brieux

6th arr. - 48, rue Jacob - 42 60 21 98
Open 10 a.m.-1 p.m. & 2 p.m.-6:30 p.m. (Sat. 2 p.m.-6 p.m.). Closed Sun., Aug. & holidays.

Here one finds astrolabes (compact instruments used to observe the position of celestial bodies before the invention of the sextant) of course, but collectors from all over the world depend on Alain Brieux as a source for medical and scientific antiques: wooden anatomy models, anatomical tables, surgical or optical instruments. Brieux takes great care in his selections, and is currently one of the important figures in his field.

Galerie Atlantide des Cinq Sens

1st arr. - 3, rue Sauval 42 33 35 95
Open 11 a.m.-7:30 p.m. (Sat. 1:30 p.m.-7:30 p.m.). Closed Sun., 2 last wks. of Aug. & holidays.

The objects in this shop constitute a veritable nautical history. Among the treasures are handsome ships in bottle and scale-model reproductions, porthole covers, sea chests and seascapes in watercolors or oils. The shop also provides a restoration service for ship models and paintings.

Olivier Roux-Devillas

7th arr. - 12, rue Bonaparte - 43 54 69 32
Open 10 a.m.-noon & 2 p.m.-7 p.m. (Mon. 2 p.m.-7 p.m.). Closed Sun. & holidays. No cards.

A superb shop with the lovely patina of graceful age, it presents a remarkable collection of marine, optical and scientific instruments. Look too for antique nautical charts, maps and documents concerning scientific and geographical subjects.

SILVER & GOLD

J.P. de Castro

4th arr. - 17, rue des Francs-Bourgeois - 42 72 04 00
Open 10:30 a.m.-1 p.m. & 2 p.m.-7 p.m. (Sun. 11 a.m.-1 p.m. & 2 p.m.-7 p.m.). Closed Mon. No cards.

This is a magical place for lovers of old silver. It's full of delightful objects to give or to keep, all at reasonable prices. The recent enlargement of the shop now permits display of one of the largest arrays of silver in Paris. Every style is represented: Victorian, Napoléon III, bistro and classic. Collectors in search of the hard-to-find piece will find happiness here in the forms of samovars, chafing dishes, rare tableware and silver-plated cutlery sold by the kilo.

Eléonore

8th arr. - 18, rue de Miromesnil 42 65 17 81
Open 10 a.m.-noon (noon-2 p.m. by appt.) & 2 p.m.-6 p.m. Closed Sat., Sun., July 15-end Aug. No cards.

Claude-Gérard Cassan and Sophie de Granzial are walking catalogs of French silver—from the Renaissance to the 1880s—and they offer a remarkable range of old silver and curiosities. The two regularly exhibit their best pieces at the Paris shows: stamped silver from the eighteenth century with full documentation. They also offer restoration work.

A l'Epreuve du Temps

7th arr. - 88, rue du Bac - 42 22 11 42
Open 10 a.m.-6:30 p.m. Closed Sun. & Aug.

If you're in the mood for shopping for charming old pieces, little boxes, knickknacks and period jewelry, all at reasonable prices, this is the spot. Restoration services, as well as the manufacture of silver-plated flatware, are also available.

Jacques Kugel

8th arr. - 279, rue Saint-Honoré 42 60 86 23
Open 10 a.m.-1 p.m. & 2:30 p.m.-6:30 p.m. (Mon. 2:30 p.m.-6:30 p.m.). Closed Sun., Aug. & holidays.

Devotees the world over speak with pride simply for having had the good fortune to visit this illustrious establishment and witness one of the most magnificent displays of silver and gold objects ever assembled. Since Jacques passed on, Nicolas and Alexis (his two sons) have carried on the family tradition. The shop's three levels brim over with lordly silver pieces, seventeenth-century paintings, furniture and all sorts of rare and curious objects of great beauty.

Au Vieux Paris

2nd arr. - 4, rue de la Paix - 42 61 00 89
Open 10 a.m.-12:30 p.m. & 2 p.m.-6:30 p.m. (Mon. 2 p.m.-6:30 p.m.). Closed Sun. & Aug. No cards.

Founded in 1849, this is the oldest establishment of its kind in Paris. Michel Turisk has a reliable eye for old gold and presents a selection of old work, such as gold boxes from the Regency and Empire periods and watches and precious objects of interest from the seventeenth, eighteenth and nineteenth centuries.

TOYS, GAMES & DOLLS

Robert Capia

1st arr. - 24-26, galerie Véro-Dodat - 42 36 25 94
Open 10 a.m.-7 p.m. Closed Sun. & holidays. No cards.

This expert, known far and wide by collectors, is the city's foremost specialist in antique dolls. He has set up shop in one of the most picturesque passages of Paris, the Véro-Dodat gallery, which was opened in 1826 by charcutiers Véro and Dodat. His dolls are all signed by the top names of yesteryear (Jumeau, Steiner, Bru, Rohmer, Gaultier, Schmitt) and are available for rental. The prices are high, but justified by the quality. Also on display are charming toys: ivory dominoes, construction sets with engraved illustrations and some mechanical toys. The workshop takes care of all after-sales service. We also particularly enjoyed the large selection of phonograph cylinders that played Sarah Bernhardt and Enrico Caruso for us.

Aux Soldats d'Antan

7th arr. - 67, quai de Tournelle 46 33 40 50
Open 2 p.m.-7 p.m. Closed Sun., Aug. & holidays. No cards.

Jacques Stella boasts one of the best collections in the antique-toy soldier business; his sideline is chivalric medals and insignias, of which he is a noted connoisseur.

La Tortue Electrique

5th arr. - 5-7, rue Frédéric-Sauton 43 29 37 08
Open 2 p.m.-7 p.m. Closed Sun., Mon. & holidays. No cards.

The electric turtle referred to in the shop's name is actually an obstacle-course game. Stacked into this shop opposite Notre-Dame are games of strategy or skill, chess pieces, puzzles, tops, target games and antique coin-activated games to boot.

Vieille France

1st arr. - 364, rue Saint-Honoré 42 60 01 57
Open 10:30 a.m.-6 p.m. Closed Sun., Mon. & holidays. No cards.

This place more than lives up to its name (which, of course, translates as "Old France"); it is packed with lovely sets of the kings of France, heroes of the Ancien Régime, military paintings, medals and insignias, antique flags and more. The France of yesteryear lives again, here among miniatures of the great moments of its history.

UMBRELLAS & WALKING STICKS

Antoine

1st arr. - 10, av. de l'Opéra - 42 96 01 80
Open 10 a.m.-7 p.m. Closed Sun., & holidays.

In 1745 Monsieur and Madame Antoine moved up from the Auvergne and set themselves up at either end of the Pont-Neuf and rented out umbrellas to bridge-crossing pedestrians. In 1760 they opened a shop in the galleries of the Palais-Royal, specializing in canes, umbrellas and parasols. Today the worthy descendant of this dynasty, Mme. Lecarpentier-Purorge, offers a collection of antique umbrellas, canes and crops, and enjoys the steady stream of artists that come through her shop.

Lydia Bical

92200 Neuilly - 31, rue de Chartres - 46 24 14 30
Open 3 p.m.-7:30 p.m. Closed Sun., Mon., Aug. & holidays. No cards.

This remarkable spot features hundreds of canes produced in the years preceding 1930: canes by Dandy with gold knobs, canes carved by doughboys in the trenches, canes identifying the owner as a Dreyfus supporter, canes depicting Georges Clemenceau. Then, of course, there are the sword canes, rifle canes, cosh canes (a weighted weapon similar to a blackjack) and professional canes (undertakers and police, among them). And we must not forget the absinthe canes, the blow-gun canes, fire-starting canes and the rather salacious model with a set of mirrors that permits the voyeur to peek beneath ladies' skirts.

Madeleine Gély

7th arr. - 218, bd Saint-Germain 42 22 63 35
Open 9:30 a.m.-7 p.m. Closed Sun., Mon. Aug. & holidays. No cards.

Madeleine Gély offers hundreds of canes in astonishing forms—from antique canes and collector's items to utilitarian canes and ceremonial canes. Equally fascinating are the dual-function canes, such as watch canes, pipe canes, cigarette-holder canes, horse-measurer canes and a whisky cane with the original flask, stopper and glass intact. Her selection of antique and new umbrellas is the most complete (and attractive) in town.

AT YOUR SERVICE

■ BABY-SITTERS

Ababa

15th arr. - 8, av. du Maine - 45 49 46 46
Open 7:45 a.m.-8 p.m. Closed Sun. & holidays.

Ababa leaves us agaga: It comprises Ababa "show" (organizing children's parties), Ababa "granny" (elderly ladies' companions), Ababa "clean" (housecleaning, particularly day-after-party cleanup), Ababa "grosses têtes" (tutorial support in all subjects), Ababa "commensal" (practicing foreign languages) and Ababa "tonus" (getting in shape). Although

Two reliable au pair services are:

L'Accueil Familial des Jeunes Etrangers, 23 rue du Cherche Midi, 6th arr., 42 22 50 34, open 10 a.m.-4 p.m. (Sat. until noon), closed Sun.; and L'Amicale Culturelle Internationale, 27, rue Godot-de-Mauroy, 9th arr., 47 42 94 21, open 10 a.m.-12:30 p.m. & 1:45 p.m.-5:30 p.m., closed Sat. & Sun.

we haven't yet had the opportunity to personally try every one of their services, the word-of-mouth reports are excellent. There is a fixed price per month or per quarter, plus hourly charges such as babysitting at 28 francs.

■ BEAUTY & HEALTH

Ismery-James Agency

9th arr. - 55, rue La-Bruyère - 48 74 33 16
Open daily 24 hours.

Put your feet up at home and have them pampered by professionals. Pedicures and manicures are among the services provided by the Ismery-James Agency.

■ CLOTHING REPAIR

Mermoz Retouches

8th arr. - 21, rue Jean-Mermoz 42 25 73 36
Open 9 a.m.-6 p.m. Closed Sun., Mon. & Aug.

This is an address to hold on to, since good alterations specialists are so rare. Nothing daunts them, whether it's a matter of lengthening, shortening or inserting shoul-

der pads. Prices are made according to estimate.

■ DRY CLEANERS & LAUNDRY

Delaporte

8th arr. - 62, rue François-Ier - 43 59 82 11
Open 9 a.m.-7 p.m. (Sat. until 5 p.m.). Closed Sun.

The Delaporte dry cleaning shop is owned by Jean-Claude Lesèche, a famous name in Paris dry cleaning specializing in garments that need special attention such as those decorated with lace and sequins. His mother taught him everything, on the job, and he was an excellent student. All the tailors and dressmakers on avenue Montaigne call on him.

Gallois

1st arr. - 215, rue Saint-Honoré 42 60 44 00
Open 9 a.m.-12:30 p.m. & 1:30 p.m.-6 p.m. Closed Sat. & Sun. No cards.

These cleaners will give your spots and stains the care they deserve. They'll cope with the trickiest problems, but the best doesn't come cheap...

Huguet

16th arr. - 47, av. Marceau - 47 20 23 02, 47 23 81 39
Open 9 a.m.-7 p.m. Closed Sat. & Sun.

Behind the imposing facade lies a eighteenth-century shop interior that is home to seemingly perfect dry cleaning services, which are relied upon by the haute couture neighbors and all the Paris celebrities, at astonishingly reasonable prices, including free delivery. And there's an extra attraction: hand-washed and ironed men's shirts for 40 francs.

Letourneur-Lesèche

17th arr. - 8, bd de Courcelles
47 63 24 33
*Open 8:30 a.m.-6 p.m. Closed
Sat., Sun. & holidays. No cards.*
Excellent, speedy work and
some of the fairest prices
around. This shop is happy to
handle delicate fabrics, suede,
leather and lampshades—and
delivery is free.

Vendôme

1st arr. - 24, rue du Mont-Thabor
42 60 74 38
*Open 8 a.m.-5:30 p.m. (Sat.
8 a.m.-4 p.m.). Closed Sun.*
Just as in the previous century, the laundry maids here
wash by hand, using soap
flakes, and hand-iron delicate
finery, Chantilly lace and all. A
cambric handkerchief is
laundered for 15 francs, but a
baptismal robe costs
500 francs. Vendôme also
takes care of embroidered
tablecloths and men's shirts,
and, best of all, they deliver.

■ GENERAL REPAIRS

Réparation-Service de Lazuli

9th arr. - 39, rue Saint-Georges
42 85 24 46
*Open 1:30 p.m.-6 p.m. Closed
Sat., Sun., Aug. & holidays.*
17th arr. - 9, bd Péreire - 42 27
02 70
*Open 1:30 p.m.-6 p.m. (Sat.
from 2 p.m.). Closed Sun., Aug.
& holidays.*
Before throwing out any-
thing that is broken or doesn't
work, ask these experts if they
can fix it. You could be
pleasantly surprised.

■ HIRED HANDS

Les Grooms de Paris

16th arr. - 73, av. Paul-Doumer
45 04 45 05
*Open 9 a.m.-8 p.m. Closed Sun.
(Delivery 24 hours).*
A batch of bellboys in livery
from this elegant stable will
give your parties a certain style
and cost you 800 francs for an

evening. And while you might
find it over the top to hire one
of their high-class delivery men
just for a bottle of Roederer
Champagne, it would be more
than appropriate for a piece of
Van Cleef jewellery. Les
Grooms de Paris will deliver
within three hours after you
call, every day until midnight.
Within the city they charge
180 francs, to which you must
obviously add the cost of the
gift. Catalogue of services
available on request.

Ismery-James Agency

9th arr. - 55, rue La-Bruyère - 48
74 33 16
Open daily 24 hours.
Originally a hairdresser's,
this business has expanded
into an institution. After moving from the occasional home
hairdo to a team of "flying
stylists", they incorporated
manicures, make-up, leg-wax-
ing and massage before
becoming a business willing to
tackle anything. Nowadays
services include delivering
flowers, Champagne or
cigarettes (even at 2 a.m.),
baby-sitting, walking the dog,
organizing children's tea parties, painting, housework or
gardening. They'll send a cook
to concoct the exotic dish of
your choice or a student to
wait in for the meter reader.
You can subscribe to some
services for 200 francs a
month or 1,000 francs a year.
Estimates and further details
available on request.

Ludéric

16th arr. - 20, rue Pétrarque - 45
53 93 93
*Open 9 a.m.-1 p.m. & 2 p.m.-
7 p.m. (Sat. until 1 p.m.). Closed
Sun. & 1 wk. in Aug.*
The "Ludéricians" all look
like their boss, Olivier Maurey:
stylishly preppy, chic, glowing
with health and bursting with
enthusiasm. Begun in 1975,
this is the best known of the
multiservice agencies, and it
remains true to its founding

dictum, "Everything is possible." You can ask of the rapidly
growing company just about
anything. At first, when it was
Ludéric Service, they baby-sat,
shopped, chauffeured, served,
dog-sat and so forth. Some
years later Ludéric Evénement
joined the family, organizing
receptions and promotional
events. Then came Ludéric
Traiteur (caterer), when hungry Ludéric bought up a
caterer and pastry outfit. Since
then we've seen Haute Ten-
sion (for launching new products), Kiosque Théâtre (for
last-minute tickets, see p. 161),
Boutique Ludéric (for caviar,
salmon and Champagne at
low prices), and, lastly, a bit of
madcap, the historic bistro
L'Ami Louis that Ludéric
bought to preserve it intact. All
horizons are met, but by the
time you read this Ludéric will
no doubt have created a new
service to meet the needs of
some new client. The only
question that remains is
whether Ludéric can continue
to cater to individual needs in
the face of its growing corporate clientele and as they expand to the provinces and
overseas. We'll let you know
in a year or two. The yearly
membership (750 francs for
individuals, 1,900 francs for
corporate accounts) provides
access to all services.

■ HOME DELIVERY

BREAKFAST

Mille Break First

12th arr. - 7-9, pl. Abel-Leblanc
43 45 76 53
*Open daily 24 hours. Free deliv-
ery in Paris. Free newspaper.*
Ordered the night before,
breakfast is delivered any time
from 7 a.m. to 1 p.m. There
are all sorts of fixed formulas
(14), including the traditional
continental breakfast
(220 francs for two), the
"brunch" (430 francs for two)
and the "morning after,"

which includes a revitalizing cocktail of white wine, grape juice, Alka-Seltzer and a small bottle of Perrier, plus grapefruit juice (60 francs). There are breakfast or brunch menus for company and group functions (special discount). Cigarettes and flowers come free with orders priced at 580 francs and up.

FOOD

L'Asie à Votre Table
48 40 50 30
Open 9 a.m.-7 p.m. Closed Sun.
For a Chinese, Vietnamese or Thai dinner, phone your order to Laurence Nguyen in the morning. Cost is around 120 francs per person, plus 120 francs for delivery.

Aux Délices de Scott
47 63 71 36
Open 8:30 a.m.-8 p.m. (Sat. & Mon. 10 a.m.-7 p.m.). Closed Sun.
For people who like to lunch in the office or don't have time to cook, this fine caterer offers a choice of twelve meals-on-a-tray. Prices range from 90 to 145 francs per person and delivery is free in the eighth and seventeenth arrondissements when you order at least four trays.

Fauchon Service Plus
47 42 60 11 - ext. 317
Open 9:40 a.m.-9:30 p.m. Closed Sun.
Seven choices of quality cold meals-on-a-tray, costing from 150 to 400 francs. Free delivery within Paris if you spend at least 600 francs.

Les Frères Layrac
6th arr. - 29, rue de Buci - before 3 p.m.: 43 25 17 72; after 3 p.m.: 46 34 21 40
Open 9:30 a.m.-midnight. Closed Sun. & Mon.
If you can't go to the shop in the rue de Buci, home delivery is only a phone call away. Festive and varied ideas for dinners organized at the last

minute. The seafood platter at 385 francs for two is a real treat. Delivery: 100-150 F.

Jacques Hesse
40 93 05 05. By Minitel, 3615 code Jacques Hesse.
Open 9 a.m.-11 p.m. (Sat. & Sun. 6 p.m.-11 p.m.). Free delivery in Paris.
Hesse delivers to companies and individuals, changes his menu daily, and comes up with exciting specials, like the bachelor platter for the month of August. Service is fast and efficient, but the portions are on the skimpy side.

FRUIT BASKETS & FLOWERS

Interfruits Service
17th arr. - 89, av. de Wagram 47 63 10 55
Open 9 a.m.-7 p.m. Closed Sun. & Aug. 70 F delivery charge.
Baskets of in-season or exotic fruit are nicely done up and delivered. Interfruit has swiftly become a classic in its field (about 500 to 1,000 francs for a lovely basket).

Téléfleurs France
10th arr. - 15, rue Martel - 05 21 72 17
Open 8:30 a.m.-7 p.m. (Sat. until 6 p.m.) Closed Sun.
This chain of florists delivers anywhere in France, with 3,000 shops at your service.

■ LOCKSMITHS

Clé-Flash
15th arr. - 162, bd de Grenelle 47 83 33 18
Open 8:15 a.m.-12:30 p.m. & 1:15 p.m.-6:30 p.m. (Fri. until 6 p.m.; Sat. 9 a.m.-noon). Closed Sun., 15 days in Aug. & holidays.
Give them a key or lock to work from and they'll quickly make you a copy. The cost is 280 francs an hour. Estimates free.

■ MAID SERVICE

Maison Service
16th arr. - 10, rue Mesnil - 45 53 62 30
Open 9 a.m.-noon & 2 p.m.-6 p.m. Closed Sat. & Sun.
You ought to know from the start that the personnel here are top-notch—and temporary. The woman who deigns to answer the telephone will inform you in no uncertain terms that Maison Service hires only French from France between 30 and 60 years old, possessing five years of certified experience and excellent references, and ready to serve "a privileged social class." If that sounds like it fits the bill, you will pay 150 francs per hour for someone to do your ironing, your cleaning, your cooking, all for a minimum of four hours. Ladies' companions and governesses can be hired on the same basis, for four or five months, but be advised that these grand ladies of household help have never heard of volume discounts. Rates go up by 50 percent on Sundays and 100 percent on holidays.

Sélection Suzanne Reinach
92100 Boulogne - 11, rue Thiers 46 08 56 56
Open 9:30 a.m.-7 p.m. Closed Sat., Sun., Aug. & holidays. No cards.
This agency is proud of picking its butlers, servants, cooks, drivers, secretaries and so on out of the top drawer. New household staff are given a trial run before being offered a permanent contract. Registration fees vary from 6,000 to 10,000 francs, depending on the type of staff you want to hire.

Find the address you are looking for, quickly and easily, in the index.

181

■ MESSENGERS

Bunny Courses
92150 Suresnes - 3-5, rue Curie
45 06 45 06
Open 8 a.m.-6.30 p.m. Closed Sat. & Sun.

These are the people to call for urgent transport and deliveries. A messenger in Paris costs 60 francs, with an express service at 240 francs. Delivery with a driver and vehicle is possible, and transport and handling are available in Paris and the suburbs. All the firm's delivery workers keep in touch by radio.

■ RENT-A- . . .

AIRPLANE

Euralair
93350 Le Bourget - Aéroport du Bourget - 49 34 62 00
Open 24 hours.

This is a wonderful service if you have the means, and we mean the means! A Mystère Falcon 20 is yours for 11,450 francs per day, to which you add 21,600 francs per hour of flying time, as well as lodgings for the two pilots and the stewardess if you are gone more than two days. Should a Mystère be too small, ask for one of the nine Boeing 737s.

BICYCLE

Paris Vélo
5th arr. - 2, rue du Fer-à-Moulin
43 37 59 22, fax 47 07 67 45
Open 10 a.m.-12:30 p.m. & 2 p.m.-6 p.m. (until 7 p.m. during summer). Closed Sun. & holidays.

A wide range of town and mountain bikes, but nothing for children—unless they're small enough to sit in one of the kiddies' seats for hire. Daily rates go from 90 to 140 francs, a weekend costs from 160 to 220 francs and a week from 420 to 495 francs.

Deposits from 1,000 to 2,000 francs.

BOAT

Rive de France
17th arr. - 172, bd Berthier - 46 22 10 86
Open 9 a.m.-7 p.m. (Sat. 10 a.m.-4 p.m. Jan-June). Closed Sat. & Sun.

Little barges, nine meters by three meters, that sleep six are available here, for about 9,310 francs a week (in season). Weekend prices equal 60 percent of the charge for a week. A boat license is preferred. Departures from all over France.

COMPUTERS

LocaMac
11th arr. - 5, passage Turquetil
43 73 51 51
Open 9:30 a.m.-1 p.m. & 2 p.m.-7 p.m. Closed Sat. & Sun. No cards.

Various kinds of personal computer but especially Macs, famed for their user-friendliness. You can hire a Mac SE or Mac II for 48 hours, a week, a month or a year, all at very reasonable tapering rates. The machine is delivered to your home, collected at the end of your contract and exchanged immediately in the unlikely event that it goes wrong.

THE EIFFEL TOWER

Salle Gustave-Eiffel
7th arr. - Champ-de-Mars - 45 50 34 56
Open daily 9 a.m.-12:30 p.m. & 2 p.m.-6 p.m.

For a really chic reception with a panoramic view, why not hire this room on the first floor of the Eiffel Tower, 185 feet up? You can even rent a private elevator. The soundproofed, air-conditioned room will accommodate 450 people for a cocktail party, 300 attending a meeting or show, and 140 sitt-

ing down to dinner. Equipment includes cinema and projection equipment, sophisticated lighting, stages and podiums.

EQUIPPED OFFICE

Club Sari Affaires
La Défense - CNIT. 2, pl. de La Défense - 46 92 24 24, fax 46 92 24 00
Open 8:30 a.m.-7:30 p.m. (Sat. 9 a.m.-1 p.m.). Closed Sun.

Fully equipped offices measuring between 145 and 600 square feet cost from 1,000 to 3,000 francs a day. A private phone line and Minitel are already installed and a computer is provided on request, while a team of full-time secretaries will handle the mail, messages and word processing. Those who need a year-round base in the Paris area might prefer the yearly rate with additional services at 36,500 francs. Meeting rooms come in various sizes and cost from 1,100 to 4,100 francs a day. Restaurant service.

FORMAL OUTFIT

Eugénie Boiserie
9th arr. - 32, rue Vignon - 47 42 43 71
Open 10 a.m.-noon & 1 p.m.-6 p.m. Closed Sun., Mon. & Aug.

In business for over 30 years, Eugénie Boiserie carries a stunning collection of haute-couture gowns for hire (800 francs, plus a 2,000-franc deposit). The vast selection of dresses is hidden away in the back of the store (the front is given over to old-fashioned gift items), where they are shown to customers by appointment. No accessories are available, but alterations can be arranged.

The prices in this guide reflect what establishments were charging at press time.

Les Costumes de Paris

9th arr. - 21 bis, rue Victor-Massé
48 78 41 02
Open 10 a.m.-7 p.m. Closed Sun. & Mon.

Among the charming, droll and zany costumes fit for the fanciest fancy-dress ball is an enchanting collection of evening gowns by Loris Azzaro, Thierry Mugler, Diamant Noir and others, in sizes 36 to 44 (which roughly translates to American sizes 6 to 14). All these gowns are in excellent condition. The price for rental runs 500 to 2,000 francs.

Since the company started in 1952 it has created more than 20,000 costumes for cinema and television. They take up four floors and range from caveman outfits to fashions from the 1970s, and hiring one will cost you between 400 and 600 francs plus VAT for a weekend. It's best to book a week ahead in case alterations are needed. You can even have a costume made to measure —ask for an estimate.

Le Cor de Chasse

6th arr. - 40, rue de Buci - 43 26 51 89
Open 9 a.m.-noon & 1:30 p.m.-6 p.m. Closed Sun., Mon. & Aug.

Famous since 1875 and loved by several generations of Parisians, this stylish shop hires out morning clothes, top hats, tuxedos and other formal apparel for men (rental fees range between 700 and 800 francs). Shirts and accessories are offered for sale, and alterations are handled by expert tailors.

Velleda

10th arr. - 206, rue Lafayette - 42 05 81 93
Open 10 a.m.-6:30 p.m. Closed Sun.

What, absolutely nothing to wear to the masquerade ball? You must check out the incredible selection of costumes and disguises at Velleda; peo-ple have been known to rent the shop's bridal "costume" to wear to their own wedding! Just as authentic are the medieval get-ups and the swingy, beaded Roaring Twenties gowns. Rates run to 600 francs for a weekend rental, plus a deposit of 1,500 to 3,000 francs.

FURNITURE

ABC Ruby

16th arr. - 11, rue Chanez - 46 51 06 42
Open 9 a.m.-noon & 2 p.m.-6 p.m. Closed Sat. & Sun. No cards.

Furnish your apartment in 48 hours with this all-inclusive service that provides furniture, fabrics (except nets), tableware and electrical goods. Short or long-term hire. They don't have much on display so it's best to send details of what you require for an estimate.

HELICOPTER

Hélicap

15th arr. - Héliport de Paris, 4, av. de la Porte-de-Sèvres - 45 57 75 51
Open 9 a.m.-7 p.m. Closed Sat. & Sun. No cards.

See Paris and La Défense from the air, or Versailles and its surroundings, or take a trip to the Château d'Esclimont for dinner, touching down on the lawn out front. The possibilities are endless: the cliffs at Etretat on the Norman coast, Mont Saint-Michel, the castles on the Loire. By now you're probably wondering what the price for such trips could be... Versailles and the château de Loire for 15,200 francs (five people) makes a very nice gift.

HOT AIR BALLOON

Air Ballon Communication

6th arr. - 12, rue Bonaparte - 43 29 14 13
Open 10 a.m.-12:30 p.m. & 2 p.m.-7 p.m. (Mon. from 2 p.m.). Closed Sun.

For your first view of France from a balloon. You take off near the Château de Maintenon, 50 minutes' drive from Paris, but there's no telling where you'll touch down. In any case the flight lasts about an hour and there'll be a car waiting to take you back to Paris. Be sure to book several weeks ahead for an unforgettable flight over the Beauce country and the valley of the Eure. Demand varies according to the time of year. The cost, including insurance,

The mysterious shrinking tower

What would be the Paris skyline without this most Parisian of silhouettes? Yet the *Eiffel Tower*, a masterpiece of engineering conceived by the genius of Gustave Eiffel, had a close shave with the wreckers' ball in 1909. Luckily, the pioneers of radio and telephone saw the tower's potential use and came to the rescue. Interestingly, the tower's height can vary by as much as six inches depending on the temperature: the hotter, the higher. When completed in time for the World Exhibition in 1889 it was the tallest construction on earth, standing 300 meters (975 feet) high on its four steel feet. For the best view, tackle the 1,652 steps to the top (the short of stamina can take the elevators) an hour before sunset.

is 1,500 francs for one person or 2,500 francs for two, plus VAT.

LIMOUSINES

Alliance Autos

94160 Saint-Mandé - 5bis, av. Foch - 43 28 20 20, fax 43 28 27 27
Open daily 24 hours.

The new leader in chauffeur-driven limousines, Alliance Autos has conquered a demanding clientele of CEOs, film stars and media moguls. But you needn't be a celebrity to benefit from Alliance's personalized service. Harried business people and travelers touring the capital are all accorded the "star treatment." Instead of fighting for a taxi, why not arrive in Paris in a chauffeured Mercedes Class S (or a Renault Safrane)? A bilingual driver will be your guide, and facilitate your visit in any way he can. To give you an idea of the attractive prices: transfer from Roissy-Charles de Gaulle to Paris, 1,000 francs; a half-day (four hours), 2,100 francs; a full day (nine hours), 3,000 francs. You will also be able to rent any kind of vehicules at Alliance Autos (buses, trucks, vans, RV, motorcycles).

SAFE

Solon

11th arr. - 126, bd Richard-Lenoir - 48 05 08 34
Open 8:30 a.m.-noon & 1:30 p.m.-6 p.m. Closed Sat., Sun. & Aug.

A safe or strongbox is yours for 500 francs a month. This doesn't include transport, which varies according to distance, the weight of the safe and how many floors there are to walk up. Same-day opening service.

SKI & CLIMBING EQUIPMENT

La Haute Route

4th arr. - 33, bd Henri-IV - 42 72 38 43
Open 9:30 a.m.-1 p.m. & 2 p.m.-7 p.m. Closed Sun.

This is the place to hire ski equipment in winter and climbing gear in summer, for two days, a week, a month or longer. Tapering rates and reasonable deposits.

TELEVISION & STEREO

Locatel

92100 Boulogne - 31, rue de Solférino - 46 09 94 90
92300 Levallois-Perret - 16, rue Barbès - 47 58 12 00
93100 Montreuil - 13, av. Gabriel-Péri - 48 58 91 92
Open 10 a.m.-7 p.m. Closed Sun.

One of the oldest TV hire services, with ten branches in Paris and fifteen or so in the surrounding area. They'll deliver within 24 hours and lend you a set while they repair yours. The cheapest TV costs 160 francs a month to rent (for a minimum of six months), a video recorder 190 francs and a hi-fi with CD player 190 francs (minimum period two years). Locatel also hires answering machines, car telephones and satellite dishes.

TRAINS

SNCF

10th arr. - 162, rue du Faubourg-Saint-Martin - 40 18 84 24, fax 40 18 84 40
Open 8:30 a.m.-12:30 p.m. & 1:30 p.m.-5:15 p.m. (Fri. until 3:50 p.m.). Closed Sat. & Sun. No cards.

The French railroad company will rent you an 80-seat second-class car, a sleeping car, a restaurant car, a disco car or even a whole train. You have to phone them two months ahead and they'll give

you an estimate based on your requirements.

TIRES (STUDDED SNOW)

Le Relais du pneu

4th arr. - 33, bd Bourdon - 42 72 01 12
Open 8 a.m.-noon & 1:30 p.m.-6 p.m₍ (Sat. until noon; Mon. 2 p.m.-6 p.m. Closed Sun. & Aug.
12th arr. - 29, bd Diderot 43 07 46 46
Open 8 a.m.-noon & 1:30 p.m.-6:30 p.m. (Sat. 8 a.m.-noon & 1:30 p.m.-3:30 p.m.; Mon. 1:30 p.m.-6:30 p.m.). Closed Sun. & Aug. 15-30.

Hiring studded snow tires costs between 300 and 400 francs for ten days, depending on the size of the wheels.

■ SECRETARIAL SERVICES

Agaphone

17th arr. - 68 bis, bd Péreire - 44 01 50 00
Open 8 a.m.-8 p.m. (Sat. 9 a.m.-noon). Closed Sun. & holidays. No cards.

No need to miss any phone calls when you go away. For 890 francs a month plus VAT, you can have them transferred to Agaphone, who will take messages or orders and record appointments. When you return the details are phoned or faxed to you, or sent by Minitel. The firm also offers typing and word-processing services.

■ SHOE REPAIR

Central Crépins

3rd arr. - 48, rue de Turbigo - 42 72 68 64
Open 8 a.m.-2:30 p.m. & 3:30 p.m.-7 p.m. (Sat. until 1 p.m.). Closed Sun. & 2 wks. in Aug.

Bags, suitcases, saddles and clothes, Central Crépins repairs everything in leather.

Discounts are available to regulars with a membership card. (Check the address before going, since the store may move).

La Cordonnerie Anglaise

4th arr. - 28, rue des Archives 48 87 11 43
Open 9:30 a.m.-7 p.m. (Sat. from 10:30 a.m.). Closed Sun., Mon., 1 month during summer & holidays.

For a payment of 500 francs in advance, you can have your shoes waterproofed in this attractive shop using a process perfected by Goodyear.

Cordonnerie Vaneau

7th arr. - 44, rue Vaneau - 42 22 06 94
8th arr. - 34, rue Jean-Mermoz
16th arr. - 35, rue de Lonchamp
16th arr. - 8, rue Mignard
17th arr. - 51, bd Gouvion-Saint-Cyr
92200 Neuilly - 37, rue de Chézy
Open 9 a.m.-1 p.m. & 2 p.m.-7 p.m. Closed Sun. Call 42 22 06 94 for information.

The best for the finest. Vaneau is where the finest feet of Paris, shod by Lobb, Weston or Aubercy, go to have work done. Their impeccable workmanship can restore footwear that only looks fit for the garbage. It costs 550 francs to give a pair of men's shoes a new lease of life.

Pulin

8th arr. - 5, rue Chauveau-Lagarde - 42 65 08 57
Open 9 a.m.-7 p.m. Closed Sun. & holidays.

Gérard Pulin's wide range of services includes changing the color of your shoes, raising and lowering heels and mixing custom-made polish—all within 48 hours. And for 70 francs there's a home pickup and delivery service.

BEAUTY

▓ BEAUTY SALONS

Carita

8th arr. - 11, rue du Faubourg-Saint-Honoré - 44 94 11 00
Open 9 a.m.-7 p.m. Closed Sun. & Mon.

Carita's famous name now belongs to Shiseido, the Japanese cosmetics company. Completely redesigned by the divine Andrée Putman, the salon's luxurious but minimalist decor in tones of beige and brown is functional and simply stunning. The ground floor is now occupied by a reception area and private rooms. The salon's cadre of hair stylists practice their art on the upper floor, where other beauty services are also dispensed (stars and other bigwigs are pampered in royally appointed private booths). Carita treatments have fully earned their excellent reputation; expert beauticians can impart a permanent curl to eyelashes or shape eyebrows and lips with a special tattooing technique, perform facials that will make your skin look fresh and firm, or soothe muscles and stimulate circulation with professional massage. Men are welcome too at Carita, and have a realm all their own on the third floor.

Guerlain

6th arr. - 29, rue de Sèvres - 42 22 46 60
Open 9:45 a.m.-6:45 p.m. (Sat. 10 a.m.-7 p.m.). Closed Sun.
8th arr. - 68, av. des Champs-Elysées - 47 89 71 80
Open 9 a.m.-6:45 p.m. Closed Sun.
Scents & cosmetics only: 1st arr., 15th arr. & 16th arr.

Guerlain is tops in beauty care. Expert technicians dispense the very latest skin-care treatments—they'll even restructure your wrinkles—you can rest assured that your face

is in the very best hands. So lie back and enjoy the luxurious surroundings while the excellent Issima line of skin-care products is applied to your face for a relaxing hour and a quarter (495 francs, including makeup). Manicure, pedicure and epilation services are available as well. Be sure to stop at the perfume counter to try some of the enchanting house fragrances.

Lancôme

8th arr. - 29, rue du Faubourg-Saint-Honoré - 42 65 30 74
Open 10 a.m.-7 p.m. (Wed. 1 p.m.-7 p.m.). Closed Sun.

Isabella Rossellini's haunting beauty projects Lancôme's public image, but top aesthetician Béatrice Braune (director of the Lancôme institute) is the woman behind the scenes here who makes sure the products deliver what they promise. An exclusive "beauty computer" measures the skin's smoothness, elasticity, moisture level and degree of dryness and/or oiliness, then produces a prescription for personalized skin care. Services offered in the institute's handsome, comfortable salons include a Niosome treatment, a bioenergizing massage and body sloughing followed by a lymphatic drainage massage.

Ingrid Millet

8th arr. - 54, rue du Faubourg-Saint-Honoré - 42 66 66 20
Open 9 a.m.-6 p.m. Closed Sun.

Madame Millet doesn't eat the quantities of caviar she buys; no, she slathers it (in cream form) on her clients' faces. Her specialized skin-care services include a facial mask/tonic/rejuvenation treatment, an energizing facial (590 francs) and an all-over body treatment with a particularly effective sloughing action (790 francs). The salon's soothing green-and-white decor makes it an oasis

185

of calm and relaxation on the busy Faubourg-Saint-Honoré.

Sothys

8th arr. - 128, rue du Faubourg-Saint-Honoré - 45 63 98 18
Open 9:30 a.m.-7:30 p.m. (Sat. 10 a.m.-5 p.m.). Closed Sun.

How luxurious! How chic! In Sothys's fifteen private air-conditioned booths (all equipped with cellular phones), a capable staff dispenses a wide variety of beauty treatments, ranging from deep facial cleansing (260 francs) to slimming techniques (which include baths in highly carbonated water paired with hydromassage). It's quite tickly and pleasant, take our word for it!

▉ EPILATION

Ella Baché

2nd arr. - 8, rue de la Paix - 42 61 67 14
Open 10 a.m.-6:30 p.m. (Mon. 11 a.m.-6:30 p.m. & Sat. 9:30 a.m.-5 p.m.). Closed Sun.

Cold wax is Ella Bache's secret weapon against unwanted hair. The treatment starts with a mentholated disinfecting lotion, then waxing and the application of a soothing moisturizing cream. Prices? Legs, 140 francs; bikini line, 85 francs; underarms, 50 francs. Facials are performed here too (235 to 275 francs).

Institut George-V

8th arr. - 17, av. George-V - 40 70 99 70
Open 10 a.m.-6:30 p.m. Closed Sun. & Mon.

Nary an unwanted hair will survive once Antoinette gets through with you. For 25 years she has been removing unwanted hair from heavenly bodies. The salon is unprepossessing (just two rooms on the fifth floor), but the service and products are first-rate. Antoinette swears by a special pale-pink bees' wax,

made just for her by an unnamed skilled artisan; and her far-famed technique leaves legs smooth and silky for at least three weeks. By appointment only, from 180 francs.

▉ HAIR SALONS

Patrick Alès

8th arr. - 37, av. Franklin-Roosevelt - 43 59 33 96
Open 9 a.m.-6 p.m. (Wed. 10 a.m.-6 p.m.). Closed Sun. & Mon.

Patrick Alès is the mind behind the excellent "Phyto" line of hair treatments. Formerly a stylist with Carita, Alès developed the products in his spare time (in his garage, no less) with the help of his friend and collaborator, Olga. She tried each formula on herself, and numbered them according to how many times each had been tested (shampoo S88: 88 trials). Today, Alès continues to come up with new products, which you can try out for yourself at his Paris salon. Henna treatments, for example, to strengthen fine, lifeless hair, cost from 200 to 400 francs.

Alexandre

8th arr. - 3, av. Matignon - 42 25 57 90
Open 9:30 a.m.-7 p.m. Closed Sun.

Even if it's only once in your life, you really should visit this lovely old Art Deco salon, where socialites and celebrities have been elegantly coiffed for years and years. Alexandre is so passionate about hair that he has devoted a museum to it! Formal styles for weddings and gala evenings are a specialty.

Camille Darmont

16th arr. - 61, rue de la Tour - 45 03 10 99
Open Tues. & Wed. & Fri. 10 a.m.-7 p.m.; Thurs. 1 p.m.-

8 p.m.; Sat. 9 a.m.-1 p.m. Closed Sun. & Mon.*

Camille Darmont, who holds diplomas in dermatology and pharmacy, for many years was the principal assistant of hair guru René Furterer. Now on her own, she is one of the most esteemed hair specialists in Paris. A two-hour treatment in her salon includes a thorough massage of head, neck and shoulders to improve circulation, followed by a mud pack and a hot-towel wrap. The client's individual hair problems are then treated with products formulated by Madame Darmont herself.

Jean-Louis David International

8th arr. - 47, rue Pierre-Charron 43 59 82 08
Open 10 a.m.-7 p.m. (Wed. 11 a.m.-7 p.m.). Closed Sun.

Businessman/coiffeur Jean-Louis David has done it again. His most ambitious venture, on the rue Pierre-Charron, is always swarming with heads eager to wear the latest JLD style. We must say, he is a first-rate manager, and he knows how to keep his customers satisfied, notably with innovative ideas like Quick Service for women in a hurry (dry cut, mousse and gel, you're out in twenty minutes), or the Mistershop (same principle, for men). Jean-Louis David International, the top-of-the-line division, charges about 400 francs for a shampoo, cut and style, while the "diffusion" sector, less chic, charges 300 francs for the same services.

Desfossé

8th arr. - 19, av. Matignon - 43 59 95 13
Open 9 a.m.-6:30 p.m. Closed Sun.

For men only. Executives, politicians, socialites and others who pay close attention to their image frequent Desfossé. In addition to hair care (200 francs for a wash, cut and style), skin care, massage, manicure and pedicure services are offered. Pressed for time? You can grab a quick lunch right here, while having your nails buffed or your pores deep-cleansed!

Jacques Dessange

8th arr. - 37, av. Franklin-Roosevelt - 43 59 31 31 (also: 3rd arr., 4th arr., 6th arr., 7th arr., 11th arr., 15th arr., 17th arr.) *Open 9:30 a.m.-6:30 p.m. Closed Sun.*

With commendable concern for his customers' hygiene, Jacques Dessange has decreed that a brand-new brush be used for each client. Efforts have also been made to warm up what was once a pretty uppity reception. But best of all, the stylists no longer systematically impose Master Dessange's latest creation on every head that passes through the salon's front doors. Good hair treatment products for use at home; stylists can give highly effective hair masks or split-end treatments if you wish.

René Furterer

8th arr. - 15, pl. de la Madeleine 42 65 30 60 (also: 17th arr., 15th arr.) *Open 9 a.m.-7 p.m. Closed Sun.*

Back when permanents meant frizz, and hairstyles were inevitably the product of rollers and pincurls, René Furterer virtually invented the science of hair care. Now retired, he leaves an impressive legacy: an institute that bears his name, where scientific hair treatments continue to be formulated. Here specialists offer clear explanations, technical advice and a treatment program that may include massage or plant-based rinses. One is never urged to buy more than two or three products, which are always reasonably priced.

Léonor Greyl

8th arr. - 15, rue Tronchet - 42 65 32 26 *Open 9:30 a.m.-6:30 p.m. (Thurs. 11 a.m.-8 p.m.). Closed Sun.*

With the help of her husband, a chemist who formulates her products, Léonor Greyl works wonders on dull, lifeless hair with her various powders, freeze-dried roots, wheat-germ oil and sundry other secret ingredients. But make no mistake: there's nothing hocus-pocus about her hair-care treatments (shampoo, manual and electric massage, scalp packs and the list goes on), and they yield excellent results. Women pay about 300 francs, men around 200 francs for a treatment. A simple cut costs 150 francs.

Harlow

1st arr. - 24, rue Saint-Denis - 42 33 61 36 *Open 10 a.m.-7 p.m. (Wed. noon-9 p.m.). Closed Sun. & Mon.*
9th arr. - 4, rue de Sèze - 47 42 40 67 *Open 10 a.m.-7 p.m. (Thurs. noon-9 p.m.). Closed Sun. & Mon.*
16th arr. - 70, rue du Ranelagh 45 24 04 54 *Open 9:30 a.m.-6:30 p.m. Closed Sun. & Mon.*

Many women want a good haircut that doesn't require elaborate upkeep. For them, Harlow and company have come up with wash-and-wear hair. The salon's atmosphere is relaxed, and service is fast. A shampoo and styling is 150 francs; with a cut, the price is 300 francs.

Lazartigue
Traitement du Cheveu

8th arr. - 5, rue du Faubourg-Saint-Honoré - 42 65 29 24 (also: 6th arr., 9th arr., 14th arr., 15th arr.) *Open 9:30 a.m.-6:30 p.m. Closed Sun.*

Decorated in tonic tones of green and white, the Lazar-tigue salon presents the highest standard of creature comforts. Each private booth boasts a telephone and an individual closet (including, of course, a lock for your fur). The staff is perfectly charming, too. There's just one hitch: for an examination and an assessment of your hair problems, treatments and a "prescription" for Lazartigue products, the bill will come to well over 1,000 francs! Now for that kind of money, wouldn't you think that the ingredients would be listed on the label of the hair-care products you've been strong-armed into buying? We suppose that Monsieur Lazartigue wants to keep his "miracle" formulas secret.

Jean-Marc Maniatis

8th arr. - 18, rue Marbeuf - 47 23 30 14 (also: 1st arr., 6th arr.) *Open 9:30 a.m.-7 p.m. Closed Sat. & Sun.*

His first clients were photo stylists from the fashion press; they raved about the Maniatis technique of precision scissoring one tiny section of hair at a time for chic, superbly shaped cuts. His reputation grew, and now Maniatis is one of the city's best-known coiffeurs. The stylists who work with him are well trained and fast; they do a lot of work for celebrities, models, journalists and so on. The salon is friendly, noisy and always busy. Be prepared to wait. A shampoo, cut and styling cost about 500 francs for a woman, under 300 francs for a man.

Mod's Hair

8th arr. - 64, rue Pierre Charron 42 25 14 29 (also : 1st arr., 6th arr. 7th arr., 11th arr., 14th arr. 16th arr.) *Open Tues. & Thurs. & Fri. 10 a.m.-6:30 p.m.; Wed. noon-7:30 p.m.; Sat. 9 a.m.-5 p.m. Closed Sun. & Mon.*

At its salon near the Champs-Elysées, Mod's Hair caters to the younger crowd, with saucy, fashionable styles. The walls of the salon are decorated with the work of talented artists, giving you something to contemplate besides your face in the mirror.

Alexandre Zouari
16th arr. - 1, av. du Président-Wilson - 47 23 79 00
Open 9:30 a.m.-6:30 p.m. Closed Sun.

Celebrities seem to appear wherever you look in this luxurious (but ever-so-slightly gaudy) salon: their PR people insist that Alexandre Zouari is the very last word in hairstyling for the rich and famous... well, now we know! Figure on spending 350 francs for a shampoo, cut and blow-dry styling, and throw in another 100 francs for a "transformation".

■ MANICURE & PEDICURE

Carita
8th arr. - 11, rue du Faubourg-Saint-Honoré - 42 65 79 00
Open 9 a.m.-7 p.m. Closed Sun. & Mon.

Entrust your feet to Monsieur Ho, and he will work his brand of Oriental magic to make your tired tootsies feel like new again. Carita is also the place to come for an expert "French manicure": white polish is applied to the very end of the nail, resulting in an impeccably groomed finish (but don't even contemplate it unless your hands are in perfect condition).

Institut Laugier
17th arr. - 39 bis, rue Laugier - 42 27 25 03
Open 10 a.m.-7 p.m. Closed Sun. & Aug. 15-30.

The best manicures and pedicures in Paris are performed at the Institut Laugier. Hands are cared for on the ground floor, where the exclusive Supernail treatment is

yours for the asking, as are vitamin baths and artificial nails for both sexes. Downstairs, feet are pampered with massage, vibrating baths, pumice stones and a skin-sloughing treatment. Before they leave, clients are strongly encouraged to purchase a whole slew of (effective, but costly) products to prolong the benefits of the salon's treatments.

Institut Yung
9th arr. - 22, rue Caumartin - 47 42 20 63
Open 9 a.m.-7 p.m. Closed Sat. & Sun. No cards.

No mere cutters or scissors are used here: Monsieur Yung's Chinese pedicure equipment is limited to a simple series of steel blades of varying lengths with more or less sharp points. In just 30 minutes, his fancy footwork will rid you of calluses, bumps, corns and dead skin. Treatment and polish cost just 150 francs.

L'Onglerie de la Madeleine
9th arr. - 26, rue Godot-de-Mauroy - 42 65 49 13
Open 10 a.m.-7 p.m. Closed Sun. & Mon.

The house specialty is American-style artificial nails, made of the same tough resins used in dentistry. These nails are absolutely "unchewable," besides being revolting tasting! Complete manicure and pedicure services are also offered.

Revlon
16th arr. - 19, rue de Bassano - 47 20 05 42
Open 9:30 a.m.-6:30 p.m. Closed Sat. & Sun.

Revlon's reputation for nail care is worldwide and well deserved. The institute near the Champs-Elysées employs four medically certified pedicurists, as well as seven

manicurists who will take your hands in hand and make them as lovely as they possibly can be. The house products are excellent and most effective. Manicures are tariffed at 175 francs (195 francs with a hot-cream treatment), pedicures at 280 francs (nail polish included).

■ SCENT & COSMETICS

L'Artisan Parfumeur
9th arr. - 22 rue Vignon - 42 66 32 66 (also: 7th arr.)
Open 10:30 a.m.-2:30 p.m. & 3:30 p.m.-7 p.m. (Mon. 11:30 a.m.-7 p.m.). Closed Sun.

This perfumer's shop looks like a stage set, rich with gilt and velvet drapery. The fragrances are equally voluptuous, based on musk, gardenia, rose iris... not, we emphasize, the sort of scents worn by shrinking violets. His two best-sellers are L'Eau du Grand Siècle and L'Eau du Navigateur. Quite popular as well are the aromatic pomanders that diffuse these heady perfumes (200 to 350 francs and 600 francs) and an exquisite selection of gift items: jewelry, fans, combs and other decorative trifles.

Body Shop
6th arr. - 7, rue de l'Ancienne Comédie - 44 07 14 00
Open 10 a.m.-8 p.m. (Sat. 10 a.m.-11 p.m. & Sun. 2 p.m.-8 p.m.).

Anita Roddick's renowned cruelty-free cosmetics are available here. Try the banana shampoo for dry hair, the menthol lotion to refresh your tired feet, or the unscented bath oil that won't clash with your favorite perfume. The lip balms come in several tasty flavors: rum-raisin, apricot, kiwi and more!

Comptoir Sud-Pacific

2nd arr. - 17, rue de la Paix - 42 61 74 44
Open 9:30 a.m.-7 p.m. Closed Sun.

Josée Fournier has a passion for Polynesia. She was the first to market Monoï oil in Paris some years ago, and followed up that initial success with a line of perfumes that recall her beloved Pacific islands, perfumes with such delicious names as Cherry Vanilla and Barbier des Iles (a kind of Bay Rum). The scents also come in the form of candles, sprays and diffusers. A line of exotic cosmetics, travel toiletries and bath fragrance is the most recent addition to Comptoir's considerable inventory.

Diptyque

5th arr. - 34, bd Saint-Germain 43 26 45 27
Open 10 a.m.-7 p.m. Closed Sun. & Mon.

Diptyque is now over 30 years old, but the shop doesn't show its age. The marvelous, exclusive fragrances are as appealing as ever; the fresh L'Ombre dans l'Eau is a perennial bestseller; the latest addition to the line is Virgilio, a green scent with notes of basil and cedarwood. You'll find all the house scents available in candle form, and there is also a pretty selection of Shetland lap robes.

Annick Goutal

1st arr. - 14, rue de Castiglione 42 61 52 82 (also: 7th arr., 17th arr.)
Open 9:30 a.m.-7:30 p.m. Closed Sun.

Annick Goutal's unique fragrances are sold in their own elegant boutiques decorated in beige and gold tones. Our favorite scents are the deliciously citrusy Eau d'Hadrien, the romantic Heure Exquise and the ultra-feminine Rose Absolue. Goutal's soaps, bath oils and scented pebbles (to scatter in lingerie drawers) make wonderful gifts.

Grain de Beauté

6th arr. - 9, rue du Cherche-Midi 45 48 07 55
Open 10:30 a.m.-7 p.m. Closed Sun., Mon. morning & Aug.

Traditional English furniture and chintzes make an appropriate setting for traditional English scents by such renowned perfumers as George F. Trumper, Penaligon's, Floris and Czech & Speake, whose toilet waters, soaps, potpourri, and other fragrant miscellanea are featured here.

Maître Parfumeur et Gantier

1st arr. - 3, rue des Capucines 42 96 35 13
Open 10:30 a.m.-6:30 p.m. Closed Sun.

Jean-François Laporte's extravagant scents are for those who like to leave a trail of lingering fragrance in their wake. Both men and women can find intense, assertive toilet waters here, with evocative names like Rose Muskissime or Fleurs de Comores. Laporte's signature scents are also sold as pot-pourri or room fragrances. Don't miss his elegant, very dandified perfumed gloves.

Patricia de Nicolaï

7th arr. - 80, rue de Grenelle - 45 44 59 59
Open 10 a.m.-2 p.m. & 3 p.m.-7 p.m. (Sat. 10 a.m.-2 p.m. & 3 p.m.-6:30 p.m.). Closed Sun. & Mon.

Guerlain's granddaughter, Patricia de Nicolaï, perpetuates the family tradition of creating divine perfumes. To date, her collection comprises six scents for women and three for men. We especially like her Mimosaïque and Jardin Secret. Alongside perfumed candles (200 francs), room sprays and pot-pourris, you'll find delicate carved crystal flacons, which can be engraved with your name.

Sephora

16th arr. - 50, rue de Passy - 45 20 03 15 (also: 1st arr., 9th arr., 13th arr., 14th arr.)
Open 10 a.m.-7:15 p.m. (Mon. until 7 p.m. & Sat. until 7:30 p.m.). Closed Sun.

If you'd rather avoid dealing with salespeople, and prefer to read labels, look at bottles and decide for yourself what makeup you need, then Sephora, the "beauty supermarket" is for you. Cosmetics and perfumes of every type are on offer: face creams, body-care products, cosmetics and accessories (hairbrushes, barrettes, mirrors...) from major manufacturers are neatly displayed.

Shu Uemura

6th arr. - 176, bd Saint-Germain 45 48 02 55
Open 10 a.m.-7 p.m. (Mon. 11 a.m.-7 p.m.). Closed Sun.

As soon as they cross the threshold, even the most fresh-scrubbed women are suddenly possessed by the urge to try the lipsticks, powders (fluffed on with terrific bamboo brushes), pencils and shadows. A Japanese-style decor of wood and glass is the handsome setting for these no-less-handsomely packaged cosmetics, many of which come in reusable containers.

Silver Moon

8th arr. - 12-14, av. des Champs-Elysées - 45 62 94 55 (also: 1st arr., 6th arr., 7th arr., 9th arr., 15th arr., 16th arr.)
Open 10 a.m.-7:30 p.m. Closed Sun. Discounts available.

All the major brands of cosmetics and perfumes are sold (many at discount prices) in Paris's several Silver Moon shops. Sales people are generally competent and helpful. Two of the branches also provide beauty services (hair removal, facials and such).

Sur La Place

6th arr. - 12, pl. Saint-Sulpice - 43 26 45 27
Open 10 a.m.-7 p.m. (Mon. 1 p.m.-7 p.m.). Closed Sun.

An appealing range of pretty toiletries and bath accessories, reasonably priced.

■ THALASSO-THERAPY

Biocéane

19th arr. - 22, rue de Flandres - 40 36 58 01
Open 10 a.m.-7:30 p.m. Closed Sun. & Mon.

No kidding, you can actually enjoy the benefits of sun and sea in the far-flung nineteenth arrondissement! Sea-water whirlpool baths, seaweed wraps, and a wealth of beauty treatments based on elements taken from the sea will restore your skin tone and boost your morale. Traditional beauty treatments are available as well, from massage to "permanent" makeup for brows, eyelashes and lips. An in-house boutique sells natural cosmetics, vitamins, sea-shell meal and herbal teas.

Villa Thalgo

8th arr. - 218-220, rue du Faubourg Saint-Honoré - 45 62 00 20
Open Mon. noon-8 p.m., Tues. & Thurs. 10 a.m.-8 p.m., Wed. & Fri. & Sat. 9 a.m.-8 p.m. Closed Sun.

Take a sea-cure right in the heart of Paris! Below the Golden Tulip Hotel is the city's first thalassotherapy center, with a (reconstituted) sea-water swimming pool. A multitude of seaweed-based body- and skin-care treatments is offered, as well as more traditional beauty care (manicure, lymphatic draining, sauna, Turkish baths...). After a morning of pampering yourself, you can lounge by the pool and nibble at a nutrionally balanced lunch. Prices vary on the length and type of treatments; memberships are available.

BOOKS & STATIONERY

■ ART

Artcurial

8th arr. - 9, av. Matignon - 42 99 16 19
Open 10:30 a.m.-7:15 p.m. Closed Sun. & Mon. (except before Christmas), Aug. & holidays.

One floor up from Artcurial's lively contemporary art gallery, this fabulous bookstore boasts some 8,000 works on fine arts, graphics and crafts. Look here for the exquisite and erudite books on art, design and fashion from the Editions du Regard (e.g. Anne Bony's monumental series on twentieth-century design), as well as an interesting selection of works (primarily Japanese) on fashion and textiles.

Image et Page

4th arr. - 25, rue du Renard - 42 71 70 77
Open daily 10 a.m.-9 p.m.

Luxuriously produced art books and exhibition catalogs are sold at discount prices at this bookshop just steps away from the Centre Pompidou. Contemporary painting is well represented, but the oft-changing stock has works to interest just about any art buff; books in many languages are available here.

Lecointre et Ozanne

6th arr. - 9, rue de Tournon - 43 26 02 92
Open 10 a.m.-7 p.m. (Sat. until 6 p.m.). Closed Sun. & Mon.

The history of architecture will be an open book to you, after a visit to this impressive bookshop, which offers an unequalled selection of rare and important works on the subject. Catalog available.

Librairie Maeght

4th arr. - 12, rue Saint-Merri - 42 78 27 64
Open 10 a.m.-1 p.m. & 2 p.m.-7 p.m. Closed Sun., Mon. & holidays.

Vying for your attention with lithographs by the Galerie Maeght's stable of artists (more affordable, incidentally, than you might think) are all the most important books on every aspect of contemporary art. In many languages.

Nobele

6th arr. - 35, rue Bonaparte - 43 26 08 62
Open 9 a.m.-noon & 2 p.m.-7 p.m. Closed Sat. & end July-end Aug.

Belgian by birth and over 100 years old, Nobele is the bookshop of reference when it comes to the fine arts, decorative arts, works on collectible antiques and on the history of books. An extraordinary stock of old or rare art books, at astonishingly reasonable prices. Catalog upon request.

■ ENGLISH-LANGUAGE

Attica 1

5th arr. - 23, rue Jean-de-Beauvais - 46 34 62 03
Open 10 a.m.-7 p.m. Closed Sun. & Mon.

The lack of order that reigns here is either appealing or off-putting: the interpretation depends on your personality. We happen to like it, and often while away a bookish afternoon browsing through the rich and eclectic collections. Helpful, literate staff; good service.

Brentano's

2nd arr. - 37, av. de l'Opéra - 42 61 52 50
Open 10 a.m.-7 p.m. (Sat. 10 a.m.-noon & 2 p.m.-7 p.m.). Closed Sun.
Brentano's deservedly remains a favorite among Americans in Paris for its remarkable array of American, English and French books, periodicals, records and art books. Bestsellers of the week are always displayed at the entrance. And there is also a large children's-book section.

Galignani

1st arr. - 224, rue de Rivoli - 42 60 76 07
Open 10 a.m.-7 p.m. Closed Sun.
Galignani, purported to be the oldest English bookshop on the continent, was established in 1805 on the rue Vivienne by Giovanni Antonio Galignani, descendant of a famous twelfth-century publisher from Padua, Italy. In the mid-1800s Galignani moved to the rue de Rivoli, near the terminus of the Calais-Paris train, and the shop has passed from father to son and so on down the line. Featured are English, American and French hardcovers and paperbacks, lots of children's literature, plus a fabulous international selection of art books.

Le Nouveau Quartier Latin

6th arr. - 78, bd Saint-Michel - 43 26 42 70
Open 10 a.m.-7 p.m. Closed Sun.
The Nouveau Quartier Latin carries a wide selection of English, American, Spanish and German literature, plus dictionaries and paperbacks in English (over 10,000). Also featured are books on painting, design, architecture, photography, graphics and music. An entire section is given over to books on teaching or learn-

ing English. The adjacent room is equipped so that you may listen to and watch audiotapes and videotapes before purchasing them. The book-ordering service is fast and efficient, and sales go on throughout the year. Catalogs are available.

Shakespeare and Company

5th arr. - 37, rue de la Bûcherie 43 26 96 50
Open daily 11 a.m.-midnight.
Shakespeare and Co. on the quai by Notre-Dame is the late-night favorite of buyers and browsers in search of secondhand English and American books (see *Open Late*).

W. H. Smith

1st arr. - 248, rue de Rivoli - 42 60 37 97
Open 9:30 a.m.-7 p.m. Closed Sun.
This is the closest thing to the perfect self-service bookstore: it is easy to locate almost any item among the over 40,000 English and American titles, from cookbooks to travel guides to children's books, videos, cassettes... The selection of periodicals is vast. The staff is efficient and friendly... and very British.

Tea and Tattered Pages

6th arr. - 24, rue Mayet - 40 65 94 35
Open 11 a.m.-7 p.m. Closed Sun.
A charming place to browse through a wide selection of English and American used books, and to enjoy a leisurely cup of tea (see *Tea rooms*).

Tonkam

11th arr. - 29, rue Keller - 47 00 78 38
Open 10:30 a.m.-noon & 1 p.m.-7 p.m. (Sat. 2 p.m.-8 p.m.). Closed Sun.
Sylvie Tonkam is the resident expert on *bandes dessinées*—comic books and

albums. Her vast inventory includes an impressive collection of American comics, some old and collectible. T-shirts, too.

The Village Voice

6th arr. - 6, rue Princesse - 46 33 36 47
Open 11 a.m.-8 p.m. (Mon. from 2 p.m.). Closed Sun. No cards.
Nowadays the Village Voice controls the turf once so jealously guarded by Sylvia Beach's original Shakespeare and Co.—a mecca for Americans in Paris, especially writers, journalists and literary types. The Village Voice hosts well-attended poetry readings and book-signing parties, and supplies voracious readers with an intelligently chosen selection of titles. Books special-ordered on request by the friendly, literate staff.

■ FILM & PHOTOGRAPHY

La Chambre Claire

6th arr. - 14, rue Saint-Sulpice 46 34 04 31
Open 10 a.m.-7 p.m. (Mon. 2 p.m.-7 p.m.). Closed Sun. & holidays.
This bookshop is given over entirely to photography—with some 5,000 editions, it is the official supplier to several of the world's greatest museums. A truly remarkable place; some discounted books are available.

Ciné Doc

9th arr. - 43-45, passage Jouffroy 48 24 77 36
Open daily 10 a.m.-7 p.m.
This flea market–style shop in the delightful passage Jouffroy boasts an admirable jumble of publications pertaining to the cinema, plus posters, postcards and original photographs. The interesting displays in the shop windows change often and add to the already lively ambience.

Aficionados take note: Ciné Doc possesses a fascinating collection of highly literate erotica.

◼ FOOD
& COOKING

La Librairie Gourmande

5th arr. - 4, rue Dante - 43 54 37 27
Open 10 a.m.-7 p.m. (Sun. from 3 p.m.).

At La Librairie Gourmande you will find a mouth-watering array of cookbooks, for amateurs and pros alike, as well as works on the history of French and foreign cooking (some volumes date the sixteenth century). Vast collections treating traditional and nouvelle cuisine, recipes by Balzac and Dumas, plus a wide range of works on oenology make this one of Paris' most appetizing bookshops, despite the high prices. You can bank on a warm welcome and excellent service from owner Geneviève Baudon.

Librairie des Gourmets

5th arr. - 98, rue Monge - 43 31 16 42
Open 10:30 a.m.-7 p.m. Closed Sun. & Mon.

A bright and tidy shop where gourmets, gourmands and good cooks will feel right at home, thanks to the owner's warm welcome. All the latest French cookbooks are on hand, as well as a wide selection of gastronomical classics.

Le Verre et l'Assiette

5th arr. - 1, rue du Val-de-Grâce 46 33 45 96
Open 10 a.m.-12:30 p.m. & 2:30 p.m.-7 p.m. (Mon. from 2:30 p.m.). Closed Sun. & 2 wks. in Aug.

Too many chefs may well spoil the broth, but they certainly don't spoil Le Verre et l'Assiette. Feast your eyes on the window display: a

---

Tea in the Pagoda

The movies saved *La Pagode* ("the Pagoda") from the threat of demolition. Since 1931 it has been one of the city's most attractive cinemas houses. The French architects responsible for La Pagode fell under the collective fin-de-siècle enchantment with all things Oriental; the structure's elegant decor delighted guests at high-society receptions in the 1890s. Later the Chinese Embassy dropped plans to buy La Pagode (the ambassador apparently objected to some wall paintings depicting Chinese warriors being soundly trounced by the Japanese). The Oriental flavor lingers on in the tea rooms and garden, additional reasons to visit this pagoda at 57bis rue de Babylone in the seventh arrondissement. Across the street at number 68, Ciné-images sells posters and other souvenirs of the world's greatest movies.

---

potpourri of books and accessories pertaining to gastronomy and oenology—from unique corkscrews to rare editions on Celtic cooking. This is the bookshop most frequented by famous chefs, gourmets and brothers of the grape. In addition to the thousands of volumes on food and wine, there is a fine selection of gift ideas (the wine taster's ideal traveling case, for example). *Bon appétit!*

◼ GENERAL
INTEREST

Gibert Jeune

5th arr. - 23-27, quai Saint-Michel - 43 54 57 32
5th arr. - 4-6, pl. Saint-Michel - 43 25 91 19
2nd arr. - 15, bd Saint-Denis - 42 36 82 84
Open 9:30 a.m.-7:30 p.m. Closed Sun.

This multstory emporium of books is renowned among the city's huge student population for its large inventory, special sales and secondhand hardcovers and paperbacks. A fine selection of English and American books (you might

consider selling your own used or unwanted books here).

La Hune

6th arr. - 170, bd Saint-Germain 45 48 35 85
Open 10 a.m.-midnight. Closed Sun.

La Hune is a favorite among Paris intellectuals, bibliophiles and browsers. It stays open late and stocks an impressive array of books on architecture, contemporary art and design, as well as classics and contemporary literature. The mezzanine houses works on the graphic arts, photography, theater and cinema.

Librairie Delamain

1st arr. - 155, rue Saint-Honoré 42 61 48 78
Open 10 a.m.-7 p.m. Closed Sun.

Delamain is the oldest bookstore in France, founded in 1710 under the arcades of the Comédie-Française. About 100 years ago the original shop burned down, and Delamain was forced to move to its current location on the rue Saint-Honoré. Thousands of volumes on French literature, travel, history and art (French only) are available new or used. The first floor is given over to the graphic arts, photography, film and theater.

FNAC

1st arr. - Forum des Halles - 40 41 40 00
6th arr. - 136, rue de Rennes - 49 54 30 00
17th arr. - 26, av. des Ternes - 44 09 18 00
Open 10 a.m.-7:30 p.m. Closed Sun.

FNAC is the biggest bookstore chain in Europe, with a low-price policy that means you can read more for less: French books sell for 5 percent under standard retail, while foreign editions are discounted even more. Miles of shelves are packed with a vast and varied stock of volumes ranging from do-it-yourself manuals, cookbooks and guides to high-brow fiction, poetry and philosophy. The stores are immense and densely packed with book-loving humanity, particularly on weekends. The sales staff is qualified and knowledgeable, though it often seems like they are rarer than first editions (which means, however, that one can browse here for hours undisturbed!).

La Librairie des Femmes

6th arr. - 74, rue de Seine - 43 29 50 75
Open 10 a.m.-7 p.m. Closed Sun.

This is not a feminist bookshop. It is a publisher/ bookseller's showcase that highlights books written by or about women (including many books by men!). The first-floor sales area is one of the most attractive in Paris— sunny, spacious and user-friendly. The shop also organizes photo and print exhibits.

Librairie Thomas

5th arr. - 28, rue des Fossés-Saint-Bernard - 46 34 11 30
Open 9 a.m.-7 p.m. (Mon. 2 p.m.-6:30 p.m.; Sat. 9:30 a.m.-12:30 p.m. & 2 p.m.-6:30 p.m.). Closed Sun.

This charming little shop features more than 10,000 works on the natural sciences (in several languages). It has recently been remodeled and is now managed by specialists affiliated with the natural history museum. You will find nature guides, works on gardening, ecology, history and much more, plus a large children's-book section. A wealth of guidebooks is on hand as well.

La Maison du Dictionnaire

14th arr. - 98, bd du Montparnasse - 43 22 12 93
Open 9 a.m.-6:30 p.m. Closed Sat. & Sun.

This ever-expanding shop in the Montparnasse shopping center features more than 4,000 new and used dictionaries (general, technical and special-interest) in more than 100 languages. Even more astounding is the Pivothèque reading room, open to the public, in which you may sit and browse through any book before buying it.OK

▓ RARE BOOKS

Pierre Bérès

8th arr. - 14, av. de Friedland - 45 61 00 99
Open 9 a.m.-6 p.m. Closed Sun. No cards.

The grand old man of the city's rare-book trade possesses one of the world's most precious inventories, which includes illuminated manuscripts, incunabula (pre-sixteenth-century printed books) and works illustrated by contemporary artists. Even if like most mortals you lack the wherewithal to purchase one of these treasures, if you

are a true bibliophile, you owe it to yourself to visit this remarkable address.

Carnavalette

3rd arr. - 2, rue des Francs-Bourgeois - 42 72 91 92
Open daily 10 a.m.-6:30 p.m. No cards.

Some rare twentieth-century volumes are offered here for sale, but what we find most interesting is the shop's collection of museum posters, highly decorative and ready to frame.

Courant d'Art

6th arr. - 79, rue de Vaugirard 45 49 30 08
Open 9 a.m.-8 p.m. Closed Sun.

Art is the passion of bookseller Marie-Josée Grandjean. Her rue de Vaugirard shop is a showcase for books on art— from studies and monographs of painters, sculptors and artisans, to sales catalogs from Christie's, Sotheby's or Drouot (France). On display is a large collection of engravings, reproductions, exhibition catalogs, back issues of art magazines and all sorts of other unfindables. Not to mention the noteworthy collection of books on cinema and photography. In addition to her Left-Bank shop, Grandjean runs a stand at the Saint-Ouen flea market (from 9 a.m.-6 p.m. on Saturday, Sunday and Monday; Marché Jules-Vallès, 40 11 43 88).

Librairie du Cygne

6th arr. - 17, rue Bonaparte - 43 26 32 45
Open 3 p.m.-7 p.m. Closed Sat., Sun. & Aug.

The Librairie du Cygne seems to have tumbled out of a Balzac novel. The ancient oak bookcases of this austere shop groan with signed first editions and illustrated works by the greats—Stendhal, Molière, Anatole France, Maupassant, Zola and Hugo. A wide-ranging array of books on the decorative arts is another specialty of the house.

Pont-Neuf

6th arr. - 1, rue Dauphine - 43 26 42 40
Open 9:30 a.m.-noon & 2 p.m.-6:30 p.m. (Sat. until 5 p.m.). Closed Sun., Mon. & Aug. No cards.

This charming shop run by Claude Coulet features a nineteenth-century reading room, with shelves packed with first editions, illustrated works and reprints by Carteret, Vicaire and Pia. The lovely setting, just across from the Pont-Neuf, and one of the best selections of antiquarian books in Paris make the Librairie du Pont-Neuf a must-visit for bibliophiles and curious browsers alike.

■ TRAVEL BOOKS

Institut Géographique National

8th arr. - 107, rue de La Boétie 43 98 85 00
Open 9:30 a.m.-7 p.m. (Sat. 10 a.m.-12:30 p.m. & 2 p.m.-5:30 p.m.). Closed Sun.

Need a map? Of course you need a map! Those published by the IGA are meticulously detailed, and will delight travelers, tourists, hikers and bikers who like to know just where they are.

Le Tour du Monde

16th arr. - 9, rue de la Pompe 42 88 73 59
Open 10 a.m.-1 p.m. & 2 p.m.-7 p.m. Closed Sun., Mon. & holidays. No cards.

Travel-book buffs take note: Jean-Etienne and Edmonde Huret have earned their reputation as the Sherlock Holmes(es) of the book world. Their shop is chockablock with hard-to-find, out-of-print and rare works on the far-flung and the right-next-door. They also stock a fine selection of children's books.

■ STATIONERY

Armorial

8th arr. - 98, rue du Faubourg-Saint-Honoré - 42 65 08 18
Open 9:30 a.m.-1 p.m. & 2 p.m.-6:30 p.m. Closed Sun.

The desk sets and other sophisticated accessories crafted by this prestigious firm can be found in the offices of many cabinet ministers and executives with refined tastes.

Cassegrain

8th arr. - 422, rue Saint-Honoré 42 60 20 08
Open 9:30 a.m.-6:30 p.m. Closed Sun.

This venerable institution on the rue Saint-Honoré, founded in 1919, is aiming to update its image (while preserving its reputation for fine engraving, of course). A new line of "youthful" leather accessories has been introduced: brightly colored lizard date and address books, boxes covered with marbleized paper, more boxes and picture frames in burled elm and amusing gadgets for children. Cassegrain is one of the rare sources in France for the legendary notebooks from Smythson of Bond Street (bible paper, sewn bindings, leather covers—they cost a fortune, but they're worth it). Another Cassegrain store is located at 81, rue des Saints-Pères, in the sixth arrondissement.

Les Crayons de Julie

16th arr. - 17, rue de Longchamp 44 05 02 01
Open 10:30 a.m.-7 p.m. (Mon. from noon). Closed Sun.

Traditionalists who still write (literally) letters and thank-you notes love to browse in Julie's charming shop for old-fashioned fountain pens and pretty stationery.

Dupré Octante

8th arr. - 141, rue du Faubourg-Saint-Honoré - 45 63 10 11
Open 9:15 a.m.-6:30 p.m. (Sat. 10 a.m.-12:30 p.m. & 2 p.m.-6 p.m.). Closed Sun.

Every illustrator and graphic designer in Paris can be found, at one time or another, in this vast stationery shop in the Faubourg-Saint-Honoré. A considerable assortment of letter papers in lovely, exclusive colors is on view, as well as a full range of office accessories. In the equally vast shop nearby on the rue d'Artois is a complete line of drawing materials—from pencils to computer software. You can expect to find even the most arcane art supplies, but don't expect service with a smile from the staff, who we found to be rather surly.

Elysées Stylos Marbeuf

8th arr. - 40, rue Marbeuf - 42 25 40 49
Open 9:30 a.m.-7 p.m. Closed Sun. & Aug.

If it's a fountain pen you're seeking, this is the place. The selection of famous French and imported brands is quite astonishing; repairs are also performed here (though no gimcrack pens will be considered). The solid-gold pens and luxurious gold and silver desk accessories make sumptuous, impressive gifts.

Marie-Papier

6th arr. - 26, rue Vavin - 43 26 46 44
Open 10 a.m.-7 p.m. Closed Sun.

Marie-Paule Orluc launched the trend of fashionable stationery when she opened her enchanting little shop, where all the different papers are conveniently displayed on the walls at eye-level. We don't know of anyone who offers a wider choice of colored letter and note papers, albums, folders and boxes; each season brings a new crop of marvelous hues. Unfortunately, there are just a few catches here: the merchandise is extremely expensive, the atmosphere very high-hat and the salespeople we found hard put to hide their annoyance when a customer walks through the door.

Mélodies Graphiques
4th arr. - 10, rue du Pont- Louis-Philippe - 42 74 57 68
Open 11 a.m.-7 p.m. Closed Sun. & Mon.
This pretty boutique, done up in blond wood, showcases desk accessories covered in marbleized paper. The papers, ten styles in all, are made by the well-known Florentine firm, Il Papiro, according to sixteenth-century methods. A selection of unusual decorative objects—carnival masks and such—is also sold.

Papier Plus
4th arr. - 9, rue du Pont-Louis-Philippe - 42 77 70 49
Open noon-7 p.m. Closed Sun.
Both this shop and Mélodies Graphiques, just opposite (see above), carry quality stationery, but each has its specialty. In Papier Plus, you'll find writing paper sold by the kilo, blank notebooks, photograph albums and files, in a host of pastel shades.

Sennelier
7th arr. - 3, quai Voltaire - 42 60 29 38
Open 9 a.m.-6:30 p.m. (Mon. 9 a.m.-12:15 p.m. & 2 p.m.-6:30 p.m.). Closed Sun.
Appropriately located next to the Ecole des Beaux-Arts, Sennelier has, in its 100-year-old life, sold tons of art supplies to many well-known and aspiring artists. Here they find the best brands of paints and pigments, paper and sketch pads of excellent quality, canvas, easels and framing equipment.

Stern
2nd arr. - 47, passage des Panoramas - 45 08 86 45
Open 9:30 a.m.-12:30 p.m. & 1:30 p.m.-5:30 p.m. Closed Sat., Sun. & Aug. No cards.
Stern started out in 1830, when the *grands boulevards* were the epicenter of elegant Parisian life. Now known throughout the world as engraver to royalty, aristocrats and people of taste, Stern carefully conserves its traditions of using the finest papers, all crafted and engraved by hand. The firm has models available for every type of visiting or business card, invitations and announcements, but Stern's draftsmen can also produce designs to your specifications.

CHILDREN

■ BOOKS

Chantelivre
6th arr. - 13, rue de Sèvres - 45 48 87 90
Open 10 a.m.-6:50 p.m. (Mon. from 1 p.m.). Closed Sun., 1 wk. in Aug. & holidays.
Enter here, all you bibliophiles in short pants and smocked dresses. Among the some 10,000 titles to choose from are illustrated story books, fairy and folk tales and novels, as well as records and educational games. There is a small selection of books and games in English. In a back corner of the shop is an area open for children—to draw, look at books or listen to a story (in French!).

See also: Brentano's, W.H. Smith, Attica in Books, pages 190 and 191.

■ CLOTHING

Baby Dior
8th arr. - 28, av. Montaigne - 40 73 54 44
Open 9:30 a.m.-6:30 p.m. (Sat. & Mon. from 10 a.m.). Closed Sun. & holidays.
If you can afford to buy an entire set of baby clothes, wonderful; if you can't... at least let yourself get one teeny little shirt with a ruffle (400 francs), a pair of sheets for the cradle or a dressing gown. The booties (200 francs) make a darling baby present, and there are also some other nice items—picture frames (650 francs) and silver cups from about 1,450 francs. Abominably expensive smocked dresses are available in sizes up to eight years (640 to 4,000 francs, for a one-year-old).

Bonpoint
7th arr. - 67 & 86 rue de l'Université
45 55 63 70 & 45 51 17 68
7th arr. - 65 & 82, rue de Grenelle - 47 05 09 09 & 45 48 05 45
7th arr. - 7, rue de Solférino - 45 55 42 79
Open 10 a.m.-7 p.m. Closed Sun.
The styles are suited essentially for French yuppie children, but without too much chi-chi. For the last few years, Bonpoint has been trying to lower prices yet maintain its renowned high quality. Pants are lined so they won't itch, hems are huge, and fabrics are of first-rate quality. A blouse runs about 350 francs; a pair of Bermuda shorts, so well cut that they grow with the child, is also about 350 francs; and a pleated or quilted skirt is about 400 francs. The boutique specializes in children's formal dress: white gloves, hats and other such romantic attire... ravishing!

Cacharel

9th arr. - 34, rue Tronchet - 47 42 12 61

Open 10:15 a.m.-7:30 p.m. (Sat. from 9:30 a.m.). Closed Mon.

Cacharel carries parkas, jackets and blazers, as well as pleated skirts, Bermuda shorts and dresses for children ages 4 to 18 years old. Girls look fetching in Liberty-print dresses, and boys handsome in the striped shirts. A note of warning: clothes are cut small, so remember to oversize when buying.

Caddie

8th arr. - 38, rue François-ler - 47 20 79 79

Open 10 a.m.-7 p.m. Closed Sun. & holidays.

From the cradle through junior high, kids can be clothed here in designer togs with the most fashionable labels: Armani, Dior, Kenzo, Moschino, Rykiel... Luxurious sportswear by Donaldson is embroidered with Disney cartoon characters.

La Châtelaine

16th arr. - 170, av. Victor-Hugo 47 27 44 07

Open 9:30 a.m.-6:30 p.m. Closed Sat. 12:30 pm-2:30 p.m., Sun., Mon., 3 wks. in Aug. & holidays.

This is the most luxurious children's clothing shop imaginable. Dresses, vests and shirts are perfectly finished, and the babywear is the finest, most elegant in all of Paris. It is designed exclusively for La Châtelaine by Molli, a Swiss lingerie firm. Clothes for any age group can be custommade and will be delivered free of charge; alterations, too, are done gratis. This isn't so surprising when you consider

---

Budget busters

Some people, we realize, are not happy unless they've paid top dollar (or franc, or whatever) to expand their little ones' wardrobe. For that segment of the population, we list the following addresses, where the children's clothes are dependably chic et chers: *Miki House* makes absolutely adorable trendy togs for toddlers, as well as the cutest sneakers on earth (1, place des Victoires, 1st arr. - 40 26 23 00); *Claude Vell* dresses kids from 0 to 18 in a rainbow of subtle colors (8, rue du Jour, 1st arr. - 40 26 76 70); *Cyrillus* provides outfits for well-bred little ladies and gentlemen—kilts, little blazers, flannel bermudas, gorgeous plaid bathrobes (11, av. Duquesne, 7th arr. - 47 05 99 19).

N.B.: like other French retailers, these shops put on worthwhile sales in January and July.

---

that a size-five Liberty dress is priced at 1,200 francs.

Chevignon Kids

6th arr. - 4, rue des Ciseaux - 43 26 06 37

Open 10:15 a.m.-7 p.m. Closed Sun. & holidays.

This is the place to find hideously expensive children's wear inspired by the clothes American teenagers wore in the 1950s. Practically every item is stamped with the firm's logo—they should pay their customers for the free advertising!

Gina Diwan

15th arr. - 20, av. du Maine - 42 22 27 09

Open 10:30 a.m.-7 p.m. Closed Sun.

Adorable, dressy rompers for babies are featured (380 francs for a three-month-old), as well as hand-smocked dresses, embroidered shirts and blouses with petal collars.

Alongside these tiny togs are clothes for children up to fourteen years.

Jacadi

17th arr. - 60, bd de Courcelles 47 63 55 23 (also in 1st arr., 2nd arr., 4th arr., 5th arr., 6th arr., 7th arr., 8th arr., 9th arr., 13th arr., 14th arr., 15th arr., 16th arr., 18th arr., 19th arr., 20th arr.)

Open 10 a.m.-6:45 p.m. Closed Sun. & holidays.

Given the prices French parents are obliged to pay for children's clothes, Jacadi's merchandise offers pretty good value. The styles are attractive, though rather sedate...how many little American boys would dare show up at school in short formal pants? At any rate, there are some beautiful shirts and blouses, sturdy outerwear and lots of lovely accessories (headbands, socks, hats, mittens and scarves). Sizes start at birth and go to age fourteen.

Naf-Naf

17th arr. - 10, av. des Ternes - 42 67 30 30

Open 10 a.m.-7:30 p.m. Closed Sun.

If you like jogging suits, sweatshirts and dungarees,

---

trot along to Naf-Naf. Everyone knows it as much for its styles as for its recent advertising campaign: piglets in a display of doubtful taste. We think you could do better elsewhere, and price-wise, too!

New Man
6th arr. - 12, rue de l'Ancienne-Comédie - 43 54 44 95
Open 10 a.m.-7:30 p.m. Closed Sun.

From the tender age of six months babies, toddlers and older kids can wear the rough-and-ready styles of this fashionable firm's Miniman line. The offerings present a welcome compromise between sloppy sweats and restrictive (itchy!) dress-up clothes.

Du Pareil au Même
12th arr. - 122, rue du Faubourg Saint-Antoine - 43 44 67 46
Open 10 a.m.-7 p.m. Closed Sun.

This is the biggest of the chain's twelve Parisian stores. The low prices are enough to motivate mothers to dig through piles of pants, shirts, skirts, pjs and so on. Surprisingly, the clothes are of more-than-respectable quality, and stylish to boot.

Petit Faune
6th arr. - 33, rue Jacob - 42 60 80 72
Open 10:30 a.m.-7 p.m. Closed Sun. & holidays.

Flowered dresses, hand-knitted baby clothes and separates for children from birth to twelve in traditional styles to which bold, bright colors give a fashion kick. As for the prices, they really do defy good sense.

Tartine et Chocolat
6th arr. - 90 & 105, rue de Rennes 42 22 67 34 & 45 62 44 04
Open 10 a.m.-7 p.m. Closed Sun. & Mon.
Open 10:30 a.m.-1:30 p.m. & 2:30 p.m.-7 p.m. Closed Sun., Mon. & Aug. 1-15.
16th arr. - 60, av. Paul Doumer 45 04 08 94
Open 10 a.m.-7 p.m. (Mon. from 2 p.m.). Closed Sun. & Aug. 1-15.

The famous little blue and pink stripes that made the brand a success have survived, though these days they represent only three percent of the collection. Aside from the clothes (up to eight years), Tartine et Chocolat also sells lots of appealing accessories,

children's furniture and baby equipment. Little girls love the firm's fresh, innocent eau de cologne (with no alcohol), "P'titsenbon", in its pretty frosted-glass bottle.

Sonia Rykiel Enfants
6th arr. - 4 rue de Grenelle - 49 54 61 10
Open 10 a.m.-7 p.m. Closed Sun.

It took becoming a grandmother for Sonia Rykiel to realize she had nothing for her darling little Lolita and Tatiana, her two granddaughters. So she got her own daughter, Natalie, to oversee a children's line. And it's a success. Clothes are embroidered with gold-colored teddies, there's plenty of sharp red, violet, gray and fuchsia jersey, long sweaters over miniskirts and velvet jogging outfits. Now mommies can have carbon-copy little Rykiels.

SHOES

Bonpoint
7th arr. - 86, rue de l'Université 45 51 17 68
Open 10 a.m.-7 p.m. Closed Sun.

Having outfitted your children at Bonpoint No. 67, what could be easier than to cross the street to outfit their little tootsies? There are black Paraboots (extremely difficult to find anywhere else) for macho minimen, pastel-colored ballet slippers, tennis shoes, boots and classic styles for school.

Cendrine
6th arr. - 3, rue Vavin - 43 54 81 20
Open 9:30 a.m.-12:30 p.m. & 2 p.m.-7 p.m. (Mon. 2 p.m.-7 p.m.). Closed Sun., last wk. of July & 3 1st wks. of Aug., holidays.

Has your child got delicate or hard-to-fit feet? Well, if so, Cendrine is the place to go. Not that these shoes are orthopedic. On the contrary,

---

Tiny togs for less

Dents de Lait ("Baby Teeth") is a brand-new, sparkling white shop that discounts the top brands of clothing for children from birth to eight years. Here, even chic labels like Petit Faune and Baby Dior can be purchased for less (15, rue Vavin, 6th arr. - 46 33 90 92). For more cut-rate kids' clothes, try *Le Mouton à Cinq Pattes*—it's a madhouse, but the prices are lowest (10, rue Saint-Placide, 6th arr. - 45 48 20 49); *Magic Stock*, on the same street, same price policy (60, rue Saint-Placide, 6th arr. - 45 44 01 89). For excellent prices on warm outdoor and ski wear by French manufacturers, head for *Mi-Prix* (27, boulevard Victor, 15th arr. - 48 28 42 48).

these are classic styles, but Cendrine will fit your baby with a half-sole or advise you on the best model to buy. Anxious mothers emerge confident that their children are correctly shod.

Froment Leroyer
16th arr. - 50, rue Vital - 42 24 82 70 (also 6th arr., 7th arr., 8th arr.)
Open 10 a.m.-7 p.m. Closed Sun., Mon.

Froment Leroyer provides sturdy Start-Rite shoes (at about twice the U.S. price), leather slippers, blue booties with laces, canvas sandals—all those unchangeable children's styles that have become reassuring symbols of continuity. Here one can find everything from classics to the more avant-garde styles in children's shoes.

Till
6th arr. - 51, rue de Sèvres - 42 22 25 25
Open 9:30 a.m.-7 p.m. (Mon. from noon). Closed Sun.

You can be sure that your little darlings will be properly shod here. Till, the largest chain in Europe of its kind, hires only experienced salespeople and will not sell any shoes that haven't been impeccably finished. Kids' tennis shoes have spongy linings, babies' shoes are reinforced and finished in leather. Till staff will explain to you that children's feet have special requirements, and that successive generations need bigger and bigger shoes. There are 300 designs displayed—from loafers to dress shoes to sandals and slippers. This is a serious shoe-shopping stop.

> *Remember that if you spend 2,000 francs or more in a store, you are entitled to a full refund of the value-added tax (VAT). See* Basics *for details.*

■ JUNIORS & TEENS

Autour du Monde
3rd arr. - 10, rue des Francs-Bourgeois - 42 77 46 48
Open 10:30 a.m.-1 p.m. & 2 p.m.-7 p.m. (Sun. & Mon. from 2 p.m.).

All the brands that French adolescents love—Bensimon, Cimarron, Chipie, Ninos de Lorca—are sure to appeal to their American counterparts. All kinds of jeanwear, naturally, in all sorts of colors, escorted by the indispensable accessories: bandanas, thick socks, hip sunglasses and more.

Benetton
16th arr. - 82, av. Victor-Hugo 47 27 73 73 (also 1st arr., 3rd arr., 6th arr., 7th arr., 8th arr., 9th arr., 15th arr., 16th arr., 17th arr.).
Open 10:30 a.m.-7:30 p.m. Closed Sun.

Let's face it, who'd leave home without a Benetton sweater slung over his/her shoulders? Grown far beyond their just-sweater beginnings, United Colors of Benetton is a worldwide success, which, alas, appears to be neglecting quality in favor of a lot of high-profile advertising. Great colors and coordinates unfortunately do not always pass the first test wash. Well, for the price (and the colorful look), we guess it's worth putting up with.

Chevignon Girl
2nd arr. - 5, pl. des Victoires - 42 36 10 16
Open 10:15 a.m.-7 p.m. Closed Sun. & 2 wks. in Aug.

The spirit of the 1950s lives on, in the form of cotton dresses, jeans, havy-canvas trousers, motorcycle jackets and all manner of accessories. Chevignon pioneered this casual look, which we would like a whole lot more without the overdose of insignias and labels vaunting the brand's

name. Prices fluctuate between modest and prohibitive.

Chipie
1st arr. - 31, rue de la Ferronnerie 45 08 58 74
6th arr. - 49, rue Bonaparte - 43 29 21 94
Open 10 a.m.-1 p.m. & 2 p.m.-7 p.m. (Mon. from 11 a.m.). Closed Sun.

The brand's motto: "Quality and fun since 1967." Well, if that's supposed to mean that the *fun* comes from the label being pasted all over the front of the clothing, and the *quality* is in the cloth (which has a tough time surviving from one season to the next)... But who cares? This is carefully coded fashion for kids who want to look like all their friends. Prices are high; service is pushy.

Creeks
1st arr. - 98, rue Saint-Denis - 42 33 81 70
Open 10 a.m.-7 p.m. (Mon. 11 a.m.-7 p.m.). Closed Sun.

This Creeks shop in Les Halles was designed by (who else?) Philippe Starck. Marble, granite and chrome predominate, and the huge spaces are filled by blasting FM music. People buy what they recognize: old friends include the Chevignon, Liberto, Levi's, Paraboot and Bowen brands. Creeks aims essentially at the 15- to 25-year-old age group, and prefers their customers svelte.

Détails d'Hérald
1st arr. - 15, rue du Jour - 40 26 75 65
Open 10:30 a.m.-7:15 p.m. (Mon. noon-7:30 p.m.). Closed Sun.

Adèle and Patricia are two fashion-wise sisters who present an eclectic panorama of up-to-the-minute clothes ranging from streetwise to sedate. Young style mavens will love the colorful collection, and the "graffiti room" at the back of the shop.

Kenzo Enfants

1st arr. - 3, place des Victoires
40 39 72 87
*Open 10 a.m.-7 p.m. (Mon. from
11 a.m.). Closed Sun., 2 wks. in
Aug. & holidays.*

Kenzo captures the younger set with his signature prints, vivid colors and splendid accessories, priced markedly lower than his first-tier line. The clothes are of good quality, and identifiably "Kenzo".

Naf-Naf

17th arr. - 10, av. des Ternes - 42
67 30 30
*Open 10 a.m.-7:30 p.m. Closed
Sun.*

The little pink pig, Naf-Naf's mascot, has a very bright and tidy new home here, filled to bursting with relatively inexpensive, youthful clothes that exactly mirror current trends. Droll and cheerful prints cover leggings, T-shirts, bare little cotton dresses that look great on teenage girls; pretty too are the ribbed-silk T-shirts and peppy skirts and sweaters. Boys will love the baggy casual trousers and flashy print shirts. Kids willingly whip out their wallets and spend weeks' worth of pocket money on the huge range of Naf-Naf accessories.

New Man

6th arr. - 12, rue de l'Ancienne-Comédie - 43 54 44 95
*Open 10 a.m.-7:30 p.m. Closed
Sun.*

Not just for men. These two stores have recently been redecorated and, by offering extra-large men's sizes, are enjoying a a new clientele. Casual clothes with considerable cachet are crafted in denim, gabardine and cotton or *cupro*, an attractive new fiber blend.

SHOES

Free Lance

6th arr. - 30, rue du Four - 45 48
14 78
*Open 10:15 a.m.-7 p.m. Closed
Sun.*

Rusted metal seems to be the dominant note in the decor, but never mind. Free Lance has the footwear that teenagers want: lace-ups with rubber or "tire" soles, postpunk wedgies, 1950s patent leathers, pretty ballet slippers, hobnailed boots and leather sandals. May not be the most comfortable of shoes, but that's not what's important here.

Gelati

6th arr. - 5, rue de Sèvres - 42 22
68 08
*Open 10 a.m.-7 p.m. Closed
Sun. (Mon., Wed., Thurs. 1 p.m.-
2 p.m.).*

This is Italian fashion at its most fun and inventive. Prices are reasonable (from 400 francs) for some brash, vivid-colored shoes with square toes and small heels. Shoes that are destined to be worn with absolute intensity will probably last for just one season.OK

Marie Lalet

4th arr. - 16, rue du Bourg-Tibourg - 40 27 08 05
*Open 11 a.m.-7 p.m. Closed
Sun. & Mon. & 2 wks in Aug.*

Essentially a boutique for heavy-duty footwear by Doc Martens, this shop also presents some 45 other models (for men, women and children) that offer just about anything one could wish for in the way of color and style. Many different leathers too (aged, oiled, patent, suede...).

■ TOYS

Ali Baba

7th arr. - 29, av. de Tourville - 45
55 10 85
*Open 10 a.m.-1 p.m. & 2 p.m.-
7 p.m. Closed Sun. & holidays.*

Ali Baba has three floors of quality games and toys for children of all ages. The basement level is a kingdom of scale models and electric trains. The ground floor is devoted to card and board games. Do not miss the superb collection of hand-painted tin soldiers.

Jouets & Cie

1st arr. - 11, bd de Sébastopol
42 33 67 67
*Open 10:30 a.m.-7:30 p.m.
Closed Sun.*

Rather alarming, the gigantic gold baby doll that serves as this company's mascot. He presides over a vast emporium of games, scale models, toys, puzzles, costumes and, yes, dollies that sell for ten to twenty percent less than in traditional toy shops or department stores. The latest electronic games and cassettes are here, as well as outdoor games, craft sets, robots and baby toys. Shopping baskets (à la Toys 'R' Us) are a welcome convenience; special promotional sales are held throughout the year.

Multicubes

4th arr. - 5, rue de Rivoli - 42 77
10 77
*Open 10 a.m.-7 p.m. (Mon. from
2 p.m.). Closed Sun., 2 1st wks.
of Aug. & holidays.*
15th arr. - 110, rue Cambronne
47 34 25 97
*Open 10:30 a.m.-2 p.m. &
2:30 p.m.-7 p.m. Closed Sun.,
Mon. & July 20-Aug. 20 &
holidays.*

Every year sees a new collection from Erzgebirge, the land of wooden-toy makers. Some of the toys are pure marvels and quite pricey, coveted by the old and young

*Don't plan to do much shopping in Paris in August—a great many stores
are closed for the entire vacation month.*

alike. There are mobiles, yo-yos, model farms and animals, as well as dolls with real hair made by Käthe Kruse (a Bauhaus disciple); prices start at 1,200 francs. There are also lots of Yuletide decorations from Germany and Scandinavia.

Au Nain Bleu

8th arr. - 406-410, rue Saint-Honoré - 42 60 39 01
Open 9:45 a.m.-6:30 p.m. Closed Sun.
Don't be put off by the 32,000-franc price tag on the miniature Bugatti in the window. This illustrious shop does have other wonderful and less expensive toys to tempt you. On the lower level, old friends like Mickey Mouse and Babar live, and you can hop a ride on some fine rocking horses, some of which boast real leather trappings. There's a great variety of enchanting dolls and doll clothes (accessory kits start at 500 francs), plastic and china tea services, lots of remote-control cars and motorcycles and a costume and makeup section. Miniature French grocery shops start at 700 francs; stuffed animals in every size and shape cost from 250 to 3,500 francs. Many of the toys sold here are exclusive models you won't find elsewhere.

L'Oiseau de Paradis

7th arr. - 211, bd Saint-Germain 45 48 97 90
Open 9:30 a.m.-7 p.m. Closed Sun.
This is the traditional toy shop *par excellence*, chockablock from floor to ceiling. Tricycles, rocking toys and scooters hang from the rafters, and we're always greeted with a smile, no matter what we've come to buy. Apart from the standard variety of toys, there are some fine tin soldiers, handmade wooden puzzles and a collection series of

miniature cars. Electronic games are now in stock as well—a sign of the times!

Pain d'Epice

9th arr. - 29, passage Jouffroy 47 70 82 65
Open 10 a.m.-7 p.m. (Mon. from 12:30 p.m.). Closed Sun.
Tucked in the lovely passage Jouffroy, just opposite the Musée Grevin (see below) this shop is surely one of the most delightful in town. Reproductions of old-fashioned toys—tops, hoops, gyroscopes, puppets, pretty cut-outs and the like—make charming gifts for good little children.

La Pelucherie

6th arr. - 74, rue de Seine - 46 33 60 21
Open 10:30 a.m.-7:30 p.m. Closed Sun.
8th arr. - 84, av. des Champs-Elysées - 43 59 49 05
Open 10 a.m.-midnight (Sun. & holidays 11:30 a.m.-7:30 p.m.).
A boon for night owls, this stuffed-animal kingdom of soft toys stays open until midnight. You'll find everything here from the tiniest teddy bear to a gargantuan elephant in every color of the rainbow. Dogs of every breed, raccoons, bees, Bambis and Dumbos (alongside the other Disney characters) coexist in exemplary harmony here. There's also a section for newborns that sells darling baby clothes. La Pelucherie delivers within Paris and all over the world.

Si Tu Veux

2nd arr. - 68, Général-Vivienne 42 60 59 97
Open 11 a.m.-7 p.m. Closed Sun. Mail-order sale catalog.
Nestled cozily in the heart of this lovely gallery is a gold mine for children's parties. Games and toys are attractive and reasonably priced. There are wooden blocks, washable dolls, a great choice of marbles and a panoply of

appealing, educational playthings. For children's birthdays and party occasions, there are ready-to-wear as well as ready-to-make costumes (from 150 francs for a kit), easily removable play makeup, hats, magic wands and party kits for 200 francs. Right next door is a space reserved for nostalgic grownups. Remember those teddy bears stuffed with straw that you loved as a child (185 francs for the smallest)? Well, you can get those here as well as painted tin toys, little china services and charming Victorian paper dolls.

■ WHERE TO TAKE THE KIDS

MUSEUMS

The following is a list of museums of special interest to children.

Centre Georges-Pompidou

4th arr. - 120, rue Saint-Martin, entrance pl. Georges-Pompidou ou "Piazza Beaubourg" - 44 78 49 17
Open 2 p.m.-6 p.m. Closed Tues. & holidays.
This Parisian cultural center hosts a children's workshop with facilities for theater, dance, video and film shows. Children are generally delighted by the pop-art fountain by Nikki de Saint-Phalle outside the Centre.

Cité des Sciences et de l'Industrie

19th arr. - 30, av. Corentin-Cariou - 40 05 70 00, 46 42 13 13
Open 10 a.m.-6 p.m. Closed Mon.
The Cité des Sciences may make your head spin, but, curiously, we don't notice this happening with children. They delight in the "Géode," a kind of geodesic dome that houses a huge panoramic cinema

screen, and the Planetarium and the Inventorium. There are also any number of video games for hands-on play. It's a user-friendly spot where a child would be hard-put to get bored.

Musée de l'Armée
7th arr. - Hôtel des Invalides - 45 55 37 70
Open 10 a.m.-6 p.m. (Oct. 1-March 31 until 5 p.m.). Admission: 30 F, reduced rate: 20 F, children under 7: Free.
This military museum exhibits arms, uniforms and scale models of famous battle scenes, and screens films of World Wars I and II.

Musée National des Arts d'Afrique et d'Océanie
12th arr. - 293, av. Daumesnil 44 74 84 80
Open 10 a.m.-noon & 1:30 p.m.-5:30 p.m. (Sat. & Sun. until 6 p.m.). Closed Tues.
This museum located on the edge of the Bois de Vincennes (site of a terrific zoo) features the largest aquarium in Paris. Children adore the crocodile pit.

Musée Grévin
9th arr. - 10, bd Montmartre - 42 46 13 26
Open daily 1 p.m.-7 p.m.
Founded in 1882, this wax museum features historical figures and distorting mirrors to amuse those of all ages.

Musée de la Marine
16th arr. - Palais de Chaillot, pl. du Trocadéro 45 53 31 70
Open 10 a.m.-6 p.m. Closed Tues.
Exhibits and scale models on naval history and marine archaeology are favorites with older children to at Musée de la Marine. The museum also displays maritime art, as well as artifacts of the technical,

historical and scientific evolution of navigation.

Palais de la Découverte
8th arr. - av. Franklin Roosevelt 40 74 80 00
Open 9:30 a.m.-6 p.m. (Sun. 10 a.m.-7 p.m.). Closed Mon., Jan. 1, May 1, July 14, Aug. 15 & Dec. 25. Restaurant.
This museum is an excellent place for children interested in science. Experiments are conducted by staff members every afternoon for the public. A list of daily activities is posted to the left of the museum's entrance.

For more details on museums in Paris, consult the *Arts & Leisure* chapter.

Muséum National d'Histoire Naturelle
5th arr. - 57, rue Cuvier - 40 79 30 00
Open 10 a.m.-5 p.m. (Sat. & Sun. 11 a.m.-6 p.m.). Closed Tues. & holidays.
Located within the Jardin des Plantes (home to a very pleasant zoo), this museum houses fascinating exhibits on paleontology, paleobotany and mineralogy. Of greater interest to older children.

Rock'n'Roll Hall of Fame
1st arr. - Forum des Halles. Porte du Louvre 40 28 08 13
Open daily 10:30 a.m.-6:30 p.m.
When it's raining and the kids can't stand the thought of another museum, try taking them here. The history of rock, from Elvis to Madonna, is illustrated by wax mannequins, animated scenes, all-around sound and lots of special effects. Good fun.

■ PARKS & GARDENS
Here are some city parks with particular appeal for children.

Bois de Boulogne
16th arr.
Entrances are located at the Porte Maillot, Porte Dauphine and Les Sablons. This enormous wooded park, which covers part of the sixteenth arrondissement, and the suburb of Neuilly, features a lake, horseback-riding clubs, a lovely children's park and petting zoo (Jardin d'Acclimatation), a marvelous floral garden (Parc de Bagatelle) and numerous paths that wind through trees and lawns. Bicycles for adults and children are available for rental.

Jardin du Luxembourg
6th arr. - Main entrance bd Saint-Michel, near place Edmond-Rostand - 40 79 37 00
Open daily dawn-dusk.
Within these attractive gardens, situated between Saint-Michel and Montparnasse, there are pony rides, a marionette theater, sandboxes, jungle gyms and a small children's park for toddlers up to 5 years old.

Jardin des Plantes
5th arr. - Main entrance 57, rue Cuvier - 40 79 30 00
Open daily dawn-dusk.
The Botanical Gardens (Jardin des Plantes) contain

For further details about parks and gardens in Paris, as well as for information on swimming pools and other sports, see the *Arts & Leisure* chapter.

---

more than 10,000 classified plants. There is also a Winter Garden (Jardin d'Hiver), with many tropical plants, and the Alpine Garden (Jardin Alpin), which includes mountain- and polar-region plants. The open-air zoo is a big hit with youngsters.

Parc de la Villette

19th arr. - Main entrance av. Jean-Jaurès, near Porte de Pantin - 42 40 76 10
Hours vary, call for information.

Lots and lots of space, with seven themed gardens, broad lawns and a fantastic sliding board. After an educational tour of the Cité des Sciences, kids can unwind here.

Parc Floral

12th arr. - Esplanade du Château de Vincennes, Rond-Point de la Pyramide - 43 74 60 49
Open Nov.-Feb. 9:30 a.m.-5 p.m.; March & Oct. until 6 p.m.; April-Sept. until 8 p.m. Entrance: 10 F; 6-10: 5 F; 0-6, 65 & over: Free.

A small fee admits kids to a playground full of delightful things to do and try. Amusement park rides cost another five francs a pop, and the miniature golf course (dotted with reproductions of famous Parisian landmarks) commands an extra fee of 25 francs.

CLOTHING

■ CHEAP CHIC

Alaïa

4th arr. - 7, rue de Moussy - 42 72 19 19
Open 10 a.m.-7 p.m. Closed Sun.

Sexy knits and winsome accessories (shoes, gloves, hats, belts) all bearing the unmistakable stamp of the tiny Tunisian designer. The clothing comes from the previous year's collections, and sells at a 50 percent reduction from the original price.

L'Astucerie

15th arr. - 105, rue de Javel - 45 57 94 74
Open 11:30 a.m.-2 p.m. & 3 p.m.-7 p.m. (Sat. 11:30 a.m.-6 p.m.). Closed Sun. & Mon.

Previously owned but hardly worn top-label clothing for women and children is the backbone of this boutique's inventory. Insiders know that they can buy Hermès silk-twill scarves here for 700 francs, as well as Kelly bags in box calf, Vuitton luggage and the occasional Chanel accessory (all in perfect condition).

Catherine Baril

16th arr. - 14 & 25, rue de la Tour 45 20 95 21
Open 10 a.m.-7 p.m. (Mon. from 2 p.m.). Closed Sun. & 3 wks. in Aug.

Catherine Baril, a pioneer of the consignment system in Paris, ampers her elegant clientele with barely used couture and designer clothing and accessories at truly unbeatable prices. The shop at number 25 offers the lowest prices of all.

Chipie Stock

14th arr. - 82, rue d'Alésia - 45 42 07 52
Open 10:15 a.m.-7 p.m. (Mon. 2 p.m.-7 p.m. & Sat. 10 a.m.-7 p.m.). Closed Sun.

"Stock" is the way the French say "designer outlet." Chipie Stock sells seconds and previous-season models of the youthful, cheerful Chipie label: look for lots of stylish sweaters, jeans, jean jackets (285 francs) and colorful sneakers, all of which look best on the under-30 set.

Le Dépôt des Grandes Marques

2nd arr. - 15, rue de la Banque 42 96 99 04
Open 10 a.m.-7 p.m. Closed Sun.

Rack after rack of designer menswear is set out for your

Bonjour Mickey!

All the familiar Disney characters have a European headquarters now: *Euro Disneyland* opened its doors in April, 1992. Situated some twenty miles east of Paris, accessible by car or by public transportation (the RER), the park is an easy day trip from the capital. It is also a mighty expensive one. A one-day admission to the park costs upwards of 200 francs (140 francs for children eleven and under). Even the simplest meals (pizza, franks, hamburgers and the like) add up quickly to 75 or 100 francs per person. Note too that visitors are not permitted to bring in any food from the outside (no kidding: the guards will confiscate your leftover "baguette"!). If you figure on buying a souvenir or two—and what kid will be willing to leave without one?— you should plan on spending a minimum of five to ten bucks. Please turn to Marne-la-Vallée in the "Suburbs" chapter, p. 86 for restaurants and p. 127 for hotels.

inspection at this first-floor shop near the stock exchange. All the best labels are represented: Renoma, Cerruti, Louis Féraud, Jacques Fath and more, priced at an average of 40 percent under normal retail. Suits, jackets, pants, shirts and ties make up the stock. Expect to find top-name suits (Renoma, for example) from current collections, Cacharel silk ties, Harris tweed and pure cashmere jackets. Take note that the most complicated alterations will be done by in-house tailors. Lots of stockbrokers invest their clothing budgets here, but so do many executives and political types who recognize a good deal when they see one.

Les Deux Oursons

15th arr. - 106, bd de Grenelle
45 75 10 77
Open 10 a.m.-7 p.m. (Mon. 2 p.m.-7 p.m.). Closed Sun.

Pre-worn furs, many with designer labels, all in excellent condition, keep women coming winter after winter to the sign of the "Two Teddy Bears." Blue fox or mink jackets start at 2,000 francs; end lots from such prestigious designers as Ricci, Dior and Revillon go for 30 percent less than elsewhere. Some shearling and leather coats are usually in stock as well. A full range of services includes repairs, expert cleaning and installment-plan payment.

Diapositive Stock

14th arr. - 72, rue d'Alésia - 45 39 97 27
Open 10:15 a.m.-7 p.m. (Mon. 2 p.m.-7 p.m.). Closed Sun.

At this outlet store prices are slashed on attractive print bodysuits, nicely tailored wool flannel suits, leggings with colorful floral or animal motifs and much more. The clothes all date from the preceding season, but they are ticketed a full 50 percent below regular price.

Bargain City

Manufacturers' outlets present unbeatable bargains in clothes, shoes and accessories on the rue d'Alésia (14th arrondissement, between the place Victor-et-Hélène-Basch and the rue des Plantes). Head to *Dorotennis* (n°74) for sportswear by top designer *Dorothée Bis*, to *Mac Douglas* (n°120) for fashionable leather gear, to *Stock 2* (n°92) for designs by Daniel Hechter for the entire family, to *Cacharel* at n°114 (something for everyone here, too) and to *SR Store* (n°64) for greatly reduced fashions by Sonia Rykiel. Across town on the *Rue de Meslay* (3rd arr.) fine Italian footwear is sold at cut-rate prices. And discount houses stand cheek-by-jowl with the most prestigious names in tableware on the *Rue de Paradis* (10th arr.). Remember, though, that rooting out a good buy requires considerable time and patience!

Dorothée Bis Stock

14th arr. - 74, rue d'Alésia - 45 42 17 11
Open 10:15 a.m.-7 p.m. (Mon. 2 p.m.-7 p.m.). Closed Sun.

Even if the clothes are two seasons old, their avant-garde design means they still look very fashionable when you buy them—at one-quarter their regular price! Evening clothes in particular are excellent

value. Summer collections arrive in mid-December, winter clothes at the end of July. Expect to pay about 700 francs for a pretty dress in top-notch condition.

Fabienne

16th arr. - 77 bis, rue Boileau
45 25 64 26
Open 10 a.m.-1:30 p.m. & 3 p.m.-7 p.m. Closed Sun. & Mon.

A consignment shop for men's clothing is rare indeed, so here is a good one to keep in mind. The inventory changes regularly of course, but you can usually count on finding Façonnable suits, Burberry trench coasts and exclusive John Lobb shoes.

Fabrice Karel Stock

14th arr. - 105, rue d'Alésia - 45 42 42 61
Open 10:15 a.m.-7 p.m. (Mon. 2 p.m.-7 p.m.). Closed Sun.

Timeless classic knitwear that never goes out of fashion is sold here for half its original price. From June to August, prices are slashed an additional 30 percent: that's 80 percent off, girls, what are you waiting for?

Réciproque

16th arr. - 89 & 123, rue de la Pompe - 47 04 30 28
Open 10:15 a.m.-6:45 p.m. Closed Sun., Mon.

Thrifty ladies of the jet-set, show-biz and business worlds bring the clothes they no longer want (but can't bear to give away—how do you think they got so rich?) to Réciproque. Manager Nicole Morel displays only the finest designer clothing from recent collections (Chanel, Mugler, Alaïa, Lacroix...), all of it in excellent condition. The spacious, quiet store is a delightful place in which to browse; the ambience is anything but thrift shop. Men's clothing is sold at 101 rue de la Pompe.

Dépôt
Vente de Paris
20th arr. - 81, rue de Lagny - 43 72 13 91
Open 9:30 a.m.-7:30 p.m. Closed Sun. No cards.
Modern and antique furniture, knickknacks and bric-a-brac, dishes, jewelry, used appliances... everything but clothing can be bought or sold on consignment (the fee is 25 percent) at this vast old warehouse. Professionals generally cream off the best of the jewels and antiques, but if they've got a sharp eye, even nonpro shoppers can come up with some interesting bargains. New stock arrives daily.

Les Deux Portes
16th arr. - 35, rue de l'Annonciation - 45 25 31 97
Open 10 a.m.-6:30 p.m. Closed Sun. & Mon.
Designer fabrics for the home (curtains, upholstery, wallpapers) and top-of-the-line household linens are sold at extremely attractive prices at the four Paris Deux Portes

shops. Many items are manufacturers' closeouts, others are the firm's own exclusive designs. Also available is a line of sofas, custom-made draperies and a decorating service.

EYEWEAR

Gualdoni
1st arr. - 228, rue de Rivoli - 42 60 77 44
Open 9 a.m.-12:30 p.m. & 1:30 p.m.-6:30 p.m. (Mon. 2:30 p.m.-6 p.m.). Closed Sun. & 3 wks. in Aug.
16th arr. - 8, av. Mozart - 42 24 77 87
Open 9 a.m.-7 p.m. (Mon. 2:30 p.m.-6 p.m.). Closed Sun. & 1 wk. in Aug.
Gualdoni specializes in tortoiseshell. The prices vary according to thickness and color; the darker the frame, the cheaper the price (about 3,500 francs). Prices for lighter-colored frames can zoom up to 25,000 francs. Come down to earth with the eye-catching Silhouette brand, the top-of-the-line in imitation

tortoiseshell; colored plastic frames are cheaper still. There is a children's section as well as a selection of designer frames (Lafont, Cartier, Vuarnet and so forth). Lots of fashionable sunglasses, too, by Ray-Ban, Beausoleil and Persol.

Lunettes
Beausoleil
4th arr. - 21, rue du Roi de Sicile 42 77 28 29
Open 9 a.m.-12:30 p.m. & 2 p.m.-7 p.m. Closed Sat. & Sun.
Miles Davis used to wear them; Stevie Wonder and Jean-Michel Jarre still do: Frédéric Beausoleil's super-sexy specs are made to measure, personalized and utterly unique. Behind those sunglasses fashioned in "tortoiseshell" (it's really cellulose) or metal, you too can look like a star.

Alain Mikli
4th arr. - 1, rue des Rosiers - 42 71 01 56
Open 11 a.m.-7 p.m. (Mon. 2 p.m.-7 p.m.). Closed Sun.
Mikli, with its sleek blond-wood interior and comfortable armchairs, is the hottest place to shop for eyeglasses. And the selection is grand indeed. Mikli still goes in for extravagant, Hollywood-style frames in large voluptuous shapes, but a glance at the new collection shows that Mikli's classic tendencies are coming to the fore (straightforward round frames). His latest creations incorporate technical innovations such as a combination of metal and plastic in matte or glossy colors. Allow a two- to ten- day turnaround for a pair of glasses, depending on how much work is involved. And you can expect to pay between 800 francs for classic frames and 5,000 francs for a pair of the most sophisticated specs.

Marché Saint-Pierre

18th arr. - Pl. du Marché Saint-Pierre
"None priced lower!" "Sensational bargains!" "Special one-day sale!" Such are the slogans (which we've freely translated for you) that lure crowds of shoppers to the Marché Saint-Pierre, the foremost fabric discount market in Paris. On the ground floor of Tissus Reine, (open 9:15 a.m.-6:30 p.m., Mon. 2 p.m.-6:30 p.m. & Sat. until 6:45 p.m.; closed Sun.; 46 06 06 31), carrying largest choice of fabrics, look for cottons priced as low as 15 francs per meter (approximately three feet), silk, velvet, satin (29 francs per meter), and felt (perfect for lining drawers and closets). The first floor is devoted to woolens, fake fur, notions and patterns. On the second floor, upholstery and decorating fabrics are grouped; all the fabrics designers being here. On the third floor, you will find curtains material. Before you leave, look out from the store and admire the fabulous unobstructed view of Sacré-Cœur.

Latin Optique
5th arr. - 31, bd Saint Michel
43 29 31 79
Open 9 a.m.-12:30 p.m. &
2 p.m.-7 p.m. Closed Sat., Sun. &
holidays.
   The owner is a *visagiste*, which means that he specializes in suiting the glasses he makes to the specific contours and features of your beautiful face. Mr. Raymond measures and studies your mug before proposing a frame that he can (if you wish) hand-craft for you in about 48 hours. Latin Optique also has a huge stock (some 20,000) of ready-made frames and a workshop on the premises to assure quick service.

Bastille Optic
11th arr. 38, rue de la Roquette
48 06 87 00
Open 10 a.m.-7:30 p.m. Closed
Sun., Mon., 1 wk. in Aug. &
holidays.
   When Bastille trendies need glasses, this is where they come for funny or fashionable frames by Mikli, Claude Montana, Agnès B. and Alfred Paris. Don't miss the bat-wing frames by Eye-Wear; another pair mimics the Eiffel Tower—a perfect souvenir (for the nearsighted) of a Parisian holiday.

FOR HIM & HER

Agnès B.
1st arr. - 2-3-6-8, rue du Jour - 42 33 04 13
6th arr. - 13, rue Michelet - 40 51 70 69
16th arr. - 17, av. Pierre ler de Serbie (Women) - 47 23 36 69
16th arr. - 25, av. Pierre ler de Serbie (Men) - 40 70 06 98
Open 10 a.m.-7 p.m. Closed
Sun.
   Above all, Agnès B. designs an ageless collection of fashionable clothing that virtually anyone can live with. In fact, if these casual classics didn't wear out so quickly, one could keep them in one's closet for decades! However

that may be, Agnès B. presents comfortable, easy styles for the entire family at relatively affordable prices: jogging outfits, sweatshirts and sweaters for a sporty look, lots of stripes and, for more dressy encounters, silk, linen and leather pieces.

Anvers
7th arr. - 7-16, rue du Pré-aux-Clercs - 42 86 84 40
Open 10:30 a.m.-7 p.m. Closed
Sun.
   In recent years the rue du Pré-aux-Clercs has become one of the most fashionable stretches of road in Paris. The Belgian city of Anvers (Antwerp, to us) is the home of this young design firm's guiding spirits, Martine Hillen and Anne Kegels. Their two beautiful boutiques present clothes for women (at number 7) and men (number 16) crafted in fine natural fabrics—wool, cotton, linen, silk. Muted shades like beige, silvery green, sand, rust or chocolate are used for their collection of stretchy dresses (500 francs), fluid dresses (850 to 1,650 francs), trousers (745 to 1,000 francs) and nicely structured men's suits (2,900 francs).

APC
6th arr. - 4, rue de Fleurus - 42 22 12 75 (Women)
6th arr. - 7, rue de Fleurus - 45 49 19 15 (Men)
Open 10:30 a.m.-7 p.m. Closed
Sun.
   APC stands for *Atelier de Production et Création*, a label dreamed up by the creative Jean Touitou. Understated elegance is the key to his fashion vision: for women, slim pants, simple but beautifully crafted blouses, alluringly feminine suits; for men, tasteful

sweaters (not so easy to find these days) and casual pants in oiled canvas—very rugged and masculine.

Armani
8th arr. - 6, pl. Vendôme - 42 61 55 09
Open 10 a.m.-7 p.m. Closed
Sun.
   Armani's Parisian outpost is a cathedral of mirrors, furnished with cubical seating crafted of glowing wood: a cross between an Egyptian mausoleum and a hall of mirrors—and just as disorienting! Armani has a couple of thousand stores all over the planet, and hundreds of thousands of faithful customers: it's a marketing miracle, really, since the price (for example) of an off-the-rack Armani suit is about the same as a ticket on the Concorde from Paris to New York! But do go in for a look-see (the sales staff may not seem glad to see you, but never mind them), and bring plenty of money in case you find something irresistible. If you can't bear to leave the shop empty-handed, there's always the Armani cologne; it's far more reasonably priced than the clothes. A few Left Bank boutiques now offer a selection of the Emporio Armani line.

Arnys
7th arr. - 14, rue de Sèvres - 45 48 76 99
Open 10 a.m.-7:30 p.m. (Mon.
10 a.m.-1 p.m. & 4 p.m.-7 p.m.).
Closed Sun.
   Always lots of window-shoppers in front of Arny's boutique, admiring the beautifully coordinated ready-to-wear on display. Inside, you'll find a huge selection of three-ply cashmere sweaters

---

Don't plan to shop on Sundays, the vast majority of Paris stores are closed.

205

Confidential Cinema

Want to see a forgotten or rare movie from New York, New Delhi or New South Wales? Join the film buffs who haunt a host of tiny art cinemas in the area bounded by the quai Saint-Michel, boulevard Saint-Michel, rue Saint-Jacques and rue Soufflot. These theaters often feature avant-garde and foreign flicks in their original languages. Action Christine in the rue Christine is devoted mainly to Hollywood classics. The projectionist takes special pride in his work, and you can ask when buying your tickets whether the copy is of good quality. Also worth a visit: Cinoche in the rue de Condé, Saint André des Arts, in the street of the same name, and Les 3 Luxembourg, rue Monsieur-le-Prince.

in some twenty different shades, an equally vast array of men's sport jackets (3,400 to 5,000 francs), silk (1,200 francs) and cotton (800 francs) shirts, as well as a dizzying collection of limited-edition ties. Upstairs in the tailoring department, women can choose from a number of models of chic suits which can be made to measure.

Barbara Bui
1st arr. - 23, rue Etienne Marcel 40 26 43 65
Open 10:30 a.m.-7 p.m. Closed Sun.
For women, designer Barbara Bui blends European style and Oriental silhouettes, using delicate, fragile fabrics (silk, velvet, airy organza). Check out her beautiful skin-colored blouses. The shop's basement level is reserved for the menswear collection (look for cool wools, heavy cottons and linen), remarkable for its bold designs.

Cerruti 1881
8th arr. - 27, rue Royale - 42 61 11 12
Open 10 a.m.-7 p.m. Closed Sun.
Nino Cerruti runs this family business, which was es-

tablished in 1881. His self-appointed role is to keep alive the tradition of the Italian suit—as classy as a Ferrari, with its unusual color combinations and the use of top-quality fabrics: silk, linen or soft wools. A few years back, Cerruti launched a collection for women of rather austere but elegant "executive" clothing. There are also lingerie and sportswear lines for both men and women.

Charvet
1st arr. - 28, pl. Vendôme - 42 60 30 70
Open 9:45 a.m.-6:45 p.m. Closed Sun.
Charvet is an institution. It has been serving the same clientele from generation to generation. Clients' measurements are kept for decades, so the faithful can order their shirts and whatnot by telephone and have them delivered. Whether you're in search of twenty fine Egyptian cotton shirts or a simple pair of cuff links, the welcome and deference extended to you will be the same. The women's styles are classic, not to say severe (suits, blouses and blazers). Another classic is the paisley silk dressing gown, a

gift for men that women love to wear. Prices are steep.

L'Eclaireur
4th arr. - 3 ter, rue des Rosiers 48 87 10 22
Open 11 a.m.-7 p.m. (Mon. 2 p.m.-7 p.m.). Closed Sun.
For women: Dolce & Gabbana, Moschino Couture, Helmut Lang, Martine Sitbon, Ann Demeulemeester, Martin Margiela, John Galliano—all the hot, hip clothes you want right *now*. For men: Paul Smith, Juliano Fujiwara, Dries van Noten, Momento Due—togs with a definite downtown attitude. To create the proper environment in which to wear these clothes, L'Eclaireur's owners Armand and Martine Hadida present furniture and trendy bibelots by Borek Sipek, Hilton McConnico, André Dubreuil and Fornasetti (whose eerie designs are now furiously fashionable).

Jean-Paul Gaultier
2nd arr. - 6, rue Vivienne - 42 86 05 05
Open 10 a.m.-7 p.m. (Sat. 11 a.m.-7 p.m.). Closed Sun.
The welcome is astonishingly courteous, the clothes are pressed together in glass wardrobes, accessories gleam... there is electricity in the air. The salespeople know what they're talking about. Clothes are beautifully cut and yet extremely provocative: rubber sweaters, tight-knit T-shirts, shoes with astrakhan trimmings; it's an inimitable mix of materials, styles and looks. The Junior Gaultier line is a boon for Jean-Paul's younger fans on smaller budgets. The bronze-green decor with video screens built into the floor is whimsical and fun. (A new Gaultier palace is scheduled to open soon near the Bastille... Watch this space).

Monday, like Sunday, is a day of rest for many shopkeepers.

Marithée et François Girbaud– Halles Capone

1st arr. - 38, rue Etienne Marcel
42 33 54 69
Open 10 a.m.-7 p.m. (Mon. 11 a.m.-7 p.m.). Closed Sun.

The brand that American adolescents adore was born right here. This Mecca for many a fashion pilgrim is a huge, trilevel high-tech commercial space, crammed with the famous Girbaud jeans (including the Métamorphojean line), the dressier (pricier!) Sport City collection for men and women, Maillaparty knitwear and leather gear that has all the girls saving up their baby-sitting money!

Hémisphères

17th arr. - 22, av. de la Grande Armée - 42 67 61 86
Open 10:30 a.m.-7 p.m. Closed Sun.

If you want to look like all those chic French folks who wander around the Luxembourg Gardens of a Sunday in their smart casual clothes, hie yourself to this classy shop near the Etoile. Then (if you are willing to pay the price) you too can clothe yourself in top-quality cashmere, the softest corduroy shirts, chic duffle coats, parkas and more, all manufactured or selected by Hémisphères.

Kenzo

1st arr. - 3, pl. des Victoires - 40 39 72 03
7th arr. - 16, bd Raspail - 42 22 09 38
Open 10 a.m.-7 p.m. (Mon. 11 a.m.-7 p.m.). Closed Sun.

Kenzo was the first of the Japanese designers in Paris. Now he's everywhere. He designs for the whole family, has a collection of bed and bathroom linens and accessories such as watches and eyeglasses. He's also jumped into sportswear. Vivid colors, soft shapes, ethnic prints and billowing shirts remain his

trademark. N.B.: the semi-annual storewide sales in January and July lower prices by as much as 50 percent.

Michel Léger

2nd arr. - 22, pl. du Marché Saint-Honoré - 42 60 47 90
Open 10 a.m.-7 p.m. Closed Sun.

Michel Léger's talents surface equally in his designs for men and women. His supple, simple, refined clothing is made in quality materials: thick cottons lined with alpaca for coats, a wool-silk mix for suits, and viscose for knitwear. His signature style is elegant and urban. You won't find anything sporty here. The service and the welcome, like the well-lit boutique, is warm.

Magic Circle Espace Mode

11th arr. - 9, bd Richard Lenoir 40 21 01 07
Open 10 a.m.-8 p.m. (Sun. 2 p.m.-6 p.m.). Closed Mon.

An immense hangar with cold, gray stone floors, cement pillars, 70s-style orange light fixtures and graffiti on the walls is home to a host of hot designers: Etienne Brunel, Helmut Lang, Dolce & Gabbana and Philippe Model. Men and women will find exemplars of the very latest fashion trends, including clothes by English designer Helen Storey and Gossip (terrific biker-style leather gear).

Mettez

8th arr. - 12, bd Malesherbes 42 65 33 76
Open 10 a.m.-7 p.m. Closed Sun.

This venerable establishment boasts a faithful clientele, most of whom come from the world of politics or the theater. Since 1947 Mettez has consistently found buyers for their linen hunting and hacking jacket (3,500 francs), as well as Austrian jackets by Giesweisen or

Staff. Knickers (from 575 francs), capes and corduroy pants abound, as do Gloverall duffle coats from England (1,600 francs).

Missoni

7th arr. - 43, rue du Bac - 45 48 38 02
Open 10 a.m.-7 p.m. Closed Sun.

This conservative yet sumptuously crafted collection of fashion is aimed primarily at people who love contrasting colors, changing textures, novel shapes, mossy mohair and (for summer) glazed linen.

Claude Montana

1st arr. - 3, rue des Petits-Champs - 40 20 02 14
Open 10:15 a.m.-1 p.m. & 2 p.m.-7 p.m. Closed Sun.

Claude Montana cultivates an ambiguous look—his style is fierce and uncompromising; he goes in for stark, geometrical silhouettes bedecked with accessories (metal belts, lots of zippers). Double knits, quilted cottons, wide belts and acid colors remain the trademark of the Montana style of the future. The leather clothing for men and women is of the highest quality and superbly designed. Montana boutiques are uncomfortably bare, but attendants are courteous, worth mentioning because it is increasingly rare these days.

Thierry Mugler

8th arr. - 49, av. Montaigne - 47 23 37 62
Open 10 a.m.-7 p.m. Closed Sun.

Thierry Mugler's new premises, done up by Andrée Putman in blinding blue, look a bit like something from outer space. A master of such materials as whipcord, jersey, piqué and gabardine, he goes in for strict lines with no frills. His high-tech designs are for glamorous women and exuberant men; colors are gener-

207

ally muted but will flare into electric blue, tobacco brown or even pine-green. Prices, too, are fiery—but just consider your purchase an investment; the Mugler style is already beyond fashion.

Old England
9th arr. - 12, bd des Capucines
47 42 81 99
Open 9:30 a.m.-6:30 p.m. (Mon. 9:30 a.m.-12:30 a.m. & 2 p.m.-6:30 p.m.). Closed Sun.
This 100 percent French firm, founded in 1867, embodies English elegance with blazers, jackets, suits, raincoats, sweaters and myriad accessories from the British isles. At the top of the store's monumental staircase is the women's wear (blouses, cashmeres and kilts) and children's (*very* conservative) department. Traditional favorites here are the Derek Rose pajamas in lovely stripes (why not buy a gorgeous robe to go with them?), Turnbull and Asser shirts, Brigg umbrellas, Mason and Pearson brushes, and Floris or Atkinson eau-de-toilettes. Should your Chester Barrie suit need alterations, the advice of the in-house tailors is invaluable.

Sonia Rykiel
1st arr. - 70, rue du Faubourg-Saint-Honoré
42 65 20 81
6th arr. - 175, bd Saint Germain
49 54 60 60
Open 10 a.m.-7 p.m. Closed Sun.
Sonia Rykiel's fringe of flamboyant red bangs hides a piercing look. This pioneer-cum-diva of fashion lately moved to roomier premises on the boulevard Saint-Germain, bringing with her the soft silhouettes, knits, wide pants, somber colors (often shot through with gold) and striped jerseys. The men's shop has been transferred too, and is now just across the street. Inscription Rykiel, the

second-tier line, remains on the rue de Grenelle.

Scapa of Scotland
16th arr. - 38, av. Victor Hugo
45 00 31 31
Open 10 a.m.-6:45 p.m. (Mon. 1 p.m.-6:45 p.m.). Closed Sun.
Brian Redding designs these pleasingly classic collections brightening them with a touch of pastel or a colorful ribbon. The chic and attractive sportswear on offer includes long and short duffle coats, gorgeous Irish sweaters, pure wool blazers and coats. Helpful but unobtrusive service.

Ventilo
2nd arr. - 27 bis, rue du Louvre
42 33 18 67
Open 10:30 a.m.-7 p.m. (Mon. 2 p.m.-7 p.m.). Closed Sun.
Earth and wood tones dominate both the shop and the clothing on display. The latter is more than a little reminiscent of Ralph Lauren's designs, but with a Continental twist. The lower level is reserved for the menfolk, the main and first floors for women. Lots of cotton shirts and jeans are proposed for both sexes. Up on the top floor, decorative objects for the home share space with a pleasant tea room, bathed in restful light.

Gianni Versace
8th arr. - 62, rue du Faubourg Saint Honoré - 47 42 88 02
Open 10 a.m.-7 p.m. Closed Sun.
Versace's newest shop in Paris was designed by Pizzi (who creates the marvelous stage sets at La Scala opera house in Milan). This wildly extravagant decor is reason enough to wander over for a look, even if you don't want to pay 11,000 francs for a sequin-spangled mini or 1,100 for Versace jeans. If you do, well then walk upstairs for the women's wear, downstairs for the Versace tots collection;

men's clothing is displayed on the main level.

Yohji Yamamoto
1st arr. - 25, rue du Louvre - 42 21 42 93 (Women)
1st arr. - 47, rue Etienne Marcel
45 08 82 45 (Men)
Open 10:30 a.m.-7 p.m. (Mon. 11:30 a.m.-7 p.m.). Closed Sun.
"Minimalism forever" is Yamamoto's enduring credo. His faith, we note, is justified by the pure lines of his gabardine jackets and the flawless form of his classic white shirt. This year, look for blood-red mohair sweaters too, and skinny-ribbed extra-long turtlenecks, and even a few leopard prints.

AND ALSO . . .

Aquascutum
1st arr. - 10, rue de Castiglione
42 60 09 40
Open 10 a.m.-7 p.m. Closed Sun.
Since 1850, quality and comfort: suits, sweaters and the famous Kingsway trench (Bogie wore it!).

Burberrys
6th arr. - 55, rue de Rennes - 45 48 52 71
8th arr. - 8-10, bd Malesherbes
42 66 13 01
16th arr. - 56, rue de Passy - 42 88 88 24
Open 10 a.m.-7 p.m. Closed Sun.
Great trench coats, rain hats, cashmere scarves and sweaters; unbearable sales clerks.

Delaunay
1st arr. - 6, rue de l'Oratoire - 42 60 20 85
Open 10 a.m.-12:30 a.m. & 2 p.m.-6 p.m. Closed Sun. & Mon.
Beautiful handmade loafers and boots will cost up to 10,000 francs and require a two-month wait.

Ralph Lauren

8th arr. - 2, pl. de la Madeleine
44 77 53 00
Open 10 a.m.-7 p.m. Closed Sun.

Hey, if you really want to pay twice the U.S. price, who are we to hold you back? The display windows are beautifully done.

MENSWEAR

Berteil

8th arr. - 3, place Saint Augustin
42 65 28 52
Open 10 a.m.-7 p.m. (Mon. 2 p.m.-7 p.m.). Closed Sun.

Berteil clothes the upper-middle-class male in garments conceived for the active life: fishing, riding, hunting and the rest. But the handsome tweed jackets, well-cut trousers, oiled-canvas coats and nubbly sweaters are more often worn in restaurants, at the movies, to cocktail parties or for a stroll in the Luxembourg Gardens.

Hugo Boss

1st arr. - 2, place des Victoires
40 28 91 64
Open 10 a.m.-7 p.m. (Mon. 11 a.m.-7 p.m.). Closed Sun.

Philippe Starck designed this monumental trilevel boutique, with an atmosphere reminiscent of an English tailor's shop (writ—very—large). Customers come here for the immense choice offered of every item of masculine clothing, from suits to socks. Clothes and accessories are stylish and colorful.

Marcel Bur

8th arr. - 138, rue du Faubourg-Saint-Honoré - 42 56 03 89
Open 9 a.m.-12:30 p.m. & 2 p.m.-7 p.m. Closed Sun. & Aug. 15-30.

Marcel Bur's suits are the stuff dreams are made of. Bur's Saxbury "miracle fabric," made of combed, carded, blended, 100 percent pure wool, is guaranteed uncreasable. We are pleased to note that Bur's formerly conservative colors have brightened up a bit. A custom two-piece suit runs upward of 10,000 francs, but semicustom models go for much less. The ground floor boasts several beautiful cashmere items, as well as the equally fine house cologne, Marcel Bur pour Homme.

Jean-Charles de Castelbajac Hommes

1st arr. - 31, place du Marché Saint Honoré - 42 60 78 40
Open 10:30 a.m.-7 p.m. Closed Sun.

The world of Castelbajac has finally thrown open its doors to men with a collection of basics, including Ko and Co Intégral plaid coats. The so-called artsy ethnic style, with primary colors—so dear to the designer—that splash across jackets, shirts and sweaters, predominates. Knitwear, crafted along rustic lines, is a specialty of the house. The striking window displays lure customers in to buy Castelbajac's line of furniture, rugs, decorative items and luggage.

Cifonelli

8th arr. - 33, rue Marbeuf - 43 59 39 13
Open 9:45 a.m.-7 p.m. (Mon. 9:45 a.m.-1 p.m. & 2 p.m.-7 p.m.). Closed Sun. & 3 wks. in Aug.

When Cifonelli opened for business in the '30s, he introduced a light, timeless style that immediately won over worldly travelers. The elder Cifonelli's son, Adriano, has perfected his father's design. The shoulder, back and sleeve fittings are all impeccably precise. So providing the 15,000-franc tab is appropriate for your pocketbook, you, too, can have people ask for the address of your tailor. These are noble threads indeed. The ready-to-wear is no less classy, and not much less expensive.

Costardo

2nd arr. - 69, rue de Richelieu
49 27 03 79
17th arr. - 9, av. Niel - 40 55 03 55
Open 10 a.m.-8 p.m. Closed Sun.

A man could easily assemble a complete, reasonably priced and utterly fashionable wardrobe at Costardo. Suits are offered in three different cuts and a wide array of fabrics. Alterations are done in-house, quickly and at no extra charge. Shirts come in three lengths with a choice of two collar styles. For the quality, the prices here would be hard to beat.

Henry Cotton's

2nd arr. - 52, rue Etienne Marcel
42 36 01 22
Open 10 a.m.-7 p.m. Closed Sun.

An Italian take on American-style sportswear, sold in a typically trendy Parisian boutique. The clothes are classy, but rather expensive (the look is not very different from, say, J. Crew). The rainwear has a bit of Italian panache.

Christian Dior Boutique Monsieur

8th arr. - 11, rue François-Ier - 40 73 54 44
Open 9:30 a.m.-6:30 p.m. (Mon. & Sat. 10 a.m.-6:30 p.m.). Closed Sun.

Everything you need for an elegant, perfectly balanced wardrobe awaits you here; nowadays, one no longer gets the impression that donning a Dior suit is like girding oneself in a suit of armor. The moment you step into the Boutique Monsieur, you are surrounded by traditional Dior good taste: double-breasted suits in striped fabrics, glen plaid wool, cashmere and linen; shirts in cotton poplin with stripes in

209

every color of the (fashionable) rainbow. And, of course, the Dior accessories are always a good value, as they kill two birds with one stone: they are both chic and functional. The Boutique Monsieur targets the man who takes life seriously but refuses to wear boring clothes.

Façonnable
6th arr. - 174, bd Saint Germain
40 49 02 47
Open 10 a.m.-7 p.m. (Mon. 2 p.m.-7 p.m.). Closed Sun.

For work or for play (polo, cricket, golf...), these clothes create an elegant yet easy image. Typically French style distinguishes the casual wear: cable sweaters, rugby shirts, twill or canvas trousers show by their cut and color that they were not made in the U.S.A. The suits are of fine quality, but there again, the cut is definitely "Continental". The accessories (socks, ties, underwear, etc.) are attractive and well made.

Gianfranco Ferré
8th arr. - 44, av. Georges-V - 49 52 02 74
Open 10 a.m.-7 p.m. Closed Sun.

Though his major focus is the haute-couture line he designs for Dior, Gianfranco Ferré signs a line of men's clothing as well, characterized by perfect lines, irreproachable collars, light and supple fabrics. Every detail is attentively crafted, as his elegant customers doubtless demand.

Gauno et Chardin
2nd arr. - 8, rue du Mail - 42 96 22 48
Open 10 a.m.-7 p.m. Closed Sun.

In an inviting decor of warm wood, tall mirrors and leather armchairs, this Belgian manufacturer displays a remarkable collection of highly desirable leather coats and jackets. All the finishing

touches on the bikers' jackets, parkas and warmly lined car coats are sewn by hand. Most models are in suede, buttery-soft lamb or textured goatskin, in beautiful colors.

Givenchy Gentleman
8th arr. - 56, rue François-ler
40 76 00 21
Open 10 a.m.-7 p.m. Closed Sun.

Blond wood and lots of light are conducive to browsing through Givenchy's refined, beautifully finished ready-to-wear for men. If your taste runs to classic, elegant clothes for office or casual occasions, you will appreciate the superb poplin shirts, the lean-lined suits and the distinguished accessories (pigskin gloves, suspenders, wristwatches, eau de cologne), all in Givenchy's timeless, never trendy signature style.

Island
2nd arr. - 4, rue Vide-Gousset
42 61 77 77
Open 10 a.m.-7 p.m. Closed Sun.

If you've been invited to a house party in Provence and need a few things to fill out your weekend wardrobe, head over to Island. You'll find the same sort of casual gear—from polo shirts, sweaters, soft trousers and sporty parkas—that all the French guests will be wearing. Dockstep and Bass are the footwear brands of choice, but if you're smart, you'll have bought them in the U.S. for less than half the price charged here.

Lanvin Homme
8th arr. - 15, rue du Faubourg-Saint-Honoré - 44 71 33 33
Open 10 a.m.-7 p.m. Closed Sun.

The venerable Lanvin label has tailor-made itself a place at the forefront of the French menswear world. This shop, which appears on the registry of historical monuments, is a

charming product of the Roaring Twenties. A ride in the marvelous elevator alone is worth a visit. Behind the array of suits, shirts and accessories stands a small army of craftsmen who draw on 50 years of Lanvin experience. Dozens of hours of work are dedicated to each suit. Flawless quality is the key. The Lanvin ready-to-wear line is designed by Dominique Morlotti; his flannel suits with embroidered quilted-silk vests are things of beauty, and far less flashy than they sound.

Lapidus
8th arr. - 35, rue François-ler
47 20 69 33
Open 10 a.m.-6:45 p.m. Closed Sun. & 3 wks. in Aug.

Classic men's clothing with a dash of French chic that makes them interesting—but never eccentric! The accessories are of fine quality, and sufficiently timeless so that you can be sure of wearing them season after season.

Marcel Lassance
6th arr. - 17, rue du Vieux-Colombier - 45 48 29 28
Open 10 a.m.-7 p.m. Closed Sun.

For over a decade now the Left Bank's upper crust has been donning Monsieur Lassance's fashionable but discreet men's clothes. He will perhaps go down in social history as the man who helped transform President Mitterrand's sartorial habits. The attractive pants, jackets, suits, shirts and sweaters are designed for intellectuals who like comfortable but elegant clothes.

Pape
7th arr. - 4 av. Rapp
45 55 09 68
Open 10:30 a.m.-7:30 p.m. Closed Sun., Mon., Aug.

Pape is a traditional English haberdasher, ensconced in a two-level wood-paneled shop in the heart of Paris's preppy-land. In addition to the made-to-measure clothing, Pape proposes a handsome and unmistakably British selection of accessories (wonderful, expensive socks) and ready-to-wear: classic suits, nicely cut overcoats and classic sweaters in lambswool or cashmere.

Saint Laurent Rive Gauche

16th arr. - 19-21, av. Victor Hugo
45 00 64 64
Open 10 a.m.-7 p.m. Closed Sun.

This former sanctum of the saint of French fashion seems to have slipped into provincial torpor. But lift your gaze beyond the indifferent sales staff to the dizzy decor of mirrors and the maze of dressing rooms... there are suits, jackets, sportswear, bathing suits—all graced by the master's touch. Sumptuous materials come in a regal rainbow of colors: turquoise, saffron, pink, Naples yellow on a black background. Some prices: 1,850 francs for a cotton sweater, 5,000 francs for a classic jacket.

Francesco Smalto

8th - 44, rue François-Ier - 47 20 70 63; 16th - 5 pl. Victor-Hugo
Open 10 a.m.-7 p.m. Closed Sun.

Francesco Smalto, king of the extravagant fabric, was trained at the renowned Ecole Camps. He continues to uphold his well-earned title of master tailor and serve a clientele that includes celebrities and millionaires. Smalto has even perfected a type of cashmere in which the tennis stripes spell out the name of the customer! His styles appear effortless. No wonder his custom suits (with the signature Smalto pinched waist) command 25,000 francs. But take heart: beautiful, less cripplingly expensive ready-to-wear is also available.

Torregiani

8th arr. - 38, rue François-Ier
47 23 76 17
Open 10 a.m.-7 p.m. Closed Sun.

Torregiani is an authorized dealer for Brioni suits, but you will also find a wide array of other beautiful, hand-sewn suits in the finest wool (priced from 9,500 to 12,000 francs). Brioni ties are somewhat less expensive, though no less exclusive; also in stock are men's shirts in luxurious printed silk.

Ermenegildo Zegna

2nd arr. - 10, rue de la Paix - 42 61 67 61
Open 10 a.m.-7 p.m. (Mon. 11 a.m.-7 p.m.). Closed Sun.

Renowned the world over, Ermenegildo Zegna is one of the giants of Italian fashion. He invented the pure-wool, no-wrinkle "high-performance" fabric that he uses so skillfully in his custom or ready-to-wear suits, priced from 5,600 to 8,750 francs. Zegna's progressive approach to classic clothes includes lively new colors and an extended range of accessories. A sophisticated and charming welcome awaits you in this must-browse shop, a favorite with Parisian fashion plates.

ACCESSORIES

BELTS

Losco

4th arr. - 20, rue de Sévigné - 48 04 39 93
Open 11 a.m.-7:30 p.m. (Mon. 2 p.m.-7 p.m. & Sun. 3 p.m.-7 p.m.). Closed 2 wks. in Aug.

The specialist for belts. Leather, lizard, colored, braided—you name it, all the styles are right here. Pick your belt and your buckle, or choose one of the ready-made models. Excellent prices: from 75 to 390 francs; crocodile is much more, of course, but you don't want to bother with that (the hassle at customs isn't worth it).

The Regent Belt Company

4th arr. - 20, rue du Roi de Sicile
48 04 57 52
Open noon-7 p.m. (Sat. from 11 a.m.). Closed Sun., Mon. & 3 wks. in Aug.

A charming, old-fashioned shop in the Marais is headquarters for a British belt manufacturer who offers a vast array of leathers, colors, buckles and trims in an appealing array of styles. The leather for all these chic waist-cinchers comes from the north of England; the variety used to imitate crocodile (black or brown) is attractive indeed, especially when combined with a bronze buckle.

HATS

Gélot

8th arr. - 15, rue du Faubourg-Saint-Honoré - 44 71 31 61
Open 10 a.m.-7 p.m. Closed Sun.

Hats off to Gélot, the master headwear ennobled by Edward VII! Gélot has been working here, at the Lanvin Tailleur shop, since 1968. Gélot's made-to-measure fedoras start at 1,400 francs; tweed caps are priced from 600 francs.

Motsch

8th arr. - 42, av. George-V - 47 23 79 22
Open 10 a.m.-7 p.m. Closed Sun.

Mad about hats? Motsch has been making and repairing top-notch headgear for over a century. Panamas, Borsalinos, fedoras and even derbies are all hand-crafted according to traditional methods.

SHIRTS

Equipment

2nd arr. - 46, rue Etienne-Marcel
40 26 17 84
Open 10:30 a.m.-7 p.m. (Mon. from 11 a.m.). Closed Sun.

Basic white poplin shirts with *trompe l'œil* buttons,

211

China-blue embroidered shirts, denims with folksy scenes stitched on, ruffled-front specials and so forth— Equipment wreaks havoc on the classics. Things change rather drastically from season to season in this tiny boutique, but Equipment shirts are always exotic and comfortable. Prices for poplin: under 700 francs; silk shirts sell for under 1,000 francs. Sunny decor, and accommodating service.

Alain Figaret

1st arr. - 21, rue de la Paix - 42 65 04 99
7th arr. - 16, rue de Sèvres - 42 22 03 40
8th arr. - 14 bis, rue Marbeuf - 47 23 35 49
16th arr. - 99, rue de Longchamp 47 27 66 81
Open 10 a.m.-7 p.m. (Mon. from 3 p.m.). Closed Sun.

Six collar styles, three sleeve sizes, short-sleeved models, several cuff styles, hundreds of colors for thousands of shirts in 600 types of fabric... you will find—not lose—your shirt at Alain Figaret's shop (prices start at 330 francs). There's always a crowd, so don't bother to wait around for things to slow down. A word of warning: Buy your shirts a size longer in the sleeve (they shrink after the first washing). Button-down collars are often too narrow to cover a tie properly, and anyone with big biceps will probably find their sleeves tight. While Figaret may not be the king of Paris shirtmakers, he's certainly a prince.

Hilditch & Key

1st arr. - 252, rue de Rivoli - 42 60 36 09
Open 9:30 a.m.-6:30 p.m. (Sat. 9 a.m.-6 p.m.). Closed Sun.

Hilditch & Key shirtmakers, established nearly a century ago, is the last bastion of menswear shops in which refinement borders on the sublime. British poplins, fine cottons from France and heavy Japanese silk are among the 500 select fabrics to choose from. Cuffs and collars are made to measure, with extraordinary accuracy. Ready-to-wear shirts are also available. And it's impossible not to mention the celebrated Hilditch & Key sweaters and dressing gowns. Gorgeous double-ply V-neck cashmere sweaters come in 35 colors and cost 3,200 francs. There is also a marvelous selection of camel-hair pullovers, cardigans and sleeveless sweater vests.

Sulka & Company

1st arr. - 2, rue de Castiglione 42 60 38 08
Open 9:30 a.m.-6:30 p.m. (Mon. & Sat. from 10 a.m.). Closed Sun.

Sulka is the paragon of refinement, a name with a slightly pre-war ring to it. The discriminating clientele arrives from far-flung nations and provinces to order made-to-measure shirts in sailcloth, poplin, silk, flannel or wool. Timeless classics, these impeccable-quality items are handled by a courteous, deferential staff. First-time orders of custom shirts must be for six or more (at 2,200 francs each). Before filling the order, a pilot shirt is made, which you take home, wear, wash and then bring it back for Sulka to check for faults. Also available are double-ply cashmere V-necks and cardigans, five-ply cashmere jackets, polo shirts, scarves, ties, umbrellas, socks and a small selection of casual wear.

SHOES

Aubercy

2nd arr. - 34, rue Vivienne - 42 33 93 61
Open 10 a.m.-6:30 p.m. (Mon. from 11 a.m.). Closed Sun. & Mon in Aug.

Aubercy shoes has ridden out the swells of style since 1935, all the while producing excellent-quality, traditional footwear for discerning customers. Sport and casual shoes, such as the Richelieu buckle loafer, are making headway among other offerings, which cater primarily to businessmen and traditionalists. Prices are not excessive.

Carvil

8th arr. - 67, rue Pierre Charron 42 25 54 38
Open 10 a.m.-7 p.m. (Mon. from 2 p.m.). Closed Mon. in Aug. & Sun.
8th arr. - 4, rue Tronchet - 42 66 21 58
Open 10 a.m.-7 p.m. Closed Sun.

At Carvil, the only place the shoe pinches is the pocketbook. It's known as the playboys' favorite, and it's a good thing that most playboys have large bankrolls. But you do get what you pay for: excellent quality and styles ranging from the conservative to the outrageous.

Church's

8th arr. - 23, rue des Mathurins 42 65 25 85
Open 10 a.m.-8:15 p.m. Closed Sun.

These famous and indestructible shoes come in sizes from 39 to 45 in a broad range of widths, in black, bordeaux, cognac, gold and other colors. With the incomparable finishing of Becket, Grafton and Burwood, they are perennial favorites. They are not cheap (you may want to wait for the semi-annual sales), but these shoes last forever.

Michel Delauney

1st arr. - 6, rue de l'Oratoire - 42 60 20 85
Open 10 a.m.-12:30 a.m. & 2 p.m.-6:30 p.m. Closed Sun., Mon. & Aug.

Welcome to the world of marvelously comfortable, solidly built shoes. Models run from mocassins to riding boots. Michel Delauney's walking shoes are elegant and long-lived. He will find the right shoe for you according to width, arch and instep—not just try to sell you the most expensive model. Sale shoes are often an excellent deal. Custom-made models cost up to 10,000 francs and require two months of work.

Fratelli Rossetti

16th arr. - 17, av. Victor Hugo
45 01 63 33
Open 10 a.m.-7 p.m. (Mon. from 11 a.m.). Closed Sun.

In the beginning there were sportswear shoes... The Rossetti family then launched into the loafer and dress shoes market. Success was close on their heels. Nowadays the Fratelli Rossetti line boasts several audacious designs, including white or two-tone Derbys in textured pigskin, rough-cut boat shoe–style loafers or riding boots in kangaroo, zebu or calfskin. They are light on the foot, the summum of casual elegance (for about 1,500 francs).

Stéphane Kélian

7th arr. - 13 bis, rue de Grenelle
42 22 93 03
Open 10 a.m.-7 p.m. Closed Sun.

This sumptuous marble-lined boutique is the lair of Stéphane Kélian, master of the braided-leather shoe and sculptured heel. He also creates strikingly fashionable footwear for the Claude Montana label. A smaller, pricey boutique at 6, place des Victoires additionally features seductive Italian shoes by Cesare Paciotti (42 61 60 74).

John Lobb

8th arr. - 51, rue François-ler
45 62 06 34
Open 10 a.m.-7 p.m. Closed Sun.

Sublimely comfortable, perfectly proportioned shoes finished to fit the most exigent of feet. Such are the masterpieces John Lobb cobbles together for his privileged customers. There are hand-decorated, custom-made house slippers as well as classic lace-up oxfords, crafted according to traditional methods and commonly requiring a wait of over six months. Prices for custom shoes start at 14,000 francs per pair and require a six-month wait. Ready-to-wear shoes include loafers and low boots as well as classic wingtips.

Weston

1st arr. - 3, bd de la Madeleine
42 61 11 87
6th arr. - 49, rue de Rennes - 45 49 38 50
16th arr. - 97, av. Victor-Hugo
47 04 23 75
17th arr. - 98, rue de Courcelles,
47 63 18 13
Open 10 a.m.-7 p.m. (Mon. from 2 p.m.). Closed Sun.
8th arr. - 114, av. des Champs-Elysées - 45 62 26 47
Open 9:30 a.m.-7 p.m. (Mon. from 10 a.m.). Closed Sun.

Once upon a time, young men lay awake at night and dreamt of handsome, solid, superbly finished Weston shoes (which were, in fact, the finest in ready-to-wear shoes). But Weston's reputation has tarnished of late. The average life of the celebrated "180" moccasin has dropped from eight to two years. Repairs are sometimes shoddy and reports have it that the soles sometimes leak! Faithful customers have turned to the Norwegian Hunter's shoe. A curious note: If you arrive wearing anything but Weston shoes you might receive a stiff welcome. And sale shoes are white elephants made especially for the cut-price selling season. At least the prices haven't gone up (but they start at over 1,200 francs).

UNDERWEAR

Chantal Thomass

1st arr. - 1 rue Vivienne - 40 15 02 36
Open 10 a.m.-7 p.m. (Mon. from 11 a.m.). Closed Sun.

Chantal Thomass, renowned for her lady's lingerie, came up with the idea of launching a men's undergarment collection inspired by Hercules. Now that the brawny-boy look is a thing of the past, you will find several attractive lines for men in white cotton, grey chiné, houndstooth, pure black and other colors and fabrics (styles and finishing change with hue and type of material). Chantal Thomass's men's undergarments are well made, comfortable and versatile. The only drawback is the price: 250 francs for briefs, 950 francs for a T-shirt and 1,200 francs for a bathing suit.

Tous les Caleçons

7th arr. - 11, rue du Pré-aux-Clercs - 45 44 32 07
Open 10:30 a.m.-7 p.m. (Mon. from 11:30 a.m.). Closed Sun. & 3 wks. in Aug.

Trying on the merchandise here can be, well...trying. No way to hide those love handles in the form-fitting tank tops, bicycling shorts and T-shirts sold in this teeny boutique. Lots of nifty underwear, too. For men and women.

We're always happy to hear about your discoveries and receive your comments on ours. We want to give your letters the attention they deserve, so when you write to Gault Millau, please state clearly what you liked or disliked. Be concise but convincing, and take the time to argue your point.

WOMEN'S WEAR

DESIGNERS

Azzedine Alaïa
4th arr. - 7, rue de Moussy - 42 72 19 19
Open 10 a.m.-7 p.m. Closed Sun.

More women dream of pouring themselves into an Azzedine Alaïa creation than can actually—decently—do so. The tiny Tunisian's artful cutting, stretch fabrics and suggestive seaming do wonders for svelte silhouettes. What they do to less-than-heavenly bodies we will leave to your imagination. Still, if Tina Turner dares to wear Alaïa, why shouldn't we? Alaïa's huge new boutique is a must-see on the fashion circuit. While you're there, check out his newest innovation: a fabric said to ward off the evil effects of magnetic fields—so you can dress for less stress!

Balenciaga
8th arr. - 10, av. George-V - 47 20 21 11
Open 10 a.m.-7 p.m. (Sat. 10 a.m.-12:30 p.m. & 2 p.m.-7 p.m.). Closed Sun.

With the real Balenciaga long gone, the name is more a label than a creative design philosophy. The strong points of the clothes on display here are their strong colors, structured lines and sophistication. Most successful are the shapely, beautifully cut "power suits" and the rather intimidating evening gowns.

Pierre Balmain
8th arr. - 44, rue François-Ier - 47 20 35 34
Open 10 a.m.-7 p.m. Closed Sat. 1 p.m.- 2 p.m. &Sun.

The fashion world is in a tizzy since word got out that Oscar de la Renta was named couturier for the venerable House of Balmain. At the age of 60, de la Renta is fearlessly launching a new career; a double career, in fact, since he plans to continue designing for his own label (but heck, if Lagerfeld and Ferré can do it, why can't he?). Hervé Pierre, the talented young stylist who handled all the Balmain's lines since the death of Eric Mortensen, is now looking for a new job.

Etienne Brunel
7th arr. - 70, rue des Saints-Pères 45 44 41 14
Open 11 a.m.-8:30 p.m. Closed Sun.

Lyon-native Mireille Etienne designs strikingly original clothes which are also perfectly wearable. Her most recent collections have featured shimmering fabrics (satin, raw silk, wool or velvet mixed with a little Lycra), most effective for bustier tops (1,000 francs) and attractive dresses (1,000 to 4,000 francs). Suits have the polish and meticulous detailing that well-dressed women require. For those with a sense of daring (and humor!) there are some crazy little frocks made of straw, plastic, foam, terrycloth (not bad, those!), feathers and patchworks of lace.

Cardin
8th arr. - 59, rue du Faubourg-Saint-Honoré - 42 66 92 25
Open 10 a.m.-6:30 p.m. Closed Sun.

Energetic middle-aged ladies (who remember Pierre's glory days back in the 1960s) go for Cardin's city suits, cocktail dresses and nicely structured seven-eighths-length coats. Cardin's ready-to-wear collections and "licensed" accessories lack the whimsical spirit and forward-looking attitude that continue to inspire his haute-couture designs.

> *Monday, like Sunday, is a day of rest for many shopkeepers.*

Chanel
1st arr. - 31, rue Cambon - 42 86 28 00
8th arr. - 42, av. Montaigne - 47 23 74 12
Open 9:30 a.m.-6:30 p.m. (Sat. from 10 a.m.). Closed Sun.

The most famous fashion house on the face of the earth, Chanel is also the most copied. To be sure that your good money is going for the *real* house logo (and not just any old intertwined Cs), spend it here, at the mother of all Chanel stores. Yes, you'll find the authentic tweed *tailleurs*, the pearls, the bracelets, the chain-link belts, the quilted bags that the world adores. Designer Karl Lagerfeld has done much to redefine the house image (would *he* wear Chanel, we wonder?), which is now best exemplified by those ads seen on the page four of every international fashion magazine: a Chanel suit (in terrycloth, why not? Somebody will buy it!) worn by a name-brand model in biker's boots.

Chloé
7th arr. - 3, rue de Gribeauval 45 44 02 04
8th arr. - 60, rue du Faubourg-Saint-Honoré - 42 66 01 39
Open 10 a.m.-7 p.m. Closed Sun.

Martine Sitbon's designs have brought a new clientele to Chloé. Sitbon's style has matured—she's more sure of herself than in years past. Result: the clothes are youthful but rigorously styled, perfectly cut and presented in a beautiful palette of colors.

Comme des Garçons
2nd arr. - 42, rue Etienne-Marcel 42 33 05 21
Open 11 a.m.-7 p.m. Closed Sun., Aug. 1-15.

The *vendeurs* size you up as you walk in, and if they don't like your "look," you can expect a pretty frosty reception. Indeed, the store itself exudes precious little warmth. As for the clothes (which, incidentally, the sales clerks just hate to see the customers touch), well... the knits are droopy and unattractive; the colors are depressing, the seams are ripped (but yes, on purpose), the fabrics frayed (ditto). Designer Rei Kawakubo's subversive, androgynous styles are not for everyone—at a recent fashion show, even Linda Evangelista looked dowdy in a Kawakubo dress! And they are most definitely not for every budget.

Dior
8th arr. - 30, av. Montaigne - 40 73 54 44
Open 9:30 a.m.-6:30 p.m. (Sat. & Mon. 10 a.m.-1 p.m. & 2:30 p.m.-6:30 p.m.). Closed Sun.

Once you enter Dior's gray-and-white flagship store, you can spend the entire day choosing everything you need to be impeccably attired at all times. From ravishing lingerie to suits, sportswear to ball gowns designed by Gianfranco Ferré (the current Monsieur Dior), chic *chapeaux* to mink-cuffed kid gloves in a rainbow of hues, no detail is neglected. You can also dress your home and your children here.

Dorothée Bis
2nd arr. - 46, rue Etienne-Marcel 42 21 04 40
Open 10 a.m.-7 p.m. Closed Sun.

After a stint in fashion purgatory, the Jacobsons are back with an attractive collection of vampy stretch, Lycra and viscose knits (lots of openwork), fluttery '40s-style dresses and suits with a masculine, distinctly Dietrich silhouette.

Louis Féraud
8th arr. - 88, rue du Faubourg-Saint-Honoré
42 65 32 84
Open 10 a.m.-7 p.m. (Sat. from 10:30 a.m.). Closed Sun.

Arab princesses and Texas heiresses rub shoulders in these salons during the season. Louis Féraud started out in Cannes, in the south of France, in the '50s and dressed such stars as Brigitte Bardot, Kim Novak and Liz Taylor. Today he is the dressmaker of France's first lady, Danielle Mitterrand. His creations are feminine and expressive, denoting a man who loves women... His evening bags are divine.

Paco Funada
4th arr. - 17, pl. des Vosges - 40 27 94 29
Open 11 a.m.-7 p.m. (Sat. from 2 p.m.). Closed Sun.

Paco Funada has abandoned menswear (he used to design for Cacharel and Marcel Lassance) for a new career in women's fashion. His is a dramatic, minimalist style which employs a limited palette of muted colors, comfortable fabrics, superb craftsmanship and detailing. The collection is on view in an attractive shop under the arcades of the place des Vosges.

Hélène Gainville
8th arr. - Arcades du Lido, 78, av. des Champs-Elysées
43 59 32 18
Open 10:30 a.m.-7:30 p.m. Closed Sun.

Hélène Gainville designs smart city suits (for your power lunches), frothy cocktails frocks (for your romantic dinners) and gowns for your most extravagant evenings at prices close to what you'd pay

for deluxe ready-to-wear. What's more, in her lovely trilevel boutique done in soothing pastel tones and warm wood, she will provide just the right accessories to complete your look, from hats to bags to shoes. And when Prince Charming finally shows up and sweeps you off your feet, Hélène will create a magical gown for the occasion (see *Wedding Gowns*, page 222).

Givenchy
8th arr. - 8, av. George-V - 47 20 81 31
Open 9:30 a.m.-6:30 p.m. (Sat. from 10 a.m.). Closed Sun.

Any fan of Audrey Hepburn is a fan of Givenchy. Hepburn has long represented the Givenchy haute-couture look: inaccessible, regal and ethereal. Beautiful cocktail dresses (in fluid jersey), lovely accessories (silk or wool-challis shawls, costume jewelry). Givenchy, who started his career alongside Balenciaga, also produces Good Life, an urbane collection at fairly reasonable prices for us mere mortals.

Irié
7th arr. - 8, rue du Pré-aux-Clercs 42 61 18 28
Open 10 a.m.-7 p.m. Closed Sun.

Irié has created a sober yet surrealistic black-and-white setting to show off his collection of hip, sophisticated clothes. Silk, angora, wool gabardine and mousseline are the major components of this designer's ultrafeminine, close-to-the-body creations. Irié is currently one of the darlings of the Left Bank set, who adore his boutique's courteous staff ("Madame, may I say that I think you've made an excellent choice...") and the relatively reasonable prices. Recent collections have featured wonderfully gay, colorful prints (fish,

---

Remember that if you spend 2,000 francs or more in a store, you are entitled to a full refund of the value-added tax (VAT). See Basics for details.

planets, alphabets, penguins...), oversized transparent shirts in fabulous colors, leggings (of course) and soft panne-velvet tops.

Paule Ka
7th arr. - 192, bd Saint-Germain 45 44 92 60
Open 10:30 a.m.-7 p.m. Closed Sun.

Serge Coifinger's ideal of feminine beauty runs to the Grace Kelly or Jackie Kennedy type. One of his most successful creations is a short trench coat in pastel silk organza, guaranteed to turn heads at any cocktail party or theater evening. Worth a look too are the long velvet skirts and the wide array of accessories.

Michel Klein
7th arr. - 6, rue du Pré-aux-Clercs 42 60 37 11
Open 10 a.m.-7 p.m. Closed Sun. & 2 wks. in Aug.

Klein's designs have simple yet strong lines and an appealing, timeless style. Easy to wear, versatile and comfortable, his clothes are excellent investments. Lately we've admired his satin Chinese jackets in bright blue, ecru or black, and his remarkably well cut pants and leatherwear.

Hiroko Koshino
8th arr. - 43, rue du Faubourg-Saint-Honoré - 42 65 83 15
Open 10 a.m.-7 p.m. (Sat. from 11 a.m.). Closed Sun.

This Japanese fixture on the Paris fashion scene creates appealing designs that make his customers feel oh-so-pretty.

Christian Lacroix
8th arr. - 73, rue du Faubourg-Saint-Honoré - 42 65 79 08
8th arr. - 26, av. Montaigne - 47 20 68 95
Open 9 a.m.-7 p.m. (Sat. 10 a.m.-1 p.m. & 2:30 p.m.-7 p.m.). Closed Sun.

Christian Lacroix's vivid, scintillating creations cause women's heads to spin—fast

and hard. He marries Provençal folklore with fantasy prints in a his style bathed in theatricality. His ready-to-wear is dreadfully expensive, but the accessories—especially the bold, fake-gem–studded jewelry—are accessible (if not exactly affordable), and give lots of fashion "juice" for the money.

Karl Lagerfeld Boutique
8th arr. - 19, rue du Faubourg-Saint-Honoré - 42 66 64 64
Open 10 a.m.-7 p.m. Closed Sun.

Versatile, prolific Karl Lagerfeld, who has infused brilliant new life into the house of Chanel, continues to designs clothes and accessories for his personal label. Modern forms and strong colors characterize these witty, irreverent (and extremely expensive) fashions, displayed in these rather monumental premises.

Guy Laroche
1st arr. - Forum des Halles, 106, porte Rambuteau, Niveau -1 - 42 21 49 57
Open 10:30 a.m.-7:30 p.m. Closed Sun.
6th arr. - 47, rue de Rennes - 45 48 18 50
8th arr. - 29, av. Montaigne - 40 69 69 51
8th arr. - 30, rue du Faubourg-Saint-Honoré - 42 65 62 74
16th arr. - 9, av. Victor-Hugo - 45 01 82 75
Open 9:30 a.m.-6:30 p.m. Closed Sun.

True to the principles of the late Guy Laroche, the boutique proposes a vast array of accessories to vary the look of the signature Laroche suits. In daytime and dinner styles, in winter- and summer-weight fabrics, they form the backbone of the house collections.

Don't plan to shop on Sundays, the vast majority of Paris stores are closed.

Lecoanet Hemant
4th arr. - 24, rue Vieille-du-Temple - 42 65 43 37
Open 9 a.m.-6 p.m. (& by appt.). Closed Sat., Sun. & 3 wks. in Aug.

Didier Lecoanet and Hemant Sagar's creations received the haute-couture classification in 1984. The two give shows in unusual venues, and their lucky number is thirteen, the day they open their salons.

Lolita Lempicka
16th arr. - 7, av. Victor-Hugo - 40 67 15 87
Open 10 a.m.-6:30 p.m. Closed Sun.

Let's be frank, shall we? For our money, designer Lolita Lempicka is more than just a little overrated. Her fussy, pretentious clothes (stiff menswear suits, drop-dead cocktail frocks) are presented in a decor that (we suppose) is inspired by some Vincente Minnelli musical. Lolita Bis is the designer's second-tier line, more youthful, less costly and easier to wear.

Issey Miyake
4th arr. - 3, pl. des Vosges - 48 87 01 86
Open 10 a.m.-7 p.m. Closed Sun.

In a deliberately theatrical setting, Issey Miyake's extravagant, extraordinary designs seem even more dramatic. While they look rather disconcertingly like rags on their hangers, when worn these soft, draped, wrinkled, sculpted and cleverly knotted clothes prove to be impressive, even stately: Miyake's long duster coat, for example, makes even an unassuming individual look like a high priest! The prices these pieces command is terrifying—the merest T-shirt costs about 1,000 francs. His second-tier line, Plantation, is slightly more affordable.

Claude Montana
1st arr. - 3, rue des Petits-Champs - 40 20 02 14
Open 10:15 a.m.-7 p.m. Closed Sun.

Short or long, Montana's skirts and dresses show a lot of leg. Zippered sheaths, undulating asymmetrical hems, black tulle and silvery mesh compose a wardrobe for a high-tech vamp who isn't afraid to attract a little attention. The clothes are beautifully crafted (Montana's leather pants and jackets are the definitive statement on the subject).

Popy Moreni
4th arr. - 13, pl. des Vosges - 42 77 09 96
Open 10 a.m.-7 p.m. (Mon. from 11 a.m.) Closed Sun.

Popy Moreni is one of the "grandes dames" of fashion design; her multi-faceted talent extends to clothes, accessories, furniture and housewares. This versatile Italian often looks to the Commedia dell'Arte for inspiration: note the oversized Pierrot collars on tulle dresses and shantung blouses. Her spacious, white boutique is not well organized, but if one perseveres, one is sure to find something to covet (we adored a floaty bright-green silk mousseline skirt with a handkerchief hem, paired with a powder-puff angora top). Those who wish to purchase, however, should come with lots of money, for the prices are awfully high.

Hanae Mori
8th arr. - 9, rue du Faubourg-Saint-Honoré - 47 42 78 78
Open 10 a.m.-7 p.m. Closed Sun.

Hanae Mori takes her inspiration from Japanese Kabuki theater, then translates her designs into a refined and international expression of haute couture.

Thierry Mugler
2nd arr. - 10, pl. des Victoires 42 60 06 37
Open 10 a.m.-1 p.m. & 2 p.m.-7 p.m. (Mon. from 11 a.m.). Closed Sun.

The boutique, designed by Andrée Putman, puts one in mind of a futuristic comic strip. As for the clothes, they are designed for heroines: strong women, sex bombs and glamorous sirens who want structured suits that underline feminine curves. Slit skirts, geometric cutouts and brilliantly colored leather are the highlights of Mugler's latest collections.

Myrène de Prémonville
8th arr. - 32, av. George-V - 47 20 02 35
Open 10 a.m.-7 p.m. (Sat. 10 a.m.-1 p.m. & 2 p.m.- 7 p.m.; Mon. from 2 p.m.). Closed Sun.

Young, modern women love these sophisticated clothes: dressy suits, crepe pants, chic jackets with nipped-in waists in gorgeous colors (lilac, raspberry...). This designer has a great sense of graphic style, evident in her strong accessories (we saw a wonderful red-and-black checked silk scarf).

Paco Rabanne
6th arr. - 7, rue du Cherche-Midi 40 49 08 53
Open 10 a.m.-noon & 2 p.m.-7 p.m. Closed Sun., Mon.

Paco Rabanne likes to defy convention. Remember his metal dresses, his use of plastic, the paper dresses? Well, these days he favors structured suits and feminine frocks for women, displayed in his "new age" boutique, designed by Eric Raffy.

Georges Rech
16th arr. - 23, av. Victor-Hugo 45 00 83 19
Open 10 a.m.-7 p.m. (Mon. from 1 p.m.). Closed Sun., 3 wks. in Aug.

Rech makes clothes for active women with lots of per-sonality, as vivacious as they are beautiful. Check out the strapless satin or velvet cocktail dresses striped with multi-colored ribbons (1,650 francs), the angora knit dresses (ever so sexy!) bordered with ostrich plumes, city shorts-suits in various beautiful shades of fluid crepe (4,750 francs). The detailing on every item is impeccable, and the Rech sales staff is very nearly perfect, too.

Rochas
8th arr. - 33, rue François-Ier - 47 23 54 56
Open 9:30 a.m.-6:30 p.m. (Sat. 9:30 a.m.-1 p.m. & 2 p.m.-6:30 p.m.). Closed Sun.

Rochas's recently launched line of luxurious women's wear is designed with plenty of panache by Peter O'Brien. These are classic clothes given an extra spark of chic by an original approach to fabric: tweed and silk are juxtaposed, wool shows up for evening alongside mousseline and lace, organza comes out in the daylight escorted by jersey and bouclé knits. Elegant accessories—bags, jewelry, sunglasses, scarves—complete a modern, quintessentially feminine look.

Yves Saint Laurent
6th arr. - 6, pl. Saint-Sulpice - 43 29 43 00
8th arr. - 38, rue du Faubourg-Saint-Honoré - 42 65 74 59
Open 10 a.m.-7 p.m. Closed Sun.
16th arr. - 5, av. Marceau - 47 23 72 71
Open 9:30 a.m.-6 p.m. Closed Sun.

Saint Laurent is a byword for French fashion. For 30 years, Dior's successor has been the standard-bearer of Parisian elegance, with his rigorously conceived, luxuriously detailed collections. His newly redesigned showcase is now twice its former size, the better to display the full range of the Saint Laurent genius: superb furs, opulent evening clothes, incomparably elegant city attire and sportswear, jewelry and accessories. Also on hand are YSL's acclaimed fragrances, cosmetics and the new skincare line represented by the eternally gorgeous Catherine Deneuve.

Jean-Louis Scherrer

8th arr. - 51, av. Montaigne - 42 99 05 79
Open 9:30 a.m.-6:30 p.m. Closed Sun.

Heavily influenced by Yves Saint Laurent, Jean-Louis Scherrer goes in for a classically elegant style. His customers include French television personalities and the Kennedy women. His cocktail dresses and ladylike suits are the highlights of his very attractive ready-to-wear line. Ravishing handbags and jewelry.

Elisabeth de Senneville

1st arr. - 3, rue de Turbigo - 42 33 90 83
Open 10:30 a.m.-7 p.m. Closed Sun.

Elisabeth de Senneville designs easy-to-wear fashions in wonderful fabrics. Her "city sportswear" is particularly inventive and flattering, with jackets, blazers and blousons that fit close to the body paired up with wide, flowing trousers. Ecru denim is a big Senneville favorite, shown plain, printed, lined and quilted. The stores also carry an amusing selection of witty and colorful children's clothes.

Angelo Tarlazzi

6th arr. - 74, rue des Saints-Pères 45 44 12 32
8th arr. - 67, rue du Faubourg-Saint-Honoré - 42 66 67 73
Open 10 a.m.-7 p.m. Closed Sun.

Tarlazzi creates sexy, provocative designs for women with splashes of bright colors in prodigiously worked materials. Prices are stiff, but, thankfully, there is the Bataclan line to temper the

whole. This is fiery fashion that frightens off some—still, try slipping into one of his draped skirts or laced-up cocktail dresses. You'll look so good you may never take it off...

Téhen

4th arr. - 5 bis, rue des Rosiers 40 27 97 37
Open 11 a.m.-7 p.m. (Mon. from 2 p.m.). Closed Sun.

Designer Irena Gregori gets top billing in the Téhen shops with her fresh, vivid and uncomplicated styles, wearable from morning till night. Her preferences run to fluid fabrics, comfortable knits and stretchy synthetics. Prices are attractive, winter and summer, but at sale time they are downright irresistible.

Chantal Thomass

1st arr. - 1 rue Vivienne - 40 15 02 36
Open 10 a.m.-7 p.m. (Mon. from 11 a.m.). Closed Sun.

The queen of wasp-waists, form-fitting dresses, ultra-feminine suits and sexy stockings has just inaugurated this huge, new, thumb-your-nose-at-recession emporium. Here, only a stone's throw away from the trendy place des Victoires, spread out over three levels, all of Chantal's multifarious creations are on view. If you don't feel like shopping, head for the *fumoir*, the salon, the library, or the boudoir (no less).

Yuki Torii

2nd arr. - 38-40, galerie Vivienne 42 66 64 66
Open 10 a.m.-7 p.m. Closed Sun.

Don't be misled by the austerity of his boutique; unlike her designing compatriots, this Japanese stylist does not go in for dramatic, ascetic "draperies." Yuki Torii likes bright colors, exuberant floral prints and amusing details. The clothes are supple, wearable and

highly original. Pricey, too, of course.

Emmanuel Ungaro

8th arr. - 2, av. Montaigne - 47 23 61 94
Open 10 a.m.-7 p.m. Closed Sun.

Emmanuel Ungaro doesn't go in for fashion trends so much as he aims to create torrid "climates." Rousing colors and mad mixes of prints are his signatures: flowers, leopards and geometrical motifs run rampant along his curvy skirts and jackets. His Ungaro Solo Donna and Ungaro Parallèles lines are slightly more affordable than the top-tier ready-to-wear. Marvelous accessories, if you can only afford a "taste" of Ungaro.

Valentino

8th arr. - 17-19, av. Montaigne 47 23 64 61
Open 10 a.m.-7 p.m. Closed Sun.

Like Caesar, another famous Roman before him, Valentino came, saw and conquered the world of French fashion. Celebrities and commoners alike flock to his boutique in search of classic styles in everything from socks to spectacles. The superbly cut flannel suits, tweed jackets, sweaters and shawls are chic, comfortable and easy to wear. Valentino goes all out for evening, with frothy silk mousseline frocks, gowns sprinkled with sequins or jet embroidery—we understand why Liz Taylor wanted him to make her umpteenth wedding dress! Everything here is expensive, so be careful not to lose control.

Plan to travel? Look for Gault Millau's other Best of guides to Chicago, Florida, France, Hawaii, Hong Kong, Germany, Italy, London, Los Angeles, New England, New Orleans, New York, San Francisco, Thailand, Toronto and Washington, D.C.

READY-TO-WEAR & SPECIALTY SHOPS

Absinthe

1st arr. - 74-76, rue Jean-Jacques-Rousseau - 42 33 54 44
Open 11 a.m.-7:30 p.m. (Mon. from 2 p.m.). Closed Sun.

Marthe Desmoulins tracks down designers of the new generation—Dries Van Noten, Christophe Lemaire, Yoneda Kasuko, Costume Nazionale, Charlotte Nilson, among others—and brings their creations together in her hip, hot boutique. If you want to know whats news in fashion, this is a good place to start.

Inès de La Fressange

8th arr. - 14, av. Montaigne - 47 23 08 94
Open 10 a.m.-6:30 p.m. Closed Sun.

Inès, once the "face" of Chanel (until she fell out of favor with Kaiser Karl) recently launched her own boutique amid much media brouhaha. Set on the swank avenue Montaigne, the shop is a roaring success. You'll find impeccably cut wardrobe basics (suits, pants, jackets) and chic accessories (a rainbow of suede loafers, jewelry, hats), all produced, designed or selected by Inès herself. A line of household linens and decorative objects is on hand as well.

Kashiyama

1st arr. - 80, rue Jean-Jacques-Rousseau - 40 26 46 46
Open 10 a.m.-1 p.m. & 2 p.m.-7 p.m. (Sat. 11 a.m.-7 p.m.). Closed Sun.
6th arr. - 147, bd Saint-Germain 46 34 11 50
Open 10 a.m.-7 p.m. (Mon. from 11 a.m.). Closed Sun.

The windows that wrap around an entire corner of the boulevard Saint-Germain offer a tantalizing sample of what's inside: beauteous garments by the hottest designers—Dolce & Gabbana, Jean Colonna,

Romeo Gigli, Sybilla and others, all the cream of the current fashion crop. Downstairs, a lavish array of lascivious, lacy lingerie awaits. We cringe at the prices (the semiannual sales are worth your close attention), but we have nothing but praise for the helpful staff.

Maria Luisa

1st arr. - 2, rue Cambon - 47 03 96 15
Open 10:30 a.m.-7 p.m. Closed Sun.

In this buttoned-up neighborhood you're unlikely to find a more avant-garde fashion boutique than this one. Maria Luisa is Venezuelan, and she is blessed with an infallible sense of style. Her stable of designing stars includes Martine Sitbon, Helmut Lang, John Galliano and Sybilla. Accessories too are at the cutting edge of fashion, with bags by 31 Février, hats by Le Corre and glorious jewelry by Berao and Valluet.

Songeur Daiya

1st arr. - 245, rue Saint-Honoré 42 60 97 35
Open 10 a.m.-7 p.m. Closed Sun.

The Daiya group (a Japanese concern), opened this spectacular shop to showcase talented designers like Nikita Godart, Brigitte Masson, Laura Caponi and Brazilian stylist, Cristal. An international clientele comes here to look for chic, unusual (and expensive) ensembles for day and evening.

Victoire

2nd arr. - 12 & 10, pl. des Victoires - 42 61 09 02
Open 9:30 a.m.-7 p.m. Closed Sun.

For a comprehensive view of what's new in fashion, Victoire is a good place to start. Young and veteran designers alike make up the

eclectic mix of clothing and accessories that reflects owner Françoise Chassagnac's unerring taste: Romeo Gigli, Donna Karan, Callaghan and a handful of newcomers who change each season.

Zenta

8th arr. - 6, rue de Marignan - 42 25 72 47
Open 10 a.m.-7 p.m. (Mon. from 11 a.m.). Closed Sun.

Some fifteen designers are represented in this spacious boutique. In addition to confirmed talents like Popy Moreni, Chantal Thomass, Martine Sitbon, Karl Lagerfeld and Lolita Lempicka, you'll discover the creations of the up-and-coming generation (which you can be first on your block to wear!).

EVENINGWEAR

Loris Azzaro

8th arr. - 65, rue du Faubourg-Saint-Honoré - 42 66 92 06
Open 10 a.m.-7 p.m. Closed Sun.

The ground floor of the shop does nothing to prepare customers for the luxury that awaits them in the gray-marble showroom upstairs. There the imperturbable Loris supervises, while his sumptuous gowns are fitted on the fair figures of jet-set celebrities. Though he may be scoffed at by more classic *couturiers*, his customers adore the way Azzaro plunges a neckline, molds a silhouette. Predictably, his prices are far from negligible, though the ready-to-wear (dresses: 5,000 to 7,000) is more attainable than the couture (10,000 and up).

Hélène Gainville

8th arr. - Arcades du Lido, 78, av. des Champs-Elysées - 43 59 32 18
Open 10:30 a.m.-7:30 p.m. Closed Sun.

See *Designers* page 215.

Narakas

16th arr. - 5, rue Lalo - 40 67 75 96
Open 9 a.m.-6 p.m. Closed Sat. (except appt.), Sun., Aug.

Whether you need a "little" cocktail dress or a gown for a gala dinner, Alexandre Narakas will provide you with a design that won't go unnoticed. In his gilded atelier, aided by Yolande de Gourcuff, he fashions yards of silk, taffeta and satin for spectacular, one-of-a-kind creations priced from 3,000 francs.

Yvan et Marzia

1st arr. - 4, pl. Sainte-Opportune 42 33 00 56
Open 11 a.m.-7 p.m. (Mon. from 2 p.m.). Closed Sun.

If your figure is flawless, you're likely to love Yvan and Marzia's luscious gowns. The lumpy and bumpy among us, however, would do well to look elsewhere. Prices start at about 3,000 francs.

FURS

Behar

10th arr. - 45, bd de Strasbourg 47 70 12 33
Open 9:30 a.m.-12:30 p.m. & 2 p.m.-6:30 p.m. Closed Sun., Mon. & 3 wks. in Aug.

Luxuriously full seven-eighths–length coats in dark, lustrous mink are the stars of Behar's collection, but there are beautiful silver-fox coats as well, and blue-fox jackets for 4,000 francs.

Sprung Frères

16th arr. - 5, av. Victor-Hugo - 45 01 70 61
Open 10 a.m.-7 p.m. Closed Sun., 1 wk. in Aug.

Definitely not for dowagers, these superbly cut furs (some designed by Chloé Bruneton) have loads of youthful style and chic.

Révillon

6th arr. - 44, rue du Dragon - 42 22 38 91
Open 11 a.m.-6:45 p.m. Closed Sun.
8th arr. - 17-19, rue du Faubourg-Saint-Honoré - 40 17 98 98
Open 10 a.m.-7 p.m. Closed Sun.

Révillon has been the very symbol of furs since 1723. And they are still the most beautiful in the world. Here style goes hand in hand with quality. Of the fur-lined coats, muskrat suits, reversible jackets in blue mink or astrakhan displayed upstairs, none is priced lower than 50,000 francs—in fact, they're generally four times that if you're into sable or chinchilla. Prices on the ground floor are somewhat less fearsome. A men's department with coats and short jackets is housed on the lower level.

Riccardo Rozzi

17th arr. - 13, rue de l'Etoile 47 66 37 37
Open 10 a.m.-7 p.m. Closed Sun., Mon. (except Sept. 30-Feb. 28) & Aug.

Furs (including reversible models) in offbeat styles with wonderful, unique sleeves and enameled with colored copper make Riccardo Rozzi a designer for the young.

KNITS

Chandail

1st arr. - 68, rue Saint-Honoré 40 41 02 72
Open 11 a.m.-2:30 p.m. & 3:30 p.m.-7:30 p.m. (Mon. & Sat. 11 a.m.-1 p.m. & 2 p.m.-7:30 p.m.). Closed Sun.

The sweaters, exotic and eccentric, come from Peru, Norway and Austria and are decorated with dolls from the Andes or strange beasties. Comfort and folksiness is the order of the day. A more run-of-the-mill Italian knitwear collection caps the cozy ambience of this store, where

prices run from 500 to 2,500 francs.

Crimson

8th arr. - 8, rue Marbeuf - 47 20 44 24
Open 10 a.m.-7 p.m. (Mon. from noon). Closed Sun.

Men and women will find a rainbow selection of colors in lambswool, with twin sets selling for 700 to 1,400 francs, and long cardigans for 1,370 francs. There are also sweaters as soft as cashmere made from wool from the first shearing of a lamb's underside (700 francs). Roll necks, V-necks and Irish knitwear in unusual colors are also stocked here at prices from 1,400 to 1,650 francs.

Fac-Bazaar

6th arr. - 38, rue des Saints-Pères 45 48 46 15
Open 11 a.m.-7 p.m. (Mon. from 3 p.m.). Closed Sun. & 3 wks. in Aug.

Fac-Bazaar offers creative designs and attractive pullovers in low-key colors.

Christa Fiedler

16th arr. - 87, av. Paul-Doumer 40 50 84 08
Open 10:30 a.m.-7 p.m. (Mon. from 2:30 p.m.). Closed Sun.

Onetime model turned knitwear designer, Christa Fiedler marries comfort and elegance in her upbeat, elegant collections. She uses strong reds, blues and blacks in her lambswool sweaters for the winter months; soft pastel colors and cotton lisle for summer. And she stocks plenty of accessories: turbans, scarves and gloves. Every item is lovingly detailed and finished.

Richard Grand

1st arr. - 229, rue Saint-Honoré 42 60 18 75
Open 10 a.m.-7 p.m. Closed Sun.

This Paris-famed cashmere specialist has been in business now for over a quarter of a century. Nobody matches its spectacular range of 70 colors in 100 styles for ladies and men. Richard Grand also manufactures cashmere-and-silk sweaters as light as feathers in a magnificient array of colors. Because the shop controls its own manufacturing, it can offer top-of-the-line chic at prices that start around 850 francs. A must for sweater fanciers in Paris.

Joseph

2nd arr. - 44, rue Etienne-Marcel
42 36 87 83
Open 10:30 a.m.-7 p.m. Closed Sun.
A megastar in London, in Paris Joseph is just, well... Joseph. But glitter and glamour aside, we like his imaginative and colorful knit separates, especially the roomy pullovers that don't make too much of a dent in the budget.

Aux Laines Ecossaises

7th arr. - 181, bd Saint-Germain
45 48 53 41
Open 10 a.m.-7 p.m. (Mon. from 2 p.m.). Closed Sun.
Tradition reigns, as it always has, in this family-run establishment founded at the end of the last century. Current owner Paul-Emile Clarisse greets his customers warmly and guides them around the shop "to feel the wares." On sale are top-quality lambswool pullovers, Shetland sweaters (500 francs) and some double-ply cashmere (2,200 francs). Colors are conservative; classic brands include Ballantyne and Gladstone, and there are also Austrian jackets made by Astrifa (1,500 francs) and plaid dressing gowns (1,300 francs.)

LARGE SIZES

Marina Rinaldi

6th arr. - 56, rue du Four - 45 48 61 57
Open 10:30 a.m.-5 p.m. Closed Sun.
Generous curves are well served by these attractive fashions by an Italian maker. Rather than mask the fuller figure, they underscore its roundness in a most feminine way. Pretty prints, fluid fabrics and three different lines: Marina Rinaldi, the most expensive (and elegant); Marina Sport; and Persona, the least costly collection.

Rondissimo

9th arr. - 42, rue Vignon - 42 66 54 77
Open 10 a.m.-7 p.m. Closed Sun.
In French, women with fuller figures are called *rondes*, hence the name of this chain (with several stores in and around Paris). The fashionable clothes are made chiefly of knits and silky fabrics that flow over the body and flatter the silhouette.

LINGERIE

Berlé

1st arr. - 332, rue Saint-Honoré
42 60 42 87
Open 9 a.m.-noon & 1 p.m.-5 p.m. Closed Sat., Sun. & Aug.
For 70 years now, this noble house has manufactured and sold a single style of brassiere, which varies in the material used and how it is adorned. It gives contour to a generous bosom and emphasizes a small bust. Britain's Queen Mother and Princess Margaret are just two of Berlé's loyal clientele.

La Boîte à Bas

16th arr. - 77, rue de Longchamp
47 55 11 55
16th arr. - 16, av. Mozart - 42 24 89 98
Open 10:30 a.m.-7 p.m. (Mon. from 2 p.m.). Closed Sun., July 25-Sept.
It's all stockings and tights here, and all the major brands are represented: Gerbe, Dior, La Perla, Osé (the up-and-comer), Wolford and so forth. There are at least 8,000 pairs in stock and range from the coolest to the warmest (prices range from 40 to 500 francs).

Alice Cadolle

1st arr. - 14, rue Cambon - 42 60 94 94
Open 9:30 a.m.-1 p.m. & 2 p.m.-6:30 p.m. (& by appt., except Sat. & Sun.). Closed Sun. & Aug.
Al-ice Cadolle invented the brassiere in 1889. Sales have been holding up well ever since; here you can find custom-made, partly custom-made and ready-to-wear bras, lingerie and swimsuits (the latter are housed on the shop's third floor).

Les Folies d'Elodie

16th arr. - 56, av. Paul-Doumer
45 04 93 57
Open 10 a.m.-7 p.m. (Mon. from 11 p.m.). Closed Sun.
Two sisters, Catherine and Nanou, reign over the two Folies boutiques. Their collections are aimed at millionairesses who will settle for nothing less than silk and lace dressing gowns and underwear. Bed linen, wedding dresses and their celebrated blouse with a ribbed yoke are also available. If you need a tulle skirt, a satin bustier or a transparent organza coat, head over here!

Natori

1st arr. - 7, pl. Vendôme - 42 96 22 94
Open 10 a.m.-1 p.m. & 2 p.m.-7 p.m. Closed Sat. & Sun.
Seductive lingerie is the specialty here: your eyes will

pop (so just think what *his* will do!) when you get a load of Natori's silk negligees, beaded body suits, slinky nightgowns, robes and undies.

Les Nuits d'Elodie

17th arr. - 1bis, av. Mac-Mahon
42 67 68 95
See *Les Folies d'Elodie* above.

Capucine Puerari

6th arr. - 63, rue des Saint-Pères
42 22 14 09
Open 10 a.m.-7 p.m. Closed Sun.
A spacious new boutique gives Capucine Puerari lots of room to display all her designing talents: there's youthful, sexy underwear and lingerie; smoothing, flattering body-suits; and satiny, beautifully detailed swimsuits. The choice is wide, the staff is helpful, the prices (for Paris, mind!) are reasonable.

Sabbia Rosa

6th arr. - 73, rue des Saints-Pères
45 48 88 37
Open 10 a.m.-7 p.m. Closed Sun.
This boutique is happy to receive couples in search of a few grams of satin or an ounce of crêpe de chine with which to spice up an evening...

Chantal Thomass

6th arr. - 11, rue Madame - 45 44 07 52
Open 10 a.m.-7 p.m. (Mon. from 11 a.m.). Closed Sun.
This lingerie is in a class of its own: garter belts, brassieres, panties and negligees are musts for collectors.

SILK

Les Trois Marches

6th arr. - 1, rue Guisarde - 43 54 74 18
Open 12:30 p.m.-7:30 p.m. Closed Sun. & Mon.
Cathy Lullier's pocket-size boutique overflows with vintage gowns and dresses in silk,

crêpe de chine and silk mousseline. She personally tracks each treasure down, then proceeds to restore and update it by hand. There is also a delicious selection of frilly cotton and eyelet underthings. Isabelle Adjani and Catherine Deneuve have been spotted shopping here.

Pour Surah

4th arr. - 7, rue du Trésor - 42 77 11 21
Open 11 a.m.-7 p.m. Closed Sun., Mon., 2 wks. in Aug.
Maud Perl wraps women in gorgeous scarves, shawls and sarongs of purest silk, in the most divinely shimmering shades.

SWIMSUITS

A la Plage

7th arr. - 6, rue de Solférino - 47 05 18 94
Open 10 a.m.-7 p.m. (Sat. 10 a.m.-1 p.m. & 2 p.m.-7 p.m.). Closed Sun., 1 wk. in Aug.
16th arr. - 17, rue de la Pompe
45 03 08 51
Open 10 a.m.-1 p.m. & 2 p.m.-7 p.m. Closed Sun., 1 wk. in Aug.
The most beautiful swimsuits and cover-ups are available here year-round. There's a children's collection, too.

Erès

6th arr. - 4 bis, rue du Cherche-Midi - 45 44 95 54
8th arr. - 2, rue Tronchet - 47 42 24 55
Open 9:30 a.m.-7 p.m. Closed Sun.
16th arr. - 6, rue Guichard - 46 47 45 21
Open 10 a.m.-7 p.m. Closed Sun.
Erès, the swimsuit specialists, sells two-piece suits separately—a brilliant idea! There is an incredible choice of adjustable tops and bottoms to suit just about any figure. What's more, they're beautifully made and as chic as can be. The Beachwear collection includes coordinates

for before and after *la plage.* Upstairs: a lingerie section.

WEDDING GOWNS

Hélène Gainville

8th arr. - Arcades du Lido, 78, av. des Champs-Elysées - 43 59 32 18
Open 10:30 a.m.-7:30 p.m. Closed Sun.
Hélène Gainville and her fairy-fingered seamstresses will create the wedding gown you've dreamed about since you were small. Made to your measurements, hand-beaded and embroidered, in silk, satin, organza or lace, these classic timeless dresses are truly fit for a princess. Naturally, Hélène will be happy to make your veil, headpiece and other accessories too. Chic traveling clothes and ensembles for the moter of the bride can be custom-made here as well.

Monique Germain

6th arr. - 59, bd Raspail - 45 48 22 63
Open 12:30 p.m.-7 p.m. (Sat. 1 p.m.-6 p.m.). Closed Sun. & Mon.
The display window is classic and conventional—anything but exciting. But inside— surprise!—you'll see sculpted bustiers for bare-shouldered brides, sheath dresses with tulle overskirts, gowns that can be transformed into cocktail dresses after the big day. Alongside is a wealth of stylish accessories, including hats, wreaths and other pretty headgear.

■ SHOES
& ACCESSORIES

Jean Barthet
8th arr. - 13, rue Tronchet - 42 65 35 87
Open 10 a.m.-1 p.m. & 2 p.m.-6:30 p.m. Closed Sat., Sun., 2 wks. in Aug.

Most of the planet's celebrities have stuck their heads through the door of this institution—and with good reason. Jean Barthet makes hats that are refined and spectacular in their elegance. This is high fashion at over-the-top-hat prices!

Isabel Canovas
8th arr. - 16, av. Montaigne - 47 20 10 80
Open 10 a.m.-7 p.m. Closed Sun.

Accessories that lift an outfit out of the banal and into the extraordinary: ants crawl up a pair of silk gloves, cats chase each other around and around a belt, lizards slither up lapels... Nature and Africa are the twin inspirations of Isabel Canovas's fascinating creations. You'll also find lovely handbags, trim little leather envelopes that go beautifully with a tailored suit, glass-bead earrings, shawls, sarongs and much more.

Chéri-Bibi
11th arr. - 82, rue de Charonne 43 70 51 72
Open 11 a.m.-1 p.m. & 2 p.m.-7 p.m. Closed Sun., Mon. & 2 last wks. of Aug.

All manner of adorable little hats (*bibis*) hang on the walls of this trendy shop, where celebrities and anonymous followers of fashion choose their bérets, caps (we love the one with a "target" design), beanies, veiled cocktail hats and turbans.

Robert Clergerie
6th arr. - 5, rue du Cherche- Midi 45 48 75 47
Open 9:30 a.m.-7 p.m. Closed Sun.

Clergerie's much-copied wedgies, metallic faux-croco loafers and tall-girl pumps with column heels are adored by fashionable *Parisiennes*. Basic shapes vary little from season to season: the designer just changes a detail or two. But the color schemes are always inventive and up-to-the-minute, with warm, muted shades in winter, pastels and flashy brights in summer.

Un Dimanche à Venise
6th arr. - 50, rue du Four - 42 22 52 38
Open 10 a.m.-7:30 p.m. Closed Sun.

A newcomer to the footwear scene. What makes this shop worthwhile is the selection of more-or-less obvious copies of shoes by more upscale manufacturers. The quality is perfectly respectable, the styles are always right in fashion and the prices are A-OK.

Maud Frizon
6th arr. - 83, rue des Saints-Pères 42 22 06 93
Open 10 a.m.-7 p.m. Closed Sun.

Characters in Judith Krantz novels covet Maud Frizons as much as they do Cartier baubles. Styles are audacious and always feminine, with a subtle use of canvas and lizard, suede and leather. There are heels for all seasons and heights, as well as a plethora of ballet slippers, beach and evening sandals, pumps and dreamy boots. Prices, 1,750 to 2,700 francs.

Harel
8th arr. - 64, rue François-Ier - 47 23 96 57 & 8, av. Montaigne 47 20 75 00
Open 10 a.m.-6:45 p.m. Closed Sun.

If you pride yourself on your elegance, you can't afford to ignore Harel. In fact, you owe it to yourself to own at least one pair of his marvels—sheer, simple luxury: three different arches, three widths and five heel heights. Pumps, sandals and walking shoes, in a choice of satin, lizard, crocodile, ostrich, snakeskin and kid, come in twenty colors. Prices run from about 1,550 to 3,000 francs. A pair of Harel's shoes lasts a lifetime; if they don't, they'll send them to the factory for repairs.

Charles Jourdan
1st arr. - 5, bd de la Madeleine 42 61 15 89
Open 9:45 a.m.-7 p.m. Closed Sun.
8th arr. - 86, av. des Champs-Elysées - 45 62 29 33
Open 9:45 a.m.-8 p.m. Closed Sun.

There's something here for every taste, including the best. Affordable fine-quality shoes are available in over twenty colors. Figure on spending about 1,050 francs for a pair of pumps.

K-Jacques
4th arr. - 16, rue Pavée - 40 27 03 57
Open 10:30 a.m.-7 p.m. (Mon. & Sun. from 2:30 p.m.). Closed wk. of Aug. 15.

Colette, the author, launched the K-Jacques sandal in Saint Tropez, some 60 years ago. Reminiscent of the footwear you see Spartans wearing in B-movies about the Greeks, the sandal comes in every shade from natural brown to metallic turquoise. Lots of other Provençal accessories are on display: great boots like the ones sported by Camargue cowboys, straw bags, ceramics and Biot glassware (the kind with the tiny bubbles locked inside).

> *The prices in this guide reflect what establishments were charging at press time.*

223

Charles Kammer
7th arr. - 14, rue de Grenelle - 42 22 91 19
Open 10 a.m.-7 p.m. Closed Sun.

Shoes as comfortable as bedroom slippers, for trotting about the city in style. In summer, look for lovely sandals and strappy numbers; in winter, you'll find high-rising vamps and thigh boots in softest leather. Kammer gives you lots of fashion for what is, in fact, a reasonable amount of money.

Stéphane Kélian
1st arr. - 6, pl. des Victoires - 42 61 60 74
1st arr. - Les Trois Quartiers, 23, bd de la Madeleine - 42 96 01 99
3rd arr. - 36, rue de Sévigné - 42 77 87 91
7th arr. - 13 bis, rue de Grenelle 42 22 93 03
Open 10 a.m.-7 p.m. Closed Sun.
8th arr. - Galerie Point-Show, 66, av. des Champs-Elysées - 42 56 11 44
8th arr. - 26, av. des Champs-Elysées - 42 56 42 26
Open 10:30 a.m.-7:30 p.m. Closed Sun.

King of the braided-leather shoe, Stéphane Kélian has based his reputation on this technique. He also adds pizzazz to classic styles for Claude Montana. Sculptural heels, fine details, fashionable forms—and sniffy service—are found in all the city's Kélian stores. Take note that it is now Kélian, not Maud Frizon, who designs the ultrafeminine Miss Maud shoe collection (rue de Grenelle).

Sidonie Larizzi
8th arr. - 8, rue de Marignan - 43 59 38 87
Open 10 a.m.-7 p.m. Closed Sun.

Sidonie Larizzi designs for couturiers, and also produces a collection with her own label. Her boutique creations blend classicism with original-

ity. Alongside the dressy pumps you'll discover delicious boudoir mules with swan's down pompoms, and some to-drool-over handbags. Studio Larizzi is a lower-priced (but still very stylish) second-tier line.

John Lobb
8th arr. - 51, rue François-Ier - 45 62 06 34
Open 10 a.m.-7 p.m. Closed Sun.

Outrageously expensive shoes for exigent feet whose owners have money to spend. You must place your order six months in advance for a pair of sumptuous, custom-made walking shoes, golf shoes or riding boots. Remarkable footwear from all points of view. Prices are staggering.

Christian Louboutin
1st arr. - 19, rue Jean-Jacques-Rousseau - 42 36 05 31
Open 11 a.m.-7:30 p.m. Closed Sun.

You don't have to have a shoe fetish to find Louboutin's footwear irresistibly sensual and alluring. A student of the great Roger Vivier, he creates jewels for the feet—just look at the gold leaf that adorns the high heels on one of his models. Prices, predictably, are high: around 1,800 francs a pair.

René Mancini
16th arr. - 72, av. Victor-Hugo 45 00 48 81
Open 10 a.m.-7 p.m. (Sat. 10 a.m.-1 p.m. & 2:30 p.m.-6 p.m.). Closed Sun., Mon., Aug.

René Mancini first made the black-tip shoe for Chanel. In 1964 he introduced square toes. And his daughter Claire has carried on the family tradition. A portion of the collection is handmade, and it is possible to match your shoes to your dress for a mere 3,000 francs and a ten-day wait. Mancini's ready-to-wear shoes are made in Italy and are more affordable. Prices at the

boutique on avenue Victor-Hugo run 700 to 1,500 francs.

Laurent Mercadal
1st arr. - 3, pl. des Victoires - 45 08 84 44
6th arr. - 56, rue de Rennes - 45 48 43 87
8th arr. - 26, av. des Champs-Elysées - 42 25 22 70
8th arr. - 31, rue Tronchet - 42 66 01 28
Open 10:30 a.m.-7 p.m. Closed Sun.

Laurent Mercadal cobbles classic but stylish women's shoes that are always in tune with current fashion trends. A limited number of basic models is offered in a vast assortment of skins and combinations, in beautiful colors. Reasonable prices (from 650 francs).

Marie Mercié
2nd arr. - 56, rue Tiquetonne - 40 26 60 68
6th arr. - 23, rue Saint-Sulpice 43 26 45 83
Open 11 a.m.-7 p.m. Closed Sun.

The Queen of Hats. This tiny boutique is stuffed with chic and shocking *chapeaux* that are guaranteed to grab lots of attention. Marie Mercié designs fantastical headgear that is featured in the fashion shows of many top couturiers.

Philippe Model
1st arr. - 33, pl. du Marché-Saint-Honoré - 42 96 89 02
Open 10 a.m.-7 p.m. (Sat.: March 1-Sept. 30 from 11 p.m.; Oct. 1-Feb 28 from 1 p.m.). Closed Sun.
6th arr. - 79, rue des Saint-Pères 45 44 76 79
Open 10 a.m.-7 p.m. (Mon. & Sat. 11 a.m.-7 p.m.). Closed Sun.

Rare is the woman who would not look fetching in a hat by Philippe Model. His shop overflows with colorful headgear: picture hats, fedoras, feathered and beribboned models, airy straw hats and jaunty panamas. Model is currently one of the

ROUGE GOURMAND

NOUVEAU MAQUILLAGE

ROCHAS

MAFIA

brightest stars in the fashion-accessory firmament. His beautiful collection of footwear for men and women is displayed in the shop next door.

Oxymuse

7th arr. - 11, rue du Pré-aux-Clercs - 45 44 43 35
Open 11 a.m.-7 p.m. Closed Sun., Aug.

Muriel Jurman, late of Charles Kammer, has launched her own line of shoes under the Oxymuse label. Artisanal methods are used to craft her small collection of classic models in stylish colors and leathers. A single price: 650 francs.

Michel Perry

1st arr. - 13, rue de Turbigo - 42 36 44 34
Open 11 a.m.-7 p.m. Closed Sun. & 1 wk. in Aug.

Fashionable to the utmost degree (he was written up by Vogue some months back), Perry designs fresh, unusual, always glamorous looks that flatter the feet. The heels of his mules and pumps are particularly inventive.

Andréa Pfister

1st arr. - 4, rue Cambon - 42 96 55 28
Open 10 a.m.-7 p.m. (Mon. from 2 p.m.). Closed Sun.

Pfister makes fine, delicate shoes to suit the comely foot and well-turned ankle. This is Parisian elegance *par excellence*. Embroidered or sequined evening shoes sell for around 2,000. The price for a pair of elegant snakeskin shoes can slither up considerably higher. Pfister will also make shoes to measure in the style and leather of your choice. Allow seven weeks with fittings.

Fausto Santini

6th arr. - 4 ter, rue du Cherche-Midi - 45 44 39 40
Open 10 a.m.-7 p.m. (Mon. from 11 p.m.). Closed Sun.

The rue du Cherche-Midi was already chockablock with shoe stores, but Santini moved in anyway; in fact, he has made quite a reputation for himself. His handbags and shoes are outstanding for their glowing leathers in myriad hues, delicate curved lines and fashionable finishing touches.

Walter Steiger

6th arr. - 5, rue de Tournon - 46 33 01 45
Open 10 a.m.-7 p.m. (Mon. from 2 p.m.). Closed Sun., Aug.
8th arr. - 83, rue du Faubourg-Saint-Honoré - 42 66 65 08
Open 10 a.m.-7 p.m. Closed Sun.

More foreigners than Parisians pass through the portals of Walter Steiger, women who find his evening sandals, daytime pumps and weekend boots indispensable. Steiger's fake-lizard (printed on leather) is utterly convincing and much less pricey than the genuine article. Expect to pay from 1,200 to 1,400 for a pair of pumps.

François Villon

6th arr. - 58, rue Bonaparte - 43 25 98 36
Open 10 a.m.-7 p.m. (Mon. 10 a.m.-1 p.m. & 2 p.m.-7 p.m.). Closed Sun.

François Villon's high-quality footwear is beyond fashion. His boots are incomparable (around 2,500 francs). Villon carries pretty dress pumps and casual flats as well as the celebrated Brides Villon sandals with black tips. Of course, these shoes don't come cheap: between 1,500 and 2,800 francs per pair.

Remember that if you spend 2,000 francs or more in a store, you are entitled to a full refund of the value-added tax (VAT). See Basics *for details.*

DEPARTMENT STORES

BHV

4th arr. - 52-64, rue de Rivoli - 42 74 90 00
Open 9 a.m.-7 p.m. (Wed. until 10 p.m.). Closed Sun.

From Americans in search of converters for their electrical appliances, to do-it-yourselfers in need of a handful of nails, everyone in Paris eventually winds up in the BHV basement, a treasure trove of tools, hardware and home-improvement items. Whether it's a brass washer or a gold-plated faucet you're tracking down, just seek it here and you're sure to find. What's more, you can count on competent advice from the sales staff on how to use or install your purchases. Savvy artists and sculptors also appreciate the BHV's first floor, which is stocked with canvases, easels, brushes and clay at unbeatable prices. Features and services include: in-house specialists to install goods and materials, from wallpaper to floor tiles to convertible-car roofs and more; bridal registry with complimentary "house kit" and a five percent discount on anything the couple buys in the store during their first year of wedded bliss; an engraving service for adorning china and glass with initials or the family coat of arms; repairs of all sorts, done on the premises (you can have your pearls restrung or your fishing reel adjusted) purchases totaling over 1,000 francs delivered free of charge.

Le Bon Marché

7th arr. - 38, rue de Sèvres - 44 39 80 00
Open 9:30 a.m.-6:30 p.m. (Sat. until 7 p.m.). Grocery store 8:30 a.m.-9 p.m., Fri. until

10 p.m. - 44 39 81 00. Closed Sun.

The good old Bon Marché is cultivating its chic new look with sharper advertising and a greater emphasis on fashion, home decor and gastronomy. This full-service department store has vastly improved its clothing departments (check out the new first-floor women's shop), and holds frequent sales that are not to be missed. Top features (in addition to an unusually courteous staff) include an eye-popping collection of expertly chosen Oriental carpets (store number 1, third floor), and the largest gourmet grocery in Paris, which is open every day but Sunday until 9 p.m. La Grande Epicerie stocks 150 types of tea, 240 kinds of cheese and over 200 different products "imported" direct from Fauchon. Discover the "daily menu" service (they deliver) and tasty health foods from La Vie Claire. A huge and enticing array of wines is overseen by bistro-owner and winegrower Jacques Mélac. The grocery prices are competitive; in fact, Le Bon Marché pledges to reimburse the difference if you find a better deal in another Parisian supermarket. The Bon Marché also provides a convenient in-house travel agency and a ticket agency and a bank. Other services include custom-tailored clothing for men; fur storage and restoration, and Oriental-rug restoration. And, of course, there's a bridal registry, as well as birth and baptism registries.

Les Galeries Lafayette

9th arr. - 40, bd Haussmann - 42 82 34 56
Open 9:30 a.m.-6:45 p.m. Closed Sun.

On an average day, 100,000 women between the ages of 20 and 40 stroll through Les Galeries each day. What draws them is an enormous selection—three full floors—of clothing and accessories, ranging from such avant-garde designers as Jean-Paul Gaultier, Yohji Yamamoto and Azzedine Alaïa, to the classics, Cacharel, Dior and Guy Laroche. The store labels (hip "Avant-Première," "Briefing" career clothes and feminine casual clothes signed "Jodhpur") represent high fashion at attractive prices. The "Mode Plus" service offers free fashion counseling on putting together a look that fits a woman's personality and lifestyle. There's also a dazzling table and kitchenware department on the basement level—a paradise for anyone who loves to cook or entertain. Three restaurants offer a wide selection of refreshments for weary shoppers (including Lina's Sandwiches, a taste of home!), and there is a Jean-Marc Maniatis beauty salon. A separate building houses the men's store (dubbed the Galfa Club), and a spiffy new food emporium, Lafayette Gourmet. Patterned after Harrod's Food Hall, Lafayette Gourmet fairly bulges with goodies from all over. More than just a supermarket (cat food and oven-cleaner share shelf space with high-priced edibles), it is a gastro-playground, with a multitude of stands for snacking and sampling: Petrossian's for caviar and smoked salmon, Lenôtre for pastries and food-to-go, there's a Champagne bar, an oyster bar, a salad bar and a "Steak Point" serving Angus beef.

Marks & Spencer

9th arr. - 35, bd Haussmann - 47 42 42 91
Open 9:30 a.m.-7 p.m. (Tues. 10 a.m.-7 p.m.). Closed Sun.

Ever faithful to its mission, this Paris branch brings a little bit of cozy old England to the hard-edged French capital. The store is always busy, particularly at back-to-school time (the children's clothing is sturdy and adorable; older kids like the lambswool and cashmere sweaters, the tartan kilts and Oxford shirts) and at Christmas (for the traditional holiday foods, decorations and gifts). Among the features and services are all the fixings for an authentic English tea: tea, of course (loose and in bags), biscuits (cookies), marmalades, scones, crumpets, muffins and the rest. Delicious, reasonably priced packaged smoked salmon is available whole, in slices or marinated in dill. And don't miss the selection of chutneys, bottled sauces and other typically English condiments. The numerous choices of single-malt whiskies are complemented by several types of sherry and good English beer. The women's clothing is solid and stolid (oh, that no-nonsense British underwear!). Skirts are available in three different lengths and in large sizes. Men's jackets (excellent-quality Harris tweed, for instance) come in three sleeve-lengths; no alterations are done in the store. The store-wide sales in January, July and August offer some fine buys in sweaters and other knitwear.

Monoprix

9th arr. - 97, rue du Provence 48 74 37 13 (also: 2nd, 3rd, 4th, 5th, 6th, 8th, 9th, 10th, 11th, 12th, 13th, 15th, 17th, 18th, 19th)
Open 9 a.m.-8 p.m. Closed Sun.

"The basics are what we do best." That's the Monoprix motto. A big factor in the stores' success is their strategic locations in the capital's busiest neighborhoods. Monoprix has its own labels of clothing and toiletries of good quality at rock-bottom prices. Lately, successful efforts have been made to give added fashion oomph to the ready-to-wear, with lines designed by hip, young stylists. In another popular

stylists. In another popular move, Monoprix regularly puts so-called luxury goods (caviar at Christmas, for example, or cashmere sweaters in the fall) within the reach of the average consumer. The supermarket selection is constantly growing, with ready-to-eat dishes, catering services (at some stores) and the excellent Monoprix Gourmet line, which includes coffee, pasta, vacuum-packed ready-cooked entrées, low-calorie products and a new line of quick-cooking dishes for hungry folks in a hurry.

Printemps

9th arr. - 64, bd Haussmann - 42 82 50 00
13th arr. - 30, av. d'Italie, centre commercial Galaxie
40 78 17 17
20th arr. - 25, cours de Vincennes - 43 71 12 41
Open 9:35 a.m.-7 p.m. Closed Sun.

Printemps cultivates an image of quintessentially Parisian chic and elegance. The store targets a slightly less youthful clientele than its neighbor, Les Galeries Lafayette. The ideal Printemps customer is a woman of style and taste who appreciates refinement in both her dress and her surroundings. Top-of-the-line women's fashions are presented on the fourth floor in the Rue de la Mode shop; a wide and appealing array of menswear is found in the Brummel shop, a separate annex that carries everything from underwear to cashmere top coats. Features and services: the Boutique Blanche is the premier bridal registry in France; Le Printemps de la Maison is actually an entire store (eight floors) devoted to home decor and housewares, its private "Primavera" collection ranges from attractive handcrafted gift items to furniture designed by the likes of Andrée Putman and Philippe Starck. The ground floor was

recently revamped in lavish style (marble and crystal everywhere!) to create Le Printemps de la Beauté, a showcase for perfumes, cosmetics and other beauty products by top manufacturers. The Printemps's free fashion-consulting service shows customers how to put together a stylish, individualized wardrobe. Following a marathon shopping session, it's a pleasure to relax in the Brasserie Flo set up under the gorgeous stained-glass dome (Flo also runs Le Printemps's two cafés, and there is a Flo Prestige take-out shop on the premises as well).

Prisunic

8th arr. - 109, rue de la Boétie
42 25 27 46
Open 9:45 a.m.-midnight. Closed Sun.
also: 2nd, 11th, 12th, 13th, 15th, 16th, 17th, 18th, 19th, 20th.
Open 9 a.m.-8 p.m. or 8:30 p.m. depending on stores . Closed Sun.

Never content to rest on its marketing laurels, Prisunic has practiced the art of creative retailing ever since it opened up for business some 50 years ago. The newly renovated branch on the Champs-Elysées is now open until 10 p.m. (midnight in summer). Every week, its inventive merchandising team comes up with a new theme or sales promotion to spark shoppers' enthusiasm. Features include: clever, colorful housewares at affordable prices—dishes, linens, lamps and gadgets; a grocery section that offers fresh, fine-quality produce every day (Forza is the house brand of canned and packaged goods); a vast array of makeup and toiletries; and sturdy, adorable children's clothing, all at excellent prices.

Don't plan to do much shopping in Paris in August—a great many stores are closed for the entire vacation month.

La Samaritaine

1st arr. - 19, rue de la Monnaie
40 41 20 20
Open 9:30 a.m.-7 p.m. (Wed. until 10 p.m.). Closed Sun.

There's a revolution going on at La Samaritaine! Having cast off its image as a jumble of miscellaneous merchandise, the city's biggest bazaar, the four-store complex known as the "Samar" has entered the era of specialization. Every department has been overhauled, modernized and streamlined. To top it off, the interior has been spruced up and polished to its original brilliance: the etched glass, steel beams, lacquered ceramic tile and exuberant floral motifs haven't looked so good since opening day. Among the store's features is one of the finest views of Paris, enjoyed (from April to October) from the Samaritaine's rooftop terrace. The recently renovated restaurant and tea room now serve breakfast, lunch and brunch. Sporting goods and gear occupy an entire store. What's more, on the second floor you can practice your putt, scale a climbing wall, test a tennis racquet or play a little ping-pong. The pet shop, on the sixth floor, is a treat for children. On the fifth floor of the main store are the most complete sewing and notions departments in town. Just a few of the services available at La Samaritaine: golf lessons, courses in tailoring and bicycle-repair and maintenance, an in-house astrologer who'll tell you your horoscope and/or read your palm (for 450 francs; call two days ahead), lampshades made to order, resilvering of flatware, and picture framing. Mothers shopping with young children can rediaper them and warm their bottles in the store nursery. And nearly every item on sale at La Samaritaine can be ordered by mail or phone, with payment on delivery.

Aux Trois Quartiers

1st arr. - 23, bd de la Madeleine
Open 10 a.m.-7 p.m. Closed Sun.

If you haven't been near Aux Trois Quartiers for several years, you won't recognize the place! Though the name is the same, the interior was recently gutted, expanded and transformed into a deluxe, tri-level shopping mall. Formerly the preserve of tastefully dressed matrons and their prim daughters, Aux Trois Quartiers now draws crowds of customers—including a large percentage of tourists—with its critical mass of 75 chic shops. Madelios, a quality men's store, is here alongside the colorful clothing of Kenzo, Dorothée Bis and Tehen for women, Bang & Olufsen audio, restaurants, take-out shops and much more.

FLOWERS & PLANTS

■ FLOWER SHOPS

Céline et Jérôme

18th arr. - 83, rue du Mont-Cenis
46 06 30 91
Open 9 a.m.-8 p.m. (Sun. 9:30 a.m.-1 p.m.).

Simple flowers enhanced by exotic foliage and the occasional rare blossom (lotus or papyrus flowers, for instance) are arranged here into splendidly original, inventive bouquets. On weekends, bunches nearing their peak—but with lots of life still left in them—are sold on the sidewalk for bargain prices.

Patrick Divert

16th arr. - 7, place de Mexico
45 53 69 35
Open 8:30 a.m.-8 p.m. (Sat. from 9 p.m. & Sun. 10 a.m.-1 p.m.).

Subtle interplays of textures—barks, wood, moss and braids of aromatic plants—mark the style of Divert's rustic yet extremely refined bouquets. Wildflowers too add their charm to these inventive compositions.

Flowers, flowers everywhere

Some 1,800 varieties of flowers are raised in Paris's greenhouses, located in the Auteuil area, and from time to time marvelous flower exhibits are held. You can pick up exhibits schedules at the local city hall), or contact the Direction des Parcs et Jardins de la Ville de Paris, 3, av. de la Porte d'Auteuil, 16th arr., 40 71 74 00.

Elyfleurs

17th arr. - 82, ave de Wagram
47 66 87 19
Open daily 24 hours.

It's 2 a.m. and you're seized with the urge to send a sumptuous bouquet to a friend in Berlin. No problem: your thoughtful present will be delivered in France or in any major European city, in record time thanks to the efficient service provided around the clock by Elyfleurs.

Guillet

7th arr. - 99, av. La Bourdonnais
45 51 32 98
Open 9:30 a.m.-12:30 p.m. & 2 p.m.-7 p.m. Closed Sun. & Mon.

This long-established florist specializes in floral decorating schemes and, in its own workshop, creates silk flowers, centerpieces and bridal headdresses to order. Faithful clients include the Opéra and the Comédie-Française, as well as some of Paris's big department stores.

Un Jardin en Plus

7th arr. - 224, bd Saint-Germain
45 48 25 71
Open 10 a.m.-7 p.m. Closed Sun. & Mon. in July & Aug.

It's a floral, floral world. At least it is in this shop, where there are flowers everywhere: cut flowers, potted flowers, garlands, flowers on fabric, wallpaper, sheets, towels, dishes, furniture and more.

Lachaume

8th arr. - 10, rue Royale - 42 60 57 26
Open 8:30 a.m.-7:30 p.m. (Sat. until 6 p.m.). Closed Sun. & Aug.

This is probably the most famous florist in Paris, and it's been here for over a hundred years. Marcel Proust stopped by every day to pick out the orchid he wore in his lapel (you can get the same kind today for 140 francs). The quality of the flowers is perfection itself. Short of buying a bouquet, you can admire 150 varieties of flowers arranged in enormous vases in the shop window. Full bouquets start at about 400 francs.

Mille Feuilles

3rd arr. - 2, rue Rambuteau - 42 78 32 93
Open 9 a.m.-8 p.m. Closed Sun.

Arguably the best florist in the Marais, bursting with blossoms in the most delicate hues. Come here for the freshest flowers, both rare and familiar, artfully disposed in antique or contemporary vases. Like us, you'll want to buy the whole store!

Don't plan to do much shopping in Paris in August—a great many stores are closed for the entire vacation month.

228

Au Nom de la Rose

6th arr. - 4, rue de Tournon - 46 34 10 64
Open 10 a.m.-9 p.m. (Sun. 10 a.m.-1 p.m. & 3 p.m.-6 p.m.).
Dani is the name of the rose who runs this divine shop; she's an ex-pop singer who now spends her time in the fragrant company of roses, nothing but roses! From ultra-sophisticated blooms that look as if they were made of porcelain, to blowsy old-fashioned roses that bring back memories of grandmother's garden, all these flowers are sublime. You can purchase an armful for a dewy bouquet, or buy a single, perfectly graceful rose (from 20 francs).

Emilio Robba

1st arr. - 47, rue Etienne Marcel 42 36 66 48
Open 10 a.m.-7 p.m. (Sat. 11 a.m.-7 p.m.). Closed Sun.
Emilio Robba composes some exquisite artificial bouquets, but it's really his vases that will knock you out, including cloth-draped ones that can double as lamps. He has recently branched out into garden-style furniture (rattan, wrought-iron, braided leather); check out his seductive room scents.

Christian Tortu

6th arr. - 6, carrefour de l'Odéon 43 26 02 56
Open 9 a.m.-8 p.m. Closed Sun.
The darling of the shelter mags, Christian Tortu is a gifted flower designer, probably the most talented of his generation. He has an inimitable knack (and Lord knows his imitators are legion!) for blending rare and delicate flowers with simple greenery or tropical plants. Tortu's bouquets are perfect and quite natural looking, yet they're also sophisticated and somehow wild... His prices have risen quite as rapidly as his popularity with the media.

René Veyrat

8th arr. - 168, bd Haussmann 45 62 37 86
Open 8:30 a.m.-7 p.m. Closed Sun.
You'll be captivated by the window displays of this corner shop on the boulevard Haussmann. The flowers and plants are of exemplary quality, the service is charming. Large bouquets start at about 450 francs.

Vilmorin

1st arr. - 2 ter et 4, quai de la Mégisserie 42 33 61 62
Open 9:30 p.m.-7 p.m. Closed Sun. June-Feb. & Mon. July-Aug.
Gardeners should plan to spend at least a few hours browsing among the shrubs, rosebushes, bedding plants, herbs, bulbs and more on display at the biggest garden store in town. The seed department alone has been known to absorb the green of thumb for entire afternoons. Gardening accessories and house plants are on sale here as well.

■ FLOWER MARKETS

Marché aux Fleurs de l'Ile de la Cité

4th arr. - Pl. Louis-Lépine (quai de Corse)
Open 8 a.m.-7:30 p.m. Closed Sun. No cards.

Marché de la Madeleine

8th arr. - Pl. de la Madeleine (east side)
Open 8 a.m.-7:30 p.m. Closed Sat., Sun. & Mon. (except holidays). No cards.

Marché des Ternes

17th arr. - Pl. des Ternes
Open 8 a.m.-7:30 p.m. Closed Mon. No cards.

Flower supermarkets

These establishments sell remarkably fresh flowers, and they'll deliver anywhere in Paris:
Monceau Fleurs, open 9 a.m.-8 p.m. (Sun. 9 a.m.-1 p.m.) (delivery is 20 francs), 4th arr., 2 quai Célestins, 42 72 24 86; 6th arr., 84 bld Raspail, 45 48 70 10; 8th arr., 92 bd Malesherbes, 45 63 88 23; 16th arr., 60 av. Paul Doumer, 40 72 79 27; 17th arr., 2 place Général Koenig, 45 74 61 39.
A prosperous ambience can be found at *La Grange*, 6th arr., 7, rue de Buci, 43 26 19 34, open daily 9:30 a.m.-8:30 p.m. (Sun. until 7 p.m.); delivery is 35 francs, even in an emergency, and credit cards are accepted.
Other addresses: *Lamartine Fleurs*, 16th arr., 188, av. Victor Hugo, 45 04 29 50, open 9 a.m.-7:30 p.m. (Mon. 2:30 p.m.-7:30 p.m.), closed Sun.
And *Nice Fleurs*, 15th arr., 19-21, rue de Lourmel, 45 78 95 14, open 9:30 a.m.-7:30 p.m. (Sun 9:30 a.m.-1:30 p.m.), closed Mon.; 8th arr., 5, rue de Régny, 45 55 85 70, open 9 a.m.-7 p.m. (Sun. 9:30 a.m.-6 p.m.).

FOOD

Ayen for the exotic and a return to French culinary roots are the two most prominent— and paradoxical—features of the current Paris food scene. Palates titillated by travels to far-off lands crave those same foreign flavors when they get back home: hence the proliferation of stores offering foodstuffs and prepared dishes from all over the world. It's an amazing development; less than a generation ago, the chauvinistic French were particularly insular in their eating habits. But their current flirtation with foreign cuisines doesn't mean they've forsaken their native gastronomy. Au contraire, demand is increasing for fine aged cheeses and bread with old-fashioned flavor. And sales of sweets—pastry, ice cream, chocolate—are booming: People are ready to lay out lots and lots of francs to buy the very best.

■ BAKERIES

Au Panetier
2nd arr. - 10, place des Petits-Pères - 42 60 90 23
Open 8 a.m.-7:15 p.m. Closed Sat., Sun., 1 month during summer & holidays. No cards.
Even if you don't want to buy one of the old-fashioned loaves of hazelnut bread, raisin bread or the house specialty: pain de Saint-Fiacre (all baked in a wood-fired oven), this excellent bakery is worth a visit just for a look at the adorable etched-glass and tile decor.

Au Bon Pain d'Autrefois
11th arr. - 45, rue Popincourt
43 55 04 48
Open 6:30 a.m.-8 p.m. Closed Sat., Sun., end Dec. No cards.
The delicious scent of sourdough wafts forth from

this pretty bakery (designated an architectural landmark), which features superb pain de campagne (the classic country loaf), rustic rye loaves and delicious brioches. Jean-Pierre Leroy's special rotating oven also produces delectable pastries.

Le Fournil de Pierre
15th arr. - 3, rue du Commerce
45 75 16 48 (also: 2nd arr., 4th arr., 6th arr., 7th arr., 8th arr., 9th arr., 12th arr., 14th arr., 17th arr.)
Open 8:30 a.m.-7:30 p.m. (Mon. 11:30 a.m.-7:30 p.m. & Sun. until 1 p.m.).
The chain's many shops in the greater Paris area sell home-style breads whose sole flaw is that they are not always as oven-fresh as we might wish. But the variety of loaves is astonishing (there are over twenty), and we like the buns, cookies and pastries for their simple homemade goodness.

Ganachaud
20th arr. - 150-154, rue de Ménilmontant - 46 36 13 82
Open 7:30 a.m.-8 p.m. (Tues. 2:30 p.m.-8 p.m. & Sun. 7:30 a.m.-1:30 p.m.). Closed Mon. & Aug.
Bernard Ganachaud has sold his shop, but the new owner still works with the original team of bakers to produce the same fabulous breads from Ganachaud's wood-fired ovens. The nut breads sold here still contain real—fresh!—walnuts; the raisin breads continue to be loaded with fruit. And the traditional country loaf turned out fifteen to twenty times daily is still crusty perfection. Meanwhile, Isabelle and Valérie Ganachaud keep the family bread-baking tradition alive a few streets away, selling their father's renowned sourdough flûte, as well as a wonderfully chewy organic bread and a wide variety of down-home pastries and brioches (A La Flûte Gana, 226 rue des

Pyrénées, 20th arr., 43 58 42 62, closed Sun. and Mon.).

Marcel Haupois
4th arr. - 35, rue des Deux-Ponts
43 54 57 59
Open 6:45 a.m.-1:30 p.m. & 3 p.m.-8:30 p.m. Closed Thurs., Fri. & 1 month during summer.
Out of this small old-fashioned bakery emerges wonderful hand-formed loaves that rank among the finest in all of Paris. The country-style bread merits particular mention, as do the rye and other whole-grain specialties.

Poilâne
6th arr. - 8, rue du Cherche-Midi
45 48 42 59
Open 7:15 a.m.-8:15 p.m. Closed Sun.
15th arr. - 49, bd de Grenelle
45 79 11 49
Open 7:15 a.m.-8:15 p.m. Closed Mon.
Lionel Poilâne is indubitably the planet's best-known baker; he can be found hawking his famous sourdough bread in magazines and on television screens throughout the world. And even though his products are sold all over Paris in charcuteries and cheese shops, goodly numbers of Poilâne fans think nothing of crossing town and standing in line to *personally* buy their favorite bread still warm from his ovens. Poilâne's walnut bread is, in a word, delicious, and we are also particularly fond of the shortbread cookies (sablés) and the rustic apple turnover (which makes a delicious and inexpensive dessert, accompanied by a bowl of thick crème fraîche).

Max Poilâne
14th arr. - 29, rue de l'Ouest - 43 27 24 91
15th arr. - 87, rue Brancion - 48 28 45 90
Open 7:15 a.m.-8 p.m. Closed Sun. No cards.
Attractive bakery, located across from the old Vaugirard slaughterhouse, which was

recently transformed into a lush park. His bread follows the family tradition fairly closely, though we find it less tart and perhaps more pleasant than the more famous loaf baked on the rue du Cherche-Midi. Max also turns out a fine walnut bread, and his croissants, brioches and chaussons (turnovers) are huge hits with neighborhood gourmands.

Poujauran

7th arr. - 20, rue Jean-Nicot - 47 05 80 88
Open 8 a.m.-8:30 p.m. Closed Sun. & Mon. No cards.

He's a real darling, that Jean-Luc Poujauran! His bakery may be in a ritzy neighborhood, but he hasn't gone high-hat; food writers regularly wax lyrical over his talent, but his head hasn't swelled an inch. And though he bakes a wonderful country loaf with organically grown flour, he's not the type to think he's the greatest thing since sliced bread. Let's just hope he never changes. And let's hope that we will never have to give up his delicious little rolls (or his olive or his poppy seed or his walnut bread), his old-fashioned pound cake (quatre-quarts), his buttery fruitcakes and those terrific frangipane-stuffed galettes that he bakes for the Epiphany (Three Kings' Day, January 6).

René Saint-Ouen

8th arr. - 111, bd Haussmann 42 65 06 25
Open 8 a.m.-7 p.m. Closed Sun., Aug. & holidays. No cards.

René Saint-Ouen has two passions in life: bread and sculpture. He brings the two together in his bakery on boulevard Haussmann, where he makes and sells golden loaves of bread (sourdough, raisin-nut and bacon, among others) fashioned into classic and fabulous shapes. Special orders are welcome. The bak-

ery also serves light lunches and tea.

■ CATERERS

François Clerc

92210 Saint-Cloud - 3, rue Dantan - 46 02 88 88
Open 9 a.m.-7 p.m. Closed Sun. & holidays.

Backed up by a team of more than 100 professionals, François Clerc moved quickly into the top rung of French caterers. Clerc, a skilled and innovative chef, is passionate about food and cooking. Among his most notable creations, we highly recommend the magnificent pike "Harlequin" served with a subtle shellfish coulis, his unusual casserole of turbot with sea urchins and, among the sweets, Clerc's peerless coffee macaroons.

Dalloyau

15th arr. - 69, rue de la Convention - 45 77 84 27
Open 9:30 a.m.-7 p.m.

The oldest catering firm in Paris (founded in 1802), Dalloyau is also indubitably one of the best. The dishes on its appetizing menu are fit for a king (in case one is coming to your party). Choose from oysters gently stewed in Champagne, Bresse chicken with prawns, stuffed suckling pig and a thrilling selection of desserts (the famous Dalloyau chocolate macaroons are our favorite!).

Potel et Chabot

16th arr. - 3, rue de Chaillot - 47 20 22 00
Open 8 a.m.-7 p.m. Closed Sun.

Potel et Chabot is an old-established Parisian caterer—and perhaps the most successful. It handles cocktail parties, receptions and other soigné soirées for the Opéra, the prime minister's office and for the president himself! The food runs to well-wrought classic dishes (stuffed saddle

of lamb, chicken stuffed with foie gras and truffles), but of late, we've noticed some innovative specialties on the menu: tagliatelle with sea scallops, shellfish terrine served with a smooth lobster coulis, and a delicate, delicious blanquette of turbot and cucumbers.

■ CHARCUTERIE & TAKEOUT

Charcuterie Charles

6th arr. - 10, rue Dauphine - 43 54 25 19
Open 8 a.m.-2 p.m. & 4 p.m.-8 p.m. Closed Sat., Sun. & holidays.

This prize-winning charcuterie, one of the finest in Paris, is the all-city champ when it comes to boudin blanc (white sausage). During the Christmas season, when boudin blanc is a traditional component of holiday meals, Charles displays some twenty varieties, all with different flavorings (truffles, prunes, pistachios and such). Andouillette (that's chitlin's, honey) is another specialty, and we are great fans of Charles's sumptuous terrines (sweetbreads, duck breast and foie gras, herbed ham), his tarts and delicious hams.

Au Cochon d'Auvergne

5th arr. - 48, rue Monge - 43 26 36 21
Open 9 a.m.-1 p.m. & 4 p.m.-7:30 p.m. (Sun. & holidays 9 a.m.-1 p.m.). Closed Mon., Jan. 1 & Dec. 25. No cards.

José Léon really knows how to cook a juicy ham—his is certainly one of the most toothsome in town. Equal praise is warranted for his head cheese, and for the rich rillettes and confits he fashions from southwestern geese sent to Paris just for him. Do make a point of sampling his excellent sugar-free compotes, made from prime, organically grown fruits.

Coesnon

6th arr. - 30, rue Dauphine - 43 54 35 80
Open 8:30 a.m.-8 p.m. Closed Mon., Sun. (except 3 wks. in Dec.), 1 wk. at Easter school holidays, Aug. & holidays.

Because true practitioners of the charcutier's art are becoming ever harder to find, and because Gérard Robert is one of its most eminent representatives, we recommend that you make a special point of visiting this wonderful pork emporium. Robert's boudin blanc and boudin noir are legendary (his chestnut-studded black pudding has won award after award!); what's more, his salt- and smoke-cured pork specialties are top-notch—especially when accompanied by the crisp yet tender sauerkraut he pickles himself. So step up to counter with confidence, knowing that you will be competently and courteously served.

Flo Prestige

16th arr. - 61, av. de la Grande-Armée - 45 00 12 10
16th arr. - 102, av. du Président-Kennedy - 42 88 38 00
1st arr. - 42, pl. du Marché-Saint-Honoré - 42 61 45 46
Open daily 8 a.m.-11 p.m. Delivery.
7th arr. - 36, av. de La Motte-Picquet - 45 55 71 25
Open daily 9:30 a.m.-9:30 p.m. Delivery.
9th arr. - 64, bd Haussmann, Printemps - 42 82 58 82
Open daily 9:30 a.m.-7 p.m. Delivery.
12th arr. - 211, av. Daumesnil 43 44 86 36
Open daily 8 a.m.-9:30 p.m. Delivery.
12th arr. - 22, av. de la Porte de Vincennes - 43 74 54 32
Open daily 9:30 a.m.-11 p.m. Delivery.
15th arr. - 352, rue Lecourbe - 45 54 76 94
Open daily 10:30 a.m.-9:30 p.m. Delivery.

Early or late, every day of the year, you have a sure source of delicious bread, fine wine, yummy desserts—in short, of wonderful meals with Flo Prestige. The selection of foodstuffs is varied and choice, and covers a wide range of prices, from the excellent house sauerkraut to prestigious Petrossian caviar. As of this writing, there are eight Flo Prestige shops in Paris.

Gargantua

1st arr. - 284, rue Saint-Honoré 42 60 52 54
Open 8 a.m.-9 p.m. (Sun. 9 a.m.-8 p.m.). Closed May 1.

The opulent window displays of this well-known charcuterie could satisfy even the gigantically robust appetite of its Rabelaisian namesake. There are cured meats, foie gras and terrines, of course, but Gargantua also carries an abundance of prepared dishes, breads, wines, pastries and ice cream. It's a fine place to go to put together a picnic.

Layrac

6th arr. - 29, rue de Buci - 43 25 17 72
Open daily 9:30 a.m.-2 a.m.

What better place to compose an elegant late-night supper for two than this bright and inviting garden of gourmandise, which that fairly overflows with delicacies both savory and sweet. Prepared dishes can be delivered to your door.

Pou

17th arr. - 16, av. des Ternes - 43 80 19 24
Open 9:30 a.m.-7:15 p.m. Closed Sun. & Mon.

Pou is divine, an excellent charcuterie whose sober decor and rich displays resemble nothing so much as a palace of earthly delights. A look in the window is an enticing, irresistible invitation to buy and taste: black and white boudin sausages, duck pâté en croûte, glittering galantines, cervelas sausage studded with pale-green pistachios and now, sumptuous pastries too. Since everything really is as good as it looks, making a choice is quite a task. And given the prices, paying isn't so easy, either.

Schmid

10th arr. - 76, bd de Strasbourg 46 07 89 74
Open 9 a.m.-7 p.m. (Sat. 8:45 a.m.-6:45 p.m.). Closed Sun. & holidays.
17th arr. - 36, rue de Lévis - 47 63 07 08
Open 9 a.m.-7:30 p.m. (Sun. until 1 p.m.). Closed Mon.
18th arr. - 199, rue Championnet - 46 27 68 24
Open 9 a.m.-7 p.m. Closed Sun. & holidays.

Naturally, with a name like Schmid, you would expect this shop to specialize in sauerkraut. And you wouldn't be wrong. It is excellent—fine, crisp and tart. But don't overlook the aged Muenster, the light and airy Kugelhopf cake and other Alsatian treats.

Vigneau-Desmaret

6th arr. - 105-107, rue de Sèvres 42 22 23 23
Open 9 a.m.-8:30 p.m. Closed Sun.

If ever you should lose your appetite, come over to this old-fashioned charcuterie... we guarantee you'll find it. Who wouldn't salivate at the sight of succulent ham wrapped in a linen cloth and poached in aromatic broth? Who wouldn't long for a bite of perfectly aged saucisson? On hand, too, are light vegetable or fish terrines and an entire list of groceries, vegetables, cheeses and fruits.

Vignon

8th arr. - 14, rue Marbeuf - 47 20 24 26
Open 8 a.m.-8:30 p.m. (Sat. 9 a.m.-7:30 p.m.). Closed Sun. & holidays.

A rather grand marble facade sets the luxurious tone

for this respected Parisian charcuterie. Monsieur Vignon, president of the professional association, turns out a superb terrine of foie gras, remarkable galantines of chicken and duck studded with truffles or pistachios, game pâtés and delicious, old-fashioned head cheese. Parma ham–fanciers should note that Vignon stocks the excellent La Slega brand from Langhirano.

■ CHEESE

Androuët

8th arr. - 41, rue d'Amsterdam
48 74 26 90
Open 10 a.m.-1:30 p.m. & 2:30 p.m.-7:30 p.m. Closed Sun. & holidays.

Pierre Androuet, that most renowned *fromager*, having retired and sold this medieval-looking cheese shop near the Gare Saint-Lazare, nothing is quite the same. Quality varies: superbly aged cheeses sit side by side with far less worthy examples...the rule of thumb for purchasing cheese at Androuët is now "Let the buyer beware!".

Marie-Anne Cantin

7th arr. - 12, rue du Champ-de-Mars - 45 50 43 94
Open 8 a.m.-1 p.m. & 4 p.m.-7:30 p.m. (Sat. 8:30 a.m.-1 p.m. & 3:30 p.m.-7:30 p.m., Sun. 8:30 a.m.-1 p.m.). Closed Mon.

Like father, like daughter: Marie-Anne Cantin is a worthy successor to the late Christian Cantin. Her customers and her cheeses benefit from large doses of tender loving care. She is an ardent defender of real (read: unpasteurized) cheeses and one of the few merchants in Paris to sell Saint-Marcellins as they are preferred on their home turf—in their creamy prime, not in their chalky youth. And so it is with the other cheeses she sells, all of which retain the authentic flavors of their country origins.

Créplet-Brussol

8th arr. - 17, pl. de la Madeleine
42 65 34 32
Open 9 a.m.-7:30 p.m. (Sat. until 7 p.m., Mon. from 2 p.m.). Closed Sun.

Former supplier of Mimolette (a firm, nutty-flavored Dutch cheese) to General de Gaulle, Créplet-Brussol still boasts a large population of celebrities among its clientele. But what really counts here is the cheese: nicely aged Camembert, creamy Brillat-Savarin, farmhouse Reblochon and tangy faisselle (fresh cream cheese) made right in the shop. The butter, cream and crème fraîche are divine, and there is an appetizing selection of foreign cheeses.

Alain Dubois

17th arr. - 80, rue de Tocqueville
42 27 11 38
Open 8 a.m.-1 p.m. & 4 p.m.-7:30 p.m. (Sun. 8 a.m.-1 p.m.). Closed Mon.
17th arr. - 79, rue de Courcelles
43 80 36 42
Open 8:30 a.m.-1 p.m. & 4 p.m.-7:30 p.m. (Mon. from 4 p.m.) Closed Sun. & Aug.

Alain Dubois's Gruyère, aged for at least two years in his cellars, is a royal treat. And there's more: Dubois offers farmhouse goat cheeses, unpasteurized Camembert and authentic Epoisses (which he rinses religiously with marc de Bourgogne). The problem is, now that his shop has expanded, this expert cheese merchant has filled it with so many enticements that we don't know which way to turn. You will not be astonished to learn that Dubois supplies premium cheeses to such great restaurants as Lucas-Carton, Guy Savoy, Michel Rostang, Laurent and more.

Ferme Poitevine

18th arr. - 64, rue Lamarck - 46 06 54 40
Open 8 a.m.-1 p.m. & 4 p.m.-7:45 p.m. (Sun. 8 a.m.-1 p.m.).

Closed Mon., Feb. school holidays & Aug.

Jack Chapu, the cheese man, is a Montmartre personality. He serves all his clients with the same warmth, whether they're famous or not. His many perfectly matured cheeses come from all over the French countryside. We particularly enjoy the flavorful Muensters, the rich Camemberts and the tender little goat cheeses marinated in herbed olive oil.

La Ferme Saint-Hubert

8th arr. - 21, rue Vignon - 47 42 79 20
Open 8:30 a.m.-7:15 p.m. Closed Sun.

Cheese seller Henry Voy is so passionate about his vocation that he has no time for anything else. Morning and night you can find him tending to his Beauforts (aged over two years), his farmhouse goat cheeses or his exclusive Saint-Hubert. He travels all over France, seeking out the best farmhouse cheeses. For true aficionados, Voy unearths such rarities as unpasteurized butter churned with spring water, and delicate goat's-milk butter. You can sample these extraordinary wares in the restaurant next to the shop.

La Fromagerie Boursault

14th arr. - 71, av. du Général-Leclerc - 43 27 93 30
Open 8 a.m.-12:30 p.m. & 4 p.m.-7:15 p.m. (Sun. 8 a.m.-12:30 p.m.). Closed Mon.

It was here that Pierre Boursault created the famous cheese that bears his name. And it is here, naturally enough, that you will find Boursault at its creamy, golden best. Current owner Jacques Vernier has made the shop one of the most pleasant in Paris, a showcase for the rare specimens that he seeks out himself in the French hinterlands. Like incomparable Beauforts aged under his supervision in their native Alpine air; farmhouse goat cheeses (ah, those Picodons!); handcrafted Saint-Nectaire from Auvergne, which has nothing in common with the industrially produced variety; and flawless Camemberts. This is one of the few places on the planet where one may buy Bleu de Termignon, a blue-veined summer cheese from Savoie.

Ferme Saint-Aubin

4th arr. - 76, rue Saint-Louis-en-l'Ile - 43 54 74 54
Open 8 a.m.-1 p.m. & 3:30 p.m.-8 p.m. (Sun. & holidays 8 a.m.-1 p.m.). Closed Mon.

The best cheeses on the Ile-Saint-Louis are available at this recently renovated shop, now under the direction of new owner Odette Jenny. In the vaulted cellars beneath the store she pampers her Pavés d'Auge from Normandy, Epoisses rinsed in marc de Bourgogne, handcrafted Cantal from Auvergne and robust Reblochon with tender, loving care. The fresh cream cheeses, made in the shop, are a delight, as are the goat cheeses from Périgord and the Aveyron region. Mme. Jenny is doing a land-office business with her latest innovation: full prepared meals on trays, complete with wine and Poilâne bread.

Barthélémy

7th arr. - 51, rue de Grenelle - 45 48 56 75
Open 8:30 a.m.-1 p.m. & 3:30 p.m.-7:30 p.m. (Sat. 8:30 a.m.-1:30 p.m. & 3 p.m.-7:30 p.m.). Closed Sun. & Mon.

Roland Barthélémy reigns over a treasure trove of cheeses that he selects from farms all over the French countryside, then brings to perfect ripeness in his cellars. He is also the creator of several marvelous specialties that have the Who's Who of French officialdom beating a path to his door (he supplies

the Elysée Palace, no less). The Boulamour (fresh cream cheese enriched with crème fraîche, currants, raisins and Kirsch) was Barthélémy's invention, as was a delicious Camembert laced with Calvados. We also enjoy the amusing Brie Surprise. But not to worry, tradition is never neglected here, witness the rich-tasting Alpine Beaufort, French Vacherin and the creamy Fontainebleau (the latter is made on the premises). Take one of the attractive cheese trays sold here as your contribution to a dinner party: your hostess will love it!

Tachon

1st arr. - 38, rue de Richelieu - 42 96 08 66
Open 9:30 a.m.-1:30 p.m. & 4 p.m.-8 p.m. Closed Sun., Mon., July, Aug. & holidays.

Jean-Claude Benoit is a native of Sainte-Maure, just like the goat cheese of the same name. His personal network of top-quality producers stretches through all of Touraine, and down into the Poitou and the Yonne. He also stocks excellent sheep's-milk cheeses from Corsica and the Pyrenees; and to go with all of them, Benoit sells an array of handmade sausages.

▨ CHOCOLATE & CANDY

Bonbonnière de la Trinité

8th arr. - 28, rue de Miromesnil 42 65 02 39
Open 10 a.m.-7 p.m. Closed Sat. & Sun.
9th arr. - 4, pl. d'Estienne-d'Orves - 48 74 23 38
Open 9 a.m.-7 p.m. (2 Sun. in Dec.). Closed Sun. & holidays.

This charming little store dates from 1925. A real sweetshop, it stocks some 60 kinds of jam, 25 types of honey, 60 varieties of tea and countless candies. The chocolate truffles are quite good, but

for us, the irresistible attraction here is the range of bitter and super-bitter chocolates sold in great, thick slabs, that are perfect for cooking or guilty nibbling.

Les Bonbons

6th arr. - 6, rue Bréa 43 26 21 15
Open 10 a.m.-8 p.m. (Mon. from 2:30 p.m., except July 14-Oct. 1). Closed Sun., Aug. & holidays.

Mme. Lesieur's miniscule shop will bring out the child in even the most strait-laced adult: it's candyland come to life! We grant you that caramels (hard and soft), candied violets, nougats, barley-sugar sticks are terrible for your teeth, but what a lift they give your spirits! All the traditional sweets of the French provinces are gathered here: cocons de Lyon, ardoises d'Angers, bêtises de Cambrai and more, alongside divinely sticky gingerbread from Basel or Dijon, and satisfyingly substantial slabs of handmade chocolate.

Au Chocolat de Puyricard

7th arr. - 27, av. Rapp 47 05 59 47
Open 9 a.m.-7:30 p.m. (Mon. from 2 p.m.). Closed Sun., Aug. & holidays (except at Christmas).

This shop is the exclusive Parisian source of the sweet (some might say, too sweet) chocolate truffles produced by the Provençal firm, Puyricard. Like the chocolates, the delicious calissons d'Aix (almond candies) are made by hand in small batches. New this year is the *clou de Cézanne*, a chocolate with a light nougatine and pine-nut filling shaped like the paving nails used on the streets of Aix-en-Provence in Cézanne's time.

> *Don't plan to shop on Sundays, the vast majority of Paris stores are closed.*

Christian Constant

6th arr. - 37, rue d'Assas - 45 48 45 51
Open daily 8 a.m.-9 p.m.
7th arr. - 26, rue du Bac - 47 03 30 00
Open daily 8 a.m.-8 p.m.

Christian Constant is mad for chocolate; in fact, not long ago he wrote a definitive book on the subject. His brilliant innovations include a line of flower-scented chocolates (try the ylang-ylang, vetiver or the jasmine varieties...), chocolates filled with delicately spiced creams, others spiked with fruit brandies or cordials, still others incorporating nuts and dried fruit (the conquistador is loaded with hazelnuts, honey and cinnamon). Yum!

Debauve et Gallais

7th arr. - 30, rue des Saints-Pères 45 48 54 67
Open 10 a.m.-7 p.m. Closed Sun. & holidays.

With its picturesque shopfront designed by renowned nineteenth-century architects Percier and Fontaine (classified as a landmark by the Beaux-Arts) and its interior decorated with painted pillars, orange-wedge mirrors and antique lamps, Debauve et Gallais has loads of charm. Their filled chocolates, soft caramels, hazelnut pralines and chocolate truffles, all prettily displayed in glass jars, are perfectly delectable and sell for 360 francs per kilo.

Au Duc de Praslin

16th arr. - 125, av. Victor-Hugo 44 05 07 01
Open 10 a.m.-7 p.m. Closed Sun., Aug. & holidays.

Named for a seventeenth-century aristocrat whose cook invented the confection known as the praline, the Duc de Praslin specializes in crunchy caramel-coated almonds (229 francs per kilo). You'll also want to sample some of the delicious variations on that basic theme: amandas (almonds, nougatine and cocoa), mirabos (nougatine and orange, covered with milk chocolate) and passions (chocolate-coated caramelized almonds). An assortment composed of 7 varieties sells for 270 francs.

A l'Etoile d'Or

9th arr. - 30, rue Fontaine - 48 74 59 55
Open 10:30 a.m.-8 p.m. Closed Sun. & holidays (except at Christmas).

Denise Acabo does not make her own chocolate; rather, she is a true connoisseur who selects the very best handcrafted chocolates made in France, and presents them, in a laudable spirit of impartiality, to her delighted customers (while explaining to interested parties the connection between chocolate and eroticism...). The famed Bernachon chocolates from Lyon are sold in this beautiful turn-of-the-century shop, as well as Dufoux's incomparable palets and wonderful soft-centered bouchées from Voiron.

Fontaine au Chocolat

1st arr. - 193, rue Saint-Honoré 49 27 01 30
Open 10 a.m.-6:50 p.m. Closed Sun., Aug. & holidays.

Pervading Michel Cluizel's shop is a scent of chocolate so intense that your nose will flash an alert to your sweet tooth, and (we guarantee!) have you salivating within seconds. Whether you try one of the five varieties of palets au chocolat or the croquamandes (caramelized almonds coated with extra-dark chocolate), the mendiants studded with nuts and dried fruit or the bold Noir Infini (99 percent cocoa, perfumed with vanilla and spices), you're in for an unforgettable treat.

Godiva

8th arr. - 102, av. des Champs Elysées
45 62 55 17
1st arr. - 237, rue Saint-Honoré 42 60 44 64
Open 9:30 a.m.-7 p.m. Closed Sun.
16th arr. - 157, av. Malakoff - 45 00 39 24
16th arr. - 96, av. Paul Doumer 42 88 59 79
Open 10 a.m.-7 p.m. Closed Sun.

These renowned chocolates are superbly packaged, 'tis true, but we still find them (Lord knows, we've tried, and tried not to) far too sugary-sweet. The sales staffs in all the Godiva shops are uniformly courteous and helpful.

Jadis et Gourmande

3rd arr. - 39, rue des Archives 48 04 08 03
Open 9:30 a.m.-7 p.m. (Sat. from 10 a.m., Mon. from 1 p.m.). Closed Sun.
5th arr. - 88, bd de Port-Royal 43 26 17 75
Open 9:30 a.m.-7 p.m. (Mon. from 1 p.m.). Closed Sun.
8th arr. - 49 bis, av. Franklin-Roosevelt - 45 25 06 04
Open 9:30 a.m.-7 p.m. (Sat. from 10 a.m., Mon. from 1 p.m.). Closed Sun.
8th arr. - 27, rue Boissy-d'Anglas 42 65 23 23
Open 9:30 a.m.-7 p.m. (Sat. 10:30 a.m.-12:30 p.m. & 1:30 p.m.-7 p.m., Mon. from 1 p.m.). Closed Sun.

It is delightful indeed to browse around this sugarplum palace, where one is tempted in turn by delicious bonbons, hard candies, caramels and chocolate in myriad forms. The thick slabs of cooking chocolate make one want to rush to the kitchen and whip up a rich devil's food cake! Our favorite confection here is a thick braid of dark chocolate studded with candied orange peel and hazelnuts. Prices range from 210 to 320 francs per kilo.

Lenôtre

7th arr. - 44, rue du Bac - 42 22 39 39
8th arr. - 15, bd de Courcelles 45 63 87 63
15th arr. - 61, rue Lecourbe - 42 73 20 97
16th arr. - 44, rue d'Auteuil - 45 24 52 52 et 49, av. Victor-Hugo 45 01 71 71
17th arr. - 121, av. de Wagram 47 63 70 30
92200 Neuilly - 3, rue des Huissiers - 46 24 98 68
Open daily 9 a.m.-9 p.m.
16th arr. - 193, av. de Versailles 45 25 55 88
Open daily 9 a.m.-10 p.m.
8th arr. - 5, rue du Havre - 45 22 22 59
Open 10 a.m.-7 p.m. Closed Sun.
9th arr. - Lafayette Gourmet, 40, bd Haussmann - 42 80 45 75
Open daily 9 a.m.-7:45 p.m. Closed Sun.
92100 Boulogne - 79 bis, route de la Reine - 46 05 37 35
Open daily 9 a.m.-9 p.m. (Sun. until 1 p.m.).
Gaston Lenôtre's range of chocolates includes classic, intensely flavored truffles and remarkable palets d'or filled with rich, subtle buttercream. Brisk turnover ensures the freshness of all these marvelous confections. In addition to chocolates, Lenôtre produces creamy caramels, nougatines and, around Christmas, meltingly tender candied chestnuts. These beautifully packaged delights cost from 355 to 500 francs per kilo (the higher price is for liqueur-laced specialties).

La Maison du Chocolat

8th arr. - 52, rue François-ler - 47 23 38 25
8th arr. - 225, rue du Faubourg Saint-Honoré - 42 27 39 44
Open 9:30 a.m.-7 p.m. Closed Sun. & holidays.
There's something of the alchemist about Robert Linxe: never satisfied, he is ever experimenting, innovating, transforming mere cocoa beans into something very precious. His chocolates are among the finest in Paris, maybe even in the world. His renowned buttercream fillings—lemon, caramel, tea, raspberry and rum—will carry you away to gourmet heaven.

Peltier

7th arr. - 66, rue de Sèvres - 47 83 66 12
Open 9:30 a.m.-7:45 p.m. (Sun. 8:30 a.m.-7 p.m.).
7th arr. - 6, rue Saint-Dominique 47 05 50 02
Open 8:15 a.m.-7:45 p.m. (Sun. 8:30 a.m.-7 p.m.).
Peltier's palets d'or (dark chocolates filled with chocolate buttercream and topped with a daub of real gold leaf) are among the capital's finest: light, suave and balanced. The legion of filled varieties, made with superb ingredients, are at least equally as luscious (try the licorice or ginger soft centers to see what we mean!). Expect to pay between 380 and 400 francs per kilo for these prestigious sweets.

Richart

7th arr. - 258, bd Saint-Germain 45 55 66 00
Open 10 a.m.-7 p.m. (Mon. & Sat. from 11 a.m.). Closed Sun. & holidays.
A top-notch *chocolatier* from Lyon has established a Parisian outpost near the House of Parliament. This elegant emporium houses superbly presented chocolates with smooth, scrumptious buttercream fillings (380 francs per kilo) and addictive dark-chocolate bars made from Venezuelan cocoa beans.

Tholoniat

10th arr. - 47, rue du Château-d'Eau - 42 39 93 12
Open 8 a.m.-7 p.m. (Sun. 8:30 a.m.-6 p.m.). Closed Wed. & July 14-Sept. 1.
Within these walls, a master pastry chef spins, sculpts, blows and shapes sugar and chocolate into tiny people, landscapes, fruit, flowers and even wee houses (with furniture!). Incredibly enough, his creations taste as good as they look. Special applause goes to Tholoniat's delicious and unusual pear- and orange-flavored chocolates.

■ COFFEE & TEA

Betjeman and Barton

8th arr. - 23, bd Malesherbes 42 65 35 94
Open 9:30 a.m.-7 p.m. Closed Sun. & holidays.
11th arr. - 24, bd des Filles-du-Calvaire - 40 21 35 52
Open 10 a.m.-7 p.m. Closed Sun. & Mon.
The name on the sign and the shop's decor are veddy, veddy British, but the firm itself is 100 percent French, directed nowadays by Didier Jumeau-Lafond. The range of premium teas on offer is quite extensive, comprising over 150 natural and flavored varieties. Indeed, B and B's teas are of such high quality that Harrod's of London (no less) deigns to market them. To help you choose your blend, the staff will offer you a cup of tea—a comforting and highly civilized custom. Vera Winterfeldt's excellent jams and a line of refreshing fruit "waters" intended to be consumed icy-cold in summer, are worth seeking out here.

Brûlerie des Ternes

16th arr. - 28, rue de l'Annonciation - 42 88 99 90
Open 9 a.m.-7:30 p.m. (Sun. & holidays until 1 p.m.). Closed Mon.
17th arr. - 10, rue Poncelet - 46 22 52 79
Open 9 a.m.-1:30 p.m. & 3:30 p.m.-7:30 p.m. (Sun. & holidays until 1 p.m.). Closed Mon.
Coffees from all over the globe are roasted and ground to perfection in this commendable shop, which draws a clientele made up, in part, of the chic and famous. Featured is the fabled Blue Mountain

coffee from Jamaica, a rare and costly treat (380 francs per kilo). Each customer's individual blend is automatically recorded on a computer, so the recipe need never be lost or forgotten. Flavored coffees (orange, chocolate, vanilla...) are justly popular, and there are 70 kinds of tea in stock as well.

L'Espace Café
11th arr. - 89, bd de Charonne 43 70 28 92
Open 10 a.m.-7 p.m. Closed Sun., Mon., Aug. & holidays.

Michel Toutain has a futuristic outlook on coffee. The shop's computer produces a sensorial analysis that allegedly matches the customer's personality with a particular bean or blend. But, of course, one may simply go in and ask for one's preferred brew: Javanese, Moka, Negus, Mexican or any one of a number of house specialties. All beans sold are carefully selected and roasted each day.

Mariage Frères
4th arr. - 30-32, rue du Bourg-Tibourg - 42 72 28 11
Open daily 10:30 a.m-7:30 p.m.
6th arr. - 13, rue des Grands-Augustins - 40 51 82 50
Open daily 10:30 a.m-7:30 p.m. Closed Mon.

Founded by a family of explorers, one of whose ancestors participated in a delegation sent by Louis XIV to sign a trade agreement with the Shah of Persia, Mariage imports no fewer than 350 varieties of tea from 30 countries. This comprehensive selection, coupled with the firm's unceasing expansion and promotional efforts, makes Mariage Frères the high temple of tea in Paris. Top-of-the-line products include the exquisite Bloomfield Darjeeling, a splendid golden-tipped Grand Yunnan and other rarities that may be sampled in the shop's tea room, ac- com-

panied by pastries or light snacks (see *Tea Rooms*).

Le Palais des Thés
6th arr. - 25, rue de l'Abbé-Grégoire - 45 48 85 81
14th arr. - 21, rue Raymond-Losserand - 43 21 97 97
Open 10:30 a.m.-7 p.m. Closed Sun. & Mon.
16th arr. - 21, rue de l'Annon-ciation - 45 25 51 52
Open 10:30 a.m.-7 p.m. (Sun. 10 a.m.-1 p.m.). Closed Mon.

Founded in 1986 by a consortium of 45 tea lovers, this establishment has risen quickly in the ranks of Parisian tea merchants. More than 350 types of tea can be found here, and a helpful staff is on deck to guide your choice. Those fond of flavored teas (we see you purists out there frowning!) will appreciate the seven-citrus blend and the monks' tea made with ten aromatic plants. All the paraphernalia required by the tea ritual—from teapots to strainers to cups—is also in stock; true tea fanatics will go gaga over the jellies and candies perfumed with their favorite brew. Frequent customers should be sure to ask for the shop's *carte de fideli-thé*, good for a ten percent discount.

Torréfaction Valade
12th arr. - 21, bd de Reuilly - 43 43 39 27
Open 8:45 a.m.-1 p.m. & 4 p.m.-7:30 p.m. (Sat. 8:45 a.m.-7:30 p.m.). Closed Sun., Mon. & holidays. Annual closings not available.

In his modern, clean-lined shop, Pascal Guiraud celebrates his passion for coffee, a passion that he shares with his equally enthusiastic customers. Beans from Cuba, Brazil, Kenya, Costa Rica, Haiti and elsewhere release an irresistible aroma as they roast (and they are prepared only as needed, so the coffee is absolutely fresh). The house blends are marvelous as well: we like the

Italian Roast, which is one of the most popular, the Turkish Special and the spicy Orient Express. Don't overlook the shop's prestigious selection of jams, honey and condiments, or the 110 kinds of tea.

Twinings
8th arr. - 76, bd Haussmann - 43 87 39 84
Open 10 a.m.-7 p.m. Closed Sun., Mon. & holidays.

Twinings's utterly English boutique is, so they claim, the only place to procure genuine Earl Grey tea, the kind still drunk in quantity by the Grey family. Another exceedingly rare variety, Darjeeling Ringtong, is also available, for a rather more hefty sum. Regular customers have their names and favorite blends recorded in a large, bound ledger (oh so chic). Tea fanciers will be glad to learn that Twinings also sells tea in bricks, just as it was sold back in the fourteenth century.

Verlet
1st arr. - 256, rue Saint-Honoré 42 60 67 39
Open 9 a.m.-7 p.m. Closed Sun. & Mon. Easter-Oct.; Sat. & Sun. from Oct.-Easter, July 14-Aug. 20 & holidays.

The Verlet family has been roasting and selling coffee beans in their delightful turn-of-the-century shop since 1880. Pierre Verlet imports the finest coffees from Papua, Costa Rica, Colombia, Jamaica, Malabar, Ethiopia and Brazil, and he also produces several subtle and delicious house blends. He will even create one specially for you, for he is a master at balancing different aromas, different degrees of acidity and bitterness to suit personal taste. If you prefer to sample before you buy, take a seat at one of the little tables and try, perhaps, the Petit Cheval blend, a marvelously balanced and smooth Moka. Verlet also stocks a selection of teas from

237

all over the world and an appetizing array of dried fruits. At lunchtime, crowds pour into the shop for an excellent croque monsieur or a slice of cake and a cup of fragrant coffee.

▉ ETHNIC FOODS

Aux Cinq Continents
11th arr. - 75, rue de la Roquette
43 56 79 69
Open 10 a.m.-1 p.m. & 4 p.m.-8 p.m. (Sun. until 1 p.m.). Closed Sat. & holidays.

The Abramoff family reign over one of the city's most comprehensive sources of grains, cereals and imported delicacies. No fewer than fifteen kinds of rice are on stock here (including wild rice at 90 francs per kilo), along with ten varieties of dried beans (the black beans are wonderful with any kind of smoked meat) and various grades of semolina. Exotica includes a delicious dried mullet roe (called "poutargue," 350 francs per kilo), Iranian pistachios, pastrami, corned beef, chewy Central European breads and flavored vodkas. The store also boasts a fascinating supply of arcane kitchen utensils. Aux Cinq Continents is worth a visit for its nose-tickling scents alone.

Davoli
7th arr. - 34, rue Cler
45 51 23 41
Open 8 a.m.-1 p.m. & 3:30 p.m.-7:30 p.m. (Sun., Wed. & holidays until 1 p.m.). Closed Mon. & 1 month during summer.

Fresh stuffed pasta headlines the offerings: cappelletti filled with meat, tortellini filled with spinach, and scallop-stuffed ravioli to name but a trio of exemplary offerings. The Parma ham is excellent, and the rosy, unctuous mortadella hails straight from Bologna. A selection of fine Italian wines (as well as liqueurs and aperitivi) lets you

wash all the good stuff down in the proper style.

Finkelsztajn
4th arr. - 27, rue des Rosiers - 42 72 78 91
Open 10 a.m.-2 p.m. & 3 p.m.-7:30 p.m. (Sat. 10 a.m.-1:30 p.m. & 3 p.m.-7:30 p.m.; Sun. 10 a.m.-7:30 p.m.). Closed Mon. & Tues. (except holidays).
4th arr. - 24, rue des Ecouffes
48 87 92 85
Open Mon., Thurs. & Fri. 9 a.m.-1:30 p.m. & 2:30 p.m.-7:30 p.m. (Sat. 10 a.m.-1:30 p.m. & 3 p.m.-7:30 p.m.; Sun. 9 a.m.-7:30 p.m.). Closed Tues. & Wed. (except holidays).

In this pretty shop, the hospitable Sacha proposes several robust and savory Yiddish specialties. Among our favorites: the stuffed carp, chopped liver and delicious little piroshki (small turnovers or dumplings filled with a savory or sweet stuffing). For dessert, try the authentic vatrouchka (Russian cheesecake) or the poppyseed cakes. In the other shop, Sacha's daughter and her husband propose traditional Jewish dishes, all made on the premises, all perfectly yummy.

The General Store
7th arr. - 82, rue de Grenelle - 45 48 63 16
Open 10 a.m.-7:30 p.m. Closed Sun.

Tacos, tortillas and all the other traditional fixings for a Tex-Mex feast may be found in this spic-and-span little shop. But the inventory doesn't stop there: You'll find buttermilk-pancake mix, a selection of California wines (not just Paul Masson), familiar American packaged foods (Karo syrup, cream cheese, canned pumpkin, chocolate chips, Hellmann's mayo) and even fresh cranberries at holiday time. If you crave a sweet snack, look for the delectable pecan squares and cookies whipped up fresh every day. As you would expect, English

is spoken, and you can count on a warm welcome from the friendly owners (neither of whom, curiously, is American).

Jo Goldenberg
4th arr. - 7, rue des Rosiers - 48 87 20 16
Open daily 8:30 a.m.-midnight. (Sat. until 2 a.m.).

For over 60 years, this far-famed little grocery-cum-restaurant has supplied the Ashkenazi community of Paris with stuffed carp, zesty herring with a procession of sauces, smoked salmon, corned beef, smoked tongue and even caviar, which you can wash down with one of the many different vodkas.

Goldenberg
17th arr. - 69, av. de Wagram
42 27 41 85
Open daily 8:30 a.m.-midnight.

Familiar deli fare, made measurably more exotic by the fact that it's served within sight of the Arc de Triomphe. There's herring, there's corned beef, there's gefilte fish (stuffed carp), there's pastrami and that well-known Yiddish dessert, the brownie.

Heratchian Frères
9th arr. - 6, rue Lamartine - 48 78 43 19
Open 8:30 a.m.-7 p.m. (Mon. until 2 p.m.). Closed Sun.

All the mellifluous idioms of the Near East and the Balkans are spoken (and understood) at this fascinating, fragrant bazaar. The sales staff will help you to fat, purple Kalamata olives, golden thyme-blossom honey, genuine sheep's-milk feta, Salonikan yogurt (made from a mix of cow's and sheep's milk) and savory kibbeh (bulghur and ground lamb, onions and pine nuts deep-fried or—for the daring—served raw). Nice prices.

Izraël

4th arr. - 30, rue Françis-Miron
42 72 66 23
*Open 9:30 a.m.-1 p.m. &
2:30 p.m.-7 p.m. (Sat. 9:30 a.m.-
7 p.m.). Closed Sun., Mon., Aug.
& holidays.*

Solski and Françoise Izraël
are the masters of this colorful,
richly scented realm of spices,
herbs, exotic foods and condiments. Burlap sacks overflow with basmati rice from
Pakistan and Thailand; crates
host fat dates and figs from
Turkey; Greek olives soak in
barrels of herbed, lemony
marinades. Curries, chutneys
and pink lentils have jour-
neyed from India to this Paris
spot; from Mexico, tacos and
several types of fiery chiles.
Argentinian empanadas,
Louisiana pecans, Chinese
candied ginger and no fewer
than five types of coconut milk
are just some of the other
international representatives
found in this unique emporium.

Kioko

2nd arr. - 46, rue des Petits-
Champs - 42 61 33 66
*Open 10 a.m.-7:30 p.m. Closed
Sun. & holidays.*

All the hard-to-find in-
gredients that go into Japanese cuisine can be purchased
at this unprepossessing little
grocery. In addition to tofu,
taro, Japanese-style rice and
wheat noodles, Kioko stocks
good native beers, like Kirin
and Sapporo. Labels are translated from Japanese into
French to ease (!) your shopping experience.

Marks & Spencer

9th arr. - 35, bd Haussmann - 47
42 42 91
*Open 9:30 a.m.-7 p.m. (Tues.
from 10 a.m.). Closed Sun.*

The food section of this all-
British emporium provides
ample evidence that English
gastronomy is not, as Parisians
tend to think, a joking matter.
The French are genetically in-
capable, for example, of pro-

ducing good bacon. Marks &
Spencer's is wonderful: meaty,
smoky, with no nasty bits of
bone, no inedible rind. The
cheese counter features
Stilton, Cheddar, Leicester and
other delicious English dairy
products, and the grocery
shelves are crowded with all
sorts of piquant condiments
and chutneys. Teas, biscuits,
jams and marmalades are legion, of course, and a special
refrigerated case offers fresh
sandwiches for a quick lunch
on the run. Prices in the Paris
branch are considerably
higher than on Marks &
Sparks' home turf.

Mourougane France

10th arr. - 83, passage Brady - 42
46 06 06
*Open 9 a.m.-8:30 p.m. Closed
Sun.*

Over the past decade, Indo-
Pakistani cooking has conquered Paris with its sunny,
fragrant, spicy dishes.
Mourougane, set in the quiet
passage Brady, carries marvelous basmati rice, papadums,
chutneys and all the colorful
spices, chiles and curries one
might need to whip up a full-
course Indian or Pakistani
feast.

Au Régal

16th arr. - 4, rue Nicolo - 42 88
49 15
*Open 9 a.m.-11 p.m. (Sun.
10 a.m.-3 p.m. & 6 p.m.-
11 p.m.). Closed 2 wks. wk. of
Aug. 15.*

Delicacies from all the
Russias are spotlighted here:
caviar, vodkas of every
description, coulibiac (salmon
baked in a pastry crust) and
pirozhki (more pastry-wrap-
ped nibbles), marinated herring and blinis, vatrouchka
(cheesecake) and walnut tart.

---

*The prices in this guide reflect
what establishments were
charging at press time.*

Spécialités Antillaises

20th arr. - 14-16, bd de Belleville
43 58 31 30
*Open 10 a.m.-7:15 p.m. (Sat.
from 9 a.m.; Sun. 9 a.m.-noon).
Closed Mon. & 1st wk. of Jan.*

Here's a one-stop shop for
Creole fixings and take-out
foods. Among the latter, we
recommend the scrumptious
stuffed crabs, the crispy accras
(salt-cod fritters), the Creole
sausage and a spicy avocado
dish called féroce d'avocat.
The grocery section offers
tropical fruits flown in fresh
from the West Indies, as well
as a selection of exotic frozen
fish (shark, gilthead...) and an
array of rums and punches.

Tang Frères

13th arr. - 48, av. d'Ivry - 45 70
80 00
*Open 9 a.m.-7:30 p.m. Closed
Mon.*

Three times a week a cargo
plane flies into Paris bearing a
shipment earmarked for the
Tang brothers. This gastronomic dynasty runs the biggest
Asian supermarket in town,
stocked with all manner of
mysterious (to the uninitiated)
roots, powders, dried
mushrooms, canned bamboo
shoots, rice and noodles,
birds' nests, sharks' fins and so
on... and on—there are literally
thousands of items to choose
from. Don't miss the great
ready-to-eat Peking duck.

Than Binh

5th arr. - 18, rue Lagrange - 43
54 66 11
*Open 9:30 a.m.-7:30 p.m.
Closed Mon. & Aug. 15-22.*

From perfumed rice to inst-
ant soups, from fresh tropical
fruit and vegetables to dried
fish, sweet bean cakes and a
selection of prepared foods
(terrific fresh dim-sum), the
Than Binh stores stock a
staggering assortment of Chinese, Japanese and Vietnamese
food products. Throngs of
Asian shoppers come here
regularly to purchase their
culinary supplies, but the

239

crowds don't seem to faze the calm and amiable staff.

■ FRUITS & VEGETABLES

Palais du Fruit
2nd arr.- 74, rue Montorgueil
42 33 22 15
Open 8:30 a.m.-7:30 p.m. (Sun. & holidays until 1 p.m.). Closed Mon., Jan. 1 & Dec. 25.

Superb fruits and vegetables from all over the globe, beautifully presented. Even when skies are gray in France, in Chile or the Antilles gorgeous produce ripens in the sun, then is picked and packed off to this cheerful store. Wide choice, remarkable quality.

Fruits de France
4th arr. - 72, rue Saint-Louis-en-l'Ile - 43 26 83 02
Open 8 a.m.-1 p.m. & 4 p.m.-8:30 p.m. (Tues. from 4 p.m.; Sun. & holidays until 1 p.m.). Closed Mon. & summer.

Fresh, fresh, fresh: the herbs, the fruits, the vegetables are above reproach at Jean-Louis Turpin's produce stand. People in a hurry can have their veggies custom-peeled while they wait (or while they pick up their dry-cleaning down the street).

Le Fruitier d'Auteuil
16th arr. - 5, rue Bastien-Lepage
45 27 51 08
Open 6:30 a.m.-1 p.m. & 3:30 p.m.-7:30 p.m. (holidays until 1 p.m.). Closed Sun. & Aug.

Bernard Rapine, president of the Fruit Retailers' Union, has a personal and professional interest in displaying the best produce he can find. He claims —and we have seen it to be true—that any store posting the union label (the word *fruitier* printed over a basket of fruit) is honor-bound to provide top-quality merchandise and service. Rapine's shop is a fine example.

■ GOURMET SPECIALTIES

Caves Augé
8th arr. - 116, bd Haussmann
45 22 16 97
Open 9 a.m.-8 p.m. (Mon. from 1 p.m.). Closed Sun. & holidays.

Augé was one of the first shops in town (maybe the only?) where eccentric gourmets could purchase such rare delicacies as bear steaks, reindeer roasts and elephant trunks. Nowadays this rather luxurious little shop specializes in fine wines and brandies. There is still a small grocery section, which includes excellent tinned foods (always handy to have in the cupboard) and an enticing assortment of boxed cookies. But the pride of the house is its wine cellar (the oldest in Paris) which features an exceptional choice of "minor" Bordeaux, great Burgundies, Cognacs and Calvados.

Detou
2nd arr. - 58, rue de Tiquetonne
42 33 96 43
Open 8 a.m.-6 p.m. (Sat. until noon, except in Dec.: until 5 p.m.). Closed Sun. & holidays.

Home-bakers browse happily among the pastry supplies that comprise Detou's principal stock-in-trade: baking chocolate, powdered almonds, candied fruit and the like. But there are also rare and delicious jams here, as well as unusual cookies and savory canned goods (the mushrooms are particularly fine), Champagnes and foie gras. Quality merchandise at surprisingly moderate prices.

Shopping in the seventh

Ministries, embassies and well-heeled residents of the posh seventh arrondissement are lucky to live amid some of the best food shops in Paris. Quality is the rule and you can fill your market basket as fast as you empty your pocketbook in the rue du Bac, the rue Saint-Dominique and the rue Cler. On the way, give your eyes a feast too by peeking into some of the flowered courtyards tucked away behind wrought-iron gates. Try the bread from Jean-Luc Poujauran (20 rue Jean-Nicot), caviar from Petrossian (18 boulevard de Latour-Maubourg), cheese from Marie-Anne Cantin (12 rue du Champ-de-Mars), and chocolates from Debauve et Gallais (30 rue des Saints-Pères).

Faguais
8th arr. - 30, rue La Trémoille
47 20 80 91
Open 9:15 a.m.-7 p.m. Closed Sun. & holidays.

Yes, Grandmother would feel quite at home in this charming gourmet shop. A dizzying variety of temptations is set out neatly on the shelves. Old-fashioned jams, oils, honeys, cookies, spices, vinegars and condiments fairly cry out to be bought and sampled. As the shop's pervasive fragrance implies, fresh coffee beans are roasted on the premises daily.

Fauchon
8th arr. - 26, pl. de la Madeleine
47 42 60 11
Open 9:40 a.m.-7 p.m. Closed Sun.

In 1886, at the age of 30, Auguste Fauchon opened his *épicerie fine* on the place de la

Madeleine, specializing in quality French foodstuffs. The rest is history. After more than a century, Fauchon is the un-contested paragon of what a luxury gourmet emporium should be. The energetic and youthful president of Fauchon, Martine Premat, has brought a new luster and energy to the firm. All 300 employees are committed to the task of tasting, testing and selling the very finest, the rarest, the most unusual foods in the world. The number of spices alone—4,500—is enough to make your head spin. And you'll find such delicacies as black-fig or watermelon preserves, lavender or buckwheat honey, Mim tea from India or Kee-yu tea from China, lavish displays of prime vegetables and fruits, and a world-renowned collection of vintage wines and brandies. As for the pastries, well...you should know that Pierre Hermé is one of the finest *chef-pâtissiers* in the business.

Fouquet

8th arr. - 22, rue François-ler - 47 23 30 36
Open 9:30 a.m.-7:30 p.m. Closed Sun. & holidays.
9th arr. - 36, rue Laffitte - 47 70 85 00
Open 10 a.m.-6:30 p.m. Closed Sat., Sun. & holidays.

Christophe Fouquet is the most recent representative of the illustrious family of grocers who have been selling choice foodstuffs at this address since 1852. Fine chocolates are a long-standing specialty at this pretty, old-fashioned shop, but don't overlook the rare mustards (flavored with black currants, oranges or raspberries), appetizing bottled sauces, vinegars distilled according to a secret house recipe, liqueur-laced jams, fruity olive oils, imported cakes and cookies and excellent white brandies. All the items are attractively packaged and make much-appreciated gifts.

Hédiard

7th arr. - 126, rue du Bac - 45 44 01 98
8th arr. - 21, pl. de la Madeleine 42 66 44 36
16th arr. - 6, rue Donizetti - 40 50 71 94
Open 9:30 a.m.-9 p.m. Closed Sun.
16th arr. - 70, av. Paul-Doumer 45 04 51 92
17th arr. - 106, bd de Courcelles 47 63 32 14
Open 9:30 a.m.-10 p.m. Closed Sun.
16th arr. - 113, av. Victor-Hugo 44 05 09 88
Open 9:30 a.m.-8 p.m. Closed Sun.
1st arr. - Forum des Halles, 1, rue Pierre-Lescot - 40 39 98 04
Open 10:30 a.m.-7:30 p.m. Closed Sun.
15th arr. - 131, rue Saint-Charles 40 59 86 41
Open 9:30 a.m.-7:30 p.m. Closed Sun.

Only the finest, rarest foodstuffs are deemed worthy of entry into this shrine of epicureanism, founded in 1854. Distinguished smoked salmon from the best "schools," sophisticated sugars and syrups, pedigreed Ports, vintage wines and brandies, and over 4,500 carefully chosen grocery items attract virtually every cultivated palate in town. Even the ordinary is extraordinary here: mustard spiked with Cognac; vinegar flavored with seaweed; opulent fruits and vegetables, always prime, that hail from the ends of the earth. Many of the items are as costly as they are exotic, but the wines consistently offer excellent value for the money.

CAVIAR & SALMON

Caviar Kaspia

8th arr. - 17, pl. de la Madeleine 42 65 33 52
Open 9 a.m.-12:30 a.m. Closed Sun.

Caviar, it would seem, is best savored in a setting of serene austerity. Such is the impression made by the stark interior of Caviar Kaspia, where the choicest Russian and Iranian roes are sold, along with an assortment of superb smoked fish. The tender, buttery salmon is flawless, but we come for the fine smoked eel, trout or sturgeon, all of which are models of their kind. Should a hunger pang occur at the sight of these delights (how could it not?), just step upstairs to the first-floor restaurant, where all the house specialties may be ordered à la carte.

Le Coin du Caviar

4th arr. - 2, rue de la Bastille - 48 04 82 93
Open 10 a.m.-2:30 p.m. & 7 p.m.-11:30 p.m. (Sat. 7 p.m.-11:30 p.m.). Closed Sun.

No doubt about it, the neighborhood around the Bastille has become madly fashionable. The Coin du Caviar, right in the thick of things (across the street from the popular Bofinger brasserie), has made faithful customers out of the most finicky caviar and smoked salmon–fanciers. Prime Russian or Iranian caviars are featured (depending on the market); the pale, delicately smoky salmon hails from Denmark.

Comptoir du Saumon

4th arr. - 60, rue François-Miron 42 77 23 08
8th arr. - 61, rue Pierre-Charron 45 61 25 14
15th arr. - 116, rue de la Convention - 45 54 31 16
17th arr. - 3, av. de Villiers - 40 53 89 00
18th arr. - 139, rue Ordener - 42 52 80 73
Open 10 a.m.-10 p.m. Closed Sun. & holidays.

The French are crazy about smoked salmon. And it is this untempered enthusiasm that's behind the success of the Comptoir du Saumon, where Irish, Swedish, Norwegian and Scottish fish are sold at attractive prices. Also stocked are smoked trout and eel, Dutch herring, Danish marinated herring and Iranian caviar. The premium vodkas and acquavits are perfect partners for the fish, and if you really can't wait for a taste, grab a table at the shop's snack bar.

Flora Danica
8th arr. - 142, av. des Champs-Elysées - 43 59 20 41
Open 10 a.m.-10 p.m. (Sun. & holidays 11 a.m.-8 p.m.; Dec. 24 until 5 p.m.).

Does the phrase "Danish gastronomy" sound fishy to you? So it should, for salmon in myriad forms is its very foundation. Delicate pink specimens from the Baltic Sea are sold here, both smoked and marinated with dill. We suggest that you sample the delicious Danish herring—in fact, why not the entire array of sweet-and-sour sauces that go with it—then wash it all down with an icy, pale Carlsberg beer.

Dominique
6th arr. - 19, rue Bréa
43 27 08 80
Open daily 9:30 a.m.-2:30 p.m. & 5:15 p.m.-10:30 p.m. Closed 1 wk. Feb. school holidays & mid-July to mid-Aug.

Dominique has been a fixture on the Montparnasse circuit since time immemorial, and will probably remain so, despite occasional lapses in food and service. The take-out shop remains an excellent source of caviar, Danish smoked salmon and herring, as well as tender blinis, zakuski (traditional Russian hors d'oeuvres) and the accompanying heady Russian vodka.

Maxoff
7th arr. - 44, rue de Verneuil - 42 60 60 43
Open 10:30 a.m.-3 p.m. & 6:30 p.m.-10:30 p.m. (Dec. 24 & 31 until 9 p.m.). Closed Sun., Aug. & holidays

Ossetra and sevruga caviars from Iran are featured in the take-out section of this pleasant little restaurant. Smaller spenders may prefer the pressed roe (it's considerably cheaper), or the good Danish smoked salmon, smoked eel, herring (there are ten types) or the assortment of Russian dishes like koulibiac (salmon pie), piroshki and cheesecake. Everything is fresh and of good quality.

Petrossian
7th arr. - 18, bd La Tour-Maubourg - 45 51 70 64
Open 9 a.m.-8 p.m. Closed Sun.

The Petrossian family introduced sturgeon eggs to France in the 1920s, a commercial coup that won them the undying gratitude of the newly born Soviet Union. Today Christian Petrossian still enjoys the rare privilege of choosing the very best roes on site at Caspian fishing ports. In addition to sublime ossetra, sevruga, beluga and pressed caviar, there are remarkably rich and unctuous Norwegian smoked salmon, smoked eel and sturgeon, Russian salmon roe and a multitude of excellent vodkas. Splendiferous gift baskets can be composed according to your tastes and budget.

ESCARGOTS

L'Escargot de la Butte
18th arr. - 48, rue Joseph-de-Maistre - 46 27 38 27
Open 8:30 a.m.-7:30 p.m. (Sun. Sept. 1-March 31: until 1 p.m.). Closed Sun. (April 1-Aug. 31), Mon. & July 15-Aug. 15.

"It's really a shame, but there are no more escargots de Bourgogne left in France," laments Monsieur Marchal. He imports them, therefore, from Germany. But his petits-gris come straight from the Provençal countryside, and arrive still frisky at his little shop located at the foot of the Butte Montmartre. He stuffs them with a deliciously fragrant blend of pure butter, gar-lic and parsley, and they are a remarkable treat!

La Maison de l'Escargot
15th arr. - 79, rue Fondary - 45 75 31 09
Open 8:30 a.m.-8 p.m. (Sun. & holidays 9 a.m.-1 p.m.). Closed Mon. & July 14-Sept. 1.

Snail fanciers from surrounding neighborhoods think nothing of making the trek to this commendable shop. Live petits-gris and escargots de Bourgogne of all sizes are prepared with a delicious snail butter—which is not too strong, not too bland—that is made according to the specifications of a secret recipe developed here in 1894. The butter may also be purchased separately. If you want to sample the wares on the spot, cross the street to the little stand opposite the shop.

FOIE GRAS

Comptoir Corrézien du Foie Gras et du Champignon
15th arr. - 8, rue des Volontaires 47 83 52 97
Open 9 a.m.-1:30 p.m. & 3 p.m.-8 p.m. (Mon. from 3:30 p.m.). Closed Sun.

Chantal Larnaudie is an energetic young woman who comes from a long line of foie-gras specialists. The specimens she offers in her shop, whole poached fatted goose liver, preserved in a terrine, are fine indeed, and attractively priced to boot. Don't miss her wide selection of fragrant wild mushrooms, sold fresh in season, or dried.

Le Comptoir du Foie Gras (Bizac)
1st arr. - 6, rue des Prouvaires 42 36 26 27
Open 8 a.m.-7 p.m. Closed Sun.

This shop is the Parisian outpost of Bizac, a renowned foie-gras processing firm from Brive, in southwestern France.

Foie gras in cans and jars comes fully cooked or, if you prefer, lightly cooked (heated just to 90 degrees). If you wish to try your hand at preparing your own terrine de foie gras, raw duck and goose livers are available.

Divay (Au Bon Porc)

10th arr. - 52, rue du Faubourg-Saint-Denis - 47 70 06 86
Open 7 a.m.-1:30 p.m. & 4 p.m.-7:30 p.m. (Sun., Wed. & holidays 7:30 a.m.-1 p.m.). Closed Mon. & Aug.
17th arr. - 4, rue Bayen - 43 80 16 97
Open 7:30 a.m.-1:30 p.m. & 3:30 p.m.-7:30 p.m. (Sun. & holidays 7:30 a.m.-1 p.m.). Closed Mon. & Aug.

Priced at 650 francs per kilo, Divay sells the least expensive fattened goose liver to be found in the city. What's more, it's delicious. You'll find great traditional charcuterie here too.

Dubernet

1st arr. - Forum des Halles, 210, porte Lescot, niveau -2 - 42 33 88 46
Open 10:30 a.m.-7:30 p.m. Closed Sun. (except 2 Sun. before Christmas).
7th arr. - 2, rue Augereau - 45 55 50 71
Open 9 a.m.-1:30 p.m. & 3:30 p.m.-7:30 p.m. (holidays 10 a.m.-1 p.m.). Closed Sun., Mon. & Aug. 1-15.
92800 Puteaux - Centre commercial Les Quatre Temps, niveau 1 - 47 73 70 02
Open 10 a.m.-8 p.m. Closed Sun.

These foies gras come from Saint-Sever, in the Landes region of Southwestern France. Whole fatted goose and duck livers are sold fully cooked in cans or lightly cooked (just pasteurized) in jars. Prices are moderate.

Aux Ducs de Gascogne

1st arr. - 4, rue du Marché-Saint-Honoré - 42 60 45 31
Open 10 a.m.-7 p.m. Closed Sun. & Aug.

4th arr. - 111, rue Saint-Antoine 42 71 17 72
Open 9:30 a.m.-2 p.m. & 5 p.m.-8 p.m. (Mon. from 3 p.m.). Closed Sun.
8th arr. - 112, bd Haussmann 45 22 54 04
Open 10 a.m.-7:15 p.m. (Mon. from noon). Closed Sun. & holidays.
15th arr. - 221, rue de la Convention - 48 28 32 09
Open 9:30 a.m.-1 p.m. & 4 p.m.-8 p.m. (Mon. from 4 p.m., holidays 9:30 a.m.-1 p.m.). Closed Sun.
20th arr. - 41, rue des Gatines 43 66 99 99
Open 9 a.m.-12:45 p.m. & 3 p.m.-7:45 p.m. (Mon. from 3 p.m.). Closed Sun. & 3 wks. in Aug.

This multistore chain specializes in canned and lightly cooked foie gras, sold at rather steep prices, but the patron is a real charmer.

Foie Gras Luxe

1st arr. - 26, rue Montmartre - 42 36 14 73
Open 6 a.m.-noon & 2:30 p.m.-5 p.m. (Mon. from 8 a.m.). Closed Sat. (except morning in Dec.), Sun. & holidays.

This worthy establishment sells raw foie gras year-round, as well as lightly cooked fatted goose and duck livers, and marvelous cured hams from Parma, San Daniele and the Ardennes.

Les Produits Jean-Legrand

8th arr. - 58, rue des Mathurins 42 65 50 46
Open 10 a.m.-2 p.m. & 3 p.m.-6:30 p.m. (Wed. 10 a.m.-1:30 p.m. & 3:30 p.m.-6:30 p.m.) Closed Sat. (except Nov. & Dec.), Sun., 1 wk. at Easter, Aug. & holidays.
17th arr. - 11, rue Pierre-Demours - 40 55 92 20
Open 8:30 a.m.-2 p.m. & 4:30 p.m.-8 p.m. (Sun. 8 a.m.-1 p.m.). Closed Mon.

This reputable processing concern turns out a fine terrine of fresh fatted goose liver, an equally tasty poached version, duck foie gras in a terrine and

some interesting canned entrées: daube of boar with cranberries, beef goulash and lotte in mustard sauce.

HONEY, JAMS & SYRUP

Daire–Aux Miels de France

8th arr. - 71, rue du Rocher - 45 22 23 13
Open 9:30 a.m.-2 p.m. & 2:30 p.m.-7 p.m. (Mon. from 2:30 p.m.). Closed Sun., Aug. & holidays.

Renée Daire stocks a dozen of the most select French honeys: pine, oak, chestnut, heather, lavender, rosemary, thyme, acacia and more. Pollen and royal jelly are also on sale, as well as a richly honey-flavored gingerbread studded with walnuts and filberts. The delicious homemade jams that glitter enticingly on the shelves are prepared by none other than Mme. Daire herself.

Le Furet

10th arr. - 63, rue de Chabrol 47 70 48 34
Open 8:30 a.m.-8 p.m. Closed Sun.

Alain Furet is a chocolatier first and foremost, but he also makes fabulous jams from recipes developed by Monsieur Tanrade, long the top name in French preserves. Furet took over the Tanrade plant, and now turns out succulent jams (raspberry, strawberry, apricot, blackcurrant...); he is also putting the finishing touches on a recipe of his own, for confiture au chocolat—we can't wait!

Maison du Miel

8th arr. - 24, rue Vignon - 47 42 26 70
Open 9:30 a.m.-7 p.m. (Mon. until 6 p.m.). Closed Sun.

Make a beeline to this "House of Honey" to try varieties from the various regions of France. There's Corsican honey, luscious pine honey from the Vosges mountains (which comes highly recommended for bronchial irritations), Provençal lavender honey, as well as choice varieties from the Alps and Auvergne, all rigorously tested by a busy hive of honey tasters. In addition, you'll find honey "by-products," such as beeswax, candles, pollen and royal jelly, as well as a wide range of honey-based cosmetics.

A la Mère de Famille

9th arr. - 35, rue du Faubourg-Montmartre - 47 70 83 69
Open 8:30 a.m.-1:30 p.m. & 3 p.m.-7 p.m. Closed Sun., Mon., Aug. & holidays.

Founded in 1761, this adorable emporium is the dean of Paris sweetshops. Today it is still a showcase for the very best sugarplums that the French provinces produce. You'll find specialties from every region: cakes, glazed chestnuts, hard candies, exquisite jams and honeys and delicious dried fruits. The current owner, Serge Neveu, is a professional *chocolatier*: his palet guanaja is deep, dark and delicious! Excellent prices.

OILS

A l'Olivier

4th arr. - 23, rue de Rivoli - 48 04 86 59
Open 9:30 a.m.-1 p.m. & 2 p.m.-7 p.m. Closed Sun., Mon. & holidays.

In this freshly refurbished shop connoisseurs will find not only several fine varieties of olive oil but walnut oil, grilled-almond oil, pumpkin-seed oil, hazelnut oil and an incomparable top-secret blend of virgin olive oils as well. We applaud the shop's policy of selling exceptionally expensive and perishable oils in quarter-liter bottles. Fine vinegars and mustards are presented too—everything you need to mix up a world-class vinaigrette!

Jean-Claude Cornu

9th arr. - 82, rue de Clichy - 48 74 60 86
Open 9:30 a.m.-1:30 p.m. & 3 p.m.-8:30 p.m. Closed Sun., Aug. & holidays.

Inside this adorable little shop is a veritable treasure trove of top-quality oils. First pressings of all sorts are featured—from peanut, sunflower and nettle to poppy, walnut and hazelnut. Fragrant, fruity olive oil from Tunisia comes highly recommended, but conspicuous consumers may prefer the horrendously expensive variety from Provence.

PASTA

Biletta

16th arr. - 35, rue d'Auteuil - 42 88 58 88
Open 8 a.m.-1 p.m. & 3:30 p.m.-7:45 p.m. (Sat. from 7 a.m.; Sun. 8:30 a.m.-1 p.m.). Closed Mon. & Aug.

The selection is small—tagliatelle, ravioli, gnocchi, lasagne—but the pasta is golden and finely textured and wonderfully flavored. Try the fine Italian hams and salamis, too.

Cipolli

13th arr. - 81, rue Bobillot - 45 88 26 06
Open 7 a.m.-1 p.m. & 3 p.m.-7:30 p.m. (Mon. from 3:30 p.m.). Closed Sun. & Aug. No cards.

Mr. Cipolli kneads and stretches his golden dough into an appetizing array of pasta specialties. The tagliatelle and ravioli have an authentic, old-fashioned flavor, while his lasagne is nothing short of sublime. The stuffed pastas (cappelletti filled with minced beef and ham, or mushrooms, or spinach and ricotta; "priests' hats" stuffed with salmon or ricotta and ham) are tender and savory. Prices range from 43 to 75 francs per kilo.

TRUFFLES

Maison de la Truffe

8th arr. - 19, pl. de la Madeleine 42 65 53 22
Open 9 a.m.-9 p.m. (Mon. until 8 p.m.). Closed Sun.

Alongside extraordinary charcuterie, foie gras, good salmon and prepared foods, this luxurious food emporium offers truffles (both freshly dug and sterilized and bottled) at prices that are emphatically not of the bargain-basement variety. The season for fresh black truffles runs from October to late March; fresh white truffles are imported from Italy in November and December. Owner Guy Monier recently set aside a corner of his shop for tasting: customers may order from a brief menu featuring dishes made with the sublime fungus (truffes en salade, truffes en feuilleté, truffles with fresh pasta, in risotto...). Look too for the range of oils, vinegars and mustards all perfumed with—you guessed it!

■ HEALTH FOODS

Herboristerie du Palais-Royal

1st arr. - 11, rue des Petits-Champs - 42 97 54 68
Open 8:30 a.m.-7 p.m. (Sat. 10:30 a.m.-6:30 p.m.). Closed Sun. & holidays.

A venerable herbalist shop that presents a vast and fragrant array of dried medicinal plants and herb teas. The 600 varieties are stocked in a cool, dark cellar to preserve their beneficial properties. Also on hand are plant-based health, beauty and hygiene products.

Grand Appétit

4th arr. - 9, rue de la Cerisaie 40 27 04 95
Open 10 a.m.-8 p.m. (Fri. & Sun. until 4 p.m.). Closed Sat. & 2 wks. in Aug.

Mme. David is committed to healthy living and a healthy environment. Her range of macrobiotic and natural foods is supplemented by a selection of "earth-friendly" household products. Her supply of organically grown fruits and vegetables is renewed three times a week for freshness. The shop's annex restaurant (vegetarian, of course) is very popular—even more so since Elton John was spotted there!

La Vie Claire
6th arr. - 126, bd Raspail - 45 48 82 70
Open 9:30 a.m.-7 p.m. (Sat. 10 a.m.-1 p.m. & 3 p.m.-6 p.m.). Closed Sun. & holidays.
Organically grown fruits and vegetables and whole-grain breads are delivered daily to this pleasant shop, which also carries farm-fresh eggs and milk, and soy-based yogurts. Those of you on salt- or sugar-free diets will find the products you need right here, alongside cosmetics and household cleaners that don't violate the rights of animals or the environment.

Veggie
7th arr. - 38, rue de Verneuil - 42 61 28 61
Open 9:30 a.m.-2:30 p.m. & 4 p.m.-7:30 p.m. Closed Sun., 1 month during summer, & holidays. No cards.
Fresh carrot juice and soy-milk desserts attract a faithful corps of regular customers to Mme. Janson's shop. But she also supplies customers with herb teas and plant-based beverages, whole grains, oils and diet supplements, as well as a selection of cosmetics for natural beauties and environmentally sound cleaning products for concerned housekeepers. Busy vegetarians will appreciate her line of meatless take-out dishes (vegetable gratins, couscous, sweet and savory tarts...).

Monday, like Sunday, is a day of rest for many shopkeepers.

Le Bol en Bois
13th arr. - 40, rue Pascal - 47 07 07 01
Open 9:30 a.m.-9:30 p.m. Closed Sun. & holidays.
Specialists in macrobiotic fruits and vegetables, the "Wooden Bowl" also imports health foods from Europe and Japan. Whole-grain breads and rice, tofu-based foods, fresh dairy products and vegetables are selected and sold by Mr. Sakaguchi, who also cooks up tasty vegetarian dishes in his restaurant annex.

Point Nature
17th arr. - 4, rue Lebon - 45 72 11 26
Open 9:30 a.m.-7:30 p.m. (Sun. & holidays 10:30 a.m.-1 p.m.). Closed Mon.
All the best-known names in natural cosmetics and cleaning products are in stock, as well as food supplements and herb teas. But vegetarians (and others) who have a sweet tooth will be especially pleased by the homemade jams and pure honeys, the guaranteed-natural pastries and other guiltless sweets. If your natural lifestyle does not exclude the pleasures of wine, here you'll find a wealth of organically grown vintages from all over France (don't miss the vin de pays de Pezenas, in red, white or rosé, sold by the liter or in bulk).

☒ ICE CREAM & SORBET

Le Bac à Glaces
7th arr. - 109, rue du Bac - 45 48 87 65
Open 11 a.m.-7:30 p.m. Closed Sun. & holidays.
These guaranteed hand-made ice creams and sorbets are crafted of top-quality ingredients, with no artificial additives. Doubting Thomases are encouraged to watch the *glaciers* busily at work in their glassed-in kitchen. Alongside the standards, you'll find some

delicious liqueur-flavored ices and other uncommon concoctions, like Camembert ice cream and carrot and tomato sorbets. We always find it difficult to decide between the scrumptious nougat ice cream and the honey-and-pine-nut combo. All these icy delights may be taken home in cartons or enjoyed on the spot in the tiny ice-cream parlor.

Baggi
9th arr. - 33, rue Chaptal - 48 74 01 39
Open 10:30 a.m.-7:15 p.m. Closed Sun., Mon. 2 wks. Feb. school holidays & 2 wks. in Aug.
The Baggis are not newcomers to the ice cream trade. Since 1850 their shop has been a mecca for lovers of frozen desserts. Today, many aficionados consider Guy Baggi, the firm's current creative force, to be the ice prince of Paris! Guy is forever dreaming up new flavor combinations—and winning prizes for them. Who wouldn't want to pin an award on the Princesse (wild strawberry and chocolate ice creams, pear sorbet and a touch of caramel) or on the Chocolatine (a symphony in chocolate, orange and caramel), or the justly celebrated Biscuit Rothschild. The flavors and dessert creations on hand on any given day vary in accordance with the seasons and Baggi's mood.

Baskin-Robbins
6th arr. - 1, rue du Four - 43 25 10 63
Open noon-8 p.m. (Fri., Sat. & May 1-Sept. 30 noon-midnight). Closed Sun. & Feb.
The French tend to find Baskin-Robbins ice creams too sugary-sweet and unnecessarily rich; but they are genuinely intrigued by the flavors: maple-walnut, banana-chocolate swirl, peanut-butter and chocolate on summer nights, French ice cream fans come out of the woodwork to join

the tourists of every other nationality to sip good ol' American milkshakes, a Baskin-Robbins specialty.

Berthillon

4th arr. - 31, rue Saint-Louis-en-l'Île - 43 54 31 61
Open 10 a.m.-8 p.m. Closed Mon., Tues. & school holidays (except at Christmas).

Berthillon is the most famous name in French ice cream. The firm's many faithful fans think nothing of waiting in line for *hours* just to treat their taste buds to a cone or dish of chocolate-nougat or glazed-chestnut ice cream. Berthillon's sorbets are our particular weakness: pink grapefruit, fig, wild strawberry... The entire repertoire comes to some 70 flavors, including many seasonal specialties.

Glacier Calabrese

14th arr. - 15, rue d'Odessa - 43 20 31 63
Open daily noon-12:30 a.m. Closed Aug. No cards.

The owner's lilting Calabrese accent and welcoming warmth are reason enough to visit this little ice cream parlor. But don't neglect to taste his delicious creations. In addition to an assortment of classic ice creams and tropical sorbets, he makes wonderful Italian-style ices: Amaretto, Croccantino (nutty and divine), mint-flavored Straciatella and Strega (for a cone with a kick!). The prices aren't half-bad either.

Gilles Vilfeu

1st arr. - 3, rue de la Cossonnerie 40 26 36 40
Open daily winter: noon-7 p.m.; from Easter & in summer: noon-1 a.m.

Vilfeu's imaginative productions include surprising and sophisticated novelty flavors—tea, lavender and foie-gras sorbets—an ice based on Beaujolais nouveau, and ice creams flavored with licorice,

cinnamon and ginger. We strongly encourage you to also sample the sumptuous frozen desserts, notably a molded cream-cheese sorbet served with a vivid raspberry coulis.

Raimo

12th arr. - 59-61, bd de Reuilly 43 43 70 17
Open 9 a.m.-midnight. Closed Mon. & Feb.

Sorbets and ice creams produced according to time-honored methods, with strictly fresh ingredients. Raimo's strong suit is concocting seductive flavor combinations; some of the most successful are pear-filbert, ginger-honey and cinnamon-mandarin orange.

■ MEAT, GAME & FOWL

Au Bell Viandier

6th arr. - 25, rue du Vieux-Colom- bier - 45 48 57 83
Open 8:30 a.m.-1 p.m. & 4 p.m.-8 p.m. (Sun. until 1 p.m. & holidays until 12:30 p.m.). Closed Mon.

Serge Caillaud is the reigning king of Parisian butchers. (You want references? Joël Robuchon buys his meat here!) Rigorous selection and skillful preparation are the hallmarks of these meats, which hail from the best French producers. There's milk-fed veal and fine beef from the Limousin region, farm-bred pork, poultry from Bresse and Challans (including superb capons for the year-end holidays), and premium game in season. Caillaud's specialties include a truffled roast of beef, veal stuffed with apricots or studded with prunes and pistachios, any of which would garner applause as the centerpiece of a dinner party.

Boucherie Lamartine

16th arr. - 172, av. Victor-Hugo 47 27 82 29
Open 6:30 a.m.-7:30 p.m. (Sat. 6 a.m.-3 p.m.). Closed Sun. & holidays.

Christian Prosper sells some of the best meat in France in this pretty, old-fashioned butcher shop. It's not cheap, mind you, but then you can't put a price on perfection, can you? The expertly aged beef is sublime. And the milky-pink veal always cooks up to juicy perfection, unlike the more commonly available varieties, which have an annoying tendency to shrink in the pan.

Boucherie Marbeuf

8th arr. - 36, rue Marbeuf - 42 25 36 55
Open 7:30 a.m.-2:15 p.m. (Fri. until 3:45 p.m. & Sat. until 12:45 p.m.). Closed Sun. No cards.

This wonderful butcher shop has a secure place in the annals of Parisian gastronomy. Countless top-rated restaurants rely on the Boucherie Marbeuf's peerless professionals to supply them with superb beef (cuts from several elite breeds, including the rare and costly Simmenthal, said to be one of the world's finest), as well as veal from the Corrèze region, farm-raised pork from Auvergne and genuine Sisteron lamb.

Boucheries Bernard

1st arr. - 38, rue du Louvre - 42 21 12 15
Open 8:30 a.m.-7 p.m. Closed Sun.
10th arr. - 221, rue Lafayette - 40 05 07 26
Open 9 a.m.-1 p.m. & 4 p.m.-7:15 p.m. (Fri. 9 a.m.-1 p.m. & 3:30 p.m.-7:15 p.m.; Sat. 9 a.m.-7 p.m. & holidays until 1 p.m.). Closed Sun.
13th arr. - 100, bd Masséna - 45 83 58 20
Open 9:30 a.m.-8 p.m. (Fri. & Sat. from 9 a.m.). Closed Sun.

14th arr. - 55, av. du Maine - 45 38 58 83
Open 9 a.m.-7 p.m. (July & Aug. 9 a.m.-1 p.m. & 3 p.m.-7 p.m.). Closed Sun.
15th arr. - 104 bis, rue Saint-Charles - 45 77 58 46
Open 8:30 a.m.-1 p.m. & 3 p.m.-7:30 p.m. (Fri. 8:30 a.m.-1 p.m. & 2:30 p.m.-7:30 p.m.; Sat. 8:30 a.m.-7 p.m. & Sun. until 1 p.m.). Closed Mon.

Over twenty years ago the Boucheries Bernard came up with a highly successful system for selling good-quality, custom-cut meat at unbeatable prices. The chain now has stores all over Paris and the suburbs, stores that offer excellent pork and lamb. The veal isn't always as appealing, and to spot bargains in the beef section, one needs a discerning eye. But the innards-and-offal counter is admirably stocked, and the poultry selection impressive.

Le Coq Saint-Honoré

1st arr. - 3, rue Gomboust - 42 61 52 04
Open 8 a.m.-1 p.m. & 4:30 p.m.-7 p.m. (Fri. 8 a.m.-1 p.m. & 3:30 p.m.-7 p.m.; Sat. until 1 p.m.). Closed Sun. & holidays.

We might as well make it clear right away: For our money, Le Coq Saint-Honoré is one of Paris's top poulterers. It's no coincidence that the list of its customers boasts such culinary notables as Robuchon, Savoy, Senderens and Terrail of La Tour d'Argent. The refrigerated cases display choice Bresse chickens and guinea hens (fast becoming prohibitively expensive), as well as laudable Loué pullets, Challans ducks and plump rabbits from the Gâtinais region south of Paris. In season, fine selection of game, including authentic Scottish grouse—a rare and wonderful treat.

The prices in this guide reflect what establishments were charging at press time.

Maison Queulevée Rôtisserie Cambronne

15th arr. - 90, rue Cambronne 47 34 36 55
Open 8:30 a.m.-12:30 p.m. & 4 p.m.-7:30 p.m. (Sun. 8:30 a.m.-12:30 p.m.). Closed Mon.

What are the hallmarks of premium fowl? Freshness, first and foremost, because the fresher the chicken, the better it tastes. But lineage counts as well, and the birds here are pedigreed—from Loué, Périgord and other noted regions—along with ducks from Challans and, in season, one of the city's finest selections of feathered game from Sologne.

Marc Tattevin Palais de la Viande

7th arr. - 15, rue du Champ-de-Mars - 47 05 07 02
Open 7 a.m.-1 p.m. & 3:30 p.m.-8 p.m. (Sun. 7 a.m.-1 p.m.). Closed Mon. & Aug.

No mere butcher, Tattevin. No, he is a knife- and twine-wielding artist who trusses up an original and delectable roast—we salivate at the thought of his loin of veal studded with nuggets of Parma ham, and the boned leg of lamb stuffed with kidneys. It goes without saying that Tattevin's raw materials are of the finest quality. House specialties include ready-to-roast truffled chickens, duck with peaches, or leg of lamb boned and stuffed with lamb kidneys.

■ PASTRY

Bourdaloue

9th arr. - 7, rue Bourdaloue - 48 78 32 35
Open 7:15 a.m.-7:15 p.m. (Sun. until 6:30 p.m.). Closed Mon.

L'amour, toujours l'amour is what we feel for Bourdaloue's Puits d'Amour, a jam-and-puff-pastry concoction that was created here in the 1800s. We also have an enduring affection for the excellent apple

turnovers (among the best we've ever tasted in Paris), the hazelnut delights and Bourdaloue's own ice creams and delectable chocolates. Tea room.

Paul Bugat

4th arr. - 5, bd Beaumarchais - 48 87 89 88
Open 8 a.m.-20 p.m. Closed Mon. & 3 wks. in Aug.

Paul Bugat is a passionate aesthete who orchestrates sweet pastry, chocolate, sugar and cream into exquisite gâteaux. The specialties of the house are delicious, jewel-like petits fours, along with the Clichy (chocolate buttercream and mocha cream on an almond-sponge base), the Pavé de Bourgogne (almond sponge cake and blackcurrant mousse) and the Almaviva (chocolate-mousse cake). Tea room.

Christian Constant

7th arr. - 37, rue d'Assas - 45 48 45 51
Open daily 8 a.m.-8 p.m.
7th arr. - 26, rue du Bac - 47 03 30 00
Open daily 8 a.m.-9 p.m.

After a stroll in the Luxembourg Gardens, why not indulge in a treat from Christian Constant's new shop on the rue d'Assas? And one needn't feel too guilt-ridden, because these cakes are low in sugar, additive-free, all-natural and incredibly light. Try a millefeuille, or Constant's famed chocolate-and-banana tart (we agree with Sonia Rykiel that it is a minor masterpiece), or the intensely chocolate macaroons. Constant's sorbets (100 francs per liter) and frozen desserts are well worth the money. Tea room.

Coquelin Aîné

16th arr. - 1, pl. de Passy - 42 88 21 74
Open 9 a.m.-7:30 p.m. (Sun. 9 a.m.-1 p.m.). Closed Mon.

Coquelin enjoys a solidly established reputation with its

247

solidly establishment clientele. Joining the traditional pastries created for holidays (the King's Cake for the feast of the Epiphany is a neighborhood favorite) are the shop's occasionally produced, tempting, original desserts, such as the Hérisson d'Automne ("Autumn Hedgehog"), a frozen coffee- and chestnut-flavored sweet. Excellent ice creams and chocolates may be purchased here too. Tea room.

Couderc

11th arr. - 6, bd Voltaire - 47 00 58 20
Open 8:30 a.m.-8 p.m. Closed Mon., Tues. & Aug.

Michel Couderc takes pride in his toothsome candies, pastries, ice creams and chocolates, all on display in this picturesque shop just off the lively place de la République. We suggest that you at least sample the rustic "peasant" and apricot tarts, and the more sophisticated Turquois (macaroons with chocolate mousse), the Délice (sponge cake, caramelized almonds and whipped cream with vanilla and chocolate) or the Ambre (praline and chocolate mousselines with crushed nougat and walnuts). Good chocolates (350 francs per kilo), authentic Kirsch-soaked cherries and a wonderful bitter-cocoa sorbet are additional reasons to note this fine address.

Dalloyau

2nd. - 25, bd des Capucines - 47 03 47 00
Open 8:30 a.m.-7:30 p.m. (Sat. 9 a.m.-7:30 p.m.). Closed Sun.
6th arr. - 2, pl. Edmond-Rostand 43 29 31 10
Open daily 9 a.m.-6:45 p.m.
8th arr. - 99-101, rue du Faubourg-Saint-Honoré - 43 59 18 10
Open daily 8:30 a.m.-9 p.m.
15th arr. - 69, rue de la Convention - 45 77 84 27

Open daily 9:30 a.m.-7:30 p.m. (Sun. 9 a.m.-19 p.m.)

Deservedly famous, Dalloyau is a temple of *gourmandise* revered by every discerning sweet tooth in town. Among the most renowned specialties are the memorably good macaroons, the chocolate-and-mocha Opéra cake (created in 1955 and still a bestseller) and the Mogador (chocolate sponge cake and mousse napped in raspberry sauce). Christmas brings succulent glazed chestnuts and gluttonously rich Yule logs; Easter calls for chocolate hens and bunnies romping among praline eggs and bells in the adorable window displays.

Gallet

16th arr. - 10, rue Mignard - 45 04 21 71
Open 7 a.m.-1 p.m. & 3 p.m.-7:45 p.m. Closed Sun., Mon. & Aug.

A reliable source of English treats for both the breakfast and the tea tables: buns, muffins, scones and pancakes, always fresh and always delicious. Special orders are gladly accepted for holiday cakes and pies.

Jean-Paul Hévin

7th arr. - 16, av. de La Motte-Picquet - 45 51 77 48
Open 10 a.m.-7:30 p.m. Closed Sun. & Aug.

Jean-Paul Hévin is an artist whose preferred medium is chocolate. His chocolate cakes are inspired symphonies, whose deep, dark intensity is tempered by fruit, spices, nuts and caramel. Recent compositions include a millefeuille au chocolate, a chocolate-mousse ice cream and (in another register entirely) a liltingly fresh gâteau of pears and caramel on an almond-sponge base.

Lenôtre

Information: see Lenôtre page 236.

Normandy native Gaston Lenôtre opened his first shop in Paris in 1957. His pastries and elaborate desserts are now internationally recognized as classics: the Casino, the Plaisir, the Carousel... his latest creation is the Fantasme, a voluptuous fantasy in chocolate (chocolate sponge cake and bitter-chocolate mousse).

A. Lerch

5th arr. - 4, rue du Cardinal Lemoine - 43 26 15 80
Open 7 a.m.-1:30 p.m. & 3:15 p.m.-7 p.m.. Closed Mon., Wed., 2 wks. in Feb. & Aug.

Traditional Alsatian pastries hold the place of honor here, from Kugelhopf (a spongy dome-shaped yeast cake, with or without raisins) to the region's justly famed fruit tarts, featuring bilberries, blue plums or rhubarb topped with meringue. Friendly prices.

Mauduit

10th arr. - 54, rue du Faubourg-Saint-Denis - 42 46 43 64
Open 7:15 a.m.-7:30 p.m. (Sun. 7:15 a.m.-1:30 p.m.). Closed Mon. & Aug.
10th arr. - 12, bd de Denain - 48 78 05 30
Open daily 7:15 a.m.-7:30 p.m. (Sun. 7:15 a.m.-1:30 p.m.).

Mauduit's windows, with their glittering displays of flawless little cakes and confections, attract quite an audience. In summer, fruit mousses garnished with fresh fruit or fruit purées sparkle invitingly, while winter brings the delicious Cointreau-flavored Tambourin, or the Mont-Blanc with caramelized almonds; the refreshing Pacifique dessert (raspberry and lime bavarian creams) is available year-round. Prices are modest for this level of quality.

Millet

7th arr. - 103, rue Saint-Dominique - 45 51 49 80
Open 9 a.m.-7 p.m. (Sun. 8 a.m.-1 p.m.). Closed Mon. & Aug.

Jean Millet, whose shop is virtually an institution in this chic neighborhood, ranks among the foremost practitioners of the art of French pastry. With his executive chef, Denis Ruffel, he turns out superb cakes and desserts that often give starring roles to seasonal fruit. Among Millet's best-sellers are his exceptional pear charlotte, his bitter-chocolate Guanaja and the silken almond-milk Royal with raspberries, pears, oranges and a fresh-tasting raspberry purée.

Gérard Mulot

6th arr. - 76, rue de Seine - 43 26 85 77
Open 7 a.m.-8 p.m. Closed Wed. & 1 month in summer.

Mulot is an endlessly inventive personality, never happier than when he is working out a new idea to complete his line of delectable pastries. The poetically named Nuée d'Or ("Goldlen Cloud") is a divine combination of honey mousseline and candied fruit; Eté Indien ("Indian Summer") combines tea-flavored and orange-flavored mousselines. In a more down to earth vein, Mulot fashions wonderfully flaky, buttery croissants.

Le Moule à Gâteaux

15th arr. - 79, rue Lecourbe - 45 67 78 36 (also: 5th arr., 14th arr., 17th arr., 20th arr.)
Open 8 a.m.-8 p.m. (Sun. until 2 p.m.). Closed Mon.

This prospering chain specializes in traditional, home-style cakes fashioned by young pastry cooks who care about their craft. They use time-tested recipes that we wish we still had the leisure (and know-how) to prepare in our own kitchens. We love the apricot feuilleté covered with a golden short crust; the

Mamita, a poem in chocolate and crème fraîche; and the Carotin: almonds, filberts and carrots, all reasonably priced.

Peltier

7th arr. - 66, rue de Sèvres - 47 34 06 62
Open daily 9:30 a.m.-7:45 p.m.
7th arr. - 1, rue Saint-Dominique 47 05 50 02
Open daily 8:30 a.m.-7:45 p.m.

Lucien Peltier's fame as a master pastry chef is well-earned. His most noteworthy achievements include the Ambre (almond sponge cake, praline-chocolate mousse with caramelized walnuts), the Riviera (almond sponge, lime and raspberry mousses) and a textbook example of Black Forest cake, made with real morello cherries. His chocolate tart or the chestnut charlotte spiked with whisky would make smashing finales for any dinner party. Individual pastries cost between 14 and 25 francs.

Stohrer

2nd arr. - 51, rue Montorgueil 42 33 38 20
Open daily 7:30 a.m.-8:30 p.m.

The shop is decorated with rosy, corpulent allegories of

Fame painted by Paul Baudry (he also decorated the Paris Opéra) in 1860; these charming murals are pleasant to contemplate while scarfing down a few of Stohrer's divine pastries: the dark-chocolate Criollo, the refreshing Royal Menthe, the Black Forest cake, almond-filled Pithiviers and buttery croissants all come highly recommended.

■ REGIONAL FRENCH SPECIALTIES

Besnier

18th arr. - 28, av. de Saint-Ouen 43 87 65 63
Open 9 a.m.-1 p.m. & 4 p.m.-8 p.m. Closed Sun. & Aug.

Guy Besnier is a hard man to please, and only foods that win his full approval find their way into his shop, a showcase for gourmet specialties from Auvergne, Brittany and Corsica. Among them are tangy dried sausages from Chassagnard à Egletons, Corsican coppa and figatelli (garlicky liver sausage) and a superb assortment of cheeses, featuring tasty farmhouse chèvres.

A home for the Nation

The *Triumph of the Nation* is the theme of the bronze group sculpted by Jules Dalou that now stands on the place de la Nation. The work was originally planned for the *place de la République*, but an official jury decided otherwise. For a closer look at the figures, take the underground walkway to the gardens in the center of the sea of traffic that surrounds the place. Exhaust fumes were less of a problem in 1880, when the first national holiday was celebrated here on the fourteenth of July. A short walk away in the *rue de Picpus*, eminent members of the French nobility executed during the Revolution (the guillotine stood for a time on the place de la Nation) are buried in the *Picpus Cemetery*. Today, this green and placid resting place is exclusively reserved for descendants of those same noble families.

La Cigogne

8th arr. - 61, rue de l'Arcade - 43 87 39 16

Open 8 a.m.-7 p.m. (Sat. 9 a.m.-6:30 p.m.). Closed Sun., Aug. & holidays.

This firm turns out innovative food products rooted in the culinary traditions of Alsace: sweet pretzels, slices of Kugelhopf (a yeast cake) thickly dusted with cinnamon, and an unctuous cream-cheese tart. The region's classic dishes are not neglected, however—witness La Cigogne's wonderful strudel, quiche Lorraine, cherry, blueberry and damson-plum tarts and, in the savory category, cervelas (sausages), weisswurst, beerwurst and bratwurst.

Comtesse du Barry

17th arr. - 23, av. de Wagram 46 22 17 38

Open 10 a.m.-8 p.m. Closed Sun.

4th arr. - 93, rue Saint-Antoine 40 29 07 14

6th arr. - 1, rue de Sèvres - 45 48 32 04

9th arr. - 13, rue Taibout - 47 40 21 01

15th arr. - 317, rue de Vaugirard 42 50 90 13

16th arr. - 88bis, av. Mozart - 45 27 74 49

Open 10 a.m.-7 p.m. Closed Sun.

From the Gers in southwestern France comes an extensive line of regional food products: duck and goose confits, foie gras, fatted duck breasts (available fresh, vacuum-packed), as well as galantines, rillettes, excellent little pâtés, good prepared foods (in tins or jars) and frozen entrées.

La Galoche d'Aurillac

11th arr. - 41, rue de Lappe - 47 00 77 15

Open 10 a.m.-midnight. Closed Sun., Mon. & Aug.

Robust fare from Auvergne may be sampled on the spot or taken home from this colorful shop on the rue de Lappe. We highly recommend the pounti (a savory loaf of pork and Swiss chard), the saucisse d'Auvergne, the regional pot-au-feu, the tangy little cabécous goat cheeses and, for dessert, the apple tart flambéed with Calvados. Wash these specialties down with sturdy local wines like Marcillac and Saint-Pourçain. The small selection of rustic brandies includes a Lou Rouergat flavored with walnuts or peaches (70 francs).

Jean-Claude et Nanou

17th arr. - 46, rue Legendre - 42 27 15 08

Open 9 a.m.-1 p.m. & 4 p.m.-8 p.m. Closed Sun. (except Sept.-April), Mon. & July 14-Aug.

Here's the sort of country food we can never get enough of. Jean-Claude and Nanou sell flavorful sausages dried under the ashes of a smoldering fire, aromatic mountain sausage and fresh Tomme (an unmatured cheese with a distinctive "barnyard" taste).

Aux Produits de Bretagne et des Pyrénées

5th arr. - 42, bd Saint-Germain 43 54 72 96

Open 9 a.m.-10 p.m. Closed Mon. & July 1-Sept. 17.

How is it that foods from two such far-flung regions share shelf space in a single shop? Simply because François Miras hails from the Pyrénées, while Madame Miras is a native of Brittany. So alongside the superb mountain-cured bacon, sheep's-milk cheese, Tarbais beans and delicious southwestern confits, you'll find jars of cèpes preserved in oil, hearty rural breads, sausages and other fine produce from Brittany.

Chez Teil

11th arr. - 6, rue de Lappe - 47 00 41 28

Open 9 a.m.-1 p.m. & 3 p.m.-7 p.m. Closed Sun., Mon. & Aug.

This turn-of-the-century shop is home to a mouthwatering selection of authentic Auvergnat charcuterie, processed by Patrick Teil himself at his family's meat-curing plant in Cayrols. By eliminating the middle man, Teil can market his hams, sausages, spreads, pigs' trotters and pâtés at attractive prices. Try his cheeses too, along with the fine crusty flat bread (fouace) and countrified sweets on display.

Terrier

9th arr. - 58, rue des Martyrs - 48 78 96 45

Open 8:15 a.m.-1 p.m. & 4 p.m.-7:30 p.m. (Sun. 8:15 a.m.-12:45 p.m.). Closed Mon. & Aug.

For generous Lyonnais charcuterie, Terrier is the outpost in Paris. Among the typical treats on hand are sausage studded with truffles and pistachios, golden-brown pâtés en croûte, pike and salmon quenelles, Burgundy ham, head cheese and genuine rosette sausage, the pride of Lyon.

A la Ville de Rodez

4th arr. - 22, rue Vieille-du-Temple - 48 87 79 36

Open 8 a.m.-1 p.m. & 3 p.m.-7:30 p.m. Closed Sun., Mon. & July 15-Aug.

Alex-Pierre Batût has represented the earthy tradition of Auvergnat charcuterie in Paris for many years. His citron-studded fouace (flat bread) is ambrosial, his terrines are legendary, and his zesty dried sausage is among the most flavorful we've had the pleasure to taste—anywhere. Ville de Rodez is the place to find all the classic cuts of pork that simmer together with vegetables in a classic potée auvergnate.

■ SEAFOOD

Le Bar à Huîtres
14th arr. - 112, bd Montparnasse
43 20 71 01
Open noon-midnight.

At the outdoor oyster bar, you can purchase dozens of succulent oysters, opened for you free of charge by the nimble-fingered *écaillers* and neatly arranged on disposable trays (no deposit, no return). A refreshing treat, this!

Poissonnerie du Dôme
14th arr. - 4, rue Delambre - 43 35 23 95
Open 8 a.m.-1 p.m. & 4 p.m.-7:30 p.m. (Wed. & Sun. until 1 p.m.; Tues. 5 p.m.-7:30 p.m.). Closed Mon. & 1 month in summer.

The lucky residents of Montparnasse can satisfy their urge for seafood at this marvelous fish store, perhaps the best in Paris. Manager Jean-Pierre Lopez admits only "noble" fish (sole, turbot, lotte, sea bass and the like) to his classy emporium. The merchandise, from French (particularly Breton) and foreign waters, is snapped up by such eminent restaurants as L'Ambroisie, Duquesnoy and L'Apicius. Need we mention that these rare and succulent denizens of the deep command regally high prices?

■ WINE & SPIRITS

L'Arbre à Vin
12th arr. - 2-4, rue du Rendez-Vous
43 46 81 10
Open 8:30 a.m.-12:30 p.m. & 4 p.m.-8 p.m. (Sun. 8:30 a.m.-1 p.m.). Closed Mon. & 3 wks. in Aug.

This fascinating wine shop dates back to 1893. The superb vaulted cellars house Bordeaux both great and modest and a comprehensive array of Burgundies. Rounding out the selection are good country wines.

Cave de l'Ecole Polytechnique
5th arr. - 48, rue de la Montagne-Sainte-Geneviève
43 25 35 80
Open 10:30 a.m.-1:30 p.m. & 4:30 p.m.-8:30 p.m. (Sun. 11 a.m.-1:30 p.m.). Closed Mon. & Aug.

In the wine business for more than half a century, Jean-Baptiste Besse must be credited with having converted many a Parisian to the cult of Bacchus. Though the shop may look like a colossal shambles, Besse will infallibly locate just the bottle you desire, from a modest red Cheverny to a majestic Château Cheval-Blanc. His choice of dessert wines (Sauternes, Banyuls, Beaumes-de-Venises) always flabbergasts us, as does his judicious selection of Cognacs and ports.

Caves Estève
4th arr. - 10, rue de la Cerisaie
42 72 33 05
Open 9:30 a.m.-12:30 p.m. & 2:30 p.m.-7:30 p.m. Closed Sun. & Mon. (except in Dec.).
5th arr. - 292, rue Saint-Jacques
46 34 69 78
Open 10 a.m.-1 p.m. & 3 p.m.-8 p.m. Closed Sun. & Mon. (except in Dec.).

For Jean-Christophe Estève, wine isn't just a business; it's more like a sacred vocation. Endowed with a formidable palate, this Gascon native declares that every region of France produces good wines—it's just a question of tracking them down. Given his pedagogic bent (he used to be a Spanish teacher), he'll be happy to help you choose from among 250 Bordeaux, and his expanding collection of Burgundies.

La Cave de Georges Dubœuf
8th arr. - 9, rue Marbeuf - 47 20 71 23
Open 9 a.m.-1 p.m. & 3 p.m.-7 p.m. Closed Sun., Mon. & Aug.

What Lionel Poilâne is to bread, Georges Dubœuf is to Beaujolais: an assurance of quality. His Paris shop stocks excellent representative from all the villages of Beaujolais, but Duboeuf is not parochial by any means. His numerous wine-making chums all over France supply him with (for example) fine Burgundies from de Montille, de Vogüé, Rousseau and Trapet, Métaireau's Muscadets, Guigal's Côtes-du-Rhône and Alsatian vintages from Trimbach.

Caves Pétrissans
17th arr. - 30 bis, av. Niel - 42 27 83 84
Open 9:30 a.m.-1:30 p.m. & 3 p.m.-8 p.m. (Sat. 10 a.m.-1:30 p.m.). Closed Sun., 3 wks. in Aug.

For many a year this renowned Parisian *cave* has been a magnet for local oenophiles, owing to its extensive selection of fine wines. On a given day, a browser might come across an uncommon red wine from Corsica, the appealing Roussette de Seyssel from Savoie, Clos du Marquis ("second" wine of Saint-Julien's Château Léoville-las-Cases), Jaboulet's Saint-Joseph and tasty first-growth Champagne from Chigny-les-Roses. Sharing shelf space with the wines are some highly reputed Cognacs and fruit brandies, Armagnacs (vintages on hand include 1893, 1900, 1912...) and rare whiskies, like the elegant Auchentoshan from the Scottish Lowlands and the peaty, invigorating Bowmore from the Isle of Islay.

Monday, like Sunday, is a day of rest for many shopkeepers.

Les Caves du Savour Club

14th arr. - 120 or 139, bd Montparnasse - 43 27 12 06
16th arr. - 11-13, rue Gros - 42 30 94 18
Open 10 a.m.-8 p.m. (Sun. until 12:30 p.m.). Closed Mon.

The Savour Club is a wine warehouse that has managed to rise above the grayness of its underground premises (a parking garage) with a bright, light decor. Inside, you'll find bottlings appropriate for every occasion, each with a card bearing an informative description and comments. There are wines for everyday drinking (country wines for under twenty francs), as well as special treats for connoisseurs (Château Haut-Brion '82, Richebourg '84).

Jean Danflou

1st arr. - 36, rue de Mont-Thabor
42 61 51 09
Open 9 a.m.-noon & 2 p.m.-6 p.m. Closed Sat., Sun. & Aug. 1-15.

Pierre Danflou-Glotin, the third generation of Danflous to run this shop, sells absolutely exquisite, fragrant, heady eaux-de-vie (clear fruit brandies) distilled especially for him in Alsace. You must sample his extraordinary aged Kirsch, his Poire Williams, his perfumed Framboise. A line of elegant Cognacs, Armagnacs and Calvados is also proposed, along with a small selection of wines from Burgundy and Bordeaux. Prices start at around 200 francs.

Legrand Filles et Fils

2nd arr. - 1, rue de la Banque
42 60 07 12
2nd arr. - 12, galerie Vivienne
42 60 07 12
Open 8:30 a.m.-7:30 p.m. (Sat. 8:30 a.m.-1 p.m. & 3 p.m.-7 p.m.). Closed Sun. & Mon.

Even if the wines were not half so interesting as they are, Legrand's wine shop would be worth a visit for its old-fashioned charm and warm atmosphere. Lucien Legrand's daughter Francine offers a wide selection of carefully chosen, inexpensive country wines from up-and-coming growers in the South and the Val de Loire, along with a far-ranging inventory of prestigious Burgundies and Bordeaux (note the many wines from average vintage years, affordably priced). Also, a few uncommon bottlings: luscious Muscat de Beaumes-de-Venise, Vin de Paille du Jura and some excellent vintage ports.

Nicolas

8th arr. - 21, pl. de Madeleine
42 68 00 16. 250 stores in Paris.
Open 9 a.m.-8 p.m. Closed Sun.

Looking better than ever with a spruce gold-and-bordeaux decor, Nicolas's 250 stores in the Paris area continue to present a wide, diverse and appealing range of wines for every budget. The chain's monthly promotions are well worth following: featured are (for example) French wines from unfamiliar or underrated appellations—the Ardèche, Corbières or Bergerac—, imports (Spanish, Italian and even Australian bottlings) and the occasional oenological curiosity, all offered at attractive prices. The multilevel flagship store on the place de la Madeleine has a huge inventory of more than 1,000 different wines, including rare, old Bordeaux. Nicolas is also an excellent source of fine distilled spirits (check out the selection of single-malt whiskies). The avenue Wagram shop stays open until 10 p.m., the Ancienne-Comédie store until 9. Home delivery service available.

Le Repaire de Bacchus

17th arr. - 39, rue des Acacias
43 80 09 68 (also: 2nd arr., 6th arr., 7th arr., 9th arr., 15th arr., 16th arr., 18th arr.)
Open 10:30 a.m.-1:30 p.m. & 3:30 p.m.-8 p.m. Closings on Sun. & Mon. vary in the different stores.

Dominique Fenouil continues to inaugurate new branches of his sleek, dynamic chain with admirable frequency. Smart marketing isn't everything, of course: the Repaires de Bacchus owe their success to a judicious choice of wines and, perhaps especially, to the excellent advice dispensed by the sales staffs (several of whom, in our experience, speak English!). From the house-label wines to fine growers' Burgundies, from little-known "village" appellations to Bordeaux's *grands crus*, the wines are selected with an eye to quality and value. Several branches sponsor clubs (membership fee: 200 francs) where, upon occasion, one may enjoy a sip (or two) of a vintage Latour, a Burgundy from the Comte de Lafond, or even a rare single-malt whisky.

Au Verger de la Madeleine

8th arr. - 4, bd Malesherbes - 42 65 51 99
Open 10 a.m.-1:30 p.m. & 3 p.m.-8 p.m. Closed Sun.

Jean-Pierre Legras's staggering collection encompasses such unique and extravagant bottles as a Cognac Impérial Tiffon 1810, a Porto Barros dated 1833 (once the property of the French ambassador to Lisbon), a Solera Sercial Madeira from 1835 and a Clos-Peyraguey 1893. Such treasures are not for everyday drinking, but they make impressive, indeed unforgettable, gifts. All the first growths of Bordeaux (Cheval-Blanc, Pétrus...) are on hand as well, along with superb Burgundies from Montrachet and Meursault, and hard-to-find wines like Château-Grillet and Jasnières. And inexpensive offerings from the Côtes-d'Auvergne, Saint-Pourçain and Saumur.

Vins Rares Peter Thustrup

46 33 83 53
The sore will open soon. Call for location and information. In the meantime orders can be taken at the above phone number.

Peter Thustrup's unquenchable passion for old, rare vintages leads him to auction rooms all over the world, in search of such finds as antique Yquem, ancient Pétrus and Mouton-Rothschild from another age (which sell, incidentally, for about 18,000 francs—just to give you an idea). Bordeaux, obviously, is well represented, but Thustrup can also show you some exceptional Vendanges Tardives from Alsace, mature Burgundies and collectible Côtes-du-Rhône. He recently added an expanded (and quite attractive) range of younger, lower-priced bottles from the world's wine-growing regions.

GIFTS

Un Air de Giverny

7th arr. - 10, rue de Bellechasse
45 55 83 69
Open 11 a.m.-6:30 p.m. Closed Sun. & Mon.

You have a passion for the Impressionists? Then this charming boutique is a "must" stop on your itinerary. Monet's famous blue-and-yellow china is on sale here, of course, but you'll also discover a selection of decorative objects in those colors, and others that date from the Impressionists' heyday, among them household linen from Quimper, handcrafted faïence, watercolors and pretty antique curios.

Find the address you are looking for, quickly and easily, in the index.

Axis

11th arr. - 13, rue de Charonne
48 06 79 10
Open 11 a.m.-2 p.m. & 2:30 p.m.-7:30 p.m. Closed Sun.

Witty, imaginative and amusing gift ideas are the Axis trademark. But this policy does not exclude the useful: the Alessi coffeepot and the Dualite toaster are trendy as all get-out, but they also help you get breakfast on the table efficiently! Axis now produces its own collection of vases, picture frames, tableware and rugs, all sporting droll or unusual designs.

La Boîte à Musique

1st arr. - 9, rue de Beaujolais - 42 96 55 13
Open 10 a.m.-7 p.m. Closed Sun.

Music boxes tinkle merrily away in this delicious little shop under the Palais-Royal arcades. The mechanisms are Swiss, dependable and made to last, while the boxes themselves have a pleasingly old-fashioned look. Prices vary according to the complexity of the design and the number of tunes and notes the box plays. The simplest, an ideal gift for a newborn (whose name and birthdate can be engraved on the box), costs about 200 francs. The finest music box in the store, made of rare wood with a sophisticated mechanism that plays four tunes and well over a hundred notes, will set you back over 30,000 francs.

Boutique Le Flore

6th arr. - 26, rue Saint Benoît - 45 44 33 40
Open 10 a.m.-1 p.m. & 2 p.m.-7 p.m. Closed Sun.

The Café de Flore now markets an array of merchandise stamped with its famous logo. The heavy, white bistro-style china is a great success: visitors snatch up the cups and saucers to take home as souvenirs. Little silver-plated table decorations, trays, a

coffeepot and teapot complete the line. If Saint-Germain-des-Prés has a special place in your heart, you'll love the framed photos of the neighborhood, and the old-fashioned postcards depicting the terrace of Le Flore in different eras (from 85 francs).

Chaumette

7th arr. - 45, av. Duquesne - 42 73 18 54
Open 9:30 a.m.-6:30 p.m. Closed Sat., Sun. & 3 wks. in Aug.

Gérard Chaumette is no ordinary dealer in knickknacks and bibelots. He has a genuine passion for faïence (earthenware decorated with opaque colored glazes) and glass objects that reproduce and reinterpret nature. On our last visit to his enchanting shop, we found an extraordinary lamp base with mauve-tinged irises; glazed ceramic cachepots displaying bunches of grapes or vegetable still lifes; and stunning reproductions of ancient Roman glass. Prices for these small marvels range from a couple hundred to several thousand francs.

Comptoirs de la Tour d'Argent

5th arr. - 2, rue du Cardinal-Lemoine - 46 33 45 58
Open 10 a.m.-12:30 a.m. (Sun. noon-12:30 a.m.). Closed Mon.

Dinner at the Tour d'Argent may be out of reach, but you can always scrape up a few francs to purchase a small souvenir bearing the restaurant's logo! Classy, classic tableware (crystal, silver, china, embroidered napery) and lots of determinedly tasteful accessories (how about a Tour d'Argent silk tie?). The good tinned foie gras, duck confit, lobster bisque and the Brut Champagne also sport the house colors, and like the rest are high-priced.

L'Entrepôt

16th arr. - 50, rue de Passy - 45 25 64 17

Open 10:30 a.m.-7 p.m. (Sat. until 7:30 p.m.). Closed Sun.

Here's a treasure trove of clever gift items and household gadgets that will charm even the most blasé shopper. We saw a funny little alarm clock disguised as a deep-sea diver, a miniature tool chest hidden inside a model car and an impressively diverse array of stationery, tableware, clothing—even jams and jellies! A delightful bazaar, improbably located in the classy Passy neighborhood.

Forestier

16th arr. - 35, rue Duret - 45 00 08 61

Open 10:30 a.m.-7:30 p.m. (Mon. from noon). Closed Sun.

In the 1930s, this was a cheese and dairy shop, but an ex-landscape gardener has transformed the place into an original boutique that follows the rhythms of the seasons and holidays. Forestier carries all the tableware and decorative touches one would need to create a festive atmosphere for Halloween, Christmas, Valentine's Day, April Fool's and so on, as well as an attractive selection of handcrafted pottery and garden accessories for year-round use.

Homme Sweet Homme

4th arr. - 45, rue Vieille-du-Temple - 48 04 94 99

Open 11 a.m.-7:30 p.m. Closed Sun.

Despite the cutesy-pie name, this shop stocks an interesting variety of (primarily masculine) gifts in a grand range of prices (25 to 2,000 francs). Wallets in all sizes, attractive fountain pens, geometric photo holders from the 1940s and tiny tools are just a few of the clever and useful items on sale. For the man who has everything (including a sense of humor),

there's even a little fan in the form of a robot.

Rita Kim

10th arr. - 79, quai de Valmy - 42 39 82 49

Open 1 p.m.-7 p.m. Closed Sun. & Mon. No cards.

We love Rita's collection of plastic stuff from the '60s: There's tableware, campy knickknacks to accent your "day-core" and irresistibly kitsch costume jewelry—don't miss the "Jesus" watch with the name of an apostle at each hour; it's the height of taste! Lots of other hilarious items are on sale for under 100 francs.

La Maison des Artisans

12th arr.- 14, cours de Vincennes - 43 41 61 63

Open 10:30 a.m.-1:30 p.m. & 2:30 p.m.-7 p.m. Closed Sun., Mon., Aug. & holidays.

For the best in French handcrafts: the Maison des Artisans presents creative, beautifully wrought objects made according to traditional methods. Come here to admire useful and decorative objects in faïence, pewter and glass (perfume bottles from 160 francs), jewelry crafted in precious wood and silver, or in Altuglas and gilded bronze (brooches from 200 francs).

Pain d'Epices Maison

9th arr. - 35-37, passage Jouffroy 47 70 51 12

Open 10 a.m.-7 p.m. (Mon. from 12:30 p.m.). Closed Sun.

The windows of this delightful shop, situated in the picturesque passage Jouffroy, are a feast for the eyes. Accessories and decorative items that make a home feel inviting and cozy are found here (potpourri, table decorations, lamp shades...), alongside old-fashioned color prints, picture frames and cookie tins—everything is beautifully displayed.

Robin des Bois

4th arr. - 15, rue Ferdinand Duval - 48 04 09 36

Open 10:30 a.m.-7:30 p.m. (Sun. from noon).

The headquarters of the Association for the Protection of Humanity and the Environment is also a source of ecologically sound gifts for yourself or the folks back home. Vegetable ivory is carved into pretty ornaments and buttons; jojoba oil replaces whale oil in the body-care products on display, and (naturally) all the stationery is made of recycled paper.

Shizuka

2nd arr. - 25, bd des Capucines 42 61 54 61

Open 9:30 a.m.-6:30 p.m. Closed Sun.

For years the avenue de l'Opéra has been a mecca for Japanese tourists. But of late they've been joined by Parisians who want to get a look at the best in contemporary Japanese design—and that's at Shizuka, a sleek, upscale emporium. On the ground floor, clean-lined desk accessories and stationery are featured, along with robots and mechanical toys. A downstairs gallery showcases recent creations by Japanese designers, while the top floor is devoted to elegant tableware and cutlery, toilet articles and linens. It's hard to leave empty-handed, especially since prices start at the reasonable sum of 35 francs.

Tant qu'il y aura des Hommes

6th arr. - 23, rue du Cherche-Midi - 45 48 48 17

Open 10:30 a.m.-7 p.m. (Mon. from noon). Closed Sun. & 2 wks. in Aug.

Among the handsome and practical gifts for men on sale here, we particularly liked the silk boxer shorts, the luggage (with lots of detachable pockets) and leather goods that look as if they could withstand hard wear, a classic Irish crewneck sweater and a good-looking leather-trimmed jacket for rough-and-tumble types. The beautiful coordinated shirts and ties, we've been assured, make highly acceptable gifts.

Territoire
8th arr. - 30, rue Boissy-d'Anglas
42 66 22 13
Open 10:30 a.m.-7 p.m. Closed Sun.
What was once a hardware store is now a bright and spacious shop brimming with ideas for leisure activities. The stock changes with the seasons; in spring, the gardening section burgeons with Wilkinson tools and terracotta pots. In summer, sporting goods take over a greater share of shelf space (we saw an impressive foldable black canvas boat for 5,000 francs), and in winter, fireside games feature more prominently. There are plenty of amusing gifts for children, including reproductions of old-fashioned board games and some spectacular kites. Prices range from about 50 to 5,000 francs.

La Tuile à Loup
5th arr. - 35, rue Daubenton - 47 07 28 90
Open 10:30 a.m.-7:30 p.m. (Sun. until 1 p.m.). Closed Mon.
As peaceful as a village square, this exceptional shop carries traditional handcrafts from all over France. You'll find beautiful glazed pottery from Savoie, Provence, Burgundy and Alsace, and stoneware from Puisaye and Le Maine. There are handmade wooden objects, rustic tableware, wrought-iron weather vanes and decorative tiles for the kitchen, bath or fireplace. Fascinating, too, are the many books documenting popular art forms and regional history.

Michèle Wilson
14th arr. - 116, rue du Château
43 22 28 73
Open 8:30 a.m.-8 p.m. Closed Sun. & Aug.
Puzzle buffs and art lovers alike adore Michèle Wilson's hand-crafted wooden puzzles, which depict paintings or prints from the Louvre, the Musée d'Orsay, the Institut du Monde Arabe and other well-known museums. Some of the puzzles are easy to put together (60 pieces, 110 francs), while others are considerably more mind-bending (5,500 pieces, 6,182 francs). Subjects run the gamut from Persian miniatures to Impressionist paintings or maps (talk about educational!). At the workshop next door, you can look on and learn how as a puzzle is made.

HOME

■ BATH & KITCHENWARE

BATH

Le Bain Rose
6th arr. - 11, rue d'Assas - 42 22 55 85
Open 10:30 a.m.-1 p.m. & 2 p.m.-6:30 p.m. Closed Sun., Mon. & Aug.
This is the place for antique washbasins and stands dating from the turn of the century up to the 1950s. Prices are high, but everything works: the faucets, the drain, the pipes. Tiles and accessories are available as well—the lighting fixtures are particularly attractive.

A l'Epi d'Or
5th arr. - 17, rue des Bernardins
46 33 08 47
Open 11 a.m.-7 p.m. Closed Sun. & Mon.
After nearly a quarter century on the rue Saint-Jacques,

this highly reputed bath shop transferred its stock to more spacious quarters, under a vast skylight. Lovely antique and reproduction bathroom sinks are the main attraction, along with period and a few contemporary accessories. A genuine 1930s sink commands a minimum tariff of 7,000 francs, while a reproduction goes for 3,000 francs. An antique soap dish, however, will cost only about 600 francs.

CUTLERY

Isler
1st arr. - 44, rue Coquillière - 42 33 20 92
Open 9 a.m.-noon & 2 p.m.-6 p.m. Closed Sat., Sun. & Aug. No cards.
Not a single element of the shop's decor has changed in 50 years, but then neither has the excellent quality of the Swiss knives (including the world-famous Tour Eiffel brand), for which Isler is known. All the great French chefs select their kitchen knives from among the 100 models in stock; and there are 40 types of pocketknives to pick from as well. The firm's latest success is a survival pocketknife with (at least) 29 functions (multiuse pliers, ballpoint pen, mini-screwdriver—you get the idea) which comes in a leather carrying case equipped with a compass, sharpening stone, mirror... Alas, now the trusty old penknife seems awfully ordinary in comparison.

Kindal
2nd arr. - 33, av. de l'Opéra - 42 61 70 78
Open 10 a.m.-6:30 p.m. (Sat. from 11 a.m.). Closed Sun.
Faithful to its long family tradition, Kindal has carefully preserved its handsome mahogany paneling that dates back to the shop's grand opening in 1905. Knives of every sort are on view: table, hunting

and pocket representatives with wooden or precious horn handles. Prices start at about 50 francs and rise to 12,000 francs for certain collectors' items. Knives are also repaired and sharpened on the premises.

Culinarion

17th arr. - 83 bis, rue de Courcelles - 42 27 63 32
Open 10:15 a.m.-7 p.m. (Mon. from 11:15 a.m.). Closed Sun.

Culinarion is a dependable source of kitchen classics (cast-iron pots, charlotte

stocks a truly amazing range of covetable cookware, superb knives and copper pots, and every imaginable baking accessory. We suggest you come early in the day to shop here, and above all, don't be in a hurry. Some of the sales clerks speak English and are quite helpful.

Kitchen Bazaar

15th arr. - 11, av. du Maine - 42 22 91 17
Open 10 a.m.-7 p.m. Closed Sun.

Kitchenware from Kitchen Bazaar is always both high-style and high-performance. The latest small appliances are always available here, with a preference for those with the sleekest designs. There's an interesting selection of cookbooks, too.

Thank God, the architect doesn't sing

Good intentions don't always work. The *Bastille opera house* was conceived as a way of bringing opera to the masses, but as a side effect its construction has inexorably turned a traditional working-class neighborhood into a magnet for the trendy and fashionable. Art galleries and night spots are ousting carpenters, craftsmen and cabinetmakers, while many venerable buildings are being demolished to clear the way for upmarket apartment blocks. The good news is that this opera house is cheaper and more accessible than its grander counterpart, the Opéra Garnier: you don't even have to dress up. An impressive array of technical devices makes the Opéra Bastille a director's dream—and at least from the inside you can't see the grim gray exterior!

Geneviève Lethu

1st arr. - Forum des Halles, level -2 - 40 39 95 94
1st arr. - 91, rue de Rivoli - 42 60 14 90
6th arr. - 95, rue de Rennes - 45 44 40 35
14th arr. - 25, av. du Général-Leclerc - 45 38 71 30
17th arr. - 1, av. Niel 45 72 03 47
Open 10:30 a.m.-7:30 p.m. Closed Sun.

There are Geneviève Lethu shops all over Paris, presenting vast selections of bright, practical, cheerful kitchen furniture, utensils, tableware and linen. The ever-growing collections of affordably priced dishes in lots of pretty colors and patterns are coordinated with fabric or wipe-clean tablecloths. We also particularly like the attractive, inexpensive glassware in myriad shapes and sizes.

KITCHENWARE

La Carpe

8th arr. - 14, rue Tronchet - 47 42 73 25
Open 9:30 a.m.-6:45 p.m. (Mon. from 1:30 p.m.). Closed Sun. & Aug.

For some 70 years the Loiseau family has furnished chefs and knowledgeable home cooks with utensils at the cutting edge of kitchen technology. All the wares are intelligently displayed by type, so that you can find what you want quickly. The sales staff is friendly and generous with its good advice. Another store in the neighborhood, A la Petite Carpe (13, rue Vignon), carries a selection of gadgets and gizmos for the table. Catalog available upon request.

molds, tart pans) at reasonable prices. But adventurous cooks will love the selection of arcana and novelties, like the combination mills that let you salt and pepper with one hand or the shopping bag specially designed for frozen foods. We're also quite fond of the shop's handsome selection of barware and tableware.

Dehillerin

1st arr. - 18-20, rue Coquillière 42 36 53 13
Open 8 a.m.-6 p.m. Closed Mon. 12:30 p.m.-2 p.m. & Sun.

Since 1820, the cream of the French food establishment have purchased their *batterie de cuisine* at Dehillerin. More recently, they have been joined by large numbers of American and Japanese culinary enthusiasts. Dehillerin

Mora

1st arr. - 13, rue Montmartre - 45 08 19 24
Open 8:30 a.m.-5:45 p.m. (Sat. until noon). Closed Sun.

The shopfront is modern, but Mora is an old established

Depuis des siècles, verriers et tailleurs de Saint Louis soufflent le cristal et le taillent à la main. De la pureté du sable et de l'ardeur du feu naissent des pièces uniques. Au premier plan, deux nouvelles créations de Saint Louis: Tsar, à côtes vénitiennes et jambe torsadée et Crocus, en cristal taillé côtes plates, clair ou doublé rouge.

Le Grand Cristal sort tous les jours.

Les Verreries de Saint-Louis, nées au 16ᵉ siècle sont devenues Verreries Royales il y a 225 ans. A l'occasion de cet anniversaire, Saint Louis vous fait un cadeau: du 1ᵉʳ mars 1992 au 31 janvier 1993, à compter de votre date d'achat, Saint Louis s'engage pendant 2 ans, à remplacer à l'identique, 6 verres brisés sur votre service de 36 verres millésimés 225ᵉ anniversaire (12 à eau, 12 à vin, 12 flûtes ou coupes à champagne), quel que soit le prix du verre!

Vous pourrez ainsi utiliser sans crainte votre service de verres tous les jours, et même vous en offrir un second !

SAINT·LOUIS
FRANCE

Boutique Saint-Louis. 13, rue Royale, 75008 Paris. Tél. (1) 40 17 01 74.
Liste des points de vente : Saint-Louis. 30, rue de Paradis, 75010 Paris. Tél. (1) 47 70 25 70.

Catherine Baril

Two Boutiques

DELUXE
SECOND-HAND
DESIGNER CLOTHING
14, RUE DE LA TOUR
PARIS 16TH
45.20.95.21

DELUXE
SECOND-HAND
DESIGNER CLOTHING
25, RUE DE LA TOUR
PARIS 16TH
45.27.11.46

OPEN DAILY 10-7
MONDAY 2-7

VISA/CARTE BLEUE ACCEPTED

SAINT LAURENT　　　CHANEL　　　UNGARO

GUY LAROCHE　　　GIVENCHY

firm dating back to 1814. The most esoteric items of culinary equipment can be found among the astonishing collection of knives and pots and pans in stainless steel, cast iron or copper, and the very best cake and tart pans coated with new-age anti-adhesives (there are 6,000 items in stock). Amateur cooks benefit from the same low prices as restaurant and catering pros, and they are greeted with the same amiability. The cookbook section boasts over 200 titles; if you think a picture is worth a thousand words, inquire about the cooking-demonstration videos.

A. Simon

2nd arr. - 48, rue Montmartre
42 33 71 65
Open 8:30 a.m.-6:30 p.m. Closed Sun.

This long-established family firm supplies kitchen and tableware to the likes of the Hôtel Méridien, the Café de la Paix and the Ecole de Cuisine in Osaka, Japan. But it also sells its vast range of dishes, glasses and utensils at the same prices to any customer who walks in off the street. For typically French dishes (like the ones you see in traditional brasseries), the prices can't be beat. You'll also find wine pitchers, carafes and ice cream *coupes* that will add an agreeable Gallic touch to your table. The rue Montmartre store specializes in kitchen supplies, while the store around the corner on rue Etienne-Marcel (same phone) deals chiefly in tableware.

Taïr Mercier

5th arr. - 7, bd Saint-Germain
43 54 19 97
Open 11 a.m.-7 p.m. Closed Sat. 1 p.m.-2:30 p.m., Sun. & mid July-mid Aug.

Place mats in appealing shapes (fruits, animals, city skylines) cut out of brightly colored pieces of plastic are big sellers here. But we also dis-covered attractive two-tone plastic shopping bags, melamine fish platters, clear plastic knife rests and absolutely stainproof plastic-coated aprons, all of which convinced us that *plastique, c'est chic!*

■ FURNISHINGS

CONTEMPORARY FURNITURE

Academy

6th arr. - 5, pl. de l'Odéon - 43 29 07 18
12th arr. - 68, rue du Faubourg-Saint-Antoine - 43 42 19 19
Open 9:30 a.m.-1 p.m. & 2:30 p.m.-7 p.m. Closed Sun., Mon. & Aug. No cards.

Jean-Michel Wilmotte was the designer selected to decorate the space beneath the Louvre's glass pyramid, and to create the furnishings to be placed throughout the Grand Louvre. The shop that showcases his collection is austere, like the materials Wilmotte prefers: perforated sheet metal, glass slabs, chipboard. Prices for these singular pieces vary widely.

Arredamento

4th arr. - 18, quai des Célestins
42 74 33 14
Open 10 a.m.-12:30 p.m. & 2 p.m.-7 p.m. Closed Sun. & Mon.

In a spacious and handsome two-level shop, Valentine Boitel and Bernard Renaudin present a wide-ranging selection of top Italian furniture and lighting designs. Connoisseurs with a taste for contemporary Italian design (and well-lined wallets) will applaud the modular storage units by Capellini, the sofas by Zanotta (from 22,000 francs), the coffee tables from Fontana Arte and the lamps by Flos. Fine French design is represented as well, though on a smaller scale—there are some marvelous lamps by Gilles Derain.

Avant-Scène

6th arr. - 4, pl. de l'Odéon - 46 33 12 40
Open 10 a.m.-7 p.m. (Mon. from 2 p.m.). Closed Sun.

An eclectic choice of limited-edition furniture and objets d'art by young designers is on display at this beautiful shop on the place de l'Odéon. Elisabeth Delacarte presents unusual sanded-glass candle holders and light fixtures by sculptor Marco de Gueltz, as well as furniture by Mark Brazier-Jones, Frank Evennou, François Béliard. Prices start at around 100 francs (for a small gilt dish) and soar up to 45,000 francs and beyond for, say, a table by Dubreuil.

Collectania

1st arr. - 2, pl. du Palais-Royal
42 97 01 30
Open 9:30 a.m.-7 p.m. Closed Sun.

Just opposite the Louvre, Collectania is itself virtually a museum of twentieth-century architect-designed furniture. Beautifully presented in this vast space are reissues of designs by Le Corbusier, Frank Lloyd Wright, Gerrit Rietveld, Andrea Branzi and Shiro Kuramata. These exclusive pieces obviously command high prices, but the quality of the furniture and the expert advice dispensed by the staff (all professional interior designers) more than justify the cost.

Ecart International

4th arr. - 111, rue Saint-Antoine
42 78 79 11
Open 10 a.m.-6:30 p.m. Closed Sun. No cards.

The headquarters of Ecart International occupies a townhouse near the Saint-Paul church in the Marais. The bright, spacious, strikingly beautiful showroom presents reissues of pieces by the great designers of the early twentieth century, including Mallet-Stevens, Eileen Gray, Pierre Chareau and Le Corbusier. Ecart also displays work by talented young French creators (Sacha Ketoff, Sylvain Dubuisson, Patrick Naggar, Olivier Gagnère), as well as designs by its own star, Andrée Putman. Prices start at about 1,000 francs and shoot up fast to over 30,000 francs.

Edifice

7th arr. - 27 bis, bd Raspail - 45 48 53 60
Open 10 a.m.-7 p.m. Closed Sun.

Each month, Edifice dreams up a splendid setting to highlight a piece or ensemble of pieces by a favorite designer. Owner Sarah Nathan is keen on avant-garde furniture, like Mario Botta's armchair, Guillaume Saalburg's screen, Ingo Maurer's splendid lamp... The store presents almost all of Philippe Starck's creations for the home (his Costes chair and the self-supporting bookcase among them), alongside designs by Ettore Sottsass, Gae Aulenti and Borek Sipek.

En Attendant Les Barbares

2nd arr. - 50, rue Etienne Marcel 42 33 37 87
Open 10:30 a.m.-7 p.m. (Mon. 10:30 a.m.-1 p.m. & 2 p.m.-7 p.m. & Sat. 11 a.m.-6:30 p.m.). Closed Sun.

The vogue for metal furniture bristling with sharp points started here, with designers Garouste and Bonetti. A comprehensive collection of their "Barbarian Baroque" pieces is on view, alongside works by new designers like Marie-Thérèse Migeon (colorful candlesticks and ashtrays), Agnès Pottier and Santiago Santiago.

Etat de Siège

6th arr. - 1, quai de Conti - 43 29 31 60
7th arr. - 94, rue du Bac - 45 49 10 20

8th arr. - 21, av. de Friedland - 45 62 31 02
Open 11 a.m.-7 p.m. (Mon. from 2 p.m.). Closed Sun.

You are certain to find a seat to suit you among the astonishing assortment stocked here. From Louis XIII *fauteuils* to the most avant-garde chair/sculpture, Etat de Siège displays some 150 different designs, many available in a variety of colors and finishes. Prices vary according to the quality of the wood or metal in question, the workmanship (hand- or factory-finished) and the style.

Galerie Neotu

4th arr. - 25, rue du Renard - 42 78 96 97
Open 11 a.m.-7 p.m. Closed Sun. No cards.

Furniture collectors with a taste for the "neo" find this multifaceted gallery a sure source of aesthetic thrills. Some say the furniture and objects displayed here are the rare and precious antiques of the future. Whether or not that will prove to be the case, owners Gérard Dalmon and Pierre Staudenmeyer spotlight works by young artists, painters, sculptors and architects, particularly those pieces that border the realms of art and design. Most are unique or limited editions, and are thus quite expensive; but the gallery also exhibits some reasonably priced objets d'art.

Modernismes

16th arr. - 16, rue Franklin - 46 47 86 56
Open 10 a.m.-1 p.m. & 2 p.m.-7 p.m. (Sat. 11 a.m.-7 p.m.). Closed Sun. & 2 wks. in Aug.

In this stunning commercial space designed by Gilles Derain, pieces by early-twentieth-century masters (Eileen Gray, Le Corbusier and others) stand side-by-side with the work of Roberto Mariscal or Boris Sipek, of the current generation. The furniture is austere, but the atmosphere in

the shop is warm and cordial, thanks in part to a decor that features art by young painters, Eileen Gray rugs and attractive hand-thrown pottery. Naturally enough, Derain's superb lamps and decorative pieces are given top billing. A lounge chair in leather, wood and fabric, designed by Sipek for Driade, costs around 20,000 francs, but you can walk away with a handsome Derain ashtray for 500 francs.

Nestor Perkal

3rd arr. - 8, rue des Quatre-Fils 42 77 46 80
Open 10 a.m.-7 p.m. (Sat. & Mon. from 2 p.m.). Closed Sun. & Aug.

Spaniard Nestor Perkal, interior architect and designer, has a thing for bright, primary colors. So for his marvelous shop, Perkal has selected pieces from Memphis, that wild and crazy bunch of designing Italians, and from the Spanish firm Ediciones. Well before Spain and the *movida* were trendy, Perkal was showing avant-garde designs from Madrid, Seville and, of course, Barcelona.

Protis

8th arr. - 153, rue du Faubourg Saint-Honoré - 45 62 22 40
16th arr. - 22, av. Raymond-Poincarré - 47 04 60 40
Open 3 p.m.-7 p.m. (Sat. 10 a.m.-1 p.m. & 2:30 p.m.-6:30 p.m.). Closed Sun.

White walls and a gray-tile floor set the glass-and-steel furniture off to advantage. Protis presents its own designs (coffee tables in glass and black lacquered metal), Italian pieces by Cattelan, Bieffeplast, Tonon and Technolinea with a beautiful line of office furniture in walnut or rosewood) and a host of creations by noted architects. A leather-covered high-back chair by Cattelan sells for 3,000 francs or so.

Antoine Schapira

6th arr. - 74, bd Raspail - 45 48 22 80
Open 10:30 a.m.-1 p.m. & 3 p.m.-7 p.m. Closed Sun., Mon. & 2 wks. in Aug.

Antoine Schapira, a designer and cabinetmaker with a diploma from the Ecole Boulle, proposes superb contemporary furniture with a strong, singular personality. Schapira crafts and signs each sofa, armchair, bookcase and console himself, using rare and precious woods (palm wood, for example); every piece is custom-made.

VIA

6th arr. - 4-6-8, cour du Commerce Saint-André - 43 29 39 36
Open 10:30 a.m.-7 p.m. Closed Sun. & Aug.

VIA stands for *Valorisation de l'Innovation dans l'Ameublement*; in other words, an association for promoting innovative furniture design. Now housed in spacious new quarters on the Left Bank, this gallery/shop/showroom continues to give young designers a boost. VIA alumni include such luminaries as Wilmotte, Starck and Mourgue; among the up-and-coming stars now on view is Kristian Gavoille, elected Designer of the Year in 1992 by a jury of his peers.

OUTDOOR FURNITURE

Le Cèdre Rouge

1st arr. - 22, av. Victoria - 42 33 71 05
Open 10 a.m.-7 p.m. (Mon from 11 a.m.). Closed Sun.
6th arr. - 5, rue de Médicis - 42 33 71 05
Open 10:30 a.m.-7:30 p.m. Closed Sun. & Mon.

Furniture for the patio and garden, in Burmese teak or colonial-style wicker, is the specialty of Le Cèdre Rouge. But you will also find handsome little volcanic stone tables in a score of colors, and copies of eighteenth-century furniture executed in steel and canvas. We could browse for hours among the many elegant pieces of handcrafted pottery (over 2,000 in stock) from Biot, Aubagne and Tuscany. A section devoted to decorative objects for indoors includes lamps, Florentine ceramics and lovely rustic baskets.

Jardins Imaginaires

6th arr. - 9 bis, rue d'Assas - 42 22 90 03
Open 10:30 a.m.-1 p.m. & 2 p.m.-6:30 p.m. (Mon. from 2 p.m.). Closed Sun.

A medley of handsome antique furnishings full of grace and wit; a selection of modern furniture and objets d'art for sophisticated gardens and conservatories; an original selection of statuary, pottery, urns and basins... the "imaginary gardens" evoked in this wonderful shop brim over with charm, humor and taste. It's one of our very favorite shops in Paris.

SOFAS & CHAIRS

Duo Sur Canapé

1st arr. - 3, rue de Turbigo - 42 33 37 12
Open 10:30 a.m.-1 p.m. & 2 p.m.-7 p.m. (Mon. 2 p.m.-7 p.m.). Closed Sun.

Contemporary sofas and chairs by top designers. Philippe Starck's recent "Paramount" collection (commissioned by the New York hotel of the same name) is on display.

Un Fauteuil Pour Deux

6th arr. - 9, rue Corneille - 43 29 74 32
Open 10:30 a.m.-7 p.m. Closed Sun. & Mon.

Bernard Maxime updates classic French chairs and sofas by splashing them with brilliant color or upholstering them with unusual fabrics. A browse around this shop will yield scores of decorating ideas, even if you don't fancy lugging (or shipping) furniture back home. Ornamental objects and accessories are also on view, at prices ranging fro 400 to 100,000 francs.

First Time

6th arr. - 27, rue Mazarine - 43 25 55 00
Open 10 a.m.-6:45 p.m. (Mon. from 2 p.m.). Closed Sun. & 3 wks. in Aug.

Noted designer Didier Gomez heads this interior decorating firm, which manufactures chairs (7,000 to 10,000 francs) and sofas (17,000 to 20,000 francs) signed by Gomez himself, or by his equally well-known colleagues, Christian Duc and Andrée Putman.

■ HARDWARE

Garnier

12th arr. - 30 bis, bd de la Bastille 43 43 84 85
Open 9 a.m.-12:30 p.m. & 1:30 p.m.-5 p.m. Closed Sat. & Sun. No cards.

Established in 1832, Garnier is a specialist in ornamental hardware and locks. Reproductions of Louis XV, Louis XVI, Directoire, Empire and English locks and plaques are still manufactured and displayed—though not sold— here. A friendly and informative staff can provide a list of dealers who handle any model you might be interested in acquiring.

A la Providence (Leclercq)

11th arr. - 151, rue du Faubourg Saint-Antoine - 43 43 06 41
Open 8:30 a.m.-6 p.m. (Mon. 8:30 a.m.-noon & 2 p.m.-6 p.m.). Closed Sun.

This is undoubtedly the most delightful hardware store on the Faubourg-Saint-Antoine (the cabinetmaker's and woodworker's quarter). Arlette, one of France's few female locksmiths, welcomes you into her domain, where she and her colleagues fashion handmade copies of locks and other hardware, working from antique originals. Some of the hard-to-find items available here are hand-cut crystal knobs for banisters and brass plaques for 1930s armoires.

■ INTERIOR DECORATION

INTERIOR DECOR

La Chaise Longue
1st - 30, rue Croix des Petits-Champs - 42 96 32 14
Open 11 a.m.-7 p.m. Closed Sun.
3rd - 20, rue des Francs-Bourgeois - 48 04 36 37
Open 11 a.m.-7 p.m. (Sun. from 2 p.m.).
6th - 8, rue Princesse - 43 29 62 39
Open noon-8 p.m. Closed Sun.
A gay and colorful shop chock-full of amusing items to add a touch of whimsy to the house. For the kitchen, there is enameled metalware (plates, pots, pitchers and so on), multicolored glasses, special barbecue grills and piles of gadgets; for the office or *salon*, there are hammered metal picture frames, trendy wire baskets by Filo di Ferro, potpourri and papier-mâché vases. Browsing here is lots of fun.

Galerie Acanthe
16th arr. - 18, rue Cortambert 45 03 15 55
Open 11 a.m.-1 p.m. & 2 p.m.-7 p.m. Closed Sun., Mon. & Aug. No cards.
Christian Benais's shop looks like the home of a private collector, where Napoléon III furniture cohabits comfortably with Art Deco ornaments and objets d'art. Benais adores antique linens, and he has amassed a considerable selection of turn-of-the-century embroidered tablecloths, as well as some fine contemporary pieces in embroidered linen and Egyptian cotton. He is also creative director for the

Chotard-Brochier textile firm, designing marvelous fabrics (lots of swatches are on view).

Elle
6th arr. - 30, rue Saint-Sulpice 43 26 46 10
Open 10:30 a.m.-7 p.m. Closed Sun.
Chosen by the style-conscious editors of *Elle Décoration*, the dishes, lamps, lap rugs and many other decorative and useful objects on display are both lovely to look at and a pleasure to use.

Etamine
7th arr. - 63, rue du Bac - 42 22 03 16
Open 9:30 a.m.-7 p.m. (Mon. from 1 p.m.). Closed Sun. & 2 wks. in Aug.
Etamine's new bilevel boutique numbers among the trendiest home-decor shops in Paris, with a superb collection of fabrics from all over the globe: neoclassic prints and cut velvets from Timney and Fowler, a horsehair look-alike made with a vegetable fiber from the Philippines and a plethora of attractive wallpaper designs. Also on hand is a selection of sofas, lamps, objets d'art and a few choice antique pieces.

Galerie du Bac
7th arr. - 116, rue du Bac - 40 49 03 03
Open 10 a.m.-1 p.m. & 2 p.m.-6:30 p.m. Closed Sun. & Aug.
Galerie du Bac is a handsome, spacious showcase for the latest creations for the home by Missoni—linens and upholstery fabrics, sheets and towels by TJVestor and Mateb. Don't miss the gorgeous Italian wallpapers (crinkled, waxed, "pre-worn"...), or the Woodnotes paper rugs.

Christian Badin
6th arr. - 12, rue de Tournon - 43 26 00 67
Open 10 a.m.-7 p.m. Closed Sat. in July & Aug. & Sun.
A warm, urbane atmosphere reigns in this pretty shop, a showcase for a marvelous collection of fabrics, rugs and decorative objects. The rugs—dhurries, English wool carpeting in 70 different patterns (1,150 francs per linear meter) and tinted palm-fiber matting (160 francs per square meter)—can be made up in the colors of your choice. Christian Badin's beautiful fabrics are inspired by eighteenth-century designs; the patterns come in bright, slightly acidic

---

A pungent pilgrimage

Paris had a *sewer system* as early as 1370, but the waste emptied straight into the River Seine. Epidemics followed plagues, and public hygiene made little further progress until 1854, when a series of drains and aqueducts channelled the worst of the city's sewage twelve miles downstream. A vast program to eliminate and purify the last outflows from the capital was launched in 1984. Although we now take the benefits of modern waste-treatment plants for granted, it is interesting to see how a city sewer plant works—and how nasty it smells! Guided tours of the sewer system of Paris leave the quai d'Orsay side of the Pont de l'Alma on Monday and Wednesday afternoons (weather permitting); the tour lasts an hour and a quarter.

colors printed on cotton or silk. Badin's furniture is crafted in natural beech or in sycamore. The splendid decorative objects are not the sort one sees everywhere; we were enchanted by some etched Austrian wine glasses, copied from an eighteenth-century model. Decorating service available.

Juste Mauve

16th arr. - 29, rue Greuze - 47 27 82 31
Open 10 a.m.-7 p.m. (Mon. from 11 p.m.). Closed Sat. (except Nov. 1-end of Feb.), Sun. & Aug.

Anne-Marie de Ganay's shop has all the charm of a cozy English home, with its mix of mahogany (coffee tables from 6,000 francs) and flowered chintz, low stools and Chinese cachepots (900 francs), picture frames in burled elm and marquetry (650 francs). Piles of lacy cushions and a selection of ravishing lingerie lend a frothy, feminine note.

Miller et Bertaux

4th arr. - 27, rue du Bourg-Tibourg - 42 77 25 31
Open 11 a.m.-1:30 p.m. & 2 p.m.-7 p.m. Closed Sun. & Mon.

A world that is at once both fragile and rough-hewn, exotic and natural—in any case, brimming with charm and fantasy. The tree-branch lamps, palm-leaf chairs, wrought-iron tables and tulip-printed fabrics perfectly sum up the "ecology-chic" that is the dominant trend in French interior decoration today.

Nicole H.

6th arr. - 28, rue Bonaparte - 43 25 43 60
Open 9:30 a.m.-noon & 1:30 p.m.-6:30 p.m. Closed Sun., Mon. & Aug.

Nicole Hannezo designs delightful furniture with a 1930s feel: writing desks, bars, dining room tables and coffee tables, in wood washed with

ceruse (a white pigment), then lacquered or given a sharkskin finish. All the pieces are made to order, and prices are really unbeatable, considering their beauty and exquisite workmanship. An exceptional selection of fabrics from the best manufacturers is available here, as well as a decorating service.

Les Olivades

16th arr. - 25, rue de l'Annonciation - 45 27 07 76
Open 10 a.m.-7 p.m. Closed Sun., Mon. & Aug.

The wonderful warmth and charm of Provence is infused into this tiny shop tucked away behind the rue de Passy. Redolent of olive oil and lavender, bright with the colors of the Midi, Les Olivades displays, among other treasures, traditional Provençal print fabrics. If you're not handy with a needle, there are many small items already made up: bags, eyeglass cases, makeup cases, skirts, shawls and even the sunniest umbrellas imaginable.

Souleiado

6th arr. - 78, rue de Seine - 43 54 15 13
16th arr. - 83-85, av. Paul-Doumer - 42 24 99 34
Open 10 a.m.-7 p.m. (Mon. from 2 p.m.). Closed Sun.

Thanks to Charles Demery, Provençal fabrics are known and sought after the world over. Souleiado's original designs, many dating from the eighteenth century, are available in a riot of cheerful colors. Coordinated wallpaper and oilcloth (30 patterns) are on hand too, and the home-decor department also offers quilted bedspreads with matching sheets, tablecloths, fabric-covered boxes, shopping bags, picture frames and—the firm's best-seller—place mat and napkin sets. The space devoted to fashion continues to grow: wool shawls sell for around 1,000 francs, and

there are very trendy men's shirts as well.

Vivement Jeudi

5th arr. - 52, rue Mouffetard - 43 31 44 52
Open Thurs. 10 a.m.-8 p.m.

Open only on Thursdays, this absolutely charming house-within-a-house presents antiques and humbler second-hand (but first-quality) furniture, linens and decorative objects for the home. All the merchandise has been lovingly collected by the shop's two owners, assiduous frequenters of flea markets all over France.

MISCELLANY

Au Chêne-Liège

14th arr. - 74, bd du Montparnasse - 43 22 02 15
Open 9:30 a.m.-6:30 p.m. Closed Sun. & Mon.

A *chêne-liège* is a cork-oak, and cork is the specialty of this well-known Montparnasse emporium. And we've seen the most astonishing range of articles, all in cork—accessories for the wine cellar, for the desk and office, luggage and handbags and even women's clothing (believe us, nothing could be less kinky!).

Passementeries de l'Ile de France

11th arr. - 11, rue Trousseau - 48 05 44 33
Open 9 a.m.-5:30 p.m. (Fri. 9 a.m.-5 p.m.). Closed Sat., Sun. & Aug. No cards.

One of the last surviving specialists in silk braid and fringe (to trim curtains, chairs and lampshades, for example), who will design to the customer's specifications. The firm also manufactures reproductions of period trims, as well as a line of contemporary designs.

La Passementerie Nouvelle

1st arr. - 15, rue Etienne-Marcel
42 36 30 01
Open 9 a.m.-6 p.m. Closed Sat., Sun. & Aug. No cards.

When France needs new trimmings for the draperies at Versailles or Fontainebleau, it calls on La Passementerie Nouvelle. In addition to reproductions of historic pieces, the company works with period-style braids, trims and fringe specially adapted for contemporary fabrics.

SMH

11th arr. - 76, bd Richard Lenoir
43 57 47 25
Open 9 a.m.-12:30 p.m. & 1:45 p.m.-6 p.m. Closed Sun.

Single- and double-curved moldings, cornices, carved door frames, baseboards and rosettes (in pine, oak, tropical wood, polyurethane or even Styrofoam) will dress up even the plainest prefab bungalow. SMH will cut all these elements to measure, then you take them home, paint them, put them up... and presto! Good-bye suburbia, hello Versailles! SMH also sells all sorts of supplies for do-it-yourself picture-framers.

RUGS & NEEDLEPOINT

Brocard

4th arr. - 1, rue Jacques-Cœur
42 72 16 38
Open 9 a.m.-noon & 2 p.m.-5 p.m. Closed Sat., Sun. & Aug. No cards.

If needlework is your favorite pastime, do make time to stop in here. Brocard manufactures all manner of canvases in many sizes. Vintage embroideries and needlepoint receive careful restoration here.

The prices in this guide reflect what establishments were charging at press time.

Casa Lopez

6th arr. - 27, bd Raspail - 45 48 30 97
Open 10 a.m.-1 p.m. & 2:30 p.m.-6:30 p.m. Closed Sun., Mon. & 3 wks. in Aug.

Casa Lopez proposes covetable jacquard rugs in geometric patterns, many of which are reversible. Most designs are available in ten different sizes, in a range of 90 colors, for reasonable prices (8,500 francs for a two by three meter rug). Palm-fiber rugs in checkerboard, herringbone or houndstooth patterns have loads of casual charm, and we love the wool carpets with raised lozenge, diagonal or ribbon motifs. Certain designs are also available on canvas, to make coordinating petit-point chair backs and seats.

Toulemonde-Bochart

2nd arr. -10, rue du Mail - 40 26 68 83
Open 10 a.m.-7 p.m. Closed Sun. & 3 wks. in Aug.

This award-winning firm's claim to fame is its collection of contemporary rugs designed by the top names: Andrée Putman, Hilton McConnico, Christian Duc, Jean-Michel Wilmotte. Decorative dhurries, sisal and palm fiber matting are pretty too, and considerably less expensive.

WALLPAPER & FABRICS

Besson

6th arr. - 32, rue Bonaparte - 40 51 89 64
Open 9:30 a.m.-6:30 p.m. Closed Sun., Mon. & 2 wks. in Aug.

The choicest English and French decorator fabrics and wallpapers have been featured at Besson for 30 years. The range of nostalgic, romantic, exotic and rustic patterns is considerable, and the sales staff, bursting with good advice, is also gratifyingly generous with samples.

Manuel Canovas

6th arr. - 5, rue de Furstenberg
43 26 89 31
Open 10 a.m.-7 p.m. (Mon. from 11 a.m.). Closed Sun. & 2 wks. in Aug.

Textile designer and manufacturer Manuel Canovas came up with a style that revolutionized interior decorating in the 1960s. This master colorist drew his inspiration from extensive travels in India, Japan and California, as well as from imagined botanical gardens. Canovas's extraordinary chintzes are done in slightly acid tones, while muted shades are preferred on such sophisticated fabrics as moiré. Coordinated wall coverings are available as well, and in the shop next door, fashion and home accessories are made up in Canovas fabrics.

Casal

7th arr. - 40, rue des Saints-Pères
45 44 78 70
Open 9:30 a.m.-6:30 p.m. Sat. (Sept. 1-May 1) & Mon. 10 a.m.-6 p.m. Closed Sun. No cards.

Casal's signature jacquard prints, inspired by traditional paisley patterns and kilim rug designs, look terrific on sofas. But in this spacious, skylit showroom (formerly an artist's studio) you will also find fabrics by Brunschwig, Jean-Michel Wilmotte and Decortex.

Pierre Frey

6th arr. - 2, rue de Furstenberg
46 33 73 00
Open 10 a.m.-6:30 p.m. Closed Sun. & 3 wks. in Aug.

This firm is a family affair with an international reputation. Although the designers draw a good deal of their inspiration from traditional eighteenth- and nineteenth-century French patterns, Pierre Frey is also known for its vast—and ever-growing—line of contemporary fabrics and wall coverings. In the *Patrick Frey* home-decor shops, you'll find a selection of handsome bed linens, cushions, shawls, fabric-covered boxes and laminated trays, all in the Frey signature prints.

Nobilis Fontan

6th arr. - 40, rue Bonaparte - 43 29 21 50
Open 9:30 a.m.-6:30 p.m. Closed Sun.

Since it opened in 1928, this decorating firm has enjoyed a reputation for the high quality and refined taste of its design. Refined, but not conservative, Nobilis Fontan has always managed to evolve intelligently, keeping pace with contemporary designers (recent additions to the Nobilis stable: Robert Le Héros, Ravage and Miller et Bertaux). The wallpapers on display here are relatively expensive, but they are beautifully made. The fabric patterns are inspired by classic English, Japanese and Chinese models, and coordinate perfectly with the wall coverings. Nobilis has extended its line of merchandise to include designer furniture and, in a recent development, shoes and *chapeaux*.

Tissus Reine

18th arr. - Place du Marché Saint-Pierre - 46 06 02 31
Open 9:15 a.m.-6:30 p.m., Mon. 2 p.m.-6:30 p.m. & Sat. until 6:45 p.m. Closed Sun.

You will get a special attention with a decorator to guide your choice among all the fabrics designers represented here. Large upholstery department.

Zuber

6th arr. - 55, quai des Grands-Augustins - 43 29 77 84
Open 10 a.m.-6 p.m. Closed Sun. & 2 wks. in Aug. No cards.

A dynamic new owner has revitalized the venerable firm of Zuber, boosting its level of creativity to new heights.

Using time-honored printing methods and working from a library of more than 100,000 antique patterns, Zuber's is an eye-popping collection of wallpapers: trompe l'œil, panoramas, marbled and damask papers, as well as sublime friezes, cornices and borders of roses and other flowers in the subtlest of tints. Orders (excluding special orders) can be filled in 48 hours.

■ LIGHTING

Antica

7th arr. - 38, rue de Verneuil - 42 61 28 86
Open 10 a.m.-6:30 p.m. Closed Sun., Mon. & Aug. No cards.

Madame Clérin can whip up a lampshade from one of the rich and refined fabrics she has in stock in about ten days, or she'll sell you a ready-made shade (for about 30 percent less than the price of a custom-made shade). If you find yourself in a decorating quandary, she will come to your home to provide sage counsel and advice.

Artémide

11th arr. - 6-8, rue Basfroi - 43 67 17 17
Open 9 a.m.-12:30 p.m. & 1:30 p.m.-6 p.m. Closed Sat. & Sun. No cards.

If you are curious to see what sort of lamps and light fixtures the best European designers have come up with lately, come to Artémide. Mario Botta, Vico Magistretti, Ettore Sottsass and Richard Sapper are just some of the famous names represented in this huge loft showroom.

Capeline

16th arr. - 144, av. de Versailles 45 20 22 65
Open 10 a.m.-7 p.m. Closed Sun., Mon. & Aug. No cards.

In this vast workshop, known to all the best Parisian decorators, craftspeople still turn out pleated, gathered and

skirted lampshades just like in the good old days.

Ready Made

6th arr. - 38-40, rue Jacob - 42 60 28 01
Open 10 a.m.-7 p.m. Closed Sun. & Mon.

Italian halogens are the specialty of this sleek and trendy shop near Saint-Germain. Flos, Artémide and Arteluce are a few of the manufacturers on hand; we particularly admire the floor lamps designed by Jean-François Crochet in metal and Murano glass. The sister store next door exhibits furniture that is equally select, with an accent on reissues of 1930s classics by Eileen Gray, Breuer, Macintosh and Chareau.

■ LINENS

La Chatelaine

16th arr. - 170, av. Victor Hugo 47 27 44 07
Open 9:30 a.m.-6:30 p.m. (Sat. 9:30 a.m.-12:30 p.m. & 2:30 p.m.-6:30 p.m.). Closed Sun. & Mon.

For superb linens for your bed, bath and table, in satiny cotton, cotton muslin, organdy or linen, this shop comes highly recommended. All linens can be embroidered at your request, or you can have pieces specially tailored to your needs (extra-large bath sheets, odd-size tablecloths...).

Agnès Comar

8th arr. - 7, av. Georges-V - 47 23 33 85
Open 10:30 a.m.-1 p.m. & 2 p.m.-7 p.m. Closed Sun. & 3 wks in Aug.

Always bubbling with fresh, elegant ideas for the home, international decorator Agnès Comar now has a solution for your dingy living room sofa and chairs: loose, flowing slipcovers in a linen-and-cotton blend that adapt to any shape, virtually any size, and are machine washable (for

3,500 francs). She also makes table skirts to measure, with luxurious quilted borders, and felt bedspreads with adorable appliqués that coordinate with Comar's curtains and cushions. Sheets come in white or ecru, embroidered or edged with pleats or lace (matched with travel and makeup kits). Expect to pay top prices for these luxurious linens.

Fanette
15th arr. - 1, rue d'Alençon - 42 22 21 73
Open 1 p.m.-7 p.m. Closed Sun. & July 10-Sept. 6.
Fanette's specialty is vintage household linen: embroidered pillowcases, damask tablecloths and Provençal quilted bedspreads. All the pieces are in excellent condition, sold in a charming country-style shop decorated with pretty antiques, curios and baskets (all of which are for sale).

Peau d'Ange
16th arr. - 1, rue Mesnil - 45 53 78 11
Open 10:30 a.m.-noon & 2 p.m.-6:30 p.m. Closed Sun. & Aug. No cards.
A delightfully refined little boutique, Peau d'Ange is awash in frothy vintage linens (embroidered sheets embellished with openwork cost 250 francs; a sheet plus two pillowcases goes for 600 francs). Hand-embroidered tablecloths range between 300 and 6,000 francs, depending on size and quality. Another specialty: old-fashioned bridal gowns, which are altered to the bride's size, then laundered, starched and ironed just before the big day!

Find the address you are looking for, quickly and easily, in the index.

Porthault
8th arr. - 18, av. Montaigne - 47 20 75 25
Open 9:30 a.m.-6:30 p.m. (Sat. & Mon. 9:30 a.m.-1 p.m. & 2 p.m.-6 p.m.). Closed Sun.
Everyone who loves luxurious linens knows Porthault. Even if you can't afford these signature prints and exquisite embroideries (they are, of course, direly expensive—a tablecloth can cost up to 50,000 francs), you can browse, finger (discreetly!) and admire them in this tony shop on the avenue Montaigne. A lower-priced line, Porthault Studio, was recently introduced—but even lower-than-regular prices here aren't cheap. A pair of sheets and two pillowcases in embroidered cotton start at 2,500 francs and quickly climb to 35,000.

■ TABLEWARE

CANDLES

Cir-Roussel
6th arr. - 22, rue Saint-Sulpice - 43 26 46 50
Open 10 a.m.-7 p.m. (Mon. from 11 a.m.). Closed Sun.
In the wax-processing business since 1643, Cir-Roussel offers a considerable choice of candles in a variety of classic and imaginative shapes. Current bestsellers are "cake," "caviar" and "sandwich" candles. These, like any candle in the shop, may be personalized with your name or initials for a modest fee.

Point à la Ligne
7th arr. - 25, rue de Varenne - 42 84 14 45
11th arr. - 28, rue Neuves des Boulets - 43 48 45 84
16th arr. - 67, av. Victor Hugo - 45 00 96 80
Open 10 a.m.-7 p.m. Closed Sun.
You are certain to find candles to match your centerpiece or tablecloth (or your

eyes, for that matter) in this pretty boutique. There are dozens of shades available, each one coordinated with paper napkins, plates and tablecloths. Candle holders are available as well, in clear or colored glass, along with hurricane lamps and a line of candles in imaginative shapes that echo the seasons or holidays. If you wish, Point à la Ligne will custom-illuminate your house or garden for a special party.

CRYSTAL & CHINA

Baccarat
8th arr. - 11, pl. de la Madeleine - 42 65 36 26
Open 9:30 a.m.-6:30 p.m. (Sat. & Mon. from 10 a.m.). Closed Sun.
Baccarat now boasts a glittering flagship store on the place de la Madeleine. Guarding the collection of incomparably pure, superbly wrought crystal stemware, decorative items and objets d'art is a fierce 65-pound bear; he, too, is entirely crafted in crystal.

Au Bain Marie
8th arr. - 10, rue Boissy-d'Anglas - 42 66 59 74
Open 10 a.m.-7 p.m. Closed Sun.
In a setting that recalls the lobby of a palatial hotel, Aude Clément presents a vast assortment of eminently desirable tableware, kitchenware and accessories. Even the items that aren't expensive antiques look as if they ought to be: embroidered table linens, genuine crystal or just-glass glasses (initialed or not, as you wish), real and fake pearl-handled cutlery... Pieces by contemporary designers (watch for Frank Evennou's Champagne bucket) and by talented artisans (the hand-decorated faïences are superb) are exhibited alongside witty, inexpensive

treasures for the table. Don't miss the huge accumulation of cookbooks and magazines on food and wine.

Bernardaud

8th arr. - 11, rue Royale - 47 42 82 66
Open 9:30 a.m.-6:30 p.m. Closed Sun.

Since 1863, the Limoges-based Bernardaud has been a standard-bearer for French china manufacturers. Following the lead of other prestigious tableware manufacturers, Bernardaud has opened a showcase on the rue Royale to display the entire array of its collections. A recent addition is the much-admired *Les Métropoles* service, whose stylized motifs represent the cities of Paris, Berlin, Moscow, London and New York (423 francs for a dinner plate).

Cristalleries Saint-Louis

8th arr. - 13, rue Royale - 40 17 01 74
Open 10 a.m.-7 p.m. Closed Sun.

This venerable firm (founded in 1586) which long crafted crystal for the kings of France, continues to maintain the highest standards of quality. A visit to Saint-Louis's dazzling showplace on the rue Royale will have you too longing to adorn your table with mouth-blown, hand-cut crystal stemware, decanters encrusted with gold and filigreed or opaline vases...

Daum

2nd arr. - 4, rue de la Paix - 42 61 25 25
Open 10 a.m.-7 p.m. (Mon. from 11 p.m.). Closed Sun.

Daum's elegant dual-level showrooms are situated in premises formerly occupied by the great couturier, Worth. Slate-gray walls and green-glazed bronze furniture form an ideal setting for the firm's latest creations. On the ground floor are the limited-edition (200 or 300 copies) glass pieces, in luminous colors: Fassianos's cobalt-blue head, carafes with cactus stoppers by Hilton McConnico, and baroque designs by Garouste and Bonetti. The lower level is devoted to Daum's lovely crystal table services.

Devine Qui Vient Dîner

15th arr. - 83, av. Emile-Zola - 40 59 41 14
Open 10:30 a.m.-7:30 p.m. Closed Sun. & Mon.

This red-and-gray shop is known for its noteworthy assortment of late-nineteenth- and early-twentieth-century tableware, along with many finely crafted reproductions. Prices are amazingly reasonable for the antique ceramic ware, colored glasses, silver-plated table accessories and such.

Dîners en Ville

7th arr. - 27, rue de Varenne - 42 22 78 33
Open 11 a.m.-7 p.m. (Mon. from 2 p.m.). Closed Sun.

It's hard not to notice this shop, with its multiple display windows that wrap around the corner of the rue du Bac and the rue de Varenne. It's even harder not to stop and gape at the lavish tables draped in old-fashioned paisley tablecloths and set (by owner Blandine de Mandat-Gracey) with turn-of-the-century French or English dishes, colorful Bohemian crystal and antique table decorations. Inside, there are glasses in an enchanting array of tints and, on the upper floor, a section devoted to the ritual of tea, with teapots, tea services, vintage cookie jars and silver accessories.

Monday, like Sunday, is a day of rest for many shopkeepers.

La Faïence Anglaise

6th arr. - 11, rue du Dragon - 42 22 42 72
Open 10:30 a.m.-7 p.m. (Sat. from 11 a.m. & Mon. from 2 p.m.). Closed Sun.

Anglophiles and other tea fanciers will love the selection of small Victorian antiques, figurines and 1930s lamps available here. But dishes and table and tea accessories are the principal specialty of the house. Teapots, cake plates and tea caddies range in price from about 300 to 500 francs. Fifteen different models of Wedgwood china are on sale here (plates run from 56 to 152 francs each).

Gien

1st arr. - 39, rue des Petits-Champs - 47 03 49 92
Open 10:30 a.m.-2:30 p.m. & 3 p.m.-7 p.m. (Sat. & Mon. hours vary). Closed Sun. & Aug. 1-22.

The Gien faïence factory, founded in 1821, has been granted a new lease on life. Noted designers have been commissioned to create new patterns that are now on view in Gien's Paris showroom: Paco Rabanne came up with a service of square plates with delicate ridges, while Jean-Pierre Caillères designed triangular plates edged with black speckles. In a more traditional vein, Dominique Lalande painted his plates with fruit motifs and added a black-and-white border. People who prefer the Gien services that their grandmothers bought will be happy to see that they are still available.

Muriel Grateau

1st arr. - 132-133, galerie de Valois - 40 20 90 30
Open 11 a.m.-12:30 a.m. & 1 p.m.-7 p.m. (Mon. from 2 p.m.). Closed Sun. & 3 wks. in Aug.

A talented designer and woman of taste, Muriel Grateau has amassed a highly sophisticated collection of Murano glasses, Limoges china and linen napery in a superb palette of muted earth and mineral tones (superb blues, grays, purples and greens). The mix of antique and contemporary pieces on a single table is simply ravishing.

Lalique

8th arr. - 11, rue Royale - 42 66 52 40
Open 9:30 a.m.-6:30 p.m. Closed Sun.

Three generations of creative Laliques have earned an international following with their enchanting crystal designs. Marie-Claude Lalique, who succeeded her father, Marc, at the head of the company in 1977, creates marvelous contemporary pieces in the true Lalique spirit—like her Atossa vase, decorated with a circlet of amber crystal-and-opaline flowers. In the courtyard of the rue Royale shop, Lalique has opened another boutique, devoted to "the art of the table." Accompanying the Lalique crystal glasses and plates are linens, silver and china by prestigious manufacturers.

La Maison du Week-End

6th arr. - 26, rue Vavin - 43 54 15 52
Open 10 a.m.-7 p.m. (Mon. until 6 p.m.). Closed Sun. & Aug.

If your idea of a weekend treat is a shopping spree for linens and dishes to fill up your cupboards, we've got just the address for you. Old-fashioned damask tablecloths, in a range of seven pastel shades, are made to order here (from about 300 francs); damask towels sell for 278 francs with fringe, 178 francs without. You'll also find table services in faïence (earthenware) or china; the most recent addition to the line is a china tea service decorated with tiny old-fashioned blossoms. Do you

feel that what is lacking in your life is a gilded garden chair? Look no further.

Manufacture Nationale de Sèvres

1st arr. - 4, pl. André-Malraux 42 61 40 54
Open 11 a.m.-6:30 p.m. Closed Sun. & Mon. No cards.

In an ultra-contemporary setting, with glass-and-brushed-steel shelves, La Manufacture Nationale de Sèvres presents its superb hand-painted, gold-trimmed china. Every piece is a work of art; some pieces are designed by noted artists—Lalanne, Mathieu, Van Lith and Coloretti, among others. Also on display are reproductions of such extraordinary objets d'art as the dancers sculpted by Léonard and Carpeaux. Prices for plates range from 1,000 to 10,000 francs, and the most expensive vase commands 200,000 francs. Special orders are completed in one to three months.

Odiot

8th arr. - 7, pl. de la Madeleine 42 65 00 95
Open 9:30 a.m.-6:30 p.m. (Sat. 10 a.m.-1 p.m. & 2:15 p.m.-6:30 p.m.). Closed Sun.

Silversmiths in Paris since 1690, this illustrious firm maintains its traditions by continuing to reissue pieces cast in eighteenth- and nineteenth-century molds. Odiot will also execute silver or vermeil pieces as requested by a customer (a Napoléon-era desk lamp in gilded silver, priced well over 250,000 francs, is the most expensive object in the shop). For shoppers of more modest means, there are some fine items in silver-plate, china and crystal. Appealing little brooches in the form of a bee cost around 350 francs.

Find the address you are looking for, quickly and easily, in the index.

Pavillon Christofle

2nd arr. - 24, rue de la Paix - 42 65 62 43
6th arr. - 17, rue de Sèvres - 45 48 17 83
8th arr. - 9, rue Royale - 49 33 43 00
16th arr. - 95, rue de Passy - 46 47 51 27
Open 9:30 a.m.-6:30 p.m. Closed Sun.

Christofle was born in 1830, and began to produce the plated silverware that was to make the firm its fortune. Since then, Christofle has become the world's premier exporter of table silver. The current bestseller is the clean-lined, contemporary Aria setting. A recent creation, the Talisman line of Chinese-lacquered settings, owes its beauty and durability to a jealously guarded secret process. Christofle has also enjoyed notable success with reproductions of its designs from the 1920s (like the coveted tea service in silver plate with briarwood handles), and a handsome line of classic china (a dinner plate from the newest service, Orientalys, costs 300 francs).

Peter

8th arr. - 191, rue du Faubourg Saint-Honoré - 45 61 19 37
Open 10 a.m.-6:30 p.m. (Mon. from 1:30 p.m.). Closed Sun. & 3 wks. in Aug.

For a couple of centuries, Peter's exclusive silverware patterns have adorned the dinner tables of the rich and refined (the Aga Khan and Giovanni Agnelli appear on the clients list, just to give you an idea). The most sumptuous setting in the shop, fashioned of lapis lazuli and vermeil, is priced just shy of 15,000 francs. But Peter accommodates less opulent tastes as well, with beautifully designed contemporary silver, china services, crystal and small gifts (an elegant nail clipper goes for around 100 francs).

Puiforcat

8th arr. - 2, av. Matignon - 45 63 10 10

Open 9:30 a.m.-6:30 p.m. (Sat. & Mon. 9:30 a.m.-1 p.m. & 2:15 p.m.-6:30 p.m.). Closed Sun.

A few years ago, Eliane Scali, director of this world-renowned silversmithing firm had the bright idea to reissue Jean Puiforcat's stunning 1930s designs (like the table settings for the oceanliner the *Normandie*). More recently Puiforcat added a gift and jewelry department that stocks merchandise for nearly every budget. A silver-plated centerpiece sells for 1,400 francs; but a pretty silver chain bracelet sells for only 200 francs. Puiforcat continues to commission pieces from well-known designers such as Andrée Putman and Manuel Canovas.

Quartz Diffusion

6th arr. - 12, rue des Quatre-Vents - 43 54 03 00

Open 10:30 a.m.-7 p.m. (Mon. from 2:30 p.m.). Closed Sun.

There's lots of space in this shop, all of it devoted to the delicate art of the glassmaker. The objects on display are signed by such talented artists as Baldwin, Guggisberg, Bouchard, Hinz, Gilbert and others who research the possibilities of glass for the Musée des Arts Décoratifs. Not everything is terrifyingly fragile or expensive, witness the "laboratory" glass carafe and salad bowl (150 francs and 180 francs, respectively). Glass dinner plates and wine glasses are available as well as glass tabletops, screens and shelves. Quartz is the exclusive source of a layered colored glass called Décor A IV.

Remember that if you spend 2,000 francs or more in a store, you are entitled to a full refund of the value-added tax (VAT). See Basics for details.

Quatre Saisons

14th arr. - 88, av. du Maine - 43 21 28 99

Open 10:30 a.m.-7 p.m. (Mon. from noon). Closed Sun.

Here's a terrific collection of high-quality wooden table and kitchenware: carving boards, salad bowls, cheese boards (from 100 francs) and more. Pretty, inexpensive glassware (8 to 80 francs) is also on hand, along with rustic baskets and an assortment of fabric and plastic tablecloths in appealing colors.

IMAGE & SOUND

▓ PHOTOGRAPHY

Cipière

11th arr. - 26, bd Beaumarchais 47 00 37 25

Open 9:30 a.m.-12:30 a.m. & 2 p.m.-7 p.m. Closed Sun. Mon. & Aug.

Michel Cipière, a certified appraiser of photographic equipment from every era, sells new and second-hand cameras (the latter in prime condition, of course). Every imaginable brand is in stock; some of the older cameras are rarities that will fascinate collectors. Expect a warm welcome and professional advice.

FNAC

1st arr. - Forum des Halles, level -2 - 40 41 40 00

6th arr. - 136, rue de Rennes - 45 44 39 12

8th arr. - 26, av. de Wagram - 47 66 52 50

Open 10 a.m.-7:30 p.m. (Mon. 1 p.m.-7:30 p.m.). Closed Sun.

You'll find a large selection of top brands at interesting prices at Fnac stores, plus all kind of equipment for developing and printing film. The customer service is excellent. There are over 28 Fnac outlets dotted around Paris, where you can buy rolls of film, spools of super-8 film and blank video cassettes, as well as have your holidays snaps developed.

Immo-Photo-Video-Son

9th arr. - 73, bd de Clichy - 42 82 02 80

Open 11 a.m.-8 p.m. Closed Sun.

You can buy or sell (good) used cameras here, or leave your photography equipment to be sold on consignment. Professionals and hobbyists alike will find a large selection to suit specific needs. The helpful staff is often willing to bargain over prices.

La Maison du Leica

11th arr. - 52, bd Beaumarchais 48 05 77 67

Open 9:30 a.m.-1 p.m. & 2 p.m.-7 p.m. Closed Sun., Mon. & Aug.

For all the lovers of this manufacturer, the Maison du Leica sells new and used equipment and repairs all Leicas. The prices are competitive with those of the big discount store, FNAC, and the service is beyond reproach.

▓ RECORDED MUSIC & STEREO GEAR

Crocodisc

5th arr. - 42, rue des Ecoles - 43 54 47 95

Open 11 a.m.-7 p.m. Closed Sun. & Mon.

In this discount record paradise, you can find reasonably priced imports, used records and compact discs and cassettes. Every genre is represented: rock, reggae, funk, blues, country, film scores, etc. In addition, you can listen to the records, and you can also have them set aside and pay several days later.

Crocojazz

5th arr. - 64, rue de la Montagne-Sainte-Geneviève - 46 34 78 38
Open 11 a.m.-1 p.m. & 2 p.m.-7 p.m. Closed Sun., Mon. & holidays.

This is a branch of the aforementioned Crocodisc, and it specializes in jazz. Crocojazz is run on the same principles. Lots of interesting imports.

La Dame Blanche

5th arr. - 47, rue de la Montagne-Sainte-Geneviève - 43 54 54 45
Open 10:30 a.m.-1:30 p.m. & 2:30 p.m.-8:30 (Mon. 2:30 p.m.-8:30 p.m.). Closed Sun.

New and used recordings of classical music (mostly on vintage 33s) are this shop's *raison d'être.* Be alert: collectible treasures occasionally come to light here.

Disco Revue

1st arr. - 55, rue des Petits-Champs - 42 61 21 30
Open 11 a.m.-7 p.m. (Sat. 11 a.m.-noon & 2 p.m.-7 p.m.). Closed Sun. & Aug.

You may have to hunt a bit to locate this shop, tucked away in the back of a courtyard, but rock 'n' roll record collectors will find the effort well worth it. Vintage 45s and 33s are bought and sold here, and although the management's preferences run to discs from the 50s and 60s, there are examples from all eras in stock, including many rare and collectible recordings. CDs and laserdiscs imported from Japan are also on hand.

FNAC Musique

9th arr. - 24, bd des Italiens - 48 01 02 03
Open 10 a.m.-midnight. Closed Sun.

Opened just a couple of years back, this FNAC is devoted exclusively to music. All types of music are represented on the cassettes, CDs, video and laserdiscs, but rock, jazz and French pop pre-

dominate. Plus you'll find a music bookshop, sheet music and a ticket agency for concerts and musical events.

Oldies but Goodies

4th arr. - 16, rue du Bourg-Tibourg - 48 87 14 37
Open 12:30 p.m.-7:30 p.m. Closed Sun.

This shop specializes in used records, including jazz, blues, and rock and roll in French and American versions (check out the hysterical French "covers" of U.S. pop songs from the 1960s—the lyrics are even worse!). There are all sorts of goodies, old or rare

ried off its prime location on the Champs-Elysées. "Mega" only begins to describe Virgin's vast inventory of books, records, stereo gear, video paraphernalia and computer equipment. The staff is young and often only minimally competent (that's why we go elsewhere for pricey electronic merchandise), but the record department is strictly fab. The newest, the oldest, the best and the weirdest recordings can be found here; new releases are regularly hooked up to earphones, so that you can give a listen before you buy. You can gloat

---

The hole in Les Halles

Many Parisians still regret that the city's famous food market, installed here since the twelfth century, was not preserved when the merchants moved out to Rungis in 1969. The *trou* ("hole") *des Halles* dug after the market was destroyed became a tourist attraction in its own right during the 1970s, while developers argued with the municipality over what should be done with it. One idea was simply to fill it in again; another was to flood it to make a lake linked up to the Seine. A dozen or so architects had their projects rejected before the present Forum shopping center was approved and built. While indistinguishable from similar emporia worldwide, the Forum at least has the merit of carrying on the centuries-old tradition of trade. Above ground, the site has been attractively landscaped and the surrounding streets are full of echoes of the past for those who care to listen.

---

or cheap. The store boasts a clientele that includes collectors and celebrities (Eddy Mitchell, Bernadette Lafont). Recently they added compact discs, and U.S. imports are making more frequent appearances.

Virgin Mégastore

8th arr. - 56-60, av. des Champs-Elysées - 40 74 06 48
Open 10 a.m.-midnight (Fri. & Sat. 10 a.m.-1 a.m.). Closed Sun.

The FNAC's British rival scored a big one, when it car-

over your new acquisitions over refreshments at the Virgin Café, at the top of the store's monumental marble staircase.

■ **VIDEO**

Playtime

7th arr. - 44, av. Bosquet - 45 55 43 36
16th arr. - 36, av. d'Eylau - 47 27 56 22
Open noon-8 p.m. Closed Sun.

This is the place for movie buffs, where they can rent

video cassettes from the collection of more than 3,000 titles, including a good selection of films in English. A nice plus for after shopping: customers can stop for a cup of tea in the adjoining tea room and bar. The help is very friendly, and cassette tapes are also available. Non-members pay 45 francs per cassette per day.

Reels on Wheels
15th arr. -35, rue de la Croix Nivert - 45 67 64 99
Open noon-10:30 p.m. (Mon. & Thurs. 10 a.m.-11 p.m.; Fri. noon-11 p.m. & Sun. 6:30 p.m.-10:30 p.m.).
English-language films on cassette are delivered to your door by the friendly crew at Reels on Wheels. Just make sure that your VCR accepts the PAL system, and you're in business. Over 3,500 titles are available; cassettes are also offered for sale.

JEWELRY

■ ANTIQUE JEWELRY

See Antiques *section page 174.*

■ PRESTIGE JEWELRY

Boucheron
1st arr. - 26, pl. Vendôme - 42 61 58 16
Open 10 a.m.-6:30 p.m. Closed Sun.
Alain Boucheron, the current—dynamic!—bearer of the Boucheron family torch and president of the Comité Vendôme, has led his firm into new areas. In fact, with his Pluriels line of jewelry, he is expanding and developing the notion of what fine jewelry is: changeable gold settings to which one may add rings or links of acacia wood,

diamonds, coral or other gems (a Pluriel piece therefore runs 12,500 francs or so). Beautiful jewels are brought forth for inspection on plush trays, in an opulent environment of wood-paneling and friezes... such is the luxury for which Boucheron has stood for generations.

Bulgari
8th arr. - 27, av. Montaigne - 47 23 89 89
Open 10 a.m.-1 p.m. & 2:30 p.m.-7 p.m. Closed Sun.
The house of Bulgari got its start in Rome in 1881 when Sotirio Bulgari began selling jewelry (which he made at night) from a pushcart in the streets. Today Bulgari jewels pay the price of success: they are among the most copied pieces in the world. The Bulgari style is marked by piles of precious stones built up on gold mountings, or hyperrealistic objects with an implicit mocking message.

Cartier
1st arr. - 7, pl. Vendôme - 42 61 55 55
Open 10 a.m.-7 p.m. (until 6:30 p.m. in winter; Mon. & Sat. 10:30 a.m.-7 p.m.). Closed Sun.
"It is better to have authentic junk than fake Cartier," exclaims Dominique Perrin, chief executive of Cartier, the most copied name in the world. The watches can be found all over the globe, as can the wine-red leather goods (from keyholders to eyeglass cases). Besides all the *must* Cartier goods, there remains the fine jewelry that made this establishment the most famous house in the world. Traditional jeweler services combined with inventiveness and know-how have conquered the world. In its Paris shops, Cartier will make up from simple sketches engagement rings or wedding bands, or they will rejuvenate—as if by magic!—old or poorly cut stones.

Chaumet
1st arr. - 12, pl. Vendôme - 44 77 24 00
Open 9:30 a.m.-1 p.m. & 2:30 p.m.-6:30 p.m. Closed Sun.
Jeweler in Paris since 1780, Chaumet belongs to the highly select association of *Haute Joaillerie de France*, a group that fosters the traditions of French design and craftsmanship in fine jewelry. Though Chaumet's creations have beguiled such connoisseurs as Napoléon, Queen Victoria and countless maharajahs, the firm also produces elegant timepieces, gold jewelry, leather goods and writing instruments that are perfectly appropriate for fast-paced modern life. Prices for the "Boutique" line start at 4,200 francs, watches at 7,800 francs and leather accessories at 600 francs.

Mauboussin
1st arr. - 20, pl. Vendôme - 42 60 32 54
Open 10 a.m.-1 p.m. & 2 p.m.-6:30 p.m. Closed Sun.
Established in 1827, the house of Mauboussin gives off that impression of security and comfort one associates with old families, for whom the purchase of fine jewelry is the natural way to celebrate life's big moments. One is warmly welcomed into the discreet little offices where business is conducted. Mauboussin specializes in engagement rings, especially in colored gemsstones (emeralds, rubies, sapphires) set off by diamonds. They are also the creators of the famous Nadia rings in carved mother-of-pearl and gold, set with a diamond or a colored gem.

Mellerio dits Meller
1st arr. - 9, rue de la Paix - 42 61 57 53
Open 10 a.m.-1 p.m. & 2 p.m.-6:30 p.m. Closed Sun., Sat. in July, Aug. & Sept.
Marie de Medicis had no idea, of course, that she was

founding a dynasty of jewelers when she granted her loyal Lombard chimney sweeps (who, from the other side of the flue, had overheard and reported a plot against the Crown) licences first as peddlers, then street vendors and finally jewelers. Now, fourteen generations later, the great house of Mellerio is by no means resting on its ancient laurels. The oldest of all the fine jewelers of France, the Mellerio family comb the worldwide gem trade for those outstanding stones, regardless of size, that measure up to their noble tradition. Constituting one of the centers of the *haut monde* of fine jewelry, Mellerio exports half its production to the far corners of the globe.

Poiray

8th arr. - 1, rue de la Paix - 42 61 70 58
8th arr. - 46 av. Georges-V - 47 23 07 41
Open 10:30 a.m.-6:30 p.m. Closed Sat. & Sun.

The house of Poiray is the youngest of the great jewelers. If a fine jewel can be said to have a soul, Poiray endows it with a spirit of youth. The multitinted style of its famous three-gold Tresse ring (13,500 francs), already seen on some very famous fingers around town, is also available in necklaces and bracelets. There are lots of new items, such as the Three-Gold Heart and the Octogo line of gold-plated pieces, as well as the renowned Poiray watches, which come in round, rectangular or square shapes in gold, steel, gold and steel, or dressed up in precious stones. As for fine jewels, Poiray has the Cascade collection, including a bracelet of gold bangles trimmed in diamonds, rubies and sapphires for 300,000 francs and up. But there are some lovely rings at much more affordable prices.

Alexandre Reza

1st arr.- 23, pl. Vendôme - 42 96 64 00
Open 10 a.m.-1 p.m. & 2 p.m.-6:30 p.m. Closed Sun.

Alexandre Reza, of Russian descent, is a major dealer in precious stones and always seems to have the most beautiful gems around his shop. An expert collector, he has transformed his basement level into a gallery exhibiting reproductions fashioned according to traditional techniques. Take a look, for example, at the necklace of pear diamonds, all in gems by Flowliss, a stunning and priceless piece.

Van Cleef et Arpels

1st arr. - 22, pl. Vendôme - 42 61 58 58
Open 10 a.m.-6:30 p.m. Closed Sun.

The most innovative of the jewelers of the place Vendôme, and originators of the jewelled evening bag of gold and precious gems, this house boasts a unique technique for mounting stones that fades into the background, thus emphatically accenting the gem. The prices reflect the highest level of workmanship and creativity, but even more modest budgets have access to the Van Cleef Boutique where rings, earrings and butterfly pendants, starting at about 4,000 francs, can be found.

Harry Winston

8th arr. - 29, av. Montaigne - 47 20 03 09
Open 9:30 a.m.-1 p.m. & 2:30 p.m.-6:30 p.m. Closed Sat. & Sun.

American jeweler Harry Winston is one of the most prestigious diamond dealers in the world. He sells uncut diamonds from his own mines to other dealers and to retailers, as well as in his own showrooms. Many of the world's best-known diamonds have come from Winston, in-

cluding five that belong to Queen Elizabeth II and one that graced the hand of Elizabeth Taylor, dubbed the Taylor-Burton diamond. Even Marilyn Monroe, for whom diamonds proved to be a girl's best friend, liked to talk to about Harry Winston. The entrance to the establishment is discreet and quite intimidating; you must have an appointment and be ready to virtually be frisked. In the two second-floor rooms, decorated in period style, the built-in showcases display diamond jewels, ornaments, earrings and other marvelous creations in a traditional but not ornate style. How much, you ask? In the millions of dollars... these jewels are intended for an international clientele seeking a recession-proof investment.

■ FINE JEWELRY

A & A Turner

8th arr. - 16, av. Georges-V - 47 23 88 28
Open 10:30 a.m.-6:30 p.m. Closed Sun. & Aug.

Françoise Turner is one of the more recent arrivals on the fine jewelry scene. Decorated with carved wood and antique red floor tiles, her gallery is nothing if not luxurious. Her striking productions run to big rings, some hand-carved (from 5,000 francs) or necklaces of rock crystal tipped in gold (from 40,000 francs). On our last visit there, we also admired large beads in malachite, marble and slate or horn, gold and cut stones that can be worn with a pearl necklace, a large chain or simply strung on a leather thong (from 25,000 francs). More affordable is Turner's new line of solid-gold jewelry, with prices ranging around the 5,000-franc mark.

The prices in this guide reflect what establishments were charging at press time.

Arthus Bertrand

6th arr. - 6, pl. Saint-Germain-des-Prés - 42 22 19 20
Open 10 a.m.-6:15 p.m. (Sat. 10:15 a.m.-12:30 p.m. & 2 p.m.-6:30 p.m.). Closed Sun. & Mon.

Opposite the church of Saint-Germain-des-Prés, next door to the Deux Magots, stands Arthus Bertrand, a venerable forger of religious medals and academic swords. Families with a sense of tradition come here for engagement rings wrought in an utterly classic style. No one, however, comes to Arthus Bertrand for the warm welcome, which is about as friendly as a court martial. The firm also specializes in reproductions of antique jewelry displayed at the Louvre. You'll find 22-carat-gold jewelry, as well as silver and two-headed rings (lion, ram and so forth), and small refined pieces starting at 600 francs.

Chanel Horlogerie

1st arr. - 7, pl. Vendôme - 42 86 29 87
Open 10 a.m.-1 p.m. & 2 p.m.-6:30 p.m. (Mon. & Sat. from 10:30 a.m.). Closed Sun.

The decor of Chanel's newest watch boutique on the place Vendôme is reminiscent of Mademoiselle's private apartment. Japanese Coromandel screens, luscious suede sofas and lacquered furniture are reason enough to go and take a look. Within the boutique you will find the complete line of Chanel fine timepieces designed by the talented Jacques Helleu, the Chanel Art Director. The Chanel staff will let you discover this beautiful collection ranging from the signature leather and chain model to the ultimate luxury: the all diamond pavé link bracelet watch.

Cotailys

3rd arr. - 6, rue Réaumur - 42 72 23 79
Open 9 a.m.-6 p.m. Closed Sat. (except in Dec.) & Sun.

Aided by the expert advice of the friendly owner, you can select from a variety of necklaces, bracelets, rings and earrings that combine contemporary taste with timeless classicism. Diamonds, emeralds, sapphires and rubies in myriad sizes are set principally in yellow gold. The shop also takes care of repairs, will make new pieces from your old jewelry, and gladly executes special orders and designs. Wholesale prices.

Ebel

1st arr. - 2, pl. Vendôme - 42 60 82 08
Open 10 a.m.-12:45 a.m. & 2 p.m.-6:15 p.m. Closed Sun. & Mon.

Since 1911 these "architects of time" have been seeking to make the perfect watch. They have succeeded, and you can find it at their gallery on the place Vendôme (with its decor by Andrée Putman): splendid, accurate watches set with cut diamonds and sapphires. The house also offers a designer line of jewelry by Italian Alexandra Gradi, featuring her necklaces and rings fashioned from rounded, tightly linked gold chain, delightful rings composed of colored gems encircled by large gold bands (ring prices range from 2,300 to 12,000 francs; bracelets, 9,000 francs; necklaces, 77,000 francs). The prices of the watches (from 8,000 francs) are justified by the precious materials and the custom manufacture. An impeccably courteous reception is the house rule.

Fred Joaillier

8th arr. - 6, rue Royale - 42 60 30 65
Open 9 a.m.-6:30 p.m. (Mon & Sat. 9 a.m.-12:30 p.m. & 2 p.m.-6:30 p.m.). Closed Sun.

This is jewelry with a resolutely sportive spin, featuring the Force 10 and Tennis lines. Gold and steel are set with diamonds, flexible bracelets of gold are accessories for the active life. There are some watches in a combination of steel and leather (4,000 francs), and fine jewelry featuring evening bags in mother-of-pearl and precious gems in exotic shapes, butterflies or scarabs. Figure a tidy million francs for the latter. Fred Joaillier also has a boutique in the Galerie du Claridge (a shopping arcade off the Champs-Elysées).

Ilias Lalaounis

1st arr. - 364, rue Saint-Honoré 42 61 55 65
Open 10 a.m.-6:30 p.m. Closed Sun.

Here you will find braided gold, gold lions' heads, jewelry inspired by that of ancient Greece, and other creations that are much more contemporary but scarcely more affordable.

Jare

1st arr. - Cour Vendôme - 42 96 33 66
Open by appt. only.

Overrun with business, this jeweler prefers to maintain a peerless standard of quality by limiting orders. Specializing in resetting the jewels that you already own, the magic worked by Jare turns your old, tired baubles into contemporary gems.

Remember that if you spend 2,000 francs or more in a store, you are entitled to a full refund of the value-added tax (VAT). See Basics for details.

Jean Dinh Van

2nd arr. - 7, rue de la Paix - 42
61 74 49
*Open 9:30 a.m.-6:30 p.m. (Mon.
& Sat. 10:30 a.m.-6:30 p.m.).
Closed Sun.*

Jean Dinh Van was discovered twenty years ago when the fashion world made his square-link chain a must (2,000 francs in silver, 21,000 francs in gold). Since then he has become the recognized leader in modern jewelry for everyday wear. His is a sober style, often featuring square shapes with rounded corners. In the same vein are his heavy square bracelets, his link chains and his famous "handcuff" clasps (from 2,000 francs) for rejuvenating pearl necklaces. His earrings of two large bands in gold or silver (from 2,300 francs) are graceful and lovely. And he offers some very pretty necklaces in black pearls, or in steel, gold or semiprecious stones (from 10,500 francs).

O.J. Perrin

16th arr. - 33, av. Victor Hugo
45 01 88 88
*Open 10 a.m.-1 p.m. & 2 p.m.-
6 p.m. Closed Sun. & Mon.*

Elegant, easy-to-wear jewelry: we love the gold Liberty clip, the satin or leather Venetian bracelet with its wonderfully tactile braided-gold clasp, and the Méridienne ring.

La Perle

16th arr. - 85, av. Raymond-Poincaré - 45 53 07 62
*Open 10 a.m.-12:45 a.m. &
1:45 p.m.-6:30 p.m. Closed Sat.
(except in Nov. & Dec.), Sun. &
Aug.*

If you care to present your daughter with her first string of pearls or have your old string reset with precious stones, La Perle offers a variety of cultured pearls custom-strung to your liking as bracelets (5,500 francs and up), earrings, ropes or single strands. As well as transforming your old jewelry, the firm designs its own.

Phedra

8th arr. - 1, rue Royale
42 66 97 41
*Open 10 a.m.-7 p.m. Closed
Sun.*

Some magnificent Italian jewels: gold rings covered in cut stones, necklaces of pearls set in rough-finish gold and rectangular watches bordered with brilliants. The collection here includes some rare and one-of-a-kind pieces.

Pomellato

8th arr. - 66, rue du Faubourg-Saint-Honoré - 42 65 62 07
*Open 10 a.m.-7 p.m. Closed
Sun.*

The headquarters of Pomellato, a famed Milanese jeweler, is elegantly decked out in gray marble with large display windows. The clever, original collection features gold jewelry accented with silver or precious stones. Necklaces and bracelets come in various versions of fine links or in richer braided gold, always involving an invisible clasp as part of the piece. The Pomellato offerings include flat, flexible chains ornamented with cut stones (20,000 to 80,000 francs) and massive rings (6,000 to 40,000 francs).

■ COSTUME JEWELRY

Artcurial

8th arr. - 9, av. de Matignon - 42
99 16 16
*Open 10:30 a.m.-7:15 p.m.
Closed Sun. & Mon.*

For limited-editions of jewels designed by modern artists, crafted in bronze, vermeil, silver and gold, visit the fascinating shop of this famous art gallery. You'll find "violin" pendants by Arman, Paul Bury's spherical jewels, Piero Dorazio's enameled-gold ornaments and Claude Lalanne's juicy-looking clusters of glass currants and grapes.

L'Avant Musée

4th arr. - 2, rue Brisemiche - 48
87 45 81
Open 1 p.m.-7 p.m. Closed Sun.

There are 24 artisans represented here, including Di Rosa (whose badges are creating a sensation), Grosso Modo, Virginia Campion and Happy Fingers. Elbow-to-elbow in the alleyways surrounding the Pompidou Center, rings, clips, bands, necklaces and bracelets in resin, metal and other materials are sold at moderate prices. These ornaments are far from classic, but collectors already are snatching up the telephone-charge-card facsimiles designed by Toffe. Prices start at 75 francs.

Césarée

6th arr. - 43, rue Madame - 45
48 86 86
*Open 9 a.m.-1 p.m. & 2 p.m.-
7 p.m. Closed Sun.*

Laurence Coupelon takes coral, horn, jade, malachite, terracotta, bronze and glass and transforms these disparate elements into highly covetable *bijoux*. Exotic and indefinably ethnic, they don't look like run-of-the-mill costume pieces; what's more, they are not exorbitantly priced.

Alexis Lahellec

1st arr. - 14-16, rue Jean-Jacques Rousseau - 42 33 40 33
*Open 11 a.m.-7 p.m. (Mon. &
Sat. noon-7 p.m.). Closed Sun.*

Fabulous fake stones, glass beads, bogus gold and even papier-mâché go into the glorious "gadget" jewelry dreamed up by Alexis Lahellec. A very '70s look, and prices that range from reasonable to... deranged.

Lei

1st arr. - 15, rue des Petits-Champs - 42 86 00 16
Open 11 a.m.-7 p.m. (Sat. 2:30 p.m.-7 p.m.). Closed Sun.
Antonella Grammatico has a knack for choosing custom jewelry from yesteryear to suit contemporary tastes. Her collection includes huge "cocktail" rings from the '40s, Second-Empire pendants and other baubles and bangles in silver or gold. Interesting prices, from about 500 francs.

Othello

6th arr. - 21, rue des Saints-Pères
42 60 26 24
Open 11 a.m.-7:30 p.m. Closed Sun.
Sheherazade would have loved the jewelry on display at Othello. Terracotta, pink ivory-wood, coral, jade beads and even yew-tree roots are used in the creation of these exotic ornaments straight out of a fairy tale. Prices begin at 300 francs.

Yamada

2nd arr. - 30, rue Danielle-Casanova - 42 86 94 81
Open 10:30 a.m.-7 p.m. Closed Sun.
From classic pieces in ivory and to hard-lined "design" ornaments in ebony or malachite, this Japanese firm comes up with jewelry for every taste. Prices start at 400 francs.

LEATHER & LUGGAGE

Aïcha

1st arr - 19, rue Pavée - 42 77 62 65
Open 11 a.m.-7 p.m. (Mon. from 2 p.m.). Closed Sun.
Vivid colors—lipstick red, ultraviolet, cobalt blue—amusing shapes and strong, wear-resistant leathers make the hand and shoulder bags sold here an excellent fashion investment.

La Bagagerie

6th arr - 41, rue du Four - 45 48 85 88 (also: 8th arr., 15th arr., 16th arr.)
Open 10:15 a.m.-7 p.m. (Sat. 10 a.m.-7 p.m.).
Prices are rising here, we note, but La Bagagerie's colorful bags, belts, luggage and leather accessories are reliably in tune with the season's fashions. Designs run from classic to pure fantasy; we especially like the combinations of timeless shapes (envelopes, bucket bags...) and vivid shades that are the shop's specialty.

Bottega Veneta

6th arr. - 6, rue du Cherche Midi
42 22 17 09
Open 10 a.m.-7 p.m. Closed Sun.
Expect a grand reception befitting this high-quality Venetian leather-goods establishment. The braided lambskin bags lined in leather are unparalleled. And there are at least 40 models of classic, all-purpose handbags in eleven colors, including bright red and green. The lizard pocketbooks are expensive but always in fashion. To the right of the shop there's a handsome line of leather and vinyl luggage, including soft and hard suitcases. An urbane staff proffers advice on how to clean or repair old leather.

William Aimard Camus

6th arr. - 25, rue du Dragon - 45 48 32 16
Open 10:30 a.m.-1:30 p.m. & 2:30 p.m.-7 p.m. (Mon. 2:30 p.m.-7 p.m.). Closed Sun.
Handsome leather backpacks that grow softer and more supple with age are sold here at eminently reasonable prices (800 to 1,500 francs), alongside sturdy suitcases especially designed for air travel.

Gucci

1st arr. - 350, rue Saint-Honoré
42 96 83 27
8th arr. - 2, rue du Faubourg-Saint-Honoré - 42 96 83 27
Open 9:30 a.m.-1 p.m. & 2 p.m.-6:30 p.m. (Wed. 10:30 a.m.-1 p.m. & 2 p.m.-6:30 p.m.). Closed Sun.
Acres of showrooms sumptuously decorated in light marble and lemon wood display leather goods manufactured in Florence by the third generation of the Gucci family. The classic Gucci handbag for day or eveningwear comes in box calf, crocodile, ostrich and wild boar. The leather and vinyl luggage is marked discreetly with the Gucci logo, or in canvas with the distinctive red and green stripes. There's also a fine selection of small leather goods (numerous gift possibilities), as well as silver and gold accessories, costume jewelry and shoes. The store at 27, rue du Faubourg-Saint-Honoré is reserved exclusively for ready-to-wear fashions, such as a classic blazer, straight skirts, silk blouses and lots of covetable leather jackets and pants.

Henell's

10th arr. - 14, av. Claude-Vellefaux - 42 06 85 94
Open 9 a.m.-noon & 1:30 p.m.-7 p.m. Closed Sun. & Aug.
For classy leather goods, from shoulder bags to shoes, in ostrich, lizard, buffalo and other rare skins, have a look in here. No, the address is not the most fashionable in town, but the service can't be beat: any item can be custom-ordered in your choice of color and size (most articles are ready in a month's time).

Hermès

8th arr. - 24, rue du Faubourg-Saint-Honoré - 40 17 47 17
8th arr. - 42, av. George-V - 47 20 48 51
Open 10 a.m.-6:30 p.m. (Sat. & Mon. 10 a.m.-1 p.m. &

2:15 p.m.-6:30 p.m.). Closed Sun.

Hermès has been the purveyors of fine leather goods long enough to reign supreme as the undisputed leader of the pack when it comes to saddles, handbags, luggage and all the accompanying accoutrements of fine living and traveling. But what about the prices? Are they reasonable or completely beyond reality? The answer is both. Check the finish on the leather goods; think of the meticulous hand-work that went into the cutting, sewing and adjusting of these bags and luggage. You still shrug your shoulders? Then go and visit the workshop in the Hermès museum on the fourth floor (by appointment only). That settled, let's move on to the handbags. Will you be tempted by the Kelly design (1949) or the Constance (1969), the red Hermès, the grained leather, the linen-and-leather or the crocodile and ostrich, which are the pride of the house? You really can't go wrong with any of these classically chic styles. The average price for the box calfs is 12,000 francs. There is a prestigious line of handmade luggage in box calf with reinforced corners. If you want something special, such as a leather covering for your bicycle seat or the cockpit of your private jet, the house will gladly oblige.

Lancel
9th arr. - 8, pl. de l'Opéra - 47 42 37 29 (also: 6th arr., 8th arr., 17th arr.)
Open 10 a.m.-7 p.m. Closed Sun.

Chic and typically Parisian leather accessories (belts, bags, wallets, key tags...) and fashionable—though never flashy— luggage. Complete lines of the latter are available in canvas as well as leather. On the whole, the craftsman-

ship is remarkable, and prices are in line with the quality.

Loewe
8th arr. 57, ave Montaigne - 45 63 73 38
Open 10 a.m.-7 p.m. Closed Sun.

Absolutely the last word in leather and suede (clothing, bags, luggage and accessories) from a patrician Spanish firm, recently established at this swank Parisian address.

Longchamp
1st arr. 390, rue Saint Honoré 42 60 00 00
Open 10 a.m.-7 p.m. Closed Sun.

A huge selection of handbags, luggage and accessories in leather, nylon or canvas with leather trim. Attractive detailing sets these bags apart; and in addition to being fashionable, they are sturdily crafted to take a lot of heavy wear.

Didier Ludot
1st arr. - 23-24 galerie Montpensier - 42 96 06 56
Open 10:30 a.m.-7 p.m. Closed Sun.

Didier Ludot's shop is located under the arcades of the Palais-Royal, which, in and of itself, is a good enough reason to come and see how he lovingly reconditions previously owned bags from Morabito and Hermès. He also carries a line of "surgical" bags used by doctors at the turn of the century and some superb 1920s-to-'30s suitcases lined with suede in box calf or crocodile.

Mac Douglas
8th arr. - 155, rue du Faubourg-Saint-Honoré - 45 61 19 71
Open 10 a.m.-7 p.m. Closed Sun.

Are you a leather lover? If the answer is yes, then you'll want to head straight for Mac and its infinite variety: glossy or dyed lambskin, goatskin, calf- skin, suede and shearling.

There are well-cut jackets in crinkled sheepskin and calf-skin coats and dyed lambskin skirts. Prices are on the high side, but the designs are consistent in quality, well made and available in lots of colors. Good sales in January and July.

La Maroquinerie Parisienne
9th arr. - 30, rue Tronchet - 47 42 83 40
Open 9:30 a.m.-7 p.m. (Mon. 1 p.m.-7 p.m.). Closed Sun.

A huge bi-level shop filled with an enormous selection of cut-price leather goods, ranging from: coin purses, suitcases (Delsey, Samsonite, Longchamp), to canvas bags and crocodile handbags. Belts, gloves and umbrellas are also featured, and there is a 15 percent reduction on the list price. Sale time is mid-January to mid-February.

Morabito
1st arr. - 1, pl. Vendôme - 42 60 30 76
Open 9:45 a.m.-6:45 p.m. Closed Sun..

Choose between custom-made luggage and handbags in the skin you fancy (box calf, ostrich or crocodile) and the color you prefer, or a sportier line of ready-made bags in textured calf (1,000 to 6,0000 francs). The made-to-measure bags are generally ready in two to three days, and prices start at about 6,000 francs. Perfect service, of course, from this long-established firm reputed for quality.

Muriel
8th arr. - 4, rue des Saussaies 42 65 95 34
Open 10 a.m.-6:30 p.m. Closed Sun.

A wall lined with neatly organized drawers, a well-polished wooden counter: what a pleasure to buy gloves at this traditional *gantier's* shop! For dress or sport, you'll find a wonderful selection of gloves for men and women, crafted in kidskin or pigskin, trimmed with mink or lined with silk.

Renaud Pellegrino
1st arr. - 348, rue Saint-Honoré
42 60 69 36
6th arr. - 15, rue du Cherche-Midi - 45 44 56 37
Open 10:30 a.m.- 7 p.m. Closed Sun.

For the most chic and desirable bags in town, adorned with leather embroidery, grosgrain ribbon, fur and geometrical motifs, visit Renaud Pellegrino's exciting boutique. Top-quality leather in a rainbow of sublime colors are used for these expensive but unique bags, which make a definite fashion statement.

Paloma Picasso
2nd arr. - 5, rue de la Paix - 42 86 02 21
Open 10 a.m.-7 p.m. (Mon. 11 a.m.-7 p.m.). Closed Sun.

A jewel of a shop decorated by Jacques Grange is the showcase for Paloma Picasso's pricey and prestigious line of accessories. Red—Paloma's favorite color—is much in evidence in the belts, bags and small leather goods for active, elegant women.

Prada
6th arr. - 5, rue de Grenelle - 45 48 53 14
Open 10:30 a.m.-7 p.m. (Sat. 10:30 a.m.-1 p.m. & 2 p.m.-7 p.m.). Closed Sun.

Versatile bags whose simple, classic shapes move effortlessly from office to opera house are the strong suit of this renowned Italian firm.

Terre de Bruyère
17th arr. - 112, bd de Courcelles
42 27 86 87
Open 10:30 a.m.-7:30 p.m. (Mon. 2:30 p.m.-7 p.m.). Closed Sun.

Canvas, leather, or both together are the materials of

choice for a handsome range of hand-crafted bags, backpacks and attaché cases. They come in subdued, countrified shades of green, beige and gray-black and (considering the workmanship) are quite reasonably priced.

Louis Vuitton
8th arr. - 54, av. Montaigne - 44 20 84 00
8th arr. - 78 bis, av. Marceau - 47 20 47 00
Open 9:30 a.m.-6:30 p.m. Closed Sun.

Vuitton lovers, here's a test. Put your bag down at the airline counter of an airport. Watch it disappear into a crowd of other Vuittons... now try and identify it! If you haven't marked it somehow, you might be unlucky. The Vuitton madness has taken over the world. For many, the Vuitton bag has become a cult object. It consists of printed linen coated with vinyl, reinforced with lozine (which looks like leather; Vuitton jealously guards the formula) ribs, untreated leather for handles and straps, copper for rivets and hard corners. If the purchase of a Vuitton suitcase doesn't work with your budget, console yourself with a card holder or racquet cover or even a key ring.

OPEN LATE

▮ BOOKSTORES

Shakespeare and Company
5th arr. - 37, rue de la Bûcherie
43 26 96 50
Open daily 11 a.m.-midnight. No cards.

Don't confuse it with the legendary Shakespeare and Company of Sylvia Beach, though owner George Whitman claims that he is carrying on the tradition, albeit in different premises. Shelves are filled

to the bursting point in this modern Prospero's cell, with books new and old covering every subject imaginable.

La Hune
6th arr. - 170, bd Saint Germain
45 48 35 85
Open 10 a.m.-midnight. Closed Sun.

If you get an urge to reread some Breton or Baudelaire late at night, head over here. Beautiful art books, too.

Newsstand

For all you news-hounds, kiosks are open 24 hours a day at the following addresses: 33 & 52, av. des Champs-Elysées, 8th arr. - 45 61 48 01; 16, bd de la Madeleine, 8th arr. - 42 65 29 19; 2, bd Montmartre, 9th; Place Charles-de-Gaulle, av. de Wagram, 17th; 16, bd de Clichy, 18th arr.; as well as in train stations and Drugstores until 2 a.m.

▮ DRUGSTORES

Be it premium bubbly or Alka-Seltzer, a little night music or earplugs for a noiseless morning after... they've got it all here!

Drugstore Publicis
6th arr. - Drugstore Saint-Germain - 146, bd Saint-Germain - 6th arr. - 42 22 92 50
Open daily 10 a.m.-2 p.m.
8th arr. - Drugstore Champs-Elysées - 133, av. des Champs-Elysées - 47 23 54 34
8th arr. - Drugstore Matignon
1, av. Matignon - 43 59 38 70
Open daily 9 a.m.-2 a.m.

Multistore Opéra
9th arr. - 6, bd des Capucines
42 65 89 43
Open daily 11:15 a.m.-midnight.

■ FLOWERS

Elyfleurs
17th arr. - 82, av. de Wagram
47 66 87 19
Open daily 24 hours.
See in *Flowers* section, page 228.

■ FOOD & DRINK

Alsace
8th arr. - 39, av. des Champs-Elysées - 43 59 44 24
Open daily 24 hours.
Beyond the main restaurant is a catering service–cum-boutique where you can purchase essentially Alsatian specialties—sauerkraut, charcuteries, foie gras, etc. There is a take-out service should you be tempted to take home a dish for a midnight snack.

L'An 2000
17th arr. - 82, bd des Batignolles
43 87 24 67
Open 5 p.m.-1 a.m. (Sun. 11 a.m.-1 a.m.). Closed 2 wks. in Aug.
After an evening at the Théâtre des Arts-Hébertot, you can put together a nice after-theater supper with provisions from L'An 2000. All sorts of appetizing dishes are on display at this spacious emporium. From caviar to charcuterie, from bread and fresh-vegetable terrines to wine, cheese and fresh fruit, you'll find all the makings of a charming midnight feast.

Flo Prestige
1st arr. - 42, pl. du Marché Saint-Honoré - 42 61 45 46
Open daily 8 a.m.-11 p.m. Delivery. See the other branches in Food *section page 232.*
Flo boutiques are cropping up all over town. They are perfect places for late-night food shopping. Temptations include foie gras from Strasbourg, Norwegian smoked salmon, beautiful cheeses and irresistible pastries, plus Champagne or a lusty country wine to wash it all down.

Les Frères Layrac
6th arr. - 29, rue de Buci - 43 25 17 72
Open daily 9 a.m.-2 a.m.
There is a wide selection of prepared dishes, but the pride of Les Frères Layrac is its seafood platter (385 francs for two). Free delivery.

Nocto
8th arr. - 23, bd des Batignolles
43 87 64 79
Open 11 a.m.-midnight (Sun. 4 p.m.-11 p.m.).
A pleasant little supermarket for late-night shopping. The merchandise is of distinctly higher quality than most such establishments offer. Good choice of prepared salads; a take-home meal-on-a-tray costs 60 francs.

■ PHARMACIES

Pharmacie Azoulay
9th arr. - 5, pl. Pigalle
48 78 38 12
Open 9 a.m.-1 a.m. (Sun. 3 p.m.-1 a.m.).

Pharmacie Les Champs
8th arr. - 84, av. des Champs-Elysées - 45 62 02 41
Open daily 24 hours.
Note the convenient, *all-day-all-night* hours of this drugstore.

Pharmacie Lagarce
11th arr. - 13, pl. de la Nation
43 73 24 03
Open 8 a.m.-midnight (Mon. noon-midnight; Sun. & holidays 8 p.m.-midnight).

■ 24-HOUR POST OFFICE

Poste du Louvre
1st arr. - 52, rue du Louvre - 40 28 20 00
Open daily 24 hours.
The central post office is open 24 hours a day. Long-distance telephone calls can be made from the first floor, ordinary postal transactions on the ground floor. Don't be surprised to find a crowd of homeless people enjoying some late-night Muzak in the post office's warm recesses.

■ RECORD STORES

Champs-Disques
8th arr. - 84, av. des Champs-Elysées - 45 62 65 46
Open 9:30 a.m.-1:30 a.m. (Sun. noon-8 p.m.).
Let there be music! Here in this shop on the world's most beautiful avenue is a broad selection of popular and classical music.

Virgin Mégastore
8th arr. - 56-60, av. des Champs-Elysées - 40 74 06 48
Open 10 a.m.-midnight (Fri. & Sat. 10 a.m.-1 a.m.; Sun. noon-midnight).
Jazz, classical, pop and rock, on records, CDs and cassettes—but that's not all: there are books (on the lower level) too, video and audio gear, computer equipment and a terrific restaurant/bar upstairs where a piano player holds forth at night (a great place to people-watch).

SPORTING GOODS

■ CLOTHING & EQUIPMENT (GENERAL)

Chattanooga
7th arr. - 53, av. Bosquet - 45 51 76 65
Open 10:30 a.m.-1:30 p.m. & 2:30 p.m.-7:30 p.m. (Sat. 10:30 a.m.-7:30 p.m.). Closed Sun.

Skateboards, roller skates, surfboards, bodyboards, frisbees, kites and boomerangs: every bit of equipment that today's speed-crazy kids covet can be found here, alongside all the trendy togs that go with (athletic shoes—wait till you see the prices!—tank tops, bicycling shorts and the rest). Some good-quality second-hand equipment is available as well.

Ekisport
9th arr. - 38, rue Rochechouart 42 80 32 85
Open 10 a.m.-7 p.m. Closed Sun.

It's well worth seeking out this sporting goods store, hidden at the back of a courtyard. Prices are about ten percent under what you would pay in a department store for tennis equipment (racquets can be restrung while you wait) and for bicycling, camping, sailing and skiing gear. Skis can be rented for 200 francs per week.

Go Sport
1st arr. - Pte. Pierre-Lescot, Forum des Halles, level -3 - 45 08 92 96
12th arr. - 110, bd Diderot - 43 47 21 40
13th arr. - 30, av. d'Italie - 45 80 30 05
14th arr. - 68, av. du Maine - 43 27 50 50
15th arr. - 16, rue Linois - Centre Beaugrenelle - 43 47 21 40
16th arr. - 12, av. Porte de Saint-Cloud - 40 71 95 19
17th arr. - 2, pl. de la Porte-Maillot - 40 68 22 46
Open 10 a.m.-7:30 p.m. Closed Sun.

The stores in this fast-growing international chain vary drastically in size and style from one to another, but all conduct business according to the same successful formula: friendly help, professional advice and quality equipment. Some of the stores specialize in equestrian equipage (the Les Halles and Montparnasse branches). Tennis and fitness equipment are featured at every branch.

K Way
1st arr. - 3, av. de l'Opéra - 42 60 88 20
Open 10 a.m.-7 p.m. (Mon. noon-7 p.m.). Closed Sun.

K Way waterproof parkas and anoraks are lightweight, colorful and attractively fashioned, but best of all, they fold up into tiny packages that can be stowed away with ease. The entire family can be fitted out here from head to toe with foul-weather gear or ski suits.

Lacoste
1st arr. - 372, rue Saint-Honoré 42 61 55 56 (also: 2nd arr., 6th arr., 8th arr., 15th arr., 16th arr., 17th arr.)
Open 10 a.m.-7 p.m. Closed Sun.

There's lots more here besides the famous polo shirts (which come in a dizzying array of colors). The Lacoste flagship store also carries well-made clothing for all sorts of sports, as well as a full line of excellent tennis equipment.

> *Remember that if you spend 2,000 francs or more in a store, you are entitled to a full refund of the value-added tax (VAT). See* Basics *for details.*

Au Petit Matelot
16th arr. - 27, av. de la Grande-Armée - 45 00 15 51
Open 10 a.m.-7 p.m. (Mon. 2 p.m.-7 p.m.). Closed Sun.

Having celebrated its 200th birthday, Au Petit Matelot is aging quite gracefully. Striped sailor shirts are less in evidence than they once were, but the foul-weather gear is as good as ever, as are the pea coats and oiled-canvas outerwear. Ladies and gentlemen come here to dress for the hunt, the saddle or the tiller. Be advised that only sporting *clothes* are found here—you'll need to go elsewhere for your equipment.

Au Refuge
6th arr. - 44-46, rue Saint-Placide 42 22 27 33
Open 10 a.m.-7 p.m. (Mon. 2:30 a.m.-7 p.m.). Closed Sun.

Newly renovated and reorganized, Au Refuge specializes in top-quality tennis racquets (the famed Snauwaert sells here for 4,500 francs), but athletes can also find the perfect shoe (140 models to choose from), fitness buffs will be fitted with all the stretchy exercise togs they might require and downhill racers are sure to locate just the ski equipment they desire. Swimmers and dancers are outfitted here as well

■ DANCE

Repetto
2nd arr. - 22, rue de la Paix - 44 71 83 00
Open 10 a.m.-7 p.m. Closed Sun.

Repetto has served the dance community since 1947, providing baby ballerinas and professional primas with dainty practice slippers, toe shoes and tutus. Jazz dancers will find the soft footwear they need, and the leotards and tights (available in a rainbow of colors) are just as suitable

---

A village vanishes

The *rue Saint-Blaise* **was the main street of the parish of Charonne before it was swallowed up to form part of the twentieth arrondissement in 1860. The neighborhood still has a village atmosphere, and the Church of Saint-Germain-de-Charonne watching over its flock from a broad flight of steps is one of only two left in the capital with its own cemetery.**

---

for exercise class as for a session at the *barre*. High prices.

Flashdance
8th arr. - 17, rue de la Pépinière
42 93 05 71
Open 10 a.m.-7 p.m. Closed Sun.

Flashy, stretchy gear for dancing and exercising (brands include Vicard leotards and Freddy tights and slippers), as well as beautiful swimwear by Livia. A friendly, professional staff helps clients choose the most flattering fit.

■ FISHING

Au Martin-Pêcheur
1st arr. - 28, quai du Louvre - 42 36 25 63
Open 9:30 a.m.-7 p.m. Closed Sun. & Mon.

This respected establishment has changed little over the years—it is still one of the most picturesque shops in Paris. In addition to a full array of deep-sea and fly fishing equipment, there's a section for diving accessories, including an underwater-photography department.

Motillon
15th arr. - 83 bis, rue de l'Abbé-Groult - 48 28 58 94
Open 9 a.m.-7 p.m. Closed Sun. & Mon.

Professional advice is lavished on customers at this venerable institution, which sells the necessities, the accessories and the luxuries for every sort of fishing. What's more, any item can be mail-ordered from its wonderful catalog. If you were enchanted by *A River Runs Through It* but would like to try your hand at sport fishing before you invest in the equipment, Motillon rents out tackle for ten to fifteen percent of its value (plus deposit).

■ GOLF

Comptoir du Golf
17th arr. - 22, av. de la Grande-Armée - 43 80 15 00
Open 9:30 a.m.-7 p.m. (Mon. 2 p.m.-7 p.m.). Closed Sun.

A very British sort of place, right down to the reserved reception. Shoes, clubs, polo shirts and carts abound, as well as the house line of golf togs in addition to the well-known makers'.

Golf-Plus
17th arr. - 212, bd Pereire - 45 74 08 17
Open 10 a.m.-7 p.m. (Mon. 2 p.m.-7 p.m., Thurs. until 8 p.m.). Closed Sun.

Owner Laurence Schmidlin, several times the French golf champion, offers friendly assistance to his customers. Good-quality clothes and equipment are sold at friendly prices, and if you find what you bought here elsewhere for less, you can come back and receive a credit, plus 10 percent. Dependable service and advice; equipment rental.

■ HUNTING & SHOOTING

Alex
8th arr. - 63, bd de Courcelles
42 27 66 39
Open 9 a.m.-7 p.m. Closed Sun. & Mon. (except during hunting season: 4 p.m.-6 p.m.).

Traditionally a firearms dealer, Alex has taken over the shop next door and devoted it to clothing, and he has his eye on the bakery next to that. He features the finest brands of rifles, as well as good selections of optical equipment, knives and cartridges. As for hunting-related clothing, you won't find a collection like this anywhere else: wool socks, elegant and practical storm coats and, of course, Paraboots. There is also an interesting hunting-themed gift department, which includes clever little knives in the form of ducks and cuckoos. An excellent store.

Fauré-Lepage-Saillard
1st arr. - 8, rue de Richelieu - 42 96 07 78
Open 9:30 a.m.-7 p.m. Closed Sun.

A specialist in rifles since 1716, this establishment still sells its own make of double-barrel rifles. Also found here are hand-crafted knives, carbines for target shooting and competition, sights and other such accessories. For collectors, there's an array of sword-canes and rifle-canes, and, for quieter hunting, there's always the Barnett Commando crossbow for around 3,000 francs. On the upper floor, superbly elegant hunting and riding clothes are displayed.

Gastinne et Renette

8th arr. - 39, av. Franklin-Roosevelt - 43 59 77 74
Open 10 a.m.-7 p.m. Closed Sun. & Mon.

This famous emporium markets its own make of rifles. And it doesn't give them away: prices start at 20,000 francs. But there are also used guns at attractive prices. An added feature is the shooting range in the basement, which permits customers to test the merchandise. Extremely diversified, the shop also stocks books, archery equipment and security systems, along with a selection of classic clothing, though not at competitive prices. And the gift department is, of course, consistent with the hunting theme.

Tir 1000

13th arr. - 90, rue Jeanne-d'Arc 45 83 34 41
Open 10 a.m.-7 p.m. (Thurs. until 10 p.m., Sat. until 6:30 p.m.). Closed Sun. & Mon.

Tir 1000 stocks a good selection of arms, knives, sights, and offers repair services too. Meanwhile, on the basement level, there's a shooting range for handguns, which is open to members (2,000 francs for an annual membership); beginners can sign up for lessons in target shooting.

■ RIDING

Duprey

17th arr. - 5, rue Troyon - 43 80 29 37
Open 9:45 a.m.-12:30 p.m. & 1:30 p.m.-6 p.m. Closed Sat., Sun. & Aug.

Hidden away on a little street near the Arc de Triomphe since 1902, this reputable shop is a family affair upheld by three generations. Duprey riding equipment is preferred in the classiest horsey circles. The excellent and comfortable saddles, virtually custom-made, are beautifully crafted (from 9,000 francs). Stirrups, bridles, girths are on hand as well; there is no apparel for the rider, but everything in leather for your mount.

Hermès

8th arr. - 24, rue du Faubourg-Saint-Honoré - 40 17 47 17
8th arr. - 42, av. George-V - 47 20 48 51
Open 10 a.m.-6:30 p.m. (Mon. & Sat. 10 a.m.-1 p.m. & 2:15 p.m.-6:30 p.m.). Closed Sun.

Housed in the tasteful luxury of this celebrated store is a complete range of equipment for horse and rider. Hermès turns out roughly 60 saddles a month, all handmade in the firm's workshops. The store will also custom-make and sew saddles made to measure in whatever leather you wish (one well-heeled customer even had a saddle made in crocodile). Should you decide to organize your own racing team, you can have Hermès fit out your jockeys in its famous silks.

Padd

15th arr. - 14, rue de la Cavalerie 43 06 56 50
Open 10 a.m.-7 p.m. (Mon. until 6 p.m.). Closed Sun.

An excellent address for equestrians: in a functional, no-nonsense environment, you'll find every kind of saddle at every sort of price. They come from all over: Spain, England, the United States. The clothing department is well stocked with hacking jackets, helmets, boots, crops and jodhpurs. The store may not be chic (go to Duprey or Equistable for that), but the inventory is complete.

Some establishments change their closing times without warning. It is always wise to check in advance.

■ SKIING

La Haute Route

4th arr. - 33, bd Henri-IV - 42 72 38 43
Open 9:30 a.m.-1 p.m. & 2 p.m.-7 p.m. (Mon. 2 p.m.-7 p.m.). Closed Sun.

You can rent everything here but the mountain: complete ski equipment in the winter, rock-climbing gear in the summer. Camping equipment is also available for rent at utterly reasonable prices.

Passe Montagne

14th arr. - 102, av. Denfert-Rochereau - 43 22 24 24
11th arr. - 39, rue du Chemin-Vert - 43 57 08 47
Open 11 a.m.-7 p.m. (Wed. until 9 p.m., Sat. 10 a.m.-7 p.m.). Closed Sun. & Mon.

Passe-Montagne can outfit you with all the gear you need for virtually any mountain sport, be it climbing, hiking, alpine or cross-country skiing. Both stores are open Wednesday until 9 p.m. Equipment rental is available at the Chemin-Vert store only.

Le Vieux Campeur

5th arr. - 48, rue des Ecoles - 43 29 12 32
Open 10 a.m.-8 p.m. (Mon. 2 p.m.-7 p.m.). Closed Sun.

Actually housed in fourteen shops all clustered around the main address. The Vieux Campeur is definitely the place to go for all manner of sporting equipment. The latest innovations and variations on a theme arrive here first. Climbing and mountaineering remain the specialty of the house, but the reputation for quality includes everything from running shoes to tennis racquets, sold with professional advice. We suggest that you avoid a Saturday visit, as the crowds are horrendous. A climbing wall is set up to be used for trying out shoes (and your technique!) before you confront the real thing.

■ WINDSURFING

Mistral Shop

16th arr. - 24, rue Mirabeau - 45 24 38 55
Open 10 a.m.-1 p.m. & 2:15 p.m.-7 p.m. Closed Sun. & Mon.

This windsurfing shop reflects the polish of its tony neighborhood: the boards are the finest made, the swimsuits are *très chic*, and the staff consists primarily of handsome beach boys. A number of designs are available but only one choice of quality—the best. These are serious boards for the committed windsurfer.

Nautistore

17th arr. - 40, av. de la Grande-Armée - 43 80 28 28
Open 10 a.m.-6:30 p.m. Closed Sun. & Mon.

Nautistore enjoys a solid reputation with windsurfers for its discount prices on new and old windsurfing boards. But the shop can also provide your with fine footwear for boating and sailing, not to mention furred parkas for Arctic expeditions.

TOBACCONISTS

■ ACCESSORIES

Au Caïd

6th arr. - 24, bd Saint-Michel - 43 26 04 01
Open 10 a.m.-7 p.m. Closed Sun.

The charming *mesdames* Schmitt still reign over this pipe-smokers' paradise. Featured is an excellent selection of pipes in clay, porcelain, cherry and briar. Accessories include tobacco pouches and cigar cases, cigar holders and pipe racks, which the Duke of Windsor and Jean-Paul Sartre appreciated in their day. The service is renowned.

Alfred Dunhill

2nd arr. - 15, rue de la Paix - 42 61 57 58
Open 9:30 a.m.-6:30 p.m. (Mon. & Sat. 10 a.m.-6:30 p.m.). Closed Sun.

The Alfred Dunhill shop remains the domain of men—and women—who have about them the expensive aroma of Havana cigars and fine leather. Foremost among the luxurious items featured around the mahogany-paneled, turn-of-the-century shop are, of course, the famed Dunhill pipes, some of the world's best...and priciest. Collectors will not want to miss the mini-museum of clay, briar and meerschaum pipes. Dunhill is also a gift shop, with a large selection of sunglasses, necktie pins, wristwatches and pens (after all, Dunhill owns Mont-Blanc), fine leather goods and hundreds of other gift ideas at reasonable prices. But the lion's share of the shop is given over to smokers' accessories: expensive lighters, cigarette holders, cigar boxes and humidors in rare woods. Dunhill also sells classic menswear and a line of men's personal-care products.

Gilbert Guyot

17th arr. - 7, av. de Clichy - 43 87 70 88
Open 10 a.m.-7 p.m. Closed Sun., Mon. & Aug.

Gilbert Guyot is one of the three remaining master pipemakers in France. When we visit his shop, we generally find Guyot (and his son) crafting, repairing, restoring or smoking a pipe and sizing up their customers. Before selling a customer his wares, Guyot personally interviews him, because, as Guyot puts it, "The pipe is the man." All kinds of pipes in every imaginable material and in a wide range of prices are sold in an atmosphere of quality and time-honored tradition.

■ CIGARS & TOBACCO

NO BARGAINS HERE

As you will note, cigars cost an arm and a leg here. Why? The state considers them a "drug" and taxes heavily. But take heart: At the shops we have listed in this section you are sure to find a fresh, high-quality cigar and not, as too often happens, a once-cherished cheroot that has turned into a roll of stale, bitter-tasting compost.

Boutique 22

16th arr. - 22, av. Victor-Hugo 45 01 81 41
Open 10 a.m.-7 p.m. (Mon. 2 p.m.-7 p.m.). Closed Sun.

Cigar lovers consider Boutique 22 the mecca of Davidoffs (even though it is no longer owned by Zino Davidoff). You will find not only Davidoff's "1000" but every other brand of Havana cigar imported in France, including slim Joyitas and thick Hoyo des Dieux and Carousoas. Boutique 22 is big on lesser-knowns as well and has the exclusive distributorship for the Compagnie des Caraïbes. You will discover such Caribbean delights as sweet and aromatic Cerdeaus, robust Juan Clementes and claro claro/50 Don Miguels, from Cabo Verde. Also featured are 100 models of off-the-shelf humidors and vaults, plus refurbished antique models. For the made-to-measure crowd, you may order haute-couture custom vaults, monogrammed by request (they come equipped with a patented climate-control system that guarantees your cigars' freshness for one month). The accessories department groans with deluxe lighters and fountain pens (Dupont, Cartier, Dunhill, Mont-Blanc), plus crystal wares by Lalique, Daum and Baccarat.

La Cave
à Cigares

10th arr. - 4, bd de Denain - 42 81 05 51
Open 8 a.m.-7 p.m. Closed Sat. & Sun.

Owner Gérard Courtial is the inventor of the much-imitated vertical humidifier/display case. Although he is by profession a member of the *confrérie des maîtres pipiers* (brotherhood of master pipemakers), he is nevertheless a cigar connoisseur and an excellent source of information and advice. Do not miss his collection of pipes, including such brands as Chacom, Dunhill and Butz-Choquin. Also, a wide range of smoking accessories, for experts and novices.

A la Civette

1st arr. - 157, rue Saint-Honoré 42 96 04 99
Open 8:30 a.m.-7 p.m. Closed Sun.

Habitués lovingly refer to this venerable establishment as the Civette du Palais-Royal. Founded in 1763, it was the first tobacconist in Paris, for many years *the* place of pilgrimage for cigar and tobacco lovers. Although it is no longer the city's foremost, it remains among its highest ranks. Tobacco goods featured run the gamut from everyday chewing weed to the very best Havanas, including the Hoyo de Monterrey, imported directly from Cuba. La Civette was the first shop in Paris to install climate-controlled vaults for its cigars, and the first to import Monte-Cristos. Also available is a wide range of accessories: deluxe lighters and pipes (Chacom, Butz-Choquin, Dunhill), humidors in all shapes and sizes, pens, leather goods.

Drugstore
Publicis

6th arr. - 149, bd Saint-Germain 42 22 92 50
8th arr. - 133, av. des Champs-Elysées - 47 23 54 34
8th arr. - 1, av. Matignon - 43 59 38 70
Open daily 9 a.m.-2 a.m. (Sun. 10 a.m.-2 a.m.).

A large selection of good-quality humidified cigars is available at each of the three Drugstore Publicis year-round and late into the night.

Lemaire

16th arr. - 59, av. Victor-Hugo 45 00 75 63
Open 8:30 a.m.-7:30 p.m. Closed Sun.

Bernard Lecrocq presides over this century-old institution, one of France's most prestigious tobacconists. Of course you will find the cigar of your dreams perfectly preserved and presented with rare flair. Havanas and San Domingos—Zinos, Don Miguels and Juan Clementes—top the list. Lecrocq's astonishing vaults accommodate thousands of cases of cigars in ideal temperature and humidity conditions. Cigar boxes and humidors, humble or extravagant, are guaranteed for workmanship and reliability (the gamut runs from a solid cedarwood three-cigar pocket humidor to a vault the size of a writing desk). Pipe smokers will discover the entire range of tobaccos available in France, plus a large selection of pipes (all major brands, with a particularly good collection of meerschaums). Lemaire's vast array of luxurious accessories includes all major brands of lighters, cases, pouches, plus 1,100 fountain, ballpoint and felt-tip pens.

ARTS & LEISURE

ART GALLERIES

GEOGRAPHY

A gallery's address is a fairly reliable indicator of its artistic allegiance. The Right Bank, from avenue Matignon to avenue de Messine, is the place to view established contemporary artists; the Left Bank, from rue Guénégaud to rue des Beaux-Arts, is home to slightly more "advanced" art. The turf of the real avant-garde extends from Beaubourg and Les Halles to the Bastille.

FINE ART

Artcurial

8th arr. - 9, av. Matignon - 42 99 16 16
Open 10:30 a.m.-7:10 p.m. Closed Sun., Mon. (except in Dec.), last 3 wks. of Aug. & holidays.

This artistic offshoot of the L'Oréal cosmetics group is the largest gallery in Paris. Artcurial is a multifaceted gallery that boasts one of the finest art bookshops in all of Europe, in addition to collections of contemporary furniture, carpets and ceramics designed by noted artists, signed lithographs and stunning limited-edition jewelry. Works by de Chirico, Sonia Delauney, Etienne-Martin, Laurens, Masson, Miró and Zadkine may be admired—and purchased—here.

Galeries Beaubourg I et II

4th arr. - 23, rue du Renard - 42 71 20 50
4th arr. - 3, rue Pierre-au-Lard 48 04 34 40
Open 10:30 a.m.-1 p.m. & 2:30 p.m.-7 p.m. Closed Sun., Mon., Aug. & holidays.

Here, at one of the most important galleries in the Beaubourg area, Pierre and Marianne Mahon favor artists of the '50s, new realists and other contemporaries. Works by celebrated artists (Arman and César, Baselitz, Basquiat, Beuys, Boisrond, Cane, Combas, Dado, Garouste, Klossowski, Monory, Paladino, Raysse, Villeglé, Warhol and Wols, to name a few!) are sold worldwide, including to museums. Some art-lovers whisper that lately the gallery is resting on its laurels, and has lost its sense of adventure. But such talk could just be the price of the Mahons' spectacular success.

Galerie Barbier-Beltz

4th arr. - 7, rue Pecquay - 40 27 84 14
Open noon-7 p.m. (Sat. 10 a.m.-7 p.m.). Closed Sun., Mon., Aug. & holidays.

A discreet, elegant little gallery run by a man who has never hesitated to pursue such "difficult" artists as Barré, Dufour, Kallos, Messagier and Pincemin. They have lately been joined by such estimable newcomers as Barbara Thaden and Christian Sorg.

Galerie Berggruen

7th arr. - 70, rue de l'Université 42 22 02 12
Open 10 a.m.-1 p.m. & 2:30 p.m.-7 p.m. Closed Sun., Mon. & holidays.

H. Berggruen retired and handed over the reins of this traditional gallery to Antoine Mendihara. The solid stock of prints and drawings by Arroyo, Dali, Klee, Masson, Matisse, Miró, Picasso and Zao Wouki are complemented by the works of contemporary artists like Beringer, Janssen and Paguignon. The sublime little catalogs are works of art in their own right.

Galerie Claude Bernard

6th arr. - 7, rue des Beaux-Arts 43 26 97 07
Open 9:30 a.m.-12:30 p.m. & 2:30 p.m.-6:30 p.m. Closed Sun., Mon., Aug. & holidays.

In a district where fine galleries abound, this is surely one of the very best. Works by Bacon and Bonnard have graced these walls, alongside unforgettable images by Balthus, Botero, Giacometti, Hockney and Nevelson. Perhaps understandably, the gallery's atmosphere is weighty and solemn—genius is never stale, but a fresh point of view would be welcome.

Galerie Isy Brachot

6th arr. - 33, rue Guénégaud - 43 29 11 71
6th arr. - 35, rue Guénégaud - 43 54 22 40
Open 2 p.m.-7 p.m. (Sat. 11 a.m.-1 p.m. & 2 p.m.-7 p.m.). Closed Sun., Mon. & July 15-Sept. 1.

Surrealism and fantastic realism are the hallmarks of this originally Belgian gallery. Some of the biggies are here: Delvaux, Ensor, Labisse, Magritte. Also present are De Andrea, Dado, Beuys and Roland Cat.

Galerie Jeanne Bucher

6th arr. - 53, rue de Seine - 43 26 22 32
Open 9 a.m.-12:30 p.m. & 2:30 p.m.-6:30 p.m. Closed Sun., Mon., Aug. & holidays.

Faithful to the Ecole de Paris of the 1960s, and to a particularly sensitive vision of painting, typified by Dubuffet, Bissière, De Stael, Viera da Silva and Jean-Pierre Raynaud.

Claire Burrus

11th arr. - 16, rue de Lappe - 43 55 36 90
Open 10:30 a.m.-1 p.m. & 2 p.m.-7 p.m. Closed Sun., Mon., Aug. & holidays.

Claire Burrus, a pioneer in this now-hip gallery district, champions post-conceptual artists like Finlay, Thomas, Nils-Udo and Felice Varini. A few of the old-guard from her former gallery, Le Dessin, are also present: look for works by Agid, Baruchello, Degottex and Voss.

Galerie Farideh Cadot

3rd arr. - 77, rue des Archives 42 78 08 36

Open 10 a.m.-7 p.m. (Sat. 11 a.m.-7 p.m.). Closed Sun., Mon., Aug. & holidays.

Farideh Cadot owns one of the most important galleries in Paris, thanks to his provocative, perspicacious choice of artists. No sectarianism here: painting, sculpture and photography are all (well) represented, with such artists as Boisrond, Favier, Laget, Oppenheim, Raetz, Rousse and Tremblay. And Cadot is always on the prowl for new, exciting work.

Galerie Louis Carré et Cie

8th arr. - 10, av. de Messine - 45 62 57 07

Open 10 a.m.-12:30 p.m. & 1:30 p.m.-6:30 p.m. (Sat. depending on exhibitions). Closed Sun., holidays, Aug. & Dec. 25-Jan. 1.

Patrick Bongers, Louis Carré's grandson, carries on the family tradition by keeping alive the great names of this gallery's past, names like Delaunay, Dufy, Hartung, Léger, Poliakoff and Soulages. He also exhibits more contemporary work by the likes of Estève and Bitran, and even had Di Rosa paint his car!

Galerie Lucien Durand

6th arr. - 19, rue Mazarine - 43 26 25 35

Open 10:30 a.m.-1 p.m. & 2:30 p.m.-7 p.m. Closed Sun., Mon., July & Aug. & holidays.

For 30 years, Lucien Durand has been discovering young artists and organizing first exhibitions. This sensitive, eagle-eyed picture dealer introduced César and Dmitrienko to the world at large. Durand's current group of artists include Braconnier, Canteloup, Frize, Lechner, Nadaud and Vanarsky.

Durand-Dessert

11th arr. - 28, rue de Lappe - 48 06 92 23

Open 11 a.m.-1 p.m. & 2 p.m.-7 p.m. (Sat. 11 a.m.-7 p.m.). Closed Sun., Mon., Aug. & holidays.

In a new gallery space that was once a factory, Durand-Dessert display European avant-garde at its loftiest level. You'll find such international high-flyers as Richter, Beuys, Merz, Kounelis, Morellet, Garouste, Lavier and Tosani. The gallery's bookstore is a wonderful place to linger and browse through the latest art publications.

Espace Photographique de Paris

1st arr. - Nouveau Forum des Halles, Place Carrée, Grande-Galerie - 40 26 87 12

Open 1 p.m.-6 p.m. (Sat. & Sun. 1 p.m.-7 p.m.). Closed Mon. & July 15-end of Aug.

After the Palais de Tokyo (see Museums), this is the most comprehensive photographic collection in town. Jacques Lowe, Ralph Gibson, Bill Brandt, Emmet, Gowin and other major figures have shown here; retrospectives and *hommages* bring works of the masters to this fascinating gallery.

Galerie Jean Fournier

4th arr. - 44, rue Quincampoix 42 77 32 31

Open 10 a.m.-1 p.m. & 2 p.m.-7 p.m. (Mon. by appointment). Closed Sun., Aug. & holidays.

Jean Fournier has worked in his vast book-lined premises for 30 years. Though he remains a champion of the postwar abstraction movement, represented by such artists as Buraglio, Sam Francis, Hantaï, Joan Mitchell and Viallat, Fournier is also a tireless seeker of new talent. If you are in search of a rare

book on contemporary art, this is the place to look.

Galerie de France

4th arr. - 52, rue de la Verrerie 42 74 38 00

Open 10 a.m.-7 p.m. (Mon. 10 a.m.-6 p.m.). Closed Sun., Aug. & holidays.

Huge, museum-like premises that span three floors makes the Galerie de France an ideal venue for sculpture exhibits and art festivals. Artists represented here include Aillaud, Antoniucci, Brancusi, Degottex, Gonzales, Kantor, Manessier, Matta, Pincemin, Raynaud, Soulages and Zao Wou-Ki. Recent photography exhibitions have displayed works by Alice Springs, Domela and Gisèle Freund. The gallery also actively promotes contemporary Russian artists.

Galerie Maurice Garnier

8th arr. - 6, av. Matignon - 42 25 61 65

Open 10 a.m.-1 p.m. & 2:30 p.m.-7 p.m. Closed Sun., Mon., Aug. & holidays.

Since 1978 Maurice Garnier has represented a single painter: Bernard Buffet, whom Picasso believed was the most talented painter of his generation (even geniuses can have an occasional lapse). Each year, in February and March, Garnier mounts a thematic exhibition of Buffet's work.

Galerie Daniel Gervis

7th arr. - 14, rue de Grenelle - 45 44 41 90, fax 45 49 18 98

By appointment only. Closed Sun. & July 15-Sept. 1.

Daniel Gervis, co-producer of the FIAC, Paris's annual International Fair of Contemporary Art, also produces limited editions of engravings and lithographs. His taste runs toward the abstract, exemplified by such artists as Benrath, Olivier Debré,

Dubuffet, Hartung and Malaval.

Didier Imbert Fine Art

8th arr. - 19, av. Matignon - 45 62 10 40

Open 10 a.m.-1 p.m. & 2:30 p.m.-7 p.m. Closed Sun., Aug. & holidays.

Didier Imbert has transformed his gallery into a veritable museum. Exhibits of works by Brauner, Brancusi and the acclaimed *Henry Moore Intime* show, which were as intellectually stimulating as they were thrilling to view, have placed Imbert in the forefront of the Parisian art scene.

Galerie Laage-Salomon

4th arr. - 57, rue du Temple - 42 78 11 71

Open 10:30 a.m.-12:30 p.m. & 2:30 p.m.-7 p.m. (Sat. 11 a.m.-7 p.m.). Closed Sun., Mon., Aug. & holidays.

Gabrielle Salomon's outlook is broadly international. She exhibits the work of German neo-Expressionists (Baselitz, Lüpertz, A. R. Penck and Immendorf) as well as sculpture by Chamberlain (an American), England's Ackling and the French artists Cogné, Mercier, Messager and Di Rosa.

Galerie Yvon Lambert

3rd arr. - 108, rue Vieille-du-Temple - 42 71 09 33

Open 10 a.m.-1 p.m. & 2:30 p.m.-7 p.m. (Sat. 10 a.m.-7 p.m.). Closed Sun., Mon., Aug. & holidays.

Aloof and reserved, Yvon Lambert is an energetic promoter of the avant-garde. A onetime aficionado of minimalist and conceptual art, Lambert now aims in another direction. His enormous gallery is home to works by Lewitt, Oppenheim, Tuttle and Twombly, as well as

Christo, Blais, Barcelo and Combas.

Lavignes-Bastille

11th arr. - 27, rue de Charonne 47 00 88 18

Open 11 a.m.-7 p.m. Closed Sun., Mon., Aug., Dec. 25 & Jan. 1.

Since 1985 Jean-Pierre Lavignes has filled his multi-level gallery with fascinating, sometimes violent work by contemporary artists working in the Realist and Expressionist veins: Calum Fraser, Grataloup, Hahn, Lukaschewsky, Rotella, Sandorfi and, on occasion, Andy Warhol (his last Parisian show was held right here).

Galerie Baudoin Lebon

4th arr. - 38, rue Sainte-Croix-de-la-Bretonnerie - 42 72 09 10

Open 2 p.m.-7 p.m. (Sat. 11 a.m.-7 p.m.). Closed Sun., Mon., Aug. & holidays.

Allow us to forewarn you: this gallery is a little offbeat. Expect, for example, to see an exhibition of aboriginal art and works by Ben, Bissier, Dado, Dine, Michaux, Pagès, Rauschenberg, Titus-Carmel and Viallat. Photography is another major focus at this eccentric gallery, now established in a fabulous new space.

Galerie Lelong

8th arr. - 13, rue de Téhéran - 45 63 13 19

Open 10:30 a.m.-6 p.m. (Sat. 2 p.m.-6:30 p.m.). Closed Sun., Mon., Aug. & holidays.

Known as the "spiritual son" of Aimé Maeght, Daniel Lelong's prestigious gallery is one of the most important in Paris. In addition to his branches in Zurich and New York, he also runs a sideline publishing venture (you'll find the books, catalogs and lithos on the gallery's lower level). Lelong's exhibits encompass works by great twentieth-century artists: Bacon, Calder, Chagall, Lindner, Moore,

Bram Van Velde, as well as Adami, James Brown, Garcia Sevilla, Kienholz, Tàpies and Titus-Carmel.

Galerie Louise Leiris

8th arr. - 47, rue de Monceau 45 63 20 56

Open 10 a.m.-noon & 2:30 p.m.-6 p.m. Closed Sun., Mon. & holidays. Annual closings not available.

Founded by D. H. Kahnweiler, this "picture dealer of the century" (Picasso, Léger, Gris, Braque and others) is indeed a venerable and historically important gallery that should not be missed. The collections are tops in terms of quality and prestige, with works by Masson, Laurens, Beaudin and, more recently, Elie Lascaux.

Galerie Adrien Maeght

7th arr. - 42-46, rue du Bac - 45 48 45 15

Open 9:30 a.m.-1 p.m. & 2 p.m.-7 p.m. Closed Sun., Mon., Aug. & holidays.

A gallery that bears the name of Maeght is obviously going to have a prestigious catalog of the highest quality. And indeed, Adrien Maeght, son of Aimé, oversees a tremendous stock of major twentieth-century paintings housed in galleries throughout Europe, with works by Matisse, Chagall, Calder and Bram Van Velde. His daughter Yoyo, also a talented picture dealer, has brought a new generation of artists such as Kuroda and Hélène Delprat to the Maeght "stable."

Galerie Daniel Malingue

8th arr. - 26, av. Matignon - 42 66 60 33

Open 10:30 a.m.-12:30 p.m. & 2:30 p.m.-6:30 p.m. (Mon. 2:30 p.m.-6:30 p.m.). Closed Sun., Aug. & holidays.

Twice a year, Daniel Malingue mounts well-publicized exhibitions of important twentieth-century artists; recent shows have focused on Dufy, Léger, Matisse and Vlaminck, as well as César, Lobo, Matta and Moore.

Galerie Nikki Diana Marquardt

4th arr. - 9, pl. des Vosges - 42 78 21 00
Open 1 p.m.-7 p.m. Closed Sun. & Mon.

American gallery owner Nikki Marquardt displays a bold approach to contemporary art: she's willing to take a risk, and usually comes up a winner. She claims that one "doesn't need direction, just vision, to know about art." David Mach has done his special brand of sculpture installation here; sculpture by Vlugt, Flavin and works by Dunoyer, Bader and Kumrov have also been shown, to considerable critical acclaim.

Galerie Marwan Hoss

1st arr. - 12, rue d'Alger - 42 96 37 96
Open 10 a.m.-12:30 p.m. & 2 p.m.-6:30 p.m. (Sat. 10 a.m.-12:30 p.m. & 2 p.m.-6 p.m.). Closed Sun., holidays & mid July-end Aug.

Apart from a few great classics, such as Matisse, Bonnard and Calder, this gallery pipes a contemporary tune from Giacometti to Garcia with some stopovers for Gonzalez, Hayden and Zao Wou-Ki.

Galerie 1900-2000

6th arr. - 8, rue Bonaparte - 43 25 84 20
Open 10 a.m.-12:30 p.m. & 2 p.m.-7 p.m. Closed Sun., Aug. & holidays.

This gallery is best known for its eye-popping exhibitions on such themes as hyperrealism, pop art and fringe artists. Represented are Max Ernst, Hérold, Marcel Jean, Matta, Picabia, Man Ray, Gaston Louis Roux, Takis and Warhol.

Galerie Montaigne

8th arr. - 36, av. Montaigne - 47 23 32 35
Open 11 a.m.-1 p.m. & 2 p.m.-7 p.m. Closed Sun., Mon., Aug. & holidays.

Somewhat isolated here in the sanctuary of *haute couture*, this gallery combines forays into the wild world of contemporary American art with shows of such modern masters as Man Ray and Marcel Duchamp.

Galerie Montenay

6th arr. - 31, rue Mazarine - 43 54 85 30
Open 11 a.m.-1 p.m. & 2:30 p.m.-7 p.m. Closed Sun., Mon., Aug. & holidays.

Marie-Hélène Montenay is the proud possessor of one of the most beautiful spaces in her part of town. From conceptual work to figurative painting, her choices are wide-ranging and always challenging. Friedmann and Bruce Marden have their niche here, and so does Malcolm Morley.

Galerie Odermatt-Cazeau

8th arr. - 85, rue du Faubourg-Saint-Honoré - 42 66 92 58
Open 10 a.m.-6:30 p.m. Closed Sun., Aug. & holidays.

This gallery specializes in works by nineteenth- and twentieth-century masters, Impressionists and post-Impressionists and has fine sculpture displays (Germaine Richier, Gonzales, Zadkine).

Galerie Proscenium

6th arr. - 35, rue de Seine - 43 54 92 01
Open 10:30 a.m.-12:30 p.m. & 2:30 p.m.-7 p.m. Closed Sun., Mon., holidays & July 20-Sept. 5.

This very pretty gallery often hosts exhibitions of theater decor and costumes, with an accent on the early twentieth century: Bakst, Bérard, Cocteau, Dupont, J. Hugo and Wakevitch are the primary artists, though Erté, Pizzi and

even Saint-Laurent are also represented.

Galerie Denise René

7th arr. - 196, bd Saint-Germain 42 22 77 57
Open 10 a.m.-1 p.m. & 2 p.m.-7:30 p.m. Closed Sun., Mon. & Aug.

In 1945 Denise René's pioneering gallery became the rallying center for geometrical abstraction. Since then she has sung its praises the world over and adopted the offshoots of constructivism, promoting the works of Agam, Albers, Claisse, Dewasne, Herbin, Naraha, Soto and Vasarely.

Galerie Stadler

6th arr. - 51, rue de Seine - 43 26 91 10
Open 10:30 a.m.-12:30 p.m. & 2:30 p.m.-7 p.m. Closed Sun., Mon., holidays & July 10-Sept. 10.

Since its opening in 1955 Rodolphe Stadler's gallery has been a Left Bank chapel for violent, gestual abstractionist art. Naturally, then, the painters favored here include Arnulf Rainer, Saura and Antonio Tàpies—artists whose canvases display plenty of texture and relief.

Leif Stahle

11th arr. - 37, rue de Charonne 48 07 24 78
Open 11 a.m.-7:30 p.m. Closings not available.

Leif Stahle, organizer of the Stockholm Festival, came to live in Paris in 1986. His beautiful, well-lit gallery is devoted to contemporary abstract art and, according to Stahle, "not just to lyrical abstraction." Such artists as Choi, Debré, Englund, Gandin, Kallos, Kinahara, Limérat, Rosenthal and Weil have found a home here.

> *Don't plan to do much shopping in Paris in August—a great many stores are closed for the entire vacation month.*

King Louis sees the light

It's hardly surprising that Louis XIV, the Sun King, preferred light to shadow—it was he who first had the bright idea to illuminate Paris at night (notably to discourage thieves, murderers and other criminals who operate under cover of darkness). Squads of torch-bearers were therefore hired to light up the night. Centuries later, in the 1960s, it occurred to the powers-that-be that they could show off the city's monuments (and discourage unwanted visitors) by floodlighting them after dark. New forms of street lighting are illuminating the nocturnal cityscape; color has recently added another dimension, bathing the renovated neighborhood of La Villette with splashes of red and blue.

Galerie Templon

8th arr. - 4, av. Marceau - 47 20 15 02
Open 10 a.m.-7 p.m. Closed Sun., holidays & July 25-beg. Sept.

Daniel Templon has moved out of the Beaubourg area to the sleeker precincts of the eighth arrondissement. His new upstairs gallery exudes a distinctly New York style, and his choice of painters reflects a contemporary American sensibility. Alongside conceptual and minimalist works by Judd and Serra, there are paintings by Frank Stella and pieces by younger members of the avant-garde, such as Clemente, Chia and Cucchi. French art is represented by the likes of Debré, Appel, Alberola, Giorda and Rouan.

Galerie Patrice Trigano

6th arr. - 4 bis, rue des Beaux-Arts - 46 34 15 01
Open 10 a.m.-1 p.m. & 2:30 p.m.-6:30 p.m. Closed Sun., Mon., Aug. & holidays.

After a spell on rue Beaubourg, Patrice Trigano ferried his pictures across the Seine to the Left Bank where he specializes in art of the '50s. He exhibits César and Harman (he started out with them) but also Atlan, Hélion, Lanskoy, Lapicque, Schneider, Bram Van Velde and Jenkins.

Galerie Zabriskie

4th arr. - 37, rue Quincampoix 42 72 35 47
Open 11 a.m.-7 p.m. Closed Sun., Mon., Aug. & holidays.

A photographic gallery with a definite downtown (Manhattan) attitude, where photos are presented as if they were sculpture. Weegee, Klein, Friedlander, Peter Briggs and Poivret: the gang's all here, with pictures full of vibrancy and temperament.

POSTERS & PRINTS

Ciné-Images

7th arr. - 68, rue de Babylone 45 51 27 50
Open noon-7 p.m. (Sat. 2 p.m.-7 p.m.). Closed Sun., Mon., Aug. & holidays. 13-Sept. 6.

Ciné-Images is dedicated to film. According to the pros, this is an absolute "must" visit for serious movie-poster collectors. All the greats are represented.

Documents

6th arr. - 53, rue de Seine - 43 54 50 68
Open 10:30 a.m.-12:30 p.m. & 2:30 p.m.-7 p.m. Closed Sun., Mon. & 3 1st wks. of Aug.

In 1953 Michel Romand put together a collection of posters amassed by Sagot, his great-grandfather. His stock of superb original posters dating from 1875 to 1930, for sale to the public, has been responsible for his meteoric rise to success. He still has works by Toulouse-Lautrec, Mucha, Chéret, Capiello and Steinlen, among others.

Galerie Princesse, Comptoir de l'Affiche

6th arr. - 18, rue Princesse - 43 25 25 18
Open 10:30 a.m.-7:30 p.m. (Fri. & Sat. 10:30 a.m.-1 a.m.). Closed Sun. & Mon. morning. Annual closings not available.

Hand over a color slide and 150 francs, and a week later you, too, can be a pinup (about 15 by 20 inches). Framing is also done here, and there are reproductions—primarily of movie posters—for sale.

A l'Imagerie

5th arr. - 9, rue Dante 43 25 18 66
Open 10:30 a.m.-1 p.m. & 2 p.m.-7 p.m. Closed Sun., Mon. morning (Mon. in July & Aug.) & holidays.

The selection of old French and foreign advertising posters (selling for 600 to 1,000 francs and up) here is grand. There are also Belle Epoque lithographs, some 1925 stencils and Japanese prints.

Nouvelles Images

5th arr. - 6, rue Dante 43 25 62 43
Open 11 a.m.-7 p.m. Closed Sun. & holidays.

Among this wide-ranging choice of posters, there are pieces to suit everyone. In addition, you will find postcards, and books on painting, architecture and contemporary photography. Posters from the national museums as well as those issued by major galleries are for sale.

THE PASS THAT MAKES PARIS YOUR PLAYGROUND.

La carte qui vous ouvre les portes du tout Paris.

Lawton

Paris Visite is an all-in travel pass - valid for 3 or [?] days - giving you access to every part of the city and [?] surrounding areas. By metro, bus or RER, as well as [S]NCF Ile-de-France lines, to Eurodisneyland®-Resort, [Ve]rsailles, Roissy-Charles-de-Gaulle and Orly air[po]rts. Available at main metro and RER stations.

Paris Visite, c'est un forfait transport de 3 ou 5 jours pour découvrir librement Paris et sa région en métro, bus, RER et trains SNCF Ile-de-France, jusqu'au parc Eurodisneyland®, Versailles et aux aéroports Roissy-Charles-de-Gaulle et Orly. En vente dans les principales stations de métro et gares RER.

RATP

l' e s p r i t   l i b r e

A BETTER WAY FOR VISITING PARIS

PARIS the light city, the capital of France, with all its monuments, its architecture and its Parisian life, were we will be pleased to welcome you.

Here are some excursions we can offer you

PICK UP	EXCURSIONS: TOUR
9h et 14h00	Paris 1/2 day
14h00	Versailles 1/2 day
13h30	Giverny 1/2 day
07h00	Loire Valley full day
07h00	Normandy full day
21h30	Illuminations +cruise
20h00	Cruise+ "Milliardaire"
21h30	Illuminations+ Moulin Rouge or Lido.
19h30	Dinner cruise +Moulin rouge or Lido.
20h00	Dinner at the Eiffel Tower + Moulin Rouge or Lido.
19h30	Dinner at the "Paradis Latin"
21h30	Cruise + Moulin Rouge or Lido.
20h00	Dinner at the Eiffel Tower+ Grazy Horse Saloon
21h30	Cruise +Crazy Horse Saloon

TAS travel agency organizes excursions in mini-buses starting and return from your hotel by day and by night in order to help you discover the best places in Paris.

TAS voyages

For any further information,
please contact our North American reservation service:
5720 Buford Highway, Norcross, Georgia 30071 U.S.A.
Telephone: (404) 448-4079
Toll-free: (800) 423-2752
Fax: (404) 447-8475

HOBBIES & SPORTS

ART SUPPLIES

Adam Montparnasse

14th arr. - 11, bd Edgar-Quinet 43 20 68 53
Open 9:30 a.m.-7 p.m. Closed Sun., holidays (except Nov. 11), & 2 wks. in Aug.

For three generations, the Adam family has supplied artists and graphics designers with all the canvas, paper, paint and ink they need, in every possible color and size. You want references? How about Braque, Soutine and Modigliani? They all shopped here, and appreciated the sage advice dispensed by the competent staff.

Sennelier

7th arr. - 3, quai Voltaire - 42 60 72 15
Open 9 a.m.-6:30 p.m. (Mon. & summer 9 a.m.-noon & 2 p.m.-6:30 p.m.). Closed Sun. & holidays.

Appropriately situated next to the Beaux-Arts school, Sennelier has, in its century of existence, sold tons of art supplies to innumerable established and aspiring artists. Here they find the best brands of paints and pigments, paper and sketch pads of excellent quality, canvas, easels and framing equipment. Sculptors too can purchase all of their special supplies right here.

ASTRONOMY

La Maison de l'Astronomie

4th arr. - 33, rue de Rivoli - 42 77 99 55, fax 48 87 40 87
Open 9:45 a.m.-6:45 p.m. Closed Sun., Mon. & holidays.

This bookstore specializes in books, posters and sky maps pertaining to astronomy, as well as equipment for searching the heavens: telescopes, photo equipment, binoculars. There are introductory courses in astronomy as well as a course in astronomic photography.

BICYCLING

Paris By Cycle

14th arr. - 78, rue de l'Ouest - 40 47 08 04
Open daily 9 a.m.-1 p.m. & 2 p.m.-7:30 p.m.

Rent a city bike or a mountain bike by the hour (28 francs) or by the week (300 francs) from this competent, friendly team of specialists. A wide selection of bicycles is available for purchase, and there is a repair shop on the premises.

Paris Vélo (Rent a bike)

5th arr. - 2, rue du Fer-à-Moulin 43 37 59 22
Open April 1-Sept. 30: 10 a.m.-12:30 p.m. & 2 p.m.-7 p.m.; Oct. 1-March 31: until 6 p.m. Closed Sun.

Bicycle rental by the hour, day or weekend. No racing bikes here, but you'll find plenty of city bikes and mountain bikes—the most practical varieties for the local terrain.

BOWLING

Bowling Mouffetard

5th arr. - 13, rue Gracieuse - 43 31 09 35
Open daily 11 a.m.-2 a.m.

One of this bowling alley's eight lanes can be yours for 20 francs plus 6 francs for shoe-rental (afternoon rate); or 24 francs plus shoes (evening rate). On weekends and holidays, the tariff rises to 30 francs. While you await your turn, you can play pool or pinball, or grab a sandwich at the snack bar.

COOKING

Le Cordon Bleu

15th arr. - 8, rue Léon-Delhomme - 48 56 06 06
Open 9 a.m.-6:30 p.m. Closed Sat., Sun. & holidays.

Cooking buffs may attend daily demonstrations given by master chefs (English-language translation available). If you are more interested in hands-on experience, week-long courses are given in regional cuisines, pastry-making, bistro cooking and so on. Professional training leading to a Cordon Bleu diploma is also dispensed (about 30,000 francs per trimester).

Ecole de Gastronomie Française Ritz-Escoffier

1st arr. - 38, rue Cambon - 42 60 38 30
Open 9 a.m.-6 p.m. Closed Sat. & Sun. Prices: Ritz-Escoffier course 68,400 F / 12 wks.; César-Ritz course 1 to 6 wks 5,550 F / wk. for 28 h.

The school's facilities are set up opposite the very kitchens where nineteenth-century chef Auguste Escoffier exercised his incomparable art. Aspiring cooks can learn every aspect of the trade here, with professional-level courses; amateurs may register for the César-Ritz cycle, which lasts from one to six weeks. Each week, students attend four hands-on cooking and pastry-making courses, watch four demonstrations and take one theory course (cheese, wine, etc.). For 220 francs, anyone can attend a demonstration performed by a master chef. English-language courses are offered.

Princesse Ere 2001

7th arr. - 18, av. de La Motte-Picquet - 45 51 36 34
Open 10:30 a.m.-2 p.m. Closed Sat. & Sun. Prices: 580 F / course

or 3,000 F for 6 courses, lunch incl.; 650 F / course or 3,400 F for 6 courses directed by G. Sallé, lunch incl.

Regional cooking, market cooking, cuisine nouvelle and, as of this year, low-calorie cooking and the art of hospitality form the curriculum here. Courses are taught by Marie Blanche de Broglie and Gérard Sallé (chef of the Régence restaurant in the Hôtel Plaza-Athénée). In addition to French, the lessons are dispensed in English and Spanish. In August and September, the school takes up its summer quarters in Normandy (11,000 francs per week, full board included).

DANCE

Marais
4th arr. - 41, rue du Temple - 42 72 15 42
Open daily 9 a.m.-9 p.m. Prices: 78 F / course (1h30); 280 F for 4 courses; 480 F for 8 courses.

Everything is taught here— from the Argentinian tango and contemporary Japanese buto dancing to African dance, flamenco or Brazilian and Asian dances. There are 32 disciplines in all, taught in somewhat tumbledown surroundings but in a friendly, non-threatening atmosphere.

GAMES

Game's
1st arr. - Forum des Halles, level -2 - 40 26 46 06
Open 10 a.m.-7:30 p.m. Closed Sun.

This is a grown-up's game shop featuring chess sets carved in precious woods or onyx, electronic games, brain-teaser puzzles, billiards, roulette wheels, slot machines and more. Also, role-playing games complete with instruction books (in French and English) and figurines.

Jeux Descartes
5th arr. - 52, rue des Ecoles - 43 26 79 83
Open 10 a.m.-7 p.m. (Mon. 11 a.m.-7 p.m.). Closed Sun.

American games of strategy and intelligence (in English!) may be purchased here, as well as collectible historical figurines and old-fashioned board games.

Stratéjeux
14th arr. - 13, rue Poirier-de-Narçay - 45 45 45 87
Open 10:30 a.m.-7 p.m. Closed Sun.

Every Wednesday and Saturday afternoon, Stratejeux hosts demonstrations of strategy games. All the equipment needed for strategy games and role-playing games are sold in this unobtrusive little shop.

Le Train Bleu
6th arr. - 55, rue Saint-Placide - 45 48 33 78
16th arr. - 2-6, av. Mozart - 42 88 34 70
Open 10 a.m.-7 p.m. Closed Sun.

This is a luxury supermarket for toys and games. The basement level is reserved for adult games, but all ages are amused by the fun stuff for kids sold on the other three floors.

GARDENINING & FLOWER ARRANGING

Centre d'Art Floral Ikebana
17th arr. - 26, rue d'Armaillé - 45 74 21 28
Call for information. Entrance fee: 100 F / year; courses: 380 F / day (3 courses incl.).

The tradition of Japanese flower arranging was originally a religious practice developed by Buddhist monks. There are several different schools of Ikebana in Japan. At this address you will be taught the pure and simple style of Ohara. Greenery is included in

the price of the lessons, but bring your own shears.

Ecole d'Horticulture du Jardin du Luxembourg
6th arr. - 64, bd Saint-Michel - 45 48 55 55
Open Oct.-Dec.: Thurs. & Sat. 8 a.m.-noon.

Register in May for courses on decorative gardens, or on the proper cultivation of fruit trees. The courses are free, but the number of places is limited.

Société Nationale d'Horticulture de France
7th arr. - 84, rue de Grenelle - 45 48 81 00
Open Tues. & Thurs. 6 p.m.-7 p.m. Entrance fee: 145 F / year.

Only association members are admitted to SNHF courses (the membership fee is 145 francs). Eight different courses are given, including an introduction to gardening, the cultivation of roses, house plants, flower arranging and so on. This is where you can learn to graft trees or create a garden on your balcony.

GOLF

Club de Golf de l'Etoile
17th arr. - 10, av. de la Grande-Armée - 43 80 30 79
Open 8 a.m.-8:30 p.m. (Sat. 9 a.m.-5 p.m. & Sun. 10 a.m.-5 p.m.). Membership: 1,650 F / 6 months; 2,450 F / year; 60 F / 30 mn. Closed Sun. July-Sept.

Polish your putting at this lovely practice range situated in a rooftop greenhouse; you can also loosen up your drive at one of the seven practice tees, or use a video simulation to help improve your swing. Eight highly qualified pros are on hand to teach beginners the basics, as well as to give veteran players advice on how to achieve a better game. You needn't even bring your clubs:

all equipment is provided free of extra charge.

HEALTH CLUBS

Club Jean de Beauvais

5th arr. - 5, rue Jean-de-Beauvais 46 33 16 80
Open 7 a.m.-10:30 p.m. (Wed. & Fri. 7 a.m.-10 p.m.; Sat. 8:30 a.m.-7 p.m.; Sun. 9:30 a.m.-5 p.m.).

A doctor supervises your progress, a chiropractor advises you, a gym instructor personally takes charge of your training and a nutritionist supervises your diet. For those who have decided, finally, to take themselves in hand, it's a complete overhaul. For sporting types just looking for a tune-up, there's ski readiness in the fall and windsurfing prep in the spring. Annual membership rates range from 3,200 francs (for off hours) to 6,150 francs.

Espace Vit'Halles

3rd arr. - Place Beaubourg, 48, rue Rambuteau - 42 77 21 71
Open 9 a.m.-10 p.m. (Sat. 11 a.m.-7 p.m.; Sun. 11 a.m.-3 p.m.). Closed at Christmas & Jan. 1.

Nearly 120 classes per week are given by the center's 20 instructors in cardio-vascular fitness, body-building and strengthening. Hi-lo, cardio-funky and funky-step, body sculpting, stretching and localized workouts (abs and buns) are just some of the options available. For relaxing after a workout, there are saunas, a Turkish bath, Jacuzzi and massage services. Personal trainers are on hand to design individualized fitness programs (200 francs an hour); other fees vary. The facilities are well-kept and clean, pleasant to use but unpretentious. Information on short-term rates is available by request.

Gymnase Club

1st arr. - 147 bis, rue Saint-Honoré - 40 20 03 03 (also: 11th, 12th, 13th, 14th, 15th, 17th, La Défense & Neuilly)
Open 7:30 a.m.-10 p.m. (Sat. 9 a.m.-7 p.m.; Sun. 9 a.m.-5 p.m.). Closed May 1, Dec. 25 & Jan. 1. Subcription 3,200-3,650 F / year.

This chain of fitness clubs boasts centers all over Paris. Several have swimming pools and offer classes in aqua-gym, though this particular facility does not. But the menu of activities does comprise cardio-training, strengthening, body-building and modern jazz dance. Among the post-workout attractions are a whirlpool bath, a sauna and a Turkish bath. A competent staff can design a fitness program that meets individual needs, and for short-term visitors, books of tickets for a limited number of entries may be obtained at the clubs.

Thermes du Royal Monceau

8th arr. - 39, av. Hoche - 42 25 06 66
Open daily 7 a.m.-11 p.m. Membership: 15,000 F / year.

Sporting-type nymphs lounge by the pool, millionaires pedal away in a supremely outfitted, rarely crowded workout room. The personnel is discreetly attentive—from the gym instructor to the masseuse, the makeup artist to the beautician. A classical air is lent to the proceedings by a decor that features Doric columns, an oval pool under a Roman-style glass roof, mosaics, frescoes, lots of plants, cushy sofas and luxurious Turkish baths. The emphasis here is more on relaxation than on hard-core waistline maintenance. Membership for one year costs 15,000 francs.

Vitatop Club Plein Ciel

15th arr. - 8, rue Louis-Armand 45 54 79 00
Open 7 a.m.-9 p.m. (Sat. 9 a.m.-7 p.m.; Sun. 9 a.m.-5 p.m.). Closed Dec. 25 & Jan. 1.

The membership fees are high (800 francs entrance fee, plus 5,150 francs a year) but the variety of services is undoubtedly the widest in town. Vitatop members have unlimited access to all Gymnase Club centers (see above), and are accorded preferred rates at the chain's tennis courts and golf practice ranges. Vitatop's state-of-the-art fitness equipment includes Stair-masters, electronic stationary bikes, rowing machines, a Gravitron and more; and each club offers a pool (also used for popular aqua-gym classes),

---

Paradise behind the walls

You'll have a better grasp of the original meaning of paradise—"walled garden"—when you visit the flower- and fountain-filled courtyards nestled within the white walls of the *Paris Mosque*. Built in 1922 in a predominantly Moroccan style, it also houses a library, Turkish baths, restaurant and tea rooms. The interior is sumptuous, with stucco, carved wood, mosaics and carpets reminiscent of a more leisurely age. Another view of Islam is afforded by the *Institute of the Arab World* on the nearby quai Saint-Bernard, a futuristic nine-story structure of glass, concrete and aluminum that includes a museum, art gallery and documentation center.

Jacuzzi, comfortable dressing rooms and showers, a sauna and so forth. Courses are offered all day long in fitness and related disciplines (jogging, personal health/nutrition supervision) for no extra charge.

ICE SKATING

Patinoire des Buttes-Chaumont
19th arr. - 30, rue Edouard Pailleron - 42 39 86 10
Open Mon., Tues. & Fri. 4:30 p.m.-6:15 p.m.; Wed. 10 a.m.-5 p.m.; Thurs. 4:30 p.m.-9 p.m.; Sat. 10 a.m.-5 p.m. & 8:30 p.m.-midnight; Sun. 10 a.m.-6 p.m. Closed mid May-beg. Sept. Prices: adults: 25 F; under 16: 20 F; groups: 25 F (skates incl.); skates rental: 15 F.
The one and only ice-skating rink in Paris. Ice dancers and speed-skaters are given run of the rink for fifteen minutes each hour.

MUSIC

Andres Serrita
9th arr. - 25, rue de Bruxelles 42 80 40 25
Telephone information available mornings .
This is a friendly place where you can learn how to play the guitar.

François Guidon
9th arr. - 16, rue Victor-Massé 48 78 91 05
Open 2 p.m.-7 p.m. Closed Sat., Sun. & holidays.
François Guidon buys, restores and sells jazz guitars. Molded instruments command between 8,000 and 12,000 francs, while handmade guitars (constructed like cellos) go for about twice that price.

Hamm
6th arr. - 135-139, rue de Rennes 44 39 35 35
Open 10 a.m.-7 p.m. (Mon. 2 p.m.-7 p.m.), 2 Sun. in Dec.

Closed Sun. & Mon. in July & Aug., holidays.
Hamm's is assuredly one of the city's best sources for all types of musical instruments. Six floors display pianos and synthesizers, percussion and wind instruments, guitars and even a selection of antiques. Small studios are also rented here, for rehearsals or lessons.

Le Projet Musical
10th arr. - 23, rue du Faubourg-Saint-Denis - 42 46 27 26
Open 11 a.m.-10 p.m. Closed Sun., holidays & school holidays. Price: 62-120 F / h.
Instruments are taught in individual lessons, and solfège in small groups. Top-notch instruction in all instruments, classical or jazz, as well as in voice is offered at this school, which is subsidized by the City of Paris.

NEEDLEWORK

L'Atelier de la Dentellière
13th arr. - 9, rue de Patay - 45 86 14 78
Call for information.
Under the tutelage of Lysianne Brulet, professor of lace-making, you'll learn how to use linen, cotton or silk thread with finesse to make lace trim for curtains, blouses and napkins. This painstaking work teaches the lovely rewards of patience.

La Droguerie
1st arr. - 9, rue du Jour - 45 08 93 27
Open 10:30 a.m.-6:45 p.m. (Mon. 2 p.m.-6:45 p.m.). Closed Sun.
Here is a gold mine for knitting fanatics. Not only will you find the needles and wool you seek, you can also count on the sales staff to help you get the hang of an unusually difficult stitch. And that's not all: the shop stocks a dazzling selection of trims—multicolored beads, feathers, sequins and such are stored in

antique candy jars and sold by the ladleful!

R. Malbranche
9th arr. - 17, rue Drouot - 47 70 03 77
Open 9 a.m.-noon & 2 p.m.-6 p.m. Closed Sat., Sun., Aug. & holidays.
For sale here are linen sheets, muslin napkins, linen handkerchiefs and cambric placemats all delicately embroidered by hand—in short, it's the household linen of your dreams (at prices that leave you still dreaming!). You can learn how to make these masterpieces of patience yourself. Courses are taught by an award-winning needlewoman on Thursday afternoons (eight two-hour classes cost 650 francs). You'll be taught all the basic stitches plus some of the more complicated ones that require real address.

RACETRACKS

Hippodrome d'Auteuil
Bois de Boulogne, 16th arr. - 45 27 12 25
Openings vary.
The *Prix du Président de la République*, a hurdle race for French steeplechasers, is run here each year.

Hippodrome de Longchamp
Bois de Boulogne, 16th arr. - 42 24 13 29
Openings vary.
Home to the prestigious *Prix de l'Arc de Triomphe*, a highlight of the year's racing calendar.

Hippodrome de Vincennes
12th arr. - Bois de Vincennes, 2, route de la Ferme - 43 68 35 39
Openings vary.
The big event at this track is the yearly *Prix d'Amérique*.

RIDING

Centre Equestre de la Cartoucherie de Vincennes

12th arr. - Rue du Champ-des-Manœuvres - 43 74 61 25
Open 9 a.m.-noon & 2 p.m.-9:30 p.m. (Sun. 9 a.m.-noon). Closed July & Aug. Entrance fee: 150 F (life time). Membership: 400 F / year. Courses: 980 F / trimester (1 course / wk.).

Indoor and outdoor riding lessons are dispensed here, in the middle of the Bois de Vincennes. Riders who have proved their steadiness in the saddle are permitted to join groups for all-day outings in the forest. Small children may be introduced to equestrian pleasures at the Centre's pony club.

Club Hippique de la Villette

19th arr. - 9, bd Mac-Donald - 40 34 33 33
Open 9 a.m.-noon & 1:30 p.m.-9 p.m. (Sat. 9 a.m.-9 p.m., Sun. 9 a.m.-1 p.m.). Closed July, Aug. & Sept.

On the plus side, this club offers modern facilities, well-cared-for horses reputed for their gentleness, and a spacious indoor ring. Unfortunately, with no woods in the vicinity, students have no opportunities for excursions.

ROCK CLIMBING

La Samaritaine (Magasin 3)

1st arr. - Rue de Rivoli - 40 41 20 20
Open 9:30 a.m.-7 p.m. (Thurs. 9:30 a.m.-10 p.m.). Closed Sun., Dec. 25 & Jan. 1. Free.

Before tackling the Alps or the Pyrenées (or the fascinating rock formations in the Fontainebleau Forest), perfect your rock-climbing technique on this five-meter-high wall. Beginners and seasoned climbers alike will be challenged by the wall's hollows, toe-holds, bumps and projections. Equipment for a mountain holiday is also sold down here in the basement of La Samar's store number three.

SWIMMING

Aquaboulevard

15th arr. - 4, rue Louis-Armand 40 60 10 00
Open 7:30 a.m.-11 p.m. (Sat. & Sun. 8 a.m.-midnight).

Aquaboulevard made quite a splash when it opened its doors in 1989. The centerpiece of this gigantic sports, fitness and leisure complex is an "aquatic park": the biggest pool in Paris, replete with water slides, rapids, toboggans and other fun stuff that drives kids wild with joy. But water sports are only part of the action. Other possibilities include tennis, squash, bowling, billiards, bridge, ping-pong and video games. You can work out at the gym, spruce up at the beauty salons or chow down at one of several restaurants. You'll be shelling out too, to the tune of 75 francs for an adult admission on weekends (children: 55 francs), plus 200 francs per hour for tennis, 60 francs per half-hour for squash... The annual fee is 300 francs per person.

Piscine les Amiraux

18th arr. - 6, rue Hermann-la-Chapelle - 46 06 46 47
Hours vary. Entrance: 9.50 F.

This beautiful pool, vintage 1930, is an architectural landmark. Open until 7:30 p.m. on Mondays, for people who like a quick dip after work.

Piscine de la Butte-aux-Cailles

13th arr. - 5, pl. Paul-Verlaine 45 89 60 05
Hours vary. Entrance: 9.50 F.

Set in a picturesque neighborhood, this lovely Art Deco establishment offers three pools. The largest is an indoor facility, but the two others are outdoor pools, fed by an artesian well.

> Clean, attractive municipal swimming pools can be found all over Paris; locating one that is open to you at a given hour is less easy, since schedules vary greatly. A *free booklet*, available from the attendants at any of the city's 28 public pools, will give you specific addresses, opening hours and pool sizes, along with a color picture of each facility. The entrance fee for city pools is currently 10 francs. Regular swimmers can purchase a three-month pass for 146 francs. Listed below is a selection of some of the prettier pools in town.

Piscine Champerret-Yser

17th arr. - 32-36, bd de Reims 47 66 49 98
Hours vary. Entrance: Adults: 20 F (under 16: 16 F).

Bright, new and modern, with a spiral sliding board that youngsters adore, this pool is enclosed by tall glass walls. There are tennis courts on the premises.

Piscine Deligny

7th arr. - 25, quai Anatole-France 45 51 72 15
Open 8:30 a.m.-7:30 p.m. Closed Oct. 16-April 30. Entrance: 50 F (students: 40 F, under 16: 35 F, mattress: 70 F).

This privately owned pool, moored along the banks of the Seine, has earned a reputation as a hot spot to flirt. But how could it be otherwise? Given the crowds, the limited space and the bathers' skimpy attire, intimacy is the only logical result! Paradoxically, although (because?) the sun-bathing facilities are overpopulated, swimmers have plenty of room in the pool.

Piscine Henry-de-Montherlant

16th arr. - 32, bd Lannes - 45 03 03 28
Hours vary. Entrance: 9.50 F.
Set in a chic neighborhood close to the Bois de Boulogne, this municipal pool is part of a sports complex that includes tennis courts and a gymnasium.

Piscine Jean-Taris

5th arr. - 16, rue Thouin - 43 25 54 03
Hours vary. Entrance: 10 F (under 16: 5 F).
Students favor this splendid pool, which boasts a view of the Panthéon and the gardens of the Lycée Henri-IV. A special system makes it accessible to disabled.

Piscine Suzanne-Berlioux

1st arr. - 10, place de la Rotonde 42 36 98 44
Hours vary. Entrance: 20 F (under 16: 15 F).
This new, 50 by 20 meter pool in the Forum des Halles is open several evenings a week.

If you're visiting Paris and wish to play tennis without spending huge sums on private clubs, contact *Allô-Sports* (42 76 54 54), a municipal sports hotline, for information on public and municipal courts. If your French is not up to that sort of project, check the addresses listed below.

TENNIS & SQUASH

Stade Henry de Montherlant

16th arr. - 48, bd Lannes - 45 03 03 64
Call for information.
When available, these public courts can be reserved 24 hours in advance, for a small fee.

Squash Montmartre

18th arr. - 14, rue Achille-Martinet - 42 55 38 30
Open 10 a.m.-10:30 p.m. (Sat. & Sun. 10 a.m.-7:30 p.m.).
If you schedule your game in off-peak hours (10 a.m. to 5:30 p.m.) you can play at reduced rates on these fine, well-lit courts, then relax in the sauna, on the terrace or in the billiard room. Several different rate structures are offered, and trial memberships are available too.

Tennis du Luxembourg

6th arr. - Jardins du Luxembourg 43 25 79 18
Open 8 a.m.-4:30 p.m. Price: 12.50 F / 30 mn.
The six open courts are usually reserved well in advance by clubs and associations, but there is no reason not to try your luck...

MUSEUMS

MAJOR MUSEUMS

Cité des Sciences et de l'Industrie

19th arr. - 30, av. Corentin-Cariou - 40 05 80 00
Open 10 a.m.-6 p.m. Closed Mon. Cafeterias. Access for disabled.
A *cité* indeed—or maybe a citadel of knowledge. This gigantic steel, glass and concrete former meat-packing plant casts a formidable shadow across the wacky Parc de la Villette, with its geodome

---

and moats set in an enormous green swath along the Ourcq Canal in northeast Paris. It is the world's largest science and industry museum, conceived for the twenty-first century. In the outsized 120-foot-high entrance hall hangs a scale model of a space station with astronauts at work. Yet once you get over that initial dizzy spell, you'll find that the Cité is, paradoxically, made to human measure. Floors are divided into modular cells, which are shuffled around to create scenic effects. Visitors are challenged to penetrate the mysteries of science. And we've found that it is best to be curious—and daring. Get the most out of the Cité by examining and playing with the exhibits. Then sit back and contemplate. Scores of computer terminals beckon, ready to measure your knowledge, to lead you through experiments of weightlessness or the speed of sound, to activate robots, take you on a trip through outer space, heighten your senses, or put you in touch with experts in myriad fields of knowledge. Of particular interest to children are the Inventorium (Level 3) with its fascinating exhibits that make science "friendly" and fun; and the Géode movie theater. Just visiting that imposing stainless-steel sphere is a treat, but actually viewing a film projected by the Omnimax system (enhanced with holograms and lasers) is an experience no child will soon forget.

Galerie Nationale du Jeu de Paume

1st arr. - Jardin des Tuileries, corner place de la Concorde/ rue de Rivoli - 47 03 12 50
Open noon-7 p.m. (Tues. until 9:30 p.m., Sat. & Sun. from 10 a.m.). Closed Mon.
When its treasure trove of Impressionist masterpieces was ferried across the river to

the new Musée d'Orsay, the Jeu de Paume lost its *raison d'être*. Then, a few years ago, it was decided that the space could be most advantageously used as a showcase for contemporary art. Magnificently restructured by architect Antoine Stinco, the museum was relaunched in 1991 by a dynamic team of art professionals. The inaugural exhibit, dedicated to Jean Dubuffet, was a resounding success. Subsequent shows featuring Ellsworth Kelly, the Belgian poet/painter Broedthaers and the photographers Tunga and Jana Sterbak, among others, also won great acclaim. The new Jeu de Paume combines the prestige of a national art institution with the excitement of an avant-garde gallery, plugged in to the way artists work today.

Musée
d'Art Moderne
de la Ville de Paris

16th arr. - 11, av. du Président-Wilson - 47 23 61 27
Open 10 a.m.-5:30 p.m. (Wed. until 8:30 p.m.). Closed Mon. & holidays. Temporary exhibitions. Access for disabled.

The MAM—as this museum is called—has always been a whirlwind of change. But while collections may waltz in and out, the various "isms" of modern art are always represented: from Fauvism (Vlaminck and Derain) to cubism (Picasso and Braque) to cinetism (Vasarely, Agam). It is your opportunity to view a remarkable series of paintings by Rouault and Gromaire, compositions by Robert and Sonia Delaunay, works by Léger, Soutine, Chagall, Pascin and others. And, of course, also on view is the celebrated *Electricity Fairy* by Raoul Dufy and Matisse's terrific triptych, *Dance*. The fourth-level ARC (*Animation, Recherche, Confrontation*) is the liveliest section of the museum, used

primarily to showcase contemporary art forms (plastic arts, photography, poetry, contemporary music and jazz). Often, several shows and events run simultaneously, with an accent on new talent. The children's museum is designed to acquaint youngsters (and their parents) with modern art (entrance is at 14, avenue de New-York).

Musée
des Arts Décoratifs

1st arr. - Palais du Louvre, 107, rue de Rivoli - 42 60 32 14
Open 12:30 p.m.-6 p.m. (Sun. noon-6 p.m.). Closed Mon. & Tues. Temporary exhibitions. Access for disabled.

The Gallic taste for living in beauty and comfort comes vividly alive in the 100-odd rooms and galleries of the Musée des Arts Décoratifs, which traces the history of French homes from the Middle Ages to the present. One-of-a-kind and mass-produced tapestries, ceramics, tableware and furniture demonstrate how taste, form and style have evolved. The exquisite suite of 1920s Art Deco rooms was crafted for fashion designer Jeanne Lanvin. Avant-garde designs by Breuer, Perriand and others flank creations by Eames, Tallon and Paulin in a sweeping panorama of the last 50 years of French and international design. Recent additions: the delightful eighteenth- and twentieth-century toy collection, plus a handsome gift—paintings and sculptures (1942–1966) by Jean Dubuffet. Extensive reference sections cover wallpapers, textiles and patterns (by appointment only). The museum library (109, rue de Rivoli) holds a treasure trove of documentation on arts and crafts, and the museum boutique proposes an alluring collection of books and gifts.

Musée de l'Homme

16th arr. - Palais de Chaillot, pl. du Trocadéro - 45 53 70 60
Open 9:45 a.m.-5:15 p.m. Closed Tues. & holidays.

No longer a daunting jumble amassed over the years, the museum's renovated entrance hall—with its design showcases—as well as the anthropology and Africa sections, are a sparkling success. Descriptions and displays are now easy for the layman to understand. But that's just the tip of the iceberg: the Arctic room is enjoying a warm renaissance, with superb collections unfrozen from the warehouse. The heavenly planetarium whisks visitors across five continents to follow humans and their evolution, their arts and crafts, rites and religions. Don't miss the Chinese theater costumes, African masks, Indian jewelry, Eskimo sculptures and other oddities from distant lands. Alas, when will the amazing Aztec skull in polished quartz escape from its safe-deposit box?

Musée du Louvre

1st arr. - Cour Napoléon - 40 20 53 17 or 40 20 51 51 (anwsering machine in English)
Open 9 a.m.-6 p.m. (Mon. & Wed. 9 a.m.-10 p.m.). Closed Tues.

The Musée du Louvre, traditionally France's greatest museum, has become the Grand Louvre, reborn with a sparkling glass pyramid designed by Chinese-American architect I. M. Pei. The 200-plus halls and Grande Galerie, the miles of wall space, are still being remodeled and reorganized. Even the once-confusing signs indicating directions to the *Mona Lisa*, the *Venus de Milo* or, for that matter, the rest rooms, have been rethought. Why? The Louvre's three million or so annual visitors (60 to 80 percent of whom are foreigners) were dropping from exhaustion and losing their way among the museum's more than 400,000 catalogued works of art. The prestige of the museum had been in steady decline—hardly surprising since this former palace of kings had remained static for nearly 200 years (it opened August 10, 1793, as the Muséum Central des Arts). How to remedy the situation— and yet maintain the architectural integrity of the buildings (repeatedly stormed, burned, enlarged and remodeled over the last five centuries)? Pei's answer was a huge underground complex with reception and ticket areas, restoration labs, gift shops and parking facilities. In addition, the office of the Minister of Finance was transferred from the Rivoli Wing of the palace to a new site at Bercy, on the Seine. (Restoration of the Rivoli Wing and its courtyards will continue for several more years.)

Now that all the hubbub has died down, people are noticing that Pei's controversial glass pyramid rises a mere 67 Feet above the Cour Napoléon. Flanked by three smaller pyramids and several reflecting pools, it is in essence a high-tech skylight and entrance. In the vast void beneath, a futuristic helicoidal staircase-cum-elevator, plus a bank of double escalators, should help control traffic flow. From inside the pyramid, the view of Lefuel's 1853 Facades is marvelous. An unexpected bonus: archaeological excavations uncovered the foundations of the ancient Louvre palace (along with some 25,000 objects from the Middle Ages). The admirably restored crypt, now open to the public, features an imposing section of wall from 1660, the Saint-Louis hall from the thirteenth century and the Philippe-Auguste tower. Three giant temporary exhibit halls

and an auditorium round out the Cour Napoléon complex. If you've been put off by the Louvre in the past, we urge you to give it another go. You're sure to be impressed with the improvements that now make it possible to view 3,000 years worth of world art in a coherent, convenient way (though not, of course, in a single day!).

Crowds in the Louvre

Watch out, the crowds in the Musée du Louvre are heavy in the earky morning, especially during summer. To have a quiet look at the Venus of Milo, the Victory of Samothrace, the Mona Lisa or other master-pieces of the collections, come in the afternoon after 3 p.m. And if you dream of being alone—or almost alone—in the galleries, plan your visit on a Monday or a Wednesday at the end of the day: the musuem is then open until 10 p.m.

Musée de la Marine
16th arr. - Palais de Chaillot, pl. du Trocadéro - 45 53 31 70
Open 10 a.m.-6 p.m. Closed Tues. Guided tours, conferences, temporary exhibitions. Access for disabled.

Ships ahoy! The world's largest maritime collection is solidly moored at Trocadéro, where waves of enthusiastic youngsters regularly inundate the Musée de la Marine. They may sail right by the magnificent Joseph Vernet paintings, but they always go overboard for the antique and modern navigational instruments, the

sidearms and cannons, the old charts and the countless scale-model ships, which cover five centuries of maritime history: caravels (small fifteenth- and sixteenth-century sailing ships), galleys, royal vessels, yachts, frigates, trawlers, war ships and atomic submarines. A favorite is Napoléon's golden-winged longboat. Likewise, the gut-wrenching wreckage of the *Juste*, which went down in 1725 with over 500 men on board and was discovered in 1968. Deep-sea divers in a grotto, diving suits and the first sailboard to cross the North Atlantic (1985) are among the museum's fascinating flotsam. The library and photo archives are awash with documents. Before setting sail, we like to stop for a view of the Trocadéro gardens or drop anchor on the terrace of Le Totem bar/restaurant for a bracer.

Musée Marmottan
16th arr. - 2, rue Louis-Boilly - 42 24 07 02
Open 10 a.m.-5:30 p.m. Closed Mon., May 1 & Dec. 25.

This Sleeping Beauty's Castle of a museum (First Empire furniture, bibelots and paintings, admirable tapestries from the reign of Louis XII) awoke one day in 1970 in an explosion of color and light when the works of Claude Monet and fellow Impressionists burst onto the scene. More than 165 oils, sketches and watercolors by Monet were donated, a stunning complement to the Donop de Monchy gift. This is the home of Monet's *Water Lilies*, plus major works by Pierre-Auguste Renoir, Camille Pissarro, Alfred Sisley... a premier Impressionism showcase. In 1987 a new Impressionist collection, the Duhem, was installed on the first floor in newly refurbished rooms. We were as thunderstruck by Paul

Gauguin's *Bouquet de Fleurs* as we were thrilled to see Monet's *Impression, Soleil Levant* back in place (stolen in 1985, it was returned not long ago). Don't miss the Wildenstein collection of illuminated medieval manuscripts—they are extraordinary.

Musée National d'Art Moderne Centre Georges Pompidou

4th arr. - 120, rue Saint-Martin
44 78 12 33
Open noon-10 p.m. (Sat., Sun. & holidays 10 a.m.-10 p.m.). Closed Tues. & May 1. Restaurant, bar, cafeteria. Access for disabled.

When it opened on January 31, 1977, the Centre Georges Pompidou was called a hideous oil refinery, destined to rust away before the very eyes of a disgusted public. Fifteen years later, it is recognized as an architectural landmark, the embodiment of a certain "romantic" vision of hi-tech. Nearly 100 million visitors have passed through its modern art galleries, museum, cinemas, concert hall, vast library (with many books in English), exhibition spaces, industrial creation center, periodicals room and record archives (with extensive listening facilities). Since space is limited, the Centre is constantly being remodeled and enlarged. The latest metamorphosis of note: the permanent collection rooms on the third and fourth floors, which have been "rebuilt" by Italian architect Gae Aulenti (also responsible for the interior of the Musée d'Orsay). The result is a sorely needed reshuffle of the museum's 17,000 works (exhibits change several times a year). The permanent collection traces the history of modern art from 1914 on. In extent, it is rivaled only by the Museum of Modern Art in New York. One of

the two screening rooms of the Cinémathèque (National Film Archives) is located in the building. And the sloping plaza in front teems with jugglers, mimes, palm readers, portrait artists, musicians, fire-eaters and other exotic specimens of humanity. Then, there's always the astonishing view of Paris rooftops from the top-floor restaurant—the twin towers of Notre-Dame to the pearly domes of Sacré Coeur. Take note that the Centre's *Librairie* is one of Paris's best-stocked art bookstores, carrying deluxe editions published by the Centre (architecture, film, music and so forth), plus temporary-exhibit catalogs, many of which have become collector's items.

Musée d'Orsay

7th arr. - 1, rue de Bellechasse
45 49 48 14
Open 10 a.m.-6 p.m. (Thurs. 10 a.m.-9:45 p.m. & Sun. 9 a.m.-6 p.m.). Closed Mon., Dec. 25 & Jan. 1.

Tempest in a teacup department: in a league with the Eiffel Tower, the Pompidou Center and the Louvre Pyramid, the Musée d'Orsay was buffeted by a wild storm on the Seine. And now, just a few years after President Mitterrand snipped the ribbon, there is little or no sign of the appalling verbal squall that surrounded the opening of the museum. The Musée d'Orsay is a resounding success. To think that this former train station was slated for demolition, judged a prime example of horrid *fin de siècle* taste (it was designed in 1900 by architect Victor Laloux). The derelict station's exterior and frame were restored and strengthened—a careful work of preservation and enhancement. Italian architect Gae Aulenti worked her peculiar magic on the vast interior. The result is impressive. Now the Grand Central Terminal of nineteenth-century art, the

Musée d'Orsay's collections trace the jagged path of painting, sculpture, photography, decorative and industrial art from 1848 to 1914. Thanks largely to generous donations from intrepid patrons of the arts, the work of greats formerly outside the mainstream, from Gustave Courbet to Edouard Manet and the Impressionists, now have a stunning home in the Orsay. Among the Orsay's finest: Honoré Daumier's classic 36-bust series *Les Parlementaires* (1832); Claude Monet's *Rue Montorgueil* (1878), bursting with noisy life; Georges Seurat's pointillistic *Poseuse de Dos*, seemingly composed of little more than air and light; and Giovanni Boldini's Proustian *Portrait de Madame Max* (1896). The museum bookshop is large and well stocked; the gift shop displays many lovely and culturally correct trinkets sure to please the folks back home.

Musée du Petit Palais

8th arr. - 1, av. Dutuit - 42 65 12 73
Open 10 a.m.-5:40 p.m. Closed Mon. & holidays.

Built in 1900 For the *Exposition Universelle*, the Petit Palais is marked by its stone-and-iron frame, and its rococo galleries decorated with allegories and ornate cupolas are excellent examples of the architecture of the time. Its eccentric permanent collection is largely neglected, which means you'll be able to enjoy an unobscured view of the exquisite Dutuit donation (works from antiquity to the seventeenth century), featuring rare examples of Egyptian and Greek art, and the sumptuous Rembrandt self-portrait in Oriental garb. The Tuck Collection, comprising furniture, tapestries and other eighteenth-century items, is also housed here. The municipal collections boast several nineteenth-century gems: magnificent paintings by Gustave Courbet, Eugène Delacroix, Pierre Bonnard, Edouard Vuillard and Paul Cézanne, plus Impressionist works that have escaped the Musée d'Orsay dragnet. An entire hall is given over to a sublime series by Odilon Redon. Elsewhere you'll find sculptures by Auguste Rodin. The inner garden is a delightfully cool refuge during the dog days of summer.

Museum pass

The *Carte Musée et Monuments*, **Museum Pass, available at museums, monuments and main Métro stations, allows you to wander at will through every of the 62 museums and monuments in Paris and the greater metropolitain area without any need to quee. The single-day pass sells for 55 F, the three-day pass for 110 F, and the five-day pass for 160 F.**

Musée National Picasso

3rd arr. - Hôtel Salé, 5, rue de Thorigny - 42 71 25 21
Open 9:30 a.m.-6 p.m. (Wed. until 10 p.m.). Closed Tues.

This is indeed art in an artful architectural frame. The magnificent seventeenth-century Hôtel Salé, one of Paris's most spectacular Marais townhouses, was painstakingly restored to house the paintings and artworks of Pablo Picasso (donated to the state by his heirs in lieu of death duties). Here we've rediscovered one of this century's greatest artists

through a complete panorama of his favorite works— "Picasso's Picassos" (he selected five of his own paintings each year plus a copy of each lithograph; the sculptures never left his studio). The treasure trove totals 203 paintings, 158 sculptures, 16 collages, 29 montages, 86 ceramics, over 3,000 drawings and engravings, illustrated books and manuscripts, sketchbooks and other original pieces. There's even proof of Picasso's precocity: several astonishingly polished paintings done when the artist was fourteen years old—*The Barefoot Girl* and *Man with a Cap* among them. Picasso's private collection of works by his contemporaries— Cézanne, Braque, Matisse, Derain and others—is also on view. Tea room, *see Tea Rooms.*

Muséum National d'Histoire Naturelle

5th arr. - Jardin des Plantes
57, rue Cuvier - 40 79 30 00
Open 10 a.m.-5 p.m. (Sat. & Sun. 11 a.m.-6 p.m.). Closed Tues. & holidays.

Taken bit by bit, this magical, many-faceted museum-cum-garden is a marvel. The lovely Jardin des Plantes (Botanical Garden) that surrounds the natural history museum is a leafy oasis in summer, a riot of color and fragrance in spring. Its sycamore-lined gravel lanes link carefully planted and labeled flower beds and herb gardens, a small zoo and a wildly exotic tropical greenhouse. The museum's galleries tell the tale of the earth—of life and its history. The anatomy and paleontology hall is a huge, surreal world filled with skeletons and prehistoric monsters. The paleobotany hall is even odder, with plant specimens from two billion to 250 million years ago. In the cavernous mineralogy hall

there are thousands of meteorites, extraordinary crystals, cut gems, precious stones (the Salle du Trésor, or Treasure Hall, reveals an astounding wealth of emeralds, sapphires, rubies, turquoise, platinum and gold nuggets from the Bank of France's safes). A flight of fancy awaits lepidopterists (and all butterfly catchers/fanciers) in the entomology hall's collections (45, rue Buffon). In case you're wondering: the museum was originally the modest medicinal plant garden of Louis XIII, later the royal garden. It flowered from 1739 to 1788 under the scientific guidance of Buffon, then became a natural history museum in 1789 by decree of convention. Beasts are back in business, with the recent remodeling of the zoology hall and zoo. There are learning labs on birds, animal languages, minerals and more, as well as a museum bookshop.

Palais de la Découverte

8th arr. - av. Franklin-Roosevelt
40 74 80 00
Open 9:30 a.m.-6 p.m. (Sun. 10 a.m.-7 p.m.). Closed Mon., Jan. 1, May 1, July 14, Aug. 15 & Dec. 25. Cafeteria. Access for disabled.

The futuristic Cité at La Villette has nearly knocked the wind out of this exploratorium. Indeed, the palatial aspect of the Palais de la Découverte has lost lots of luster. The floor is shedding mosaics while the carpets curl and the *Sciences* and *Techniques* statues collect dust. Still, enthusiastic toddlers, eager adolescents and bemused tourists discover science in the electricity, solar system, nuclear physics and chemistry-and-biology-in-the-service-of-man galleries. We guess it's just too bad when the computers refuse to play games as programmed or when the knobs and buttons of the touch-me experiential devices come off in your hand... But the planetarium still features star-studded astrological projections. And outer space fans can admire the teeny French flag planted on the moon by the Apollo XVII crew.

Palais de Tokyo

16th arr. - 13, av. du Président-Wilson - 47 23 36 53
Open 9:45 a.m.-5 p.m. Closed Tues.

The Palais de Tokyo has finally found its true mission in life: as France's official temple of photography. Visitors may discover the nation's photographic heritage in the permanent collections, or view fascinating thematic shows (aerial photography, for example) and exhibits featuring the work of individual artists (a recent show presented celebrity portraits by Annie Liebowitz).

OFF THE BEATEN TRACK

Cabinet des Médailles et Monnaies Antiques de la Bibliotèque Nationale

2nd arr. - 58, rue de Richelieu 47 03 83 30
Open daily 1 p.m.-5 p.m.

Even hard-core numismatists are floored by this awesome collection of 400,000 coins and medals (the world's largest collection of cameos and intaglios), precious works from antiquity (including a remarkable Hellenistic torso of Aphrodite), the Middle Ages and the Renaissance, plus Persian silverwork and paintings by Boucher and Van Loo. Housed in the Bibliothèque Nationale building, it is one of the most venerable Paris museums, dating to the 1500s.

Note that national museums are generally closed on Tuesdays.

Catacombes de Paris

14th arr. - 1, pl. Denfert-Rochereau - 43 22 47 63
Open 2 p.m.-4 p.m. (Sat. & Sun. 9 a.m.-11 a.m. & 2 p.m.-4 p.m.). Closed Mon. Guided tour: Wed. 2:45 p.m. Admission: 16 F (reduced rate: 10 F). Groups w.-e. only by appointment.

The museum of Paris's catacombs is located in the former Montrouge quarry, which once beyond the city walls is now on the place Denfert-Rochereau. To improve sanitary conditions in the capital, ab out six million skeletons were brought here in 1786 From the cemeteries and charnel houses of central Paris. Open for visiting is about a one-mile, well-lit section of this immense catacomb. The entrance is in the center of the place Denfert-Rochereau.

Le Cellier des Bernardins

5th arr. - Caserne de Poissy, 24, rue de Poissy - 47 54 68 18
Open daily by appointment only.

The Poissy firehouse was once the refectory of the Collège des Bernardins, whose fourteenth-century vaulted cellar is one of the largest and finest in the Paris area. To visit, simply request permission at the firemen's guardhouse.

Espace Grévin

1st arr. - Forum des Halles, level -1, 1, rue Pierre-Lescot - 40 26 28 50
Open 10:30 a.m.-6:45 p.m. (Sun. & holidays 1 p.m.-6:30 p.m.).

The Forum des Halles branch features Paris in the Belle Epoque, a series of animated tableaux and Reynaud's Optical Theater—the praxinoscope, the predecessor of the Lumière brothers' cinematograph—which he operated in Montmartre from 1892 to 1900.

Historial de Montmartre

18th arr. - 11, rue Poulbot - 42 64 40 10
Open daily 10 a.m.-7 p.m.

We could write a book about the beauty of this museum's location, with its panoramic view across Paris. The amusing historical waxworks evoke vivid images of yesteryear in Montmartre and of famous people and places. If Madame Tussaud's is your cup of tea, you'll love this place.

Maison de Balzac

16th arr. - 47, rue Raynouard 42 24 56 38
Open 10 a.m.-5:40 p.m. Closed Mon. & holidays. Temporary exhibitions.

The rustic charm of Honoré de Balzac's modest house and verdant garden—*la cabane de Passy*, where he lived from 1840 to 1847—was only one reason the penurious novelist holed up here. The other is a discreet back entrance and escape route down the rue Berton—because when Balzac wasn't penning immortal prose like *The Human Comedy*, he was keeping his eye out for debt collectors. The flavor of his checkered life comes through in his austere study, which, entirely intact, is stuffed with letters, documents and everyday objects—an inkwell shaped like a padlock and primed for sixteen hours of work—and decorated with portraits of the women he loved and admired. Armchairs and tables entice visitors to sit down and have a good read.

Maison de Victor Hugo

4th arr. - Hôtel de Rohan- Guéménée, 6, pl. des Vosges 42 72 10 16
Open 10 a.m.-5:40 p.m. Closed Mon. & holidays.

Victor Hugo lived from 1832 to 1848 in this seventeenth-century house on the place des Vosges. He wrote several chapters of Les Misérables and scores of other plays and poems here in these seven rooms, which effectively re-create the atmosphere of the *salon rouge*, the Guernesey dining room and the death chamber of the avenue d'Eylau. Family portraits, yellowed souvenirs and piously preserved memorabilia rather blandly trace Hugo's tormented life. But the rooms do provide an excellent idea of how Hugo amused himself when he was not writing: a series of somber pen-and-ink drawings executed in a state of "almost unconscious reverie" or the eccentric wooden cabinets he cobbled together. The haunting initials V. H. seem to appear everywhere.

Musée de l'Armée

7th arr. - Hôtel des Invalides, 129 rue de Grenelle - 45 51 92 84
Open 10 a.m.-5 p.m. (April 1-Sept. 30 until 6 p.m.). Closed Jan. 1, May 1, Nov. 1 & Dec. 25. Concerts in Saint-Louis des Invalides church; cafeteria.

Arm yourself for the onslaught of countless weapons and machines of war designed to slash, club, explode, flatten, puncture and otherwise exterminate your neighbor. Every imaginable type of weaponry is on display in this extremely popular museum (right up there with the Eiffel Tower and the Château de Versailles in terms of tourist visits). Louis XIV had the Invalides built by architects Libéral Bruant and Jules Hardouin as a veterans' hospital. Mansart erected the towering Dôme church, which is visible from all over Paris. The Invalides is still considered one of the city's most handsome architectural ensembles. True to character, Napoléon appropriated the church as a monument to his own glory, and he is entombed in the elaborate carved-porphyry

Emperor's Tomb under the cupola. However, we found the astounding engraved sword by Benvenuto Cellini, the gigantic François-Ier on horseback, the 1914–1918 section, with its moving displays, and the 1939–1945 galleries, with their superb model of the Normandy landings, far more interesting. For Napoléon-trivia fans, there's the bizarre stuffed white charger he rode on Saint-Hélène and the dog that kept him company during his exile on the island of Elba. Be forewarned: you will never be able to see the whole museum in one go.

Musée d'Art et d'Histoire de Saint-Denis

93200 Saint-Denis - 22 bis, rue Gabriel-Péri - 42 43 05 10
Open 10 a.m.-5:30 p.m. (Sun. 2 p.m.-6:30 p.m.). Closed Tues. & holidays.

Winner of the coveted Prix Européen du Musée, this marvelous former Carmelite convent (seventeenth and eighteenth centuries), superbly restored in 1981, makes the trip to dingy Saint-Denis worthwhile. On display is a fine collection of religious art and archaeological finds pertaining to the city and the Carmelite order. Easy to reach (the RER express subway takes you there from central Paris in just a few minutes), it is located next door to the phenomenal Cathedral of Saint-Denis, resting place of the French kings.

Musée d'Art Juif

18th arr. - 42, rue des Saules - 42 57 84 15
Open 3 p.m.-6 p.m. Closed Fri., Sat. & Jewish holidays.

Objects used at temple services, popular art, scale models of synagogues from the thirteenth through the nineteenth century, rare books, contemporary pain-

tings and drawings (Marc Chagall, among them) are on display at this fascinating museum housed in the Montmartre Jewish Center.

Musée d'Art Naïf Max Fourny-Musée en Herbe

18th arr. - Halle Saint-Pierre, 2, rue Ronsard - 42 58 72 89
Open 10 a.m.-6 p.m. Closed Mon., Jan. 1, May 1 & Dec. 25. Tea room. Admission: 22 F (reduced rate: 16; F).

This two-in-one museum, housed in the sunny nineteenth-century Halle Saint-Pierre, is a charming place to spend an afternoon. A vast second-floor loggia houses Max Fourny's renowned collection of naïf and folk art. The ground floor features thematic exhibits for children that cover an almost infinite range of subjects. The museum also hosts a number of workshops for kids, spin-offs of the temporary shows.

Musée des Arts Asiatiques-Guimet

16th arr. - 6, pl. d'Iéna
47 23 61 65
Open 9:45 a.m.-5:15 p.m. Closed Tues. Audiovisual & conference rooms.

Ten years of remodeling and enlarging transformed this venerable temple of Asian art from a jumbled bazaar into a shining showcase. Unique treasures have finally been retrieved from the warehouse and put on display. You will be whisked across the vast territory of Oriental art: Khmer statues from ninth- through eleventh-century Cambodia; smiling gods and eyeless kings that well up in a halo of light. There is also a huge collection of Buddha paintings (from Nepal and Tibet), a cubist-like head of Kasyapa sculpted in gray chalkstone (sixth-century China) and, from the monasteries of Hadda in Afghanistan, delicate, fragile stucco and dried-earth figurines. Chinese ceramics and porcelain fill several halls.

Musée des Arts de la Mode

1st arr. - 107, rue de Rivoli - 42 60 32 14
Open 12:30 p.m.-6 p.m. (Sun. noon-6 p.m.). Closed Mon. & Tues.

This lovingly restored museum of fashion arts in the Pavillon de Marsan comprises five floors of elegant clothing, accessories, shoes, bags and hats (eighteenth- to twentieth-century collections from the Arts Décoratifs and the Union Française des Arts du Costume)—in all, about 32,000 pieces of finery. Exhibits change regularly. Don't miss the haute-couture collections by Doucet, Poiret, Chanel and Dior.

Musée Bouchard

16th arr. - 25, rue de l'Yvette - 46 47 63 46
Open Wed. & Sat. 2 p.m.-7 p.m. Closed last 2 wks. of: March, June, Sept. & Dec. Access for disabled.

Chisels and chips of stone, sketches and photos thumbtacked to the wall in delightful disarray—the liveliest sculptor's studio in town is the Musée Henri Bouchard (1875–1960). The masterful academic's work leave some cool, but the guided tours (Wednesday at 7 p.m., limited to twenty participants) and lectures on the sculptor's trade, won't.

Musée Bourdelle

15th arr. - 16, rue Antoine-Bourdelle - 45 48 67 27
Open 10 a.m.-5:40 p.m. Closed Mon. & holidays. Access for disabled.

Riotous green gardens strewn with Antoine Bourdelle's bronzes are hidden in the heart of old Montparnasse. We like to visit in the spring when the trees are bursting with blossoms. This house/museum has been suspended

in time since the sculptor's death in 1929. Bourdelle's brawny art represents a powerful reaction to the sculpture of its time (he was, when young, Rodin's assistant). Giant original plasters are featured in the exhibit hall: *The Dying Centaur, The Polish Saga* and the equestrian statue of Alvéar. The Beethoven series of bronze heads overflows with pathos. Don't miss Bourdelle's bas-reliefs (1912–1913, restored in 1987) on the facade of the Champs-Elysées theater.

Musée Bricard (de la Serrurerie)

3rd arr. - 1, rue de la Perle - 42 77 79 62
Call for information.

This unusual museum holds the key to the locksmith's ancient art. On display are locks from early Christian times, door handles and knobs, ornamental lock casings, bolts, keys, door knockers and all such devices designed to lock, enclose, seal, protect and hide. Banal? You may be surprised to find yourself getting all keyed up over these odd objects: the first rudimentary key from Gallo-Roman times, a massive medieval lock, glittering goldsmithery, seventeenth-century twelve-tooth keys, Napoléon's imperial door bolt, the Marquis de Sade's safe... The museum is in an exquisite seventeenth-century Marais townhouse (designed by Libéral Bruant, architect of the Invalides) just down the street from the Picasso museum. It was restored by Bricard, the 150-year-old French lock manufacturer, to house its immense collections.

Musée Carnavalet

3rd arr. - 23-29, rue de Sévigné 42 72 21 13
Open 10 a.m.-5:40 p.m. Closed Mon. & holidays.

A vivid panorama of Parisian history is presented here—

from the city's ancient origins to the present day. The sound and fury of years gone by, the restitching of the urban fabric, the beautification and destruction of the metropolis are captured in topographical models of neighborhoods, scale models of monuments, paintings, prints and, for the modern era, photographs. The mansion that houses the museum is itself a prime exhibit: begun in the 1500s by Pierre Lescot, floors were added by François Mansart in the seventeenth century, and further additions made in the nineteenth century. Yet it is one of the most harmonious architectural ensembles in the Marais, with a lovely inner-court garden graced by sculpted shrubs, flower beds and fountains. From 1777 to 1796 the mansion was inhabited by Madame de Sévigné, famed in French letters for her epistolary excellence. French Revolution devotees will not want to miss the blood-stained letter Robespierre was writing when the Terror turned upon him. The temporary exhibitions mounted by the museum are always worthwhile.

Musée de la Chasse et de la Nature

3rd arr. - 60, rue des Archives 42 72 86 43
Open 10 a.m.-12:30 p.m. & 1:30 p.m.-5:30 p.m. Closed Tues. & holidays. Access for disabled.

Don't be put off by the gory theme—the history of the hunt—for this is a charming museum housed in a magnificent 1654 Marais mansion built by François Mansart. Always a hit with youngsters of all ages are the fine collections of weapons—from flint arrowheads to precision firearms, carved powder horns, gold-encrusted carbines, ancient elephant guns... Impressive trophies from three continents and a superb collection of paintings by Rembrandt, Cranach, Breughel and Monet, among others, make this a museum to be sure and visit.

Musée de la Contrefaçon

16th arr. - 14 ter, rue de la Faisanderie - 45 01 51 11
Open Mon. & Wed. 2 p.m.-4:30 p.m., Fri. 9:30 a.m.-noon. Admission: free.

A curious, somber little museum, the Musée de la Contrefaçon features famous counterfeits and fakes, from chocolate (*Meinier* instead of Menier) to perfume (*Chinarl* instead of Chanel). Wines, liquors, jewelry, clothing, luggage and so forth—every imaginable item and its dubious double.

Musée du Crystal

10th arr. - 30bis, rue de Paradis 47 70 64 30
Open 9 a.m.-6 p.m. (Sat. 10 a.m.-noon & 2 p.m.-5 p.m.). Closed Sun. & holidays.

After stocking up on china, silver and crystal on the rue de Paradis, where the foremost manufacturers of French tableware cluster in confraternal companionability, do make time to visit the Musée du Cristal. You'll gasp in amaze at Baccarat's most impressive creations, from stemware and perfume bottles to opaline objets d'art and sumptuous chandeliers.

Musée Ernest Hébert

6th arr. - 85, rue du Cherche-Midi - 42 22 23 82
Open 12:30 p.m.-6 p.m. (Sat, Sun. & holidays 2 p.m.-6 p.m.) Closed Tues., Dec. 25 & Jan. 1.

Onward, the intrepid! This is the unjustly unknown museum of forgotten painter Ernest Hébert (1817–1908), the rage of his day. Here, we rediscovered the pricey painter of the princesses of the imperial court, winner of the Prix de Rome and countless

accolades, the worldly portraitist of the Comtesse Greffulhe, immortalized by Marcel Proust... Well, if Hébert's old-fashioned art leaves you cold, at least come and see the admirable eighteenth-century mansion furnished with Princess Mathilde's Louis XVI best.

Musée Eugène Delacroix

6th arr. - 6, rue de Furstenberg 43 54 04 87
Open 9:45 a.m.-12:30 p.m. & 2 p.m.-5:15 p.m. Closed Tues.

Anyone with a 100-franc bill already owns a valuable Delacroix (1798–1863). In a secret garden off the place Furstenberg, romantic as can be, the Eugène Delacroix home/museum (the painter's apartment and sunny studio are linked by a curious footbridge) is one of Paris's great little-knowns. There are no masterworks here but rather a fine series of drawings, watercolors and pastels (plus studies for such famous paintings as *The Death of Sardanapalus*), an astonishing self-portrait, the palette and easel this Romantic artist used to paint his early works, pages from his journal and various other oddities of the artist. We like to follow up with a visit to the nearby church of Saint-Sulpice, where Delacroix, advanced in years, decorated the Saints-Anges chapel.

Musée de la Franc-Maçonnerie

9th arr. - 16, rue Cadet - 45 23 20 92
Open 2 p.m.-6 p.m. Closed Sun. & holidays. Admission: free.

This is no ill-lit hideaway for regicides and fearful freethinkers, but a modern, rather stark museum of French Freemasonry. Displayed in glass cases in a somber hall are paintings, sculptures, engravings and medals, pertaining primarily to political

figures, intellectuals and military leaders. You will discover scores of illustrious names on the roster: Philippe-Egalité (a royal supporter of the French Revolution who was guillotined during the Reign of Terror), Voltaire, Montesquieu, Marshal Joffre, the Comte de Bourbon-Condé and, surprise, even a Roosevelt.

Musée Grévin

9th arr. - 10, bd Montmartre - 42 46 13 26
Open daily 1 p.m.-7 p.m.

You and the other 650,000 annual visitors to the Musée Grévin will either chuckle at or pale among the petrified personages assembled here. The delirious decor of this monumental waxworks (the fourth most frequently visited museum in Paris) ranges from the Cabinet Fantastique, a charming little theater done up by Bourdelle and Chéret, to a madcap mob that includes Leonid Brezhnev and Presidents Reagan and Mitterrand all dressed as astronauts with the ever-haggard Woody Allen as space cadet floating above. The ground floor features current celebrities. The basement galleries groan with scenes from France's long and eventful history.

Musée Gustave Moreau

9th arr. - 14, rue La Rochefoucauld - 48 74 38 50
Open 10 a.m.-12:45 p.m. & 2 p.m.-5:15 p.m. (Wed. 11 a.m.-5:15 p.m.). Closed Tues.

"If you want to get a job done right, do it yourself,"thought Symbolist painter Gustave Moreau (1826–1898). So he erected this Renaissance Revival building on the lovely place Saint-Georges, a temple to his own posterity. It is worth a visit just to see the spectacularly baroque spiral staircase that links the third and fourth floors, where an enormous workshop and grand gallery house Moreau's works. Surrealist writer André Breton was for decades the sole defender of Moreau's prodigious talents, but the admiration of Matisse (whose teacher he was) brought Moreau wider admiration. We've spent hours rummaging through the nearly 5,000 drawings, studies and watercolors that verify Moreau's fertile creativity.

Musée de l'Histoire de France

3rd arr. - 60, rue des Francs-Bourgeois - 40 27 61 78
Open 1:45 p.m.-5:45 p.m. Closed Tues. & holidays. Annual closings not available.

What could be more precious than the history of a nation? Which explains the choice for the National Archives: the magnificent Hôtel de Soubise, considered by many to be the finest eighteenth-century townhouse in Paris. In these exquisite apartments, decorated by some of the most illustrious artists of the time—Boucher, Natoire, Van Loo and Adam—are cases containing medieval manuscripts covering the period from the Merovingians (the dynasty of Frankish kings that flourished from the fifth century to 751) to the Hundred Years War, as well as an impressive collection of documents pertaining to the French Revolution (the *Declaration of the Rights of Man*). Long-running exhibits generally feature some sort of

written document, so a working knowledge of French is helpful. Regardless of language, a stroll through the townhouse and inner gardens are worth the visit.

Musée Jean-Jacques Rousseau

95160 Montmorency - 5, rue Jean-Jacques Rousseau - 39 64 80 13
Open 2 p.m.-6 p.m. Closed Mon.

The wandering philosopher and scribe Jean-Jacques Rousseau settled down from 1757 to 1772 in this modest abode and penned *La Nouvelle Héloïse*, *L'Emile* and the *Lettre à d'Alembert*. Rousseau's furniture, various letters and manuscripts are among the memorabilia. The charming garden's path of ancient lime trees—tradition has it that Rousseau planted two of them—leads to a tiny pavilion that houses the philosopher's workroom.

Musée du Jouet

78300 Poissy - 2, enclosure of l'Abbaye - 39 65 06 06
Open 9:30 a.m.-noon & 2 p.m.-5:30 p.m. Closed Mon., Tues. & holidays.

This museum is nothing to toy with—you can look but not touch! Overflowing with thousands of exquisite but fragile toys—from porcelain dolls to lead soldiers and mechanical merry-go-rounds from the nineteenth century. It is housed in an attractive former priory in suburban Poissy.

Musée Lambinet

78000 Versailles - 54, bd de la Reine - 39 50 30 32
Open 2 p.m.-6 p.m. Closed Mon. & holidays. Admission: free.

No pomp and circumstance, as in the neighboring Château de Versailles. Here you will find a delightful eighteenth-century townhouse lost in a restful green garden, collections of Sèvres and Saint-Cloud porcelain, sculptures by Houdon, eighteenth-century paintings, period furniture plus nineteenth-century statuettes and works by painters Dunoyer de Segonzac and André Suréda, all charmingly displayed.

Musée Mémorial Ivan Tourgueniev

78380 Bougival - 16, rue Ivan-Tourgueniev - 45 77 87 12
Open March 22-Dec. 22: Sun. 2 p.m.-6 p.m. & weekdays by appointment.

This delightful *dacha* was the great Russian writer's slice of home (so what if it looks more like a Swiss chalet!). Turgenev lived here happily, near friends Louis and Pauline Viardot (his pavilion is actually located in their garden; pretty Pauline was his secret lover). And he died here in 1883. A pleasant pilgrimage for Turgenev devotees.

Musée de la Mode et du Costume

16th arr. - Palais Galliera, 10, av. Pierre-Ier-de-Serbie
47 20 85 23
Temporary exhibitions only. Open during exhibitions 10 a.m.-5:40 p.m. Closed Mon. Annual closings depending on exhibitions. Access for disabled.

Housed here is one of the world's richest wardrobes: 5,000 costumes in a 50,000-piece collection of fashions for men, women and children of all social classes—from the eighteenth century to the present. Interested in the remark-

---

Museum tours

La Réunion des Musées Nationaux, which organizes most of the exhibitions at the national museums in Paris, offers guided tours of the Louvre and other museums and art galleries. For details phone 40 20 51 77 for the Louvre and 40 13 48 00 for the other national museums.

---

able wardrobes that once belonged to the Countess of Greffulhe (Marcel Proust's muse) and the Countess of Castellane? Popular recent exhibits have focused on the designs of Dior, Givenchy and jewelers Van Cleef and Arpels.

Musée de la Monnaie

6th arr. - 11, quai de Conti - 40 46 56 66
Open 1 p m.-6 p.m. (Wed. until 9 p.m.). Closed Mon.
The end of the rainbow for numismatists: a staggering array of precious coins and medals housed in the gorgeous Hôtel des Monnaies. A mere 200 years or so after its creation (1768 by Louis XV), the mint has been reborn as a museum. On display are coins from ancient times to the present, paintings of coin presses, plus scales, tools and books pertaining to minting techniques. The mansion's court of honor and the many superb salons are alone worth the visit.

Musée de Montmartre

18th arr. - 12, rue Cortot - 46 06 61 11
Open 11 a.m.-5:30 p.m. Closed Mon., Jan. 1, May 1 & Dec. 25. Temporary exhibitions.
Relive the notorious Montmartre Bohemia of politicians and artists (which include the likes of Picasso, Utrillo and Renoir) in this sunny, charming museum that overlooks the hillside Clos Montmartre, one of the city's last remaining vineyards. Watch for the excellent temporary exhibits (a recent show on Modigliani was a great hit).

Musée National des Arts d'Afrique et d'Océanie

12th arr. - 293, av. Daumesnil 44 74 84 80
Open 10 a.m.-noon & 1:30 p.m.-5:30 p.m. (Sat. & Sun. 10 p.m.-

6 p.m.). Closed Tues. Access for disabled.
Kids love this place, with its crocodile pits and an immense aquarium swimming with piranhas. On the edge of the Bois de Vincennes at the Porte Dorée, the massive 1931 former Musée des Colonies is a remarkable example of the architecture of its age. Outside is an gigantic bas-relief of some riotously rich colonial kingdom of flora and fauna. Inside are the marvelous collections of African masks, statues in wood and bronze, jewelry and finery from Africa and Melanesia.

Musée National des Arts et Traditions Populaires

16th arr. - 6, av. du Mahatma-Gandhi, Bois de Boulogne - 44 17 60 00
Open 9:45 a.m.-5:15 p.m. Closed Tues. Access for disabled.
Another favorite among the young, this is the sort of museum that captivates some and loses others right off. Collections of objects from popular traditions trace the development of rural civilization in France. Arranged with startling precision and displayed in huge plexiglas cases are a blacksmith's forge, a cooper's shop, the interior of a Breton peasant's house, a wheelwright's and carpenter's workshop, a trawler with sail spread and numerous other life-size models, and various regional costumes, implements and decorative items. Impressive temporary exhibits, archives, library and other research facilities are available to researchers.

Musée National de la Coopération Franco-Américaine

02300 Blérancourt, Château-(16) 23 39 60 16
Open 10 a.m.-noon & 2 p.m.-5 p.m. (in winter 2 p.m.-7 p.m.). Closed Tues. Parking available.

Restaurant. Admission: 12 F, 7 F on Sun., free for children under 18, ages 18-21 & over 60: 7 F.
This museum of Franco-American friendship, located in the lovely Château de Blérancourt, belongs to the French National Museums group. The seventeenth-century château was designed by Salomon de Brosse, architect of the Luxembourg Palace in Paris. Although it has undergone many changes over the centuries, Brosse's ornamented portals, pavilions and portions of the *corps de logis* (the main part of the building) have survived. In 1915 Ann Morgan, daughter of American financier J. P. Morgan, set up a Red Cross infirmary in the château. After World War I she began the painstaking restorations that have only recently been completed. Blérancourt's permanent collection comprises some 50 paintings from the United States and France, formerly displayed at the Musée d'Orsay and the Pompidou Center, plus a sculpture garden and landscaped grounds. Situated minutes from the forest of Compiègne, where the Armistice was signed, and Viollet le Duc's spectacular Pierrefonds Château, Blérancourt is also a charming Picardy village. Trains from the Gare du Nord stop at Noyon; a taxi will transport you the rest of the way.

Musée National des Monuments Français

16th arr. - Palais de Chaillot. 1, pl. du Trocadéro - 44 05 39 10
Call for information: temporary exhibitions. Access for disabled.
This cathedral-size museum is chockablock with monumental yet scrupulously accurate phonies—repro-ductions of France's sculptural monuments from pre-Roman times to the nineteenth century.

Musée National du Moyen-Âge

5th arr. - 6, pl. Paul-Painlevé - 43 25 62 00
Open 9:30 a.m.-5:15 p.m. Closed Tues.

All you need to know about the Middle Ages, from religious relics to everyday objects, is on display in the superb fifteenth-century Hôtel des Abbés de Cluny. Collections include ivory works, wood sculptures, paintings, stained-glass windows, furniture, jewelry, ironwork, tapestries and such. In the Gallo-Roman baths next door are the barrel-vaulted frigidarium ("cold bath") and other impressive halls (filled with statuary and masterpieces of goldsmithery) restored with rare flair. Do not miss the famed series of fifteenth-century unicorn tapestries, *The Lady and the Unicorn*.

Musée National de l'Orangerie des Tuileries

1st arr. - Jardin des Tuileries, corner quai des Tuileries/place de la Concorde - 42 97 48 16
Open 9:45 a.m.-5:15 p.m. Closed Tues.

Claude Monet's dazzling *Water Lilies*, painted in Giverny between 1890 and his death in 1926, hang here in the two oval basement rooms, custom-designed according to the wishes of the artist. Upstairs, the Walter-Guillaume collection contains just one Monet but several undisputed masterpieces from the end of the nineteenth and the beginning of the twentieth century (by Modigliani, Renoir, Cézanne, Matisse, Picasso, Soutine).

Find the address you are looking for, quickly and easily, in the index.

Musée Nissim de Camondo

8th arr. - 63, rue de Monceau 45 63 26 32
Open 10 a.m.-noon & 2 p.m.-5 p.m. Closed Mon., Tues., Jan. 1, May 1 & Dec. 25.

This grand 1914 townhouse is a nearly exact replica of the Petit Trianon at Versailles. Count Moïse de Camondo built it on the edge of the Parc Monceau and filled it with his priceless collection of eighteenth-century furniture (designed by such master craftsmen as the Jacob brothers, Riesener and Leleu), paintings (by Vigée-Lebrun and Hubert Robert) and sculptures (by Houdon and Pigalle). Sèvres porcelains, Beauvais tapestries and rare Savonnerie carpets round out the exquisitely harmonious ensemble, perfectly restored and presented as the count knew it. A true labor of love. The only drawback is that you're almost forced to purchase a catalog in order to follow the exhibits, which lack adequate description.

Musée du Pain

94220 Charenton-le-Pont - 25 bis, rue Victor-Hugo - 43 68 43 60
Open Tues. & Thurs. 2 p.m.-4 p.m. Annual closings not available.

This delightful little museum kneads you in all the right places as it recounts the history of bread as art. Installed in the granary of a flour mill, the only thing missing is the smell of baking bread. It's up to you to add that pinch of imagination.

Musée Pasteur

15th arr. - 25, rue du Docteur-Roux - 45 68 82 82
Open 2 p.m.-5:30 p.m. Closed Sat., Sun., Aug. & holidays.

The apartment where the great scientist and inventor Louis Pasteur lived is movingly simple, quite a contrast to the Byzantine chapel in which he is buried. The room that dis-

plays the souvenirs of science is wonderfully nostalgic.

Musée de la Poste

15th arr. - 34, bd de Vaugirard 42 79 23 45
Open 10 a.m.-6 p.m. Closed Sun. & holidays.

A first-class museum, recently rejuvenated, for philatelists and anyone interested in the history of the postal service. Displays range from Roman wax tablets to featherweight airmail paper, from mailboxes to high-tech video encoders. On our last visit, our favorite piece was a rural mailman's bicycle from the nineteenth century. A word to the wise: bring a magnifying glass for a proper view of the stamp collections.

Musée de la Publicité

1st arr. - 107, rue de Rivoli - 42 60 32 14
Temporary exhibitions only. Open during exhibitions 12:30 p.m.-6 p.m. (Sun. noon-6 p.m.). Closed Mon. & Tues. Documentary center Mon.-Fri. noon-6 p.m.

The incredibly imaginative, colorful sallies inspired by the profit motive. Thousands of slogans, thousands of posters dating from 1750 to the present are displayed in temporary public exhibits (researchers are not permitted to handle the fragile paper posters but are provided the opportunity to view slides). A recent addition: TV and movie-theater commercials, plus a collection of press, radio, TV and movie documents and items used as advertisements.

Musée Auguste Rodin

7th arr. - Hôtel Biron, 77, rue de Varenne - 47 05 01 34
Open 10 a.m.-5:45 p.m. (Oct. 1-April 30 until 5 p.m.). Closed Mon., Jan. 1, May 1 & Dec. 25. Cafeteria in the park.

Come when the roses in the courtyard bloom around Auguste Rodin's *The Thinker*, then wander through the

305

eighteenth-century garden. Along the lanes stand the sculptor's monumental bronzes The Burghers of Calais, The Hell Gate and the imposing Balzac, to name just a few. The 1728 rococo townhouse belonged to the Duchesse du Maine and the Maréchal de Biron before it was divided into apartments where the likes of Matisse, Cocteau and Rilke spent time. Rodin moved in at the peak of his career, and his presence saved the house from demolition. Also on display is an impressive array of sketches and studies. Don't miss the excellent jade carving Les Bavardes, by Rodin's lover and fellow-sculptor, Camille Claudel. (See the following entry for the Rodin museum annex.)

Maison d'Auguste Rodin
92190 Meudon - Villa des Brillants, 19, av. Auguste-Rodin 45 34 13 09
Open June-Sept. 1:30 p.m.-7 p.m..
This is the must-see Rodin annex, housed in the red-brick Louis XIII Villa des Brillants. The pastoral setting on a hill is one of the most enchanting locations in the Paris area. Studies for Rodin's masterworks are displayed here.

Musée de la Sculpture en Plein Air
5th arr. - Jardin et quai Saint-Bernard
Open year-round. Admission: free.
This monumental sculpture garden covers a half-mile stretch of the Seine between the Pont d'Austerlitz and Pont de Sully, featuring works donated or loaned by artists Gilioli, César, Ipoustéguy, Arman and Etienne-Martin. A breath of fresh air in a lovely green setting.

> Note that national museums are generally closed on Tuesdays.

Musée de la Vie Romantique Maison Renan-Scheffer
9th arr. - 16, rue Chaptal - 48 74 95 38
Open 10 a.m.-5:45 p.m. Closed Mon. & holidays. Temporary exhibitions.
Ary Scheffer (1795–1858) was Louis-Philippe's court painter. Ernest Renan (1823–1892), the renowned writer, was Scheffer's nephew. But, surprise, this museum is given over to yet a third celebrity: George Sand. There are a few Scheffer paintings, nothing at all by Renan and an interesting collection of Sand memorabilia that includes furniture and portraits, plus a plaster cast of Sand's and Chopin's hands. The real attraction is the house—a handsome Restoration-period mansion with a charming garden at the end of an ivy-draped lane—where time stands still.

Musée Zadkine
6th arr. - 100 bis, rue d'Assas 43 26 91 90
Open 10 a.m.-5:40 p.m. Closed Mon. & holidays.
The Russian sculptor Zadkine (1911–1967), creator of the celebrated La Femme à l'Eventail, lived and worked here most of his life. Today, a forest of sculptures stands in the tiny garden, an idyllic enclave on the edge of Montparnasse. We like it best in the spring when the daffodils are in bloom.

PARKS & GARDENS

Bois de Boulogne
16th arr. - 40 71 03 43
This immense park, which spreads over more than 2,000 acres in the city's western reaches, is a vestige of the primeval forests that once surrounded Paris. Long a royal

domain, the Bois was presented to the capital with imperial munificence by Napoléon III, who stipulated that it be landscaped and maintained with municipal funds. Today the Bois is a paradise for runners, bikers, riders and strollers. Dogs and kids alike love to come to the Bois for a romp along the many miles of hiking trails and lawns. Among the myriad attractions are a children's park with a little zoo (Le Jardin d'Acclimatation), a sumptuous rose garden (Le Jardin de Bagatelle), and a lake (le Lac Inférieur) for boating. Also situated within the park's ample precincts are two racetracks (Longchamp and Auteuil), the Roland-Garros tennis stadium where the French Open is held each spring, equestrian clubs and a couple of first-rate restaurants: Le Pré Catelan and La Grande Cascade (see Restaurants).

Nature walks

Paris isn't made only of asphalt and stone; nature thrives in parks, squares and odd corners of each arrondissement. For guides to the city's flora and fauna, and some suggested itineraries that will allow you to discover them, pick up a Sentiers Nature guide at the local mairie (town hall).

Bois de Vincennes
12th arr. - 44 06 51 00
Even larger than the Bois de Boulogne, the Bois de Vincennes is similarly endowed with bike and bridle trails, nature paths and sporting facilities. But it is also home to the city's sole Buddhist tem-

ple (complete with a 30-foot statue of Buddha), a world-class zoo where 1,100 animals frolic in naturalistic surroundings, an arboretum and a fascinating museum of African and Oceanic arts. Our favorite features, though, are the Ferme Georges-Ville, a working farm open to the public on weekends and holidays, where city kids can get up close and personal with barnyard animals; and the Parc Floral, with its bouquet of thematic gardens (herbs, perennials, azaleas, aquatic plants...), its incredible "Valley of Flowers" rich with 100,000 plants, and its superb sculpture garden.

Jardin Albert-Kahn

92100 Boulogne - 1, rue des Abondances and 14, rue du Port 46 04 52 80
Open 11 a.m.-6 p.m. (from May 1-Sept. 30: 11 a.m.-7 p.m.). Closed Mon.

One of Paris's prettiest parks, this landscape garden on the banks of the Seine was created in the early twentieth century by wealthy banker and philanthropist Albert Kahn, who dreamed of bringing together all his favorite scenes of nature in a single park. You may wander through a freshly renovated Japanese garden, a Vosges forest, a formal French garden, a placid lake bordered by trees, a romantic English garden as well as a coniferous and a deciduous wood. We particularly like to visit here from March to June, when the daffodils, hyacinths, azaleas, rhododendrons and roses are in bloom.

Jardin du Luxembourg

6th arr. - Main entrance bd Saint-Michel, near place Edmond-Rostand - 40 79 37 00
Open daily dawn-dusk.

Head for the Luxembourg Gardens when you need to entertain a couple of energetic kids; or you yearn to sit or stroll

in leafy solitude; or you decide to take the pulse of Parisian life on a sunny Sunday afternoon. The Luxembourg offers activities galore for youngsters, from swings and sandboxes to pony rides and racing cars, not to mention a pond for launching little sailboats (the sort one pushes with a stick) and puppet shows manage to amuse even children who don't speak French. Elsewhere, quiet paths wind through lawns and flower beds ornamented with statues that honor the artists and statesmen of France (many of these allegorical tributes are unintentionally hilarious). Inveterate people-watchers should note that the area of the garden closest to the boulevard Saint-Michel is a veritable vivarium of vaguely arty, intellectual Left-Bank types—it's an ideal place to observe Parisians in their natural habitat.

Jardin du Palais-Royal

1st arr. - Main entrances beg. rue Montpensier & after 1, rue de Valois - 42 60 16 87
Open April 1-May 31 7 a.m.-10:15 p.m., June 1-Aug. 31 7 a.m.-11 p.m., Sept. 1-30 7 a.m.-9:30 p.m., Oct. 1-March 31 7:30 a.m.-8:30 p.m.

For all its serene beauty, this garden maintains an almost secret air; never crowded, it is protected from urban noise by the noble houses that enfold it with their sculpted facades. In summer, it's an enchanting place to sit and watch pigeons bathe in the fountains with little black swifts just flown back from Africa; or listen to tiny French toddlers twitter in the sandboxes. The architecture embraces the seventeenth, eighteenth, nineteenth and twentieth centuries: Richelieu lived in what was known as the Palais-Cardinal, later promoted to royal rank when Anne of Austria and the future Louis XIV moved there from the Louvre. The elegant

arcades that run around three sides of the garden date from just before the Revolution, but the buildings behind them, now occupied by the Ministry of Culture and the Constitutional Council, were not completed until the Restoration. The current era is represented (alas!) by the controversial black-and-white columns designed by Daniel Buren, and the polished steel fountains by Pol Bury.

Jardin des Plantes

5th arr. - Main entrance 57, rue Cuvier - 40 79 30 00
Open daily dawn-dusk.

Once upon a time, herbs and medicinal plants were cultivated here to treat royal ailments. In 1641 Louis XIV graciously opened his botanical gardens to the public. Ever since, Parisians have promenaded en masse among the charming shaded walks of the maze which encircles the Belvedere, the park's sole surviving edifice from before the French Revolution (note, however, that the garden's centerpiece, a stupendous cedar of Lebanon, also predates that war: it was planted in 1734). You will discover rare species of trees, flowering shrubs and countless other plants from cold climes (in the Jardin d'Hiver, or Winter Garden) or warm (in the huge greenhouse, a jungle of tropical flora and cacti). Reptiles, deer, bears, apes and birds of prey are housed in quaint Second Empire buildings, which have been recently renovated. (See *Museums, Muséum d'Histoire Naturelle.*)

Jardin des Tuileries

1st arr. - Main entrances place de la Concorde & place du Carrousel - 42 60 27 67
Open 7 a.m. (Sat., Sun. & holidays 7:30 a.m.) -10 p.m. (winter 8 p.m.).

When work is completed in 1995, the Jardin des Tuileries

and adjoining Jardin du Carrousel will link the Louvre and the place de la Concorde with an uninterrupted avenue of lawns, walks, flowers, fountains and statuary. For now, this historic area is in a state of disarray. Excavations around the Louvre yielded an unexpected bonanza in the form of a large section of Philippe-Auguste's defensive wall, along with innumerable medieval artifacts. Preserving that archaeological bounty has meant considerable delay in the reconstruction of the Tuileries Gardens. But soon, authorities assure us, the Tuileries will be a revitalized, coherently landscaped space worth of its central place in the capital's geography and the nation's history.

Parc André-Citroën

15th arr. - Main entrances rue Montagne-de-la-Fage & rue Balard - 45 33 51 97
Open 7:30 a.m. (Sat. & Sun. 8:30 a.m.) to 30 mn before dusk.

With the Parc de la Villette (see below), the 35-acre Parc André-Citroën is the most ambitious project of its kind since the Second Empire, the "Golden Age of Parisian Parks." From the spectacular view of the Seine to the multitude of fountains, the canal and ornamental ponds, water is a dominant theme in this imaginative landscape. Don't look for your garden-variety herbaceous borders here: the visionary architects who designed the park have composed thousands of trees, shrubs and flowers into fantastic themed gardens of extraordinary botanical richness. The dark foliage of the Black Garden sets off the fragrant perennials of the White Garden; the *Jardin des Métamorphoses* changes with the seasons to reflect the alchemical transmutation of lead into gold; then there are the Moss and the Rock Gar-

dens, as well as a series of six gardens, each themed to a different color, metal and sense (the Blue Garden, associated with mercury, is redolent of mint; fruit trees bloom in the Red Garden; a spring bubbles up in the Japanese-inspired Green Garden...). The rarest plants are housed in two tall glass-and-wood conservatories which close the perspective from the Seine. Officially opened late in 1992, the park is still a work in progress. Future plans include the landscaping of the river banks that abut the park, and the construction of a footbridge linking the gardens to the sixteenth arrondissement.

Parc de Belleville

20th arr. - Main entrance rue Piat, in front of rue des Envierges 43 43 97 27
Open year-round. Hours vary, call for information.

This brand-new park in far-flung Belleville boasts an impressive pergola, an orangery, an open-air theater and hills landscaped with waterfalls.

Topping it all is a panoramic point—the highest in Paris—with a knock-your-socks-off view of the city.

Parc des Buttes-Chaumont

19th arr. - Main entrance place Armand-Carrel - 40 36 41 32
Open daily 7 a.m.-9 p.m. (summer 11 p.m.).

This wildly romantic park at hilly Buttes-Chaumont is cross-cut by creeks and roaring waterfalls fed by the nearby Ourcq Canal. A tiny Greek Revival temple perches on a peak in the middle of a swan-filled lake. The temple and panoramic point is reached from below, via a suspension bridge, or from above, by crossing a narrow walkway 100 Feet above the lake. The park's main cascade tumbles into a stylized grotto, newly renovated and open to the public for the first time since 1945. This former quarry and dump was, in the late nineteenth century, transformed into one of Paris' most fashionable public gardens.

Computerized Trees

Despite the ravages of pollution, dogs and Dutch elm disease, Paris still has more trees than any other European capital. Nearly 200,000 trees line its streets and grace its parks and gardens, not to mention another 300,000 in the Bois de Vincennes and Bois de Boulogne. Plane trees are the most common, making up 43 percent of the total, and one of their number is the city's tallest tree, standing 136 feet high in the avenue Foch. Chestnuts, sophoras and lime trees are also well represented. But if we look on the shady side, the figures also show that 25 percent of Parisian trees will have disappeared by the year 2000. In an attempt to stop the rot, the city government is keeping a close watch on its woody heritage: every single tree now has a computer file detailing its surroundings, vital statistics and state of health. An experimental greenhouse has been set up to study the effects of traffic pollution on different species, and 4,200 new trees are being planted every year.

The mark of the park's designer, Baron Haussmann, is evident in the cast-concrete railings and benches sculpted to resemble tree branches. Over $1 million have been spent to restore the Buttes-Chaumont to its original splendor. A job well done!

Parc Georges-Brassens

15th arr. - Main entrance at carrefour rue des Morillons & rue de Cronstadt - 45 33 51 97
Open 7:30 a.m. (Sat. & Sun. 8:30 a.m.) to 30 mn before dusk.

The twin bulls who guard the entrance to this spacious park are survivors, so to speak, of the slaughterhouse that stood on the site until 1975. Other elements from the abattoir were also integrated into the landscape, such as the bell tower that dominates the center of the park, and the Grande Halle, once a horse's last stop before the glue factory, now the scene of a weekly used-book market. Other opportunities for peaceable pursuits are provided by the park's fragrance garden, a collection of 80 aromatic and medicinal herbs, a vineyard planted with Pinot Noir (memento of the now-vanished Clos Morillon, a famed Parisian*cru*) and a honey-producing beehive. Children are not forgotten: there are several playgrounds, a puppet theater and a special wall on which kids and adults too may hone their rock-climbing skills.

Parc Monceau

8th arr. - Main entrance bd de Courcelles, in front of place de la République-Dominicaine - 40 53 00 15
Open daily: Nov. 1-March 31 7 a.m.-8:30 p.m.; April 1-Oct. 31 7 a.m.-10 p.m.

The verdant *allées* of this picturesque park attract large crowds on weekends. But since most of the Sunday strollers are well-mannered inhabitants of the surrounding *beaux quartiers,* no untoward jostling ever seems to occur. Late in the eighteenth century, the artist and stage designer Carmontelle was hired by a princely patron to create "an extraordinary garden" on this site. Taking his mission to heart, he erected bogus Greek and Egyptian ruins, a Gothic castle, a Dutch windmill and a minaret. Today only a pyramid and an ornamental lake with a colonnade remain of those imaginative edifices. The city of Paris acquired the Parc Monceau in 1860, and is now responsible for its maintenance. We hope that the current replanting and releveling of the park's grounds will not disturb the stately great maple or the Oriental plane tree (note its 22-foot girth), which have spread their branches here for 130 and 170 years respectively.

Parc Montsouris

14th arr. - Main entrance at the corner of av. Reille & rue Gazan 45 33 51 97
Open 7:30 a.m. (Sat. & Sun. 8:30 a.m.) to 30 mn before dusk.

Tat energetic architect and engineer, Adolphe Alphand, whose legacy includes the Bois de Boulogne, the Bois de Vincennes, the Buttes-Chaumont, the Parc Monceau and the Square des Batignolles, also supervised the construction of the Parc Montsouris. The lovely English-style gardens were created at the behest of Napoléon III, but were completed only after the fall of the Second Empire, in 1878. On opening day, the artificial lake which was the park's principal attractions, suddenly and inexplicably drained dry. The engineer responsible did the only proper thing under the circumstances: he committed suicide. But why let that tragic occurrence spoil your enjoyment? Concentrate instead on the charmingly serpentine paths shaded by Virginia tulip trees, an immense cedar of Lebanon, an American redwood and Siberian elms.

Parc de la Villette

19th arr. - Main entrance av. Jean-Jaurès, near Porte de Pantin - 42 40 76 10
Hours vary, call for information.

Water, light and greenery guided Bernard Tschumi's design for the Parc de la Villette. The result is an enchanting, indeed poetic "urban park for the 21st century." A long, winding avenue leads visitors through a succession of themed gardens: a bamboo grove signals the Energy Garden, ornamented with sculpture and Bernhard Leitner's *Sound Cylinder;* the Trellis Garden, with its grape vines, hops and perennials, is dotted with seven sculptures by Jean-Max Albert; and the Water Garden is made even dreamier by F. Nakaya's *Cloud Sculptures.* Along the way are scattered some 30 blood-red "follies" (the color recalls that La Villette was once the city's abattoir), which house, variously, a snack bar, a restaurant, a gazebo... Philippe Starck is responsible for the benches, lights and other fixtures that strikingly combine function with elegant form. Though the park is difficult to reach from central Paris, your kids will thank you for herding them out here, where lawns may be walked and picnicked upon and where imaginative playground activities abound (do not under any circumstances miss the *Jardin du Dragon* with its wonderfully scary sliding board).

Square des Batignolles

17th arr. - Place Charles-Fillion 40 53 00 15
Open 7:30 a.m. (Sat. & Sun. 9 a.m.) to 30 mn before dusk.

Another example of the ubiquitous Alphand's art (see above), the Square des

Batignolles delights visitors with its winding paths, running stream and its waterfall edged by weeping willows and ash trees. Hundreds of comically obese ducks paddle on a little lake, where equally gluttonous carp and goldfish also dwell. The only jarring note in this otherwise harmonious ensemble is the incongruous statuary group called *Vultures* that rises up, black and forbidding, from the middle of the water. On weekends a carrousel often opens for business, creating a "village fair" atmosphere that is utterly charming. Before you go, do walk around to the place Charles-Fillion for a look at Sainte-Marie-des-Batignolles. With its triangular pediment and Tuscan columns, the church resembles a small Greek temple mysteriously set down in a Parisian square.

Montmartre by train

A delightful way to discover the village atmosphere of old Montmartre is from the little train that winds through this attractive neighborhood. Trains leave every day from 10 a.m. to 7 p.m. (midnight on weekends and in summer) from place Blanche (in front the Moulin Rouge) every 30 minutes and the trip takes 40 minutes. You'll pass and hear about all the places that have mattered in Montmartre's history: the Moulin Rouge—home of the Can-Can, Saint Peter's Church—one of the oldest in Paris, the Jewish Art Museum, the Sacré Cœur Basilica with its exceptional views, the Montmartre Museum, Place Pigalle and the charming Place du Tertre. Adults 25 francs; children 15 francs.

OUT OF PARIS

INTRODUCTION

Those lucky Parisians! Not only do they have the rare good fortune to live in a glorious city; that city is ringed with equally glorious forests and accessible countryside. Here are our suggestions for ten easy excursions in the Ile-de-France region, all calculated to combine fresh air and greenery with visits to places of notable historic and/or cultural interest. And naturally Gault Millau wouldn't dream of taking you anywhere without first scouting out the best places to dine and spend the night!

The French monarchy's abiding passion for the hunt dates back to the days when the French were still the Franks. Owing to this regal obsession and to the intense personal interest that kings took in their *chasses royales* (private hunting grounds), the forests of the Ile-de-France, with their ancient stands of oak, beech and hornbeam, have been uncommonly well-preserved and responsibly managed over the centuries.

Hugues Capet, founder of the Capetian line and ancestor of the Valois and Bourbon dynasties, was elected king in 987 at Senlis, a thickly forested royal estate north of Paris famed for its excellent hunting. And hunting, in fact, was what made Capet's election necessary in the first place: his predecessor, Louis V (the last of the Carolingians), while in hot pursuit of a stag, had taken a fatal tumble from his horse.

The neighboring domain of Chantilly, for centuries home to some of France's most powerful lords—the Bouteillers, the Montmorencys, the Condés—was also celebrated for its densely wooded forests, alive with game. The châteaux at Fontainebleau, Rambouillet (where Renaissance monarch François I departed this world with his hunting boots on) and Saint-Germain-en-Laye were all particularly beloved by their royal proprietors for the sport they enjoyed there. Even Versailles, that epitome of regal grandeur, was, before the Sun King transformed it, the preferred (and rather swampy) hunting ground of his father, Louis XIII.

So, like generations of royalty who could pop off to their country castles whenever they got that atavistic urge to bag a boar (or when things got too hot for them in Paris—and we don't just mean the weather), present-day Parisians can hop on a train and, an hour or so later, alight near one of a half dozen splendid forests, all complete with magnificent châteaux.

But even if they don't fancy the forest primeval, nature lovers will find lots to like in the environs of Paris. Admirable parks like those at Ecouen and Rambouillet, and elegant gardens like Le Nôtre's seventeenth-century *jardins à la française* at Saint-Germain-en-Laye, Vaux-le-Vicomte, Chantilly and Versailles will please those who prefer more manicured landscapes.

Travelers in search of a rural antidote to city stress can head for the farmlands of the Beauce region, southwest of the capital. The soothing sameness of these wheat-bearing plains is broken only by grain-gorged silos (this is the bread basket of France) and by the dramatic spires of the Chartres cathedral. Northwest of Paris, along the meanders of the Seine, where the Ile-de-France meets Normandy, lies the Vexin, a region of farmlands and river valleys overflowing with bucolic charm. Here Claude Monet spent the last years of his life, painting in his garden at Giverny.

Thus by venturing just 20, 30 or 50 miles beyond the Paris city limits and the bleaker *banlieues* (suburbs), one can discover a bounty of gently beautiful scenery, bathed in the unique light that inspired not only Monet and the Impressionists, but also Corot, the Barbizon painters, Derain and the Fauvists. Punctuating these luminous landscapes are fascinating historic monuments and landmarks, as well as masterpieces of religious, civil and domestic architecture—any of which would make an ideal destination for a fair-weather *promenade*.

CHANTILLY

R eflected in the shimmering blue waters of its surrounding moat, the Château de Chantilly looks like a fairytale castle, almost too perfect to be true. And in a way, it is: The Renaissance-style Grand Château isn't much more than 100 years old (though the adjoining Petit Château dates from the sixteenth century). The castle that previously stood on this site was razed during the Revolution by angry citizens for whom Chantilly (about 50 kilometers north of Paris by Autoroute du Nord A1, exit at Survilliers), fief of two ancient warrior families, the Montmorencys and the Condés, symbolized aristocratic privilege and military might.

The Grand Château houses the Musée Condé and its gem of a collection which ranges from the curious—a wax head of King Henri IV, the pink Condé diamond—to the sublime—Piero di Cosimo's *Portrait of Simonetta Vespucci*, Raphael's *Virgin of Loreto*, works by Botticelli, several pictures by Poussin, two masterpieces by Watteau, a splendid series of Renaissance portraits by the Clouet brothers (including the famous *Catherine de Medici* and *Henri III*) and an admirable collection of illuminated manuscripts. Arranged just as the Duc d'Aumale, the last owner of Chantilly, left it (with orders that it never be changed), the museum has the personal and agreeably eccentric style of a private collection.

Connoisseurs of fine horseflesh also know Chantilly as the site of a famous racetrack and Thoroughbred training center. A fascinating "living museum" devoted to horses occupies the colossal eighteenth-century stables. From an architectural viewpoint, these Grandes Ecuries are more imposing than the château itself (not so surprising, perhaps, if one considers that the Prince of Condé, who built the stables, was convinced that he would be reincarnated as a horse).

The château's majestic park, complete with a canal, gardens and pools planned by seventeenth-century landscape artist André Le Nôtre, is crisscrossed by shady walks and velvety lawns. But the immense (nearly 16,000-acre) Chantilly forest, with its hiking paths and ponds (the étangs de Commelles), is by far the best choice for a long woodland ramble. Take care, however, between 9 a.m. and noon—that's when 3,000 Thoroughbreds thunder into the forest for their morning workout!

*The **Château de Chantilly** is open daily, except Tuesday, from March 1 through October 31, 10 a.m. to 6 p.m.; from November 1 through February 28, 10:30 a.m. to 5 p.m. Reservations: (16) 44 57 08 00, Monday to Friday from 9 a.m. to noon, fax (16) 44 51 70 31. Admission: Château and park 35 F, children under 12 9 F; park 15 F, children under 12 9 F.*

*The **Musée Vivant du Cheval** is open daily, except Tuesday, from   10:30 a.m. to*

6:30 p.m.; from November 1 to March 31 2 p.m. to 7:30 p.m. weekdays, and from 10:30 a.m.to 6:30 p.m. on week-ends. Call (16) 44 57 40 40 for information, fax (16) 44 57 29 92. Admission: 42 F, children under 16 32 F.

RESTAURANTS & HOTELS

 Campanile

60270 Gouvieux, 3 km N on N 16, rte. de Creil (16) 44 57 39 24, fax (16) 44 52 10 05
Open year-round. 47 rms 258F. Restaurant. Parking.
At the edge of the Chantilly forest, the Campanile is quiet, modern but not always well maintained. Restaurant.

 Château de Montvillargenne

60270 Gouvieux, 3 km W on D 909, av. F.-Mathet - (16) 44 57 05 14, fax (16) 44 57 28 97
Open year-round. 10 stes 780-980 F. 140 rms 450-490 F. Restaurant. Half-board 440 F. Pool. Tennis. Parking.
Set in extensive grounds, this magnificent nineteenth-century castle boasts warm wood paneling and a series of elegant linked lounges. Renovated, well-equipped rooms and various leisure facilities.

12/20 **Les Etangs**

8 km SE, 60580 Coye-la-Forêt, 1, rue Clos-des-Vignes - (16) 44 58 60 15, fax (16) 44 58 75 95
Closed Mon. dinner, Tues., Jan. 15-Feb. 15 & Sept. 6-14. Open until 9:30 p.m. Terrace dining.
Summer visitors should slip under the bower leading to the garden to sample the slightly conventional but well executed cuisine. Top-quality ingredients go into the home-made foie gras, brill sautéed in goose fat, and duck with orange. The wines are good but costly.

A la carte; 270-350 F. Menus: 140 F (except holidays), 200 F (holidays only).

 Hostellerie du Lys

60260 Lamorlaye, 7 km S on N 16, 63, 7e-av., Lys-Chantilly, Rond-Point de la Reine (16) 44 21 26 19, fax (16) 44 21 28 19
Closed Dec. 18-Jan. 4. 35 rms 185-510 F. Half-board 350-703 F. Parking.
A beautiful, cozy weekend inn with comfortable rooms and a quiet, pleasant ambience. Tennis, golf and swimming are nearby.

Le Relais Condé

42, av. du Maréchal-Joffre - (16) 44 57 05 75
Closed Mon. dinner off-season & Tues. Annual closings not available. Open until 9:30 p.m. Terrace dining.
The nicest and classiest restaurant in Chantilly is located near the racetrack, under the frame of a nineteenth-century Anglican chapel. Jacques Legrand, formerly of La Saucière at Tourcoing (14/20), has just taken over in the kitchen. We look forward to his elegant and carefully-prepared dishes like lobster and crunchy vegetable terrine, duck breast with spices and honey, and mint-scented peach soup.
A la carte: 300-430 F. Menus: 180 F, 280 F.

COMPIEGNE

 Auberge de la Forêt

60350 Trosly-Breuil, 11 km E on N 31, 19, place

des Fêtes - (16) 44 85 62 30, fax (16) 44 85 60 27
Closed Tues. dinner & Wed. Open until 9:30 p.m. Terrace dining.
Gérard Magnan's traditional cuisine has the personal touch and enough originality to provide agreeable surprises. A former colleague of Michel Guérard and a friend of Alain Senderens, he uses only the finest ingredients in the morel mushroom ragoût topped with a poached egg, succulent, bacon-flavored pike steaks, and veal fillet with pears and tarragon. A smiling Monique Magnan will help you choose a bottle from the carefully constructed wine list.
A la carte: 330-440 F. Menus: 140 F, 180 F and 280 F (except holidays), 250 F (holidays only).

 Château de Bellinglise

14 km N on D 142, Route de Lassigny, 60157 Elincourt-Ste-Marguerite (16) 44 76 04 76, fax (16) 44 76 54 75
Open year-round. 3 stes 1,500-1,620 F. 47 rms 680-1,370 F. Restaurant. Half-board 563-753 F. Tennis. Parking.
This immense Louis XIII–era castle on a 600-acre estate has been remarkably preserved and restored; guests can stay in one of the attractive rooms in the hunting lodge. Pond, tennis, horse-riding, archery and conference facilities. Fine wood-paneled restaurant.

See also "Senlis," below.

Red toques signify modern cuisine; white toques signify traditional cuisine.

CHARTRES

Long before Christianity had penetrated the Ile-de-France, before Caesar marched into Gaul—even then, Chartres was a holy place. Legend has it that every year Celtic druids assembled in Chartres (90 kilometers southwest of Paris by Autoroute A10) to celebrate their mysteries around a sacred wellspring now immured in the cathedral crypt.

What is certain is that from the fourth century on, a sanctuary consecrated to the Virgin Mary brought the faithful to Chartres. When, in 876, Charles the Bald endowed the church with a precious relic (said to be the Virgin's tunic or veil), it gained even greater importance as a shrine, drawing pilgrims from all over Christendom in a steady stream that neither invasions, fires nor revolutions have stanched. Even today, Catholic students organize a pilgrimage to Chartres each May in honor of the Virgin.

The ancestor of the current cathedral, a Romanesque structure built in the eleventh and twelfth centuries, was ravaged by fire in 1194. The flames spared only the crypt, two towers and the lower portion of the western facade, with its majestic Portail Royal (royal entrance). But the people of Chartres very quickly set about rebuilding their cathedral, with so mighty a collective will—and generous contributions from rich lords and wealthy townspeople—that it was completed in the impressively short span of just 30 years. It is to the builders' speed that the cathedral owes its exceptional stylistic unity. And it is to their skill in applying new architectural advances—notably the flying buttress—that Chartres owes its soaring height and rare luminosity. Since the buttresses shouldered weight that would otherwise have fallen on the walls, the builders could make the walls higher, with taller windows.

It would be impossible for us to do justice here to the aesthetic and spiritual riches of Chartres. A visitor with plenty of time, patience, curiosity and an observant eye will find innumerable sources of pleasure and interest. Here, however, are a couple of features worth noting, one outside and one inside the cathedral.

The Portail Royal, unscathed by the fire of 1194, represents one of the oldest examples of Gothic sculpture in existence. While the emphasis of the ensemble is on the figure of Christ, depicted in infancy and in majesty above each of the three doors, viewers often feel irresistibly drawn to the nineteen elongated figures, a combination of statue and column, that stand aligned on either side of the doors. Interestingly, these Old Testament figures belong to two different eras, the Romanesque and the Gothic; they are the survivors of the old cathedral and, at the same time, heralds of the new sculptural style that first emerged at Chartres. In their extraordinarily sensitive faces, in the contrast between their expressive features and their rigid, stylized bodies, a visitor can trace the mysterious passage from one age—one way of viewing and representing human reality—to another.

Inside the cathedral, among the ravishing, jewel-like shadows and colors of stained glass, there are three windows and a portion of another that, like the Portail Royal, escaped the fire of 1194. They are the windows inserted in the western facade, which depict the genealogy, life and resurrection of Christ, and, to the left, the fragment known as Notre Dame de la Belle Verrière (*The Madonna of the Window*), one of Chartres's most venerated images. They merit your special

315

attention because they are the sole remaining examples of the miraculous *bleu de Chartres*, a blue tint rich (as we now know) in cobalt and copper, but which for centuries no one successfully reproduced.

In medieval times, Chartres was a flourishing town, its wealth based on cloth and farming. It was also an intellectual center, with a renowned philosophy school. Investigating the many ancient houses and churches in the Old Quarter (the fifteenth-century Maison Saumon and the Hôtel de la Caige; the medieval church of Saint-Pierre, with its striking stained glass) can be an extremely rewarding way to spend an afternoon.

Agriculture still thrives hereabouts, and the prosperous Beaucerons are fond of the table. Between a tour of the cathedral and a stroll through the town, hungry visitors will find any number of excellent eating places where they may relax and restore themselves.

*The **cathedral** is daily open from 7:30 a.m. to 7:30 p.m. from April 1 to September 30; and until 7 p.m. from October 1 to March 31. For additional information, contact the Office du Tourisme, place de la Cathédrale, (16) 37 21 50 00.*

RESTAURANTS & HOTELS

 Le Grand Monarque
22, pl. des Epars
(16) 37 21 00 72,
fax (16) 37 36 34 18
Open daily until 9:45 p.m. Terrace dining.

The huge dining room with its handsome wood paneling and beautiful bouquets is just the same and so, unfortunately, is the ultra-classic cuisine of Michel Menier. No doubt it's what the local gentry enjoys, but we're beginning to tire of the same old dishes, especially as they were not all up to scratch during our last visit: we found grit in the mussel salad and the lamb noisettes with tarragon were on the dry side. The pineapple savarin was excellent though, and the wine cellar is just as thick with fine Loire vintages. We're awarding a point less this year because for such high prices, we think the cooking ought to be less ordinary.

A la carte: 400-450 F.
Menus: 198 F, 288 F.

 Le Grand Monarque
(See restaurant above)
Open year-round. 5 stes 860-1,220 F. 49 rms 460-700 F. Air cond 1 rm.

The best hotel in Chartres has charming new rooms in two turn-of-the-century buildings surrounding a garden. Nice modern suites. Excellent breakfasts.

 Le Manoir du Palomino
28300 Saint-Prest, 10 km NE on N 154 & D 6 (16) 37 22 27 27, fax (16) 37 22 24 92
Closed Dec. 23-Feb. 15. 20 rms 250-550F. Restaurant. Half-board 305-550F. Tennis. Golf. Parking.

A fine weekend escape from Paris, for relaxing or for conferences. The 40-acre estate provides golf and tennis facilities, and the spacious, quiet, luxuriously decorated rooms have charm, flowers, beams and fine views of the landscape.

12/20 **Relais de la Tour**
28630 Nogent-le-Phaye, 8 km on D 4, N

10, Le Bois-Paris
(16) 37 31 69 79
Closed Tues. dinner, Wed. & July 27-Aug. 15. Open until 10 p.m. Air cond. Parking.

The pleasant service helps customers forget the noisy highway and boring decor, and concentrate on the generous portions of salmon tartare, duck breast with cranberries (slightly overcooked) and delicious crème brûlée. Reasonably priced and well-chosen wines.

A la carte: 160-250 F. Menus: 75 F (weekdays and Sat.), 105 F, 162 F, 175 F.

 La Sellerie
28630 Thivars, 7 km S on N 10, 48, rue Nationale
(16) 37 26 41 59
Closed Sun. dinner (off-seas.), Mon. dinner, Tues., Jan. 4-12 & Aug.3-24. Open until 9 p.m. Terrace dining. Parking.

Imagination is not Martial Heitz's strong point, but his traditional cuisine is elegant and well prepared. The smiling welcome and excellent Bordeaux add to the enjoyment of a rabbit pâté with tender carrots, stuffed mutton tripe and fresh pasta, and bitter chocolate soufflé. The decor mixes refinement with rustic charm, and there's a pleasant garden for summer lunches.

A la carte: 250-380 F.
Menus: 130 F, 270 F.

ST-SYMPHORIEN-LE-CHATEAU

 Château d'Esclimont
(16) 37 31 15 15,
fax (16) 37 31 57 91
Open daily until 9:30 p.m. No pets. Parking.
This attractive restaurant could still do better, but our most recent visits have helped to dispel some earlier disappointments. Chef Patrick

Guerry is paying more attention to the freshness of his vegetables: we really enjoyed the tender, tasty baby lamb served with asparagus tips and broad beans, although such excellence did make the heavy crème brûlée even harder to bear! The wine list is as magnificent as the Renaissance castle and surrounding countryside. And as for the prices, they seem to scale new heights every year.

A la carte: 400-450 F.
Menus: 320 F, 495 F.

Château d'Esclimont
(See restaurant above)
Open year-round. 6 stes 1,800-2,700F. 48 rms 580-1,500F. Half-

board 1,015-1,285 F. Air cond 1 rm. Heated pool. Tennis.
The 48 rooms and six suites of this château are classic, comfortable and well situated in the middle of a 150-acre expanse of completely walled-in grounds at the bottom of a valley, which is traversed by a river and situated near the road that connects Rambouillet and Chartres. Some rooms have been refurbished this year. Guests can play tennis, swim in the heated pool and attend wintertime musical evenings. There's even a helipad. Relais et Châteaux.

> The prices in this guide reflect what establishments were charging at press time.

ECOUEN

One needn't travel all the way to the Loire Valley to view a superb French Renaissance château. Just 20 or so kilometers north of Paris, (Autoroute du Nord A1, exit n°3), stands Ecouen, an admirably preserved castle built between 1538 and 1555 for François I's closest comrade-in-arms, Constable Anne de Montmorency (who also commissioned the first château at Chantilly).

As befitted a great feudal lord and powerful military chief, the constable made Ecouen a formidable fortress. Situated on a hill overlooking the broad plain below, surrounded by moats and fortified by steeply sloping walls, Ecouen was designed to withstand even artillery fire—a wise precaution on the eve of the Wars of Religion, which ravaged the region in the later sixteenth century.

Yet the constable and his wife, Madeleine de Savoie, were also humanists and patrons of the arts, who engaged the best architects and sculptors of the day to embellish their home. Framed in the portico that leads to the grand courtyard, an equestrian statue of Anne de Montmorency in Roman warrior garb proclaims the constable's taste for antiquity. That taste is also reflected in the château's architecture. Niches in the monumental colonnade of the southern (left) wing once housed Michelangelo's *Slaves* (now in the Louvre), presented to the constable by King Henri II.

In 1632, the constable's grandson, Henri II de Montmorency, was accused of conspiracy against the Cardinal de Richelieu, and beheaded. Ecouen then reverted to the Condé family, but they spent little time there, preferring their estate at

Chantilly. During the Revolution, the contents of the castle were confiscated by the state, and eventually dispersed.

Since 1962, Ecouen has housed the Musée de la Renaissance, a unique collection of period French, Italian and Flemish furniture and decorative arts. The most dazzling exhibit is surely the 246-foot-long tapestry displayed in the Galerie de Psyché. Woven in Brussels in the early sixteenth century, this masterpiece of silk, wool and silver thread relates the story of David and Bathsheba.

What makes all the objects on view particularly interesting is their setting in the château's authentic, beautifully restored Renaissance interior. Do take the time to examine and admire the immense fireplaces, decorated with biblical scenes, for which Ecouen was famous in its glory days. And nothing gives a better idea of the grandeur of a Renaissance lord's castle than the Grande Salle, where the Montmorencys received their vassals. A visitor cannot help but be impressed with the monumental fireplace of porphyry and polychrome marble; or with the magnificent gold-and-cerulean tile floor displaying the entwined initials of Anne de Montmorency and Madeleine de Savoie.

We like to wind up a tour of Ecouen with a stroll in the garden; the park affords an impressive, sweeping view of the plain below. Hardier souls may go explore the forest that borders the château.

The **Château d'Ecouen** is open daily from 9:45 a.m. to 12:30 p.m. and 2 p.m. to 5:15 p.m., except Tuesday and holidays; call 39 90 04 04 for information.

FONTAINEBLEAU

Just as Versailles was created at the whim of young Louis XIV, Fontainebleau owes its splendor to the sudden caprice of Renaissance monarch François I, who in 1528 decided to transform a neglected royal manor near the forest of Bière into a personal residence fit for a king. After his humiliating two-year captivity in Madrid, the Roi Chevalier wanted to prove to Emperor Charles V and King Henry VIII of England (who were then erecting spectacular palaces at Grenada and Hampton Court, respectively) that he could equal, indeed surpass, them in magnificence.

Every aspect of the new château in Fontainebleau (65 kilometers south of Paris by Autoroute du Sud A6) was calculated to glorify France's first absolute ruler (he was the first, for example, to be addressed as "Majesty," a title previously reserved for the emperor). Today, François I's spirit is still tangibly present at Fontainebleau.

Over the centuries the actual architecture of the palace has undergone considerable alteration. The Galerie François I, the most celebrated decorative ensemble of the French Renaissance, was constructed between 1528 and 1530 and embellished with marvelous stuccowork and frescoes by Florentine artist Il Rosso, a pupil of Michelangelo. The recently restored frescoes illustrate a complicated and fairly obscure symbolic scheme. One remarkable figure is an elephant emblazoned with fleur-de-lis and sporting a salamander (François I's emblem) on its forehead, which signifies the royal virtue of wisdom. Other scenes commemorate the king's Italian campaigns or his role as a patron of art and literature.

The Salle de Bal (ballroom) is another impressive Renaissance creation. Commissioned by François I, it was completed under the supervision of his son, Henri II, by architect Philibert Delorme (who also worked on the Louvre). Here the frescoes—superbly restored—were designed by Il Primatice and executed by Niccolo dell'Abbate, two of the foremost Italian artists of what came to be known as the first Fontainebleau school. The ballroom created such a sensation in its day that painters and engravers came from all over to record its sumptuous decoration. Even now, the room provides a fairly accurate idea of the opulence of the Valois court.

Though Fontainebleau was relatively neglected during the second half of the sixteenth century, it flourished once again under Henri IV. Dated from this era are the Cabinet de Théagène (marvelously preserved, it's the birthplace of Louis XIII) and the Chapelle de la Trinité, decorated with biblical frescoes by Mathieu Fréminet, a French master of the baroque.

The Bourbons made a habit of spending the autumn at Fontainebleau, and continued to embellish and enlarge the palace even after the court officially took up residence at Versailles. Marie-Antoinette, who loved Fontainebleau, completely redecorated several rooms, including the Salon du Jeu (Gaming Room) and the charming Boudoir de la Reine, which was designed by Mique, her favorite architect.

Napoléon too was fond of Fontainebleau, and refurnished the palace entirely. Today it boasts Europe's finest collection of Empire furniture, as well as extensive holdings of Napoleonic relics and memorabilia culled from various national museums.

The palace is surrounded by what is surely one of the most beautiful forests in France. In autumn and winter, hunters still gallop through the russet groves of oak, riding to hounds just as French kings did centuries before them. Less bloodthirsty nature enthusiasts prefer to explore the innumerable bridle and hiking paths, or scramble around the spectacular rock formations, cliffs and gorges that make the Forêt de Fontainebleau an excellent and highly popular training ground for aspiring alpinists.

*The **Château de Fontainebleau** is open daily (except Tuesday) from 9:30 a.m. to 12:30 p.m. and 2 p.m. to 5 p.m.; the park and gardens are open from dawn to dusk. Call 64 22 27 40 for further information.*

*The **Musée Napoléonien** is open from 2 p.m. to 5 p.m. (closed Sunday, Monday, September and holidays). Call 64 22 49 80 for further information.*

RESTAURANTS & HOTELS

12/20 Chez Arrighi
53, rue de France
64 22 29 43
Closed Mon. & Jan. 8-25. Open until 10 p.m.
Some Corsican specialties are still available but traditional French food now tends to be the mainstay of the menu. Prune-stuffed young rabbit, fillet of veal with mushrooms, and crunchy caramel croustine are freshly prepared and generously served.
A la carte: 230-300 F. Menus: 110 F, 139 F, 180 F.

 ### Le Beauharnais
27, pl. Napoléon-Bonaparte, 64 22 32 65
Closed July 14-aug. 13 & Dec. 23-30. Open until 9:30 p.m. Garden dining. Parking.
Chefs come and go here but the cuisine is so classic it's hard to see the join. Here's a typical 220F menu from this year's new face in the kitchen, Remy Bidron: attractively presented salad of pike roulade, cod in crumb with mushrooms, a fine cheeseboard, and tasty apple tart. The cellar is superb but too expensive, like the à la carte prices, and the splendid setting would seem more luxurious if the staff could bear to smile.
A la carte: 320-420 F. Menus: 220 F, 300 F.

L'Aigle Noir
(See restaurant above)
*Open year-round. 7 stes 1,200-
2,000 F. 49 rms 950F. Air cond.
Heated pool.*
Facing the garden or the château, the luxurious rooms are individually decorated in Louis XVI, Empire or Restoration style. Modern comforts include satellite TV, books in English, a gym and sauna. Courteous service.

 **Hôtel Legris
et Parc**
36, rue du Parc - 64 22 24 24, fax 64 22 22 05
Closed Sun. off season, Mon. & Dec. 20-Jan. 28. 5 stes 525-575 F. 26 rms 265-525F. Restaurant. Half-board 385-510 F.
This pleasantly renovated old building is well situated in front of the entrance to the château's grounds. The best of the extremely comfortable rooms look out on the flowers of an interior garden.

BARBIZON

 Le Bas-Bréau
22, rue Grande - 60 66 40 05, fax 60 69 22 89
Closed Jan. 4-30. Open until 9:30 p.m. Garden dining. Parking.
A weekend in the most beautiful inn in the Fontainebleau forest will obviously cost you an arm and a leg, but you'll be rewarded with a veritable feast for the eyes. This is where Robert Louis Stevenson wrote *Treasure Island*. The food prepared by Alain Tavernier is pricey but savory: fillets of red mullet and green lentils, lobster salad dressed with olive oil and balsamic vinegar, coriander-scented turbot cooked on the bone and served with artichokes, baby veal chop and button onions, and fine desserts. In winter the log fire crackles away cheerfully and

summer meals can be enjoyed in the shady garden. This place is practically an enchanted forest in itself.
A la carte: 450-700 F. Menus: 300 F and 360 F (weekdays and Sat. lunch only, wine incl.), 360 F (dinner only).

 Le Bas-Bréau
(See restaurant above)
Closed Jan. 4-30. 8 stes 1,700-2,800 F. 12 rms 950-1,500 F. Pool. Tennis.
This Fontainebleau inn, one of the most refined in the Paris region, is where Robert Louis Stevenson wrote *Treasure Island*. Located on the edge of the forest and surrounded by roses and century-old trees, it has a simple, pleasant atmosphere. There's one deluxe, astonishingly comfortable bungalow at the back of the vegetable garden and owner Jean-Pierre Fava has recently added a superb heated pool. Relais et Châteaux.

12/20 Les Pléiades
21, rue Grande - 60 66 40 25, fax 60 66 41 68
Closed 3 wks in Feb. Open daily until 10 p.m. (10:30 p.m. in summer). Garden dining. Parking.
On a flower-laden terrace on the street or in a quiet garden out back, you'll enjoy a pleasant meal prepared by the latest chef: roulade of pike served cold, turbot with cockles, and a crisp apple dessert with caramel sauce. The service is slow though, and the bill a bit steep.
A la carte: 270-350 F. Menus: 200 F (weekdays only), 190 F, 295 F.

 Les Pléiades
(See restaurant above)
Closed 3 wks in Feb. 1 ste 680 F. 23 rms 290-490 F. Half-board 460-500F.
The former house of painter Daubigny has attractive, com-

fortable rooms, and the hotel boasts a beautiful, large flower garden on the edge of the Fontainebleau forest.

See also Melun in "Vaux-le-Vicomte" below.

Le Corbusier's design for living

Architect and urban planner *Le Corbusier* is probably best remembered for his rather joyless efforts to rationalize living space into modular units. However, at an earlier stage in his career he made a living by designing houses for the rich. One, the Villa Laroche, (10 impasse du Docteur-Blanche in the sixteenth arrondissement), is open to the public and affords a glimpse of an architect more concerned with space and light than with political correctness. The house was designed in 1923 for a collector of modern art, its pure lines intended as a backdrop to the works of Braque, Picasso and Ozenfant. You can still see examples of Le Corbusier's furniture there, along with a few Cubist paintings and some striking sculptures.

Ask us for a glimpse of France before you've even landed.

AIR FRANCE, SERVICE À LA FRANÇAISE.

AIR FRANCE
ASK THE WORLD OF US

Let THEM get restless

→ Normal fare : 42 F*, Orly-Paris.

→ One-Day "LIBRE ACCES" Pass : 95 F*, giving unlimited access to the métro ORLYVAL and the whole Parisian Public Transportation System (zones 1-3).

→ At Orly South, the ORLYVAL terminal is located near the Baggage Claim Area, **Door E-F.**

* Starting September 1st 1992

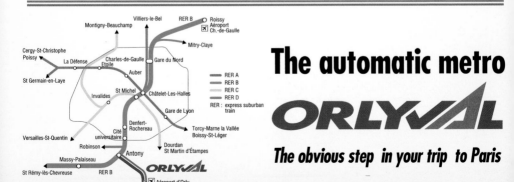

The automatic metro

ORLYVAL

The obvious step in your trip to Paris

GIVERNY

It isn't a palace or royal legend that brings travelers to this tiny village 75 kilometers northwest of Paris (55 km on Autoroute A 13, 10 km on N 13BIS and 5 km on D 5), on the border of the Ile-de-France and Normandy regions; what draws crowds to Giverny is the artistic legacy of Claude Monet. From 1883 until his death in 1926, Monet lived and worked in these sublime surroundings, a setting he created largely by and for himself. Giverny provided the light, the multifaceted landscape and the meandering Seine that the painter so loved. But Monet himself supplied the grand design, as well as 40 years of unrelenting efforts to make his ravishing garden a reality. It soon became the central motif of his pictures, and in the end, his garden was the only subject that Monet chose to paint.

Shortly before his death, assailed with doubts about the value of his pictures despite public acclaim for them, Monet came to regard the garden at Giverny as his ultimate creation. He kept six gardeners hard at work in it, full-time. The painter's garden had slowly gone to seed for half a century when in 1977 the American Versailles-Giverny Foundation undertook to restore it, along with Monet's house and studio. Well before Europe recognized his genius, America had embraced Monet at his first New York show in 1889. Now, owing in large part to American generosity, Monet's admirers may visit the house where he worked and entertained fellow artists Mary Cassatt, the poet Mallarmé and many more.

Nothing less resembles a formal French garden than Giverny's glorious, painterly composition of flowers, water and greenery. Ordinary fruit trees were banished from the orchard where the flower garden now blooms; Monet replaced them with exotic Japanese strains of ornamental cherry and apple. With the arrival of spring, perennial beds lose their disciplined, linear look under an exuberance of bright blossoms. Interestingly, except for the roses and peonies, all the flowers at Giverny are humble varieties: iris, foxglove, poppies and lupine. Yet they are planted so artfully and their colors, textures and shapes are arrayed to such advantage that an observer's eye roams over the banks and borders of the garden with as much pleasure as it does over Monet's *Water Lilies*, which hang in the Orangerie in Paris.

At the far end of the winding central path—take care not to trample the nasturtiums, which grow pretty much wherever they please—is the famous pond that Monet always insisted on showing off to his guests after lunch (he had paid a not-so-small fortune to have it installed). In spring, a curtain of languid wisteria nearly hides the "Japanese bridge," which looks out over a hypnotizing profusion of water lilies. Massed on the surface of the pond, they seem to form a huge artist's palette of delicate tints: white, yellow, pink, blue and mauve.

The house and three studios at Giverny—including one Monet had built specially to paint *Les Nymphéas*—give the haunting impression of being actually inhabited; it's as if the people who lived and worked there have only just stepped out for a moment. Everything is exactly as it was on an ordinary day at the turn of the century, from the pots and pans set out in the kitchen (Monet loved rich, complicated cooking), to the master's fascinating collection of Japanese prints. To borrow a phrase from Marcel Proust, Monet's contemporary and admirer, the evocative atmosphere of Giverny rewards the pilgrims who journey there with a sense of time recaptured.

The *Musée Claude Monet is open every day but Monday—the gardens are open from 10 a.m. to 6 p.m.; the museum is open from April 1 through October 31, 10 a.m. to 6 p.m. Admission: 30 F the house and the gardens; 20 F for the gardens. Call (16) 32 51 28 21 for further information, fax (16) 32 51 54 18.*

Visit also the **Musée Américain***, 99 rue Claude-Monet. The museum, funded by Chicago art patrons Daniel and Judith Terra, is open every day but Monday from April 1 through October 31, 10 a.m. to 6 p.m. Call (16) 32 51 94 65 for further information, fax (16) 32 51 94 67.*

RESTAURANTS & HOTELS

PACY-SUR-EURE

 Château de Brécourt

27120 Douains, by D 181 - (16) 32 52 40 50
Open daily until 9:30 p.m. Parking.

Admire the exterior of this lovely seventeenth-century château at the gateway to Normandy rather than reading the menu outside: the one you'll be given in the comfortable dining room is completely different. The 225-franc fixed-price menu is the most interesting: smoked salmon and crab pancakes, carefully cooked cod steak, a good cheeseboard, and a refreshing mango and wild strawberry dessert.

A la carte: 350-450 F. Menus: 350 F (Fri. dinner only), 225 F, 340 F.

 Château de Brécourt

(See restaurant above)
Open year-round. 4 stes 1,200-1,400 F. 21 rms 480-990 F. Half-board 730-945 F. Heated pool. Tennis.

Amenities include spacious, comfortable, stylishly furnished rooms (though the bathrooms are a bit small). Most have good views of the marvelous grounds. Conference facilities. Relais et Châteaux.

VERNON

12/20 **Les Fleurs**

71, rue Carnot
34 51 16 80,
fax 32 21 30 51
Closed Sun. dinner, Mon., Feb. school holidays & July 20-Aug. 20. Open until 9 p.m.

Flowers brighten up the walls and chair covers as well as filling vases in the pretty and cheerful dining room. The owner-chef offers an interesting 160-franc menu that includes six oysters (a tad too salty), correctly cooked but under-seasoned pepper steak, and an excellent Grand Marnier soufflé omelet. Enjoyable Coteaux d'Aix served by the carafe.

Menus: 125-240 F (wine incl.).

 La Gueulardière

78270 Port-Villez, Lieu dit Le Village
34 76 22 12
Closed Sun. dinner & Mon. (except holidays). Open until 9:30 p.m. Terrace dining. Air cond.

This picturesque site on the Seine, just across from Monet's house and gardens at Giverny, provides a perfect setting for Claude Marguerite's attractive dishes: small snails in sorrel, langoustines and braised bell peppers, John Dory with asparagus tips, and

veal kidney cooked in truffle juice. Excellent wines.

A la carte: 350-400 F. Menu: 160F (weekdays and Sat. only).

 Les Jardins de Giverny

27620 Giverny, 6 km E on D 5, chemin du Roy
32 21 60 80,
fax 32 51 93 77
Closed Jan. 4-Fev. 2. Open until 9 p.m. Terrace dining. Parking.

A stone's throw from Claude Monet's house, this fine Norman residence is surrounded by roses and rare trees. The owner-chef, Serge Pirault, bases his cuisine on the seasons: foie gras with apple brandy, hot oysters and seaweed butter, tajine of young turbot, fresh fruit gratin with fluffy sabayon sauce. Michèle Pirault will give you a warm welcome.

A la carte: 300-350 F. 120 F (weekdays and Sat. only), 180 F, 240 F.

 Normandy

1, av. Pierre-Mendès-France - 32 51 97 97
Open year-round. 47 rms 380-400 F. Restaurant. Half-board 485 F. Garage parking.

This modern, convenient hotel has just opened in the town center. The rooms in back are the quietest; all are comfortable if somewhat lacking in originality. Breakfasts are plentiful and the welcome courteous.

RAMBOUILLET

Although it is now the peaceful summer retreat of the president of France, the château at Rambouillet has witnessed some of the more dramatic moments in the nation's history. In 1547 François I, who enjoyed hunting in the nearby forest, died in a tower of the castle (which then belonged to the captain of his guards). Forty years later, Henri III, driven out of Paris by the League, took refuge at Rambouillet (located about 50 kilometers from Paris by Autoroute Chartres–Orléans A10). In 1815, before his departure for exile, Napoléon spent a last night of melancholy reflection at Rambouillet. It was there, too, that Charles X learned of the Revolution of 1830 and announced his abdication. And it was from Rambouillet, in August 1944, that General Charles de Gaulle gave the order for Leclerc's armored division to liberate Paris.

Yet Rambouillet has seen more tranquil times as well. Today, little remains of the sixteenth-century château, save the cool red-and-gray Salle des Marbres (marble room). The eighteenth century and Empire are the periods now best represented at Rambouillet. The Count of Toulouse, a legitimized son of Louis XIV, purchased the château in 1705. He enlarged the existing structures and had the new west wing decorated with enchanting rococo woodwork. For the garden, he commissioned a system of canals and artificial islands on which magnificent *fêtes* were held throughout the century. The count's son, the Duke of Penthièvre, completed the canals and, in the English garden, had an incredibly kitsch cottage constructed of seashells and slivers of mother-of-pearl.

In 1783, Louis XVI purchased Rambouillet for the exceptional hunting the nearby forest afforded. Marie-Antoinette was less than enthusiastic: She called the place "the toad hole" and longed for her Trianon at Versailles. To appease her, in 1785 Louis had the neoclassic *laiterie* (dairy) constructed, where ladies of the aristocracy came to sip new milk and sample fresh cheese. Today the dairy is no longer in operation, but the *bergerie* (sheepfold), built the following year, is still home to some 800 sheep, including 120 merinos descended from a flock presented to Louis XVI by the king of Spain (and those *moutons* of course will have nothing to do with the other 680).

Rambouillet was virtually abandoned during the Revolution, and its furniture removed and sold, but Napoléon took a fancy to the château and decided to restore it. Today, visitors may admire the emperor's study, his private apartments ornamented with "Pompeiian" frescoes and the grand dining room—still used for state dinners—with its enormous, 550-pound bronze chandelier.

The densely treed forest of Rambouillet, a great favorite with hunters and mushroom gatherers, covers close to half a million acres and begins virtually at the door of the château.

*The **Château de Rambouillet** is open daily, except on Tuesday and when the president is in residence, from 10 a.m. to 11:30 a.m. and 2 p.m. to 5:30 p.m. (until 4:30 p.m. from Oct. 1 through March 31).*

*La **Laiterie de la Reine Marie-Antoinette** is open daily, except Tuesday, March 15 through October 31, from 10 a.m. to noon (last tour: 11 a.m.) and 2 p.m. to 6 p.m. (last tour: 5 p.m.), November 1 through March 14, from 10 a.m. to noon (last tour: 11 a.m.) and 2 p.m. to 16:30 p.m. (last tour: 15:30 p.m.). Call 34 83 00 25 for further information.*

RESTAURANTS & HOTELS

12/20 Le Cheval Rouge

78, rue du Général-de-Gaulle
30 88 80 61
Closed Sun. dinner & July 15-Aug. 4. Open until 9:30 p.m. Garden dining. Air cond.

The flower-filled garden of this pleasant inn is just the place to enjoy traditional dishes prepared from the freshest ingredients: crab ravioli, turbot in butter sauce, kid sautéed with garlic purée.

A la carte: 250-350 F. Menus: 120 F (weekdays and Sat. only), 200 F.

Resthôtel Primevère

ZA du Bel-Air, rue J.-Jacquard - 34 85 51 02
Open year-round. 42 rms 245-260 F. Restaurant. Pets allowed. Parking.

Set back from the highway, this brand-new hotel offers bright, pleasant rooms and buffet breakfasts. The forest is nearby.

MONTFORT-L'AMAURY

La Toque Blanche

78490 Mesnuls,
12, Grande-Rue
34 86 05 55
Closed Sun. dinner, Mon. & Aug. Open until 10 p.m. Garden dining. Pets allowed. Parking.

Jean-Pierre Philippe, a burly chef with a booming voice, is what you might call a "charac-ter" and his clients enjoy distinctive and original cuisine. A native of the coast town of Paimpol, he is at his best when cooking seafood dishes like the basil-scented langoustine ragoût, sea bass and leeks, mussel soup, and John Dory served with fried parsley. None of which come cheap, but the delightful setting helps to take the edge off the bill.

A la carte: 400-450 F. Menu: 360 F.

See also Saint-Symphorien-le-Château in "Chartres," above.

> Remember to call ahead to reserve your table, and please, if you cannot honor your reservation, be courteous and let the restaurant know.

SAINT-GERMAIN-EN-LAYE

In 1862 Emperor Napoléon III, an ardent archeology buff (his great boast was that he had discovered the site of the Battle of Alésia, where Caesar defeated Vercingetorix, leader of the Gauls, in 52 B.C.), established the Musée des Antiquités Nationales at Saint-Germain-en-Laye (about 20 kilometers west of Paris by Autoroute de Normandie A13). The oldest artifacts unearthed on French soil are housed in this fascinating museum, which follows the course of French history up to the time of the Merovingians, the first Frankish dynasty. Today, nothing could be simpler than to take this journey back in time, for the RER links Saint-Germain to the center of Paris in a matter of minutes.

On the museum's vast mezzanine, exhibits document the millennia that preceded Rome's occupation of Gaul. It is strangely moving to contemplate these age-old vestiges of human artistry. Most of the pieces are quite small, like the Dame de Brassempouy, the oldest-known representation of a human face, which is thought to predate Christ's birth by about 20,000 years; or the famous bone carving of a Bison Licking Its Fur, from Dordogne (16,000 B.C.); or the many images that remind us that in France too the buffalo roamed and the deer (and antelope) played—at least until the end of the Ice Age.

Even visitors with only a mild interest in archeology will be riveted by artifacts discovered in the tombs of Celtic princes of the first Iron Age (Hallstatt period), particularly the funeral chariots, which indicate that the entombed were of noble rank, the iron swords, carved daggers and personal ornaments. Other finds verify that Gaulish tribes traded with Greece and Etruria, thus invalidating the theory that Gaul lived in isolation before the Romans burst on the scene. The very existence of coins minted by the principal Gallic tribes, of amphoras and other luxury goods, bears witness to the wealth of Gaul's aristocracy, and to their links with the Mediterranean world.

Exhibits on the upper floor illustrate the period of Roman colonization and include a model of the Battle of Alésia, which marked the end of Gaul's independence. The number of statues representing Gaulish divinities underscores Rome's generally tolerant attitude toward foreign religions, while an abundance of manufactured goods—ceramics, glass objects—give us a picture of France's earliest industries. The barbarian invasions that followed this period of prosperity are evoked by jewels and impressively worked weapons excavated at Frankish tomb sites.

Though Saint-Germain-en-Laye is now synonymous with prehistory, it holds a significant place in the history of France. A prestigious royal château, it was the birthplace of Kings Henri II, Charles IX and Louis XIV (who preferred it to all his other palaces until he built Versailles). From the twelfth century through the nineteenth, extensive building and remodeling altered the château's appearance many times over. What the visitor sees today is the Vieux Château, rebuilt under François I. This first important example of brick-and-stone architecture in the Ile-de-France, was heavily restored in the nineteenth century).

The former splendor of Saint-Germain is perhaps best translated by Le Nôtre's magnificent gardens, and the Grande Terrasse bordered with linden trees. Moreover, with its 8,500 acres of flat, sandy paths, picturesque hunting pavilions and majestic stands of oak, the Forest of Saint-Germain offers ideal hiking terrain within easy reach of Paris.

The Musée des Antiquités Nationales is open daily, except Tuesday, from 9 a.m. to 5:15 p.m. Call 34 51 53 65 for further information.

See also "The Suburbs" in the Restaurants (page 94) and Hotels (page 130) chapters.

SENLIS

When you walk through the narrow medieval streets of Senlis (50 kilometers north of Paris by Autoroute du Nord A1), don't be surprised if you suddenly recognize the set from your favorite French costume drama. This compact, well-preserved town on the border of the Ile-de-France and Picardy offers a fascinating glimpse into the history of pre-Revolutionary France. Understandably, it is a popular location with film-production companies.

North of the town, the Jardin du Roy (king's garden) lies in what was once the moat surrounding a Gallo-Roman defensive wall. The garden affords a marvelous overall view of Senlis, and of one of the best-preserved Roman fortifications in France. About 13 feet thick and 23 feet high, the wall dates back to the barbarian invasions of the third century. It once linked together 28 watch towers, 16 of which have survived.

The nearby Château Royal, despite its grandiose name, is now nothing more than a park scattered with romantic ruins that date from antiquity to the Renaissance. Built on the site of a first-century Roman fortress, the château was a royal residence from the time of Clovis, in the fifth century, until the reign of Henri IV, early in the seventeenth century. It was there, in 987, that the Capetian line of monarchs was established, with the election of Hugues Capet, Duke of the Franks, to the throne of France.

If you cross the pretty square in front of the Cathedral of Notre-Dame, you can best admire the monumental portal with its celebrated Gothic sculpture. Begun in 1153, ten years before Notre-Dame de Paris, the cathedral at Senlis served as a model for those at Chartres, Amiens and Reims. Yet by the sixteenth century, recurrent fires had made it necessary to rebuild the northern and southern facades practically from scratch. The work was directed by Pierre Chambiges, who created one of the finest (and last) examples of flamboyant Gothic architecture. Crowning the northern portal are the initial and emblematic salamander of François I.

After visiting the cathedral, we always take the time to wander through the winding, ancient streets of Senlis: rue de la Tonnellerie, rue du Châtel, rue de la Treille and rue de Beauvais all boast sixteenth-century houses and mansions with splendid carved entrances (many of which are open to visitors in odd-numbered years, during the month of September for the Rendez-vous de Senlis). You'll end up at the thirteenth-century church of Saint Frambourg, restored through the efforts of pianist and composer George Cziffra, and now used as a concert hall.

If you have time and a car, drive a few kilometers north to the Italianate Château de Raray, built in the seventeenth century, where Jean Cocteau filmed his magical *Beauty and the Beast.* Who knows? Perhaps, as you stand admiring the fantastic hunting scenes sculpted on Diana's Gate, your own Beauty—or Prince Charming—will suddenly appear!

*The **Château Royal** and **Musée de la Vénerie** are open daily, except Tuesday and Wednesday morning, from 10 a.m. to noon and 2 p.m. to 5 p.m.*
*The access to the **Jardin du Roy** is permanent.*
*The **cathedral** is open from 7 a.m. to 7 p.m. Call (16) 44 53 00 80 for further information.*

RESTAURANTS & HOTELS

 Les Gourmandins
3, pl. de la Halle
(16) 44 60 94 01
Closed Mon. dinner & Tues. (except holidays) & Aug. 5-25.
Open until 9:30 p.m.
Other restaurant guides seem slow in "discovering" Sylvain Knecht's excellent cuisine. Never mind, we'll continue to pay tribute to his perfect sense of timing, the subtlety of his sauces and contemporary creations like a Champagne-flavored lobster and scallop mold, lotte sautéed with chanterelle mushrooms or an olive-studded lamb charlotte. Marie-Christine Knecht makes you feel at home in the cozy dining room.
Menus: 120 F (weekdays only), 210 F, 310 F.

11/20 **Auberge de Fontaine**
60300 Fontaine-Chaalis,
8 km SE by D 330,
22, Grande-Rue
(16) 44 54 20 22
Closed Tues. dinner, Wed. & Feb.
Open until 9 p.m. Garden dinning.
This charming inn, tucked away in a delightful village, stresses simplicity and sincerity both in the dining room and in the kitchen. Salad of baby rabbit, seafood ragoût and veal kidneys with shallots are among the highlights of the menu.
A la carte: 210-320 F.
Menus: 120 F, 190 F.

 Auberge de Fontaine
(See restaurant above)
Closed Tues. & Wed. 8 rms 240-330 F.
Rooms as restful as you could wish for, with flowered wallpaper, wood beams and superbly comfortable beds.

See also Chantilly and Compiègne in "Chantilly," above.

Red toques signify modern cuisine; white toques signify traditional cuisine.

VAUX-LE-VICOMTE

A s we stand in the unfinished Grand Salon of Vaux-le-Vicomte, looking out over the intricate gardens designed by Le Nôtre, we can almost picture the scene: The dog days of August 1661... Nicolas Fouquet, France's brilliant finance minister, is entertaining his young sovereign, Louis XIV, at an indescribably lavish reception. A thousand fountains play in the magnificent Jardins à la Française, while Molière's troupe performs the comic ballet Les Fâcheux. Courtiers applaud the water jousts, the concerts, the fireworks... At dinner—prepared by Vatel, the foremost chef of his day—the king and his retinue are served on solid-gold plates. According to legend, the dinner did not sit well with Louis, whose suspicions—and envy—were aroused by such luxury. Historians claim that Colbert, Fouquet's rival for control of the royal treasury, had calumniated Fouquet, insinuating that he was raiding the king's coffers. Or it may have been that the king set Fouquet up himself: wangling an invitation to Vaux, then watching the vainglorious minister flaunt his riches, and thus be hoist by his own petard!

Whoever laid it, the trap was sprung that August day at Vaux-le-Vicomte (about 60 kilometers south of Paris by Autoroute de Sud A6). A few weeks later, Louis sent d'Artagnan, the captain of his musketeers, to arrest Fouquet at Nantes. He then sent workmen to pack up the finest tapestries, furnishings and paintings from Vaux and carry them straight into the royal collection. Louis summoned Fouquet's architect, Le Vau, his decorator, Le Brun and his landscape designer, Le Nôtre, and ordered them all to begin work on the royal showplace at Versailles.

After a trial that dragged out over three years, the courts handed down a sentence of banishment for Fouquet. Louis, implacable, overruled them, and condemned his former minister to life imprisonment. Fouquet was, in all probability, a rascal. Yet the story of his fall and miserable end (after nineteen years in prison) still colors our view of Vaux's splendors with a tinge of melancholy.

It is largely thanks to Alfred Sommier, a sugar-refining magnate who purchased a dilapidated Vaux-le-Vicomte in 1875, that we can now see the château and gardens much as they were on that fateful day in 1661. He spent prodigious amounts of money and energy to rebuild sagging roofs and walls, to furnish the nearly empty house with seventeenth-century antiques, and to restore the gardens to their former beauty. That last task alone took a good half century. Using Le Nôtre's plans and contemporary engravings, Sommier was able to reconstruct the terraces, pools and the complex system of pipes that feed the fountains. He planted acres of trees and bushes, and acquired antique statuary for the garden, as well as commissioned pieces from modern sculptors to replace the statues confiscated by Louis XIV.

In addition to the gardens, three levels of the château are now open to the public. On the upper floor are the Fouquets' private living quarters—studies, boudoirs and bedrooms—handsomely fitted out with period furniture and hung with tapestries and reproductions of paintings from the minister's (confiscated) collection. Above the fireplace in Mme. Fouquet's study is Le Brun's famous portrait of a smiling Nicolas Fouquet.

For us, the most appealing aspect of the reception rooms downstairs (the Grands Appartements) is Le Brun's decoration. Actually, the term *decoration* is not adequate to describe this virtuoso performance with paint, stucco, carving and gilt. The scores of rosy nymphs, cherubs, squirrels (Fouquet's emblem) and other allegorical figures that populate the ceilings and woodwork of the Salon des Muses and Cabinet des Jeux (Gaming Room) fill these formal rooms with a rapturous charm. Le Brun's stucco-and-fresco decor in the Chambre du Roi (Royal Chamber) is the model for what later became known throughout Europe as the "French style," which reached its apotheosis at Versailles.

Bereft of its intended decoration, the Grand Salon demonstrates the measure of architect Le Vau's genius; the eye, unsolicited by bright allegories and visions, is naturally drawn outside, to the harmonious perspectives of the gardens, Le Nôtre's masterpiece. In their more modest way, the workrooms and staff quarters on the lower level are also quite interesting. The kitchens (in use until 1956) display a dazzling collection of copper pots and pans scoured to a high polish.

Those in search of rare sensations and exquisite atmospheres will surely want to visit Vaux-le-Vicomte by candlelight on a Saturday evening in summer. The scene is unforgettable—indeed, it is enough to rouse the envy of a king!

*The **Château de Vaux-le-Vicomte** is open daily (except Christmas Day) April 1 through October 31, from 10 a.m. to 6 p.m.; November 1 through March 31, from 11 a.m.-5 p.m., except from November 16 to December 18 and January 4 to February 12 when the château is closed. **Candlelight tours** are held Saturday evenings from May through September (Sunday evenings in July and August), 8:30 p.m. to 11 p.m. **Fountain displays** are scheduled the second and final Saturday of each month from April through October. Call 60 66 97 09 for further information.*

RESTAURANTS & HOTELS

MELUN

 ### L'Ecurie
77176 Nandy, 9 km NW by N 446, Ferme de Nandy, 1, rue Arqueil
60 63 63 63
43 rms 300-330 F. Restaurant. Half-board 453 F. Parking.
This solid stone hotel between Melun and Corbeil houses comfortable, well-soundproofed rooms with full bathrooms. Fitness center.

Gault Millau's ratings are based solely on the restaurants' cuisine. We do not take into account the atmosphere, decor, service and so on; these are commented upon within the review.

 ### Grand Monarque
Melun-la-Rochette, av. de Fontainebleau
64 39 04 40
Open daily until 9:30 p.m. Garden dining. Parking.
In the middle of the forest stands this restaurant, with well-dressed tables, a cheery and comfortable modern decor and a terrace by the pool. Service is attentive and the cooking brings out the best in fine ingredients: duck foie gras cooked with green cabbage, shark steak and basmati rice, and a bitter chocolate dessert coated in orange sauce.
A la carte: 280-400 F. Menu: 145 F (weekends only, wine incl.), 190 F.

Concorde Grand Monarque ♣♥
(See restaurant above)
Open year-round. 5 stes 700-750 F. 45 rms 450-550 F. Half-

board 462-512 F. Heated pool. Tennis.
The small but perfectly equipped rooms open onto the park. Conference facilities. Excellent service.

12/20 La Mare au Diable
77550 Moissy-Cramayel, 5 km N on N 6, parc Plessis-Picard
60 63 17 17
Closed Sun. dinner & Mon. Open until 10 p.m. Garden dining. Pool. Tennis. Parking.
Overlooking romantic grounds, this charming inn has warm, rustic decor. The cooking is simple and honest, with succulent broiled meats as the main attraction. The 150-franc menu offers salmon salad, entrecôte steak with shallots, andouillette sausage, and île flottante. The service is pleasant, the bill less so.
A la carte: 270-470 F. Menus: 200 F (lunch only), 150 F, 230 F, 300 F.

VERSAILLES

Versailles, undoubtedly the world's most famous palace, has been a favorite destination for day-tripping Parisians since 1833, when King Louis-Philippe turned the château, which had been abandoned since the Revolution, into a "museum of the glories of France." Today, Versailles (about 25 kilometers west of Paris by Autoroute de Normandie A13) offers pleasures at every season, in every kind of weather. Visitors can amble through parks dotted with romantic statuary, admire a wealth of art, furniture and architecture—comparing Louis this with Louis that—or simply spread out a blanket and picnic beside the Grand Canal.

It took Louis XIV just 40 years to build the palace and its park around a hunting lodge erected by his father, Louis XIII. And though his successors made many changes, Versailles still bears the unmistakable stamp of the Sun King, who, from 1682 on, made it the official residence of the court, the sole seat of royal power and the political capital of France. The court's permanent presence explains the colossal proportions of the palace, which housed the royal family, the princes of the blood, the courtiers, the king's councilors, everyone's servants... it's little wonder that the western facade of the palace stretches out nearly 2,000 feet.

Lodging his considerable household and entourage was not all that Louis had in mind when he built Versailles. He also saw the palace as a powerful propaganda tool, a monument to the glory of the French monarchy and a showcase for masterworks by French artists and craftsmen. Versailles was open to all. The humblest subjects of the realm could wander freely through the Grands Appartements to gape at the cream of the royal collections. Classical statues and busts stood in marble-lined halls; paintings from the French and Venetian schools hung on walls covered in velvet, damask and brocade. Today's tourists are the descendants of those visitors who, at the end of the seventeenth century, marveled at the dazzling Galerie des Glaces (Gallery of Mirrors) or the Salon d'Apollon before attending the king's supper or submitting a petition to Louis XIV as he made his way to mass at the royal chapel.

But we have the advantage over those tourists of long ago, for we can visit parts of Versailles that were then off-limits to the public, even to courtiers. Among the most beautiful of the private quarters is the Petit Appartement, fitted out for Louis XV just above his official suite, a place where he could relax alone—or with friends (like Madame du Barry, who had her own room there).

A similarly intimate mood and scale are evident in the two Trianons, situated about half a mile from the main palace. The Grand Trianon was built in 1687 for Louis XIV, who spent many a quiet summer evening there surrounded by his family. Today it houses heads of state on official visits. The Petit Trianon is an exquisite neoclassic structure designed by Gabriel in 1764 for Louis XV, who wished to live closer to his beloved botanical garden. It was also the preferred residence of Marie-Antoinette, whose spirit still pervades the place. There, on October 5, 1789, she learned of the Parisians' march on Versailles.

In fine weather, the gardens of Versailles are an irresistible invitation to wander. They cover over 200 acres with an enchanting variety of landscapes. The classical French *parterres* (flower beds), with their broad perspectives, pools and lawns, were designed by Le Nôtre at the height of his powers; his is also the genius behind the marvelous *bosquets* (coppices) that combine thickly massed greenery and spectacular waterworks. Scattered throughout are hundreds of marble and bronze statues, many inspired by the myths of Apollo, with whom the Sun King strongly identified. If you happen to be in Versailles between May and September, make a point of touring the gardens when the Grandes Eaux are scheduled: all over the gardens, in every bed and *bosquet*, the fountains put on a magical display.

And in summer, it is well worth the effort to obtain tickets for a performance at the Opéra Royal, an architectural masterpiece by Gabriel, inaugurated in 1770 for the marriage of the future Louis XVI and the Archduchess Marie-Antoinette. The elegance of its proportions, its superb acoustics and the splendor of its decoration make it perhaps the most beautiful theater in the world.

*The **Château de Versailles** is open daily, except Monday and holidays, from 9 a.m. to 6 p.m. (until 5 p.m. from October 1 to April 31). The **park and gardens** are open daily from dawn to dusk. Fountain displays are scheduled on two or three Sundays a month from May through September at 4 p.m. to 5 p.m. Call 30 84 74 00 for further information.*

◼ RESTAURANTS & HOTELS

See "The Suburbs" in the Restaurants (page 96) and Hotels (page 130) chapters.

◼ SIGHTS

Following is a highly condensed list of Versailles's most noteworthy sights.

The **Château de Versailles** (a must!), with more than four million visitors per year (from May to September its parks host the Grandes Eaux and the Fêtes de Nuit); the **Trianon Palaces**; the **Salle du Jeu de Paume**; **Notre-Dame** church (designed by Hardouin-Mansart); the **king's vegetable garden** (school of horticulture); the **Carrés Saint-Louis** (modest lodgings during the time of the Old Régime); the **antiques** and **secondhand market** (passage de la Geôle, next to the colorful market at Notre-Dame); the **Hôtel des Ventes** (former home of the Light Cavalry); the delightful **Musée Lambinet** (with beautiful eighteenth-century paintings, see *Museums* section page 303); the **Couvent des Récollets**.

BASICS

GETTING AROUND

Paris is a rationally designed city divided into twenty *arrondissements*, or districts. Essential to getting around Paris is a knowledge of the excellent transportation system and a pocket-size street index called *Paris par Arrondissement*. Available in most bookstores and at major newspaper stands, it includes comprehensive maps of Paris, the subway system (Métro and RER) and bus routes.

■ BUSES

Riding the bus is a great—and cheap—way to tour the city. The n° 24 bus, for example, passes by many historical monuments. Buses take you almost everywhere within the metropolitan area for just two tickets (one ticket is good for two zones). You can purchase tickets (6 francs) on the bus or a book (*carnet*) of ten tickets (36.50 francs—an economical investment) at Métro stations or in some tobacco shops. Special three- or five-day tourist passes (*Paris Visite*) allow unlimited travel on buses, the Métro, the RER express line and the SNCF Ile-de-France lines and are sold at major Métro and RER stations. Major bus routes operate from 7 a.m. to 12:30 a.m. every day. These bus numbers are indicated by a colored number inside a white disk at the bus stops. The less important routes, marked by a white number inside a colored disk, do not run on Sundays or holidays, nor does the service go on much after 8 or 9 p.m. There is an excellent late-night service (*Noctambus*): Buses leave Châtelet from special stops marked with the night owl–logo every hour on the half hour. Every bus stop in Paris posts fares, times, routes and bus numbers. When you enter the bus, punch your ticket(s) in the machine next to the driver. Do not punch passes or orange card coupons: simply hold them up for the bus driver to see. When you wish to get off, signal the driver by pressing the red button near your seat. Getting around by bus is a good deal easier than it may sound; and listening to an irate Parisian bus driver caught in rush-hour traffic is also an excellent way to learn some interesting French words that you won't find in the dictionary!

A convenient way to get to the different Paris airports is to take the *Air France Bus*. It leaves every 12, 15 or 20 minutes depending on the destination, from 3 different points in the capital: the Aérogare des Invalides, Esplanade des Invalides, 7th arr., 43 23 84 49; Le Palais des Congrès, place de la Porte Maillot, near the Air France agency, 16th arr., 42 99 25 00; and near the Arc de Triomphe, at the beginning of

avenue Carnot, 17th arr. The bus makes the same stops on the return journey from the airports.

■ LIMOUSINES

See *Alliance Autos*, p. 184

■ MÉTRO

Getting the knack of the Métro system is a cinch. You'll find a Métro map posted at each station, outside on the street and inside as well. Let's imagine you want to go from the Gare du Nord to Saint-Germain-des-Prés. Locate the two stations on your map and check whether they are on the the same line (each line is indicated by a different color). In this case, they are, so follow the line from your station of departure to your station of arrival, then note the name of the station at the end of the line (in this instance it's the Porte d'Orléans). That means that Porte d'Orléans is the name of the direction you will be taking. Inside the station, look for signs indicating "direction Porte d'Orléans," and when you reach the platform, check again on the sign located in the middle of the platform. If you must change lines to reach your destination, consult a Métro map to ascertain which stop offers the relevant *correspondance*, or interchange.

A single ticket will take you anywhere on the Métro system and within zones 1 and 2 of the RER system (see RER, below). Don't forget to keep your ticket until you leave the bus or Métro, for you may be asked to produce it by an R.A.T.P. official. Tourist or not, if you don't have it, you will have to pay an on-the-spot fine if you're caught.

> The *R.A.T.P.* runs the Métro, the buses and the RER. Information line: 43 46 14 14 from 6 a.m. to 9 p.m.

■ RER

The *Réseau Express Régional* is a network of fast commuter services linking the center of Paris to destinations all over the Greater Paris Region. Quite a number of interesting places to visit are accessible by RER, and you can pick up brochures listing these from any Métro information kiosk. There is also a very good bicycle-hire service (*Roue Libre*) run by the RER that allows you to explore some beautiful woodlands around Paris (like the Chevreuse Valley, the Forest of Saint-Germain-en-Laye and so forth). The flat-rate system on the regular Métro does not apply to the RER (unless you are traveling within the city), so you must consult the diagrams on the automatic ticket machines to determine the cost of your ticket. It is possible to get round-trip tickets, and the machine will give change on any coins you care to use (though it doesn't take bills).

■ TAXIS

There are some 14,700 taxis available in Paris (until you really need one!). There are three ways of getting yourself a taxi: The first is simply to flag one down (it is available if its roof light is fully illuminated); the second is to go to a taxi stand (*Tête de Station*); the third is to call up a radio taxi that will arrive five to ten minutes later at your address (the meter will already be running, but don't get in if it's more than 30 francs). Normally, you pay 11 francs to get in the cab and about 2.79 francs per kilometer during days hours (7 a.m.-7 p.m.) and 4.35 francs during night hours (7 p.m.-7 a.m.). You'll be charged a supplement if the taxi leaves from a train station (5 francs), if a fourth person is aboard (5 francs), and for each item of baggage (5 francs). The fare scale is higher on expressways (keep this in mind if you take a taxi to or from an airport). Tip the driver 10 to 15 percent. If you wish to report a problem or lodge a complaint, you can call 45 31 14 80, or write to Service des Taxis, 36, rue des Morillons, 75732 Paris cedex 15, indicating the taxi's licence number as well as the date and time you were picked up.

Alpha-Taxis	**Artaxi**
45 85 85 85	42 41 50 50
G7 Radio	**Taxis-Radio "Etoile"**
47 39 47 39	42 70 41 41

TOURS

■ BY BUS

Cityrama
1st arr. - 4, pl. des Pyramides - 42 60 30 14
Open daily April 1-Oct. 31: 6:30 a.m.-10 p.m.; Nov. 1-March 31: until 8:30 p.m.
Cityrama's double-decker, ultracomfortable tour buses whisk visitors all around Paris morning, noon and night (call for schedules and fares). A recorded commentary describes monuments, landmarks and points of interest in the language of your choice. For early-risers,

there is a superb crack-of-dawn tour in spring and summer.

Panam' 2002
8th arr. - 5, rue Lincoln - 45 04 36 78
Open daily 9 a.m.-7 p.m. Guided tours: 1 p.m. & 9 p.m. Fee: 240 F.
A hostess will provide a running commentary while you tour Paris in the comfort of a luxuriously appointed coach. From the place de la Concorde to the Opéra, the Eiffel Tower, the Champs-Elysées and onward, you can even nibble on a prepared dinner as you admire the cityscape and watch the locals hustle and bustle about their business.

Paris et son Histoire
9th arr. - 82, rue Taitbout - 45 26 26 77
Open 10 a.m.-noon & 2 p.m.-6:30 p.m. Closed Sun. & holidays. Fee: 330 F, 480 F per couple.
As the name indicates, this association specializes in the history of Paris (and the surrounding Ile-de-France region). Members attend lecture tours throughout the year; and from March to October, bus trips are organized to points of interest in the Paris area. Annual membership fees are 330 francs (480 francs for couples) and include a monthly bulletin of events. Meeting times and other information are provided by phone, or at tourist offices.

Walking tours

Discover the city on foot during a three-hour stroll with a theme. You can choose from luxury fashion, avant-garde fashion, Left Bank fashion, designer fashion, antiques and art galleries, or gift ideas. Cost is 180 francs per person, which includes the services of a bilingual guide and a tea or coffee break. Call *Shopping Plus* at 47 53 91 17 for further details, fax 44 18 96 68.

Paris Passion
17th arr. - 34, rue Chazelles - 42 67 20 73, fax 40 53 85 54
Open 9 a.m.-1 p.m. & 2 p.m.-6 p.m. Closed Sun. Prices vary.
If you like the idea of an informed guided tour but don't want care for buses, give Emanuelle Daras a call. This smart young woman has created a series of small, first-class, personalized tours. In a luxurious minivan (stocked with Champagne, no less), a maximum of five

people at a time are taken to such places as artists' ateliers, foie-gras makers, the Cartier workshops and much more.

Paris-Vision

1st arr. - 214, rue de Rivoli - 42 60 31 25
Open daily 8 a.m.-10 p.m.
Paris-Vision conducts guided tours of the city in just about any language you can think of.

R.A.T.P.

8th arr. - Pl. de la Madeleine (behind the flower market) - 40 06 71 45
Open 9 a.m.-7 p.m. (Sat. & Sun. in summer 6:30 a.m.-7 p.m.); winter: until 5 p.m. Closed Sun.
Guided bus tours conducted in every imaginable language.

T.A.S.

43 80 56 56, fax 43 80 04 34
Open daily 7:30 a.m.-midnight.
T.A.S.: a new way to travel. Specialized in tours of Paris and the surrounding area, T.A.S. will pick you up at your hotel in a minibus holding 8 to 15 passengers and escort you on a guided tour conducted in your own language, for a day or half-day, morning, noon or night.

■ BY BOAT

Les Bateaux-Mouches

8th arr. - Port de la Conférence, Pont de l'Alma, rive droite - 42 25 96 10
Call for information.
These whales of river cruisers go nosing down the Seine packed with thousands of tourists, often eliciting a sarcastic smirk from Parisians. But the laugh is on the cynics. These fast, smooth boats provide one of the few ways to see Paris from a new angle. Take an early-morning or dusk cruise, when the light is at its loveliest. On night cruises, the Bateaux-Mouches' floodlights unveil a phantasmagoric cityscape that fascinates tourists and seen-it-all Parisians alike. Lunch and formal dinners are available on board at reasonable prices, considering the incomparable view that accompanies your meal.

Canauxrama

19th arr. - 13, quai de la Loire - 42 39 15 00
One day cruise March 15-Nov. 15: 8:30 a.m.-6 p.m.; 3 hours cruise: 9:45 a.m. & 2:45 p.m. Closed Dec. 25 & Jan. 1. Admission: 70-195 F, reduced rate for children.
Did you know that the Saint-Martin and the Ourcq Canals flow from the Seine in central Paris as far (upstream) as Meaux? Well, now you do. So why go by bus or subway when you can take a boat back from La Villette's Cité des

Sciences? Canauxrama's cruises are one of the city's most pleasant, unhurried, uncrowded excursions. The view of Paris and the Ile-de-France from a comfortable canal boat (sunroof, onboard bar, guided tours) has a special softness. Canauxrama offers a day-long trip on the Canal de l'Ourcq through the charming countryside between Paris and Meaux, with a stopover at Claye-Souilly for a picnic or bistro lunch. Also featured is a tour of the exciting La Villette neighborhood, which includes passage through the deepest lock in the Paris region. Departures take place at the pier opposite 5 bis, quai de la Loire (nineteenth arrondissement) and from the Paris-Arsenal canal port opposite 50 boulevard de la Bastille (twelfth arrondissement), just down from the new Opera house.

Paris-Canal et Quiztour Continental

9th arr. - 19, rue d'Athènes - 48 74 75 30
Open 9 a.m.-6:30 p.m. (Sat. 10:30 a.m.-4 p.m.). Closed Sun. Admission: 90-200 F, reduced rate for children.
Quiztour offers Canal Saint-Martin and Seine cruises from April 1 to November 13 on board the *Patache* and the *Canotier*, two comfortable riverboats that carry between 50 and 100 passengers. The ambience is particularly fine in the off-season. Boats are also available for receptions or private cruises, and there are houseboats and canal boat/hotels as well.

Les Vedettes de Paris-Ile-de-France

15th arr. - Port de Suffren - 47 05 71 29
Open daily April 1-Sept. 30: 10 a.m.-11 p.m.; Oct. 1-March 31: 10 a.m.-6 p.m. (Sat. & Sun. until 10 p.m.).
A summery dance-hall atmosphere reigns on these tea-dance cruises with such themes as historic Paris or the Val-de-Marne.

Les Vedettes du Pont-Neuf

1st arr. - Square du Vert-Galant - 46 33 98 38
Open daily 10 a.m.-11 p.m.
For anyone who knows Paris well, the tour commentary (in several languages) is somewhat bewildering. Les Vedettes du Pont-Neuf runs medium-size boats and is centrally located. Its one-hour pleasure cruises and run up and down the Seine. Departures take place every 30 minutes from 10 a.m. to noon and from 1:30 p.m. to 6:30 p.m. From May through October there are illuminated tours from 9 p.m. to 10:30 p.m. (departures every half hour). From November to March, call for the hours. Tours for groups (minimum 50 persons) and parties can be arranged upon request.

AT YOUR SERVICE

■ TOURIST INFORMATION

For all the brochures and other "literature" that the sage sightseer might need:

Eiffel Tower Office
7th arr. - 45 51 22 15
Open May 1-Sept. 30 11 a.m.-6 p.m.

Bureau Gare d'Austerlitz
13th arr. - bd de l'Hôpital - 45 84 91 70
Open 8 a.m.-3 p.m. Closed Sun.
Located at the international arrivals area.

Bureau Gare de l'Est
10th arr. - bd de Strasbourg - 46 07 17 73
Open 8 a.m.-9 p.m. (off-seas. until 8 p.m.). Closed Sun.
Located at the arrivals lobby.

Bureau Gare de Lyon
12th arr. - 20 bd Diderot - 43 43 33 24
Open 8 a.m.-9 p.m. (off-seas. until 8 p.m.). Closed Sun.
Located at the exit of the international lines.

Bureau Gare Montparnasse
14th arr. - 15, bd de Vaugirard - 43 22 19 19
Open 8 a.m.-9 p.m. (off-seas. until 8 p.m.). Closed Sun.
Located opposite track 18.

Bureau Gare du Nord
10th arr. - 18, rue de Dunkerque - 45 26 94 82
Open 8 a.m.-9 p.m., Sun. 1 p.m.-8 p.m. (off-seas. until 8 p.m.). Closed Sun. off-seas.
Located at the international arrivals area.

Office de Tourisme de Paris
8th arr. - 127, av. des Champs-Elysées - 47 23 61 72, fax 47 23 56 91 (after April 1 '93: 49 52 53 54, fax 49 52 53 00)
Open 9 a.m.-8 p.m. Closed May 1, Dec. 25, Jan. 1.

24-Hour Information Line
47 20 88 98 (after April 1 '93 49 52 53 56)
In English, of course.

■ ORIENTATION

Here are a few facts of French life for foreign visitors:

Remember that in France, the **ground floor** (*rez-de-chaussée*) is what Americans call the first floor; the French first floor (*premier étage*) corresponds to the American second floor, and so on.

When dining out, the **service charge** (15 percent) is always included in the bill. An additional tip can be left if you are satisfied with the service. Hairdressers are generally given a 10 to 15 percent tip. Porters, doormen and room service are tipped a few francs. A hotel concierge makes all sorts of reservations for you (theater, restaurant, plane, train and so on) and can offer advice about getting around in Paris; don't forget to tip him afterward for his or her considerable services. Ushers at some movie houses, sporting events, ballets and concerts expect a tip, and can be vengeful if you fail to shell out a couple of francs.

French and American **voltages** differ, so your electrical appliances (shavers, hairdryers) will require a transformer. You will doubtless also need an adapter for the round prongs of French plugs. These items can be obtained in the basement of the Samaritaine or the BHV department stores. (See *Department Stores* in the Shops chapter.)

Hallway lighting systems are often manually operated. Just to one side of the entrance, in a conspicuous place on each landing or near the elevator, you'll find a luminous switch that is automatically timed to give you one to three minutes of light. To enter many buildings, you must press a buzzer or a numerical code usually located at the side of the front door.

The French telecommunications services (FRANCE TELECOM) have created plastic **telephone cards** to be used instead of coins in public phone booths. They sell for 96 francs or 40 francs and may be purchased at the post office, cafés and some bookstores. Their microchip technology gives you a certain number of units, which are gradually used up as you make your calls. Don't count too heavily on using telephones in cafés and restaurants unless you have a drink or meal there.

Most modern pay phones have instructions in English printed on them. A local call costs 1 franc. You can **phone abroad** from most pay phones using either your plastic card or a large reserve of 5-franc coins. Collect calls can be made from pay phones by dialing 19, then 33 after the tone, and then the code for the country you want (Australia, 61; Britain, 44; Canada and the United States, 11).

The Louvre **post office** (52, rue du Louvre, 1st arr., 40 28 20 00) has a 24-hour international telephone/telegraph/fax service. Also note that Paris telephone numbers have eight figures. If you should come upon an old-style Parisian number with only seven digits, you must dial 4 before the number.

■ USEFUL ADDRESSES

Here are some addresses and phone numbers of particular interest to English-speaking travelers:

CHURCHES

American Cathedral in Paris
8th arr. - 23, av. George-V - 47 20 17 92

American Church
7th arr. - 65, quai d'Orsay - 47 05 07 99

Christian Science
14th arr. - 36, bd Saint-Jacques
47 07 26 60

Church of Scotland
8th arr. - 17, rue Bayard - 47 20 90 49

Great Synagogue
9th arr. - 44, rue de la Victoire
45 26 95 36

Liberal Synagogue
16th arr. - 24, rue Copernic - 47 04 37 27, fax 42 27 81 02

St. George's (Anglican)
16th arr. - 7, rue Auguste-Vacquerie
47 20 22 51

St. Joseph's (Catholic)
8th arr. - 50, av. Hoche - 42 27 28 56, fax 42 27 86 49

St. Michael's English Church
8th arr. - 5, rue d'Aguesseau - 47 42 70 88

EMBASSIES

American Embassy
8th arr. - 2, av. Gabriel - 42 96 12 02, fax 42 66 97 83

Australian Embassy
15th arr. - 4, rue Jean-Rey - 40 59 33 00, fax 40 59 33 10

British Embassy
8th arr. - 35, rue du Faubourg-Saint-Honoré - 42 66 91 42, fax 42 66 98 96

Canadian Embassy
8th arr. - 35, av. Montaigne - 44 43 32 00, fax 44 43 34 99

New Zealand Embassy
16th arr. - 7 ter, rue Léonard-de-Vinci
45 00 24 11, fax 45 01 26 39

City lights

Admire Paris in all its splendour during a night-time visit. Hundreds of the city's buildings and monuments are cloaked in illuminations when the sun goes down to show them at their best. Sparkling fountains, shining façades, glowing towers—you'll see the city in a new light. Monuments: Sun.-Fri. from dusk to midnight; Sat. & eves of holidays until 1 a.m. Fountains: Daytime April 1-Dec. 31 from 10 a.m. to dusk; Nighttime April 1-Dec. 31 Sun.-Fri. from dusk to midnight; Sat. & eves of holidays until 1 a.m.

ENGLISH-SPEAKING ORGANIZATIONS

American Center
12th arr. - 51, rue de Bercy - 44 73 77 77, fax 43 07 11 11
Open 9 a.m.-7 p.m. (Sat. until 2 p.m.). Closed Sun.
Until the Center's exciting new home, designed by architect Frank Gehry, is completed in September 1993, English courses only are taught (at a temporary address). The other classes for which the Center is known —yoga, dance, theater and exercise—will be offered again once the building is complete; at that time dance and theater performances will be scheduled as well.

American Chamber of Commerce
8th arr. - 21, av. Georges-V - 47 23 80 26
Open 9 a.m.-5 p.m. Closed Sat. & Sun.

American Express
9tht arr. - 11, rue Scribe - 47 77 70 00
Open daily 24 hours.
Here you'll find traveler's checks and American Express card and travel services. You can also arrange to pick up mail and wire money or have money wired to you.

American Library

7th arr. - 10, rue Général-Camou
45 51 46 82
Open 10 a.m.-7 p.m. Closed Sun., Mon., French hols., July 4 & Thanksgiving.
This privately run establishment houses the largest English-language library on the continent. There is also a selection of records and cassettes. You must, however, be an official resident of France (with a *carte de séjour*) to take books out of the library. A membership fee is required.

British Council

7th arr. - 9, rue Constantine - 49 55 73 23
Open 11 a.m.-6 p.m. (Wed. 7 a.m.). Closed Sat. & Sun.
The council sponsors a wide-ranging library of English books and records.

Canadian Cultural Center

8th arr. - 5, rue Constantine - 45 51 35 73, fax 47 05 43 55
Open 9 a.m.-5 p.m. Closed Sat. (except exhibitions) & Sun.
This Canadian cultural center offers dance, theater and musical performances, as well as a library, art gallery and a student-exchange-program office.

HOSPITALS (ENGLISH-SPEAKING)

Hôpital Américain
American Hospital of Paris

92200 Neuilly sur Seine - 63, bd Victor-Hugo
46 41 25 25, fax 46 24 49 38
A consultation here is more expensive than at most hospitals in Paris. You can pay in dollars. Dental services are also provided, and there is a 24-hour English-speaking emergency service.

Hôpital Franco-Britannique (British Hospital)

92300 Levallois-Perret - 3 rue Barbès
47 58 13 12
This hospital provides complete services.

PHARMACY

Swann Pharmacy

1st arr. - 6, rue Castiglione - 42 60 72 96, fax 42 60 44 12
Open 9 a.m.-7:30 p.m. Closed Sun.
This is the only pharmacy in Paris where your English-language prescription will be translated

and an equivalent medicine made up by a pharmacist.

■ PHONE DIRECTORY

Police/Help
17

Fire Department
18

SAMU (Ambulance)
45 67 50 50

S.O.S. Médecins
43 37 77 77 or 47 07 77 77, fax 45 87 13 47
These doctors make house calls at any hour of the day or night, for about 250-300 francs.

S.O.S. Crisis Line (in English)
47 23 80 80
Open 3 p.m.-11 p.m.

S.O.S. Psychiatrie
47 07 24 24
Emergency psychiatric care.

S.O.S. Dentaire
43 37 51 00
An operator will direct you to a dentist offering emergency care in your neighborhood.

Centre Anti-Poisons
40 37 04 04
Poison Control Center.

■ DUTY-FREE SHOPPING

The bad news is that just about everything in France is subject to Value Added Tax (VAT). The charge is 18.6 percent on most items. The good news is that people living outside Europe can get a 100 percent VAT rebate on items they export from France. To qualify for a rebate, you must spend more than 2,000 francs in one shop.

To get reimbursed, have the store fill in the Détaxe Légale form (make sure the shop carries it before you make the purchase). Bring your passport, because you'll be required to show it. Along with the form, the store will supply you with an envelope bearing its address.

When you leave France, show the forms at the Bureau de Détaxe or at Customs and have the Customs officer stamp them. Then seal the forms in the envelope supplied by the shop and mail it back. Keep your receipt.

The rebate can be credited directly to your account. Some stores charge a commission for this service, while others (especially the tax-free shops on the Champs-Elysées and the avenue de l'Opéra) charge no commission. For futher information, call 47 57 26 48.

GOINGS-ON

As an international city, Paris is the site of many artistic festivals, trade fairs and sporting events. Exact dates vary from year to year, so we've simply listed the month in which they occur.

French national holidays are January 1, May 1, May 8, July 14 and November 11; religious holidays fall on Easter, Easter Monday, Ascension Thursday, Pentecost Sunday and the following Monday, Assumption Day (August 15), All Saint's Day (November 1) and Christmas. A word of warning: Banks and some shops will close early the day before a public holiday, and often a three-day weekend will become a four-day weekend when holidays fall on a Tuesday or a Thursday.

■ JANUARY

Prix d'Amérique
12th arr. - Hippodrome de Vincennes
49 77 17 17
End Jan.
One of the most prestigious prizes in horse racing.

■ FEBRUARY

Antiquités-Brocante à Champerret
17th arr. - Porte de Champerret, espace Champerret
Mid-Feb.
Antiques and bric-à-brac.

Foire à la Ferraille de Paris
12th arr. - Parc Floral de Paris, Bois de Vincennes
End Feb.
An amusing collection of taste treats and "junque".

■ MARCH

Foire du Trône
12th arr. - Pelouse de Reuilly, Bois de Vincennes
End March-beg. June. Open 2 p.m.-midnight (Fri. & Sat. until 1 a.m.)
All the fun of a fair.

Jumping International de Paris
12th arr. - Palais Omnisports de Bercy,
8, bd de Bercy - 43 46 12 21
Mid-March.
International horse-jumping trials.

Salon International de l'Agriculture
15th arr. - Parc des Expositions, Porte de Versailles
Beg. March. Open 10 a.m.-7 p.m.
Bring the kids to this international agricultural show.

Salon du Livre
15th arr. - Parc d'Expositions, Porte de Versailles
Mid-March. Open 9:30 a.m.-7:30 p.m.
A mammoth book fair.

Salon de Mars
7th arr.- Place Joffre (in front of Ecole Militaire)
Mid-March. Open noon-8 p.m. (Thurs. 11 p.m.), Sat. & Sun. 10 a.m.-8 p.m.
Top-of-the-line antiques.

Salon Mondial du Tourisme et des Voyages
15th arr. - Parc des Expositions, Porte de Versailles
Mid-March.
World tourism and travel.

■ APRIL

Expolangues
15th arr. - Parc des Expositions, Porte de Versailles
End Jan. Open 9:30 a.m.-7 p.m.
Everything connected with foreign languages.

Foire de Paris
15th arr. - Parc des Expositions, Porte de Versailles
End April-beg. May. Open 10 a.m.-7 p.m.
Food, wine, household equipment and gadgetry.

Marathon International de Paris
Departure avenue des Champs-Elysées, 8th arr; arrival avenue Foch, 16th arr.
End April.
26 miles or 42 kilometers, it's all the same to the runners.

■ MAY

Championnats Internationaux de France de Tennis (French Open)
16th arr. - Stade Roland Garros,
2, av. Gordon-Bennett - 47 43 48 00
End May-beg. June
Top international tennis championship.

Foire du Trône
12th arr. - Pelouse de Reuilly, Bois de Vincennes
See *March.*

Les Cinq Jours de l'Objet Extraordinaire (Carré des Antiquaires Rive Gauche)
7th arr. - rues du Bac, de Beaune, de Lille, des Saints-Pères, de l'Université, de Verneuil & quai Voltaire
Mid-May - 10 a.m.-10 p.m.
Paris's top antiques shops hold open house: rare and unusual objects.

JUNE

Course des Garçons de Café
1st arr. - Departure & arrival at L'Hôtel-de-Ville - 40 07 30 12
Beg. June
Waiters race in the Paris streets holding a tray with a full bottle and a full glass of beer.

Fête de la Musique
Streets of Paris - 42 20 12 34
June 21. All day, all night.
Anyone who wants to can blow his horn on Music Day.

Foire du Trône
12th arr. - Pelouse de Reuilly, Bois de Vincennes
See *March.*

Paris Villages
Various Paris neighborhoods - 42 74 20 04
From mid-June through summer.
Local festivities with a working-class flavor: parades, drum majorettes, folk dancing, fun and games for all.

Prix de Diane Hermès
60500 Chantilly - Hippodrome de Chantilly - (16) 44 62 41 00
Mid-June.
Wear your classiest *chapeau* to this elegant day at the races, attended by the cream of Parisian society.

Salon International de l'Aéronautique et de l'Espace
93350 Le Bourget - Parc des Expositions du Bourget - 48 35 91 61
Only in odd-numbered years. Open 9:30 a.m.-6 p.m.
Air shows by daredevil pilots; aircraft displays.

JULY

Arrivée du Tour de France Cycliste
8th arr. - av. des Champs-Elysées
End July.
The Tour de France cyclists triumphantly cross the finish line.

Bastille Day Eve
July 13. In the evening.
A jolly evening: dance to rock, tango and accordion bands in public squares and at neighborhood firehouses. The largest *bal* is the one on the place de la Bastille, 12th arr.

Bastille Day
8th arr. - Avenue des Champs-Elysées
July 14.
In the morning, a military parade on the Champs-Elysées celebrates the French national holiday. Fireworks display in the evening in the Jardins du Trocadéro, 16th arr.

AUGUST

Virtually everything is closed in August, but true Paris-lovers regard this as the best month of the year to be in their favorite city.

SEPTEMBER

La Biennale des Antiquaires
8th arr. - Grand Palais, av. Winston Churchill.
End Sept.-beg. Oct.
This major antiques show is held every two years, in even years—so look for it in 1994 and 1996.

OCTOBER

Fête des Vendanges
18th arr. - Butte Montmartre, corner of rue des Saules & rue Saint-Vincent
First Sat. in Oct.
A grape harvest at the only working vineyard within the city limits.

Foire Internationale d'Art Contemporain (FIAC)
8th arr. - Grand Palais, av. Winston Churchill
Mid Oct. Open noon-7:30 p.m. (Thurs. 11 p.m.), Sat. & Sun. 10 a.m.-7:30 p.m.
An international contemporary-art show.

Journée du Patrimoine

44 61 21 50/51
One w.-e. mid Sept.

A celebration of France's architectural heritage: 300 monuments, ministries, town houses and public buildings open to visitors.

Mondial de l'Automobile

15th arr. - Parc des Expositions, Porte de Versailles
Only in even-numbered years. Beg. Oct. Open 10 a.m.-10 p.m.

The second world-largest international automobile show.

Salon Meubles et Décors

15th arr. - Parc des Expositions, Porte de Versailles
Mid Oct.

A trade show highlighting the latest innovations in home furnishings and decor.

■ NOVEMBER

Salon d'Automne

8th arr. - Grand Palais, av. Winston Churchill
End Oct. Open 11 a.m.-7:30 a.m. (Thurs. 10 p.m.).

New artwork by budding talents.

2,000 years of history

The past comes to life in Paristoric, a spectacular show in which Paris displays its history and monuments on a giant screen. Open 365 days a year at 78 bis, boulevard de Batignolles, 17th arr., tel. 42 93 93 46, fax 42 93 93 48. Shows start every hour, on the hour, from 9 a.m. to 6 p.m. (9 p.m. in summer). Adults, 70 francs, children and students, 40 francs.

SICOB

93420 Villepinte - Parc des Expositions, Paris-Nord
48 63 30 30, fax 48 63 31 36
Beg. Oct. Open 9 a.m.-6:30 p.m.

International office machinery, computers and supplies.

Open de la Ville de Paris

12th arr. - Palais Omnisports de Bercy,
8, bd de Bercy - 43 46 12 21
Beg. Nov.

The City of Paris Open Tennis Championships.

Prix de l'Arc de Triomphe

16th arr. - Hippodrome de Longchamp
Beg. Oct. - 49 10 20 30

A day at the races and a chance to win a lot of money.

Salon International de l'Alimentation (S.I.A.L.)

93420 Villepinte - Parc des Expositions, Paris-Nord
48 63 30 30, fax 48 63 31 36
Only in even-numbered years. Mid Oct.

An international food-products exhibit.

■ DECEMBER

La Crèche

4th arr.- Place de l'Hôtel de Ville
Dec. 4-Jan. 4. Open 10 a.m.-8 p.m.

A giant nativity scene, with moving figures and music, set up on the esplanade outside City Hall.

Salon du Cheval et du Poney

15th arr. - Parc des Expositions,
Porte de Versailles
Beg. Dec. Open 10 a.m.-7 p.m.

Horses and ponies galore, and all the accompanying trappings.

Salon Nautique International

15th arr. - Parc des Expositions,
Porte de Versailles
Beg. Dec. Open 10 a.m.-7 p.m. (Thurs. until 11 p.m.)

International boat show.

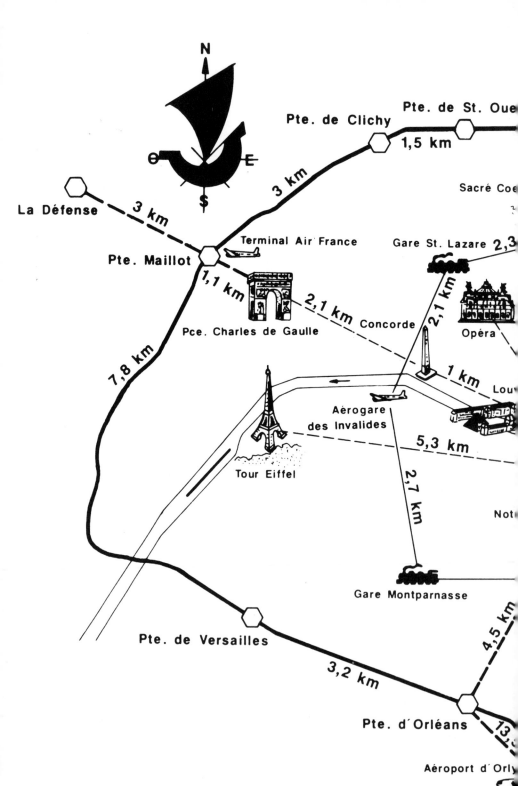

N

O E

S

Pte. de Clichy

Pte. de St. Oue

1,5 km

La Défense

3 km

3 km

Sacré Coe

Terminal Air France

Gare St. Lazare 2,3

Pte. Maillot

1,1 km

2,1 km

2,1 km Concorde

Opéra

Pce. Charles de Gaulle

7,8 km

1 km

Lou

Aérogare
des Invalides

5,3 km

2,7 km

Tour Eiffel

Not

Gare Montparnasse

4,5 km

Pte. de Versailles

3,2 km

Pte. d'Orléans

13,

Aéroport d'Orl

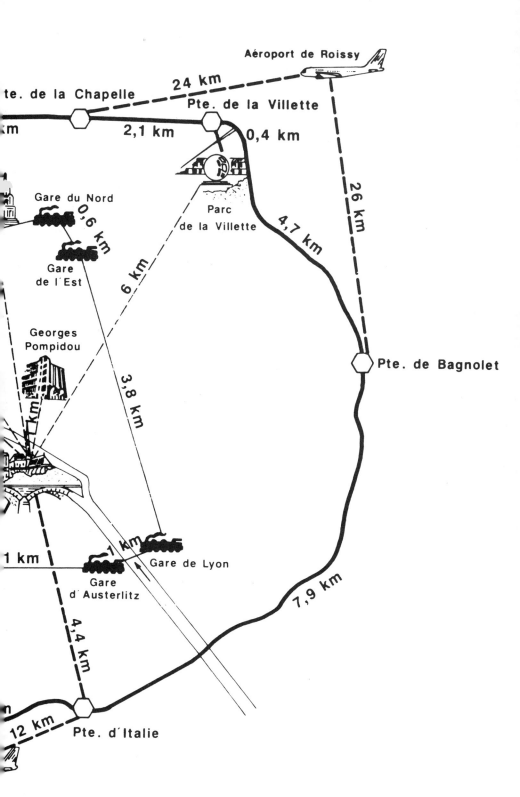

Aéroport de Roissy

24 km

te. de la Chapelle

Pte. de la Villette

2,1 km

0,4 km

km

26 km

Parc
de la Villette

4,7 km

Gare du Nord

0,6 km

6 km

Gare
de l'Est

Georges
Pompidou

3,8 km

Pte. de Bagnolet

km

7,9 km

1 km

1 km

Gare de Lyon

Gare
d'Austerlitz

4,4 km

12 km

Pte. d'Italie

n